PRAISE FOR *CONFRONTING FAILURES OF JUSTICE: GETTING AWAY WITH MURDER AND RAPE*

"When a person shouldn't be punished, or is punished too much, the injustice done is easy to see. Harder to see is the injustice at work when those who should be punished are never found, their crimes never solved. Paul Robinson, Jeffrey Seaman, and Muhammad Sarahne do a great service bringing this invisible injustice to light, identifying its many causes, and offering commonsense proposals for reform. Highly recommended."
> —**Stephen P. Garvey**, A. Robert Noll Professor of Law, Cornell Law School

"Criminal-law icon Paul Robinson and his esteemed colleagues have produced a text that flips the threadbare contemporary-academic discussion on its head—asking whether a modern-liberal society that seeks to improve the life and circumstances of all its members must take as seriously its moral obligation of imposing just punishment on wrongdoers as it does avoiding unjust punishment on the innocent. So often modern-intellectual discourse is an echo chamber of rut-digging commentary that ignores multitudes of alternative paths. *Confronting Failures of Justice* systematically explores those other avenues. Kudos for producing such a thoughtful analysis."
> —**Robert Steinbuch**, law professor, University of Arkansas at Little Rock

"This comprehensive, exhaustively researched book by Robinson, Seaman, and Sarahne probes the issues facing criminal justice today, primarily in the English-speaking world. Highly recommended for everyone committed to a just society."
> —**George P. Fletcher**, Cardozo Professor of Jurisprudence, Columbia University School of Law

"*Confronting Failures of Justice* is comprehensive and thoroughly researched but wears its erudition lightly, offering a vivid and highly readable account of criminal law's failings—and possible ways to mitigate or avoid them—that will engage and inform academics and general readers alike. With numerous compelling real-world illustrations, this book surveys a wide range of grave and troubling injustices yet leavens its tragic tales with hopeful proposals for reform."
> —**Michael T. Cahill**, emeritus president and dean, Brooklyn Law School

"*Confronting Failures of Justice* brilliantly and nonideologically interweaves criminal law theory, substance and procedure, painstaking investigation of the criminal justice system, massive statistical research, and illustrative case studies to convincingly document the regular, immensely costly failures of the criminal justice system to do justice. It canvasses the causes of such injustice, and equally important, it offers sensible solutions to the problems created at each stage of the system. It is a balanced, magisterial work that is indispensable for those who seek to understand and improve American criminal justice."
> —**Stephen J. Morse**, Ferdinand Wakeman Hubbell Professor of Law and professor of psychology and law in psychiatry, University of Pennsylvania

Confronting Failures of Justice

Getting Away with Murder and Rape

PAUL H. ROBINSON
University of Pennsylvania Carey Law School

JEFFREY SEAMAN
University of Pennsylvania

MUHAMMAD SARAHNE
Criminal Department, State Attorney's Office, Israel

ROWMAN & LITTLEFIELD
Lanham • Boulder • New York • London

Associate Acquisitions Editor: Becca Beurer
Assistant Acquisitions Editor: Sarah Rinehart
Sales and Marketing Inquiries: RLtextbooks@bloomsbury.com

Published by Rowman & Littlefield
An imprint of The Rowman & Littlefield Publishing Group, Inc.
4501 Forbes Boulevard, Suite 200, Lanham, Maryland 20706
www.rowman.com

86-90 Paul Street, London EC2A 4NE

British Library Cataloguing in Publication Information Available

Library of Congress Cataloging-in-Publication Data

Names: Robinson, Paul H., 1948- author. | Seaman, Jeffrey, author. |
   Sarahne, Muhammad, 1989- author.
Title: Confronting failures of justice : getting away with murder and rape
   / Paul H. Robinson, University of Pennsylvania Carey Law School; Jeffrey
   Seaman, University of Pennsylvania; Muhammad Sarahne, Criminal
   Department, State Attorney's Office, Israel.
Description: Lanham : Rowman & Littlefield Publishers, 2024. | Includes
   bibliographical references and index.
Identifiers: LCCN 2024021098 (print) | LCCN 2024021099 (ebook) | ISBN
   9781538191767 (cloth) | ISBN 9781538191774 (paperback) | ISBN
   9781538191781 (ebook)
Subjects: LCSH: Criminal justice, Administration of—United States. |
   Discrimination in criminal justice administration—United States. |
   Judicial error—United States.
Classification: LCC KF9223 .R625 2024 (print) | LCC KF9223 (ebook) | DDC
   364.973—dc23/eng/20240602
LC record available at https://lccn.loc.gov/2024021098
LC ebook record available at https://lccn.loc.gov/2024021099

∞™ The paper used in this publication meets the minimum requirements of
American National Standard for Information Sciences—Permanence of Paper
for Printed Library Materials, ANSI/NISO Z39.48-1992.

To my students.
—PHR

To all victims of justice failures.
—JCS

To my loving parents, Tawfeek and Alya, to whom I owe everything.
—MS

Brief Contents

Contents

Acknowledgments

OUR GREATEST DEBT IS TO SARAH McAlpine Robinson, who has been the primary researcher on this project for the three plus years it has been underway. This book would not have been possible without her. We would also like to thank the many other people who over several years worked hard to bring this book forward, especially Catherine W. Lewis, Dushaun Thompson, Erin E. Kelly, Melissa N. Nong, Hannah Agarwal, and Josef Weitzman, all of the University of Pennsylvania law school or undergraduate classes of 2022, 2023, or 2024. Special thanks go to Andrew Lang, of the Penn Law Library, for his creative problem solving with our endless requests for his research expertise. For technical assistance with the photographs, we thank Atticus Robinson.

As the project touches on a wide range of topics and specialties, we often needed to get advice from other academics. It is with much gratitude that we thank University of Pennsylvania law professors Stephen Morse, Sandra Mason, and Paul Heaton; Vanderbilt University law professor Chris Slobogin; and Rutgers University philosophy professor Doug Husak, none of whom are responsible for the views expressed in this volume.

Many of the images that are used in this book were provided by individuals touched by these stories. Heather Peters of MLive is the source for the photograph of Shannon Siders's mother by her daughter's grave. Harry MacLean, author of *In Broad Daylight: A Murder in Skidmore, Missouri*, which gives the full account of McElroy's death, allowed us to use the photograph of McElroy's ruined truck. The photograph from the Watts Riots and of William Bonin's victims were both made available through the Los Angeles Public Library. Chris Helms of the Jamaica Plains News kindly gave permission to use the photograph of the Zachery crime scene. The photograph of Earl Bradley is used courtesy of the Delaware State Police and that of Larry Eyler was provided by the Indiana State Police. The image of young Vincent Chin was provided courtesy of Helen Zia and the estates of Vincent and Lily Chin. Latasha Shaw's sister, Charnette Grayson, allowed us to use her sister's image and took the time to explain how the loss has continued to affect the family. Tim Ide is the creator of the photograph with the wreckage of the beauty salon in Ferguson. Matt Garceau, owner of Camelot Photography, allowed us to use his image of the fires in Minneapolis. And our thanks to a Philadelphia police officer who asked to be acknowledged as P/O Fidler#4666-PPD, who permitted us to use his image from the funeral of Officer Wenjian Liu. The Prison Policy Initiative generously allowed us to use their graphic concerning the prison population in America. And, finally, Julain Mark and Lydia Chavez of Mission Local allowed us to use the organization's image of the storefronts in San Francisco.

CHAPTER 1

Getting Away with Murder and Rape

A. INTRODUCTION: FAILURES OF JUSTICE

MOST KILLERS GET AWAY WITH MURDER. In 2020, there were around 22,000 murders in America, and police solved just over 10,000—less than 50 percent.[1] Commonly, almost half of these solved cases result in no homicide conviction.[2] Even more troublingly, homicide has the best victimization-conviction ratio of any offense. Most other crimes are rarely punished. Of more than 980,000 aggravated assaults annually, only around 7.4 percent end in a conviction.[3] Of more than 460,000 rapes and sexual assaults annually, 97.2 percent end in no felony conviction.[4] Hundreds of thousands of murderers, assaulters, and rapists remain free. What explains these regular failures of justice?

This book attempts to answer that question by examining the doctrines, practices, and conditions in the criminal justice system that allow serious criminals to escape the punishment they deserve. There are few simple fixes. Our analysis of the many justice-frustrating rules and practices does not conclude that all such doctrines should be eliminated. Most of these rules and practices are not irrational. Almost all are designed to protect some legitimate societal interest. However, there is reason to believe that lawmakers and system actors seriously undervalue the societal costs of failing to do justice and the societal benefits of doing it.

This volume examines the competing costs and benefits of justice-frustrating doctrines, including such topics as limitations on police investigative procedures, investigative errors, restraints on the use of investigative technology, witness intimidation, poor police-community relations, the exclusionary rule, plea bargaining, the use of anti-justice distributive principles in criminal law codification and sentencing, executive clemency, and many more. In each instance, we consider the nature and extent of the justice-frustrating problem, evaluate the competing interests, discuss reforms that could strike a more appropriate balance between the competing interests, and ultimately recommend what we think is the most important and feasible reform to make in each area. As will become clear, many of these justice-frustrating rules and practices exist not because their creators have miscalculated the balance of interests but rather because they have done no balancing at all and instead have focused on one interest to the exclusion of all others. Our analysis suggests that for most issues there are ways to protect and promote the legitimate interests upheld by the status quo in ways that avoid or reduce the current justice-frustrating effect.

There is a particular need to address the issue of failures of justice (where offenders escape the punishment they clearly deserve) because academic attention has focused almost exclusively on the problem of the justice system doing injustice (instances of undeserved liability or overly harsh punishment).[5] This focus is certainly understandable. Avoiding injustice is critical not only for its own sake but also for improving the criminal law's moral credibility with the community and thereby its crime-control effectiveness.[6] But as the following analyses show, especially in chapter 3, a modern liberal society that seeks to improve the life and circumstances of all its members must take seriously its moral obligation, and the practical crime-control importance, of imposing just punishment and not simply avoiding unjust punishment.

B. THE CAUSES OF JUSTICE FAILURES

Our examination of justice failures is organized around four categories: failures caused by legal rules governing the assignment of criminal liability and punishment, failures caused by limitations on criminal investigation, failures caused by rules or practices in the criminal adjudication process, and failures caused by social or political factors.

Criminal Liability Rules

Chapter 2 examines how justice sometimes fails because the law prevents prosecution. The double jeopardy rule allows previously acquitted offenders to escape justice even if new, compelling evidence (such as DNA) is discovered. Statutes of limitation dictate that serious crimes (such as rape) cannot be prosecuted after a given number of years even if compelling evidence exists. Diplomatic immunity allows foreign diplomats and some of their staff to avoid prosecution for even serious crimes. Finally, the legality principle (especially in the context of the rule of strict construction) prevents conviction for an offense even if it was clear to everyone—including the offender—that the conduct was criminal, so long as the statutory offense is susceptible to more than one interpretation.

Chapter 3 examines the importance of the legal system doing justice by considering the effect of anti-justice distributive principles such as general deterrence and incapacitation of the dangerous, which seek to promote crime-control goals other than just desert when assigning punishment. When justice in the form of desert is not recognized as the primary criterion for imposing criminal liability, the moral credibility of the law declines as some offenders may be punished too much and others too little.

Limitations on Criminal Investigation

Chapter 4 examines how justice can fail due to poor investigative strategies and practices such as failures to collect and analyze forensic evidence. Chapter 5 looks at the issue of financial limitations that often lead to underfunded, undertrained, and underequipped crime investigation and prosecution. Chapter 6 examines how limitations on criminal investigations designed to uphold privacy and personal liberty (such as search and seizure limitations and suspect interrogation restrictions) can cause justice to fail. Chapter 7 builds on chapter 6 by looking at the issue of restrictions on the use of promising new technologies such as DNA databases and surveillance systems that have the potential to catch thousands of serious offenders.

Criminal Justice Adjudication Procedures

Chapter 8 examines procedural rules that lead to the exclusion of reliable probative evidence at trial because it was gathered in violation of judicial rules (such as search and seizure restrictions) or because it is deemed prejudicial to the defendant. Chapter 9 deals with pretrial procedures such as pretrial release and speedy trial rules that can allow serious offenders to go unpunished. Chapter 10 examines how the common practice of plea bargaining regularly allows serious offenders to get off with only a fraction of the punishment they deserve, and that the law prescribes. Chapter 11 looks at the similar issue of unchecked judicial sentencing discretion, which can lead to inadequate and often wildly disparate sentences. Chapter 12 examines how justice can fail even after conviction through processes such as early or compassionate release that allow some offenders to go free well before serving the sentence they deserve. Chapter 13 looks at the related issue of executive clemency that has allowed even heinous criminals to go free based on personal or political connections.

Social and Political Influences

Social and political factors can also cause failures of justice. Chapter 14 examines the consequences of citizen non-cooperation with investigators caused by such influences as witness intimidation, "no snitch" codes, distrust of police, and legal cynicism.[7] Chapter 15 looks at the parallel problem of police non-intervention, when police pull back from proactive policing for reasons ranging from political interventions to voluntary decisions not to risk triggering violent reactions, negative publicity, or personal harm or sanction (the so-called Ferguson Effect). Chapter 16 examines how political ideology can lead to failures of justice through policies of decarceration,

decriminalization, non-prosecution, and the creation of sanctuary cities.

All these policies and more can make it easier for serious offenders to escape punishment no matter the intentions of policymakers. It is worth noting again, however, that there are often good reasons behind many of these justice-frustrating rules and practices. This book is meant to consider the competing societal interests and to imagine possible reforms. It is quite possible to believe some rules or practices need reform while others are a justifiable compromise. Chapter 17 offers a perspective on which causes of justice failures are most troubling and which reforms are potentially most important.

C. THE FREQUENCY AND SERIOUSNESS OF JUSTICE FAILURES

The previous causes produce frequent and serious failures of justice, as evidenced by low and decreasing clearance rates and low and decreasing conviction rates for even the most serious crimes such as homicide and rape. The low clearance and conviction rates in turn fuel more crime and even lower clearance rates.

Clearance and Conviction Rates: Homicide

It's a good time to be a killer in America. The majority of murderers walk away from their crimes without any punishment. According to the FBI's Uniform Crime Report data, there are at least 250,000 unsolved murder cases (known as "cold cases") in the United States, and each year, that haunting number grows by roughly 6,000.[8] As daunting as these numbers are, they only tell part of the story. Illinois and New York only provide partial data to the FBI's database, and so the number of unsolved crimes is likely even higher than the available data suggests.[9] As more murders go unsolved, available investigation time to dedicate to each case dwindles and existing investigative resources are stretched thinner. Failures of justice are then compounded when these uncaught killers go on to kill again. The chance of this massive backlog of cold cases ever being solved is slight as only 7 percent of the nearly 18,000 law enforcement agencies in the United States even have designated cold case units.[10]

Despite significant advances in the forensic sciences, the problem of homicide clearance rates has significantly worsened over recent decades and shows no signs of improving. Nationally, homicide clearance rates (the percentage of cases that police declare solved) decreased from 72 percent in 1980[11] to just over 40 percent in 2020,[12] and there is good reason to suspect that the true homicide clearance rate is in fact significantly lower.[13] However, this national average obscures dramatic variation among states. In New Mexico (where 152 homicides occurred in 2018), the homicide clearance rate was 36.84 percent, and in Maine (where only 23 homicides occurred in 2018), the homicide clearance rate was 95.66 percent.[14] Similarly vast differences can be observed on local levels. For example, the Philadelphia Police Department saw 447 fatal shootings in 2020 and only cleared 37 percent of these crimes.[15] Virginia's Fairfax County Police Department only had fourteen murders to respond to in 2018 and a clearance rate of 100 percent.[16] Generally, the more murders that occur in a jurisdiction, the lower the clearance rate tends to be. Some cities are plagued by the chronic inability to solve murders, such as Chicago, which had a homicide

clearance rate of 15.7 percent in 2017, making its 44 percent clearance rate in 2020 an almost respectable performance by comparison.[17] Gun homicides, and street shootings in particular, have a disturbingly low clearance rate. In Philadelphia in 2020, fewer than 30 percent of all fatal shootings were solved. However, this low number is roughly twice as high as the clearance rate for non-fatal shootings in the city, indicating a city-wide crisis in solving violent crime mirrored in other localities across the country.[18]

But low clearance rates actually understate the problem of justice failures. Police count cases as "cleared" even when the perpetrator hasn't been charged, much less convicted. Suspects who have successfully fled, died, or plea bargained for a non-homicide conviction are counted as "cleared" in calculating the clearance rate despite the fact that no homicide conviction has occurred.[19] Police may also count cases as cleared when they are confident they have found the perpetrator but do not possess the necessary evidence for a charge. In none of these cases has justice been done.

These low clearance and conviction rates for killings are not an inevitability of living in a modern society. In Japan, for example, the clearance rate for homicide is around 95 percent.[20] Countries that experience more violent crime than Japan also do better than the United States. The most recently available UK statistics, for example, suggest a homicide clearance rate of 66 percent, even despite a recent downturn (it used to commonly be 90 percent).[21]

Clearance and Conviction Rates: Rape and Aggravated Assault
As low as they are, homicide clearance and conviction rates around the coun-

try are dramatically higher than for any other offense, even serious crimes such as rape and aggravated assault. According to the Rape, Abuse, and Incest National Network (RAINN), out of every 1,000 sexual assaults, only 310 are reported to the police, leading to fifty arrests, yielding twenty-eight felony convictions, with only twenty-five sentences imposed that cause the offender to spend at least a day in jail.[22] In other words, the conviction rate for sexual assault is less than 3 percent. Moreover, some researchers suggest that this is an overly generous assessment and that the true conviction rate for sexual assault could be less than 1 percent.[23] With close to half a million sexual assaults occurring each year in the United States, justice is failing to an extraordinary degree when it comes to sexual violence.[24]

The statistics for other serious crimes, such as aggravated assault, are similarly dismal. In 2006 (the last year for which the US Justice Department reports state court conviction data[25] [see chapter 17C for more on how government agencies sometimes do not report inconvenient statistics]), there were an estimated 1,344,280 aggravated assaults in the United States,[26] but only 100,560 convictions for it,[27] meaning 93 percent of offenders escaped the justice they deserved. Available state conviction data for 2021 suggests conviction rates remain dismal. For example, Minnesota had an estimated 23,841 aggravated assaults in 2021[28] but only 1,400 convictions,[29] for a conviction rate of about 6 percent, similar to the 7 percent conviction rate in the 2006 national data.

The Vicious Cycle of Increasing Crime and Decreasing Clearance Rates

Low clearance rates for serious crimes are serious failures of justice by themselves, but they can also fuel a vicious cycle that continuously increases crime and decreases clearance rates even further. Justice failures can increase when rising crime overwhelms police and prosecutors, leaving less time spent investigating and prosecuting each individual case (which is one reason why higher murder rates usually go together with lower clearance rates).[30] Much of this additional crime comes from criminals escaping justice and reoffending. A study conducted by the US Sentencing Commission estimated that almost one-half of federal offenders were rearrested within eight years of release.[31] About one-fourth of those rearrested had assault as their most serious charge.[32] One can imagine that the recidivism rate among those criminals who are never caught would be even higher.

Low clearance rates also affect crime rates in other ways. Low clearance rates signal that future crimes may also go unsolved, and so deterrence against crime in general is weakened. A study of homicide in major US cities revealed that a lower clearance rate one year was often followed by a greater homicide count the next year.[33]

The connection between high crime and low clearance rates can be seen in the murder surge of 2020. Data from seventy major US cities found that fifty-seven police agencies experienced an average increase in murder rates of 36.7 percent between 2019 and 2020.[34] At the same time, clearance rates fell across the country. For example, the 55 percent increase in homicides in Chicago in 2020 corresponded to a 6-percentage-point decrease in clearance rates.[35] Similarly, a 54 percent increase in homicides in Houston sparked an 11-percentage-point decrease in clearance rates.[36] Nationally, the 15,449 homicides reported to the FBI database in 2019 had a clearance rate of 61.4 percent,[37] while even the most conservative estimate for homicides in 2020 (20,250) had a clearance rate of less than 50 percent.[38]

Sometimes the cycle of rising crime and falling clearance rates can be broken by increased public scrutiny and additional resources. For example, Chicago's horrifically low homicide clearance rate of 29 percent in 2016, which was caused in part by a massive surge in homicides, sparked intense scrutiny and new funding that helped the clearance rate rebound to around 50 percent in 2019.[39] Other times, increased resources are not enough to solve the problem. In Houston, murder clearance rates have yet to improve despite the police department's budget increasing by roughly $300 million to $930 million between 2013 and 2021.[40]

The larger point is that increasing crime commonly means lower clearance rates, which necessarily means increased justice failures and vice versa.

Today's Rising Crime and Justice Failures: More Important than Ever

Some activists have sought to deny that there exists a growing violent crime problem today,[41] arguing instead that America is enjoying historically low serious crime rates as the triggers of criminality dry up. Why bother about failures of justice if serious crime is plummeting? Obviously, such an argument ignores the substantial costs associated with the large number of offenders escaping the punishment they deserve, but if correct it would suggest failures of justice are a shrinking problem.

However, the truth is that America is not enjoying historically low rates of crime, and serious crimes such as murder, rape, and aggravated assault are on the rise again, especially in urban jurisdictions, after falling from their peak in the early 1990s.[42] If the graph showing crime rate trends is framed to start in the 1970s, 1980s, or 1990s, this may suggest that America is enjoying historically low crime rates. But, in reality, those three decades represented America's abnormal highs in crime. If one looks at the broader historical record, it becomes clear that when compared to before the devastating crime wave starting in the late 1960s, our current crime rates are higher today. For example, comparing the FBI's crime data reported by the Library of Congress from 1960 with 2019 (the last year the Library of Congress chose to report these inconvenient statistics) shows that total offenses per 100,000 increased from 1,887 to 2,489, a 32 percent increase.[43] Violent crime increased even more dramatically, as shown in table 1.1.[44] Modern violent crime rates are well above double the 1960 benchmark, mainly due to the explosion in aggravated assault.

This data does not even account for the recent surge in homicides since 2019, which saw the murder rate rise by nearly 30 percent from 2019 to 2020.[45] Even the 2019 data understates the size of the problem as the murder rate compari-

Table 1.1. Violent Crime Rate in the United States in 1960 versus 2019, Broken Down by Offense

Year	Total Offenses per 100,000	Violent	Murder	Forcible Rape	Robbery	Aggravated Assault
1960	1,887.2	160.9	5.1	9.6	60.1	86.1
2019	2,489.3	379.4	5.4	42.6	81.6	250.2

son is deceptive: enormous advances in emergency medical care since 1960 have dramatically improved the survivability of a shooting or aggravated assault. Victims now arrive at hospitals sooner due to better ambulance and helicopter response times, and most hospitals now have dedicated trauma centers skilled in treating severe wounds. For example, serious gunshot wounds treated in hospitals increased almost 50 percent between 2001 and 2011 even as the death rate decreased, causing the murder rate to drop from 5.6 to 4.7.[46]

Studies show that if 1960s medical technology prevailed today, the murder rate would be more than five times higher than it is.[47] In 2020, 24,567 homicides took place in America.[48] Without modern technologies, this number would be closer to 122,855.[49] America is not in a period of historically low violent crime but rather a period of advanced emergency care saving many victims from death despite steady or increasing severe violence in some jurisdictions.[50] Addressing failures of justice is more important now than ever as America is caught in a vicious cycle of rising violence and falling clearance rates.

D. CASE EXAMPLES AND THE PUBLIC REACTION TO THEM

Reviewing the statistical data on failures of justice for serious crime is important, but it ultimately gives a sanitized picture of the situation. Unlike many if not most academics, who are more concerned with false convictions than false acquittals, research shows ordinary people consider both equally important.[51] The ordinary citizen cares deeply about seeing justice done, and when justice fails, people and communities respond with outrage, advocacy, or even violence.

What follows are six illustrative cases that sparked public outrage. Some are famous, others are not. They are simple illustrations of how deeply the public cares about having justice done. More than fifty additional real-world examples are scattered throughout the book to illustrate the justice failures discussed in every chapter and subchapter.

- *Cari Lightner—Outrage Provokes Reform.* On May 3, 1980, thirteen-year-old Cari Lightner is walking with a friend to a church carnival in Fair Oaks, California.[52] The neighborhood street is quiet until a car comes roaring around a turn, veers off the road, and hits Cari, throwing her into the air. She lands 125 feet away, with her internal organs crushed to a pulp. Her killer is Clarence Busch, a habitual drunk driver who is legally allowed to drive despite four previous offenses. Busch is convicted of vehicular manslaughter and given a two-year sentence. Cari's mother, Candace Lightner, is outraged by the lack of justice. In California, littering carries higher penalties than drunk driving. Lightner founds Mothers Against Drunk Driving and works to rally the nation in demanding justice for drunk driving victims. People across the country agree with Lightner about the importance of doing justice, and a wave of stricter punishments for drunk driving are enacted.
- *Fred Ortiz—Outrage Provokes Vigilantism.* Forty-one-year-old Fred Ortiz is on parole, and he regularly beats his pregnant girlfriend.[53] The families of the couple are aware of the abuse, but reporting past violations has only served to anger Ortiz and parole authorities have not revoked his parole, so they no longer inform police. On June 14, 2021,

Figure 1.1. After her daughter was killed, Candice Lightner did much to bring attention to the problems of impaired driving, 1984. Photo from Mi Ae Lipe, "Guest Profile: Candace Lightner, Founder of MADD and We Save Lives," Driving in the Real World, January 2019, https://drivinginthereal world.com/guest-profile-candace-lightner-founder-of-madd-and-we-save-lives/.

a group of family members and friends of Ortiz's girlfriend visit her and find she has suffered a particularly brutal beating with obvious injuries. When Ortiz arrives, the angry group, who sees the criminal justice system as having repeatedly failed to punish or protect, attacks the man. They chase him, hit him with a car, and beat him with pipes and boards. Ortiz dies of his injuries.

- *Shannon Siders—Justice Failures Are Not Forgotten.* On July 18, 1989, eighteen-year-old Shannon Siders is murdered after leaving a party in Newaygo, Michigan, but the case quickly goes cold.[54] Her town does not forget her though, and for the next twenty-two years, police con-

tinue to receive hundreds of tips. A documentary about Siders's unsolved murder is made and shown at her old high school to remind people of the importance of bringing her killer to justice, and a Facebook page is created in her memory. Several private citizens continue to sift through the evidence and try to gather clues. In 2011, a local man who went to high school with Siders, and is now the police chief, creates a cold case unit devoted to finding Siders's killer. After conducting over three hundred new interviews, investigators finally solve the case. Brothers Matthew and Paul Jones are convicted in 2015 of murdering Siders twenty-six years earlier.

Figure 1.2. Fred Ortiz was beaten to death by community members outraged over his assaults upon his pregnant girlfriend, 2021. Photo from Facebook, in Jack Longstaff, "Mob Beat Domestic Abuser to Death After He Gave His Pregnant Girlfriend a Black Eye," Metro, June 17, 2021, https://metro.co.uk/2021/06/17/mob-beat-domestic-abuser-to-death-after-he-gave-his-girlfriend-a-black-eye-14789365/.

Figure 1.3. Shannon's mother places a Native American medicine pouch in the grave of her daughter, 2012. Photo from Heather Lynn Peters, "Reburial of Newaygo Homicide Victim, Shannon Marie Siders Brings Some 'Peace' to Family, Closure to Some (Video)," Mlive, October 15, 2012, https://www.mlive.com/news/muskegon/2012/10/reburial_of_newaygo_homicide_v.html. Reprinted with permission of Heather Peters and MLive.

The men promised to take her home from a party but then took turns raping and beating her. That the town spent twenty-six years finding the killers says much about the importance they put on doing justice.

- *Polly Klaas—Outrage Provokes Reform Providing Excessive Punishment.* Richard Davis has a long criminal career that includes armed bank robbery and multiple attempts to kidnap and rape women. On October 1, 1993, the thirty-nine-year-old is on parole, having served half of a sixteen-year sentence for kidnapping and armed robbery. He breaks into a house and kidnaps twelve-year-old Polly Klaas.[55] The abduction makes national news as thousands of Americans assist with the search in sympathy with Polly's frantic parents. When the child's body is finally found, it is determined that she was raped and strangled. There is intense public outrage at the crime and fury over the fact that Davis was free to kill Polly, despite having been convicted of so many serious and violent offenses. Davis is caught and convicted, but the public demand for justice morphs into widespread support for "three strikes" laws that would have kept Davis off the street. As discussed further in chapter 11, however, the new "three strikes" statutes, which commonly provide for automatic life imprisonment upon a third

Figure 1.4. The case of Polly Klaas became a national news story, 1993. Police resource photo by Petaluma Police Department, from Larry Magid, "Larry Magid: Polly Klaas Tragedy Changed How We Look for Missing Children," The Mercury News, October 5, 2023, https://www.mercurynews.com/2023/10/05/polly-klass-tragedy-led-to-changes-in-how-we-look-for-missing-children/.

(even non-serious) felony, can regularly produce excessive punishment. This is one reason why even those primarily concerned with injustices should care about reducing failures of justice as the public reaction to serious criminals escaping punishment can result in unjustly harsh criminal penalties.

- *Elie Nesler—Outrage Provokes Distraught Mother.* On April 2, 1993, Elie Nesler sits in the courtroom because her young son is to testify at a pretrial hearing for Daniel Driver, a thirty-five-year-old man who molested four boys at the summer camp where he worked, one of whom was Nesler's eight-year-old son.[56] Driver is in the courtroom and appears to be smirking through the questioning of the children. The children are not good witnesses because they cannot

keep track of details and times. During a break, the parents talk about the reality that Driver may escape justice even after the children suffer the added trauma of testifying in court. Nesler, overwhelmed by these realizations, walks up behind Driver in court, pulls out a pistol, and shoots him five times in the head. Nesler is charged with murder but becomes a hero to thousands of victims everywhere who see the system as failing to do justice. At her trial, a crowd rallies to chant "Free Ellie" outside the courtroom. Many mourn her ten-year sentence.

- *Casey Anthony—Outrage Undermines System's Credibility.* In June 2008, twenty-two-year-old Casey Anthony suffocates her two-year-old daughter, Caylee, by wrapping her face in duct tape.[57] When the

Figure 1.5. Ellie Nessler with her son Bill in 1999. Photo courtesy of Frank Weber.

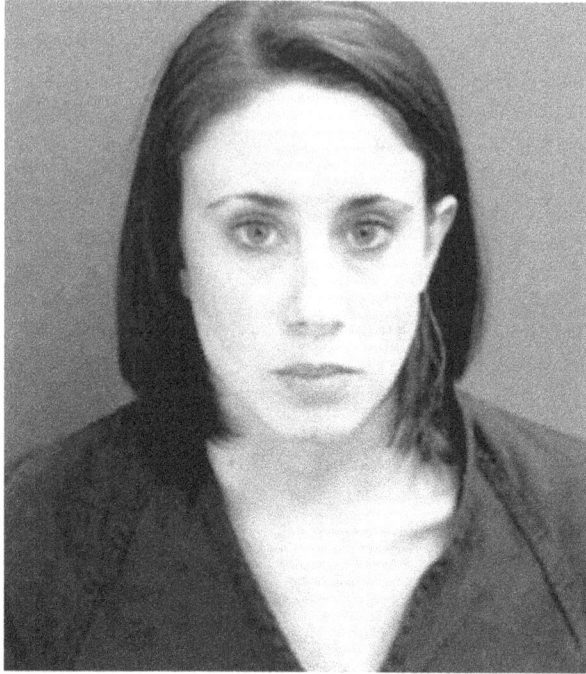

Figure 1.6. Casey Anthony mug shot, 2008. Photo from Orange County Sherriff's Office, Orlando Metropolitan, FL, "Police Custody Booking Photo of Casey Anthony (Public Release)," 2008, Orlando Sentinel, https://commons.wikimedia.org/wiki/File:Casey_Anthony.jpeg.

body is found, Anthony lies to investigators repeatedly, but she is soon charged with first-degree murder. The heartless case of a mother killing her helpless child generates national news coverage, and public calls for justice make prosecutors decide to seek the death penalty. Against all odds, Anthony is acquitted in a 2011 trial after her defense attorney spins an outlandish tale of framing to instill confusion and doubt in the jury. After the trial, additional conclusive evidence of her guilt surfaces. For example, she did computer searches on how best to kill her baby through suffocation. (Investigators had checked her Google searches but not her Firefox searches.) People across the country are shocked by the clearly false verdict, and the case is dubbed "O. J. Number 2" by hundreds of angry protestors outside the courtroom demanding justice for Caylee.

It is hard to review these cases without coming away with a sense of how deeply ordinary people care about doing justice and how outraged they can be about failures of justice.

E. THE COSTS OF JUSTICE FAILURES

As this volume will make clear, failures of justice carry enormous costs to society that justify making their reduction a policy priority.[58] One set of costs is moral, as those who believe in deserved punishment as a moral imperative see justice failures for serious offenses as a serious wrong that must be put right. But aside from these abstract morality costs, failures of justice also have clear practical societal costs that any good utilitarian should recognize.[59] These costs affect victims, families, neighborhoods, and society generally.

Personal Costs to Victims and Families

Many serious, violent crimes leave victims alive but scar them with emotional trauma, especially when justice is not served. Surviving a rape or attempted murder is merely the beginning of suffering for most victims. A victim may well find some measure of solace and healing in the thought that their attacker has been caught and punished, but most victims of serious crime never experience that comfort, as the abysmal conviction rates discussed previously show.[60] It is impossible to quantify the suffering victims experience when their victimizers escape justice, but the cost is real and significant. Recall from the previous case examples the instances in which victims and their families are so pained by the justice failure as to lash out through vigilantism.

Depression, self-harm, posttraumatic stress disorder (PTSD), and panic attacks are all common among survivors of violent crime, and at least 89 percent of all victims of sexual assault suffer from some physical or mental distress afterward.[61] Roughly one-third of sexual assault victims develop PTSD within their lifetime, and victims of sexual assault are 6.2 times more likely to develop PTSD than others.[62] Furthermore, 33 percent of women who are raped contemplate committing suicide and 13 percent attempt suicide.[63] These traumatizing effects of rape are exacerbated when justice fails. Studies have found that rape victims are more likely to experience PTSD if they have "negative experiences with the criminal justice system" compared with those who have positive experiences with the system or even those who had no interaction with

the system.[64] The knowledge that one's attacker still walks free can be infuriating and crippling to many victims.

Rape victims illustrate another cost when justice fails: after reporting a crime and cooperating with investigators, a victim can feel revictimized by the justice system when their additional suffering caused by an investigation ends up being for nothing. Over 50 percent of survivors of sexual assault have described their experiences with the system as "harmful, unsatisfactory, unfair, and in some cases, more harmful than the assault itself."[65] Reporting a crime like rape especially requires a willingness to lay oneself open to investigation, questioning, and constant reliving of the initial crime. To see all that effort wasted for nothing when justice fails can sometimes feel worse than the initial victimization.

Even worse, when justice fails, individuals and communities often engage in victim blaming or question whether a crime ever took place. This type of victimization can sometimes be the worst of all, when a failure of justice turns into a punishment of the victim. In a particularly egregious case, a judge dismissed rape charges against a man who raped a four-year-old girl because she supposedly was a "promiscuous young lady."[66] Less extreme examples are common. A failure of justice commonly leads many people to believe that the victim was at fault. This is one key reason so few rapes are reported to police in the first place, because the perceived high chance of a justice failure and revictimization makes the personal cost not worth the risk.[67]

Rape is not the only crime with enormous personal costs. When a murderer or other serious violent offender gets away without deserved punishment, the victims' families and friends are emotionally scarred. The relatives and friends of someone lost to homicide are often referred to as "covictims," a term that acknowledges that victimization extends far beyond the person killed.[68] Anyone who has had a friend or a family member murdered will have to deal with lifelong grief, but a failure of justice adds anger, upset, and fear to that pain through the constant knowledge that the killer is free. In the United States, it is estimated that roughly 9 to 15 percent of adults are covictims of homicide and that roughly 8 to 18 percent of youths are covictims of homicide.[69] Because justice fails in more than half of such cases, around 5 percent or more of the population suffer from the knowledge that the killer of their loved one got away with murder. Worse, the covictimization rates are staggeringly higher for other crimes, such as rape or aggravated assault, where the punishment rates are extremely low, even trivial.

Just as victims may experience increased trauma due to justice failures, covictims may as well. Some victims have isolated themselves from their communities, battling debilitating depression spurred first by the murder of a loved one and again by the lack of closure because of the failure of justice. Studies reveal covictims who experience failures of justice are more likely to experience anxiety, depression, and other mental health problems, including PTSD.[70] Unsolved murders also cause enormous personal trauma to covictims beyond PTSD, including "eating and digestive problems, difficulty sleeping, frequent crying, heart palpitations and flashbacks."[71] One mother of a homicide victim explained, "I really feel if the police was doing their job, I could live. I died when my son died."[72] Youth are emotionally dam-

aged by justice failures in unique ways. Studies have shown that "teenage family members deal with suffering with an impulse to act and take action, resulting in violent behaviors driven by the desire for revenge, quest for justice and suffering relief."[73] The increased need for "retaliation" and "revenge" among young covictims prevents youth from properly processing the grief that comes from murder and failures of justice and can have long-term mental health impacts.[74]

Part of the reason that failures of justice are particularly painful to covictims is because they "often look to the criminal justice system—police, prosecutors, lawyers, and judges—for help in making sense of the murder" of their loved one.[75] In other words, they hope that the legal system can insert some reason or justice into an otherwise senseless situation. Many covictims go through a process of "meaning making" in order to make sense of murder, and the criminal justice system plays an essential role in either assisting covictims with this process or denying them the ability to properly heal and reckon with their tragedy.[76] Covictims of cold cases have reported feeling that their "loved one was not valued," increasing the existing trauma and grief.[77] A sense that the system is indifferent to justice and certainly an outright failure of justice may contribute to the "revictimization" or "secondary victimization" of covictims.[78]

Similarly, a failure of justice can also prevent surviving family members from mourning the death of their loved one and may only deepen their pain when the case is not "resolved in a manner that appeals to the co-victim's sense of justice, further complicating their emotional and psychological reactions."[79] Some covictims are simply unable to begin mourning until "the court [has] passed its final judgement," which may delay the process indefinitely for some.[80]

By contrast, when justice is delivered, it can help covictims achieve closure. A "strong correlation has been established between survivors' level of satisfaction with the disposition of the criminal case and their levels of clinical depression and anxiety."[81] As it turns out, transparency between covictims and legal authorities is the most important issue to covictims.[82] Just knowing that the legal system really is working to deliver justice can help, regardless of case disposition. Sympathy or "tears of a judge" have helped covictims heal by acknowledging their suffering.[83] If the criminal justice system helps covictims make sense of homicide and positively contributes to their "meaning making," it may be "therapeutic" and extremely beneficial for the mental health of covictims.[84] Ultimately, justice represents society's attempt to bring some balance out of the horrific moral and emotional disruption of crime, but when justice fails, those scales remain unbalanced forever, a hanging reminder of a harm never punished and a hurt never healed.

Costs to the Neighborhood

Failures of justice can also covictimize entire neighborhoods when people begin to fear that the justice system is unable or unwilling to help them. While a single failure of justice can have painful consequences for the family, a series of failures of justice can inflict deep, lasting wounds on an entire community.[85] One study of the tight-knit community of Five Points, Colorado, which saw some of the highest homicide rates and lowest clearance rates in the state between 2010 and 2017, found community-wide emo-

tional and physical responses to justice failures that inflicted terror and grief.[86] Children are especially prone to these risks, as "children exposed to the adversity and trauma of an unsolved murder when their brains are still forming can develop an ongoing stress, known as toxic stress."[87] Trauma over unresolved crimes has also manifested in a form of PTSD, impacting people's appetite, ability to sleep, mental function, and cardiac function.[88]

Minority communities are at particular risk of experiencing community-wide trauma due to failures of justice from historically ineffective policing and low clearance rates for violent crimes, and this has often resulted in widespread mistrust of police and a sense of abandonment.[89] Such trauma and disillusionment with the justice system can be passed down generationally, fostering a sense of powerlessness.[90] These feelings commonly result in decreased crime reporting within these communities, which further exacerbates failures of justice and increases community suffering.[91] (See chapter 14D for more on the negative effects of community-wide legal cynicism.)

Societal Costs: Uncaught Offenders Mean More Crime

Failures of justice commonly leave the uncaught criminal free to reoffend, thus adding to the cost of crime, which is estimated at a staggering 2.6 trillion dollars each year in America.[92] Criminals rarely escalate from nothing to murder, and most serious crimes are committed by repeat offenders who have escaped justice repeatedly in the past. If the justice system was more effective in solving and punishing crime, repeat offenders would often have their careers ended earlier, avoiding a string of later crimes. Given the enormous costs of repeat criminals to society (even excluding the costs to victims and covictims of letting offenders go free), allowing criminals to escape justice is unlikely to save societal resources on net. Doing justice ultimately more than pays for itself in the long run, especially when one considers the societal damage of justice failures to the law's moral credibility, discussed shortly.

Societal Costs: Reducing the Criminal Law's Moral Credibility with the Community Means More Crime

While the personal costs to victims, covictims, and neighborhoods adds an enormous sum to any attempt to calculate the social cost of justice failures, even more significant costs come from the effects of the criminal justice system's loss of credibility with the community generally. Communities that witness repeated failures of justice commonly lose faith in the criminal justice system, which undermines the criminal law's ability to gain compliance, deference, and assistance, and, perhaps most importantly, to get people to internalize its norms. Instead of inspiring cooperation, a criminal justice system with reduced credibility provokes resistance, subversion, and rejection. This leads to increased lawbreaking and can provoke a justice-seeking backlash in the form of vigilantism, as noted earlier, where members of the community take the law into their own hands and undertake to do justice where the system seems unwilling or unable to do it.[93] Of all the pernicious effects of failures of justice, the criminal justice system's loss of moral credibility with the community may be the most damaging because it creates a vicious cycle in which lost credibility produces more crime and less justice, which in turn reduces the system's credibility further.[94]

The Disillusionment-Noncompliance Dynamic

The disillusionment-noncompliance dynamic, in which a community loses its respect for the criminal justice system and responds with increased lawbreaking, has been repeatedly demonstrated by historical events as well as experiments in social psychology. Various historical moments illustrate the strong causal connection. For example, in the 1920s, the American public's trust in the law plummeted during the Prohibition era. As citizens sought alcohol illegally, experienced little or unjust enforcement of the law, and witnessed government officials and many of their fellow citizens partaking in the illegal distribution of alcohol, laws far beyond the scope of the Eighteenth Amendment lost their credibility and individuals committed an increasing number of crimes unrelated to alcohol.[95]

Various social psychologists have also undertaken controlled experiments that demonstrate the existence of the disillusionment-noncompliance dynamic. Numerous studies have found that even a small increase in one's trust in the legal system results in a large increase in the likelihood that one will believe that deference to the law is a good thing. Perhaps more importantly in our context, studies shows that even small decreases in the system's credibility with the community produce predictable reductions in compliance. Chapter 3 reviews these studies in some detail.

Every failure of justice chips away at the criminal justice system's credibility and erodes the public's willingness to comply. To prevent the massive costs of increased crime, a society ought to place great importance on those measures that will avoid failures of justice and thereby improve the system's credibility with the community.

Sparking Vigilantism

One final cost of failures of justice is vigilantism. It was the legal system's perceived lack of ability or willingness to deliver justice that led Elie Nesler to shoot her son's abuser and Fred Ortiz to be killed by the friends of his victim, in the previous case examples. In addition to this classic form of vigilantism, in which the citizen takes the law into their own hands to impose deserved punishment, there exists another form that has been called "shadow vigilantism," in which people disillusioned by failures of justice do not openly punish the unpunished offender themselves but rather subvert and manipulate the criminal justice system to bring about the justice they think is deserved.[96] Shadow vigilantism can take a number of forms. One example is "testilying," where police officers lie or shade the truth during in-court testimony to ensure that incriminating evidence is not excluded on what the officers consider to be a mere technicality.[97] Prosecutors can perform shadow vigilantism through overcharging and judges through abuses of their discretion in sentencing. But shadow vigilantism is not limited to institutional players in the criminal justice system. Ordinary citizens can engage in shadow vigilantism in the jury room by ignoring their legal instructions and substituting their own notions of justice, on the streets through witness intimidation, and at the ballot box by voting for laws that impose unjust draconian punishments that people would never support

if the system was perceived as already doing justice.[98]

The special danger of shadow vigilantism comes partly from the fact that it is impossible to fully measure or quantify. Because shadow vigilantism is generally unseen, it can introduce arbitrariness and disparities among similar cases that are difficult to detect, let alone prevent or deter.[99] Even if an individual instance of shadow vigilantism seems morally justified, it contributes to undermining the criminal justice system's moral credibility. When shadow vigilantism is at work, it is necessarily inconsistent in where and whether it is applied, and the system naturally will be seen as more inconsistent and unpredictable. As noted earlier, that increased arbitrariness will undermine the criminal justice system's credibility, which will in turn undermine compliance and internalization of its norms, which in turn will increase the motivation for further shadow vigilantism.[100]

All these issues surrounding the system's loss of credibility are discussed further in chapter 3.

Racial and Economic Disparate Effects of Justice Failures

One final factor that makes the societal cost of justice failures all the more tragic and unjust is its disparately large impact on racial minorities and the economically disadvantaged. This disparate impact plays out in several ways.

First, the violent crime rate is disproportionately higher in poor neighborhoods,[101] and the people who live in those areas are often racial minorities. Thus, the criminogenic effect of lost credibility from justice failures is highest in these neighborhoods and disproportionately suffered by minorities. For example, several studies, including one by the Department of Justice, found that from 2008 through 2012, Americans living in households at or below the Federal Poverty Level (less than $15,000 for a couple) had more than double the rate of violent victimization as persons in higher-income households ($75,000 or more).[102] In 2020, one-third of violent crimes reported to police had a Black victim—almost 20 percentage points higher than the Black share of the population.[103] This means that even if police have the same clearance rates and prosecutors have the same conviction rates for crimes in poor and minority neighborhoods as they do in wealthier neighborhoods, poor and minority communities would experience dramatically more failures of justice simply by virtue of the fact that more crime is happening in their neighborhoods.

But the reality is much worse. Crime clearance rates are significantly lower in poorer areas with high racial minority populations than they are in White middle-income and high-income areas.[104] The recent decline in nation-wide murder clearance rates noted previously in this chapter is almost entirely due to failures to solve the killings of Black victims.[105] The recent murder surge has also mainly been driven by Black victims, with the murder rate for White victims increasing by 0.4 per 100,000 between the 2018–2019 and 2020–2021 periods while the rate for Black victims increased by 9.7 per 100,000—twenty-five times more than for White victims.[106] In 2022, over 54 percent of homicide victims were Black.[107] The situation is even worse in urban areas. A *Washington Post* investigation of murder trends in several large cities found that "Black people made up more than 80 percent of the total homicide victims [in those cities] in 2020

and 2021,"[108] and most of these murders have gone unsolved. And the racial disparity in solving homicides is not new. One analysis of fifty-two of the United States's largest cities found that police arrested someone in 63 percent of homicides that killed White victims, compared with just 47 percent of homicides of Black victims, a 16-percentage-point difference in clearance rates.[109] Data from Chicago indicates that homicide cases involving a White victim are solved 47 percent of the time, cases involving a Hispanic victim are solved 33 percent of the time, and cases involving a Black victim have a clearance rate of a mere 22 percent.[110] There are several factors that likely contribute to these disparities (such as the type of killing, with street shootings being especially hard to solve),[111] but regardless of the causes, the effect is clear: poor neighborhoods and minority communities suffer failures of justice at highly disproportionate rates to their share of the population.[112]

Finally, the problem of justice failures is exacerbated by the fact that poorer communities tend to be less equipped with resources to help people in coping with and recovering from the cost of justice failures. Underfunded schools serving low-income children are far less likely to have adequate counseling available for children dealing with trauma,[113] and healthcare facilities typically cannot provide the individualized level of care that victims receive in wealthier neighborhoods.[114] Families with lower incomes are also less likely to have health insurance,[115] adding yet another barrier to providing victims of crime and justice failures with needed care and treatment. So not only are the poor more likely to experience failures of justice, the mental and emotional harms that result from such failures are likely to be greatest for poorer communities. For anyone who takes racial and economic justice seriously and wishes to close unjust disparities, tackling failures of justice is essential. Too often the same advocates who protest against police violence and decry the injustices caused by systemic racism in the legal system are nowhere to be found on the issue of solving and punishing crime.

F. SYSTEMIC INDIFFERENCE TO JUSTICE FAILURES

Despite the prevalence and costs of justice failures, America's criminal justice system often seems largely indifferent to them.[116] While the rest of this book examines this problem in terms of the wider policies of the justice system, this indifference is often best seen in individual judicial decisions. Next are seven examples of the kinds of trivial or nonsensical procedural reasons, or simply appalling judgment, that lead judges to show a tragic indifference to the importance of doing justice by letting offenders escape the punishment they deserve.

Case Examples
- *Jean Packwood.* In 1979, San Francisco bank robber Jean Packwood shoots Janette Pimentel execution style.[117] Packwood enters a plea deal in 1980 where he confesses to multiple robberies and receives immunity in the Pimentel murder case so long as he fully and truthfully cooperates with investigators. During this cooperation, Packwood tells investigators he refused to help his fellow robber, Donald Desbiens, murder Pimentel. Later on, however, he confesses that he did in fact help in the murder. Because he lied to investigators, Packwood is charged with

murder. Yet a California judge decides Packwood did not violate the plea agreement because even though he obviously misled investigators and is guilty of murder, it is theoretically possible that, as Packwood claims, he refused to help with the murder the first time he was asked—thus his statement to investigators was technically true—even though he did agree to kill Pimentel upon a second request. Packwood is never punished for the murder.
- *Gary Ault.* On December 27, 1984, Gary Ault breaks into a home in Arizona and makes his way into a six-year-old girl's bedroom.[118] He unzips her pajamas and begins molesting her until she wakes up screaming. He flees into the rainy night, leaving muddy footprints behind. The victim identifies Ault in a photo lineup, and police knock on his front door to request Ault go to the station for questioning. Ault agrees but goes to his bedroom to grab some clothes, followed by the police officers. The officers notice muddy tennis shoes and seize them. The shoes match the crime scene footprints perfectly, and Ault is convicted at trial. An appeals court overturns Ault's conviction, claiming the police should not have followed Ault into his bedroom without a warrant. The court declines to apply the inevitable discovery doctrine because Ault's roommate would have had time to destroy the shoes if the police had spent time getting a warrant.
- *Julius Wideman.* In 1971, Julius Wideman savagely beats James Allen before shooting him to death on a Philadelphia street.[119] Police bring Wideman to the station for questioning, where he receives his Miranda warnings twice and denies involvement in the murder. After

taking a nap and undergoing a polygraph test, however, Wideman confesses that he did murder Allen. Wideman is convicted but appeals on the basis that his confession should have been excluded because when he confessed it had been several hours since he was last read his Miranda rights. An appeals court agrees, suppresses the confession as evidence, and overturns Wideman's conviction.

- *Trido Rogers.* On August 29, 2003, Trido Rogers and two other men beat Derrick Floyd in the head before leaving him on a street in Columbus, Ohio, to die of severe brain damage. A tip leads police to request a warrant to search Rogers's apartment, and the judge grants the warrant.[120] During the warrant search, they find pants with Floyd's spattered blood and charge Rogers with murder. At trial, a judge excludes the pants because he disagrees with the judge who issued the warrant about whether there was probable cause. Without the pants as evidence, Trido Rogers and his accomplices are acquitted of murder. Floyd's mother screams "they still killed my son."[121]
- *Stacey Rambold.* In 2007, forty-nine-year-old high school teacher Stacey Rambold rapes his fourteen-year-old student, Cherice Moralez, in Billings, Montana.[122] Moralez initially stays silent but eventually reports the crime to her mother and the police. She is viciously bullied in school after the rape becomes known and commits suicide. A judge sentences Rambold to fifteen years in prison but suspends all but thirty days of the sentence. He justifies the leniency by claiming the fourteen-year-old girl was "as much in control of

the situation"[123] as her forty-nine-year-old teacher and "older than her chronological age."[124] Besides, the crime against the now-dead girl "wasn't this forcible beat-up rape."[125]
- *Timothy Becktel.* On February 25, 2009, Timothy Becktel attempts to murder an acquaintance, Stephen Kozmiuk, with a large, serrated kitchen knife after an alcohol-fueled quarrel.[126] He severely injures Kozmiuk and leaves him for dead, but his victim survives. Becktel is convicted and sentenced to up to forty years in prison for attempted murder. A Michigan appeals court agrees Becktel is guilty but overturns his conviction because the trial judge forgot to administer a second oath to the selected jury after administering a first oath to all prospective jurors.
- *Joyce Garrett.* On the evening of September 22, 1977, at a trailer park in Carizzo Springs, Texas, Joyce Garrett tracks down and attempts to shoot the man who shot her dog.[127] She misses and kills a woman in a nearby trailer. Garrett is charged with murder under the common law theory of transferred intent, which uses the defendant's intention to kill a person as adequate to satisfy the intention required for murder when a different person is killed. The jury convicts Garrett of murder. She appeals, claiming that the legal charging document did not explicitly mention the doctrine of transferred intent so the prosecutor should have had to prove that she intended to kill the person who died. An appeals court agrees and overturns her conviction and bars a retrial. Garrett is never punished.

The frustrating tragedy of the previous examples is that they are not exceptional.[128] They are routine symptoms of a legal system that is systemically indifferent to whether justice is actually done.

G. A NEW LOOK AT THE COMPETING INTERESTS AND IMAGINING REFORMS

If failures of justice are so harmful to so many people, why do so many justice-frustrating mechanisms exist? It would be easy to assume from the seeming indifference of the legal system to doing justice that their existence reflects the system's arbitrariness or corruption, but justice-frustrating rules and practices are rarely without some core of merit. They commonly protect or promote some legitimate, even important, interest. The goal of this book is not to reject a rule or practice simply because it frustrates justice but rather to revisit each with an appreciation of the personal and societal costs of the justice failures and to ask these two questions:

1. *In weighing the societal costs from the justice-frustrating rule or practice against the benefits it provides, is it still justified?*

2. *If so, is there a non-justice-frustrating or a less-justice-frustrating way of protecting the interests at stake?*

In other words, the purpose of this project is not to convince readers that every justice-frustrating rule should be abolished but rather to help people think more clearly about the balance that ought to be struck in keeping or reforming the current rules. What is unacceptable is tolerating justice-frustrating rules simply because no one has seriously thought about the costs they inflict or the balance of interests they reflect.

The chapters that follow describe reforms that have been suggested by others, some of which have been implemented in some jurisdictions. The chapters also brainstorm about other possible reforms that would avoid or reduce justice failures. And for each justice-frustrating cause, the chapters recommend one particular reform proposal that we believe is the most important and feasible for policymakers to consider. It is our hope that this volume will illustrate why justice fails, illuminate what interests are at stake, and inspire reforms that can make our justice system more truly just.

Part I

CRIMINAL LIABILITY RULES

CHAPTER 2

Legal Bars to Prosecution

THE MOST INTENTIONAL SOURCES OF justice failures in the criminal justice system are the formal legal defenses that bar prosecution of even obviously guilty serious offenders. These "non-exculpatory defenses," as they have been called,[1] are examples of the law attempting to promote other societal interests at the expense of justice, but some of these rules may be outdated or frustrate justice to an unnecessary degree. This chapter examines the most significant of these legal bars: statutes of limitation, the double jeopardy rule, diplomatic immunity, and defenses based upon the legality principle, in particular the rule of strict construction.

A. STATUTES OF LIMITATION
Statutes of limitation specify the length of time during which a crime may be prosecuted and after which it may not, regardless of even conclusive evidence of guilt. American statutes of limitation originated from early English practice. Centuries ago, physical evidence could not be preserved in a reliable manner, and old cases were difficult to defend or prosecute because of the fading memories and unavailability of witnesses, justifying the need for statutes of limitation. Interestingly, murder has never had a statute of limitation due to its seriousness, which suggests statutes of limitation were always an attempt to balance justice against other interests.

The practical situation has changed with time. Fairer trial procedures now make it much easier for defendants to discredit old evidence or witness statements that may have become unreliable over time. Additionally, advances in forensic science, such as the advent of DNA analysis, make it possible to show guilt with high certainty even in old cases. Thus, the original justifications for statutes of limitation may no longer apply. Many people now argue that statutes of limitation for serious crimes have outlasted their usefulness, and the decision to prosecute should be made solely on the quality of the evidence instead of on how much time has elapsed since the crime.[2] Why should the perpetrator of a rape or a debilitating aggravated assault go free simply because he has escaped detection and capture for five years while a similar offender goes to prison for committing the same offense four years ago? Why should eluding investigators for a fixed period entitle an offender to walk free for his crime? With an increasing number of crimes being solved after statutes of limitation expire due to the advent of modern technologies and more organized police forces, the societal costs of such statutes are rising, making a reconsideration of the balance of interests essential.

Case Example: Donna Palomba
On September 11, 1993, thirty-six-year-old Donna Palomba puts her two

young children to bed and goes to sleep in her house in Waterbury, Connecticut. Her husband is away on a trip. Around 1:00 am, a masked man breaks into her house and binds her with her own stockings before brutally raping her. After he leaves, Palomba calls the police and goes to the hospital for a forensic examination. The investigation goes nowhere. Finally, in 2004, police arrest John Regan, a former friend of Palomba's husband, for attacking one of his female employees. Regan's DNA matches that of Palomba's rapist, and, in fact, he proves to be a serial rapist. But Connecticut's statute of limitation for rape is five years, so Regan is never punished for raping Donna Palomba.[3]

Case Example: Lori Kustudick

On March 16, 1978, sixteen-year-old Lori Kustudick is dropped off by her mother at a dance club in Glenview, Illinois.[4] Kustudick plans to meet some of her friends there for a St Patrick's Day Eve party, but her friends never show up. Around 10:30 p.m., a kindly looking man offers her a ride home in his friend's car. The two men look unthreatening, and she accepts. Instead of taking her home, the man savagely attacks and rapes Lori in the backseat while his friend drives around aimlessly. When they stop the car at a gas station, the girl manages to escape, but she is so traumatized she can only tell the most basic details to a police officer who finds her. Police quickly discover that Herbert Howard was the man who offered her a ride home as the club doorman remembers checking his ID and seeing him leaving with Kustudick. When the victim is asked to identify him, however, she is so traumatized that her memory blanks and she flees the room. Prosecutors are obliged to drop the case.

In 1993, after much therapy, Kustudick has recovered from much of her trauma and is now able to testify about the attack. Police show her a photo lineup that includes their prime suspect at the time, and she immediately identifies Herbert Howard. But the five-year statute of limitation for rape has run, so her rapist escapes justice.

Competing Interests

One can identify valid interests in support of retaining statutes of limitation and interests in support of abolishing or lengthening them.

INTERESTS SUPPORTING KEEPING STATUTES OF LIMITATION

- *Efficiency.* Statutes of limitation increase efficiency by making the justice system focus on recent crimes instead of working on older cases. There are limited investigative resources, so it makes sense to focus on more recent cases that are likely easier to solve. Statutes of limitation also encourage victims to report crimes earlier rather than later and force prosecutors to act in a timely fashion.
- *Reducing False Charges and Convictions.* Statutes of limitation can reduce charges and convictions based on false or misremembered claims about occurrences long ago. Memories become less reliable as time passes. Moreover, crucial witnesses may not be available after long periods of time. Statutes of limitation can also prevent malicious harassment in the form of false accusations leading to charges for long-ago supposed crimes.
- *Finality and Repose.* Statutes of limitation provide finality and repose for those who have committed crimes or fear that they may be charged with a crime. On the other hand, the societal interest in finality decreases as the se-

riousness of the crime increases, and it is likely only an important societal interest in more minor cases. While it may be in the interest of society for citizens not to worry about loitering twenty years ago, it is likely not in the interest of society for a citizen not to worry about raping someone twenty years ago.

- *Rehabilitation.* Some argue that after a long enough time, the offender may have been rehabilitated, reformed, or incapacitated so as to pose no future threat. As the years pass, the offender may become a different person. Punishing long-past wrongdoing in such cases may not serve larger societal interests and might sabotage the offender's chances to reintegrate into society. However, this argument is valid only to the extent that one discounts the societal value of doing justice. (More on this in the next chapter.) Perhaps most problematic for this interest is the fact that nothing in statutes of limitation inquire into whether the offender has been rehabilitated or not. An offender who has been committing a serious offense every six months will still escape conviction for older offenses under such statutes.

INTERESTS SUPPORTING ABOLISHING OR LENGTHENING STATUTES OF LIMITATION

- *Justice.* Statutes of limitation prevent even clearly guilty criminals from being punished for even serious offenses. The blameworthiness of an offender and the seriousness of a crime do not decay over time, so it makes little sense that a criminal should escape deserved punishment simply because he was lucky enough to be caught only after an arbitrary amount of time. The importance of doing justice is such that no statute of limitation exists for murder, so why should it thwart justice for rape, aggravated assault, or other serious crimes?

- *New and Reliable Forms of Evidence in Old Cases.* The development of new forms of evidence conclusively proving guilt in long-past crimes, such as DNA,[5] and better storage of old evidence means statutes of limitation are blocking vastly more easily prosecutable cases today than when they were first introduced. Perhaps statutes of limitation struck an appropriate balance of interests in the past, but circumstances have fundamentally changed. Other legal rules have been changed to reflect advances in science,[6] and updating statutes of limitation may be another example of legal changes called for by scientific advances.

- *Public Trust in the Justice System.* The public is outraged when the justice system is unable to accomplish its primary role of delivering justice because of an arbitrary deadline. For example, when rapists escape due to statutes of limitation, victims and the public are likely to lose faith in the justice system, with a resulting drop in the criminal law's ability to gain compliance and internalization of its norms. (See chapter 3.)

- *Protecting Society from Criminals.* Statutes of limitation allow dangerous criminals to walk free, at times to commit more crimes. Prosecuting such offenders would better protect society by incapacitating known, dangerous offenders and removing them from the community. Some statutes of limitation also endanger society by encouraging certain types of crime, like child sex abuse, which are unlikely to be reported within the existing limitation period.

The Nature and Extent of the Problem

Statutes of limitation differ as to their length and exceptions, but all frustrate justice to some degree.

DIVERSITY IN STATUTES OF LIMITATION
There is significant diversity in how states formulate their statutes of limitation, perhaps reflecting the lack of a clear justification for them. Seven states have dropped a statute of limitation for all felonies (Kentucky, Maryland, North Carolina, South Carolina, Virginia, West Virginia, and Wyoming),[7] and nineteen states have no statute of limitation for any form of homicide (manslaughter remains statutorily limited in all other states).[8] Thirteen states have a statute of limitation of ten years or less for their most serious sex crime, eight states (and DC) have a limitation between eleven and twenty years, twenty-two have a limitation of twenty-one years or more, and seven states have abolished statutes of limitation for all felony sex crimes.[9] Some states, like Arkansas, have abolished statutes of limitation for specific crimes such as rape or sexual assaults against a minor while retaining them for most other serious crimes.[10] Statutes of limitation also vary based on whether or not the victim reported the crime promptly.[11] At the federal level, statutes of limitation do not exist for crimes that can carry the death penalty, terrorism, or sex offenses. The majority of other federal crimes have a five-year statute of limitation.[12]

EXCEPTIONS TO LIMITATION PERIOD   In addition to diversity in the length of statutes of limitation, states also vary by whether they allow exceptions. So far, twenty-eight states have adopted a variety of exceptions to statutes of limitation.[13] These include an exception suspending the statute of limitation for crimes where DNA evidence is discovered,[14] a crimes against minors exception abolishing the time limit or granting additional time to report, a confession exception allowing a confession to obviate the statute of

limitation,[15] and a special rule for crimes like fraud that starts the time limit clock only after discovery of the offense.[16] The ways these exceptions are implemented also vary by state. For example, in Indiana the statute of limitation is only extended to one year after the state first discovers DNA evidence sufficient to charge the perpetrator.[17] In Connecticut, if the crime has been reported within five years and the defendant is identified by DNA evidence, then there is no time bar.[18]

In the vast majority of states, if the offender leaves the state, the statutes of limitation are tolled (suspended) until the offender returns.[19] Similarly, certain states suspend or change the statute of limitation when the defendant is "actively concealing himself or evidence of the crime."[20] For example, in Tennessee, the law states that "no period during which the party charged conceals the fact of the crime, or during which the party charged was not usually and publicly resident within the state, is included in the period of limitation."[21]

Many states retain restrictive statutes of limitation for at least some crimes, often with little rhyme or reason. Maine has no statute of limitation for sexual abuse of a minor under the age of sixteen but retains a statute of limitation of just three to six years (depending on the felony class) for sexual abuse of a minor aged sixteen or older.[22] Colorado has no statute of limitation for forgery but maintains a statute of limitation for vehicular homicide of three to five years.[23] Short time periods for sex crimes are particularly frustrating due to the nation-wide backlogs in rape kit testing that may lead to a suspect being identified only after the statute of limitation has run.[24] Even in states with relatively long statutes, such as Ohio, where the time limit for rape is twenty-five years,[25] prosecutions are still regularly foiled by statutes of limitation. The Sexual Assault Kit (SAK) testing initiative in Ohio, which ended in 2018, revealed a total of sixty-one sexual assault cases with DNA matches that could not be pursued due to the statute of limitation.[26]

OLD LAWS IN SEARCH OF A JUSTIFICATION
With the increasing use of DNA evidence and other forensic advances, the number of known guilty offenders who walk free due to statutes of limitation will only increase. Rapists—especially child predators—are particularly likely to benefit from retaining tight statutes of limitation. While estimating the number of justice failures caused by statutes of limitation is difficult, it is probably in the thousands or tens of thousands, with many more victims discouraged from even reporting in the first place. Simply extending the time limit for some crimes may not be enough. For example, one-third of victims of childhood sexual abuse come forward much later in life (the median age being fifty-two), long after the statute of limitation has expired even in states that have extended their limitation period for crimes against minors.[27]

The fact that there is such diversity among state statutes of limitation suggests that the justifications for such statutes are less than clear. As noted earlier, the assumption that delay increases the chance of wrongful conviction no longer stands. Under modern trial and evidence rules, the passage of time makes delayed prosecution harder for prosecutors, not defense counsel, because the prosecutor has the burden of proving the offense beyond a reasonable doubt. The justification that the passage of time may have resulted in the offender's reform or rehabilitation is simply inconsistent with existing statutes of limitation, which apply to the recidivist and the rehabilitated equally. The offender who has been committing the same offense regularly during the limitation period will still escape justice. This justification is also inconsistent with the fact that some states have extremely short limitation periods during which a serious offender is unlikely to have reformed.

The only justification that seems to have any continuing traction is the very general sense that society should not be obsessed with minor wrongs in the past, wrongs that even the victims are no longer concerned with. But that rationale would seem to support a statute of limitation for only lesser offenses. Because the justifications for statutes of limitation appear so lacking or limited, it is no surprise that state laws vary so widely in attempting to implement these uncertain justifications. In truth, most existing state statutes of limitation simply reflect the persistence of an old law that would never be enacted today.

Public Complaints

Because so many failures of justice caused by statutes of limitation involve sexual assault cases, public complaints have commonly focused on calls to reform or abolish time limits that make it easier for rapists to escape justice. As society moves to take sexual assault more seriously and new forms of evidence become more common, there has been increasing public support for ending or extending statutes of limitation for sexual assault, often driven by victim complaints that such statutes are an unjustifiable relic of the past. Statutes of limitation on child sex abuse have provoked particular frustration. As one sexual abuse survivor and advocate put it: "It is undeniable that statutes of limitation do nothing to protect children and show no respect for survivors."[28] Many in the public feel that statutes of limitation devalue survivors who must bear the costs of abuse their entire lives while their perpetrators receive a free pass from society after an arbitrary amount of time.

Calling for the reform of statutes of limitation is almost universal among sexual assault survivor advocacy groups and has gained some bipartisan support at both state and federal levels. Public complaints about statutes of limitation are almost entirely on the side calling for reform, with the opposition mainly coming from political inertia rather than any counter-advocacy or public opinion. This inertia has angered many victims. "We're not going to take this anymore. Sexual assault is as important as murder. And we're going to find out who you are and we're going to come after you," said William Dinkel, a child sexual abuse survivor and advocate for reforming statutes of limitation.[29]

High-profile cases of justice failures caused by statutes of limitation have also sparked public ire and motivated change. Serial abusers and rapists such as Harvey Weinstein[30] and Bill Cosby[31] largely escaped accountability for many of their crimes due to statutes of limitation on sexual assault that left prosecutors with only one or no cases to pursue against men who had attacked dozens of women.

Victims are sometimes successful at turning their complaints into reform. For example, Donna Palomba, the Connecticut woman denied justice in the earlier case example, launched a lobbying campaign to change Connecticut's law in 2007, leading the state to create a DNA exception to its statute of limitation.[32] This sort of victim advocacy has also led to other reforms in states such as Indiana and Florida.[33]

Reforms

There have been several implemented or proposed reforms to statutes of limitation that strike a balance between the competing interests in a less-justice-frustrating way.

Eliminating or Extending Statutes of Limitation for Serious Crimes. As the tide of public opinion and advocacy slowly advances, more states are abolishing or extending their statutes of limitation for rape and child sexual assault. For example, in 2019, Illinois enacted a law eliminating the statute of limitation for rape.[34] And "since 2002, at least 29 states have amended their prosecution deadlines so victims of child sexual abuse have more time to pursue criminal cases as adults—including 15 states that now have no cutoff for prosecuting any felony sexual assault of a minor."[35] In October 2021, a bipartisan bill was introduced in the US Senate to incentivize states to abolish their statutes of limitation for child sex abuse, but it did not pass.[36] Ten states have also abolished the statute of limitation for all felony sex crimes. Other states are likely to follow.

Something important to note about changes to statutes of limitation is that they do not apply retroactively to crimes whose time limit has already passed, but they can apply to crimes that at the time of the reform are still prosecutable under the old statute of limitation. This makes reforming statutes of limitation an urgent issue as every year that passes puts more cases permanently beyond the reach of justice.

Use of John Doe Warrants. Even in states with strict statutes of limitation, policies have been put in place by some local officials to reduce the practical effect of the statute of limitation.[37] Because the statute of limitation clock is stopped when an arrest warrant is issued even if the arrest is made later, police can obtain warrants for unknown suspects based solely on their DNA to keep a case open beyond the statute of limitation. Such a John Doe warrant is "an arrest warrant issued for a suspect who is identified only by genetic information. In lieu of the suspect's name, the warrant will be filed against 'John Doe' and will cite only the DNA profile."[38] This has the effect of stopping the statute of limitation clock. "Once an individual is matched to the DNA profile, the suspect may be apprehended and charged with the crime at any time."[39] This is an ingenious way for investigators to circumvent statutes of limitation, and the process has been upheld in various courts, but it only works in cases where DNA evidence is discovered within the statute of limitation period. At least ten states have used John Doe warrants in cases where DNA evidence is available.[40]

Recommendation: Abolish Limitation Periods for Serious Felonies and for Others Restart the Clock Upon Any New Felony

In reforming statutes of limitation, we think it is best to aim to honor both sets of competing interests through clear new rules as opposed to creating workarounds or narrow exceptions that paper over the archaic nature of many such statutes. We recommend a two-part reform that would see statutes of limitation abolished for serious crimes while preserving the statutes of limitation for lesser crimes. However, even where the statute of limitation is kept, its time clock would restart at any point that the offender commits a new felony—or at least a violent, sexual,

or similar felony, depending on the legislature's decision—during the limitation period, thus making clear that the passage of time has not brought rehabilitation (one of the underlying justifications offered in support of statutes of limitation).

The first part of the reform is warranted because some crimes are sufficiently serious that it is always in the interests of society to pursue their prosecution, no matter how much time has passed. Historically, this was the reason murder was never statutorily limited despite concerns about deteriorated evidence. Given the vast improvements in evidence and trial procedures, it makes sense to expand the list of serious crimes exempt from statutes of limitation. The exact crimes included on such a list may vary, but it should at least include all forms of murder, attempted murder, kidnapping, forcible rape, and child sex abuse. Indeed, the limitation period might well be abolished for all felonies, or at least all violent felonies. Such a reform would avoid the kind of justice failures seen in the cases of Donna Palomba and Lori Kustudick discussed earlier.

Such a reform is by no means unprecedented as some states have already abolished statutes of limitation for all felonies, while others have already abolished them for select serious crimes such as kidnapping and forcible rape, and as mentioned earlier, ten states have abolished statutes of limitation for all felony sex crimes.[41] Internationally, the European Union has also abolished statutes of limitation on the most serious criminal offenses including murder and rape.[42]

The second part of our proposed reform seeks to honor those societal interests of finality, efficiency, and recognizing the possible rehabilitation of some past offenders by keeping limitation periods for lesser crimes but allowing the time limit to restart if the offender commits a new felony.

The new felony provision would be triggered by prosecutors proving that the offender committed a new felony during the limitation period of the original offense. For example, if an offender commits third-degree sexual assault that has a statute of limitation of five years, then during that five-year period commits another felony, the limitation clock on the original offense would restart from the date of the new felony, giving prosecutors five years from that time to prosecute the original third-degree sexual assault. It seems clear that an offender who commits a new felony is not rehabilitated. This clock-restarting mechanism is similar in some respects to existing provisions that allow postoffense conduct to alter the running of the limitation clock, such as when the clock is tolled while the offender is out of state.

Such a provision would allow for the chaining of prosecution periods to punish serial offenders such as Harvey Weinstein or Bill Cosby. However, such a provision would not threaten any offender who had indeed been rehabilitated by remaining felony free during the limitation period. The reform would also have the useful effect of discouraging uncaught offenders from committing an additional offense that would extend their period of exposure to prosecution for their past offense.

B. DOUBLE JEOPARDY

Double jeopardy is a legal rule that protects a person from being tried twice for the same crime.[43] The doctrine was a component of Roman law, became a cornerstone of English common law, and is enshrined in the Fifth Amendment to the US Constitution, which provides that no person shall "be subject for the same offense to be twice put in jeopardy of life or limb."[44] Notably, while the Fifth Amendment bars the same sovereign from prosecuting a defendant acquitted of the crime,[45] it does not prevent both the state and federal governments from prosecuting a person independently for the same criminal conduct if it violates both state and federal law.[46] Unlike in the United Kingdom and some Commonwealth countries, the American rule of double jeopardy has been interpreted to mean that there is no compelling new evidence exception, and so once a criminal is acquitted, no number of smoking guns or bragging confessions can bring a murderer to justice. The double jeopardy rule in the United States has also been interpreted to mean that jury acquittals are not subject to appeal, even if a legal error has been made by the trial judge during the proceedings and that error caused the wrongful acquittal.[47]

When first formulated in the Roman Empire, and even later when adopted in the US Constitution, double jeopardy was a cutting-edge legal innovation created during periods when the justice system was often the domain of vindictive rulers more concerned with punishing the individual than the crime. And the rule rarely caused justice failures because the lack of professional and systematic investigative police forces meant that the chance of turning up new evidence years after the commission of a crime was negligible. There were no police bureaus to keep cases open and no effective ways to store evidence or keep track of suspects and witnesses. A second prosecution for the same crime would almost certainly have been an attempt to obtain a different verdict on the same evidence. Such an attempt would likely be an individual official trying to override the decision of a jury they disagreed with, and so double jeopardy was a way to uphold the power of juries and protect individuals from powerful vindictive governmental actors. While changes in the legal system professionalizing most investigative and prosecutorial decisions have made the concerns behind double jeopardy less relevant, it still serves to signify the power of the jury and to shield defendants against potential government harassment.

But the double jeopardy rule has become more justice frustrating due to the increasing likelihood of finding new reliable evidence in old cases, making it appropriate to revisit the rule.[48] As noted in the previous section on statutes of limitation, DNA has allowed for even decades-old cold cases to be solved. DNA analysis is not the only innovation raising the costs of double jeopardy. Something as simple as a photograph or video establishing guilt might be discovered today. The ever-increasing interconnectedness of police forces, the proliferation of new long-lasting evidence, and the ability of police to store evidence and keep cases open for decades means wrongful acquittals are far easier to identify and prove than in the past. As a result, it seems likely that the number of cases where *known* offenders are escaping justice because of double jeopardy is rising. Victims and their families often ask what form of justice is served when conclusive evidence arises linking an acquitted murderer or rapist to their crimes, and the justice system stands by, incapable of delivering justice or protecting society.[49]

Case Example: Melvin Ignatow

On September 24, 1988, fifty-year-old Melvin Ignatow is angry because his fiancé, thirty-six-year-old Brenda Schaef-

fer, has broken off their relationship.[50] Schaeffer does not feel safe around Ignatow, but he is able to lure her into a last meeting in Louisville, Kentucky. Ignatow enlists the help of a previous girlfriend, Maryanne Shore, to teach Schaeffer a lesson. Ignatow tells Shore that Schaeffer was "frigid" during their relationship. He wants to use Shore's house to administer some "sex therapy" to his former fiancé. Schaeffer is brutally raped by Ignatow while Shore takes pictures. When the torture session is over, Ignatow kills Schaeffer and buries her body in Shore's backyard. The police investigation quickly centers on the two, and Shore agrees to testify against Ignatow in exchange for being charged with only evidence tampering. Ignatow's defense fabricates a claim that Shore is a bitter ex-girlfriend who murdered Schaeffer by herself to get revenge on the younger woman for stealing her boyfriend. The jury is taken in by the defense's lies and acquits Ignatow. Months later, the photographs of the rape and torture are discovered in a heating duct by the new owners of Ignatow's house, conclusively proving his guilt for the crime. Double jeopardy nevertheless shields him from being retried for the brutal rape and murder.

Case Example: Michael Lane

On February 10, 1991, Jennifer Watts leaves her two-year-old son, PJ, in the care of her boyfriend, twenty-seven-year-old Michael Lane, while she goes to church in Salt Lake City.[51] Despite promising to take good care of PJ, Lane becomes furious when the child's crying prevents him from sleeping. Exasperated, Lane grabs the little boy and smashes him into the floor repeatedly until the noise stops. Watts comes home to find her dead son in his crib, while her boyfriend is asleep in another room. All evidence points to Lane, but Watts stands by him at trial, and her emotional testimony persuades the jury to acquit. By 2005, Lane has become religious and is troubled by his memories of his crime. He goes to the police and confesses everything, saying he is willing to go to jail that very day. However, due to double jeopardy, Lane cannot be tried again.

Competing Interests

There are a variety of legitimate interests that ought to be considered when deciding how the constitutional double jeopardy protection should be interpreted.

INTERESTS SUPPORTING THE CURRENT INTERPRETATION OF DOUBLE JEOPARDY

- *Finality.* The concept of finality in the legal system means that a criminal case should have a clear conclusion, at which point no further action can be taken on it. Finality prevents government harassment in the form of continual new trials for the same offense and reduces the chance of government officials weaponizing the legal system against their enemies through reviving an old case for a new trial. It also upholds the preeminence of jury trial by making a single jury the definitive and final decider of guilt. Finality also encourages prosecutors to direct their attention to more current cases instead of constantly reevaluating whether to revive old cases for

Figure 2.1. Michael Lane went to the authorities and admitted to killing young PJ, 1991. Photo by Salt Lake City Police Department, from Pat Reavy, "Acquitted Man Says He's Guilty: Utahn Cites Conscience in Admitting He Killed S.L. Toddler in 1991," Deseret News, January 19, 2006, https://www.deseret.com/2006/1/19/19933580/acquitted-man-says-he-s-guilty. Courtesy CNN.

another trial. (Recall that statutes of limitation also relied in part upon a finality rationale.)

- *Efficiency.* Finality promotes efficiency as well. When the government knows it only has one chance at prosecution, it is unlikely to prosecute a case too quickly before conducting a full and thorough investigation. This encourages the government to hire qualified investigators and competent prosecutors and to build strong cases before proceeding to trial. If double jeopardy did not exist, prosecutions might become less efficient as more unripe cases would be rushed to trial with the knowledge that any case ending in a false acquittal could always be retried with more effort. The "one strike and you're out" rule of prosecution forces the government to be efficient at when and how it brings cases to trial.

- *Justice and Fairness.* Double jeopardy ensures that the prosecution does not wield an unfair leverage over the defendant through jury shopping and continual strategy refinement. Otherwise, prosecutors could keep trying a case in hopes of finding the right combination of jury and arguments necessary to secure conviction. If the prosecution was allowed to jury shop, this would almost certainly lead to more innocent people being wrongfully convicted as all it would take is a prosecutor mistakenly convinced of a defendant's guilt to keep trying a case until a successful conviction is secured. More probably, such a determined prosecutor could get an innocent defendant to agree to a plea bargain simply to end the continual trials.

INTERESTS SUPPORTING LOOSENING THE CURRENT DOUBLE JEOPARDY RULE

- *Justice.* Double jeopardy currently protects acquitted criminals from being brought to justice for their crimes even when compelling new evidence is discovered. The inflexibility of double jeopardy in the United States means no amount of additional evidence can bring even the most heinous murderer or rapist to justice. As a fairness matter, some argue that if a convicted defendant may file a motion for a new trial on the grounds of newly discovered material evidence, then by the same token the state should be allowed, under certain circumstances, to retry an acquitted defendant because of new evidence.[52]

- *Protecting Society from Criminals.* Double jeopardy allows dangerous criminals to walk free, commit more crimes, and continue posing a threat to public safety. Permitting reprosecution in some instances would better protect society by removing dangerous offenders from society.

- *Public Trust in the Justice System.* Every time a clearly guilty criminal evades justice, the credibility of the justice system suffers. The public wants guilty and dangerous individuals convicted and put behind bars regardless of whether they previously managed to obtain a wrongful acquittal. Instances of criminals escaping due to double jeopardy have invariably led to public outrage.

- *New Forms of Evidence.* The development of new forms of evidence such as DNA and better storage of old evidence means double jeopardy is creating far more apparent justice failures today than in the past.

The Nature and Extent of the Problem

A significant percentage of acquittals are of guilty offenders, and new forms of evidence make it easier to identify these cases than in the past, raising the question of whether it is time to revisit the interpretation of the constitutional double jeopardy protection.

THE CRIMINALS THAT DOUBLE JEOPARDY PROTECTS: ODDS OF A GUILTY ACQUITTAL Estimating the cost of double jeopardy to justice requires calculating how many guilty offenders are acquitted because double jeopardy harms justice by protecting such individuals from ever being retried. Studies provide a baseline estimate that at least 6.7 to 19 percent of all acquittals at trial are of guilty individuals.[53] While there is no completely accurate way to determine the true percentage, these estimates are calculated based on "the levels of disagreement in acquittal decisions between juries and the presiding judges in those trials."[54] Studies show that "juries acquit 19% of defendants that the judge would have convicted instead," providing basis for an upper bound of the estimate.[55] The lower bound derives from the 6.7 percent of jury acquittals that the presiding judge views as totally "without merit" and is unable to understand how or why the jury reached their decision.[56]

Of course, these estimates of wrongful acquittals do not even consider the many cases where a guilty offender is acquitted with both judge and jury agreeing there is insufficient evidence presented at trial (but where compelling evidence might later appear). This is especially a problem in cases hinging primarily on conflicting testimony. Sixty-five percent of charged rapists who go to trial are acquitted,[57] and because it seems unlikely that so many victims in cases that make it to trial lie, many if not most of these acquitted rape defendants are likely to be guilty yet are protected by double jeopardy. Similarly, 40 percent of robbery defendants who go to trial are acquitted and 61 percent of assault defendants are acquitted.[58]

Given that prosecutors generally only go to trial with cases that have been thoroughly vetted (with unconvincing cases being dropped), the actual percentage of guilty acquittals would probably be significantly higher than the previous estimates, but it is impossible to know how high.

Of course, in only a small percentage of such wrongful acquittals does compelling incriminating evidence later come to light, so the cost to justice in absolute terms from double jeopardy is probably more measurable in hundreds of serious criminals escaping rather than thousands. However, better forensic technology means those numbers will rise. But perhaps more damaging to society is the loss of credibility the justice system suffers from high-profile failures of justice caused by double jeopardy.

A CONSTITUTIONAL PROBLEM Remedying the problems caused by double jeopardy is especially difficult because protection against double jeopardy in America is based upon a constitutional provision rather than a procedural rule or legislative enactment. This makes it extraordinarily difficult to make any reform to double jeopardy through the legislative process because the number of cases where justice is perverted by the rule would likely not generate the political will needed to pass a constitutional amendment. This contrasts with the United Kingdom, which was able to change its double jeopardy rule purely through an act of Parliament (see more on the UK reform in the reforms section that follow).

However, the US double jeopardy rule is capable of change through judicial reinterpretation. The constitutional language is in fact very broad: no person shall "be subject for the same offense to be twice put in jeopardy of life or limb."

It is the courts, not the constitutional language itself, that created the contours of the modern American double jeopardy rule, which recognizes a wide variety of exceptions. For example, as noted earlier, both state and federal courts can convict an offender for the same offense.[59] For another example, if a defendant's conviction is reversed on appeal, he can commonly be retried for the same offense without violating the double jeopardy rule[60]—even though the constitutional language itself provides no basis for recognizing such an exception. Commentators stress that "retrials in these instances are justified by society's interest in punishing the guilty. Defendants' countervailing interests are considered inferior when a conviction rendered by 12 jurors is overturned for reasons unrelated to guilt or innocence."[61] Courts have also read into the double jeopardy clause a protection against prosecutors appealing an acquittal (even if the trial judge erred on a matter of law), showing how open the clause is to interpretation. If courts, using logic and taking account of practical consequences, can recognize these exceptions and others, why not recognize an exception for something as important as compelling evidence only recently discovered through no fault of the prosecutor?

Public Complaints

There is commonly a public outcry against the double jeopardy rule when it causes a confirmed failure of justice.[62] In Britain, public complaints were a key driver behind the reform that loosened the double jeopardy rule.[63] In America, which has made no such reform, public complaints against the rule continue. Some of the most poignant protests arose after fourteen-year-old Emmett Till, a Black boy, was lynched by two White men for whistling at a White woman in 1955. His murderers were acquitted but later confessed to his killing in a 1956 magazine article (for which they were paid $4,000). It was a confession with little consequence, however, as the double jeopardy rule prevented a retrial. Even fifty years later, Till's family still finds the murderers' bragging confessions and the justice system's inability to act as "salt" rubbed into their "still-fresh wounds."[64]

Another case that spurred debate and public complaint regarding double jeopardy was that of O. J. Simpson.[65] When Simpson was acquitted in 1995 after being tried for the murder of his ex-wife Nicole Brown Simpson and her friend Ron Goldman (due in part to investigative and prosecutorial errors), much of the public was suspicious and outraged, having been quite certain of his guilt, a suspicion that seemed to be confirmed when he was found liable for the murders at a civil trial. Another round of public outrage was sparked when it was revealed that Simpson was writing a book titled *If I Did It*, which included descriptions of how the murders could have "hypothetically" occurred had Simpson been the perpetrator. As familiarity with the DNA evidence implicating Simpson increased over time, many wondered why an obviously guilty man should go free no matter how compelling the evidence might become.[66]

The most obvious supporters of reform are victims and their families who feel betrayed when their demands for justice are tossed aside in favor of protecting defendants from theoretical abuses. The United Kingdom's reform allowing reprosecutions in narrow circumstances has brought many families hope of finally bringing justice to the killers of their loved ones. One mother whose daughter was murdered previously felt "let down by the criminal justice system."[67] However, after the United Kingdom's reforms to the double jeopardy rule, she felt that families can now "eventually see justice."[68]

Reforms

It is a reexamination of the balance of competing interests in light of changing circumstances that has led to a number of reforms of the double jeopardy rule in other countries, including the United Kingdom where the American rule originated.

Double Jeopardy Reform in Other Countries. As noted earlier, in 2003, the United Kingdom passed the Criminal Justice Act, which permitted acquittals to be reversed and the acquitted to be retried in England and Wales if new evidence such as blood tissue, DNA, witness testimony, or confessions came to light.[69] Only crimes that had a significant impact on the victim or on society are eligible for a retrial (for example, homicide, kidnapping, and sex offenses).[70] The British reform applied retroactively, and Britain's first murder retrial occurred in 2005, sentencing William Dunlop, who murdered his ex-girlfriend in 1989, to life in prison.[71]

That reform is especially useful in the wake of the development of technology that allows for crimes to be solved with DNA testing.[72] For example, Russell Bishop was originally acquitted for the double murder of nine-year-old girls Karen Hadaway and Nicola Fellows in 1986. However, with the help of DNA testing that confirmed Bishop was the killer and the revision of the United Kingdom's double jeopardy rule, Bishop was finally convicted for the murders in 2018.[73] The UK reform has been critical in bringing murderers to justice.

Other Commonwealth countries have followed the United Kingdom's lead with Australia and New Zealand adopting similar reforms. In Canada, prosecutors can reopen a case under the consideration of three factors: if the submission of new evidence would significantly affect the case's outcome, if reopening the case would lead to the possibility of the opposing party calling evidence in reply and the court's consideration of the relevance and necessity of the proposed evidence, as well as the effect that reopening the case will have on the integrity of the trial process.[74]

Furthermore, many other Western countries have different versions of a double jeopardy rule that minimizes the chance of failures of justice in the first place. In France, the prosecution can appeal an acquittal, while in Germany, retrials of acquitted defendants are allowed in certain circumstances. While common law countries are updating their double jeopardy rule to recognize the increasing chance of convincingly proving guilt following a wrongful acquittal, no such reforms have been implemented or even seriously considered in the United States because the constitutionalization of the rule tended to freeze it in place, leaving it to judges to update the rule to adapt to changed circumstances.

Recommendation: Recognize an Exception for Compelling New Evidence of a Serious Felony Only Recently Discovered Through No Fault of the Prosecution

We support adoption of the double jeopardy reform implemented by the United Kingdom and other Commonwealth countries, which show that it is possible to remedy the identifiable justice failures caused by the rule without significantly undermining the rule's protections. The interests protected by double jeopardy are important, and there is no doubt that to avoid governmental harassment or abuse, retrying an acquitted defendant should only be allowed in limited circumstances. Only clearly guilty defendants should ever be targeted for a retrial. We propose a retrial be allowed only when the following conditions are met:

1. A prosecutor obtains compelling evidence not known to the prior prosecution through no fault of the government.
2. The case in question is a serious felony (for example, murder or rape).
3. The prosecutor obtains approval to request a retrial from the jurisdiction's attorney general.
4. A judge grants a motion for retrial after reviewing the nature of the crime and certifying the new compelling evidence would likely change the verdict. (The defendant can, of course, appeal this court decision.)
5. After a retrial occurs, if the defendant is acquitted, the government must pay the defendant's legal fees and is barred from any further attempt to retry the case.

This proposed reform, based closely on the proven UK model,[75] would have allowed retrial and conviction in both the Melvin Ignatow and Michael Lane cases in the previous examples, but it does not appear to open any significant avenue for harassment of innocent defendants or allow jury shopping on the part of prosecutors.

Such a reform could be adopted as an appropriate interpretation of the Constitution's broad double jeopardy language, just as the federal courts have done for a variety of other specific exceptions, as discussed earlier.[76] Such a compelling new evidence exception would take a page from other constitutional provisions such as the Fourth and Fourteenth Amendments that have been broadened in response to changing circumstances in order to honor the intended extent of their protections. The double jeopardy clause was meant to protect the innocent from government harassment, so a stringent new evidence exception would not interfere with that original purpose. The courts should be urged to update the interpretation of the double jeopardy rule just as they have with other constitutional protections.

C. DIPLOMATIC IMMUNITY

Some statutory bars to prosecution are clearly necessary. Stable and effective diplomacy requires diplomats to enjoy at least some security from harassment, and so diplomatic immunity has a long tradition dating back to ancient times. In the United States, foreign diplomats, ambassadors, and sometimes their family and staff are granted immunity from prosecution while they are in the United States. The Vienna Convention of Diplomatic Relations states that "a diplomatic agent shall enjoy immunity from the criminal jurisdiction of the receiving state." The United States codified the provisions of the Convention through enacting the Diplomatic Relations Act in 1978.[77]

When dealing with a criminally offending official who is under the protection of diplomatic immunity, the only official recourse provided in international law is to demand that the offending diplomat leave the country, typically by classifying them as *persona non grata*. However, the diplomat's sending country may revoke the offender's diplomatic immunity and allow prosecution by the host country because the grant of immunity is to the sending state and not to the diplomat personally. Additionally, a protected diplomat may be prosecuted in their sending state for a crime committed abroad. Oftentimes, however, diplomatic criminals go entirely unpunished for serious and violent offenses.

Case Example: Manuel Ayree

In 1981, Manuel Ayree is a serial rapist preying on women in New York City.[78] He follows women into their apartment buildings, pushes in as they unlock their doors, and then rapes them at knife point. Several women have gone to the police to report the attacks, and the police are doing everything they can to identify a suspect. So far, police are aware of ten attacks, all in the same neighborhood.

One of the victims, particularly traumatized by the attack, regularly walks the neighborhood streets with her boyfriend to search for her attacker. When the couple spots him one day, they seize and hold him until the police arrive. Ayree tells police he has diplomatic immunity. At the station, additional victims are called in to aid in the identification. Several women confirm that Ayree is their rapist. Members of the Ghanaian mission also arrive. The rapist is indeed the son of the Ghanaian mission's third attaché. Because the police cannot hold him, Ayree is released. As he exits the building, he laughs tauntingly as he walks past several of his victims. The Ghanaians promise to do a full investigation, but Ayree is allowed to return home, and the matter is never pursued.[79]

Competing Interests

There are clear compelling reasons for maintaining diplomatic immunity even at some costs to justice.

INTERESTS SUPPORTING CURRENT DIPLOMATIC IMMUNITY RULES

- *Facilitating International Relations.* Diplomatic immunity respects the sovereignty of other countries over their own diplomatic legations. Countries would be far more hesitant to engage in diplomatic relations unless they were confident their legations would not be subject to potentially false and harassing charges overseas.
- *Avoiding Injustice.* Many countries have extremely unreliable legal systems or unreasonable laws that other countries would consider deeply unjust. Diplomatic immunity ensures that diplomats are not subject to the injustices produced by many foreign legal systems.
- *Protecting Embassy Staff.* Without diplomatic immunity, US diplomats and staff would be in danger of politically motivated harassment, blackmail, and potential imprisonment and might end up being used as bargaining chips in international relations.

INTERESTS SUPPORTING REDUCING THE REACH OF DIPLOMATIC IMMUNITY

- *Justice.* Diplomatic immunity allows crimes committed by diplomatically protected persons to go unpunished. While diplomatic immunity is sometimes waived, it more frequently is not, leading to criminals escaping justice purely due to their diplomatic status. Crimes committed with impunity by immune diplomats can't help but have a damaging effect on the criminal law's moral credibility with the community.
- *Increasing Deterrence.* Reduced diplomatic immunity would deter diplomatic personnel from committing crimes because of the possibility of prosecution by the local justice system.

- *Reducing Public Frustration with Foreign Countries.* When a country refuses to waive diplomatic immunity, the receiving nation's public often feels outraged by the failure of justice. This can lead to resentment and anger at other countries and their citizens and jeopardizes the quality of the diplomatic relations between the two countries.

The Nature and Extent of the Problem

In 1961, the Vienna Convention on Diplomatic Relations established the rules of diplomatic immunity, and 187 countries, including the United States, formally bound themselves to the terms of the Convention.[80] In the United States, there are roughly 200,000 individuals under the protection of diplomatic immunity, whether they are diplomats or the family or staff of a foreign diplomat.[81] Every year, at least forty to fifty of these protected individuals are known to commit a crime in the United States.[82] Some of these crimes result in the death of innocent victims. The true number of violent offenses committed by immune diplomats is largely unknown, however, partly due to government reluctance to disclose details of diplomatic offenses. In 2014, the US Department of State released a partial list just of driving offenses committed by individuals with diplomatic immunity.[83] Some of these cases were quite alarming. In some cases, the driver was speeding at over one hundred miles per hour, and other cases involved hit and runs or driving under the influence—highly dangerous offenses.[84] But the most shocking examples of justice failures appear when diplomatic immunity provides a license to commit serial crimes, as in the Manuel Ayree case earlier.

One source of largely unreported diplomatic crimes comes from foreign workers in embassies in the United States. Thousands of "individuals from low-income countries, especially women, have entered the US with A-3 and G-5 visas to work as domestic employees in the residences of diplomats, consular officers, and officials to international organizations."[85] There is evidence to suggest that some of these employees are routinely subjected to crimes ranging from withholding wages to illegal confinement and rape.[86] There is also evidence of human trafficking. While Article 32 of the initial Vienna Convention allows sending states to waive diplomatic immunity, there is no enforcement mechanism to compel such a waiver,[87] and so in practice, immunity is rarely waived even between allies or in cases of serious crime.[88]

While the absolute numbers of such cases are not large compared to other kinds of justice failures, high-profile cases continue to highlight the problem both in and outside the United States. For example, in 2019, Anne Sacoolas, the wife of an American CIA agent in Britain, killed nineteen-year-old Harry Dunn while she was driving on the wrong side of the road in the United Kingdom.[89] British police applied for a waiver of diplomatic immunity, but the United States refused to waive immunity, and Sacoolas quickly returned to the United States. The United States refused to waive any of her protections or to extradite her, despite pleas from then Prime Minister Boris Johnson.[90] This has deeply upset Dunn's family, who argue that they "are unable to obtain closure until Sacoolas faces trial."[91] The United States also maintained the diplomatic immunity of Col. Joseph Hall after he killed a motorcyclist in Pakistan with his car.[92] Perhaps one reason some in the United States are hesitant to waive diplomatic immunity in these cases is to avoid setting a precedent that would increase the pressure for waivers in other cases in the future.

Public Complaints

As with double jeopardy and statutes of limitation, complaints against diplomatic immunity are loudest from the victims of the crimes. However, larger public opinion also reveals negative sentiments regarding widespread application of diplomatic immunity. After the death of Harry Dunn, a poll found that "84% of Britons and 63% of Americans agree that diplomatic immunity should not be invoked in the case of Dunn's death."[93] Other complaints question why diplomatic immunity is extended to the family or staff of diplomats,[94] which only seems to increase the potential for failures of justice because it is usually those associated with diplomats, and not the diplomats themselves, who commit crimes.[95] Others are angered by the secrecy involved with protecting guilty diplomats. The US Department of State does not release the names of these offenders, but many argue that releasing such information should be standard to create at least some public accountability.[96]

Reforms

While a form of diplomatic immunity must remain, the interests in support of limiting it have led to some reforms and proposals that might better serve justice. An important backdrop to any reform proposal is the fact that any reform enacted by the United States toward foreign diplomats will almost certainly be enacted reciprocally by foreign countries toward US diplomats. Still, one can imagine a variety of reforms that could be made to diplomatic immunity.

Allow for Verdicts of "Guilty But Not Punishable." Part of the problem posed by diplomatic immunity could be solved by allowing prosecutions that could end in verdicts of "guilty but not punishable," providing a recognition of the offender's guilt without the infliction of criminal punishment. Such verdicts would signal that a morally blameworthy violation had occurred as well as publicly shaming the offender involved and offering some vindication for the victim. This reform would also address the secrecy surrounding the identity of guilty diplomats, making the public aware of who has engaged in criminal conduct. The primary difficulty with this attractive proposal is that such a trial in most instances would have to be conducted without the cooperation or presence of the defendant, which would raise questions about the fairness of the procedure and the reliability of the verdict. Of course, if the defendant and their sending country were given every opportunity to participate in any way that they chose, the potential unfairness could be reduced. Also, just as the vast majority of cases do not go to trial but rather are settled by plea agreement, the "guilty but not punishable" disposition could be reached by agreement of the parties without a trial. Making such a case disposition available would not require sending states to accept the blanket jurisdiction of receiving states, and so it might provide a useful compromise that both the sending and receiving state could accept in resolving diplomatic crimes with unwaived immunity.

Establish an International Court for Diplomatic Crimes. A different approach to diplomatic immunity would be to allow host countries to charge diplomats in an international diplomatic court invested with the power to convict and punish for certain serious crimes (such as murder, rape, manslaughter, robbery, sex trafficking, etc.). This might alleviate sending countries' concern about politically motivated convictions against their diplomats, which partly underlies the need for diplomatic immunity.

While the reform would take a great step toward reducing the damaging effect of justice failures caused by diplomatic immunity, it would be difficult to implement for two reasons. First, it would require the assent of nations to subject their diplomats to the jurisdiction of the international court, and the United States is notorious for maintaining its sovereignty in all matters. (It has not, for example, ratified the treaty to join the International Criminal Court.)[97] Second, even if convicted, a diplomat would still have to be extradited by their country, so a foreign country could always shelter a diplomat from punishment if desired. Obviously, penalties would have to exist for non-compliance, but this makes it even less likely that countries would agree to the establishment of such a court. *Limit Full Diplomatic Immunity to Only Diplomats.* One way of reducing diplomatic failures of justice would be to limit the pool of those granted full criminal immunity. For example, staff and family members might be excluded from any criminal immunity. But again, such a proposal could create significant practical difficulties for running an effective diplomatic mission and therefore is likely to be unattractive to most sending countries.

A more limited proposal of a similar sort would allow immunity for most crimes to the same group as currently eligible but would limit criminal immunity for serious offenses to just the diplomats themselves. In 1987, the proposed "Dip-lomatic Immunity Abuse Prevention Act" sought to subject "certain members of foreign diplomatic missions and consular posts in the United States . . . to the criminal jurisdiction of the United States with respect to crimes of violence."[98] Under the act, only diplomats themselves would remain totally immune to criminal liability; their staff and families would be subject to prosecution for violent crimes.[99] The Department of State strongly opposed the bill, claiming that it undermined the intent of diplomatic immunity, and it did not pass.[100] Certainly one problem with such a reform lies in the reciprocity from other nations that would put US diplomatic families and staff at risk in foreign countries.

Recommendation: Impose Collateral Sanctions on Offending Diplomats and the Officials Who Shield Them from Deserved Punishment for a Serious Offense

While it seems unlikely that the official rules governing diplomatic immunity can be significantly altered, there do exist other mechanisms by which the United States could punish diplomatic offenders who have committed serious offenses. The United States is in a fortunate position of already having an extensive personal sanction regime for international criminals who are beyond the reach of American jurisdiction. The United States should make a policy of imposing personal sanctions on diplomatic offenders with unwaived immunity as well as sanctioning foreign officials who refuse to investigate, prosecute, or waive the immunity of said offenders in serious cases.

The United States has previously used three major kinds of sanctions against individuals outside American jurisdiction: travel bans, asset freezing, and prohibiting dealings with US-affiliated entities. Travel bans are the lightest kind of sanction and prevent entry to the United States temporarily or permanently. Asset freezes are a harsher economic sanction allowing the United States to block sanctioned individuals' access to any of their assets held in the United States. Such assets include physical property, bank accounts, investment accounts, and any other source of value held within the legal jurisdiction of the United States. The most severe form of sanction is to prohibit any US entity, including companies and individuals, from engaging in dealings with the sanctioned individual even abroad. In rare cases, this may mean preventing the sanctioned individual from any dollar transaction, a sanction recently imposed on top Russian officials following the Russian invasion of Ukraine.[101]

Depending upon the diplomatic offender and the nature of the offense, the United States could choose to use any of these collateral sanctioning mechanisms, or even some combination of them. Such collateral sanctions could also be used against those foreign officials in the sending country who refuse to punish their offending diplomat for serious violent offenses.

The use of such collateral sanctions would not constitute a breach of the Vienna Accords, as diplomats, their families, and their staff would still remain protected from criminal and civil liability in US courts. While other countries could well impose similar personal sanctions on US diplomats given unwaived immunity, this would not significantly damage US interests. The United States's position in the global community, and in particular its preeminent control of financial infrastructure, gives it a collateral sanctioning ability that other countries simply do not have (and so would not be able to use to punish US diplomats). Moreover, implementing such sanctions would require little extra administrative work. The Office for Foreign Assets Control (OFAC), a branch of the Treasury Department, maintains and publishes a Sanctions List, which consolidates several specific lists of individuals and companies that the US government wishes to punish. Additionally, the Bureau of Industry and Security within the Department of Commerce maintains a list of "Denied Persons," made up of foreign governments, corporations, groups, and individuals that have been denied certain privileges.[102] Adding diplomatic offenders to such lists would be easy.

The United Kingdom provided some precedent for this kind of approach to sanctioning diplomats when it passed an extensive set of personal sanctions laws in 2018, with options for sanctions to be applied against foreign diplomats. The sanctions regime provides a detailed process for administering sanctions against individuals and includes provisions that lay responsibility on diplomats when they commit a crime and procedures to impose sanctions on them regardless of their immune status. Per the Sanctions Act, however, the government may only sanction diplomats after special approval from Parliament.[103]

While such personal sanctions would not give victims the satisfaction of a criminal conviction, it would at least impose direct personal costs on diplomats who commit crimes. Being unable to ever enter the United States or engage in financial dealings with US entities would constitute a major punishment for otherwise immune lawbreakers.[104] To make sure the previous sanctioning policy does not damage US relations with foreign countries by seeming like an unfair use of US sanctioning power, the United States should also publicly commit to fully investigate and either prosecute or waive the immunity of US diplomats who seriously offend abroad, or provide a clear justification for why the diplomat is innocent.

Recall the Manuel Ayree case discussed earlier, where US authorities were unable to punish a brutal serial rapist because Ghanaian authorities refused to waive his immunity or to sanction him on their own. Under our proposal, the United States could have imposed sanctions against Ayree including banning him from ever visiting the United States or interacting with any US entity abroad. It also could have imposed a variety of collateral sanctions on Ghanaian officials who protected Ayree from local investigation and punishment, a move that might have made the officials reconsider their decision to protect him.

D. THE LEGALITY PRINCIPLE AND THE RULE OF STRICT CONSTRUCTION

In addition to the previous constitutional and statutory bars to prosecution, there is a broader principle that serves to prevent culpable actors from facing deserved punishment. The legality principle in its original Latin reads "nullum crimen sine lege, nulla poena sine lege,"[105] which means "no crime without law, no punishment without law."[106] In its modern form, the legality principle bars criminal liability and punishment that is not based upon a prior legislative enactment of a prohibition expressed with adequate precision and clarity. The principle is not itself a legal rule but rather a legal concept embodied in a series of rules and doctrines, such as the constitutional pro-

hibition against *ex post facto* laws and the constitutional void for vagueness rule.[107] These doctrines impose important procedural safeguards governing when and how the government can criminalize behavior and punish perpetrators.[108]

Most aspects of the legality principle are unquestionably essential to a just and ordered society. Together, the rules embodying this fundamental principle impose important limitations on the government's ability to use its most powerful mechanism of control, the threat of criminal liability. Few people will want to dispute that the balance of interests favor keeping most legality principle doctrines even if they do sometimes frustrate justice.

Competing Interests

The interests in favor of the legality principle are fivefold.[109]

INTERESTS SUPPORTING THE LEGALITY PRINCIPLE

- *Fair Notice.* Fair notice ought to be required as to the contours of a criminal prohibition if a person is to be punished for its violation. Laws are meant to guide individual decisions in line with societal judgments of permissible behavior, and so it would be unfair to punish someone unless the person had a chance to decide their course of behavior in light of the law.
- *Compliance.* Unless an action is clearly criminalized by a clear statute, it is less likely that the law can gain compliance because people simply will not be able to know the nature and scope of the prohibited conduct.
- *Democratic Accountability.* It makes sense to reserve criminalization decisions to the legislature that represents the will of society as opposed to unelected judges. This is a separation

of powers concern that if judges are allowed to make criminalization decisions, they are performing a legislative function. Requiring the codification of criminal laws ensures that the legislature will retain control of criminalization decisions.

- *Uniformity.* Uniformity in application is important to uphold because the entire criminal justice system loses credibility if different judges apply different views of what constitutes an offense. Uniformity in application is difficult without a single codified definition of crimes that govern all criminal adjudications.

- *Avoiding Judicial Abuse.* The interest in uniformity ties into the additional interest of avoiding the abuse of judicial discretion. If the criminalization of an act is based on non-legislative discretion, all sorts of potential abuses arise. For example, a judge could take into account characteristics of the defendant such as their race, gender, or class—a problem already seen in judicial sentencing but one that would be even more serious when deciding what conduct is punishable in the first place.

INTERESTS OPPOSING THE LEGALITY PRINCIPLE (IN SOME CASES) The interests against the legality principle's application chiefly rest on the idea that justice should be served for egregious wrongs even without a codified law as long as the person knew or should have known that their conduct was reprehensible.

- *Satisfying Society's Demands for Justice.* The legality principle prohibits criminal liability even if the condemnable nature of the conduct is clear to all, including the offender. If a person's moral blameworthiness is clear to all (and all agree the wrong deserves societal punishment), in-cluding the offender, the criminal justice system's failure to impose deserved punishment not only undermines deterrence but also damages the criminal law's moral credibility and thereby its crime control effectiveness. Therefore violating the legality principle (see the Nuremberg example shortly) may sometimes be the correct way to minimize the harm done to the law's credibility.

Before turning to examine the specifics of the doctrines making up the legality principle, consider several case examples that illustrate the justice-frustrating operation of the principle, one resulting from the rule of strict construction and one from the prohibition against *ex post facto* laws.

Case Example: Ray Marsh

Ray Marsh owns a crematorium in Georgia that breaks down in 1997. Rather than fix it, Marsh simply begins to toss the dead bodies into the woods behind the crematory to rot. He believes that what he is doing is illegal, but he continues to stack the dead on the dead for years until a local dog pulls up a skull and authorities are alerted. Authorities find nearly three hundred discarded bodies, and the community is outraged. (Police have Marsh wear a bulletproof vest at court appearances out of fear that he will be shot.) People are adamant that Marsh must pay for his crime, which has brought terrible upset to so many families. However, the court applies the rule of strict construction to interpret the statute against defacing corpses as requiring a body to be "defaced" in a technical sense and concludes that Marsh did not actually "deface" the dead bodies in this narrow sense (as he left them to rot instead). Thus, Marsh cannot be crimi-

Figure 2.2. As remains were collected from the Tri-State grounds, they were sorted into individual evidence bags, 2002. Photo from Staff Report, "Tennessee Supreme Court Upholds Crematory Verdict," *Chattanooga Times Free Press*, September 22, 2012, https://www.timesfreepress.com/news/2012/sep/22/tennessee-supreme-court-upholds-crematory-verdict/.

nally convicted for his shocking treatment of hundreds of bodies.[110]

Case Example: Nuremberg

With the invasion of Poland in 1939, Nazi Germany under the leadership of Adolf Hitler wages a new type of warfare: a warfare that wipes out entire classes of people, uses massive amounts of slave labor, and slaughters POWs. When Nazi leaders are brought to justice before an international tribunal at Nuremberg, the most serious charge is that of aggressive warmaking. (Hitler kills himself rather than face capture and trial.) But complicating matters is the fact that, before the war, aggressive warmaking had not been recognized by international law as a crime, and convicting the Nazi leaders of it would violate the legality principle because it would be an *ex post facto* application of criminal law. Faced with

the choice of allowing Nazi leaders to go unpunished for this most fundamental offense or setting aside the legality principle (which requires that the conduct be declared a crime before the offense occurred), the tribunal elects to convict the leaders.[111] If the legality principle had not been set aside at the Nuremberg trials, some of the worst crimes in modern history might have gone unpunished.

A Closer Look at the Doctrines of the Legality Principle

One doctrine instantiating the legality principle holds that the power to criminalize is vested exclusively with the legislature, and this has led to the modern abolition of common law offenses and the prohibition against judicially created crimes. American jurisdictions with modern criminal codes bar prosecution for an offense if it has not been codified,

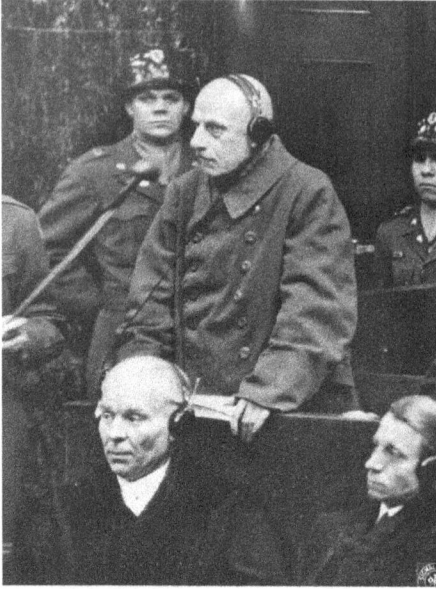

Figure 2.3. German Fieldmarshal Wilhelm Leeb pleads not guilty during the Nuremberg Trials, 1947. Image from the Gen. Eugene Phillips Nuremberg Trials Collection at the University of Georgia, https://digitalcommons .law.uga.edu/trial_photos/51/. Reprinted with permission.

while under common law, judges could theoretically decide to punish acts that are sufficiently repulsive and injurious to society even if those acts are not explicitly criminalized in statutes. Some American criminal codes that missed the Model Penal Code–based recodification movement in the 1960s and 1970s still allow the prosecution of uncodified common law offenses.[112]

A second doctrine instantiating the legality principle is that a violation may be punished only prospectively, meaning after its adoption as a legal rule. This rule applies to US legislatures through the constitutional prohibition against *ex post facto* laws.[113] This has been interpreted to prohibit the punishment of conduct that was not criminal at the time it was performed and to prohibit the imposition of a level of punishment greater than that

which existed at the time of the criminal conduct. Under this rule, courts are barred from making retroactive judicial interpretations that expand crimes or increase punishment.[114]

Recall the refusal of the Nuremberg court to apply this aspect of the legality principle when it convicted the Nazi leaders of the previously undefined crime of aggressive warmaking. One may criticize this failure as something that weakens the protective promise of the rule. On the other hand, one might argue that if it takes a crime as extreme as genocidal warfare to justify an exception to the rule, such an exception may not have much effect in undermining the rule. The "Nuremberg exception" would be a hard standard to meet.

Another doctrine instantiating the legality principle is that criminal offenses must be drafted so as to provide sufficient precision and clarity in the definition of the offense. This requirement is embodied in the Due Process Clauses of the Fifth and Fourteenth Amendments to the US Constitution, prohibiting vague and overbroad statutes.[115] The doctrine requires that statutes define "the criminal offense with sufficient definiteness that ordinary people can understand what conduct is prohibited and in a manner that does not encourage arbitrary and discriminatory enforcement."[116] Otherwise, a statute may be declared void for vagueness. However, a statute is not unconstitutionally vague merely because one of its elements calls for a matter of judgment or is subject to multiple interpretations. If a provision defines the prohibited conduct with some specificity yet is subject to two or more interpretations, then it is termed ambiguous, rather than vague, which is not itself necessarily unconstitutional.

THE RULE OF STRICT CONSTRUCTION VERSUS THE RULE OF FAIR IMPORT There is one rule whose origin derives from the legality principle that is controversial and deserves close examination: the so-called rule of strict construction. The rule requires any ambiguity in the statutory definition of an offense be interpreted to define the offense narrowly, or as best benefits the defendant. This "rule of lenity," as it is also called, can regularly lead to failures of justice. For instance, in *People v. Nunez*,[117] a prisoner injured a guard during an escape while awaiting transport to a state prison to serve a life sentence. He was charged with an offense under the California Penal Code that punishes assault by a "person undergoing a life sentence in a state prison."[118] However, the appellate court applied the rule of lenity and quashed his conviction because although he assaulted someone while he was sentenced to serve life in state prison, the prisoner was at the time of the assault not yet "in a state prison" but only on his way there.[119]

Consider a more severe example involving sexual assault. Jane Doe, a thirteen-year-old who is wheelchair bound, is at home alone with her father, Curtis Davis, when he sexually assaults her. Davis takes his daughter into the bedroom, picks her up from her wheelchair, and places her on the bed. She resists, strikes her father, and screams for help. Davis sexually assaults her multiple times. Doe reports the incident to the police, and Davis is arrested and charged with the rape of a person who is "physically helpless." At trial, the jury finds Davis guilty. Davis appeals, claiming that he was accused under the wrong law because his victim is not "physically helpless." While Doe has muscular dystrophy and may be "physically helpless" in one

sense, she is not "physically helpless" in the narrow sense that the court gives the statutory language because she was capable of attempting resistance. Davis's conviction is overturned. In place of his sixty-year sentence, he is convicted of misdemeanor battery with a sentence of time served, and released.[120]

The Model Penal Code (a model code drafted by the American Law Institute that has been the model for criminal code reform in three-quarters of US states)[121] tries to mitigate the failures of justice produced by the rule of strict construction by providing a code with greater clarity and precision. Having done so, the Model Code drafters felt it was appropriate to switch the rule of strict construction to what is commonly called the "rule of fair import," directing courts to interpret the code's provisions "according to the fair import of their terms but when the language is susceptible of differing constructions it shall be interpreted to further the general purposes stated in this Section and the special purposes of the particular provision involved."[122] In other words, instead of interpreting any ambiguity in favor of the defendant, no matter how awkward that would be, ambiguities are to be interpreted according to the fair meaning of the terms and the legislative intent of the law.[123]

Public Complaints

Failures of justice from the rule of strict construction are often the kinds of cases that outrage the public and confirm their view that the law is obsessed with technicalities and indifferent to the importance of doing justice. Complaints from members of the public in the case examples mentioned earlier reflect this public distrust of the criminal justice system. For example, Lee Curtis

Davis's acquittal by technicality for the rape of his daughter sparked widespread outrage, with editorials condemning the legal system's reliance on technicalities. One infuriated columnist called the legal system "helpless" to do justice and dared its defenders to tell the thirteen-year-old victim that "the system works."[124]

Reforms

While the legality principle itself is not in need of reform and no one has seriously proposed eliminating it, the rule of strict construction has attracted proposals to soften its application.[125] For example, the rule only applies if there is an ambiguity, and it is for the court to decide whether an ambiguity exists in the first place. Thus, a court could cut down on the justice failures that the rule produces by setting a higher standard of what counts as an ambiguity that will trigger application of the rule.

Similarly, the rule of strict construction can and has been tempered by judicial interpretations that have found a statute is "not to be construed so strictly as to defeat the obvious intention of the legislature"[126] or "to override common sense."[127] Nor is it necessary that a statute be given its narrowest possible meaning or a "forced, narrow or over-strict construction."[128] Still further, the Supreme Court has limited the rule of strict construction by applying it only after all efforts to ascertain the statute's meaning—such as canons of construction and legislative history—have been exhausted, leaving ineradicable ambiguity.[129]

In our view, however, there exists a significantly better means of avoiding the justice failures of the rule of strict construction than judicial interpretations that limit its worst excesses.

Recommendation: Adopt the Fair Import Test (After Adopting a Code Using MPC's Modern Drafting Techniques)

Our recommendation is to replace the rule of strict construction with the more flexible fair import rule, a reform already adopted by many states. This reform is desirable, of course, only if the jurisdiction has adopted a code designed to provide clear guidance as to what is criminal, but this can easily be done by using the modern drafting techniques of the American Law Institute's Model Penal Code. Such criminal code improvement is an essential aspect of this proposal, as the adoption of the rule of fair import without the clarity and specificity of a modern code could create significant confusion. However, with a modern code in place, adoption of the fair import test can avoid the justice-frustrating failures of strict construction without opening the way for confusion or unfairness.

For an example of the significant difference in clarity between a Model Penal Code drafting approach and older techniques, consider section 850 in title 11 of the Delaware Code, which defines the offense of "use, possession, manufacture, distribution and sale of unlawful telecommunication and access devices." The text is long, complex, and messy and runs to more than two thousand words. Beyond its verbose and technical language, the provision also relies upon a series of special definitions created only for this offense that differ in meaning from the same term used in other contexts. In contrast, using the modern drafting techniques of the Model Penal Code, the gravamen of this offense could be captured in a simpler and clearer codification by criminalizing, as the Draft Delaware Criminal Code proposes, whoever "knowingly obtains without consent services that the person knows are available only for compensation."[130] The terms used here have their ordinary meaning or have a legal definition that applies to all instances in which the term is used in the criminal code. This simplicity would be reason enough to adopt a modern code, but an added benefit is the rule of strict construction is no longer necessary because any ambiguities can be interpreted consistent with the clear purpose of the law and the way specific terms are used throughout the rest of the criminal code.

Both the Ray Marsh case in Georgia and the Lee Curtis Davis case in Florida ended as failures of justice because of the rule of strict construction[131] and would have come out differently under a rule of fair import. For example, recall in the Davis case that a man who repeatedly sexually assaults his daughter with muscular dystrophy cannot be convicted because under the rule of strict construction his daughter was not held to be "physically helpless" as the statute required. However, under the fair import rule, courts would have been able to look beyond a claimed ambiguity in the strict meaning of the phrase "physically helpless" and instead look at the overall sense of what the law criminalizes.[132] Unfortunately, as of this writing, a number of states still use the rule of strict construction.[133]

Anti-Justice Distributive Principles

As the previous chapter illustrates, criminal law contains many rules (for example, statutes of limitation) that regularly and predictably produce justice failures for serious offenses. These justice-frustrating rules are not without reason, but they do raise the important question of what the preeminent goal of the criminal law and justice system should be. What governing principle should be used in assessing criminal liability and punishment? Before turning to examine other causes of justice failures in later chapters, we pause here to justify the claim that the criminal justice system's primary governing principle should be to do justice, that is, to impose punishment in proportion to each offender's relative blameworthiness, which necessarily includes an assessment of the seriousness of the offense and the culpability and capacity of the offender when committing the offense. Some argue the whole notion of "justice" has no real discernible meaning and is of little practical significance. But the evidence is to the contrary.

First, most people believe that doing justice is demanded as a matter of morality.[1] Moral philosophers have provided detailed accounts of what is and is not "just" criminal liability and punishment, each explanation painstakingly reasoned from basic principles of right and good. Doing justice in this "deontological desert" sense, as it has been called, is important simply because it is the right,

moral thing to do.[2] (This view that doing justice is a moral imperative is strongly held among ordinary people. Recall the case of Shannon Siders, mentioned in chapter 1, where the town of Newaygo, Michigan, worked for twenty-two years to solve a single murder, showing just how strongly ordinary individuals valued justice.[3]) Part B of this chapter examines the issue of deontological desert and its implications for constructing criminal law rules.

Second, even if one were inclined to ignore the demands of morality in constructing a criminal law, there are strong practical reasons to care deeply about doing justice as ordinary people understand it, or what has been called "empirical desert." Empirical studies make clear that people's willingness to support and assist criminal justice activities, to cooperate and acquiesce in the law's demands, and to internalize the law's norms increase with the criminal law's reputation among the public for being just. The more the criminal law is perceived as unjust or failing to do justice, the more it will provoke resistance, subversion, and vigilantism. Further, empirical studies make clear that the criminal law's reputation for being just—its "moral credibility," as it has been called—depends in large part upon whether the system is seen as imposing punishment in a pattern that tracks the community's shared intuitions of justice (that is, "empirical desert").[4]

Thus, even utilitarians who chiefly value effective crime control should want the criminal law to distribute liability and punishment in a way that tracks ordinary people's shared intuitions of justice, which includes avoiding failures to convict and punish where empirical desert calls for liability. Part C examines this further.

Unfortunately, the criminal justice system's dominant distributive principles of punishment for the past half-century and more have been general deterrence and incapacitation of the dangerous, both of which seriously conflict with empirical desert, thereby reducing the criminal law's moral credibility with the community. Such non-desert distributive principles obviously cause injustices by punishing offenders too harshly in order to deter or incapacitate, but they also lead to justice failures. If dangerousness is the primary punishment criterion, people who have committed serious offenses, such as murder or rape, will avoid liability and punishment if they are no longer dangerous. Similarly, if criminal law rules are structured to maximize general deterrence, they will punish more when there is an opportunity to maximize the general deterrent message—for example, in high-profile cases—and less when there is less likelihood that others will hear of the case. But these considerations, such as publicity level, are entirely inconsistent with ordinary people's judgments of justice. Doing justice according to empirical desert would instead focus exclusively upon the seriousness of the offense and the culpability and capacities of the offender. Part D discusses the problems inherent in using general deterrence or incapacitation of the dangerous as distributive principles.

The available evidence strongly suggests that the criminal law ought to prioritize doing justice (operationalized as empirical desert) and therefore avoiding justice failures. For those who value a moral criminal law, this is necessary because it is the right thing to do. For those who care most about effective crime control, doing justice is essential because building the law's moral credibility is most effective in increasing its crime control success. Perhaps these reasons explain why the American Law Institute amended its Model Penal Code, which is the foundation for criminal codes in three-quarters of US states, to change the general principles provision in 2007 to set desert as the dominant, inviolable distributive principle over all other principles for distributing punishment.[5]

A. DEONTOLOGICAL DESERT AS A DISTRIBUTIVE PRINCIPLE

Deontologists commonly argue for making deontological desert (that is, justice as reasoned out by moral philosophers) the dominant distributive principle for criminal liability and punishment. While philosophers provide good reasons for why we should care about doing justice, constructing a practical distributive principle for determining punishments based purely upon philosophical conceptions of justice is simply not feasible.

Deontological desert is appealing as a distributive principle because it, by definition, represents the true transcendent truth about justice. Its strength comes from the fact that its conclusions are based upon carefully reasoned analysis. However, what is to be done when two moral philosophers disagree on an issue where one or both must be wrong? The only way to keep the transcendent truth advantage of deontological desert is to have some universally recognized reasoned mechanism to determine which philosopher is right. Alas, there is no way for humans to do this, or there would be no disputes in moral philosophy. We might determine which philosopher's reasoning is better than another's on several grounds, each producing a different result. We might use our own personal assessment or accept the majority view among philosophers at the current moment. Whatever approach we take, it cannot be one that is a purely objective analysis from universally recognized principles of right and good (which are themselves disputed), and thus any attempt to turn differing conceptions of deontological desert into a single governing principle of punishment loses its claim to transcendent truth from pure reason that makes deontological desert attractive. Deontological desert—defined as true transcendent justice—is a beautiful aspirational goal, but it simply cannot be operationalized without losing its transcendent truth.[6]

B. DOING JUSTICE AS THE MOST EFFECTIVE MEANS OF CONTROLLING CRIME: MAXIMIZING THE CRIMINAL LAW'S MORAL CREDIBILITY WITH THE COMMUNITY

While deontological desert cannot be operationalized, the law can track the desert principles reflected in ordinary people's shared intuitions of justice (that is, empirical desert). When the community observes the criminal law as regularly failing to do justice or doing injustice as defined by their shared intuitions, the law's reputation as a reliable moral authority suffers. As mentioned in chapter 1, this loss in moral credibility reduces people's willingness to defer to the criminal law's demands and undermines the law's ability to make people internalize its norms, as well as provoking vigilan-

tism.[7] While all of this is common sense, it is worth devoting some space to reviewing the empirical evidence in support of three facts:

1. Ordinary people have strong and nuanced shared intuitions of justice based on desert, which they believe the criminal justice system should uphold.
2. When community members see the criminal law regularly deviating from their shared intuitions of justice, the moral credibility of the law declines.
3. As the moral credibility of the law declines, its crime control effectiveness also declines.

These three facts taken together provide a compelling utilitarian case for why the criminal justice system should primarily concern itself with doing justice as the community sees it and why failures of justice are such a serious matter in need of attention. In fact, as some scholars have noted, the best way to measure the success of a criminal justice system is based on how much people trust it to actually do justice.[8]

Some oppose empirical desert by pointing out that the public's shared intuitions of justice on an issue may sometimes be unjust (in a deontological sense), and so tracking community views may entrench injustice. However, the correct solution to this problem is to change public views of justice before changing the law. To seek to change the law first would not only be deeply undemocratic (reflecting the beliefs of a powerful elite minority instead of the people) but would also undermine the credibility of the rest of the (admittedly just) criminal law. For example, laws against sodomy were repealed or struck down in the United States only after societal beliefs had significantly shifted on the topic. If such laws had been changed earlier by a visionary moral elite—say in the nineteenth century—the result would only have been strong democratic resistance and a loss of credibility for the entire criminal law. The fact that society's justice judgments may be incorrect at a particular point in time is not an argument for an undemocratic criminal law (as powerful elites are often morally wrong as well) but rather a call for continual openness to changing the law as public views change. Moral activists can do a valuable service by changing people's beliefs, but they must resist the authoritarian urge to become philosopher kings and dictate a criminal law society finds unjust.

1. Ordinary People Have Strong and Nuanced Shared Intuitions of Justice Based on Desert, Which They Believe the Criminal Justice System Should Uphold

We know from empirical studies that ordinary people think of criminal liability and punishment in terms of desert—offenders should get the punishment they deserve rather than the punishment that might best deter others or best incapacitate dangerous offenders. Consider, for example, two empirical studies that tested the factors that drive ordinary people's criminal liability and punishment judgments.

One study focused on whether ordinary people thought general deterrence or desert was the proper basis for imposing punishment. Participants were given short vignettes of a wrongdoing, with varied factors of the wrongdoing that could affect the sentence. Subjects were then asked to recommend a punishment severity on two scales, ranging from not

at all severe to extremely severe, and then not guilty to life sentence. The degree to which the subject's sentence recommendation was influenced by each of the factors of wrongdoing provides insight into the respondent's underlying motivation (that is, distributive principle) for the punishment given.[9]

The vignette variables that would have a significant influence if respondents used a general deterrence principle included the seriousness of the offense, the difficulty of detecting the particular crime type, and the publicity that the sentence received. These variables are all highly relevant in distributing liability and punishment when maximizing general deterrence.[10] The variables used that would be highly relevant to a desert-based principle included the seriousness of the offense, conditions of moral mitigation (for example, whether or not the offender expressed remorse), and whether or not the offender committed their crime for ostensibly noble purposes.[11]

Several studies were conducted using these basic parameters, controlling for various components to determine the validity of the results.[12] In their responses, participants appeared insensitive to general deterrence factors but highly sensitive to desert factors.[13] For example, while the offender's expression of remorse reduced the severity of the participants' recommended punishment, the publicity of the case did not have a similar effect. Although participants expressed support for deterrence as a general goal of having a criminal justice system on an abstract level, they failed to assign punishment in a way that was consistent with using general deterrence as a distributive principle for criminal liability and punishment.

A similar study tested whether ordinary people are more inclined to assign punishment according to desert or in- capacitation of the dangerous.[14] Subjects in the study were given descriptions of a variety of harmful actions and were asked to assign punishments using a seven-point Likert-type scale that asked for severity of punishment and a more elaborate thirteen-point scale that pro- vided actual prison sentences.[15] In the various vignettes, the seriousness of the crime as well as the likelihood that the actor would commit other harms in the future were varied.[16] The authors exam- ined the weights that participants gave to desert or incapacitation consider- ations as they assigned punishments to wrongdoers.[17] The results indicated that respondents' natural inclinations more closely resembled just deserts judgments than incapacitation judgments.[18] The seriousness of the act, demonstrated in large part by the degree of moral outrage it provokes, determined the degree of punishment respondents assigned.[19]

In a second part of the study, respon- dents were given three test cases to de- termine whether they would be willing to incapacitate a dangerous offender rather than assigning him a just desert pun- ishment.[20] In each vignette, a previously mild-mannered individual attacked and killed another person. In the control case, the actor killed out of a work-related jealousy; in another case, the actor killed a stranger because a previously undis- covered brain tumor caused the violent act, but the brain tumor was inoperable; and in the last case, the tumor was op- erable, so the individual was expected to become less dangerous if he received treatment. After reading the vignettes about the three offenders, the subjects were asked whether they would recom- mend incarceration in a prison, incar- ceration in a mental hospital, or whether

they would set the person free.[21] In the jealous rage case, a strong majority of subjects (86 percent) would send the of- fender to prison, as desert would require. In the brain tumor cases, where a ma- jority of respondents saw the tumor as responsible for the offense rather than the actor, few subjects would send the of- fender to prison, whether the tumor was inoperable (7 percent) or operable (21 percent).[22] In other words, the vast ma- jority of respondents again saw criminal punishment (prison) as appropriate only where they considered the offender to be blameworthy for the offense; danger- ousness might be appropriate to civilly commit the person to an institution but was not a basis for criminal liability and punishment.

Various other studies have found sim- ilar conclusions regarding peoples' intu- itions on punishment. Among these are a 2006 study demonstrating that people are overwhelmingly drawn to retributive punishment,[23] another 2006 study indi- cating that individuals are more likely to support restorative justice practices that include retributive features,[24] and a 2008 study showing that individuals are more likely to inherently support retribution despite self-reporting their preference for alternative distributive principles.[25] It seems clear from this research that ordi- nary people normally expect and want criminal liability and punishment to be distributed according to an offender's desert rather than according to principles of general deterrence or incapacitation of the dangerous. Thus, where offenders are overpunished or underpunished accord- ing to laypeople's intuitions of just des- ert, one would expect laypeople to view the punishment as unjust.

Additionally, laypeople's intuitions of desert are closely correlated to one another, allowing the criminal law to use these shared intuitions as the basis of a criminal code. For example, one study asked participants to rate the seriousness of fifty-one offenses relative to bicycle theft, which was given a starting seriousness value of ten (so a crime twice as serious as bicycle theft would be given a twenty). The researchers concluded that "the most strongly supported conclusion . . . is that all the raters . . . tended to assign estimations [so] that the seriousness of the crimes is evaluated in a similar way, without significant differences, by all the groups" and, further, that a "pervasive social agreement about what is serious and what is not appears to emerge."[26] This societal agreement on the relative seriousness of crimes holds up across multiple subgroups. For example, a different study that asked people to rate eighty offenses according to nine ranked categories of seriousness found that the correlation of ratings between Whites and Blacks, males and females, and more and less educated people was all around 0.9, indicating an impressive societal consensus across subgroups.[27] Other studies have also confirmed that intuitions about the relative seriousness of crimes and their appropriate punishments do not vary significantly based on characteristics such as sex, race, age, income, or education.[28] People really do appear to have strong shared intuitions about what justice means in a criminal context.

Not only do people have shared intuitions about what justice means, they also have a strong innate desire to see it done, even if they have no personal interest in the case. As several scholars note in a metanalysis, "Unfair treatment triggers a desire to punish the offender, both among victims (i.e., 'second-party punishment')

and among uninvolved observers (i.e., 'third-party punishment'). This finding is so universal and robust that it does not require any more replication studies."[29] The same scholars' metanalysis of a wide range of studies showed that this desire for punishment was intuitively retributive (that is, based on desert) as opposed to other distributive principles of punishment.[30] Studies have shown that even preverbal infants display a third-party desire to punish offenders—demonstrating just how deep and instinctual the human desire for desert-based justice is.[31] And experimental evidence shows both children and adults will sacrifice their own resources to punish offenders in cases they are not directly involved with.[32] The human propensity to engage in costly third-party punishment shows people care deeply about justice and are willing to sacrifice much to achieve it.

2. When Community Members See the Criminal Law Regularly Deviating from Their Shared Intuitions of Justice, the Moral Credibility of the Law Declines

This claim is just common sense, but it is also borne out by clear empirical evidence. For example, the next section will present a wide variety of studies in which experimenters varied the subjects' perception of the criminal law's moral credibility in order to observe the resulting shift in the subjects' willingness to defer, acquiesce, and comply with the criminal law and to internalize its norms. How do researchers typically manipulate the extent to which subjects determine the criminal law's moral credibility? Answer: by exposing subjects to more (or fewer) cases where the criminal law's results conflict with the subjects' own sense of justice, or by exposing subjects to cases where the conflict with their intuitions of justice is greater (or lesser).[33] This standard experimental method has been shown to work reliably and predictably. The greater and more frequent the conflict with subjects' justice judgments (either in the form of perceived injustices or justice failures), the greater the loss of the criminal law's moral credibility in their eyes.[34]

Even beyond this common mechanism for manipulating the criminal justice system's moral credibility with subjects, a separate set of studies have independently shown the same dynamic. For example, a 1988 study found that defendants' confidence and trust in the criminal justice system increased when they felt that their sentence was fair or proportional to their crime,[35] and a 1972 study indicated that plea bargaining in particular heavily degraded defendants' trust in the criminal justice system and eroded the criminal law's moral credibility because the outcomes of the plea bargains did not seem to be based on actual desert.[36]

These empirical studies reinforce the common sense notion that regular conflicts with community views as to the just allocation of criminal punishment will reduce the criminal law's moral credibility.[37] It is widely acknowledged that prevalent injustices (instances of overpunishment or punishing the innocent) erode the moral credibility of the justice system, but it is important to recognize that ordinary people care as much about preventing justice failures (where the guilty escape their deserved punishment) as they do about preventing injustices. As noted in chapter 1, research shows that ordinary people consider wrongful convictions and wrongful acquittals as "equally important," unlike many academics who pay dramatically more attention to wrongful convictions.[38]

3. As the Moral Credibility of the Law Declines, Its Crime Control Effectiveness Also Declines

The claim that the criminal law's reduced moral credibility causes reduced deference and compliance is also just common sense. If a criminal law is widely viewed as unjust or unenforced, why would anyone assume that this perception has no effect on the community's deference to the law? In what world would citizens be indifferent to such a poor performance in doing justice? The evidence from history shows that when such disillusionment over the criminal law does set in, lawbreaking rises. This is because the law's compliance effect comes in significant part from the law's reputation as a reliable indicator of what society genuinely condemns.[39] If the law is seen as unrepresentative of society's justice judgments, then its ability to harness the powerful forces of social influence are correspondingly reduced.[40]

Natural Experiments Showing the Disillusionment- Noncompliance Dynamic

No governments are likely to let experimenters degrade the credibility of their criminal justice systems in order to see the resulting rise in crime, but there have been a variety of natural experiments in which a justice system's moral credibility has been noticeably degraded, with a corresponding reduction in compliance. Consider a few examples, which are not meant to be comprehensive or exhaustive:

American Prohibition. In 1920, Congress prohibited the sale, manufacture, and transportation of alcohol within the

United States with the passage of the Eighteenth Amendment. Demand for alcohol remained high, however, and illegal stills, bootlegging operations, and speakeasies flourished. When even government officials openly ignored the rules of Prohibition, this overt disrespect for the criminal law reinforced public disillusionment with the Prohibition movement. As trust in the law eroded, Americans openly violated the law to an ever greater extent. Most importantly, the disillusionment tainted not only the alcohol-prohibition rules, but it also reduced compliance with criminal law rules generally,[41] including those unrelated to alcohol.[42]

Spanish Flu. To give an example with present-day COVID-19 relevance, in 1918, as the Spanish Flu swept through the United States, communities across the country instituted public health measures to slow the spread. Foremost among these was mask wearing.[43] However, many people were unpersuaded that the inconvenience and intrusiveness of the government action was justified by its supposed health benefits. When some local governments imposed mandatory mask ordinances and punished those who flouted the law with jail terms and fines,[44] many in the community resisted through protest or political organizing. The sense that the mask mandates were excessive and the punishments unfair sparked protests en masse across the country.[45] Irritated as they were by the mask ordinances and their associated criminal penalties, people took more and more liberties, hosting large gatherings, and refusing to wear a mask properly (or refusing to wear a mask at all) even when under the scrutiny of officers.[46] And, as with Prohibition, this increased public unlawfulness morphed into increased lawbreaking in other areas of life, pro-

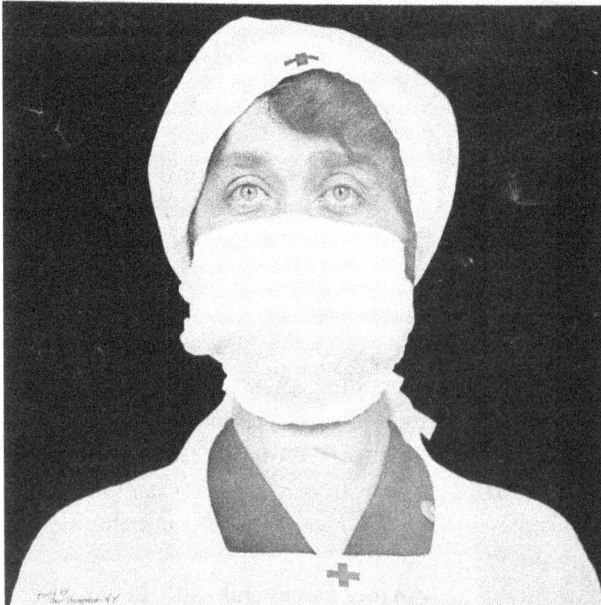

Figure 3.1. Spanish Flu was understood to be a threat to public safety, 1918. Photo by Paul Thompson, "To Prevent Influenza!" New Haven: Illustrated Current News 1, no. 785 (December 18, 1918), https://commons.wikimedia.org/wiki/File:Illustrated_Current_News-1918-Thompson,_Paul.png.

ducing increases in prostitution, drug consumption, and even attacks on immigrants.[47] Without acquiescence from the community generally in the rightness of the law, greater enforcement served only to provoke greater resistance and reduced compliance.

The Watts Riots. In the 1960s Watts neighborhood of Los Angeles, violations of the criminal law were increasingly met with charges and sentences that seemed to residents grossly disproportionate. The aggressive policing and punishment did not reduce crime, as intended, but rather increased it,[48] as the criminal law's moral credibility within the neighborhood diminished. In August 1965, this tension came to a boiling point after a Watts resident's violent encounter with the police inspired the community to take to the streets. An official investigation of the Watts riots found that the riots were a result of the Watts's community's long-growing discontent with criminal justice system.[49]

Gilded Age of New York City. In the Gilded Age of New York City, at the end of the nineteenth century, the legislative process in New York was notoriously corrupt: even valuable and legitimate legislation could not be passed unless the right political players were paid off.[50] The result was a criminal law that simply failed to address and punish the full range of conduct that social mores at the time saw as condemnable, such as pornography, abortion, and gambling.[51] As the criminal law came to be seen as increasingly out of touch with community norms, crime rates escalated.[52] Street

Figure 3.2. After the riots ended, the police response was criticized as being too much and too little, 1965. Photo from the Los Angeles Public Library Collection, https://www.flickr.com /photos/bethnoe/19924044423/. Courtesy of Beth Noe.

gangs proliferated and even shoplifting among middle-class women rose.[53]

Cold War Berlin. The dynamic between the law's credibility and compliance can be seen in a wide variety of societies. Berlin at the beginning of the Cold War was divided into occupation zones controlled by the United States, Great Britain, and France—West Berlin— and the Soviet Union—East Berlin. In 1948, after negotiations between the Allies and the Soviets broke down, the Soviets restricted the delivery of food, coal, and other crucial supplies into the Allied sectors and controlled distribution within East Berlin according to political ideology.[54] Only those who professed allegiance to the Kremlin received provisions.[55] The restrictions created a thriving black market, which the Soviets worked to prevent with increasingly harsh penalties for unauthorized dealings.[56] But as the penalties for such offenses went up, the stigma surrounding such lawbreaking declined and lawbreaking actually increased.[57] Despite the greater scarcity in the Allied sectors, which was being blockaded by the Soviets, more and more East Berliners escaped to West Berlin, in part because they felt they could better trust the government and police.[58] Under a justice system they perceived as more trustworthy, escaped East Berliners committed fewer crimes, notwithstanding the greater shortage of goods.[59]

Empirical Studies Showing the Disillusionment-Noncompliance Dynamic

In addition to these historical case studies, social psychology research suggests that the relationship between the system's moral credibility and community deference and compliance is widespread and nuanced. Even small incremental losses in moral credibility can produce corresponding incremental losses in deference and compliance.[60]

Consider a study published in 2010 using a within-subjects design in which subjects were asked a number of questions relating to various ways in which moral credibility is thought to affect deference, compliance, and the internalization of the law's norms. Will a citizen assist police by reporting a crime? Will they assist in the investigation and prosecution of a crime? Do people take the imposition of criminal liability and punishment as a reliable sign that the defendant has done something truly condemnable? Do people take the extent of the liability imposed as a reliable indication of the seriousness of the offense and the blameworthiness of the offender? With a baseline established on these issues, subjects were then disillusioned by exposing them to real accounts of the system's failures of justice and injustices. Later retesting showed that the measures of deference, compliance, and internalization of norms had decreased among the disillusioned subjects.[61]

A follow-up study used a between-subjects design, giving different levels of disillusionment to three different groups and then testing their levels of deference, compliance, and internalization.[62] The results confirmed the conclusions of the earlier within-subjects design: the greater the disillusionment, the greater the loss in deference, compliance, and internalization. A third study analyzing responses in preexisting large datasets came to a similar conclusion using regression analysis.[63]

The results in these studies are particularly striking because in each case, subjects came to the study with preexisting views on the legal system's reputation for being just. The experimenters, within the context of the study, could only nudge those preexisting views slightly. Yet even that incremental disillusionment produced a corresponding incremental reduction in willingness to defer and comply. This is a particularly important finding because it means that no matter the current state of a criminal justice system's moral credibility with the community, any incremental reduction in credibility can produce an incremental reduction in deference, and any increase can produce an increase in deference.

A 2002 study on the "flouting thesis"—the idea that the perceived justice of one law can influence compliance with unrelated laws—found that rules regarded as unjust have "subtle but pervasive influences on people's deference to and respect for the law."[64] The experiment consisted of two parts. First, participants were exposed to a set of laws, which were chosen because of their apparent justness or unjustness.[65] Exposure was conducted via newspaper stories, which varied in their discussion of civil forfeiture, income tax, and landlord/tenant laws so as to emphasize the fairness or unfairness of the proposed laws.[66] Next participants were told that they would be participating in a separate study in which they were asked to indicate their willingness to engage in particular types of future lawbreaking.[67] These items included drunk driving, parking in a no-parking zone, failing to pay taxes, and drinking alcohol under age twenty-one.[68] Non-compliance in the second study served as an indication of so-called flouting behavior.[69] The study found that there was an overall trend for participants primed with unjust laws to demonstrate a higher probability of engaging in criminal behavior.[70] That is, perceptions of an unjust law activated

a more general attitude about the unjustness of the legal system and a willingness to disobey it.[71]

A host of other empirical studies have confirmed this disillusionment-noncompliance dynamic, including a 2007 study on traffic laws in the European Union,[72] a 2006 study on illegal alcohol consumption in Sweden,[73] a 2003 tax enforcement study in Europe,[74] and a 2009 study using survey data from multiple African countries on citizens' perceptions of the government.[75] Other studies document the same dynamic.[76]

Other Evidence that Reputation Affects Compliance: Law Enforcement Legitimacy and Community Compliance

There exists a separate literature on these points demonstrating that the fairness of the process—even apart from the justness of the results—has a similar effect on compliance, with increases in fairness and professionalism increasing people's willingness to defer and acquiesce to the criminal law's demands.[77] These studies in the context of law enforcement legitimacy are worth examining because they show how the reputation of a system can have important effects on compliance.

Evidence supporting the notion that the criminal justice system's reputation has a direct and measurable effect on crime control effectiveness is seen in studies relating to community perceptions of the fairness of the criminal justice system's adjudication procedures and the professionalism of police. Tom Tyler and other scholars have shown that a decline in the system's reputation for fairness and professionalism—what he calls its perceived "legitimacy"—commonly translates into reduced compliance, deference, and acquiescence.[78] The claim that the system's reputation for "legitimacy" affects its crime control effectiveness is directly parallel to the studies by Robinson and others that find the system's "moral credibility" in distributing criminal liability and punishment directly affects its crime control effectiveness.[79]

Tyler and colleagues found that people were willing to voluntarily accept the decisions of judges where those decisions appeared both neutral and respectful.[80] If the decision-making process appeared to lack bias, focus on objective facts, recognize citizen rights, and treat people with dignity, then people were more likely to defer to the decisions of legal authorities. "People depend heavily upon their inferences about the intentions of the authority," the authors wrote. "If the authorities are viewed as having acted out of a sincere and benevolent concern for those involved, people infer that the authorities' actions were fair."[81] Similarly, Tyler has found that law-abiding behavior can be encouraged where police exercise their authority over citizens through fair processes and with appropriate respect. In a study of adults in Chicago, Tyler found that a feeling of obligation to obey the law and allegiance to, or support for, the relevant authority were the single most important determinants in people's deference to the law.[82] Similarly, in a study of 1,656 adults in Oakland and Los Angeles, Tyler found that 30 percent of the variance in subjects' overall assessment of the justice system's legitimacy was derived from perceptions of their own interactions with the police. Ultimately, both studies suggest that the divergence between people's perceptions of how the police should act versus how the police actually act is one of the most important indicators of law-abiding behavior.[83] This same effect is seen cross culturally in empirical studies from South Korea and Australia.[84]

The dynamic between perceived legitimacy of law enforcement and compliance with the law has also been observed in a variety of historical examples, including the relationship between police and communities in Nigeria in the twenty-first century;[85] the police shooting of Michael Brown in Ferguson, Missouri;[86] invasive crime control efforts in Mexico City in 2003;[87] distrust of the federal government among Native American communities;[88] and tensions between law enforcement and citizens in Northern Ireland in the 1970s.[89]

Disillusionment Expressed as Vigilantism

Another source of evidence suggesting that a reduction in the criminal law's moral credibility results in less compliance is the fact that vigilantism is often sparked by the disillusionment of justice failures.[90] Some of those who care strongly about doing justice sometimes turn to appointing themselves jury, judge, and even executioner when the criminal justice system seems unable or unwilling to do justice.[91] (One reason for the low clearance rate for fatal shootings in many cities is that the witnesses to shootings often refuse to cooperate with police from a sense of disillusionment about the law's ability to serve justice, preferring instead to take justice into their own hands through retaliatory vigilante killings.[92]) Recall the case of Elie Nessler, mentioned in chapter 1, where a mother shot her son's abuser in court from a disillusioned belief that the system would fail to punish him appropriately. The following case examples similarly show the vigilante dynamic of disillusionment at work.[93]

CASE EXAMPLE: KEN REX MCELROY Ken McElroy, a Missouri resident, has committed dozens of felonies, including assault, child molestation, rape, arson, hog and cattle rustling, and burglary.[94] He is indicted twenty-one times but escapes conviction each time by use of intimidation, false alibies, and local connections.[95] In 1981, McElroy is finally convicted of shooting and seriously injuring the town's seventy-year-old grocer, Ernest "Bo" Bowenkamp. Pending his appeal, he is released on bond and undertakes a harassment campaign against Bowenkamp. Many people In town are highly sympathetic to the old grocer and disgusted by McElroy's previous manipulations of the system, which they see as utterly unable to deliver justice. McElroy appears at a local bar, armed with a rifle and bayonet and threatening to kill Bowenkamp. When McElroy comes to town the next day, a group of thirty to forty people surrounds his pickup truck in the middle of town. He is shot to death in front of the crowd by at least two different shooters. Despite the very public nature of the killing, no person in the crowd is willing to identify either of the shooters or otherwise cooperate with police.

CASE EXAMPLE: WILLIAM MALCOLM William Malcolm lives in East London with his wife and her two children, a six-year-old stepdaughter and a nine-year-old stepson.[96] He sexually abuses both children on a regular basis and is eventually charged. During the trial, it comes to light that Malcolm had been abusing his stepdaughter since she was three years old. Convicted of serial child abuse, Malcolm is given only a two-year jail term.

Upon his release, Malcolm returns to the same house to resume life with the two children whom he had been convicted

Figure 3.3. Ken Rex McElroy was killed by several people in his community while sitting in his truck, 1981. Photo courtesy of Harry MacLean.

of abusing. Before the end of the year, Malcolm is again charged with abusing his stepchildren, as well as other young victims in the neighborhood. He is convicted and sent back to jail.

Released again, Malcolm moves in with a girlfriend and her five children. Malcolm continues to abuse the children in that household as well as other children in the neighborhood. Malcolm is once again charged with sexually abusing children.

Prior to prosecution on these latest charges, Malcolm undergoes a psychological evaluation. The report describes him as having pedophile tendencies of a "strongly sadistic nature." The social workers state that he is "incurably psychopathic and violent." At trial, the judge describes the crimes as "unspeakable" but concludes that there could be no trial for the new offenses because his earlier offenses made a fair trial impossible: at a trial on the present charges, the child

Figure 3.4. William Malcolm was well known in his community as an abuser of children. Photo from *Witness plea after paedophile killing*, February 19, 2000, BBC News, http://news.bbc.co.uk/2/hi/uk_news/648475.stm.

victims in the present case would inevitably mention the defendant's prior abuse of them, which the judge finds would prejudice the jury.[97]

Malcolm now moves to an apartment that overlooks a playground. The neighbors know who Malcolm is and they know that the courts are not going to do anything about him. One night, when Malcolm answers his door, he is shot in the face and killed instantly. Despite the numerous neighbors likely aware of the planned event and the number of witnesses in the dense block of flats, the police cannot find a single person willing to admit to seeing or knowing anything about the shooting.

THE DANGERS OF VIGILANTISM Some individuals feel vigilantism is morally justified when the system fails.[98] While classic vigilantism is often romanticized in blockbuster movies and television shows,[99] in real life it can bring tragic consequences.[100] Consider, for example, the case of Steve Utash, who was driving his pickup in Detroit when a child stepped in front of the vehicle and was hit. Utash jumped from the truck to aid the child, but a group of bystanders decided that Utash was in the wrong and didn't trust the justice system to bring justice. The crowd beat Utash so badly that he was placed into a medically induced coma. Vigilante action commonly occurs without gathering all facts or adhering to basic principles of blameworthiness proportionality.[101] Other case examples (see note) illustrate more dangers of vigilantism.[102]

Even more problematic is what has been called "shadow vigilantism," in which actors within the criminal justice system—officers, prosecutors, judges, jurors, and others—do not extrajudicially punish the perceived wrongdoer as the classic vigilante does but rather manipulate and distort the criminal justice system in order to achieve their vigilante purpose. Shadow vigilantism in many ways is more dangerous and more intractable than classic vigilantism and can do more to undermine the criminal justice system's credibility with the community.[103]

The only way that a criminal justice system can avoid the destructive effects of shadow vigilantism is to make clear to the community that it is well aware of the importance of doing justice and to publicly commit itself to doing all that it can to avoid failures of justice.

The larger point is that, whether it is avoiding vigilantism or reducing regular crime, designing a criminal justice system that does justice as society sees it is important from a purely utilitarian crime control perspective as well as a moral perspective. Reducing justice failures should be a priority because such failures have an enormous social and moral cost to society.

C. THE PROBLEMS WITH GENERAL DETERRENCE AND INCAPACITATION OF THE DANGEROUS AS DISTRIBUTIVE PRINCIPLES

As the previous section made clear, there are compelling reasons to adopt a distributive principle designed to maximize the criminal law's moral credibility with the community by tracking its shared intuitions of justice. Those reasons are both deontological—it is the right thing to do (at least in the eyes of most people)—and utilitarian—it is the most effective way of controlling crime.

Some people will still argue, however, that at least as to the second point, other distributive principles would be better at controlling crime, namely gen-

eral deterrence and incapacitation of the dangerous. (Rehabilitation is not a separate distributive principle because even though it makes a fine correctional policy regardless of why an offender is sent to prison, it cannot independently guide who should be subject to prison for how long.[104] To the extent it does offer such guidance by recommending prison for the unrehabilitated, it is subsumed under the principle of incapacitation.) But as mentioned previously, both general deterrence and incapacitation as distributive principles have significant crime control costs because, by focusing on factors irrelevant to desert, they regularly fail to do justice and also regularly do injustice, which also undermines the law's moral credibility. This damage to the law's credibility is likely to undo any benefits reaped through deterrence or incapacitation beyond that sanctioned by desert. The accumulating evidence of the past several decades has shown that these classic utilitarian coercive crime control principles not only conflict with desert but also fail to provide the crime control effectiveness they were once believed to possess.

Deterrence and incapacitation are certainly good justifications for having a criminal justice system that punishes criminal conduct, but the evidence suggests that they are counterproductive when used as distributive principles within that system instead of desert to decide who should get punished how much.

1. Justice Failures Caused by General Deterrence

General deterrence is mostly known for causing injustices by overpunishing certain crimes in an attempt to deter them (commonly unsuccessfully, as discussed shortly).[105] A classic example of general deterrence in action is mandatory minimum sentencing laws that attempt to deter certain crimes by setting inflexibly high punishments for them regardless of the desert-relevant factors in a specific case. While general deterrence–generated injustices can have terrible effects on the credibility of the legal system, general deterrence also causes failures of justice when deterrence logic suggests liability or punishment that is less than deserved. Consider a case example.

CASE EXAMPLE: JOHN WALKER John Walker commits an armed bank robbery in 1987, is convicted, and serves fourteen years in prison.[106] A few years after getting out, Walker commits a second armed bank robbery and is convicted again in 2004. After being released in 2009, he collects a string of convictions for drug-related crimes. In 2014 he is convicted of two additional bank robberies. He asks for and receives a postponement for sentencing to help his family move out of state. While on presentence release, he collects a DUI conviction.

After the DUI and before sentencing, Walker asks and is granted permission to go to a residential treatment program. According to the court's calculations, Walker's guideline sentence for his latest two bank robberies ranges from 12.5 to 15.5 years in prison. (The statutory maximum for the offense is twenty years. Consecutive sentences for the two most recent bank robberies would provide a maximum of forty years.)

Departing from the guidelines, the judge sentences Walker to time served, thirty-three days, plus three years of probation, and restitution of what he stole, $3,695. The government appeals the lenient sentence, but the Tenth Circuit notes that "effective general deterrence comes from better visibility of policing, which increases certainty of punishment, rather than increasing the severity of punishment on the back end." They let stand Walker's sentence of thirty-three days in jail for his third and fourth bank robberies.[107]

2. Justice Failures Caused by Incapacitation of the Dangerous

As with general deterrence, incapacitation of the dangerous is most noted for its ability to cause injustices with disproportionally harsh sentences (for example, through measures such as "three strikes" laws that target repeat offenders). However, it can also cause failures of justice when the legal system decides a given offender is not dangerous and so gives a more lenient sentence than is deserved. Consider two case examples.

CASE EXAMPLE: ALBERT FLICK In 1979, thirty-six-year-old Albert Flick brutally murders his wife in front of her twelve-year-old daughter, but his relatives testify to his fundamentally good character (and thus his likely future nondangerousness). He serves twenty-one years in prison for the vicious murder and is then released. In 2007, Flick is sent back to prison for stabbing his girlfriend with a fork. Out of prison again in 2010, he puts another woman in a headlock and beats her repeatedly with the butt end of a knife. When she gets free, he chases her with a screwdriver. The prosecutor seeks the maximum eight-year sentence for the crime, but the judge disagrees, and despite the prior record of violence gives less than half the maximum,[108] reasoning that Flick is not likely to be dangerous in the future because he is almost seventy and will surely "age out of his capacity to engage in this conduct."[109]

After his release in 2014, Flick violates his probation by again making violent threats and is returned to prison for two years. After his next release, Flick becomes enamored with forty-eight-year-old Kimberly Dobbie but is then enraged when she decides to move away from the area. On July 15, 2018, the seventy-seven-year-old Flick stabs Dobbie to death in front of her eleven-year-old twin boys. Unlike all of Flick's previous presiding judges, the judge this time sentences purely based on just deserts, and Flick goes to prison for the rest of his life.

CASE EXAMPLE: WILLIAM BONIN In November 1968, twenty-one-year-old William Bonin begins kidnapping and raping boys around Los Angeles who capture his fancy. In 1969, he is caught and labeled a "mentally disordered sex offender." A judge sentences him in 1971

to an indefinite period of rehabilitation at a state hospital. The psychiatrists decide Bonin is incurable and send him to prison to be kept safely out of society. After a few years, the prison doctors set him free, reporting that he is "no longer a danger to the health and safety of others."[110]

After his release in 1974, Bonin kidnaps and rapes another boy, and in 1975 he is given an indeterminate sentence of up to fifteen years. Prison authorities decide to release him after three years believing he is rehabilitated.

Punishing Bonin based on a flawed determination of dangerousness instead of desert has terrible consequences. Between 1979 and his capture in 1980, Bonin goes on to become a prolific serial killer—kidnapping, raping, and murdering around forty boys, many as young as twelve.[111]

Figure 3.5. Albert Flick was released from prison when a judge decided he was too old to be a danger to the community, 2019. Photo by Andree Kehn, from Christopher Williams, "Prosecution and Defense Rest in Murder Trial of Alber Flick," *Sun Journal*, July 16, 2019, https://www.sunjournal.com/2019/07/16/prosecution-and-defense-rest-in-murder-trial-of-albert-flick/. Courtesy of Judy Meyer, Sun Journal.

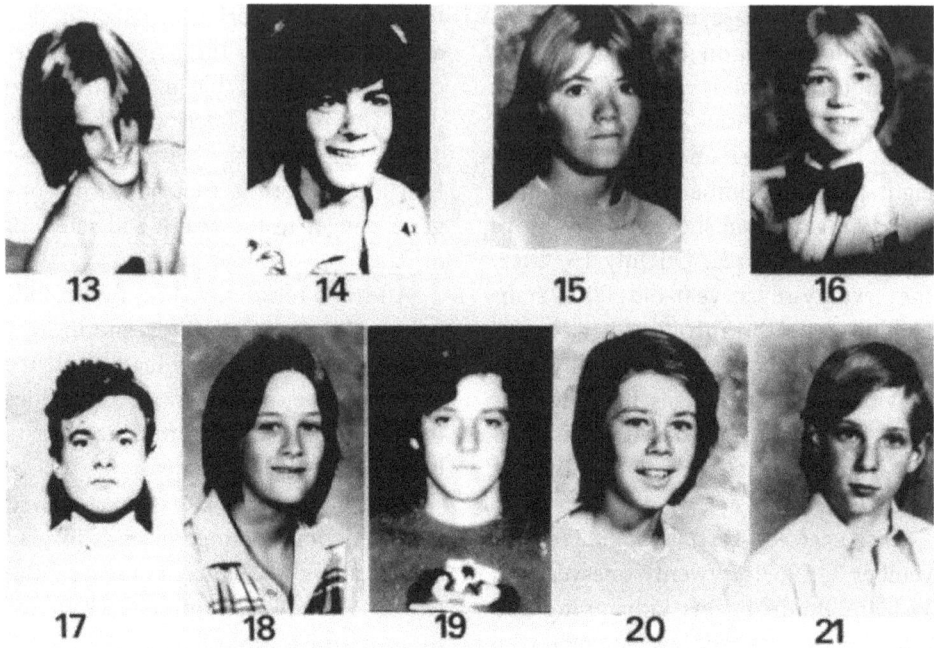

Figure 3.6. An array of photos showing Bonin's known victims. Photo by Los Angeles Sheriff's Department, https://www.ocregister.com/wp-content/uploads/migration/lvh/lvhnpa-b7888450z.120111130113249000g8013righ.2.jpg?w=1200.

3. The Crime Control Problems of General Deterrence and Incapacitation of the Dangerous

Even beyond failing to do justice, both these distributive principles also fare badly as mechanisms of crime control because both have serious flaws in their operation. That is, using general deterrence as a distributive principle—that is, setting criminal liability and punishment rules to maximize general deterrence—is a hopelessly unworkable enterprise. Similarly, using incapacitation of the dangerous as a distributive principle is similarly doomed to fail on its own terms.

A. GENERAL DETERRENCE Assigning punishments to maximize general deterrence is popular because it can be a highly efficient and effective crime control mechanism in principle, but unfortunately it rarely works well in practice.[112] While having a criminal justice system that imposes punishment for wrong-

doing does have an important general deterrent effect, what is problematic is *setting punishments for individual offenders* so as to maximize or at least increase the general deterrent effect on other potential offenders. In other words, general deterrence makes sense as a justification for having a criminal justice system but not as a distributive principle for assigning punishment to individuals.

For a punishment scheme to effectively produce general deterrence, it must meet at least three prerequisites. First, the intended audience (that is, potential offenders) must know the deterrence-based rule. Second, the intended audience must be rational calculators who can and will behave in a way that promotes their self-interest in light of the rule. And third, the intended audience's cost-benefit analysis under the rule must suggest that the cost of the contemplated violation outweighs its benefit.

Unfortunately, these prerequisites rarely exist in the real world. First, empirical research suggests that the target audience of potential criminals rarely knows the law. Even when they think they do, they commonly have it wrong.[113] Academics and politicians agonize over the formulation and adoption of general deterrence doctrines such as the felony murder rule, the three strikes rule, the use of strict liability, and other crime control doctrines, but when a drug addict is standing outside a convenience store deciding whether to go in and rob it, what are the chances he knows whether his jurisdiction has a felony murder rule and, if so, which particular variation of the rule it has adopted? The answer is practically no chance at all.[114]

Second, even if the target audience did know the legal rules and punishments they would incur, available research suggests they are rarely rational calculators. Instead their decisions are heavily influenced by mental or emotional disturbance; drug use or addiction; group influence, especially by gangs; impulsiveness; and an indifference or inattentiveness to consequences.[115]

Finally, even if the target audience did know the legal rules and were rational calculators, a general deterrent effect is possible only if rational calculation suggests that the costs of the wrongdoing outweigh the benefits. Yet the capture and punishment rate for most offenses is so low—sometimes less than one in one hundred for offenses other than homicide—that the target audience commonly sees the immediate benefit, such as getting that next fix, as outweighing the vague and minor future risk of actually being caught and convicted. More importantly, the result of the calculation depends not on the reality of the situa-

tion but rather on the potential offender's perception of it. Empirical evidence suggests that many, if not most, potential offenders overestimate their ability to avoid detection and punishment, so punishments designed by general deterrence would have limited effect even if actual punishment rates were higher.[116]

Moreover, general deterrence as a distributive principle has an added problem when one observes that the prospect of receiving just deserts already provides a deterrent effect under an empirical desert distributive principle. General deterrence as a distributive principle can only provide a more general deterrent effect than that inherent in an empirical desert distribution *by deviating from desert*. Yet such deviation from desert creates several new special difficulties. First, general deterrence as a distributive principle has an additional educational barrier to overcome as studies show most people assume the criminal law tends to align with their view of justice based on blameworthiness (empirical desert).[117] Second, even if the community learns of the special general deterrence-based rule, the deviation from desert incurs the crime control cost that follows from reduced moral credibility and reduced compliance when people do not see the legal system as implementing what they see as true justice.

General deterrence also has disturbing ethical implications because it divorces the rationale for punishment from an individual's blameworthiness. For example, total reliance on general deterrence could technically justify framing and punishing an innocent person for a crime to reap the societal benefits in deterred crime. Obviously, no advocates of general deterrence would support such actions, but that only goes to show

how general deterrence cannot provide a morally acceptable basis for punishment without reference to individual blameworthiness and desert.

B. INCAPACITATION OF THE DANGEROUS Incapacitation of the dangerous is a simple principle in theory: put dangerous offenders in prison until they are unlikely to commit further crime. While incapacitation of the dangerous is proven to work in many specific cases (unlike general deterrence), it is problematic for different reasons.[118] Behavioral scientists are at present relatively poor in reliably predicting future criminality in a specific individual, and so false positive and negative rates are high when incapacitation is used as a distributive principle, which creates enormous costs and intrusions on personal liberty with no crime control benefit. Furthermore, it is difficult to implement a consistent principle of incapacitation in the United States based on behavioral predictions due to constitutional limitations imposed by courts on the use of preventive confinement.[119] Incapacitation as a distributive principle essentially calls for preventive confinement based on the likelihood of future dangerous actions, but the same things that make people uneasy about the broader use of civil commitment similarly give pause when punishing a person for a crime they have not yet committed.[120] So instead of being able to openly evaluate an offender's predicted future dangerousness at sentencing, the legal system commonly uses substitutes like the presence of a prior criminal record, which is an unreliable predictor of future dangerousness.[121]

Even if incapacitation could be implemented in a clear and consistent way, its only advantage over a distributive principle of empirical desert would be when

its preventive sentences for offenders deviated from desert by either providing shorter or longer sentences than the community believes are just, as was the case with general deterrence as a distributive principle. But such preventive detentions in conflict with desert will have even worse effects on the credibility of the law than general deterrence-based deviations from desert because they may completely ignore the seriousness of the offender's past offense. In contrast, general deterrence at least follows a proportionality principle of sorts by giving greater punishments to more serious crimes. But incapacitation is more likely to tie its sentence to the duration and degree of the offender's future dangerousness. For example, incapacitation might punish a repeat robber more harshly for his new offense than a one-time murderer who seems unlikely to repeat his crime.

The result can be almost ludicrously unjust sentences as shown by "three strikes means life" laws designed to take dangerous repeat offenders off the streets. For example, the third-time offender in the 1980 case of *Rummel v. Estelle* was sentenced to life in prison for pocketing $230 after he promised to use the money to buy parts to repair an air conditioner.[122] Meanwhile, murderers and rapists routinely escape with far less time.

Thus, incapacitation of the dangerous is a poor distributive principle because it ignores the offender's blameworthiness for their offense in favor of predicting future criminality. Logically, if one embraced incapacitation of the dangerous over desert, then there would be no need for an offender to even commit an initial crime so long as the system had reason to believe he would in the future. Of course, few advocates of incapacitation support arresting and sentencing people whose backgrounds make them likely future criminals, but this only goes to show that incapacitation cannot be used as a substitute for a distributive principle of desert.

Additionally, any benefits of incapacitation in violation of desert are likely offset by the costs associated with the criminal law's loss of moral credibility when society sees people receiving unjust sentences.

State Penal Codes

States began to adopt "purpose of punishment" sections in their penal codes during the Model Penal Code–inspired code reform movement of the 1960s, with most following the lead of the Model Code at that time in choosing to focus on utilitarian reasons for punishment such as deterrence or incapacitation in addition to desert. However, there has since been a nation-wide trend of revising codes to prioritize desert principles, with codes that were adopted

or revised after the 1960s tending to be somewhat more desert focused.[123]

Given the overwhelming preference among people, whether lawbreakers or law abiders, for a desert-based distributive principle, it is surprising how often other distributive principles still appear in practice. As of 2018, as seen in figure 3.7, thirty states include desert as a basis for punishment in the language of their penal codes, but only five states have code provisions that appear to operate exclusively based on desert.[124] Other states employ a mix of distributive principles with goals of deterrence and incapacitation being quite popular.

Judicial Rulings on Distributive Principles

Given the importance of distributive principles in the formulation of criminal law, it is no surprise that courts have been involved in their interpretation and application. Over a century ago, the Supreme Court in *Weems v. United States*

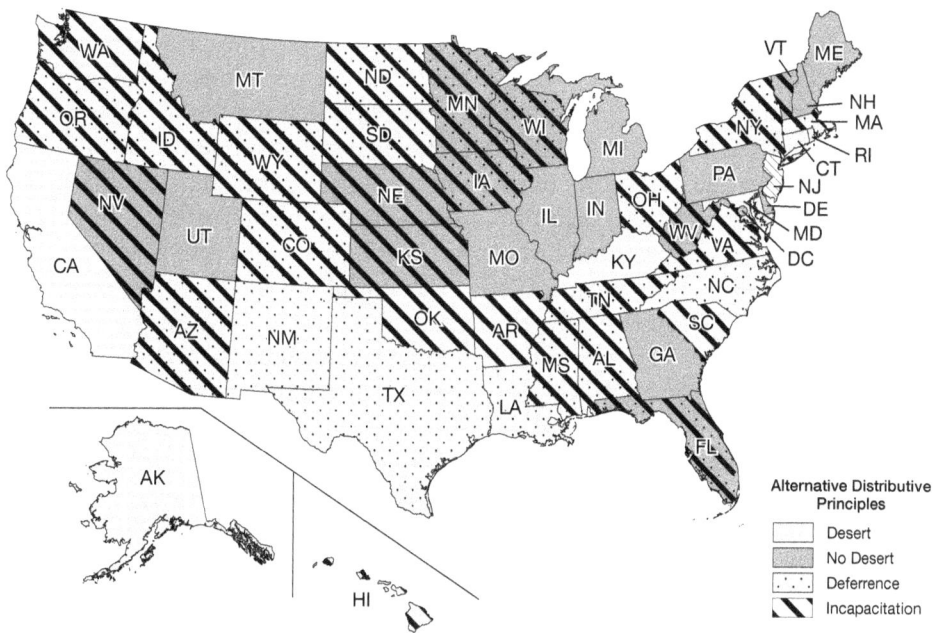

Figure 3.7. Alternative Distributive Principles. Graphic by Paul H. Robinson.

interpreted the Eighth Amendment as embodying a concept of desert-based proportionality, stipulating, "it is a precept of justice that punishment for crime should be graduated and proportioned to the offense."[125] For this reason, the court held that a sentence of fifteen years of hard labor for falsifying a public document was cruel and unusual.

However, the Supreme Court shifted away from supporting a purely desert-based distributive principle around the middle of the twentieth century when emerging scientific discoveries in the social sciences seemed to promise the possibility of new ways of dealing with crime and offenders.[126] Already in 1949, in *Williams v. New York*, Justice Black announced, "retribution is no longer the dominant objective of the criminal law. Reformation and rehabilitation of offenders have become important goals of criminal jurisprudence."[127]

Since then, the Court has never clearly agreed on one constitutionally mandated distributive principle and has appeared to recognize the constitutional validity of multiple conflicting distributive principles. The lion's share of Supreme Court discussion of distributive principles has focused on cases involving capital punishment. The fight over the constitutional status of distributive principles in justifying punishment came to a head in the 1972 case of *Furman v. Georgia*, which temporarily halted all death penalty sentences. In *Furman*, the justices disagreed upon the legitimacy of desert—or "retribution" as they termed it—as a goal of punishment. Every justice in the majority wrote a separate opinion, with Justice Marshall arguing a revisionist position that "retaliation, vengeance, and retribution have been roundly condemned as intolerable aspirations for a government

in a free society,"[128] and that "the history of the Eighth Amendment supports only the conclusion that retribution for its own sake is improper"[129]—a conclusion previous courts would likely have found surprising.

However, most justices rejected Marshall's radical view and acknowledged the role of retribution as a justification for punishment. Justice Stewart in his concurring opinion stated that he could not "agree that retribution is a constitutionally impermissible ingredient in the imposition of punishment. The instinct for retribution is part of the nature of man, and channeling that instinct in the administration of criminal justice serves an important purpose in promoting the stability of a society governed by law. When people begin to believe that organized society is unwilling or unable to impose upon criminal offenders the punishment they 'deserve,' then there are sown the seeds of anarchy—of self-help, vigilante justice, and lynch law."[130]

Also agreeing on the legitimacy of desert was Chief Justice Burger, with whom three other justices joined in dissent. Burger wrote, "there is no authority suggesting that the Eighth Amendment was intended to purge the law of its retributive elements, and the Court has consistently assumed that retribution is a legitimate dimension of the punishment of crimes."[131] Burger noted, "it would be reading a great deal into the Eighth Amendment to hold that the punishments authorized by legislatures cannot constitutionally reflect a retributive purpose."[132]

But even when the Supreme Court recognized the permissibility of a desert-based distributive principle, as most justices did in *Furman*, it only did so concurrently with other values and made clear that desert was not the sole—and not even the primary—distributive principle justifying the constitutionality of a given punishment. In the 1976 case of *Gregg v. Georgia*, Supreme Court Justices Stewart, Powell, and Stevens wrote a plurality opinion that argued the death penalty was permissible because it satisfied the purposes of retribution and deterrence,[133] but the death penalty solely for the sake of retribution would not be valid. They were likely influenced by legal experts at the time who considered retribution barbaric. As the American Correction Association noted in its 1966 *Manual of Correctional Standards*, "Punishment as retribution belongs to a penal philosophy that is archaic and discredited by history. . . . Penologists in the United States today are generally agreed that the prison serves most effectively for the protection of society against crime when its major emphasis is on rehabilitation. They accept this as a fact that no longer needs to be debated." As noted shortly in the reforms section, that conclusion no longer commands broad support among legal scholars.

Perhaps somewhat ironically, the Court has often used the blameworthiness proportionality principle inherent in a desert-based distributive principle to strike down punishments as unconstitutional without recognizing that this makes a principle of retribution founded on just deserts the dominant constitutional principle. After all, it makes little sense to inquire into proportionality under a utilitarian principle of deterrence or incapacitation, which care very little about making the punishment proportional to the offense. However, the Court has chosen to develop a framework for assessing the constitutionality of punishment that recognizes multiple distribu-

tive principles. In *Coker v. Georgia*,[134] the Supreme Court opined—following *Gregg*—that according to the Eighth Amendment, a punishment is excessive, and thus unconstitutional, if it makes no measurable contribution to any of the acceptable goals of punishment, which could be utilitarian or retributive in nature. The Supreme Court in *Enmund v. Florida* also held unconstitutional the use of the death penalty for the driver of a getaway car in a robbery-murder case, commenting that neither deterrence nor retribution was a sufficient justification for executing the defendant, and "unless the death penalty . . . measurably contributes to one or both of these goals, it 'is nothing more than purposeless and needless imposition of pain and suffering,' and hence an unconstitutional punishment."[135] The *Enmund* Court appeared to view a punishment as constitutional so long as it is justified on either retributive or utilitarian grounds.

Later, in the early 1990s, the Supreme Court addressed the issue of the acceptability of specific distributive principles more directly. In *Harmelin v. Michigan*, the Court acknowledged that the "fixing of prison terms for specific crimes involves a substantive penological judgment that, as a general matter, is 'properly within the province of legislatures, not courts,'" and that reviewing courts "should grant substantial deference to the broad authority that legislatures necessarily possess in determining the types and limits of punishments for crimes."[136] The Court recognized that the federal and state justice systems have granted different weights at different times to penological objectives of retribution, deterrence, incapacitation, and rehabilitation, and the Eighth Amendment does not mandate adoption of any one penological theory.[137] Eventually, after a close analysis of its past decisions, the Supreme Court held that the Eighth Amendment does not require a strict proportionality between crime and sentence but only prohibits extreme punishment that is grossly out of proportion to the crime (as judged by societal standards).[138] As a result, a desert-based distributive principle is not constitutionally mandated but can be used by the Court to strike down grossly unjust punishments.

Under *Harmelin*, a criminal sentence will generally be constitutional if it furthers any of the four main purposes of punishment mentioned by the Court: desert (retribution), deterrence, incapacitation, and rehabilitation (a complement to incapacitation) so long as the sentence does not grossly violate blameworthiness proportionality (a feature of desert) in the direction of overpunishment. More recent cases have affirmed *Harmelin*'s finding of four constitutionally acceptable purposes of punishment.[139]

D. PUBLIC COMPLAINTS REGARDING ANTI-JUSTICE DISTRIBUTIVE PRINCIPLES

Public complaints against non-desert distributive principles have largely focused on their ability to cause injustices, with the overly harsh punishments distributed by mandatory minimums and three strikes laws garnering a great deal of attention (see chapter 11 for more on the controversy and reforms surrounding mandatory minimums). However, anti-justice distributive principles have also outraged the public when they fail to deliver a sentence the public sees as adequate, even when those lenient sentences are justified by non-desert theories of punishment. For example, public outcry was sparked when it was discovered that Maine murderer Albert Flick was only able to kill again after being given a previous lenient sentence because his advanced age suggested (incorrectly) that he was no longer dangerous, as discussed in the previous case example.[140]

Non-desert distributive principles have commonly led to sentences the public and victims consider a justice failure in cases of rape and sexual assault. In 2016, a respected California judge, Aaron Persky, sentenced Stanford sexual assault perpetrator Brock Turner to only six months in jail, while the maximum punishment was fourteen years, because the judge concluded that a longer sentence did not make sense given that Turner was unlikely to be dangerous and could complete a rehabilitation course in the six months. But an outraged public viewed the situation quite differently and successfully voted to recall Judge Persky from the bench in 2018. Truthfully, Persky was not an unethical judge conniving to let "boys be boys" but was simply following the probation office's sentencing recommendation, which ignored the demands of desert.[141] Persky was a victim of the disconnect between the public's perception of and demands for justice and the non-desert distributive principles used by some criminal justice professionals.

E. REFORMS

Not recognizing desert as the governing distributive principle of punishment can lead states to adopt flawed criminal codes with punishments that erode the credibility of the law. Reforming these codes and explicitly acknowledging doing justice as the purpose of the criminal justice system is important if governments are to take failures of justice seriously. After all, it is harder to ignore justice failures under a criminal code that specifically calls for doing justice than under a code that lacks a clear commitment to desert. Several reforms have been undertaken or proposed to promote reliance upon desert.

Alter Specific Statutory Punishments that Conflict with Blameworthiness. While many states have changed their statutory punishments in a desert direction, a host of criminal penalties are still based on factors other than desert. One can imagine a long list of specific statutory revisions to specific criminal penalties that would better focus on blameworthiness proportionality. Some legislatures have worked to roll back non-desert-focused punishments such as three strikes laws aimed at incapacitation and deterrence. As of 2014, more than half of states had taken steps since 2000 to roll back mandatory sentencing laws such as three strikes.[142] Legislatures have also undertaken a host of amendments to criminal code offense definitions that introduce grading criteria that take account of offense variations suggesting different levels of blameworthiness.[143]

Change Sentencing Guidelines to Focus on Blameworthiness. Given that some judges still look chiefly to non-desert factors in deciding sentences, one useful reform would be for states to create clearer sentencing guidelines for judges that prioritize desert instead of asking judges to juggle thoughts of deterrence, rehabilitation, and incapacitation. Such desert-focused sentencing guidelines would make it harder for judges to justify giving non-desert sentences that would offend the community. Note that because a desert-based sentence concerns itself primarily with the total punitive bite of the sentence rather than the method of sanctioning, it would be entirely consis-

tent with a desert distribution to prefer non-incarcerative sanctioning methods as long as the total punitive bite of those sanctions placed the offender in their appropriate blameworthiness rank among all offenders.

Delegate More Sentencing to Juries. One possible way to better implement a distributive principle of empirical desert might be to allow community members (that is, juries) to contribute more to the sentencing decision. While some states allow juries to decide on death sentences, it would be possible to give juries more involvement in the sentencing process to help the process better reflect community views on what a just sentence might look like. Several states now do this.[144] However, without the influence of sentencing guidelines, one would need to worry about significant sentencing disparities between different juries. (More on the problem of judicial sentencing disparities and the value of sentencing guidelines in chapter 11.)

F. RECOMMENDATION: ADOPT THE MPC REVISION THAT SETS DESERT AS THE INVIOLATE DISTRIBUTIVE PRINCIPLE

As noted earlier, recent decades have seen significant changes in the relative popularity of different distributive principles, in part because of the lessons learned from social science studies, including studies about the superior crime control effectiveness of desert-based principles. Perhaps the most significant reform seeking to prevent the failures of justice that occur from non-desert distributive principles was the 2007 revision to the Model Penal Code (MPC). The MPC was first promulgated in 1962 by the American Law Institute to serve as a guide to legislatures in creating modern criminal codes. The 2007 revision, which was the first revision to Model Code since its promulgation in 1962, changed section 1.02, "Purposes; Principles of Construction," which provides the principles governing sentencing. Previously, the MPC suggested that a variety of distributive principles be considered in sentencing. The long list of recognized purposes to be served is listed in the note.[145]

In the 2007 revision, however, the American Law Institute dropped the undefined multiple goals approach and adopted desert as the inviolable dominant distributive principle:

REVISED MPC SECTION 2.01 (2007)

(2) The general purposes of the provisions on sentencing, applicable to all official actors in the sentencing system, are:

(a) in decisions affecting the sentencing of individual offenders:

(i) to render sentences in all cases within a range of severity proportionate to the gravity of offenses, the harms done to crime victims, and the blameworthiness of offenders;

(ii) when reasonably feasible, to achieve offender rehabilitation, general deterrence, incapacitation of dangerous offenders, and restitution of crime

Table 3.1. Alternative Distributive Principles Summary

DP	Strengths/ Advantages	Weaknesses/Disadvantages
GD	• Under right conditions can avoid crime • Can have effect beyond offender at hand	• Works only when prerequisite conditions exist, which may not be common: knowledge of deterrence-based rule, capacity and inclination to rationally calculate what is in one's best interest, perception that costs of crime exceed benefits • Can give punishment other than what is deserved
SD	• Under right conditions can avoid crime by offender at hand	• Works only on the offender at hand • Works only when prerequisite conditions exist • Can give punishment other than what is deserved
RH	• If successful, can avoid crime by offender at hand • May have value in itself, in making person's life better	• Works only on the offender at hand • Only modest success in only limited cases • Can give punishment other than what is deserved • Problematic as sole distributive principle; must combine with another • Forcibly changing person's nature may raise ethical questions about intruding upon personal autonomy
Inc	• No doubt effective at reducing crime by offender at hand	• Works only on the offender at hand • Commonly inaccurate in predictions, which causes wasted costs and unjustified detentions • Can give punishment other than what is deserved • Can better reduce prevention costs, reduce damage to system's moral credibility, and increase accuracy by operating as open civil preventive detention system
ED	• Seen as most just, thereby optimizing criminal law's normative influence	• May do injustice that is not apparent to the present community • Failure to deviate from empirical desert can miss special crime control opportunities (for example, deterrence prerequisites present and high deterrent effect possible, reliable prediction of high probability of an offender's serious future offense)
DD	• Does justice	• Fails to prevent avoidable crime • Difficulty in operationalizing because of common disagreement among moral philosophers

victims, preservations of families, and reintegration of offenders into law-abiding community, provided these goals are pursued within the boundaries of proportionality in subsection (a)(i); and

(iii) to render sentences no more severe than necessary to achieve the applicable purposes from subsections (a)(i) and (ii); . . . .

The MPC revision makes clear that criminal punishment should not stray from the distributive principle of desert, stating that "the general purposes of the provisions on sentencing . . . are . . . to render sentences in all cases within a range of severity proportionate to the gravity of offenses, the harms done to crime victims, and the blameworthiness of offenders."[146]

In our view, adopting this new statutory language is the best way for states to make clear that the justice system should be concerned above all with doing desert-based justice. Adopting the MPC's new language can have benefits beyond sentencing. By expressly recognizing desert as the dominant inviolate distributive principle, the code language can lay the groundwork for remedying other failures of justice by explicitly making justice the top priority. While worthy goals such as incapacitation, deterrence, and rehabilitation can all be achieved within the constraints of doing justice, such goals should never be sought at the expense of justice.

Part II

LIMITATIONS ON CRIMINAL INVESTIGATION

CHAPTER 4

Investigative Errors

FAILURES OF JUSTICE ARE OFTEN CAUSED by external limitations placed on police investigations, such as a lack of funding or legal limitations on investigative procedures (issues discussed in the next three chapters). But internal police procedures can also generate justice failures, usually due to problems with evidence. This chapter considers three areas of criminal investigations where police errors produce failures of justice: errors in collecting, analyzing, and maintaining evidence. These evidentiary errors are often caused by understaffing, lack of training, or poor leadership in police departments.

In each instance, the competing societal interests are the same: doing justice versus the potential economic costs of providing better training, equipment, and recruiting more and better investigators and police administrators. Given the importance that ordinary people place on doing justice, citizens would probably be prepared to pay more in support of such activities if they fully understood the justice-frustrating costs of insufficient support—an issue examined more fully in the next chapter on inadequate financing. But even with adequate financing, effective investigation and prosecution requires attentive, devoted, and trained investigators and analysts working under competent leadership to implement best practices. Unfortunately, these conditions often do not exist in police departments across America, and thousands of

serious criminals slip through the cracks opened by investigative errors.

A. CASE EXAMPLE: O. J. SIMPSON

On June 12, 1994, football superstar O. J. Simpson attempts to reconcile with his ex-wife, Nicole Brown, at their

Figure 4.1. O. J. Simpson holding his infant daughter, Honolulu, 1986. Photo by Alan Light, February 1986, Kahala Hilton Hotel, Honolulu, Hawai'i, via flickr, https://www.flickr.com/photos/alan-light/2101359333.

daughter's dance recital, but she rejects him.[1] That evening, Simpson arrives at Brown's home and viciously stabs her to death along with her friend, Ron Goldman. Brown's and Goldman's blood are found on Simpson's car, and a glove with Brown's, Goldman's, and Simpson's blood is also found in his backyard, matching another glove found at the crime scene. Simpson tries to flee arrest by leading police on a televised freeway chase but is eventually taken into custody and tried for murder. His defense team points out numerous errors in the police handling of evidence such as contaminating the crime scene, not properly entering evidence into the chain of custody, and storing evidence in poor conditions. They argue Simpson was framed for the murders by a racist detective, and the poor investigative techniques introduce just enough doubt to allow the jury to acquit, despite experts agreeing that Simpson's guilt was never in doubt. Simpson is later found liable for the deaths at a civil trial and writes a book titled *If I Did It* revealing all the "hypothetical" details of how he got away with murder.

B. CASE EXAMPLE: KENNETH "EXXON" DAVIS

On August 5, 2000, eighteen-year-old Quortez Jackson, who is known and loved in his Baltimore community, is gunned down execution style outside his mother's townhouse in broad daylight. Many witness the crime. With four separate witnesses bravely stepping forward to identify the killer, the police arrest Kenneth "Exxon" Davis for the murder. However, at trial the defense shows long response-time delays in investigators arriving at the crime scene, mishandled evidence, incomplete reports, and lack of witness interviews, leaving the jury

to conclude that they cannot find guilt beyond a reasonable doubt. While Davis is still almost certainly guilty (as O. J. Simpson was), the sheer number of police errors creates a strong perception in the jury that they can't quite be sure. A local newspaper reports, "Davis joined a long list of murder suspects acquitted after . . . police blunders."[2] The variety of failures suggests a department-wide administrative failure to implement best investigative practices. With the Baltimore police department failing so miserably in its murder investigations, the trial judge is forced to appeal to divine justice as he enters the defendant's official acquittal, warning Davis, "I hope that you don't think this is something you have gotten away with because . . . I believe there is a God whose business is justice."[3]

C. COMPETING INTERESTS

As noted earlier, the only societal interests in tension with effective investigation are the opportunity costs of the money spent on improving justice through better investigator training, equipment, and hiring.[4] That is, money spent on these activities cannot be spent on other societal goods. The complex issue of competing interests over financial resources is discussed in the next chapter.

D. THE NATURE AND EXTENT OF THE PROBLEM

As noted earlier, investigative errors leading to justice failures arise most commonly in the collection, analysis, or maintenance of evidence. Each is examined in turn.

Failure to Collect Evidence

A slow police response or inadequate evidence collection at the scene of a serious crime (including not identifying witnesses) can threaten justice by allowing evidence to be contaminated or go uncollected.[5] The failure to obtain evidence often leads to the perpetrator going unidentified, and even if an arrest is made, prosecutors regularly decline to prosecute due to inadequate evidence. Gauging the full extent of failed evidence collection is difficult because failing to collect evidence usually results in no arrest, so no data on the subject is available. But to get a sense of how broad the problem could be, consider that of those cases where evidence collection is adequate to trigger a felony arrest, even here federal prosecutors decline to prosecute around 36 percent of violent offenses,[6] and about half of these refusals are due to witness problems and insuf-

ficient evidence.[7] Given the dramatically low clearance rates for even serious offenses, as discussed in chapter 1, it seems likely that effective evidence collection can and does make the difference in prosecution success for a wide variety of serious offenses. Assuming just 18 percent of serious arrests are not prosecuted because of evidence issues, this would suggest at least ninety thousand serious failures of justice a year are caused by investigative errors because police make about five hundred thousand arrests for violent crime each year.[8] But, of course, investigative errors also lead to failures to even make an arrest in many serious criminal cases. If we conservatively assume that an equal number of cases are lost due to investigative errors in cases

Figure 4.2. Collecting evidence is an exacting, time-consuming, and expensive process. Photo by Bobby Jones, US Air Force, Forensic Experts Identify Keys to Crimes, May 18, 2006, Office of Special Investigations, https://www.osi.af.mil/News/Photos/igphoto/2000556402/.

without an arrest as are lost in cases with an arrest, then investigative errors likely account for close to two hundred thousand serious justice failures every year. It is worth noting that the failure to collect evidence is not confined to forensic evidence alone. Recall the case of Casey Anthony, mentioned in chapter 1, who suffocated her daughter to death. During the investigation, officers examined only her Google searches, finding no incriminating materials. Had they searched properly and thoroughly, including her Firefox searches, they would have found Anthony had searched how best to kill her baby through suffocation—evidence that would likely have led to her conviction. If police departments across America performed at the highest possible level of detective work and investigative effectiveness (a proposition that would likely require significantly greater funding), it is likely that hundreds of thousands of additional serious crimes would end with justice being served. More realistically, incremental increases in investigative effectiveness across the worst-performing departments would still eliminate many thousands of serious justice failures.

THE SPECIAL PROBLEM OF INADEQUATE EVIDENCE COLLECTION IN RAPE CASES Police have an unfortunate history of repeated investigative failures in cases of rape and sexual assault. When investigating rape, evidence is primarily obtained through rape kits and interviews. Historically, in many instances rape cases were dismissed without significant attempts to collect evidence. Police departments sometimes deter victims from reporting in order to "meet statistical goals" regarding crime and clearance rates.[9] For example, between 1995 and 2010, the Baltimore Police Department drastically underreported rape cases when reporting

crime data to the FBI's Uniform Crime Reports (UCR). During that period, Baltimore reported a 77 percent decline in rape cases after systematically dismissing cases prior to investigation.[10] Dozens of other major police departments have similarly been found to have underinvestigated rape complaints, vastly skewing UCR data.[11]

When police do attempt an investigation, the victim interview usually becomes an investigator's primary source of evidence, but investigators often poorly handle such interviews through expressing skepticism, disinterest, or hostility. If a victim feels judged or doubted, they are less likely to disclose critical information.[12] Studies indicate that police officers are often skeptical of the validity of rape claims despite the fact that false reports of rape are relatively rare.[13] Research indicates that it was common for law enforcement officers to "disbelieve victims of sexual assault more than victims of any other type of crime"[14] and that police officers believed in "rape myths" at a higher rate than the general population.[15] Harmful myths include the notions that "only bad girls get raped," that "women ask for it,"[16] and the inherent unreliability of rape accusations made by prostitutes or women deemed to be "promiscuous."[17] Investigator attitudes have been shown to be the greatest contributing factor to an interview's success when engaging with a sexual assault victim.[18] Better rape interview training is especially important for male officers, who significantly outnumber female officers and who tend to have greater levels of rape myth acceptance.[19]

When investigators drop a rape case prior to full investigation or create a hostile environment while interviewing a victim, they ensure a failure of justice and perpetuate a feeling of mistrust between officers and sexual assault victims. This in turn leads to further non-reporting of rape and a sense of legal cynicism where victims do not believe the law offers a significant chance at justice (legal cynicism is explored more in chapter 14).

Failure to Analyze Evidence

One of the most frustrating and shockingly prevalent causes of justice failures is a systemic failure to analyze probative evidence once collected. For example, in 2012, over four hundred thousand rape kits across the country were reported to have never been tested to reveal potential suspects.[20] Similarly, forensic evidence from thousands of unsolved homicide cases, including DNA evidence, was never submitted to crime labs for analysis.[21] Reasons investigators do not analyze evidence include a lack of funding, available labs, and, ironically, the failure to identify a suspect (though the untested evidence might pinpoint the perpetrator).[22] The truth is that thousands of rapists and murderers get away with their crimes despite leaving behind clues the police find.

Failure to analyze available evidence is not a small problem. Results of a national survey of 2,250 state and local law enforcement agencies from 2003 to 2007 identified at least 12,548 unsolved rape and homicide cases containing DNA evidence that had not been sent for testing.[23] The study estimated at least 31,570 unsolved rape and murder cases had some form of untested evidence, a number that has only continued to grow over the years since 2007.[24] The number 31,570 was likely a vast underestimation even at the time given later studies showing hundreds of thousands of untested rape kits, but the survey still provided

useful information about why evidence goes untested. When asked why this evidence was never tested, 44 percent of law enforcement agencies responded that a suspect had not been identified and 12 percent responded that a suspect had been identified but not charged and therefore analyzing the evidence was not seen as a priority.[25] Seventeen percent of law enforcement agencies reported that they did not submit evidence for testing because they did not believe it would be useful, 9 percent cited insufficient funding for evidence analysis, and 6 percent reported that forensic laboratories were no longer accepting evidence submissions due to backlogs.[26]

Once again, these investigative problems disproportionately affect rape investigations. As previously mentioned, hundreds of thousands of rape kits in the United States have never been tested.[27] Currently, thirty-four states have legislation requiring the testing of both backlog rape kits and all new rape kits; several of these states enacted their legislation only recently.[28] In states where testing is not mandated, it is often up to the discretion of individual officers or agencies as to whether kits are sent to laboratories for testing.[29] While there have been efforts in recent years to solve the massive backlog of untested rape kits, many states have still failed to find a solution.[30]

Part of the problem of untested rape kits stems from the fact that most police departments have not established a uniform policy to send kits for testing and so the decision to test is often made on a case-by-case basis by potentially skeptical officers or financially strained department heads.[31] Even when states pass laws mandating testing certain types of evidence like rape kits, authorities still sometimes find ways around the directive.

In 2019, 10 percent of rape kits in Minnesota continued to go untested despite a state law requiring testing because a loophole allowed evidence to be discarded if the county attorney was consulted prior to doing so (a decision some prosecutors might see as a way to minimize their caseload). The failure to test evidence for rape (and other serious offenses) continues to be a systemic problem within the criminal justice system.

Failure to Maintain Evidence
Even when evidence is collected and analyzed, failures of justice occur when that evidence is not properly maintained until trial. Sometimes this occurs because police departments destroy the evidence, accidentally or otherwise. In other cases, the chain of custody is broken. The chain of custody refers to the documentation of how and where evidence is maintained from the time it is collected to the time it is submitted in court. A proper chain of custody is essential to show that evidence has not been tampered with, falsified, or contaminated along the way, and maintaining a proper chain of custody is an essential prerequisite to having the evidence introduced at trial. Many police departments are rife with chain of custody problems, with evidence being submitted late, lost, or contaminated at some point.[32] As one scholar notes, "There are too many cases in which evidence is 'thrown away' or destroyed and in which inexplicable gaps in the chain of custody exist."[33] When these gaps exist, evidence becomes inadmissible and guilty offenders may walk free.

DESTRUCTION OF EVIDENCE Around the country, thousands of rape kits and other forms of evidence are destroyed by authorities for a variety of reasons, such as to save space or simply by ac-

cident. In 2002, the Los Angeles Police Department accidentally destroyed more than one thousand rape kits.[34] Between 2010 and 2015, police departments in the Baltimore region intentionally destroyed 250 rape kits.[35] Even after the Maryland General Assembly enacted a rule that mandated rape kits be stored for at least twenty years, agencies continued to destroy evidence.[36] Such destruction often was the result of individual departments' poor policies. While Baltimore County destroyed hundreds of rape kits, police in neighboring Montgomery County destroyed none, reflecting a stark difference in internal procedures.[37]

This contrast in department policies reflects a national split as well. A CNN investigation sent records requests to 207 police departments across the country, and nearly half reported they had destroyed rape kits.[38] An investigation of police departments across the country found that rape kits for hundreds of cases were destroyed "before the statutes of limitations expired or when there was no time limit to prosecute," and much of the evidence was discarded by police only weeks after it was obtained.[39] Eighty percent of the evidence was "never tested for DNA" and "twenty-five agencies in 14 states destroyed kits tied to cases while they could still be prosecuted."[40] The agencies involved argued that the cases were closed and that the evidence was no longer worth storing when space could be made for evidence in new or ongoing investigations. In response to widespread destruction of potentially useful evidence, in 2017, the US Department of Justice recommended that "rape kits in 'uncharged or unsolved' cases be kept for at least 50 years," but many jurisdictions around the country have disregarded the recommendation.[41]

When detectives believe that a case is closed, they often have the power of deciding when to destroy evidence. In some cases, the destruction of evidence results from police ignorance. The LAPD destroyed DNA evidence in various rape cases "because they were unaware that the statute of limitations for rape cases was lengthened in 2001 from six years to 10."[42] Once the evidence is gone, there is no hope for bringing justice even if new developments occur.[43]

CHAIN OF CUSTODY PROBLEMS In addition to destruction, vital evidence is also jeopardized when the police chain of custody is broken. Failures in the chain of custody can occur when a "form or evidence bag is mislabeled, if the transfer takes an unreasonable amount of time, or if the evidence falls into the wrong hands."[44] For example, the O. J. Simpson murder trial was almost certainly lost for the prosecution due in significant part to failures in the chain of custody and poor evidence handling by police.

Statistics on chain of custody problems are hard to come by, but mistakes are ubiquitous and only solvable by better training and administration. Even when police know better, they sometimes cut corners under the press of business, leading to failures of justice. Unfortunately, many departments simply have no adequate monitoring system. For example, an officer in Tempe, Arizona, "knowingly botched 10 cases—including murder and rape—by keeping evidence in his garage and failing to write reports."[45] He also improperly stored crime scene photographs, case notes, and interview recordings and failed to submit a rape kit from a seventeen-year-old victim. Sadly, the Tempe police department's unorganized chain of custody policies and lack of oversight are not unique.

Understaffing

A major contributor to the failure to collect, analyze, and maintain evidence is the shortage of investigators. A recent study indicates that 86 percent of police chiefs nation-wide report a shortage of sworn officers; nearly half report that the shortage was only getting worse over time.[46] These shortages have seriously affected clearance rates. Studies show homicide cases have the greatest chance of being solved when three to four investigators are working on the case, when investigators arrive at the scene within thirty minutes of the murder, and when investigators attend the postmortem exam.[47] If not enough detectives are available or are overworked with too many other cases, clearance rates are bound to fall. (More on the problem of police officer shortages and their causes in chapter 15.)

Understaffing often results in organizational disorder as police departments try to spread too few investigators across too many crimes. For example, in 2019, the Chicago Police Department did not have a detective unit devoted specifically to homicides and had no consistent way of assigning caseloads, meaning that officers were often unclear about who was working on each case and how many cases they were assigned to.[48] Such disarray resulting from a failure to deal with manpower shortages inevitably allows serious crimes to fall through the cracks and produces preventable justice failures.

Lack of Training

Another contributor to the failure to collect, analyze, and maintain evidence is inadequate investigator training. For example, in 2002, Baltimore lost up to 44 percent of its homicide prosecutions because investigators had not properly secured crime scenes, not interviewed witnesses soon enough, not been trained well enough to organize essential case details, or not taken steps to ensure accuracy in witness identifications.[49] The disastrous state of Baltimore's homicide investigations in the early 2000s illustrates a deficit of training that afflicts many investigative forces. A 2013 study for the Bureau of Justice Assistance found that police departments with the highest homicide clearance rates offered continuing training for all homicide officers. The study showed that better training generally means better evidence collection, analysis, and maintenance.[50]

The lack of proper investigator training is also evident in how searches and interrogation of suspects are conducted, where police sometimes fail to follow judicial rules due to a lack of awareness. (Chapter 6 discusses discusses these rules.) As a result, such improperly gathered evidence can be suppressed, thus letting serious offenders offenders go free (chapter 8 discusses the exclusionary rule) or forcing prosecutors to cut a lenient plea deal (plea bargaining is examined in chapter 10).[51] Understaffing and lack of training complement each other in that understaffing often leads police departments to assign poorly trained officers to cases they are not equipped to handle. As one police chief has noted, "There's a shortage of detectives to do the routine detective work, and very often it's being farmed out to people who do their best but are not trained at the same level."[52]

Poor Administration

As is already evident from the previous discussions, many investigative failures are due less to errors by individual investigators or analysts and more to poor administration of the investigative procedures and resources by police administrators. In any organization, including police departments, leadership and policies made by leadership matter immensely to outcomes. Sometimes police administrators directly cause failures of justice by setting departmental policies that actively make solving criminal cases more difficult. For example, department policies that mandate the destruction of viable evidence or the dismissal of cases preinvestigation must ultimately be blamed on police leadership. More often, poor police administration causes justice failures by failing to adopt investigative best practices. For example, police departments where leadership allows individual investigators to decide on the destruction of evidence are failing to adhere to best practices when it comes to preserving evidence. Another instance would be when the police administration fails to ensure adequate training for the entire investigative force or neglects to provide standard operating procedures (discussed more in the reforms section shortly). There are numerous other examples of police administrators failing to adopt best practices either because of ignorance, inertia, or incompetence. For example, chapter 7 explores the usefulness of new technology in criminal investigations, but many police administrators fail to take advantage of the new technology even though it is commonly not only a more effective investigative tool but also more cost efficient than their current practices.

Poor administration also contributes to justice failures by creating or allowing structural inefficiencies within police departments. For example, as mentioned previously, Chicago's police department did not have a dedicated homicide detective unit in 2019 because of administrative failures to efficiently assign caseloads. Police departments, especially large ones, require good channels of communication between different internal departments and subgroups, with every individual knowing their specialized roles and having sufficient training to fulfill them. A confused administrative scheme can snarl a department's investigative effectiveness and eat up precious time that could be spent solving crime.

Police administrators may also cause failures of justice through prioritizing other goals above solving crime. For example, police leadership might focus on maximizing revenue by expanding traffic enforcement and asset seizure at the cost of reducing investigative personnel, or leadership might decide that aggressive crime prevention is more important than the investigation of serious crimes. Even if administrators do not intentionally deprioritize solving crime, they may still cause justice failures by failing to undertake strategies to improve investigative performance.

Of course, the presence of justice failures caused by investigative errors does not mean that a department necessarily has poor leadership—unusual mistakes, bad apple officers, and a lack of resources are hard to solve by even the most competent administrators. However, when departments display a pattern of investigative errors, at least some—if not most—of the blame lies with poor police administration.

E. PUBLIC COMPLAINTS ABOUT INVESTIGATIVE FAILURES

Investigative errors often cause the public and media to express concerns about the competence and good faith of law enforcement, and so failures to collect, analyze, and maintain evidence may undermine the credibility of the criminal justice system even more than other causes of justice failures. This is clearly the case with rape-related evidence where police investigative failures have led to a culture of legal cynicism among rape victims and massive public outcry. For example, in 2009, when investigators discovered almost twelve thousand untested rape kits in a Detroit warehouse[53] (more on this case in the next chapter), public outcry led to a mix of private and public funding to test the backlog, which was only completed ten years later. Similar discoveries across the country have led to the public and victim advocacy groups demanding reform in the way police conduct rape investigations. Rape victims have even taken to suing state and local officials over the mishandling of rape-related evidence, with lawsuits being launched in Texas, Maryland, Illinois, Connecticut, New York, and Tennessee.[54] Whenever a new trove of untested evidence is discovered by the media, outrage inevitably follows. For example, Marci Hamilton and Steven Berkowitz writing for CNN in 2018 summed up the general feeling when they noted that "the mishandling of child rape kits uncovered by CNN is an outrage, and the destruction of rape kits while prosecutions were still possible is an atrocity."[55] Mistakes happen in any system, but mistakes that allow serious offenders to escape justice are seen by the public as inexcusable.

F. REFORMS

Many reforms have been undertaken or proposed to help minimize investigative errors. This section presents some of those specific reforms before offering a recommendation to ensure best practices across all facets of criminal investigation.

Improving Chain of Custody and Evidence Maintenance. After O. J. Simpson's case became infamous for law enforcement's mishandling of evidence, police across the country implemented better evidence maintenance and chain of custody procedures. The crime lab and the scientific investigation division of the LAPD were deemed a "cesspool of contamination" by Simpson's defense attorney, Johnnie Cochran, and the lab soon received increased funding and staff and gained proper accreditation in 1997.[56] Now the lab "uses barcodes to scan and track evidence" and crime scenes must be handled by "two fully trained criminalists" rather than trainees (who handled the crime scenes in the Simpson case).[57] New policies also sought to avoid the specific errors in the Simpson case. For example, in that case an investigator carried a vial of Simpson's blood in his pocket for hours before submitting the vial to evidence, prompting the defense to argue that this was indicative of a framing. Officers today are not "allowed to re-enter a crime scene with evidence," and evidence must be submitted as soon as possible to limit problems in the chain of custody.[58]

Designing better storage facilities for evidence can also help prevent evidence from being lost or degraded. For example, before the Maplewood Police Department in Missouri renovated its evidence storage room, "everything from drugs and guns to bicycles and even a tombstone—were housed haphazardly in a 4-by-10 foot space."[59] In 2009, the disorganized space was transformed to include a "pass-through lock system, including a refrigeration unit for the storage of fluid and DNA evidence."[60] The department also adopted eTWIST, a "bar-coded evidence-tracking system" to better maintain evidence and avoid

failures in the chain of custody.[61] These changes, which were funded by the US Department of Justice's Edward Byrne Memorial Justice Assistance Grant, have significantly improved the department's ability to store and track evidence, thus enabling evidence to be more effectively used at trial.[62]

Adopting Standard Operating Procedures. Standard operating procedures (SOPs) can help eliminate investigative errors by giving police a manual and even checklists for how to conduct investigations. They can greatly reduce the number of errors of ignorance, but they also serve as useful reminders to even knowledgeable and conscientious investigators at times when things become hectic, as often happens immediately after a crime is discovered. While numerous different SOPs exist, they usually share many common features. For example, the following key principles come from *Practical Homicide Investigation* by former Bronx Homicide Taskforce Commander Vernon J. Geberth. The manual, first published in 1983, has gone through several editions and is considered something of an authoritative text as far as homicide SOPs go. Here, for example, is a general SOP for handling crime scenes:

> The three basic principles involved in the initiation of an effective homicide investigation are as follows.[63]
>
> 1. Rapid response to the homicide crime scene by patrol officers. This is imperative in order to protect evidentiary materials before they are destroyed, altered, or lost.
> 2. Anything and everything should be considered as evidence. Whether this evidence is physical or testimonial, it must be preserved, noted, and brought to the attention of the

investigators. The only evidence collected at this point of the investigation is eyewitness accounts or spontaneous statements of a suspect at the scene. After the scene is secured, immediate and appropriate notification must be made to the homicide investigators.

3. The importance of preserving the homicide crime scene and conducting an intelligent examination at the scene cannot be overemphasized. If a murder case ends in failure or an officer is embarrassed in court, the primary reason may very well be an inadequate examination of the homicide scene or a failure to implement good basic crime scene procedures as outlined in this text.

Those are just general principles, of course, and a well-written SOP will have specific details for responding officers to check off as they investigate the scene.[64] Almost all police departments have some form of SOPs, but making sure these are updated regularly and understood by all is an area that can use further improvement.

Mandate Testing of Forensic Evidence. As noted previously, many states (thirty-four) and local police departments have adopted laws or policies mandating the testing of forensic evidence, especially rape kits.[65] Such mandated testing may lead to some unnecessary evidence testing, but many will argue that this downside is likely outweighed by the prevention of justice failures that occur under a discretionary testing policy.

Implement Improved Technology and Testing Procedures. To address the immense backlog in DNA testing, Congress passed the Rapid DNA Act of 2017 "to subsidize the use of rapid DNA testing, which can cost as little as half of what a lab-based DNA test costs."[66] Rapid DNA testing machines do not require evidence to be sent to laboratories for analysis and can be operated by police officers (even those who are not trained in forensics) at a crime scene, which vastly decreases wait times. However, rapid DNA tests are not as reliable as laboratory testing and "the few studies done to validate the equipment suggest an inability to examine mixed samples and a high percentage of cases in which evidence is consumed."[67] Thus, while the machines can be extremely valuable, they should be used selectively when more thorough testing options are not feasible. There are currently nineteen states that do not allow rapid DNA testing.[68]

In 2000, the Tallahassee Regional Operations Center in Florida also used technology to reduce its test backlogs. The center developed a system of "process mapping" that has better organized the evidence database through barcoded and automatic labeling.[69] These changes eliminated the testing backlog by 2002, "even though their sample submissions had increased by 31 percent that year."[70] "By 2006, the sample analysis time had decreased from 30 days to 8 days despite an approximately 85 percent increase (since 2000) in the number of samples received."[71] The initiative, which streamlined and organized the testing process, did not require the hiring of additional staff and actually saved the laboratory roughly $300,000 each year.[72] Such changes to laboratory procedures can be useful at reducing backlogs and saving money.

Laboratory Quality Assurance. Police are not the only ones who make mistakes, and crime laboratories also require quality assurance. Some proposals suggest hiring staff to focus specifically on the issue throughout laboratories.[73] Many scientists have argued that the lack of standardization and accreditation of forensic crime laboratories is a significant barrier to crime investigation. Eric Lander, who served as an expert witness in one of the first court cases involving DNA evidence, claimed that "forensic science is virtually unregulated, with the paradoxical result that clinical laboratories must meet higher standards to be allowed to diagnose strep throat than forensic labs must meet to put a defendant on death row."[74] While the regulation of laboratories has improved since this argument was made, the problem remains. Currently, roughly "25% of all Federal laboratories [are] unaccredited" and roughly 15 percent of publicly funded federal, state, and local forensic laboratories are not accredited.[75] Even if the majority of laboratories are accredited, the standards and policies vary greatly depending on the accrediting body. There is no nation-wide standard of accreditation procedures.[76]

Independent Forensic Laboratories. Today, the majority of crime labs operate under the control of law enforcement agencies. Apart from the potential appearance of bias and the potential opportunity for police officers or prosecutors to influence laboratory findings, it is also detrimental from a scientific standpoint as investigators and prosecutors usually lack the proper background and are not qualified to operate forensic laboratories. As Michael Kusluski, a criminalist and an assistant professor at Penn State University, described it, "this control may be as simple as setting budgets and priorities, but often involves setting policies and procedures . . . decisions are being made by nonscientists who influence millions of cases annually."[77] The National Academy of Sciences recommended in 2009 the removal of public forensic laborato-

ries from the administrative control of police departments and prosecutors' offices, and others have voiced similar proposals. Yet this reform is far from being widely implemented.[78]

Increase Resources and Training for Homicide Detective Units. After suffering from relatively low homicide clearance rates compared to the national average during the early 2000s, the Boston Police Department attempted to revamp its homicide investigation unit by implementing the Boston Homicide Clearance Project in 2012.[79] The BPD established a Homicide Advisory Committee consisting of homicide detectives, prosecutors, forensic and intelligence analysts, and other field experts. The BPD also hired an investigative consultant from the United Kingdom to learn about investigative best practices that could be adopted in the United States. After these collaborative efforts, the department expanded the homicide detective unit by over one-third. The department also increased the training of detectives and forensic analysts. By expanding the department's homicide units and dedicating more resources to training, the BPD increased its adjusted homicide clearance rate by 18.4 percent.[80] As the first study of its kind, the Boston Project demonstrates the power of collaborative reform processes and the direct impact of increased personnel and resources on homicide investigative success.

G. RECOMMENDATION: CREATE A NATIONAL CENTER FOR CRIME INVESTIGATION EFFECTIVENESS (CCIE) TO ESTABLISH BEST PRACTICES AND ASSIST DEPARTMENTS IN MEETING THEM

Many, if not most, of the previous investigative reforms would be worth pursuing to reduce failures of justice, but what is truly needed is a way to inform and assist police departments in adopting these and other possible reforms. Thus, our recommendation is to create a national body of experts, including criminologists, detectives, and forensic scientists, to draft and continually update a set of best investigative practices aimed at reducing failures of justice. And, perhaps more importantly, to help the worst-performing departments move toward compliance with those best practices.

The organization, which might be called something like the Center for Criminal Investigation Effectiveness (CCIE), could be created and funded by Congress or the Department of Justice but, if so, should be strictly non-partisan. Alternatively, it could be created and funded privately, although contributions to it ought to never come with strings attached. The center's work would not be aimed at police practices generally, which can become highly political, but rather would focus strictly on the challenge of ensuring better and more effective police investigation of serious offenses. Its goal would be to reduce failures of justice in serious cases rather than to promote better policing or crime control, thus its members would be selected for their technical expertise in investigation.

Ideally, grants would go not to those police agencies best at grant writing but rather to those agencies most in need of improvement. Thus, the funding process would not be one based upon applications but one where the center itself, through its own research, identified those departments most in need of help. Where the investigative problems exist because of a lack of state or local financial support, the center could advertise that fact and help encourage proper funding

by local governments. Where the problem is not inadequate funding but rather a lack of effective leadership that provides needed training and organization, the center's charge would be to help the leadership see the need for reform and to help bring those reforms about.

In creating a code of best practices for criminal investigation, the center would not be starting from scratch. In 2005, the federal government provided funding for and directed the National Academy of Sciences to create a report detailing the current state of forensic science, including assessing the present and future needs of the forensic science community, identifying potential scientific advances that might assist investigators, and disseminating the best practices and guidelines for forensic evidence practices.[81] The National Academy of Sciences employed "members of the forensic science community, members of the legal community, and a diverse group of scientists" to oversee the project, conducting meetings to hear expert testimony and review published materials.[82] Their findings were compiled in a report published by the National Academies Press, but it was a one-time effort. Our recommended center would generate guidelines for best practices across all areas of investigation and would continue to update and refine such guidelines as needed.

Establishing best practices is likely to be the easiest and least demanding part of the center's work. Most of its focus will be on identifying those departments most in need of investigative improvements and developing strategies to help those departments. It would be most convenient, of course, if the center had access to funding that it could provide directly through grants, but that seems unlikely and is not essential. There already exist several federal agencies involved in grant funding to local law enforcement agencies, the most important being the Office of Justice Programs (OJP). The Bureau of Justice Assistance office within the OJP provides a wide range of resources, both financial and informational.[83] The center could help the local departments most in need of improvement to apply for such federal funding or for state or local funding. But unlike these and other government funding sources, the center's panel would be immune from the increasingly common political pressures triggered by all matters related to policing. The panel's sole charge would be to help the worst-performing investigative units reduce justice failures caused by investigative shortcomings in serious cases. If such a panel had existed before the O. J. Simpson case in Los Angeles or the Kenneth "Exxon" Davis case in Baltimore, for example, it could have identified many of the flawed investigative procedures used by those departments and helped replace them with best practices that would avoid such justice failures.

CHAPTER 5

Inadequate Financing

A. INTRODUCTION

AS THE PREVIOUS CHAPTER DISCUSSED, inadequate financing is the cause of many investigative errors, from understaffed detective units to laboratory backlogs for forensic testing. This chapter examines inadequate financing in more detail and how it produces a wide range of justice failures. In addition to causing under-staffing and testing backlogs, inadequate financing prevents the purchase and use of effective crime detection and investigation equipment, such as CCTV cameras and modern fingerprint readers. For example, in 2003, the Los Angeles Police Department had over six thousand murder cases in which fingerprint analysis had not yet been done due to the department's inability to afford modern fingerprint analysis equipment.[1] (See more on the importance of employing modern technology in chapter 7.) Similarly, inadequate financing can leave police unable to use modern technologies like GPS trackers to monitor defendants released pretrial. (See more on pretrial release in chapter 9.) Inadequate financing also affects prosecutors and courts, forcing more criminal cases to be dropped or resolved through unjustly lenient plea bargains. (See more on plea bargaining in chapter 10.) The decision to provide more financing raises opportunity costs, but because inadequate financing threatens effective investigation and prosecution at almost every level, it may well be worth additional investment in proven areas to ensure greater justice.

Police investigations are funded at three levels. Local police departments are primarily funded by municipal budgets, tied to such revenue sources as sales and property taxes.[2] States also maintain state police forces and crime laboratories and sometimes offer aid to local police budgets. However, state governments currently spend surprisingly little on policing, with police department expenditures constituting a mere 1 percent of states' total budget allocation. By contrast, local governments spend about 3.7 percent of their budgets on policing.[3] This leaves municipalities to pay for the vast majority of investigative costs, a situation that often produces significant inequalities as poorer communities, which may have higher crime rates, end up suffering greater rates of justice failures.

The federal government also maintains federal law enforcement agencies as well as funding some crime laboratory testing and offering grants to local and state police. Overall, 87 percent of police expenditures come from local jurisdictions, though in recent years, the federal government has increased its share of funding.[4]

Police departments are not the only parts of the justice system to suffer from poor financing. Underfunded prosecution offices have resulted in a shortage of qualified prosecutors across the country, with the result being excessive prosecutorial caseloads, more dropped cases, and unjustly lenient plea bargains letting serious offenders escape deserved punishment by the thousands. Local and state prosecution offices, which handle the vast majority of serious crime, are almost entirely funded by state and local governments, with very few federal grants.[5]

While inadequate financing is usually a result of legislative decision making, executive and judicial actors also make decisions with financial implications for criminal investigations. For example, courts may create limitations on investigation that raise the difficulty and cost of delivering justice. (More on judicial limitations on investigation in chapter 6.) Additionally, executive actors like police chiefs or chief prosecutors have some discretion in how budgets are spent and may direct money away from justice-related activities, thereby reducing financing for investigations. No matter the cause of the inadequate financing, poor funding threatens justice in a multitude of ways. Consider three case examples.

Case Example: Detroit Rape Kits
On November 18, 1995, eighteen-year-old Ardelia Ali is walking to her grandmother's home in Detroit when a man forces her into a vacant lot at knifepoint. The attacker rapes the terrified young woman several times before disappearing into the night. Ali goes to the police, where a rape kit is used to collect

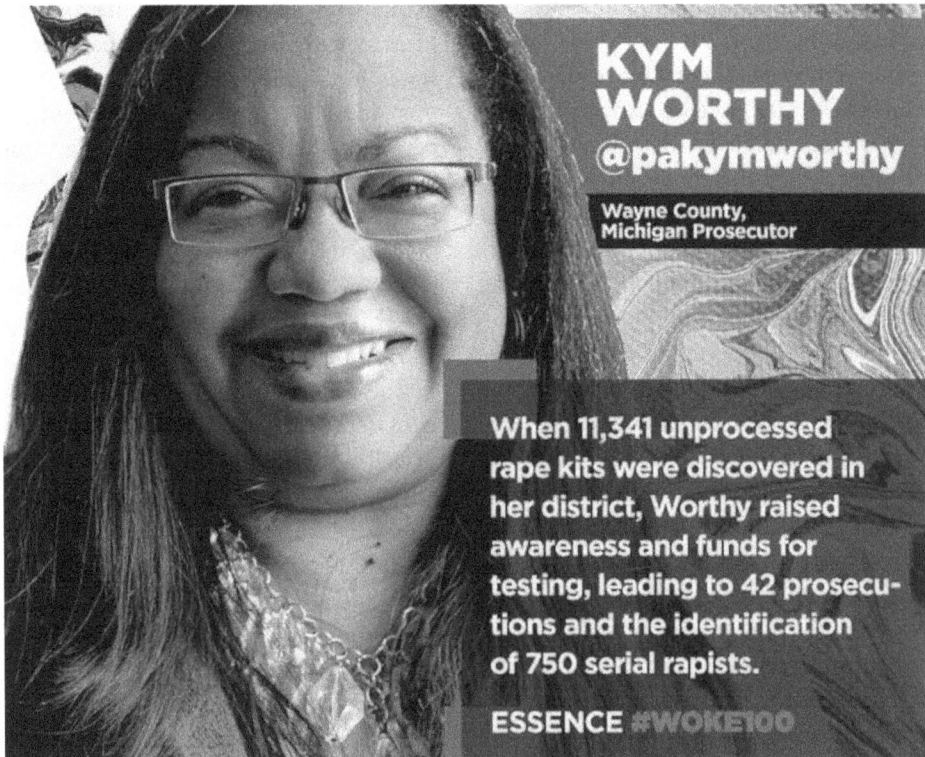

KYM WORTHY @pakymworthy
Wayne County, Michigan Prosecutor

When 11,341 unprocessed rape kits were discovered in her district, Worthy raised awareness and funds for testing, leading to 42 prosecutions and the identification of 750 serial rapists.

ESSENCE #WOKE100

Figure 5.1. Kym Worthy became the champion of justice by forcing the backlog of untested rape kits to be processed, 2020. Photo graphic from Sickle Cell Disease Association of America, Michigan Chapter, Inc., https://www.scdaami.org/about-us. Copyright © 2020 by Sickle Cell Disease Association of America, Michigan Chapter, Inc.

evidence. Police promise to investigate but simply close her case and shelve her rape kit in a warehouse with thousands of other untested kits to reduce costs. In 2009, an assistant prosecutor discovers 11,341 untested rape kits dating back to 1984 in an old police warehouse. For the next ten years, the Wayne County prosecutor Kym Worthy battles to find funding to test all the kits. Over eight hundred serial rapists are discovered, and two hundred new convictions are obtained, with hundreds of other cases ongoing. Ali finally gets her call from police twenty years after the attack. Her rapist is Marshall Alan White, whose DNA was found in her kit and the kits of two other women. If police had tested Ali's kit back in 1995, White could have been convicted then, as his DNA was already in a state database. White escaped justice for twenty-five years due to these failures.[6]

Case Example: Dennis Kurasz

In 2021, Dennis Kurasz, a forty-four-year-old convicted felon, is arrested for domestic violence and illegal possession of a firearm. His victim, Amanda Ducharme, tells police she is afraid of Kurasz because he has threatened to kill her if she complains to police. Despite his threat making, Kurasz is quickly released on $250 bail and ordered to stay away from Ducharme. To enforce the order, Kurasz is required to wear a GPS tracking bracelet. However, because of inadequate funding, Milwaukee County has only ninety GPS bracelets, so almost two hundred people with bracelet orders, including Kurasz, are released with no bracelet. Several months into his unmonitored release, Kurasz beats Ducharme to death with a piece of concrete.[7]

Figure 5.2. Dennis Kurasz, left, killed his girlfriend, Amanda Ducharme, while out on bail for domestic violence, 2021. Photos (*left*) from Pinterest profile photo, dennis449716, https://www.pinterest.com /dennis449716/; (*right*) from LinkedIn profile photo, Katharine Kucharski, https://www.linkedin.com/in/kath arine-kucharski-7b568844/; in Jessica McBride, "Milwaukee DV Murder Suspect Was on GPS Waiting List, Out on $250 Bail," *Wisconsin Right Now*, December 29, 2021, https://www.wisconsinrightnow.com/dennis-kurasz/.

Case Example: Stockton Investigator Layoffs

In 2008, Stockton, California, had twenty-four murders.[8] The year also brought a national recession. Inadequate financing forced the police department to lay off a quarter of its personnel, institute pay cuts, and reduce pension contributions.[9] The narcotics force was closed entirely, and community policing became an unaffordable luxury.[10] The arrest rate for homicides saw an immediate decline from 68 percent in 2008 to 24 percent in 2009.[11] And the situation continued to grow worse. By 2012, the city filed for bankruptcy, and the killings hit a record high.[12] There were six people left in the homicide department to work on the ever-growing mountain of unsolved cases.[13] Many people felt that the cuts led to "an emboldened criminal element" as would-be offenders correctly reasoned the police were too underfunded to effectively prevent or solve crime.[14] In 2020, the number of murders had climbed further.[15] The city police force was still at least 25 percent below pre-2008 levels, and Stockton is currently the most dangerous city in the State of California.[16]

B. COMPETING INTERESTS

The competing interests in deciding whether to invest additional funds in criminal justice investigation and prosecution are somewhat different than for most other justice issues discussed in this volume. Unlike most other causes of justice failures, in this instance there are no societal interests upheld by allowing failures of justice caused by inadequate financing. The competing interest is the opportunity costs for other uses of the needed additional funding: What interests might have been served by alternative uses for the funds? But given the high

societal costs and high rate of justice failures, not to mention the government's foundational responsibility to ensure justice and safety, the better long-term investment in most cases would likely be to allocate more financing where the expenditures really will reduce justice failures for serious offenses.

Others have argued that public funds are better spent on social programs that aim to prevent crime in the first place (and thus also the potential for justice failures). Anti-poverty programs are particularly touted due to the widely accepted claim that poverty causes crime. However, equating crime and poverty rates does not withstand scrutiny. Violent crime rates decreased during the Great Depression while the poverty rate increased, and crime rates increased between the 1960s and 1990s even as the poverty rate decreased.[17] In 1967, the first year the government started collecting the SPM (supplemental poverty measure accounting for government benefits), the poverty rate was 26 percent and the violent crime rate was 253 per 100,000.[18] In 2021, the SPM poverty rate was down to 7.8 percent, but the violent crime rate was up to 395 per 100,000. Combatting crime requires more than just reducing poverty because while offenders are more likely to be poor, most poor people are not likely to be offenders. Crime—particularly violent crime—is a choice, not simply a product of circumstances.

However, even if expensive social programs could effectively combat crime, the sums required for that long-range goal of social restructuring, like ending poverty or drug abuse, are enormous compared to the sums required to significantly improve the investigation and prosecution of serious offenses today. As a result, the cost of funding better crime investigation and prosecution—more DNA analysis, more detectives, etc.—would likely be significantly more cost effective at reducing justice failures in comparison to social programs indirectly reducing crime. This is especially true because decreasing justice failures through more effective investigation and prosecution has positive crime control benefits, as discussed in chapter 3, meaning that each dollar spent on doing justice also goes to reducing crime. Additionally, safer and more just communities are likely to be more prosperous, given the serious economic costs of crime and justice failures.[19] Considering the relatively poor track record that expensive social reorganization programs have at improving crime or justice, as seen in the tragically high victimization levels and low clearance rates common in poor neighborhoods, the comparatively minor criminal justice funding increases called for here would seem likely to be considerably more successful and efficient.

How Should Societal Resource Allocation Decisions Be Made?

People have different beliefs about how the government should spend money. Even if everyone agreed that the justice system needed more funding, how much of an increase should be granted before diminishing marginal returns would make it best to shift funds to other sectors? As today's acidic political environment makes clear, different people—and different legislators—have dramatically different values and beliefs about what is best for society.

Some may argue this means there is no correct answer to the allocation of societal resources, as different individuals have different interests. In other words, there is no correct answer, just conflicting values. But that view is unjustifiably

cynical. While it may be difficult to find, there is in fact a correct answer in resource allocation questions. Certainly our present political decision-making process (financial or otherwise) is influenced by majoritarian views subject to the strong influences of special interests and personal idiosyncrasies, but the imperfections of the current process do not mean that there is no right answer we ought to strive for.

Rational well-intentioned people should agree on at least a general decision-making principle that considers the interests of everyone in a democratic society. John Rawls, for example, describes a process in which the decision maker stands in the "original position" under a "veil of ignorance"—that is, a mental test in which the decision maker does not know what their place in society will be, not knowing whether they will be a criminal offender, a victim, or someone else. From this perspective, what allocation decisions and rules would they make? Performing this exercise in an intellectually honest way can be a challenge, especially for those people with strong ideological commitments, but it does make clear that good faith actors can approach these decisions to come to a "correct" decision for society.

We believe that such an exercise applied to American society would lead to greater funding for securing justice in serious crimes given how many people in society are negatively impacted by justice failures and the broader negative societal effects of such failures. Those policymakers responsible for denying additional justice funding are usually not personally affected by justice failures, but if they seriously considered the perspective of those who are, they might make different funding decisions.

Unfortunately, there are those who do not care about making decisions in the best interests of society but merely about achieving a minority's interests—often at the majority's expense. Perhaps one reason the justice system is underfunded is because there are few powerful private lobbies that stand to gain anything from greater justice—particularly in poor and minority neighborhoods. Those who would benefit the most from greater justice system funding often have the least political power.

C. THE NATURE AND EXTENT OF THE PROBLEM

Inadequate financing generates regular avoidable justice failures through numerous mechanisms. This section considers four common examples: underfunded police departments, laboratory backlogs, failures to implement new technology, and underfunded prosecution offices.

Underfunded Police Departments

It would be easy to overlook the problem of police underfunding because, while police budgets have remained at a steady 3.7 percent[20] of local budgets for decades, the dollars spent have grown by 179 percent since the mid-1970s.[21] Lost in these numbers is how much the demands on the police have grown. Since the mid-1970s, the population of the United States has grown by 50 percent, and policing has undergone significant mission creep. By the mid-1970s, most inpatient facilities for the mentally ill were closed and former patients were largely without support, causing police to become more involved in responding to mental illness. In addition, domestic violence laws began to appear in the 1970s.[22] The early 1980s marked the emergence of what now may be considered the mod-

ern era of homelessness, which requires significant police attention.[23] In the wake of the September 11 attacks, 70 percent of police agencies reported additional demands related to terrorism.[24] Cybercrimes and identity theft were unheard of in the 1970s but are now an ongoing criminal threat. Human trafficking prevention and response efforts also consume law enforcement resources in a way they did not in the 1970s.[25] Perhaps most importantly, since the 1970s, illegal drug use has become an epidemic in the United States, with police being forced to fight an expensive war on illicit drug distribution.

As a country, we call 911 and expect to receive help, no matter what the issue is. As a society, our standards for investigators have increased—we want college-educated officers and top-notch evidence processing and the certainty of expensive DNA testing. It is also an uncomfortable truth that "as governments, local and federal, attempt to address social problems they often do so by passing laws with criminal penalties. The police are pulled into social control roles ever more deeply, expanding their mission beyond fighting traditional violent and property crimes."[26] Police are required to do far more today despite receiving the same fraction of societal resources they did in the 1970s. Adjusted for mission creep, police funding—far from rising—has likely fallen as departments try to stretch the same tight money across a far wider range of responsibilities.

Practically everywhere one looks, one can find examples of police departments lacking the funds to engage in adequate investigations. Despite rising murder rates around the country, police departments are still battling budget cuts that cause understaffing. In Philadelphia, for example, overtime spending has been significantly reduced. In 2017, many officers experienced a decrease in overtime pay by up to $10,000 as compared to their overtime pay the previous year.[27] Overall, the city's budget for homicide detectives was reduced from roughly $6 million to $4.5 million.[28] This decreased funding had serious repercussions on investigations, and detectives noted that the cuts meant "less time to prepare for trials, and restrictions on their ability to interview witnesses who turn up during off hours."[29] The unit already suffered from inadequate technical support, lacking "basic technology, like voicemail or email accounts for detectives."[30] In 2020, the homicide unit was still using typewriters.[31] That year, 499 people were murdered in Philadelphia, and the official clearance rate was only 42 percent.[32] Underfunding means it is no wonder that Philadelphia police have been unable to effectively respond to record high shootings, with one Philadelphia homicide captain calling the decreasing clearance rate a "law of averages" when too few detectives are spread across too many cases.[33] Scarce resources mean there is little police can do. Philadelphia's police commissioner added just twelve detectives to the homicide taskforce in 2020 in response to the violence and low clearance rates.[34] The extra detectives barely registered. Philadelphia's homicide count soared to a record-breaking high of 561 in 2021, with most killings going unsolved.[35] In the first half of 2022, 1,400 people were shot in Philadelphia, more than 300 fatally—a number higher than in Los Angeles and New York despite those cities' larger populations.[36] When detectives are overworked, inadequate attention is given to each case and investigators may not be able to respond fast enough to crime scenes, risking the deterioration or destruction of critical evidence.

As one might expect, police departments with higher caseloads consistently have lower arrest rates.[37] As noted in chapter 4, research indicates that homicides are more likely to be solved if detectives arrive at the scene within thirty minutes and if three or four detectives are initially assigned to a case, yet these are all impossibilities in many departments due to underfunding.[38] The case study of Stockton, California, discussed earlier, illustrates the problem well. A similar dynamic is observable in every state. After significant budget cuts and layoffs, Atlantic County, New Jersey, had the worst homicide clearance rate in the state in 2010.[39]

Even cutting budgets for non-investigative police personnel has consequences. When Houston cut funding for "civilian support positions," which would normally handle various administrative and paperwork duties, the result was "much of the red tape and paperwork [had] to be handled by classified officers at a far greater expense."[40] Shifting officers to administrative duty commonly has negative effects on clearance rates.

In 2011, former Chicago mayor Rahm Emanuel sparked public concern when he decreased the police department's budget by $190 million.[41] In response to the significant budget cut, the president of the Chicago police lieutenants union remarked, "They've already laid off civilian employees, laid off everybody they can and now we're to the point where watch secretaries (sworn officers) are going out to buy office supplies."[42] Between 2008 and 2012, the Chicago police force fell from 13,359 to 11,944,[43] likely further contributing to dismal homicide clearance rates, which took a turn for the worse around 2010 and have dipped below 20 percent in some years.[44]

Inadequate financing for police departments also significantly hinders police officers' training. In Massachusetts, for example, the state's fifteen thousand police officers normally undergo forty hours of training each year, but a state auditor concluded that "there are only enough [funds] to pay for about 5,000 officers' training."[45] Apparently, "Massachusetts doesn't have enough money to fund the training, the facilities are really old, and there aren't enough trained instructors and there's 'not enough space to train police officers consistently after they graduate and because of that there's no uniformity across the cities and towns.'"[46] Some law enforcement agencies around the state have had no money to pay for any training.

While the status quo has left many police departments chronically underfunded, investigators have faced even greater challenges due to recent politically motivated budget cuts in the wake of George Floyd's murder in 2020. Of the nation's fifty largest cities, twenty-two have cut their police budgets in the wake of protests against police, with cuts reaching up to 15 percent in the case of New York City.[47] These budget cuts occurred despite surging violent crime and homicides and likely led to more crime and justice failures. (Chapter 15 examines these developments in greater detail.)

Perhaps most tragically, the societal costs of inadequate financing falls disproportionately on poor and minority neighborhoods, as noted in chapter 1. Many of these marginalized communities are desperate for more and better criminal investigations, not less—a need commonly ignored by those pressing for cuts in police budgets. As one distinguished Black professor observed in a *Washington Post* op-ed: "Police agencies serving low-crime, affluent neighborhoods . . . will continue to enjoy healthy operating budgets, inadvertently sanctioning age-old structural inequality. And it will be poorer people living in higher-crime neighborhoods who have to live with the consequences of whatever lawmakers decide to do."[48]

Inadequate police financing can turn entire neighborhoods into "no-go zones" where innocent residents are victimized with impunity.[49] An extreme example is Seven Mile Road in Detroit, Michigan, which is "one of the most dangerous no-go zones in the USA."[50] With violent crime rates in Seven Mile Road "five times higher than the rest of the US," police refuse to enter at night.[51] It would take highly armed and guarded patrols to restore order and solve crimes in such areas, but overstretched police have to prioritize use of their limited resources. Of course, neighborhoods like Seven Mile Road are far removed from where policymakers who make funding decisions live—or those funding decisions might be very different.

Laboratory Backlogs

Underfunding investigations is often visible when it causes extreme backlogs in evidence testing at crime laboratories. Most forensic laboratories are administered by their state's Attorney General's Office or Department of Public Safety and commonly lack adequate funding.[52] For example, as far back as 2003 when the Senate held hearings on the funding of forensic laboratories, the Alabama Department of Forensic Sciences "ha[d] a drug chemistry analysis backlog of 11,917 cases, a firearm evaluation backlog of 700 cases, and a DNA backlog of over 2,000 cases."[53] Similarly, the New Hampshire State Forensic Laboratory "ha[d] a thirteen-month fingerprint backlog."[54] In Phoenix, the fingerprint backlog was 5,900 cases and the DNA backlog 342 cases.[55] According to an old Bureau of Justice Statistics study of the country's fifty largest forensic labs, there was a 270,000-case backlog by the end of 2002.[56] The report found that "manpower shortages are the biggest concern of the forensic community and directly impact on the ability of crime laboratories to address casework backlogs."[57]

Far from improving since the early 2000s, these backlogs have only increased even as the number of labs has grown. The backlog of DNA evidence at crime labs almost doubled between 2011 and 2017. The average turnaround time for a testing request was five months—often guaranteeing a case will go cold.[58]

Backlogs are not a one-time problem caused by delays accumulating but rather a rolling, systemic issue for the justice system.[59] Currently, for every one piece of evidence being tested nationally, 1.2 more pieces replace it.[60] Demand for testing simply exceeds supply of testing capabilities either because of inadequate investment in testing capabilities or inadequate financing of conducting tests. The American Society of Crime Lab Directors, the Consortium of Forensic Science Organizations, the American Academy of Forensic Sciences, the National Association of Medical Examiners, the College of American Pathologists, the International Association for Identification, state prosecutors, and state and local law enforcement have all agreed that a lack of funding has "created a crisis for State laboratories" and has significantly contributed to evidence backlogs.[61] These

backlogs translate into justice failures as investigators are often unable to effectively manage delayed investigations, and case backlogs ensure thousands of rapes and murders remain unsolved.

Funding problems in laboratories often manifest through the inability to hire qualified staff, or any staff. In Mississippi, state funding for forensic evidence analysis did not even suffice to cover technician payroll. In fact, at one location, "fewer people worked in the Crime Lab now than did in 1994, even though crime has increased exponentially. Salaries are virtually unchanged since 2007. A crime analyst, requiring a master's in chemistry, starts at $33k per year."[62]

Staff shortages and lack of training funds commonly means that many existing forensic laboratory staff are not adequately trained. In fact, as a National Institute of Justice report found, "the United State requires at least 850 board-certified forensic pathologists, roughly double the current number. Many autopsies are now performed by individuals without needed training in general pathology and forensic pathology."[63] Mississippi, for example, has been experiencing an extreme lack of qualified staff. When the *Washington Post* investigated this ongoing issue they wrote: "When you don't budget enough to attract competent doctors to perform autopsies, the need for autopsies doesn't go away. It's just met by doctors who are less competent. Now you have less-than-competent doctors testifying at murder trials or investigating police shootings and deaths in custody. The disastrous consequences ripple through the criminal justice system, the medical community, and public health."[64]

A major factor in the continuing manpower shortages in laboratories is the way in which attempts to solve the problem revolve around one-off grants to clear backlogs that will return once the temporary funding is gone. [65] Only a long-term, substantial increase in base funding levels will solve backlogs and the justice failures they cause.

Failing to Make Use of Modern Technologies

Inadequate financing also means police departments are unable to make use of available modern technologies that can more effectively—and more cost efficiently—improve clearance and conviction rates and avoid crime altogether. The previous case example concerning Dennis Kurasz and the shortage of tracking bracelets in Milwaukee illustrates the point. When departments struggle with funding, basic operations like detective work, investing funds in new technologies—or enough ankle bracelets—will be a lower priority, with significant negative consequences on justice and safety.

Some modern technologies, such as increased surveillance capabilities, can be controversial due to privacy concerns (as discussed in chapter 7), but other technologies would help optimize law enforcement functions without infringing on privacy, yet they go unadopted for cost reasons. For example, as noted previously, the Los Angeles Police Department in 2003 had "over 6,000 murder cases in which fingerprints have not yet been evaluated because it cannot afford to update its fingerprinting analysis equipment."[66] As of 2014, the backlog remained.[67] Consider also the usefulness of technologies enabling pretrial and parole monitoring through GPS ankle bracelets or smartwatches that allow such offenders to be released without intensive, and more expensive, human oversight.

If departments struggle to find funds to invest in such widely used technology, it is no surprise they often do not get ahead of the curve on adopting cutting-edge devices[68]—such as biosensors for extracting identifying material from formerly unreadable fingerprints,[69] or breathalyzer ignition devices or other alcohol monitoring systems for probationers that cost less than $10 a day and provide much more effective monitoring than human officers ever could.[70]

Underfunded Prosecution Offices

Police departments are not the only part of the justice system to suffer from underfunding. Prosecutors play a critical role in securing justice for serious crimes, but many prosecution offices are overworked and understaffed—leading to more criminal cases being dropped or cleared through unjustly lenient plea bargains.

There are two basic levels of prosecution offices: ninety-four US District Attorney offices that prosecute federal crimes and over 2,300 district or county attorney offices that prosecute state and local crimes. All such offices not only employ a chief district attorney but also dozens or hundreds of deputies and line prosecutors who handle everything from charging and plea bargaining decisions, preparing witnesses for trial, guiding victims through the court system, paying for expert witnesses, and arguing cases before juries.[71] While federal district attorney offices are better funded and such federal jobs are seen as stepping stones to lucrative careers in private law, state and local prosecution offices have chronically struggled with a lack of funds and staff. "We're seeing a prosecutor shortage throughout the country; it's not limited to large jurisdictions versus small jurisdictions," Nelson Bunn, director of the National District Attorneys Association, lamented in 2022.[72]

Much of this staffing shortage is because of poor prosecutor pay. According to a report from the Association of Prosecuting Attorneys, "the average salary for entry-level state prosecutors in 2020 was $68,056. Starting salaries for associates at large law firms have soared to $215,000 as of January [2022]."[73] As a result, prosecution offices struggle to attract and retain talented lawyers. Without competitive salaries, "inadequately trained prosecutors who are worked to their limit" often fail at trial. As one New Mexican prosecutor, Raul Torrez, stated: "Simply put, we lack both the personnel and the basic resources necessary to provide adequate justice to the citizens of this community."[74]

While the problem of overworked public defenders is more publicized, research shows prosecutors and public defenders should have fairly equivalent caseloads, with the national advisory board setting that load at around 150 felonies or 400 misdemeanors per year.[75] In reality, prosecutors in some jurisdictions are assigned more than one thousand cases annually.[76] For people looking at the issue, it appears that "many prosecutors are asked to commit malpractice on a daily basis by handling far more cases than any lawyer can competently manage."[77] Many of the serious felony cases police refer to prosecutors are dropped not because they could not be won but simply because underfunded prosecution offices must prioritize time and resources by focusing on the easiest cases to prove.[78] Given the current state of prosecutorial funding, it is easy to see that the effectiveness of prosecution in serious criminal cases could be massively improved at only modest, even trivial, cost. Consider that the total estimated budget for state and local prosecution across the entire United States in 2007 (the last year the BJS reported this number) was just $5.8 billion.[79] This represented just 0.2 percent of the $2.6 trillion state and local governments spent that year.[80] Even an increase of less than a billion dollars, nationally, could go far toward solving the problem.

D. PUBLIC COMPLAINTS

In cities across the country, inadequate financing has produced public fear and frustration at the resulting toll on justice and safety. Even many of those who protest against current police policies and advocate for significant reforms in police hiring and training acknowledge that budget cuts to police departments are a threat to justice. Residents of Oakland, California, for example, have recently expressed their frustration with the city's rising violence and the lack of law enforcement response. After her daughter was fatally shot and her case remained unsolved, Chalinda Hatcher argued, "I do not think we need to take cops off the streets, because these streets are absolutely nuts."[81] While Oakland Mayor Libby Schaaf previously pledged to decrease funding for the police department in the wake of George Floyd's murder, she recently revoked that plan due to the city's rising violence and public outcry.[82]

The majority of citizens across the country agree that slashing budgets and cutting police forces will bring more harm, suffering, and failures of justice. Many Americans now share a desire for increased police funding. A poll in October 2021 revealed 47 percent of Americans support additional funding for police in their local area, while only 15 percent wanted it decreased.[83]

E. PAST REFORM EFFORTS

There have been many past moves toward increasing funding for specific areas of criminal investigation such as hiring more investigators or increasing laboratory funding. While every additional dollar can help, many reforms tend to be sporadic temporary increases or one-off grants meant to take the immediate edge off the problem while doing little to nothing to solve the long-term insufficient funding level.

Increase Funding to Hire More Staff. Just as cities have shown that cutting police officers decreases homicide clearance rates, other cities have proven the reverse. Between 2018 and 2019, the majority of states increased staffing in their police departments.[84] By January 2022, half of the largest twenty cities in the United States passed bills to increase police funding following increased crime rates in 2021.[85] In Chicago in 2017, three hundred additional detectives were hired, and the city's homicide clearance rate increased from only 30 percent in 2016 to over 46 percent in 2017.[86] Large increases in police funding have also occurred at the federal level in the past. The 1994 federal crime bill aimed to provide funding to hire one hundred thousand additional police officers across the country.[87] Also included in the 2009 Recovery Act were funds to allow jurisdictions around the country to hire more police officers.[88] More recently, the Biden administration announced "that cities can use part of the $350 billion American Rescue Plan relief money to hire more officers to combat gun violence. Cities—big and small—are jumping on that offer, with claims that

their police departments are running out of officers."[89]

Increase Funding to Analyze More Evidence. Some influxes of money have focused on clearing testing backlogs, but usually only temporarily. In 2013, Memphis mayor A. C. Wharton announced an executive order to clear the backlog of 12,164 untested rape kits as soon as possible.[90] In order to accomplish this, evidence would have to be processed in a private lab and would cost roughly $6.5 million. To support the effort, the US Department of Justice's Bureau of Justice Assistance (BJA) awarded the City of Memphis $1.9 million in 2015 and the Manhattan District Attorney's Office awarded Memphis almost $2 million.[91] In 2017, the BJA awarded the city an additional $1 million.[92] The additional funding had a positive effect on justice, as 2,612 investigations were begun and 270 requests for indictment were issued as more kits were tested.[93] However, the backlog will likely reappear after the funding runs out.

Similarly, Cleveland implemented a "test everything" policy in 2010 and began submitting all rape kits, even those for cases that had already been investigated, for testing. Cuyahoga County, which contains Cleveland, was awarded $1.9 million from the BJA in 2015, $2 million in 2016, $2.1 million in 2017, and $2 million in 2018, and temporarily increased the laboratory workforce in order to continue to reduce the backlog.[94] As of 2021, Cuyahoga County has completed analysis on 7,025 sexual assault kits, which has resulted in the identification of 511 serial rapists, 850 serial sexual offenders, and 826 indictments.[95] But once again, the backlog is likely to return without permanently increased funding levels.

Detroit has similarly benefited from grant funding. Since 2015, the BJA has awarded the Wayne County Prosecuting Attorney's Office millions of dollars to address the testing backlog.[96] As of April 2022, "the crime lab has completed analysis on 11,341 kits from Wayne County and ended the known backlog in Detroit. The efforts resulted in 2,616 DNA matches, the identification of 840 serial rapists, and 229 convictions."[97] Increased funding has immediate positive impacts on arrest and conviction rates and can drastically decrease justice failures.

Initiatives to increase DNA testing and reduce backlogs have also been taken at the national level. In 2003, President Bush allocated $1 billion over five years to reduce DNA testing backlogs in federal, state, and local forensic labs.[98] In 2004 alone, $92 million went toward crime labs around the country to analyze untested DNA and rape kits.[99] The DNA Initiative also supported increased forensic laboratory training. In 2004, Congress passed the Justice for All Act, which allocated half a billion dollars to clear forensic testing backlogs.[100] This initiative was inspired by Debbie Smith, a woman from Virginia who had to wait six years for her rapist's DNA to be tested. In 2017, the Department of Justice allocated $119 million in grants to forensic laboratories across the country to reduce backlogs;[101] in 2021, it granted $210 million for the same purpose.[102]

In some states, including Washington,[103] Wisconsin,[104] Virginia,[105] and New York,[106] defendants pay fees when their DNA is collected and tested, which helps cover the costs of crime laboratories.[107] In some states, "all criminal defendants are initially charged a small fixed fee (say $50) for DNA testing and will thereafter be charged a much larger fee (say $600) if a DNA test is actually conducted in connection with their case."[108] However, one could argue that billing defendants raises constitutional concerns because the government should be responsible for conducting proper investigations and bearing their costs, especially where the investigation does not lead to a criminal conviction.

As valuable as these special funding efforts have been, the inevitable conclusion they suggest is that the normal baseline budgeting for investigative testing is wholly inadequate. What is needed is not a continuing string of special grants to fix appalling backlogs after they have been created but rather the establishment of adequate ongoing support for investigative testing that avoids the backlogs in the first place.

F. REFORM POSSIBILITIES

Beyond the kind of traditional grant and funding possibilities described earlier, what new approaches might be useful in producing better funding for more effective crime investigation?

Raise Money through Charities and Private Donors. One funding source police have more frequently pursued in recent years is private charities and donations to police foundations, which most major city police departments maintain.[109] Just as philanthropists fund education and health initiatives, there has been an effort to foster a culture of giving around law enforcement investigations or specific initiatives such as testing rape kits, funding crime labs, buying new technologies, or hiring more detectives.

Institute Statewide Revenue Sharing for Law Enforcement. Local police departments receive their funding primarily from local taxes, which often creates large disparities within a state in the funding of police departments.[110] Often it is wealthier, low-crime neighborhoods that have the best-funded police departments, while poorer neighborhoods with the greatest need of better funding have underfunded police. As one study found, "analysis reveals widespread inequality in American police departments—some well-funded and some underfunded—often in a manner that bears no real relationship to the kind of public-safety challenges faced in each respective community."[111] States could adopt revenue-sharing laws essentially redistributing local taxes meant for police on a basis of crime rates. This could also be accomplished through funding local police departments entirely through state taxes with additional local police taxes possible if residents wished to pay more for more protection. This would mirror the way many states attempt to redistribute funding for education. However, such a reform would raise significant opposition from lower-crime areas that would end up subsidizing safety and justice in higher-crime areas. Still, even those traditionally opposed to government redistribution may acknowledge that guaranteeing justice and safety is a fundamental duty of government, which it fails if some communities are allowed to be ravaged by unpunished crime. A person's access to justice should not depend on their zip code.

Have Donors and Police Administrators Give Funding Priority to Effective Investigation. Increased funding for police departments does not guarantee an increase in investigative effectiveness unless the money actually goes toward investigation. Donors and police

administrators must first recognize the special importance of improving investigative outcomes. Buying better squad cars, uniforms, and guns is unlikely to help decrease justice failures. More investigative staffing, better investigative training, improved evidence handling and testing, increased access to modern technology, and all the other investigative funding needs discussed earlier are required to decrease failures of justice in serious cases. No doubt there are legitimate occasions where emergency situations demand the diversion of funds to non-investigative police activities, such as the need to pay increased overtime at times of social unrest. But apart from immediate public safety concerns, there should be a priority in police budgeting for reducing failures of justice for serious offenses. As shown in chapters 1 and 3, even if one's focus is on reducing crime rates, those rates will to a significant extent depend upon police's ability to catch offenders and the community's perception of the criminal justice system's moral credibility. Doing justice is the most effective path toward long-term crime control.

Separate Budgeting for Enforcement and for Investigation. In today's political climate, there is often hostility toward increasing funding for law enforcement because of allegations of police brutality and racism. (Details on this in chapter 15.) One way to potentially avoid this obstacle for policymakers would be to provide separate police budgeting for enforcement and investigation activities. The former triggers pushback by some concerned about aggressive policing, but few oppose the investigation of serious crimes. This might make it easier to get political support for the funding of better crime investigation without triggering resistance by those opposed to financing "oppressive" policing.

G. RECOMMENDATION: CREATE A NATIONAL CENTER FOR CRIME INVESTIGATION EFFECTIVENESS (CCIE) TO ASSIST DEPARTMENTS IN OBTAINING FUNDING TO MEET BEST PRACTICES

The simplest solution to the problem of underfunding is increasing funding for the justice system. However, this is easier said than done. Besides large and sustained increases in spending, the best solution to inadequate financing of criminal investigation is devising a means whereby funds can be directed to where they are most needed. Recall that our recommendation in chapter 4 was to create a national body of experts—which might be called something like the Center for Criminal Investigation Effectiveness (CCIE)—that would set, update, and refine best practices in criminal investigation but would devote most of its energies to helping the departments implement strategies to achieve these practices, including by helping departments obtain funding from whatever source possible. While the focus of that earlier chapter was on reducing investigative errors, through providing better training and procedures, the same CCIE approach could work effectively for directing funding to all means of improving investiga-

tion effectiveness, such as increasing the number of detectives, reducing laboratory backlogs, and increasing the use of modern technologies. As discussed in chapter 4's recommendation, the center's charge would include not just arranging funding from currently available grant sources but also advertising the failings of current investigative departments and the enormous societal costs they bring.

The center should focus on helping the worst-performing investigative agencies, not the ones cleverest at writing grant proposals. It will often be the case that the worst investigative performers will have the lowest sustained financial support from the state and local government, so the center's largest challenge will be to create the public support and the political will needed to improve permanent funding. The best means of doing this will frequently be, first, to show how poorly the investigative agency is performing in comparison to others; second, to make clear the significant social, institutional, and personal costs that stem from the continuing stream of resulting justice failures; and third, to show how additional funding could reduce those societal costs. Inadequate financing largely results from political ignorance or inattention, not from public indifference about the importance of doing justice. What is needed is an institutional lobbying force in favor of doing justice for serious crimes, and our proposed center could be such a force.

CHAPTER 6

Legal Limitations on Police Investigation

SOCIETY FACES MANY TRADEOFFS IN creating criminal justice system rules. One of the most pervasive dilemmas is how to strike the proper balance between protecting personal liberties, including the right to privacy, and the importance of doing justice. Criminal investigations commonly require some intrusion into personal liberty and privacy, whether it is searching personal property, monitoring online traffic, or interrogating suspects. Society imposes limitations on the techniques investigators may use, limitations that seek to strike a balance between these interests. But each additional limitation imposed can come at the cost of increasing justice failures. On the other hand, the more unrestricted the investigations, the greater the potential for unjustified infringement upon liberty and abuse of power.

While society must strike a balance, that balance ought to be open for reconsideration if changes in societal circumstances result in the present balance producing undesirable results. And it should arguably be ordinary citizens, who must live with the results, who should decide the ultimate balance. However, it is judges, commonly unelected, who create the legal rules that strike the liberty-justice balance that binds us all. These judicially created rules are rarely changed, even if societal circumstances change, as they are said to be based upon the court's interpreta-

tion of constitutional requirements. Another downside to the present practice of constitutionalizing these balances, especially by the federal judiciary, is that it forces a single rule upon all communities no matter how distinct their situations may be. It is highly likely that different communities would prefer to strike the balance of interests differently, and a federal system should welcome such democratic variation. Although courts have largely removed the issue of striking the liberty-justice balance from legislatures, it is nonetheless worth examining these issues to see how the current judicially imposed balance creates significant justice failures and what reforms might move toward a better balance that imposes fewer societal costs.

This chapter is divided into two parts. The first explores the current legal limitations on searches and seizures; the second examines the rules regarding the interrogation of suspects. The next chapter (chapter 7) examines the state of the justice-privacy balance regarding the use of new investigative technology and advancements, such as DNA analysis, surveillance cameras, facial recognition, and cellphone tracking. The limitations on justice discussed in this chapter are largely the result of judicial decisions, while the limitations discussed in the next chapter are largely the result of legislative or executive decisions.

A. SEARCH AND SEIZURE RULES

The overarching limitation on criminal investigation in the United States is found in the Fourth Amendment to the Constitution, which declares:

> The right of the people to be secure in their persons, houses, papers, and effects, against unreasonable searches and seizures, shall not be violated, and no Warrants shall issue, but upon probable cause, supported by Oath or affirmation, and particularly describing the place to be searched, and the persons or things to be seized.[1]

The Fourth Amendment departed from English common law, which allowed for "writs of assistance," or general warrants, to be issued permitting law enforcement to enter any building to search for illegal goods regardless of whether probable cause or even reasonable suspicion existed. The use of such general warrants by British customs officers to search American colonists' goods for contraband sparked great resentment and helped lead to the American Revolution.

While the Fourth Amendment clearly bans such general warrants, the proper interpretation of the amendment is not obvious in other aspects, such as exactly when a warrant is needed in the first place and how this relates to reasonableness and probable cause.[2] For example, is a search necessarily or even presumptively unreasonable if it is conducted without a warrant? In practice, such questions have been determined by American courts, raising questions for some about the democratic legitimacy of such rules. Particularly problematic in this approach is that constant judicial refinement and additions have produced a system of rules so complex that often no one really knows beforehand which

searches and seizures are permitted and which are not. Some of these judicial rules seem to have little relation to rational policy ends and would likely never have been adopted by a legislature. For example, judicial rulings have variously allowed police to search a car but not the driver and to arrest a suspect but not search the bag he is carrying.[3] Even if a lawyer could master the full complexity of search and seizure rules, the chance of busy police officers doing so, who are usually not legal experts, is slim.

The resulting response by police is often to refrain from undertaking searches and seizures where there exists ambiguity, which is common in a complex system based upon subjective concepts of what is "reasonable" or whether there is "probable cause."[4] This inevitably results in many serious crimes going unsolved. Furthermore, if the police do go ahead with a search and make a mistake, potentially crucial evidence can be excluded under the Supreme Court's 1961 decision in *Mapp v. Ohio*,[5] ruling that evidence gathered in contravention of court-imposed rules must be excluded at trial whether at the state or federal level.[6] (See chapter 8 for more on the exclusionary rule.) It should be no surprise that imposing increasingly strict and complicated search and seizure rules on criminal investigations in the 1960s contributed to a rise in crime and a decline in clearance rates.[7]

Consider several examples of the justice-frustrating application of search and seizure limitations.

Case Example: Earl Bradley

Earl Bradley, a pediatrician, is first accused of inappropriate contact with patients in 1994 after Thomas Jefferson University Hospital in Philadelphia investigates patients' complaints of sexual misconduct.[8] The hospital is unable to sufficiently prove the allegations to support criminal liability. Bradley moves his practice to a small, low-income community in rural Delaware. Accusations of sexual misconduct with patients are soon leveled against Bradley again, but he tells investigators that his patients are simply trying to extort money from him. In 2004, Bradley's sister, who serves as his medical office manager, alerts the state medical society that parents have complained to her about inappropriate touching of their children by Bradley. Several doctors also report complaints about long and unnecessary vaginal exams of young female patients. But when police in Milford, Delaware, seek a warrant to arrest him in 2005 for inappropriately touching a child patient, the Attorney General's Office concludes there is insufficient evidence for a warrant.

This is the history when, in 2008, additional patient complaints are filed, and investigators request a warrant to search his medical office. The court denies the warrant application as lacking sufficient supporting evidence. More complaints of sexual abuse continue to be filed.

In December 2009, a court finally agrees to issue a search warrant to the Delaware State Police.[9] Among the materials police find is an entire four-gigabyte thumb drive containing images of Bradley abusing children after the original warrant request was denied.[10] It turns out that Bradley has been abusing patients almost constantly, victimizing more than 1,200 children. Their average age was three, while the youngest was three months old. Bradley is ultimately charged with 529 criminal counts, which are consolidated into a single indictment upon which he is convicted of twenty-four offenses, including fourteen convictions for rape. (He is sentenced to fourteen consecutive life terms plus 165 years in prison without the possibility of parole.)

Figure 6.1. Earl Bradley was accused of assaulting children several times before the police were able to get a warrant to arrest him, 2009. Photo by Gary Emeigh, Georgetown, Delaware, *The News Journal*, December 18, 2009. From James Fisher, "Earl Bradley Moved to Prison Out of State," Delaware Online, June 13, 2016, https://www.delawareonline.com/story/news/local/2016/06/13/bradley-moved-prison-out-state/85659834/.

Case Example: Junead Khan

In 2014, twenty-four-year-old Junead Khan begins planning to join the Islamic State from his home in Luton, England.[11] Khan is a follower of radical Islamist preacher Anjem Choudary, and police visit Khan's home four times to offer him deradicalization resources as part of an anti-extremism program. Khan turns them down each time and strategizes with ISIS fighters online to kill American servicemen stationed in Britain. He plans to crash his truck into a vehicle with American airmen before killing as many as possible with a knife. If escape proves impossible, he plans to blow himself and others up with a backpack bomb. British police grow increasingly suspicious, and based on collected information amounting to probable cause, he is arrested by undercover officers who trick him into handing over his unlocked phone by pos-

Figure 6.2. Junead Khan was arrested for planning a terrorist attack in the United Kingdom after British police obtained his cellphone containing evidence of the plan, 2014.
Photo by the Crown Prosecution Service, from Daniel Sandford, "IS Supporter Junead Khan Guilty of US Airman Death Plot," *BBC News*, April 1, 2016, https://www.bbc.com/news/av/uk-35941296.

ing as company managers. UK law allows police to search a suspect's person, home, and phone upon his arrest (the probable cause required to justify the arrest is judged as sufficient justification for the searches).[12] Investigators find over sixty-six thousand messages that reveal the details of his plot. Khan is convicted of plotting terrorism and sentenced to life in prison.

In the United States, police may well have been barred from this search. Even if they had probable cause to arrest the suspect, they cannot search house, computer, or phone unless they also can affirmatively show probable cause that these contain evidence of his crime.[13] Without Khan's phone messages, the US authorities might have been unable to prove Khan's plot or even stop it.

The more demanding US search requirements have allowed terrorists to kill in the past, as in August 2001 when the FBI has al-Qaeda hijacker-in-training Zacarias Moussaoui in custody. The FBI has reliable information that suggests Moussaoui is an extremist working on a plan to hijack a plane. Because he is in violation of his visa, the FBI arrests him. Over a period of several days, field agents do everything in their power to try to obtain a warrant to search Moussaoui's computer. Despite the escalating urgency of the field agents' requests, the authorities in Washington repeatedly state that there is insufficient probable cause to show evidence of a crime would be found on the laptop.[14] As a result, the 9/11 plot goes undiscovered; the unsearched evidence might have led investigators to all the 9/11 hijackers.

Competing Interests

The issue of search and seizure rules presents an instance where legitimate societal interests exist on each side of the balance.

INTERESTS SUPPORTING THE CURRENT SEARCH AND SEIZURE RESTRICTIONS

- *Privacy Protection.* Current search and seizure rules recognize the importance of individual privacy interests. The right to privacy should not be undervalued. Police intrusions on personal space violate the "negative" freedom to be free of government interference in one's daily life.
- *Guarding Against Police Abuse.* Current legal limitations on the ability of police to search and seize can help protect against police abuse of power and the unjust government harassment of individuals. If police could freely search people and premises whenever they felt like it, there would be enormous opportunity to abuse that power. Strict warrant requirements do much to protect against such abuse.
- *Efficient Use of Police Resources.* Rigorous search rules requiring particularized warrants issued only on probable cause may save police resources by preventing investigators from engaging in time-consuming and resource-intensive wild goose chases and fishing expeditions that ultimately go nowhere.
- *Judicial Superiority in Fair Decision Making.* It can be argued that judges are in a better position to make fair rules regarding searches and seizures because they are likely to be more sympathetic to the rights of suspected criminals than legislators, who are likely more sympathetic to victims or innocent members of society.

INTERESTS SUPPORTING LOOSENING THE CURRENT SEARCH AND SEIZURE RESTRICTIONS

- *Greater Justice.* Current search and seizure limitations prevent police from solving many crimes that would be solvable under more expansive investigative authority. Loosening search and seizure rules would almost certainly lead to more criminals being apprehended and punished, thus ensuring greater justice.
- *More Deterrence and Less Crime.* Bringing more criminals to justice will deter future crime as well as prevent specific caught criminals from immediately reoffending.
- *Simplicity and Common Sense.* Current search and seizure rules are often highly complex, defy common sense, and are difficult to learn and follow by police officers in the field. Needless complexity is never a good thing in the law, especially in something as routinely necessary to investigation as searching is. Simplifying the law around search and seizure rules would help officers know what is legal. Equally important, simplified search and seizure rules make it easier for citizens to know their rights, and to know under what circumstances they may exercise those rights.
- *Democratic Accountability.* The status quo of search and seizure rules is almost entirely generated by unelected judges and does not necessarily reflect what society would choose in balancing the competing interests. Many argue search and seizure rules should reflect the compromise between liberty and justice that citizens and their representatives would strike and not the private opinions of judges.

The Nature and Extent of the Problem

Current search and seizure restrictions on investigators are potentially justice frustrating in several ways, such as by requiring warrants to be based on probable cause with high particularity (showing that there is probable cause that the specific thing to be searched contains evidence of a crime), by being so complex as to be difficult for police to follow with confidence, by having largely unaccountable federal judges set minimum requirements that bind state judges, and by having concrete negative effects on clearance and crime rates. Each of these issues is addressed here.

PARTICULARITY AND PROBABLE CAUSE
American police are required to obtain warrants based on probable cause. This means police must show a reasonable basis for believing that a person has committed a specific crime (for an arrest warrant) or that there is a reasonable basis to believe evidence of a specific crime would be found in a particular place (for a search warrant). Even when exigent circumstances allow police to act without a warrant, there must be probable cause for the officers to conduct the search.[15]

What constitutes a "reasonable" basis in probable cause is somewhat unclear, and the Supreme Court has acknowledged it is not possible to precisely articulate the requirement.[16] The Court found in the 1949 case of *Brinegar v. United States* that probable cause exists whenever the facts and circumstances within the officer's knowledge, based on reasonably trustworthy information, "are sufficient in themselves to warrant a man of reasonable caution in the belief that an offense has been or is being committed."[17] Of course, "reasonably trustworthy" and "reasonable caution" create enough ambiguity to leave the matter mostly up to the discretion of individual judges.

In addition to being based on probable cause, warrants are required to be particular in that police cannot search a location, such as an arrestee's house, for whatever potentially incriminating

evidence might be there. Police must know what they are looking for. For example, in the United States, police cannot get a search warrant for a known criminal's electronic devices under the reasonable belief that there will be records of some illegal activity on the devices unless they can state specifically what they expect to find—whether that be specific incriminating text messages or child pornography. The same goes for searching a house. US police cannot obtain a general warrant to search a suspect's home, even if they have probable cause to arrest him for a crime, without listing specifically what they expect to find in the house.

The particularity requirement in the Fourth Amendment was an obvious reaction to highly invasive general searches conducted by British authorities before the American Revolution. However, the Court's present interpretation of the Fourth Amendment's search requirements may be an overreaction in the sense that it bans any non-particular search irrespective of the strength and quality of the evidence against the suspect or the seriousness of the offense. Note that the current UK rules offer an alternative balance by automatically allowing the search of a person, their property, and their possessions upon arrest,[18] as in the Junead Khan case above. In the United Kingdom, the protection from governmental overreach is provided by the probable cause requirement for arrest. Once that is established, the balance of societal interests shifts. It is not unreasonable to conclude, as the United Kingdom has, that the privacy interests of a person for which there is probable cause to believe that they have committed an offense may be weighed differently from those of ordinary citizens.

While warrants are normally required to make arrests or engage in search and seizures, the Court has delineated six major exceptions that allow police to act without a warrant.[19] The *search-incident-to-arrest exception* allows police to search a lawfully arrested suspect and the area immediately under their control to an extent necessary to neutralize threats to officers' safety and to preserve evidence from destruction. The *plain view exception* allows police to seize evidence of a crime that is in plain view of an officer who is lawfully present. The *consent exception* allows police to engage in any search if the owner of the property consents. The *stop-and-frisk exception* (a *Terry* stop) allows police to stop and question an individual on the basis of statable facts giving rise to "reasonable suspicion" (a standard less than probable cause but higher than mere suspicion). The officer may also frisk the suspect if there is reason to believe they may be carrying a weapon. The *vehicle exception* allows police to search any movable vehicle on the basis of probable cause that the vehicle contains evidence or fruits of a crime. A warrant is not required because delay could allow the vehicle to escape and evidence to be destroyed, but the warrantless search must be restricted to areas where the police could reasonably expect to find the evidence they are looking for. (For example, police could not search the glove compartment of a car they have probable cause to suspect is carrying a trafficked child, but they could search it if they were looking for drugs.) Finally, the *exigent circumstances exception* "applies when 'the exigencies of the situation' make the needs of law enforcement so compelling that a warrantless search is objectively reasonable under the Fourth Amendment."[20] In practice, this allows police to seize without a warrant evidence that would likely be removed or destroyed as well as authorizing police to enter a location in lawful pursuit of a suspect. However, for the exception to apply, there must have been probable cause at the time of the police action.

Of course, these exceptions have limited effect in the real world because they all require judgment calls by police, often under rapidly changing and difficult circumstances, and any error in judgment means that the evidence obtained will be excluded from use by the prosecution at trial. The reality is that these exceptions to the warrant requirement are not used in many, if not most, of the situations in which they apply.[21] Any warrantless search or seizure may be challenged, and investigators must convince a court that their actions were authorized under one of the exceptions.

In contrast to America's reliance on warrants, other Western countries have not adopted such requirements.[22] Many European countries, such as France and Germany, do not generally require warrants but prioritize acting on reasonable suspicion in order to follow promising leads.[23] In Germany, "The contrast with American search and seizure law is striking. Searches may be performed on mere 'suspicion,' rather than probable cause, and a written search warrant is frequently not used at all in Germany."[24] German police can conduct any search without a warrant if there is a danger that evidence might be lost with delay. As a result, the majority of searches occur without a warrant.[25] In France, search warrants are not required when investigating serious crimes, and police are allowed to conduct any search that could reasonably aid the investigation, with rules governing how the search may be conducted. And, as noted previously, even in the United Kingdom, the originator of many of America's warrant requirements, police have greater latitude, such as being allowed to search an arrestee's property without an additional warrant, as in the Junead Khan case. Many European countries are examples of societies that highly value privacy but strike a different balance on search and seizure rules to better facilitate crime investigation. It should be no surprise that such countries also enjoy higher homicide clearance rates.[26]

COMPLEXITY AND VAGUENESS The complicated nature of America's judicially created search and seizure rules leads to general incomprehension of the rules among police officers and many accidentally illegal searches, as well as an unwillingness by police to engage in some searches due to the fear of conducting an unlawful search. One study of more than 450 police officers found that they performed "better than chance" on only one of six questions about search and seizure rules.[27] Other studies have found that the "average officer did not know or understand proper search and seizure rules" and that officers demonstrate a "widespread inability to apply the law of search and seizure or police interrogation."[28] The Supreme Court recognizes a "good faith" exception to the exclusionary rule for searches made under a judicial warrant later held to be improperly issued. However, this exception applies only to errors by judges and not to good faith errors made by police officers in conducting a warrantless search, and some state courts do not recognize any "good faith" exception at all.[29]

THE FEDERAL JUDICIAL NATURE OF SEARCH AND SEIZURE RULES The Supreme Court's 1961 decision in *Mapp v. Ohio* radically shifted the landscape of search and seizure restrictions, marking the launch of what some have referred to as the "criminal procedure revolution."[30] Before *Mapp*, the power to decide the scope of search and seizure restrictions was left largely to the states—at least as far as criminal proceedings were concerned.[31] Although states were not free to "affirmatively" endorse police conduct that ran afoul of Fourth Amendment restrictions as interpreted by federal courts, the means of enforcing Fourth Amendment violations were left up to the states.[32] In *Wolf v. Colorado*, the Supreme Court recognized "varying solutions which spring from an allowable range of judgment" on Fourth Amendment issues and declined to impose the exclusionary rule on the states just twelve years before *Mapp* did so. Before *Mapp*, states had the practical ability to balance the interests at stake in making decisions on search and seizure rules and how strictly to enforce them. The variety of approaches taken by states—which was documented by the Supreme Court in both *Wolf* and its 1960 decision in *Elkins v. United States*[33]—reflects the considerable variation in the relevant value judgments across different communities.

After *Mapp*, however, the balancing decision was made for states by the Supreme Court, and all evidence obtained through an illegal search *as defined by the Court*, no matter how reliable or incriminating the evidence and no matter how serious the offense, was subject to the exclusionary rule. States could create additional restrictions on searches, but they were bound by the federal restrictions, which already set demanding requirements limiting investigation. Some on the Court, such as Justice Burger, criticized this move for "[inhibiting] the development of rational alternatives" by states that would strike a different balance of the competing interests at stake.[34]

The federal courts' usurpation of states' role in setting search and seizure rules is problematic as there are strong arguments for why search and seizure rules should be created by individual states. Nearly every state has an affirmation of the Fourth Amendment in its State Constitution.[35] Why shouldn't each state be free to act for its own community in converting the broad language of the Fourth Amendment into specific rules? Doesn't it seem likely that different state populations would want to strike the privacy-justice balance somewhat differently?

Indeed, this same observation argues for having a democratically elected legislature rather than judges strike the balance.[36] Legislatures are arguably more responsive to changes in those societal judgment than courts and more likely to evaluate and revise rules based on changing practical effects.[37] By contrast, the judicial doctrine of *stare decisis* means old decisions on police investigation often continue to govern society even if relevant societal circumstances change and even if the effects of the rules cause a state's population to desire a significantly different balance of interests. Such legislative rules would also probably be simpler and easier for police to apply. Virtually all these arguments apply not only to making search and seizure rules but also to rules governing the interrogation of suspects (see the second half of this chapter) and use of new technologies (see chapter 7).

Stripping legislatures of their ability to make fundamental decisions on how to limit police investigation is especially problematic because there is no evidence

legislatures would not properly consider the liberty interest of their citizens. Indeed, legislatures have shown themselves clearly willing to restrict police in ways the courts have not. Almost every state has varying additional rules on police power beyond what is established by the Supreme Court. For example, Delaware forbids warrants from being executed between 10:00 p.m. and 6:00 a.m. unless a judge rules it necessary. Illinois requires a warrant to be executed within ninety-six hours of its issuance. New Hampshire classifies canine drug sniffers as a search and requires police to have probable cause to use them.[38] Some scholars, activists, and special interest lobbyists continue to push for tighter state legislative restrictions on search and seizures than the federal rules, demonstrating the unfoundedness of fears that legislatures will ignore privacy rights.[39] Just as legislatures can create *additional* restrictions on police investigation, they should also be able to reconsider existing judicial restrictions in light of changing circumstances.

CONCRETE EFFECTS ON JUSTICE The nature of the American warrant requirement leads to justice failures by frustrating investigators' ability to follow reasonable leads (that do not amount to probable cause with particularity) and by delaying searches even when particularity and probable cause are satisfied. Quantifying the effect of warrant requirements on justice is difficult, however, as there is almost no data on the subject.

Processing times can be an issue because "drafting and submitting a warrant application may take as long as half a day."[40] If police are forced to take the time to draft and submit a warrant and wait for it to be approved, justice delayed may become justice denied when evidence is lost or destroyed. But while this effect exists, no statistics are kept as to how much evidence may be lost due to the delay from the warrant requirement, and it may not be feasible to gather such data.

Additionally, 8 percent of warrant applications are denied, and 5 percent of issued warrants are later deemed invalid, often halting the possibility of further investigation and prosecution.[41] An estimated one hundred thousand search warrants are issued in the United States each year, which means that though denials and invalidations are small percentages, these numbers translate into thousands of cases where investigations were likely stymied[42]—eight thousand search warrants denied and five thousand later invalidated. Courts also strike down warrantless searches (conducted by investigators in a belief they are covered by the court-authorized exceptions) in the thousands or tens of thousands each year. (See chapter 8, section A, for more on the frequency of the exclusionary rule's application, which is mainly used to exclude evidence obtained via warrantless searches.)

However, by far the greatest effects on justice created by search and seizure restrictions are the tens or hundreds of thousands of unrecorded instances where investigators need to search but do not apply for a warrant (because it is unclear that the warrant would be granted) or conduct a warrantless search (because the officers correctly or incorrectly believe the search would not meet judicial scrutiny). Many of these searches that do not take place could have brought justice in cases of serious crime, which means the costs of the search and seizure restrictions are invisible but significant. Trying to measure the number of unconducted searches is difficult, but one study compared the vehicle stop and search rate in

Los Angeles, where officers have great discretion in such searches, to the rate in Pittsburgh where the requirements for a vehicle search are almost warrant-like. In Los Angeles, fifty-three such searches per thousand people were conducted, compared to just six such searches in Pittsburgh per thousand people,[43] even though the latter had a higher violent crime rate.[44] It appears that tightening search requirements leads to an enormous drop off in the searches police even attempt to perform—certainly more than halving such searches.

The evidence supports the obvious assumption that more restrictive search and seizure rules produce more crime. When the federal search and seizure rules along with the exclusionary rule were imposed on the states in 1961, it caused dramatic effects on crime and clearance rates. A recent empirical study on the effect of the *Mapp* decision found that assault increased by 18 percent and violent crimes increased by 27 percent in suburban localities,[45] suggesting hundreds of thousands of additional victimizations occurred that could have been prevented by looser search rules.[46] Instead of risking violating complex rules, police simply declined to search and thus caught fewer criminals, leading to more crime as deterrence lessened and the same criminals reoffended. Such increased crime rates have the effect of decreasing clearance rates,[47] which, as discussed in chapter 3, creates a vicious cycle of more crime, more justice failures, and reduced moral credibility of the system, which creates more crime, and so on.

Public Complaints

The societal costs of limiting police searches are largely invisible to most Americans because the failures of justice caused by them are not likely to make headlines. There are exceptions to this, such as the case of al-Qaeda terrorist Zacarias Moussaoui, where if a search warrant had been issued, it might have stopped the 9/11 attacks. But most of the time, the public is unaware of any specific failure of justice caused by a lack of search authority. The case of Moussaoui and public fears about terrorism did lead to a discussion about loosening the rules around searches through laws like the PATRIOT Act (2001), which was designed to make investigation of suspected terrorism easier.

This legislative expansion of search authority, which was not resisted by the courts, met with public approval in the wake of the 9/11 terrorist attacks. A survey after the act's passage found that 48 percent of the public claimed that the PATRIOT Act was "about right"[48] and only 22 percent believed that the PATRIOT Act had gone "too far" toward restricting individual liberties for antiterrorism purposes.[49]

The public often adjusts to the status quo, especially on complicated legal matters like search and seizure, so perhaps a more accurate gauge of public opinion would be to look at the reaction to the Supreme Court opinions that created the current set of judicial rules back when they were not the status quo. That reaction was largely negative, with public outrage being sparked by the Warren Court's seeming disregard for the importance of doing justice and of public safety in favor of increasingly detailed limitations on police.[50]

Public concern today over search and seizure rules is usually generated by special interest groups, the majority of which are dedicated to advancing privacy rights. While there are many such groups

advocating for further restrictions on search rules, there is no similar-sized lobby pressing for expanding search and seizure authority. This is largely because the justice failures caused by search and seizure restrictions are mostly invisible to the public and not necessarily because the public understands or supports the current balance of interests enshrined by judicial search and seizure rules.

Reforms

As with other judicial rules, significantly reforming search and seizure limitations would require the Supreme Court to revise its jurisprudence. The court has occasionally done so in the past, for example, in recognizing six major exceptions to the warrant requirement, as discussed earlier. Additionally, legislatures can make some changes to streamline the warrant procurement process. Discussed here are other reforms that have already been undertaken, and the end of the section presents some more ambitious reform proposals.

Recognize Exceptions to Suppression of Evidence Under the Exclusionary Rule. Even if the search and seizure warrant requirements are not loosened, the Supreme Court could reduce the societal damage of these requirements by abolishing or limiting the exclusionary rule. While the direct effect of this would not be to improve investigative success, it would at least be likely to improve prosecution success by allowing reliable and probative evidence to be admitted at trial. (Obviously, some alternative mechanism would be required to encourage police compliance with existing restrictions.[51]) On the other hand, it is possible that this shift might reduce the number of instances in which officers presently decline to pursue a search or seizure because, while they think it is authorized, they don't want to risk permanently hobbling the investigation if they are later held to have been mistaken. (See chapter 8 for more on the exclusionary rule.)

Simplify the Process of Obtaining Search Warrants. Some legislative reforms have attempted to simplify the process of obtaining a warrant in the interest of efficiency and justice. For example, police commonly search for criminals who are "sexually exploiting children and uploading videos of that exploitation for others to see—but concealing their locations through anonymizing technology."[52] The recordings are located in several jurisdictions, and the investigators would typically need search warrants in each jurisdiction in order to remotely access the contents of the computers there. To lighten this burden, in 2016, Rule 41 of the Federal Rules of Criminal Procedure was amended by Congress to allow judges to issue warrants to members of law enforcement for the remote search (hacking) of computers or electronics outside of the jurisdiction in which the warrant was issued.[53]

Additionally, warrants sometimes get held up in review at police departments before being sent to judges. Some jurisdictions have implemented reforms that speed up the forwarding of warrant applications, usually by utilizing electronic approval processes that can allow department supervisors to review search requests much faster.[54] Forty-five states have also implemented some form of electronic court submission for warrants.[55] In Utah, for example, electronic warrant applications can be processed and sent to judges within minutes.[56] Besides warrant applications, some jurisdictions now use electronic forms and accept electronic affidavits and other

digital forms of evidence. A minority of jurisdictions have implemented entirely electronic processes.[57]

A number of bolder reforms have been imagined but not yet implemented.

Recognize Additional Exceptions or Revisions to the Current Rules. Some commentators have suggested that a consideration of crime severity be added to the Fourth Amendment requirements that would allow greater freedom to search in serious cases (for example, by reducing the particularity or probable cause requirements) as is already the case in France.[58] Thus, an invasive search of someone accused of murder would be viewed by courts as more permissible than an invasive search of someone accused of a non-violent or less serious crime. This could be done either by reducing the extent of probable cause required in serious cases or by increasing the extent of intrusion permitted upon finding probable cause, as in allowing the search of a suspect's phone incident to a probable cause arrest for a serious offense. Similarly, some scholars advocate for a homicide scene exception that would allow police to conduct a warrantless search of the surroundings of a homicide scene.[59] Implementing these exceptions might enhance the ability of police to investigate the most serious cases and prevent failures of justice. But these reforms, and many others, may be unlikely because they would require the judiciary to amend current constitutional interpretations.

Educate Judges on the Societal Costs of Current Judicial Interpretations and on Changes in Circumstances Since the Judicial Interpretation Was First Adopted. Given the existing judicially controlled system for striking the privacy-justice balance, it could be useful to educate judges on the effect of their interpretations by providing data-driven analysis of the real-world costs of such interpretations. Such information might include the effects on crime of certain investigative or interrogative rules, the investigative benefits of new technologies, the availability of alternative interpretations of the broad Fourth Amendment language that would strike an updated balance between justice and privacy, and so on. This kind of education would recognize the basic legislative function judges are now playing in limiting police investigation and would strive to provide judges with the kind of information any lawmaker would think appropriate in exercising such a balancing function.

Recommendation: Legislatively Codify Existing Search and Seizure Rules

One useful way of clarifying existing search and seizure rules and reasserting some degree of legislative involvement would be for state legislatures (as well as Congress on the federal level) to codify existing search and seizure rules and exceptions into a single comprehensive investigative code. For the most part, the current rules governing search and seizure are embodied in court precedents, rendering them narrow in scope and often leaving gray areas in the law. They do not provide the confidence, breadth, and clarity that a legislative enactment can. The proposal is for legislatures to review existing court precedents and to use them as the basis for enacting a comprehensive investigation code that spells out in one place, with clarity and authority, investigators' powers and limitations. The legislative code would work to fill in gaps in precedent, clarify gray areas, and potentially even push the bounds of some judicial precedents that seem unwise and

malleable. Courts may be willing to accept a boundary-pushing legislative rule because courts commonly prefer to avoid overturning democratic enactments. The current status quo of judicial rules results more from legislative abdication of responsibility over search and seizure law than a direct attack on the power of legislatures by courts.

This recommended reform is best suited to reducing justice failures for several reasons. First, by having some degree of legislative involvement in codifying and clarifying search and seizure rules, the rules may end up better reflecting the balance of interests that the community would support, or at least would be seen as more legitimate. Second, even if no restrictions are removed, the clarity provided by a legislative code would likely make police more efficient and decisive in performing searches within their authority. There would be fewer occasions where investigators would not search, even though the law actually allows it, because they are unsure about the exact location of the legal boundary (and the costs of exceeding it can be impunity for serious offenders). The clarity of such a legislative code would also make the job of courts easier by giving judges a firmer basis for their adjudication of individual cases. Finally, it is much easier to change a legislative code in response to changing circumstances than it is for courts to reverse past outmoded opinions on their own, given the general judicial obligation to follow precedent.[60] Nothing in the proposal would take away the courts' current authority to declare a search or seizure unconstitutional.

Some jurisdictions have already implemented such a reform. Internationally, the United Kingdom began a comprehensive codification of its court precedents with the Law Commissions Act of 1965[61] and later specifically codified its search and seizure laws in the Search, Seizure, and Detention Crime Act of 2002.[62] It is the United Kingdom's judicial and parliamentary stance that codification provides clarity and safeguards for law enforcement that court precedents fail to guarantee.[63] In fact, the United Kingdom has adopted what has been called "Police Acts," which are a body of laws that essentially codify the rules governing most aspects of an officer's daily conduct.[64]

While US states do not possess the power of parliament to override courts, at least ten states, including New York, Texas, and Florida, have codified at least some search and seizure exceptions into statutory law.[65] Such codification has even been used to clarify gray areas in court precedent. After the Supreme Court found that a cellphone could not be searched incident to arrest in the 2014 case of *Riley v. California*, Texas codified the circumstances under which police may search a cellphone without a warrant. These include circumstances such as the phone having been reported as stolen, an existing life-threatening situation, or if the phone is in possession of a known fugitive or previously convicted criminal.[66] Courts have so far not overturned this legislative rule governing the search of cellphones without a warrant, generally finding that the various situations in which such cellphone searches are undertaken might arguably be justified under one or another of the warrant exceptions currently recognized. This would seem to support the previous suggestion that courts are likely to give a certain deference to democratically enacted search and seizure rules, especially if they seem within the general range of existing constitutional interpretations.

The proposed comprehensive codification could have potentially prevented failures of justice in cases like Earl Bradley, mentioned earlier, and tragedies like 9/11. Considering that multiple complaints of unnecessary sexual touching were filed against Bradley, it is possible that a codified law on search warrants would have made clear that such multiple complaints, especially those alleging suspicion of child abuse, a serious offense, are sufficient for a search warrant of the suspected predator's electronic devices. Additionally, a search code could have made clear that in cases of reasonably suspected terrorist activity on the part of an already arrested suspect, a search of the suspect's electronic devices and communications should be authorized. Such a clarification might have prevented 9/11.

Regardless of one's beliefs on the proper balance between liberty and justice in search and seizure laws, a codification of such laws can only be beneficial by providing some degree of democratic input, informed by practical consequences and shifts in technology and culture. It would always remain the case, of course, that courts would have the constitutional authority to reject any aspect of the legislative rules.

B. CUSTODIAL INTERROGATION RULES

Probably every American knows from television that the police cannot simply interrogate a suspect in custody without first reading them their "Miranda rights." These include the right to remain silent, a warning that any statement can and will be used against them in court, and the right to have a lawyer present during questioning. Only if a suspect acknowledges they understand and waive these rights can custodial questioning proceed. Statements or confessions obtained without such a waiver will likely be excluded from evidence under the exclusionary rule no matter how volitional and no matter how reliable they are. Moreover, postarrest silence cannot be used against a defendant even to impeach an "ambush defense"—an exculpatory story or alibi carefully constructed after arrest to be consistent with the facts the prosecution will be allowed to present at trial and mysteriously never mentioned previously to investigators.

American arrest warnings were designed by the Supreme Court in the 1966 case of *Miranda v. Arizona* to uphold procedural justice by informing people of their constitutional rights, specifically the Fifth Amendment right against self-incrimination and the Sixth Amendment right to legal counsel. The Miranda warnings largely replaced the Court's previous voluntariness test that dated back to common law and focused on excluding only unreliable confessions where there was an indication of coercion.[67] Many have questioned who benefits most from the replacement of this standard by *Miranda*. As one scholar notes, the Miranda warnings go "far to protect noncooperation and cover-up by the most knowledgeable, cunning, and steely criminals, while providing only minimal safeguards for those who are uneducated, unintelligent, or easily coerced."[68] This view is supported by the fact that juvenile suspects, who are less likely to have criminal records, waive their Miranda rights at notably higher rates than their adult counterparts.[69]

Evidence suggests confessions are the basis for conviction in almost a quarter of all cases,[70] and measures that limit reliable voluntary uncoerced confessions or incriminating statements will regularly lead to avoidable failures of justice. This fact moved Justice Byron White to dissent from the *Miranda* decision, stating, "in some unknown number of cases the Court's rule will return a killer, a rapist or other criminal to the streets and to the environment which produced him, to repeat his crime whenever it pleases him."[71] The extent of these justice failures has become clearer since the advent of *Miranda*. Research on the decline in confessions and crime clearance rates reveals thousands of justice failures are routinely caused by the Miranda warning.[72] Suspects have a right to remain silent, but society may wish to reconsider the consequences of so aggressively encouraging silence.[73] Consider two examples of the costs.

Case Example: Swedi Iyombelo

Swedi Iyombelo has been communicating with an eighteen-year-old woman online. In February 2019, the two agree to meet in Bingham County, Idaho. When the teen arrives, however, she is confronted by a group of four men who gang rape her. She goes to the police, and all four are arrested and, when interviewed, make incriminating statements. The defendants' attorneys argue that the county sheriff who arrested the men did not use the proper language in advising them of their Miranda rights. According to the sheriff's office, "One of our deputies made an error while telling two of the four suspects their Miranda rights when he told them they had a right to an attorney 'in court'—instead of just saying they had a right to an attorney." Based on the wording error, the court suppresses the incriminating statements, and instead of facing life in prison, the four men are

Figure 6.3. Swedi Iyombelo was one of four suspects arrested for the attack, 2019. Court pool photo from CBS 2 News Staff, "16-Year-Old Kuna Gang Rape Suspect Charged as Adult, Transferred to Ada County Jail," Idaho News, March 22, 2019, https://idahonews.com/news/local/16-year-old-kuna-rape-suspect -charged-as-adult-transferred-to-ada-county-jail.

allowed to plead guilty to a misdemeanor and put on probation. A spokesman for the office writes, "It was an honest mistake that had a horrible consequence."[74]

Case Example: Brian Argent

On August 18, 1995, Brian Argent goes to a nightclub in East London with his wife. At some point, an intoxicated Tony Sullivan asks Argent's wife to dance.[75] Argent is furious. Sullivan slips away. When Argent leaves the club, he sees and stabs the unresisting Sullivan seven times with a knife before leaving him to die in the gutter. Later that day, police arrest Argent at his house for the killing and ask him for his side of the story. Argent refuses to answer any questions then or at any subsequent time during the investigation. At trial, he offers an elaborate story, worked out with his wife, about how he left the club early and never met Sullivan. Prosecutors argue that, if that were the case, why wouldn't Argent ever have mentioned any of this to police when they first came to arrest him for stabbing Sullivan? The prosecution argues that he never mentioned any such story because it was fabricated after the fact as the best story he could come up with consistent with the facts that would be presented at trial. English law allows postarrest silence to be used to impeach a defendant's credibility, so the jury is allowed to hear about Sullivan's failure to ever mention his story, and they choose to disbelieve him. They convict him of murder. In the United States, however, Argent's failure to mention any part of his elaborate story when asked by investigators would have to be hidden from the jury, so the prosecution could not effectively impeach the credibility of his fabricated alibi.

Competing Interests

Citizens will want to consider both sides of the competing interests because it is they who will suffer the consequences of either too many or too few restrictions on interrogation rules.

INTERESTS SUPPORTING THE CURRENT RE-STRICTIONS ON INTERROGATION

- *Encouraging the Use of Fifth and Sixth Amendment Rights.* Current interrogation rules centering on the Miranda warnings encourage suspects to invoke their right to remain silent and consult a lawyer. To the extent this is considered an interest society values, then the status quo upholds it to at least some degree. Perhaps encouraging the use of such rights is innate to respecting human dignity, but that is not entirely clear because it might be argued that respecting human dignity merely requires not engaging in coercion.
- *Preventing False or Coerced Confessions.* Current interrogation rules may help prevent false or coerced confessions, although there is little evidence that Miranda warnings do this. The standard of voluntariness in confessions, established by the Supreme Court long before *Miranda v. Arizona*, already prevented police from using coerced confessions in court regardless of whether Miranda warnings were given.[76]
- Some may argue that Miranda warnings constitute an extra care in interrogation that is important because wrongful conviction rates in the United States are supposedly so high, in part due to suspects falsely incriminating themselves. Consider a few popular estimates: "One in every 8.3 people put on death row has been wrongfully convicted and sentenced to death in the U.S. since executions have resumed in the 1970s."[77] "Studies estimate that between 4–6% of people incarcerated in US prisons are actually innocent."[78] "Between 2% and 10% of convicted individuals in US prisons are innocent."[79] But these numbers are highly dubious, with a more careful non-ideological analysis suggesting that, in reality,

the true rate of wrongful convictions is something around 0.031 percent,[80] and this results from a wide range of errors in the system, not just unreliable incriminating statements.[81]

- *Forcing Police to Rely on Better Evidence.* By making confessions harder to obtain, interrogation rules such as the Miranda warnings may force police to rely on better evidence and build stronger cases, thus benefiting justice as a whole and preventing false convictions. However, while non-confession convictions might be attractive, most serious offenders will not voluntarily confess after getting a Miranda warning, and many if not most serious offenses cannot be successfully prosecuted without relying to some extent upon an offender's incriminating statements. Further, as to the quality of the evidence, some would argue that there is no stronger evidence than a reliable voluntary confession (or admission of damaging information).

INTERESTS SUPPORTING RELAXING CURRENT RESTRICTIONS ON INTERROGATION

- *Doing Justice.* Encouragement to stay silent mainly benefits guilty criminals, whose interests are adversarial to those of society, and there is no societal value in criminals staying silent. Encouraging suspects to talk to police is likely to lead to more crimes being solved by confessions or damning admissions. Historical confession rates suggest *Miranda* led to a drop in confessions. (See a more detailed discussion of this effect in a subsequent subsection.) Thus, replacing Miranda warnings with other rules could lead to a rise in the confession rate and an increase in justice for serious offenses.
- *Miranda's Apparent Ineffectiveness.* *Miranda*'s stated justification was reducing illegal coercion in interrogation, but there is little evidence to

suggest that *Miranda* warnings reduce such coercion. After all, police can still illegally threaten suspects before, during, and after *Miranda* warnings. If judged by its own aims, *Miranda* does not appear to be a success.[82] To be clear, *Miranda* does reduce the number of reliable voluntary confessions or damaging statements by warning criminals to act in their self-interest (an interest adversarial to society), but it does nothing to prevent police from wringing false confessions by lying, threatening, or brutalizing suspects. While proponents of *Miranda* may claim it reduces coercion by reducing the stress and pressure of a normal police arrest or interrogation (thereby giving criminals a chance to plan how best to escape justice), it is not this normal psychological pressure of being arrested or interrogated by police that is unconstitutional but rather illegal acts such as threatening violence or brutalizing suspects—acts not prevented by *Miranda*.

- *Greater Deterrence and Less Crime.* Increasing clearance rates through encouraging reliable confessions would contribute to deterring future criminals and make society safer.
- *Saving Justice System Resources.* Proving a crime via confession or damaging statement is the most cost-effective means of obtaining convictions. Even if investigators and prosecutors manage to prove a crime without such statements, such non-confession investigations take more time, use more resources, and are less likely to end in plea agreements, thus necessitating more expensive trials.

The Nature and Extent of the Problem

This section examines four problematic issues relating to *Miranda*: its ef-

fect on confession and clearance rates, its protection of ambush defenses, its inflexible judicial nature, and its ineffectiveness measured by its own aims.

MIRANDA'S EFFECTS ON CONFESSION AND CLEARANCE RATES   The best available evidence suggests *Miranda*'s requirements contributed to a notable decrease in confession rates, thus reducing the success of police investigations, resulting in lower crime clearance rates and fewer convictions. When caught, criminals often panic and make incriminating statements either confessing to the crime or attempting to deny the crime in a way that reveals damaging information. *Miranda* warnings are a saving grace to many offenders by giving them an opportunity to calculate how best to escape justice. Only about 20 percent of arrestees invoke their *Miranda* rights, thus refusing to answer any questions, but even if guilty suspects choose to waive their rights and talk to police in a bid to mislead investigators, as many do, the *Miranda* warnings still put suspects in a tactical mindset and prime them to cease answering questions during the interrogation.[83] In essence, *Miranda* warnings could have been taken straight from a criminal's best practices handbook. And criminals have been taking full advantage of *Miranda*.

Some studies suggest confession rates may have fallen from 55 to 60 percent before the *Miranda* decision to 30 to 40 percent after *Miranda*'s implementation, a reduction of 20 to 25 percentage points.[84] Another estimate suggests that confession rates dropped by roughly 16 percent.[85] Interestingly, a similar drop in confession rates was observed after Britain's adoption of the 1984 PACE Act, which required police to read arrest warnings similar to those of *Miranda*.[86] This suggests that Miranda-type warnings do indeed affect confession rates. Some pro-*Miranda* scholars have estimated that *Miranda* has only reduced confession rates by as little as 4 or 9.1 percent, but even these extremely conservative estimates show *Miranda* as having a non-trivial effect in tens of thousands of cases.[87]

Statistics on the number of US felony cases resolved by confession are not kept, except by a few cities, and even those few statistics are hardly current, but they are consistent at a rough estimate of 33 percent of cases.[88] Because police make about 500,000 violent crime arrests each year, this would suggest about 167,000 violent crimes each year are resolved by confession.[89] In other words, even if *Miranda*'s confession loss rate was only 10 percent, it would mean that *Miranda* is producing around 18,000 fewer confessions just in cases of violent crime each year.[90] If the loss rate is actually 25 percent, it would mean a loss of more than 55,000 violent crime confessions a year. These calculations do not even consider the much greater loss of confessions for crimes categorized as non-violent such as for theft, arson, fraud, certain sex offenses, and many others.

Such decreases in confession rates have in turn reduced crime clearance and conviction rates. It is estimated that confessions are necessary to obtain a conviction in about 24 percent of cases involving interrogation.[91] Assuming that *Miranda* caused a decrease in confessions by 16.1 percent, one scholar and former federal district court judge estimates that convictions in 3.8 percent of cases involving an interrogation were lost purely due to *Miranda*.[92] He estimated that *Miranda* caused the clearance rate for violent crimes to decrease by 6.7 percent, or 28,000 a year,[93] with even more sig-

nificant decreases for non-violent crimes (where investigators would be less likely to spend limited resources proving the crime if they could not get a confession).[94] More recent empirical work upped these estimates, with research suggesting up to 213,000 additional violent crimes (other than murder and rape) might have been cleared in 2012 alone without *Miranda*.[95] Much more conservative estimates suggest that *Miranda* only decreased convictions by 1.1 percent, but even that conservative figure means 4,700 lost violent crime convictions a year.[96]

Regardless of which estimates are used to determine how many convictions have been sacrificed, *Miranda* has clearly had tangible implications on confession rates, clearance rates, and conviction rates. Since *Miranda* was adopted in 1966, the overall justice costs of the decision have been staggering for society. Even using the most conservative estimates available, at least 260,000 serious violent criminals since *Miranda* have escaped conviction purely due to the decision.[97] More reliable estimates would put that number well over a million. Considering that most of these violent criminals who escaped because of *Miranda* almost certainly reoffended, the overall cost to society is incalculable in terms of human misery. If the *Miranda* court could have seen the full costs of its decision—as Justice White foresaw in his dissent—a very different decision might have been made.

THE PROBLEM OF AMBUSH DEFENSES The Supreme Court has found that the Fifth Amendment right against self-incrimination includes a right not to have post-Miranda silence used to impeach a defendant's testimony at trial.[98] This encourages a popular technique among guilty defendants: the ambush defense. An ambush defense is where a defendant will stay silent until they are aware of the prosecution's case, at which point they will construct a believable story to present at trial that fits as well as possible the prosecution's admissible evidence, as in the Brian Argent case. Guilty defendants often make the mistake of speaking too soon and telling false stories to police that do not account for all the facts that will become known to investigators. The ambush defense can be a powerful tactic for obtaining a false acquittal unless prosecutors are able to point out to the jury that the defendant inexplicably never mentioned any of this exculpating story to investigators. Of course, once the jury knows they are dealing with an ambush defense, the credibility of the defendant is in question unless the defendant can provide some reasonable explanation for why they said nothing to investigators about these compelling exculpatory facts.

As noted, the US rule prohibits prosecutors from making any reference to the defendant's earlier silence, so prosecutors have no way of impeaching an ambush defense. This makes it particularly difficult to prosecute rape cases, where an ambush defense alleging consensual sex is all but impossible to disprove without bringing up the defendant's previous failure when questioned to explain such a consensual encounter. Unlike the United States, the United Kingdom's interrogation rules limit the possibility of ambush defenses by allowing postarrest silence to be used to impeach a defendant if they choose to testify with a new story at trial. As a result of this, the UK variation of arrest warnings includes a right to remain silent but also a warning that staying silent can harm a suspect's defense if they do not mention now something they later rely on in court.[99]

THE JUDICIAL NATURE OF THE RULES The judicial nature of interrogation rules raises its own problems, as mentioned in the earlier part of this chapter relating to search and seizure. Requiring Miranda warnings was an act of judicial policymaking, as acknowledged by the court itself, directed at reducing coercion in interrogation. Such blatant lawmaking provoked outrage at the time[100] and still raises separation of powers concerns. While courts should prevent the use of coerced confessions at trial, it is less clear why they, instead of legislatures, should decide on the exact procedures by which coerced confessions should be avoided. Letting the legislature set the specific procedures would not take away from the court's authority to exclude any confession that it thought was coerced, as courts already did before *Miranda*. Setting the specific procedures to avoid coerced confessions, which involves striking the balance between shielding suspects and promoting justice, is arguably better done by legislatures because they are in a better position to evaluate the effects of one policy approach versus another, and in a better position to adapt to changes in societal circumstances, including resulting significant reductions in clearance and conviction rates for serious offenses. The judicially imposed nature of Miranda rules also largely prevents state legislatures from exploring alternative reforms aimed at better preventing coercion and promoting reliable confessions. The constitutionalizing of *Miranda*'s quasi-legislative policy has prevented useful experimentation with any other variations in interrogation rules across the country.[101]

MIRANDA'S INEFFECTIVENESS Regardless of who should make interrogation rules, many if not most legal scholars agree that Miranda failed to produce its intended benefits of stopping coerced confessions.[102] A quick word of warning about one's rights will not help much if police are determined to make a suspect's life miserable until they get a confession. Further, the fact that juveniles waive their rights at higher rates than adults indicates that the warnings do little to shield those most likely to be manipulated or coerced.[103] Police can easily rattle off Miranda rights while threatening the suspect with an iron poker, metaphorically or literally. It is hard to see the logic behind thinking that a Miranda warning will stop false confessions, but it is self-evident that it will stop many guilty criminals from providing reliable confessions and incriminating statements. There is a general sense that *Miranda* is a failed fix of the coercive interrogation problem. The only clear advantage *Miranda* has to the legal system is allowing the court to primarily look at a simple box check (whether the defendant was read and waived their rights) in determining whether a statement was coerced. Even if a statement was truly coerced, so long as the defendant was read their Miranda rights, it is possible the court might simply not investigate other aspects of the confession because the formula was followed. This has even led some proponents of defendants' rights to call for reforming *Miranda* due to its lack of substantive protections against coercion.[104]

Public Concerns

There was an initial public outcry at the *Miranda* decision in 1966, which was seen as yet another example of an out-of-touch court's soft-on-crime policies.[105] "Even certain supporters of the Warren Court had admitted that *Mapp* and *Miranda* were among the Court's

'self-inflicted wounds.'"[106] North Carolina Democratic senator Sam Ervin complained that "enough has been done for those who murder, rape and rob. . . . It is time to do something for those who do not wish to be murdered, raped or robbed."[107] Senate hearings on *Miranda* saw a stream of witnesses who vigorously criticized the decision.[108] The public outrage led to Congress's attempt to overrule *Miranda* in a 1968 law allowing confessions obtained without a Miranda warning to still be admitted as evidence as long as they were not coerced. The Supreme Court responded by overturning the law.[109]

Over time, however, the American public has become accustomed to police warning suspects of their rights.[110] Americans ultimately want incompatible things. People would like to have the assurance that if they end up in the hands of the law, they will have the best chance of escaping conviction through a smart use of their rights. At the same time, people would like to maximize the chance of others getting convicted when they commit crimes.

Reforms

Reform is not impossible. The Supreme Court has recognized exceptions to its interrogation rules, and other policies have been put in place to reduce coercion that might be capable of replacing *Miranda*. Other countries also offer alternative models of interrogation rules designed to avoid coerced confessions but still allow use of reliable confessions and damaging admissions.

Recognize a Public Safety Exception to Miranda. The Supreme Court has agreed over time that there are, in fact, valid situations in which officers should not be obligated to read a suspect their Miranda rights due to public safety concerns. The public safety exception originated from *New York v. Quarles*. The exception covers any "situation where concern for public safety must be paramount to adherence to the literal language of the prophylactic rules enunciated in *Miranda*."[111] State courts have followed suit in adopting the exception. For example, the New York Court of Appeals upheld the public safety exception in *People v. Doll*, in which Scott Doll was arrested after police saw him walking the street with wet blood stains on his clothes, hands, and shoes. Fearing that someone was gravely injured, they continued to question Doll despite his request for legal assistance. Doll was charged and convicted of second-degree murder; his appeal failed.[112] In these cases, the safety of bystanders or other at-risk individuals is deemed more important than the reading of Miranda rights. One could argue this same logic undermines *Miranda* in other ways as a suspect's silence and ability to mount an ambush defense to serious offenses significantly endangers public safety and justice.

Record All Interrogations. Police officers in the United States have found that audio or video taping interrogations is useful by providing evidence that no coercion took place and thus increasing the chances that a confession will be admitted at trial (if Miranda warnings were given). Additionally, 59.8 percent of police departments surveyed during a National Institute of Justice study found that the implementation of taping "increased the amount of incriminating information obtained from suspects."[113] Some scholars argue that recording interrogations should entirely replace *Miranda* as videotapes allow for a better judgment to be made whether a confession was coerced while not encouraging suspects to stay silent. As of May 2021, twenty-seven states and the District of Columbia require custodial interrogations to be recorded.[114]

International Approaches to Police Interrogations. Other countries also have arrest warnings and interrogation rules, but they are usually less justice frustrating. In the United Kingdom, as noted previously, the arrest warning includes a warning that staying silent can harm a suspect's defense if they do not mention now something they later rely on in court. A criminal suspect's post-arrest warning silence may also be used to draw negative inferences, as in the Argent case, in several countries beyond the United Kingdom, such as Australia, Singapore,[115] and Israel.[116]

In addition to its less-justice-frustrating arrest warning, UK solicitors (synonymous to the counsel that one is entitled to when invoking US Miranda rights) are instructed not to prevent questioning during an interrogation but rather ensure that "interviews" are conducted fairly.[117] Some US scholars call for lawmakers to take inspiration from this particular instruction to counsel.[118]

While an estimated 108 countries or jurisdictions around the world have adopted arrest warnings of some sort, the exact nature of these warnings differ.[119] In addition, the United Nations has adopted the International Covenant for Civil and Political Rights (ICCPR), which specifically mentions the right to remain silent during interrogations. Importantly, the ICCPR does not require countries to tell detained individuals about this right so long as it is respected if invoked.[120] As of December 2018, 172 countries have ratified the covenant.[121]

More ambitious reforms have also been proposed.

Incentivize Talking to Police. One proposal to strike a different balance between individual liberties and justice is informing all suspects of their Miranda rights while at the same time incentivizing them to give statements and confessions by reducing the severity of sentences by a certain percentage if they do so.[122] While this may prevent a criminal receiving their "just deserts" by failing to give a full sentence, it could also prevent a complete justice failure in which an offender walks away with no sentence at all. The logic of this tradeoff is mirrored in the United States Sentencing Commission sentencing guidelines that formally authorize a specific downward departure where an offender pleads guilty,[123] and such discounts for guilty pleas are of course standard practice in the United States through plea bargaining.

Eliminate Miranda and Allow Legislative Alternatives. Some scholars argue that Miranda is a hopelessly failed policy that should be discarded because it increases crime and failures of justice without reducing coercion. Eliminating Miranda warnings would in some sense not be a radical step for the Supreme Court, which has found that Miranda warnings are not a personal constitutional right but rather a judicially mandated prophylactic measure against coercion.[124] The Court would merely have to find its prophylactic measure ineffective, which it arguably has been, to return the issue of interrogation rules to state legislatures, which could then come up with alternative arrest warnings and interrogation rules. Regardless of the resulting legislative interrogation rules, the courts would still have the authority to reject any confession that was coerced,

as judged by a due process voluntariness standard that is already used to reject coerced confessions made after Miranda warnings.

Recommendation: Adopt UK Version of the Miranda Warning (Allowing Defendant's Silence to Be Used to Impeach an "Ambush Defense")

A tried and true reform that would be feasible to implement without overturning the Miranda framework would be to adopt the United Kingdom's version of arrest warnings, which mention the right to stay silent but allows for and warns suspects that postarrest silence can be used to undermine the credibility of a defendant's testimony at trial. The United Kingdom adopted its current arrest warnings in the Criminal Justice and Public Order Act of 1994, which authorized the current arrest warning, which says, among other things:

> You do not have to say anything, but it may harm your defense if you do not mention when questioned something which you later rely on in court. Anything you do say may be given in evidence.[125]

The UK law outlines several situations where adverse inferences can be made at trial based on the accused's silence. We propose allowing such inferences only in the instance where the accused fails to mention an important fact that he later states in testimony and that he could have been reasonably expected to mention at the time of interrogation.[126] Importantly, under the UK system, a conviction cannot be based solely upon silence, and our recommendation similarly would only allow a defendant's silence to be used to impeach his testimony at trial—not used as affirmative proof of guilt.[127] The advantages of this approach are exemplified by the Brian Argent case mentioned earlier. Prosecutors were allowed to cast doubt on Argent's false alibi, arguing that, if the alibi were real, Argent would have quickly given it to police when first questioned about the murder.

While courts have allowed post-Miranda silence to be used at trial in a few special situations (such as when a suspect initially waives their Miranda rights but then fails to answer a question),[128] allowing post-Miranda silence to call into doubt an ambush defense would require the Supreme Court to overturn the 1976 case of *Doyle v. Ohio*, but the Court might be willing to reevaluate its old precedent if state legislatures were to enact the UK version of Miranda. It is not at all obvious why the Fifth Amendment right against self-incrimination is violated by allowing prosecutors to introduce the fact of the defendant's previous silence if the defendant specifically chooses to testify in an ambush defense. This is especially the case because the Court does allow for pre-Miranda silence to be used

to impeach a defendant. For example, if a murderer later claims self-defense at trial, a prosecutor can cast doubt on that story by bringing up the fact that he did not suggest this to police at the time of his arrest but before he was read his Miranda rights. The current distinction in US jurisprudence makes little sense and expanding the ability to impeach trial testimony based on prior unreasonable silence could help avoid false acquittals, especially in cases like rape where credibility is often the main issue at focus for the jury.

The advantages of our recommended reform are several. First, it would make fabricated ambush defenses harder and rarer. Second, it is not radical because it allows the Court to maintain the Miranda framework, which makes adjudicating cases of alleged coercion easy by looking to whether police have checked the box of arrest warnings. Third, the addition of a warning that staying silent may be harmful could incentivize some criminals to talk, thus increasing rates of incriminating statements or confessions and reducing failures of justice.

CHAPTER 7

Restraints on Use of Technology

TECHNOLOGY CONTINUES TO RAPIDLY change our world, and the criminal justice system is only beginning to exploit these new opportunities. A hundred years ago, investigators relied solely on witness and suspect questioning and obvious physical evidence such as an abandoned weapon or footprints. Today, technology allows investigators to review surveillance footage, pinpoint suspects' locations using location tracking, utilize artificial intelligence (AI) algorithms to instantly identify faces, and employ the tiniest fragments of DNA evidence to search millions of profiles to find criminals. Technological advancement is opening a brave new world for law enforcement, but this world is full of debates on how to balance the interests of justice and privacy. Many shudder at the notion of increased police and government surveillance. This fear has resulted in an array of corporate, cultural, and legal restrictions on law enforcement's ability to utilize technology in solving crimes. In addition to public concerns about privacy infringements, police are often slow to adopt helpful technologies because they are unaware or unable to acquire new technology due to budgetary constraints. Despite these barriers, new technologies have the potential to significantly reduce justice failures, and it should be up to society to determine how to best balance the competing interests over their use. This chapter examines the competing interests raised by using new technology and the public's conflicting opinions on it, before examining restrictions on its use in the three areas in which it could provide the greatest potential investigative benefit: biometrics (focusing on DNA evidence), surveillance systems (such as CCTV cameras), and data analytics (focusing on facial recognition algorithms).

A. COMPETING INTERESTS

There are numerous important interests in tension when formulating proper restrictions on investigative use of technology, but they might be summarized this way.

Interests Opposing Investigative Use of New Technologies

- *Privacy.* New technologies, especially surveillance technologies, may encroach on citizens' personal privacy. Many Americans intrinsically dislike being surveilled or having their data recorded and kept in government databases. While most people accept sacrificing privacy when investigators already have enough evidence to obtain a warrant for such intrusion, many are concerned with how new technologies allow police to gather more information without a warrant. Privacy advocates also worry about the collection and use—warrant or no—of uniquely personal information such as DNA. Everyone has a slightly different definition and valuation of privacy, but there is clearly a tension between government investigative power and a sphere of personal privacy. However, questions remain such as whether society should even recognize an offender's privacy interest in covering up their crime and whether innocent people should be willing to sacrifice privacy in certain areas if it brings significant increases in doing justice. People are likely to come to different conclusions on these questions, often based on purely subjective, cultural, or generational considerations.

- *Limited Government.* Closely connected to privacy concerns is the value of limited government. If the police can know practically everything a person does, this allows the government to have a potentially tyrannical control over the populace. The current surveillance and police state in China is a warning of how governments can weaponize the gathering of information against their citizens. At the same time, it is not entirely clear that keeping information out of the hands of the government will prevent tyranny because a government resolved to tyrannize its citizens can quickly find a way. Most modern governments possess the technical abilities to become police states with disturbingly little trouble; it is their lack of resolve to do so generated by democratic accountability that prevents them. There is also a separate interest in keeping information out of even the most trustworthy government's hands if that information could be used by individual bad actors within the government to humiliate, extort, or blackmail individual citizens. However, in either case, it may be that limited government is not so much achieved by limiting the technical abilities of the state to collect information but rather by creating and enforcing legal limitations on the use of that information.

- *Concerns over Fairness, Accuracy, and Reliability.* New technologies that involve big data and AI, be they facial recognition technology or predictive crime algorithms, raise questions of fairness and reliability in their outputs. Any data program is only as good as its inputs, as well as the fairness and accuracy of its analytics. For example, facial recognition technology could, depending upon input data, be more accurate for Caucasians than African Americans, resulting in racially disparate results. Some new technologies still raise questions over reliability and accuracy, though these fears are often overblown, as shown later in this chapter's examination of facial recognition algorithms. Additionally, there are concerns that new technology may encourage shoddy police work by lending a veneer of accuracy to claimed results (such as police claiming CCTV footage showed something clearly when it did not).

- *Concerns over Effectiveness and Cost.* Adopting new technology is often expensive and time consuming. Police have limited resources, so the decision to invest in new technology carries with it the opportunity cost of using those resources in other ways. For example, it might serve some police departments better to simply hire more detectives instead of installing expensive CCTV cameras or license plate readers. Some new technologies are clearly cost effective (such as expanding and integrating DNA databases), but others may represent a more speculative investment (such as creating specialized AI programs to sort through gathered data). New technology is often flashy, but scarce resources mean police must consider the opportunity costs involved. Moreover, new technology is often only as good as the investigators using it, meaning it cannot replace the need for competent and trained investigators.

Interests Supporting Investigative Use of New Technologies

- *Greater Justice Through Apprehending More Criminals.* New technologies make it easier to catch and convict criminals in many circumstances, thus ensuring that more crimes end in arrest and conviction. Improved forensic science and better DNA databases have already led to significant improvements in crime-solving capabilities. Along with increased justice comes greater public faith and confidence in the legal system as better adjudication of justice increases the law's moral credibility with the community. It may well be worth some privacy incursions to increase justice, especially for serious crimes.
- *Monitoring the Public Sphere, Not the Private.* While a private sphere is important, privacy has always had limits. Many new technologies simply better monitor things done in the public sphere as opposed to shrinking the private sphere. For example, many things done publicly in the past (such as walking outside one's house or driving on the roads) were not so much private as simply not normally recorded. The use of CCTV cameras and automatic license plate readers have arguably not made the private public but merely ensured that *public* activities can be recorded and potentially used in criminal investigations. Offenders committing inculpatory deeds in

public were always at risk of being seen by police or witnesses, and new technologies have simply increased that risk. Few would argue that offenders have a right to retain better odds of not being caught.
- *Greater Deterrence and Public Safety.* As more criminals are caught, and the perception grows that new technology makes it harder to get away with crimes, deterrence may increase and crime rates may correspondingly fall. New technology can even prevent crimes about to be committed. For example, CCTV cameras can let police see a crime is about to occur or an ankle bracelet can alert police to a parolee violating their terms of release. By decreasing crime, new technologies also reduce the worst possible violations of liberty and privacy for citizens— serious crime. Many may believe it is worth sacrificing a small amount of perceived privacy to investigators in exchange for reducing the chance that others and themselves are forced to suffer crimes like murder, rape, or robbery.
- *Increased Reliability of Evidence.* New forms of evidence such as DNA and surveillance footage are more reliable than witness testimony, which research has shown is often surprisingly fallible. New technology not only helps catch offenders, it also minimizes the risk of wrongful convictions based on less reliable forms of evidence. For example, reviewing surveillance footage can easily show who was the aggressor in a violent altercation instead of forcing investigators to sort through a hash of conflicting stories.
- *Shielding Innocents from Privacy Intrusions.* Related to the previous point, new technologies can actually shield innocent would-be suspects from investigative intrusions

by sending police down fewer rabbit trails. For example, CCTV footage or DNA results can quickly rule out potential suspects, thus preventing lengthier investigations into innocent suspects' private lives as might have occurred in the past. New technologies such as DNA testing can even clear previously wrongly convicted and imprisoned suspects, thus ending the worst possible form of government intrusion on liberty and privacy.

- *Efficiency and Saving Resources.* New technology often represents a more efficient and less costly way to gather evidence and conduct investigations. For example, it is easier to simply review CCTV footage than to question all potential witnesses in a neighborhood. Algorithms can also automate data collection and review, allowing human effort to be spent elsewhere on police investigations where only human judgment will suffice. While adopting certain technologies may be costly in the short term, they can decrease costs in the long run.
- *Publicly Discussed Implementation versus Slow Creep.* History suggests that new, useful technologies are often eventually adopted by law enforcement even in the face of opposition, so it makes sense for society to have a robust discussion of the issue now and arrange a clear and agreed upon implementation of new technology rather than leaving adoption to the inevitability of a slow, haphazard, and inefficient creep. In any democratic society, the views of ordinary people should decide the proper balance of competing interests when striking compromises on whether and how a new technology should be used.

B. PUBLIC VIEWS ON INVESTIGATIVE USE OF TECHNOLOGY

The most publicly debated competing interests in determining the proper investigative use of technology pits privacy against justice and safety. These competing interests are reflected in divided public opinion. But while ordinary people usually instinctively understand how new technology may affect privacy, they may not realize how useful such technology is in achieving justice and safety.

Public Support for Prioritizing Safety and Justice over Privacy

Most people want the best of both worlds: use of available technology to catch criminals with no infringement upon their own personal privacy. Because this is not achievable, there are balances that must be struck. On some issues, the public supports prioritizing justice and safety over privacy—especially when it comes to the privacy of offenders. For example, in 1998, a poll found that 66 percent of people believed that "police should . . . be allowed to collect DNA information from suspected criminals, similar to how they take fingerprints," and another survey in 2000 found that 88 percent supported "a national DNA databank with DNA collected from all criminals."[1] Evidently, a vast majority of citizens would not agree with many of the current restrictions limiting the collection of DNA from arrestees. The public view is more complicated when it comes to using innocent people's DNA, but data from 2020 indicates that 48 percent of Americans believe that DNA testing companies should "share customers' genetic data with law enforcement to help solve crimes," while only 33 percent are opposed.[2]

More Americans than not appear comfortable with an expansion of police use of DNA beyond the limits of current restrictions. Such restrictions have often provoked confusion and opposition among law enforcement and commentators. For example, Ann Coulter, a commentator hardly known for favoring government power, summed up opposition to policies preventing investigators from accessing ancestry DNA databases: "I'm sorry, but why? . . . [DNA companies don't] want to lose the business of skittish serial killers?"[3] The privacy arguments against access to DNA databases often appear paranoid to those who point to the obvious concrete benefits to justice and safety of allowing law enforcement to search all available records. After all, if one is not a criminal, how much does one have to fear from police searching for a match in a database containing one's DNA?

When it comes to surveillance, public opinions shift based on the exact extent of the surveillance and its purpose. The greatest public support is for anti-terrorism surveillance even if it means sacrificing the privacy of all. For example, a 2019 poll found that 49 percent of Americans believe "it is acceptable for the government to collect data about all Americans in order to assess potential terrorist threats," compared with 31 percent who felt that was unacceptable.[4] However, other surveys have found less support for monitoring internet traffic, and about two-thirds of Americans oppose warrantless surveillance of phone, email, and text messages.[5] When it comes to CCTV surveillance of public spaces, however, a clear majority (78 percent) are supportive.[6] Of course, the value of opinion surveys that ask unnuanced questions about surveillance, without specifying context, is limited. For example, people may feel very differently about the warrantless collection of personal data from a murder suspect when compared to a mass data collection program targeting all citizens.

Public Support for Prioritizing Privacy over Justice

However, privacy advocates and many in the public continue to prioritize privacy over the crime-solving potential of modern technologies, often because of fears that new technology may be abused. These fears are often grounded in specific instances where police surveillance technology has been used to target and track individuals without any legal justification. In Detroit, for example, police officers have been caught, on occasion, using surveillance technology for personal purposes, including stalking women and "estranged spouses."[7] Some worry about how surveillance cameras have allowed individual bored officers to voyeuristically watch civilians (albeit in public spaces).[8] Such cases have led many to fear CCTV surveillance. Fears about the abuse of license plate recognition technology exist as well, rooted in the case of a DC police officer who used license plate readers to identify and blackmail individuals at a gay club in 1997.[9] Privacy advocates usually generalize from such specific, usually already illegal, instances to create fears of mass abuse based on the wide reach of technology. For example, the executive director of the Center on Privacy and Technology at Georgetown Law warns against license plate reading technology because "it's powerful stuff, and it's not under control."[10] Such claims may be vague, but they often resonate with the public.

Sometimes public opposition to new technology is based on a faulty understanding of data, as is the case with fears over the potential inaccuracy or racial bias of facial recognition technology. As discussed more in section F, the fact that some facial recognition algorithms are more accurate in identifying Caucasian than African American faces is largely irrelevant because the best available facial recognition algorithms have false positive rates of 0.01 percent for White males, and no more than 0.03 percent for Black faces regardless of gender.[11] While this may generate a frightening headline about African Americans being "three times more likely to be falsely identified," the actual error rate is negligible for any race.

Members of the public may also oppose the use of new technology out of fears over a lack of transparency. For example, some privacy advocates point to the fact that police and prosecutors rarely disclose their use of facial recognition technology, potentially making it "difficult, if not impossible to ensure that defendants are able to exercise" their constitutional rights.[12] The public generally is ill informed about police use of technology and has little understanding of how it works. Such opposition could potentially be overcome with more openness, which would not interfere with the benefits of such technology.[13]

Others in the public simply fear the effects of increased surveillance or monitoring based on the claim that "when citizens are being watched by the authorities—or aware they might be watched at any time—they are more self-conscious and less free-wheeling."[14]

Americans appear evenly split as to their level of concern about privacy versus justice and safety, at least as far as generic surveillance is concerned. A poll found that 52 percent of Americans are very or somewhat concerned about government surveillance, while 46 percent are not very or not at all concerned about such surveillance.[15] Of course, this even split on a generic question about surveillance obscures actual public support or disapproval for specific new investigative technologies. For example, one might support increased use of DNA, CCTV, and facial recognition technology while still being concerned about excess government surveillance and strongly opposing warrantless surveillance of personal internet activity. A common mistake is assuming that there is a single "pro" or "anti" privacy or surveillance position when most reasonable people would prefer a balance that involves increased use of technology in some areas while maintaining or establishing strong restrictions in others.

It is also easy for privacy advocates to present the public with the stark choice of unlimited use of a new technology or a complete ban. But it need not be all or nothing: the most publicly popular option may be to pursue new technology while also adding appropriate legal safeguards. The public is most likely to support the use of new technology when they believe it is being adopted with safeguards in place. For example, 83 percent of American voters support Congress passing a national data protection bill to ensure Americans' sensitive data is used properly by government agencies.[16] This suggests advocates of new technology should push for its adoption within the context of commonsensical regulation designed to assuage public fears over potential abuse.

C. RESTRAINTS ON THE USE OF BIOMETRICS AND FORENSICS (SUCH AS DNA)

The greatest advance in investigative technology over the past century has been the proliferation of forensic and biometric data collection and analysis, most commonly through the use of fingerprints and DNA evidence. For such evidence to be effective at solving crimes, police need databases large enough to include potential suspects. This process is well advanced for fingerprints as the FBI created the Integrated Automated Fingerprint Identification System (IAFIS) in 1999, establishing a "national, computerized system for storing, comparing, and exchanging fingerprint data in a digital format."[17] The IAFIS currently contains fingerprint data for over 185 million individuals (collected from arrestees, federal job applicants, military personnel, and aliens, among others).[18] Information from this database is used annually to identify in excess of three hundred thousand fugitives.[19]

The use of DNA databases is not as advanced. The Combined DNA Index System (CODIS), which is managed by the FBI, is an umbrella term describing the search software and support infrastructure for the criminal justice system's DNA databases at the federal, state, and local level. In 2021, CODIS added its twenty millionth DNA sample.[20] Since its inception in 1998, CODIS has aided in 545,000 investigations.[21] All states participate in CODIS, but the regulations on whose DNA may be collected for investigative purposes is determined by the individual state, with some taking DNA from all arrestees while others only collect the DNA of individuals convicted of serious offences.[22] Laws governing investigator use of private genetic ancestry databases, by which police can identify a perpetrator directly or through a relative's DNA, also differ by state. Some states have proposed banning police searches of private databanks entirely, while others have moved to make their use a more regular part of investigation.[23] While privacy advocates fear a world in which citizens' DNA is accessible to law enforcement, such a world would make it significantly harder for murderers and rapists to escape justice. Research has shown that allowing the police access to larger pools of DNA samples is directly correlated with increased crime-solving effectiveness and that as fewer DNA samples are added to databases, correspondingly fewer serious crimes are solved.[24]

As in most cases of police use of technology, there is a tradeoff between privacy and justice. But police databases only record those particular DNA alleles necessary to uniquely identify an individual as opposed to the whole of a person's genetic code with information about their health, personality, etc. Thus, the DNA recorded in police databases is akin to a genetic fingerprint, not a complete genetic analysis of the individual.[25] This makes the privacy intrusion from a DNA database little more than the intrusion from a fingerprint database, but with even greater crime-solving abilities. Unlike a fingerprint, DNA can allow for familial searching to reveal a killer's relatives, allowing investigators to zero in on a perpetrator even if their individual DNA is not in any database. While most police databases are not currently configured for familial DNA searching, it can solve otherwise impossible cases and catch even the cleverest criminals. Consider how one of America's worst killers was found after escaping justice for decades.

Case Example: Golden State Killer

From 1974 to 1986, a killer-rapist stalks the California night, committing at least thirteen murders, over fifty rapes, and some 120 burglaries.[26] He is known by many names—the Visalia Ransacker, the East Area Rapist, the Night Stalker, and the Golden State Killer.[27] Police simply cannot find him. The man's preferred crime is targeting couples. His modus operandi (MO) is breaking into a home and raping the woman for hours while her bound partner listens from another room. The attacker often takes breaks during the rape to eat from the couple's refrigerator, ransack their house, and threaten them with death. He then kills them both and vanishes into the night. In 1986, the attacker retires. His only mistake is leaving DNA evidence, but even when the use of DNA analysis becomes feasible, searches of the available police databases produce no results. In 2018, California forensics specialist Paul Holes has the idea of uploading the attacker's DNA to the ancestry tracing website GEDmatch to find the killer through his relatives. Based on the results, Holes draws up twenty-five possible family trees and eliminates suspects one by one until he finds former police officer Joseph James DeAngelo, now seventy-two. After his DNA is found to match the killer's, DeAngelo is convicted and sentenced to life in prison. An earlier advent of familial DNA searching could have avoided the enormous human suffering caused by DeAngelo's crimes. But privacy advo-

Figure 7.1. Joseph DeAngelo, also known as the Golden State Killer, was arrested in 2018 with the help of GEDmatch, an online genetic ancestry database, 2018. Photo by Santiago Mejia, San Francisco Chronicle via Associated Press, from Don Thompson, "Apology at Sentencing Deepens Mystery of Golden State Killer," Associated Press, August 21, 2020, https://apnews.com/article/ap-top-news-ca-state-wire-us-news-08a241b485d1d7be03f62293e2da3277.

cates are furious at the police use of the ancestry database, and a combination of new government rules and private DNA company policies make it much harder in the future for police to find and stop such killers using ancestry tracing.

The Nature and Extent of the Problem

Past practice has shown DNA databases are extremely useful at bringing serious offenders to justice, but there still exists an enormous disparity in the breadth of DNA samples collected when compared to fingerprints, with rules varying widely by state. The fact that DNA samples are not collected from all arrestees in most states, while fingerprints are, is a costly anachronism that allows thousands of serious criminals to escape justice each year.

THE EFFECTIVENESS OF DNA DATABASES AND DANGER OF RESTRICTIONS Restrictions on the construction and use of DNA databases are particularly problematic because such databases are often the only way to solve many serious crimes, especially cold cases. DNA databases not only offer ways to catch dangerous repeat offenders, but some research suggests they also may deter crime more broadly as criminals fear the results of increased crime investigation effectiveness.[28]

Increased DNA collection and investigative access to DNA databases has improved success in identifying offenders for serious crimes even when that DNA is collected from those convicted of less serious crimes. New York's criminal DNA database has mostly been collected from those convicted of minor crimes, and when DNA from New York murder investigations without a suspect were analyzed, 82 percent of positive matches led back to DNA previously placed into the system from an offender convicted

of a "lesser" offense.[29] Offenders typically do not go from law-abiding citizen to murderer or rapist without any intermediate arrests or convictions for less serious crimes. Over one third of all alleged rapists have prior convictions,[30] and over 70 percent of arrested murderers have been previously arrested.[31] Collecting DNA from all those convicted or even arrested for lesser crimes increases the likelihood that serious offenders will be caught. When Arizona implemented arrestee DNA collection for all felonies and some misdemeanor charges, criminal DNA match rates almost doubled.[32]

California provides a case study in the dangers of restricting the collection of arrestee DNA. In 2011, California's intermediate appellate court decided in *People v. Buza* that the collection of DNA from felony arrestees without a warrant or probable cause of the offender having committed past crimes violated the Fourth Amendment.[33] In the months immediately following the decision, the state's DNA uploads decreased from 19,294 to 7,946 per month (a 59 percent decrease), and police DNA matches decreased from 501 to 215 per month (a 57 percent decrease), showing how essential arrestee DNA collection had been in solving crime.[34] Hundreds of criminals, many of them serious offenders, escaped justice every month as a result of the new restrictions. The California Supreme Court eventually reversed the appellate court's decision and allowed felony arrestee DNA collection in 2018, but the benefits of this reversal were largely mitigated by California passing Proposition 47 in 2014, which reclassified many felonies as misdemeanors.[35] Because California's DNA collection laws do not allow DNA collection from misdemeanor arrestees, the growth of the state's DNA databases was significantly curbed. As one might expect, after the passage of Proposition 47, fewer cold cases were solved due to the resulting limitations on DNA collection.[36]

STATE DIVERSITY IN COLLECTION OF DNA
In the federal system, every arrestee has their DNA collected, regardless of crime severity or whether the arrest ends in conviction.[37] According to the US Supreme Court, states and the federal government have wide constitutional latitude in authorizing the collection of DNA from offenders and arrestees.[38] However, despite this wide legal latitude to construct arrestee DNA databases, many states have lagged behind the federal government in taking advantage of the crime-solving potential of DNA collection. This is particularly problematic because almost all serious violent crimes are state, not federal, offenses, and so state rules are the major determiner of the size of DNA databases.[39]

In 2013, twenty-six states had enacted laws allowing DNA collection from arrestees of serious crimes.[40] By 2018, after the Supreme Court's decision specifically authorizing such collection, the number had increased to thirty states.[41] As the figure 7.2 illustrates, as of 2021, thirty-three states allow DNA collection from at least some arrestees.[42] Among these thirty-four states, fifteen generally allow collection from only arrestees of certain serious felonies, twelve allow collection from any felony arrestee, and six also allow for collection from misdemeanor ar-

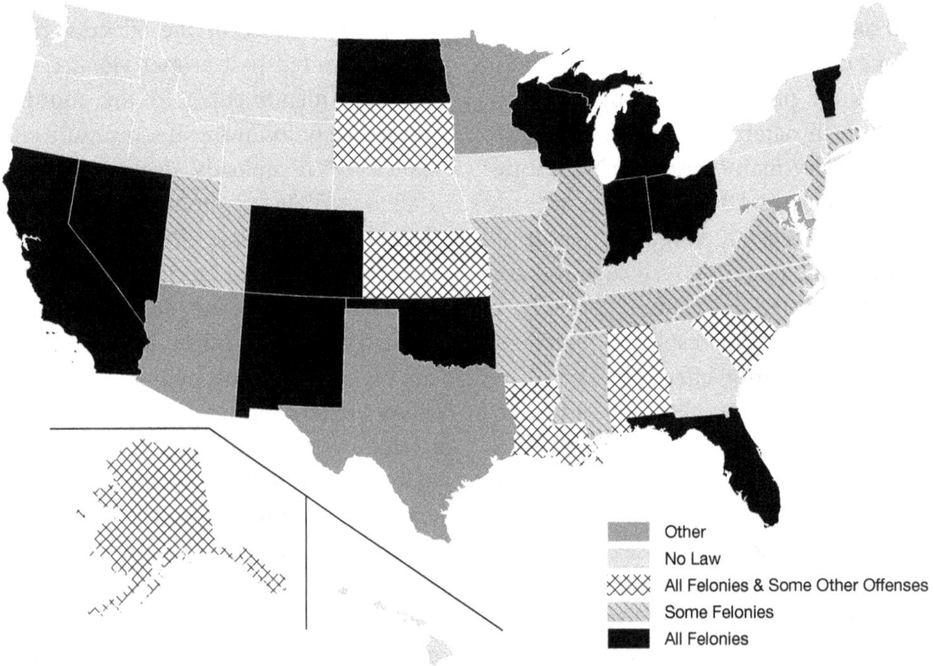

Figure 7.2. Type of arrest that qualifies for DNA collection, by state, 2021. Figure by Charlotte Anne Spencer, "What Is the Arrestee DNA Collection Law in Your State?" Biometrica, May 27, 2021, https://www.bio metrica.com/what-is-the-arrestee-dna-collection-law-in-your-state/. Copyright © 2021 by Biometrica. Reprinted with permission from Deepti Govind. *Note*: Spencer largely based this map on source data from https://www .ncsl.org/research/civil-and-criminal-justice/dna-laws-database.aspx and legal research on FastCase to check for laws that had changed since the original source data from NCSL was put together.

restees.[43] The rules across the remaining sixteen states range from barely utilizing DNA collection to allowing it for all convicted offenders: four states limit DNA database additions to only felons convicted of enumerated sexual offenses,[44] while eleven states add to their database all persons with even misdemeanor convictions.[45] There are additional state-by-state differences with respect to issues such as juvenile offenders and whether DNA records are automatically expunged if charges are not filed or the case ends in acquittal.[46]

There is also the problem of patchwork DNA databases because some jurisdictions do not cooperate or consolidate with the national CODIS network. Some areas of the country, such as Palm Beach County, Florida, and Bensalem Township, Pennsylvania, have historically maintained local DNA databases that only collaborated with nearby jurisdictions.[47] While many states and localities are gradually passing laws to expand their DNA databases, such databases are still often fragmented and prevent nation-wide searches, which is where DNA evidence has the maximum potential to solve serious crimes.

A MORE EFFICIENT SYSTEM: THE EXAMPLE OF THE UNITED KINGDOM Large countries are not doomed to inefficient and patchwork DNA collection systems, nor do they have to embrace authoritarianism to construct broader national DNA databases. The United Kingdom has a vast national DNA database (NDNAD) from previous offenders and arrestees that includes 10 percent of the UK population.[48] In 2001, the passage of Britain's Criminal Justice and Police Act allowed the United Kingdom to maintain the DNA even of individuals who had been acquitted or whose cases had been dropped, and an-

other amendment in 2003 authorized the current practice of collecting DNA from all arrestees.[49] These expansions proved to be extremely useful for solving serious crimes and increasing clearance rates, as the newly stored DNA profiles matched to more than eighty-eight murders and 116 rapes in the five years after the 2001 law was implemented. In the two years after the 2003 amendment, four more murders and three more rapes were solved by analyzing the expanded DNA (of individuals who were arrested but never charged).[50] Hundreds more extremely serious crimes have been solved since then, and tens of thousands of other crimes besides murder and rape have been solved thanks to the United Kingdom's expanded DNA database.

RESTRICTIONS ON ACCESS TO GENETIC ANCESTRY DNA DATABASES Privacy advocates have successfully lobbied some states, as well as private DNA ancestry companies, to restrict investigative access to DNA samples stored in ancestry databases. After the identification of the infamous Golden State Killer with genetic ancestry tracing from the website GEDmatch in 2018, some states restricted investigative access. In Maryland, investigators are only allowed to access such DNA databases with a judge's permission and then only for cases of rape and murder.[51] In Montana, investigators need a search warrant to access the database.[52] A proposed bill in Utah aimed to entirely ban genetic genealogy searches by police, but it ultimately failed to pass.[53] The Department of Justice has also restricted the use of such ancestry databases by federal investigators.[54]

Genetic ancestry companies have also taken action to limit investigative access. GEDmatch, which was used to identify the Golden State Killer, now restricts law enforcement from using its services and allows police access only to those records that users have expressly opted in for law enforcement use.[55] Only about 14 percent of GEDmatch users have affirmatively opted in, substantially reducing the data available to police.[56] Of course, that percentage would likely have been much higher if the company set the default as allowing law enforcement access and asked customers to opt out if they wished to. Three other DNA testing companies have jointly lobbied Congress for increased restrictions on law enforcement access to their databases. After GEDmatch restricted police access to customer DNA profiles, the chief of forensic services at the Florida Department of Law Enforcement emphasized that the change simply meant that now, as a direct result, "there are cases that won't get solved or will take longer to solve."[57]

These efforts to restrict police access are not supported by a majority of the public. As mentioned earlier, a 2020 study by Pew Research Center found that 48 percent of those polled believe that DNA testing companies should "share customers' genetic data with law enforcement to help solve crimes,"[58] while only 33 percent of those polled opposed such data sharing. Carol Dodge, whose daughter's killer was found using GEDmatch, spoke for many when she argued that "people who have a clean conscience shouldn't have a problem" with law enforcement's use of ancestry databases to solve crimes.[59]

Reforms

Several reforms have been proposed or undertaken to expand and integrate investigative use of DNA databases.

Collect DNA from More Offenders. As mentioned earlier, many states have slowly expanded the range of offenders from whom DNA may be collected. Thirty-four states and the federal government have laws allowing DNA samples to be collected from individuals arrested (but not convicted) of some or all crimes.[60] A conservative reform proposal is to expand DNA collection to all those convicted of any offense (even misdemeanors). A more impactful proposal is collecting DNA from all arrestees, as is done by the federal government, some states, and the United Kingdom.

Encourage Citizens to Join DNA Databases. While there are many restrictions on police use of genetic ancestry databases, there are also groups working to convince Americans to voluntarily join such databases and opt in to allowing police to search their profiles. For example, the Institute for DNA Justice is an advocacy group that strives to get all twenty-six million Americans who have taken DNA tests to upload their results to services like GEDmatch or FamilyTreeDNA and to opt in to allowing police use. If even a small proportion of people did this, the resulting DNA coverage would allow many more criminals to be found through relatives.[61] As noted previously, such an expanded database would not only assist in finding criminals but also shield innocent persons by ruling them out as potential suspects.

Consolidate DNA Databases. One major advantage that UK investigators have over US police is the country's consolidated police database. Currently, many but not all state and local police DNA databases are incorporated into the CODIS network. Incorporating all government DNA databases into CODIS would involve little privacy infringement because the information is already being stored in a state or local database and may already be accessible to local investigators, but consolidation would significantly improve the crime-solving benefit of the database for all investigators, including local ones.

Update Police Database Software and Guidelines to Allow for Familial Searching. Typical police DNA databases do not use software enabled to run a familial search (such as the one used to identify the Golden State Killer), unlike ancestry databases that are specifically configured for this purpose. For example, CODIS (the software used by the FBI's national DNA database) does not allow familial searching but only individual identification. There have been efforts to update database software, but so far with limited success, in part because of strict guidelines around familial DNA searches. Such a software update would substantially increase the chance of investigators finding a lead. The United Kingdom has already updated its software to run such familial searches, but police are allowed to conduct a familial DNA search only in serious cases.[62] Running familial searches on existing criminal DNA databases is likely to be particularly useful because criminality is correlated within families (that is, having a close relative engaged in crime increases an individual's chance of also engaging in crime).[63] As a result, the odds are good that even a first-time serious offender may have a relative's DNA already in the database.

Recommendation: Enlarge Databases But Limit Their Use to Investigation of Serious Offenses

Expanding the reach of police DNA databases is as critical to advancing justice in the twenty-first century as fingerprint databases were in the twentieth century. At the same time, many in the

public are wary of unchecked police DNA access, even as a majority favors expanding DNA databases. Thus, we believe the best reform to balance justice and privacy may be for states to mandate the collection of DNA from all arrestees (and the uploading of such DNA to the national CODIS database) but to limit the use of such an enlarged DNA database to only the investigation of felonies, or perhaps even serious felonies. In 2012, the United Kingdom passed the Protections of Freedom Act that limited the use of DNA to the investigation of felonies.[64]

To the extent that people see DNA collection as a privacy intrusion of some sort, this approach would respect that perceived interest and ensure that the perceived privacy sacrifice had a significant payoff in doing justice in serious cases. The limitation might also assure people that their DNA would not be used to link them to minor crimes they might have committed or could imagine themselves committing. With such limitations in place, measures to expand the database (as suggested in some of the reforms and proposals discussed earlier) could perhaps be taken as well. The most valuable such additional reform would be to authorize familial searching of present law enforcement DNA databases, as is allowed in the United Kingdom for serious crimes, thus greatly expanding the investigative effectiveness of existing DNA records.

Law enforcement and governments should also do more to educate the public on the critical fact that police DNA databases only store a genetic fingerprint—with the possibility for familial matching—instead of more personal DNA data such as information on health conditions.[65] This knowledge, combined with the existence of the previously discussed legal safeguards about investigative use of DNA, should allay most of the public's privacy concerns, especially when the expanded databases have a significant effect in catching serious offenders. Such knowledge might even motivate some to volunteer their DNA. The United Kingdom has a standing policy of calling for volunteers to submit their DNA samples to be added to the NDNAD, a successful venture that has prompted much participation including by many crime victims.[66] States should also consider requiring government job seekers to provide DNA samples just as they are required to provide fingerprints (the provision of such DNA would allow for better background checks by seeing if a job seeker's DNA matches an unsolved crime).

Looking back at the Golden State Killer case, it is clear how an expanded DNA database could ensure such serial killers would be caught much sooner in the future. Under our recommended reform, a modern DeAngelo—who was a former government employee—would have been required to submit his DNA when hired and would have been immediately caught as soon as DNA was pulled from a crime scene. Moreover, if any of a modern DeAngelo's relatives were arrested or hired by the government, their DNA would allow police to narrow in on the killer without having to use private ancestry databases.

Consider how one man was able to wreak such destruction—at least thirteen murders, over fifty rapes, and some 120 burglaries—because police failed to catch him early in his criminal career. As noted earlier, most murderers and rapists have previous arrests or convictions, making it critical to collect such offenders' DNA at the time of their first arrest. Catching

offenders at the beginning of their serial criminality could avoid tens or hundreds of thousands of serious offenses. People have good reason to care about their privacy, but one would have to be hard hearted to oppose the minor privacy intrusion of being in a DNA database when doing so could avoid so much human misery and destruction.

D. RESTRAINTS ON THE USE OF SURVEILLANCE TECHNOLOGIES (INCLUDING CCTV)

Big Brother is watching, but he often solves crimes with what he sees. The rise of surveillance technology in the form of CCTV cameras, license plate readers, and phone tracking has opened a wealth of new clues for solving crimes, but these technologies often remain unused due to unfamiliarity with their investigative effectiveness or opposition from privacy advocates. CCTV cameras have been around for decades, but their crime-solving and crime-deterring potential is only beginning to be fully realized. In addition to generally reducing crime by spreading the notion that police are watching,[67] surveillance cameras are now an essential part of finding suspects, building cases, and making arrests.

A study of homicide investigations in Vancouver using a sample of solved cases revealed that police reviewed surveillance footage for clues in 90 percent of investigations (and the footage was the direct source for identifying the perpetrator in 13 percent of the homicide cases).[68] The London borough of Hackney, an early adopter of CCTV cameras, reported cameras were involved in producing twenty-seven thousand arrests over the course of twelve years of use. Today, surveillance footage is an essential part of the modern police toolkit.

Even when witnesses exist for a crime, CCTV has the benefit of providing a more reliable version of events in court than witness testimony, which experts recognize is often far more flawed and biased than many realize.[69] CCTV footage is not subject to witness intimidation, and existence of usable footage can do a great deal to alleviate fear that witnesses may feel.

Similar to CCTV, automated license plate readers (ALPR) are specialized cameras designed to recognize the license plates of all passing cars and to check those plates against those of fugitives or of plates associated with a recent crime. License plate readers have been crucial in solving a wide range of serious crimes, including murder.[70] Such plate reading technology is particularly effective when placed in police squad cars allowing them to automatically spot cars that police are searching for, as is often done in the United Kingdom. Obtaining meaningful results with fewer resources benefits everyone, and license plate reading technology clearly does this. One study found that such automated plate readers have resulted in "six to seven times the national average arrest rate per officer and two to three times the number of OBTJ [offenses brought to justice] compared to conventional policing."[71]

However, the swiftest, most effective, and most concerning form of location tracking derives from the device most people carry in their pockets. Police can pinpoint a mobile phone's location via triangulation, allowing police to view a suspect's location and movements if they know their phone number. Police can even use a device known as the "stingray" to search an area for all nearby phones and then use these collected phone numbers to identify who the numbers belong

to. Between 2008 and 2015, Baltimore police alone used phone triangulation to help solve 176 homicide cases, 118 shootings, and 47 rapes in addition to hundreds of other crimes.[72] Tracking suspects' cellphones is an increasingly common form of police investigation across the country. "It's how we find killers," the FBI's director noted in 2015.[73]

Regardless of the technology in question, when police are slow in utilizing new forms of surveillance technology, or are legally prevented from doing so, criminals who could have been caught escape justice.

Case Example: Josiah Zachery

On February 11, 2015, eighteen-year-old Josiah Zachery receives a text from a fellow Franklin Hill gang member who works on a snow shoveling crew in Boston.[74] Twenty-one-year-old Kenny Lamour, a member of the rival Thetford Ave gang, has just joined the shoveling crew, and Zachery has been instructed to dispose of the man. Zachery rides the Boston subway with his MBTA Charlie Card, which tracks his movements whenever he swipes it in a station. At 10:30 am, Zachery arrives in Jamaica Plain and calmly walks up to the shoveling crew. He guns down Lamour then takes off running through neighboring yards. Police arrest Zachery as a potential suspect for being in the location, but he denies being involved and tells a false story. Police then use his Charlie Card number to access the MBTA data on his movements that morning and review CCTV footage of what he was wearing and carrying in the stations. The evidence disproves Zachery's story and allows police to get a warrant to search his phone, where they discover further evidence of the murder plot. Zachery is convicted of murder but appeals on the grounds that the MBTA data on him should not have been searched without a warrant. While Zachery loses his appeal, privacy advocates persuade the Massachusetts state legislature in 2021 to ban police from accessing MBTA location data without a warrant, thus making justice less likely in similar cases. Under the new law, police would likely not have had probable cause to search Zachery's phone, as it was the warrantless search of the MBTA data that gave them probable cause for the phone search warrant.

Case Example: Nelson Mora

On December 6, 2017, Massachusetts police install a pole camera outside the home of suspected drug dealer Nelson Mora.[75] The camera runs continuously for 169 days and allows police to monitor Mora's front door and the sidewalk next to his house to discover his contacts. As a result, police find the other members of Mora's drug ring and put their houses under surveillance with similar pole cameras to keep unraveling the criminal organization. On May 22, 2018, police raid multiple locations across Massachusetts, arresting thirteen people, including Mora, and seizing thousands of oxycodone and fentanyl pills, stashes of heroin and cocaine, and almost half a million dollars in cash. Mora seeks to have all the evidence excluded, claiming the pole cameras were an illegal search, even though they were directed only at locations in public view. The Massachu-

Figure 7.3. Josiah Zachery was arrested for the murder of a rival gang member, 2017. Photo by Chris Helms, from David Ertischek, "Life Terms with Possible Parole for Two Convicted in Jamaica Plain Murder," *Jamaica Plain News*, December 4, 2017, https://www.jamaicaplainnews.com/2017/12/04/life-terms-with-possible-parole-for-two-convicted-in-jamaica-plain-murder/29704. Courtesy of Chris Helms, Jamaica Plain News.

setts Supreme Court agrees and finds warrantless pole cameras a violation of Massachusetts's state constitution, and reverses Mora's conviction.[76]

The Nature and Extent of the Problem

Many US jurisdictions currently restrict a variety of surveillance technologies, including the use of CCTV, automatic license plate readers, and cellphone tracking. All these technologies have proven useful in obtaining reliable and compelling evidence in cases of serious crimes, but their adoption has been resisted to some extent in the United States by privacy activists and others. Compared to the United States, some European countries, especially the United Kingdom, have done more to use surveillance technologies and reap their justice and crime control benefits.

RESTRICTIONS ON USE OF CCTV In the United States, the two biggest restraints on the installation and use of CCTV cameras are financing and privacy concerns.[77] The Fourth, Fifth, and Fourteenth Amendments, which "consider issues of privacy, anonymity, and equal protection under the law" may inhibit the installation of CCTV cameras aimed at certain locations (such as private homes) and may limit police access to privately owned and operated CCTV cameras.[78] While cameras aimed at purely public spaces (such as an intersection) are clearly constitutional, courts have issued conflicting rulings on the constitutionality of their use when aimed at spaces where there might be some expectation of privacy. For example, in 2018, a federal district court in Massachusetts ruled that police violated the Fourth Amendment when they used a surveillance camera to track visitors to a home over an eight-month period, only for this decision to be reversed in 2020

by the US Court of Appeals for the First Circuit.[79] While the court's precedents leave some uncertainty with respect to the use of surveillance cameras, their increasing prevalence and usage strengthen the argument in favor of their constitutionality based on a decreasing expectation of privacy (the expectation of privacy being a key factor in the constitutional analysis).[80] Given that such pole cameras are only observing a public space that a police officer would be free to observe, it is not immediately obvious why using the camera rather than a live officer leads to a privacy violation.

Even when there is no legal bar to cameras—as is the case for most CCTV street cameras—public opinion in some communities can limit their use. When Washington, DC, installed more cameras in high-crime neighborhoods in 2006, some community members were concerned that their privacy would be violated and that the "cameras would be subject to misuse."[81] However, the community's concerns were allayed by guidelines preventing the targeting of people "based on their race, gender, sexual orientation, disability, or other distinguishing characteristics."[82] Many of the concerns over CCTV are ultimately concerns over preventing its abuse by individual bad actors, but that is an argument for careful monitoring of police, not for a ban on CCTV installation that could produce reliable and compelling evidence leading to more justice and less crime.

Partly due to opposition from privacy activists, CCTV coverage in many US cities lags behind other parts of the world, especially Asia. Perhaps typical for a US city would be New York's 7.88 cameras per 1,000 people,[83] compared to London's 13.21 and Singapore's 17.94 cameras per 1,000 people.[84]

Studies show that CCTV surveillance footage has helped solve numerous serious crimes including kidnapping, murder, and assault and has been especially useful when other forms of evidence such as DNA are not available.[85] A study in Milwaukee found that clearance rates were 82 percent higher for violent crimes occurring on street intersections with PTZ (pan-tilt-zoom) cameras than at intersections without the cameras.[86] Washington, DC's Metropolitan Police Chief Peter Newsham explained that CCTV camera technology is "one of the advances in technology that has been most significant in helping law enforcement," noting that CCTV footage advanced the investigation in 70 percent of homicide cases and "contributed to closing 40%" of homicide cases in DC in 2018.[87] In Vancouver, Canada, murder suspects are tracked with CCTV footage in 41 percent of cases and CCTV identifies murder suspects in 13 percent of cases, as noted previously.[88]

While there is little doubt that increased CCTV coverage does improve clearance rates, it is hard to identify the exact extent of improvement, but even a small increase would have a significant impact in absolute numbers. For example, if the United States adopted more blanket CCTV coverage resulting in a mere 4-percentage-point increase in the clearance rate, that would translate to *an additional fifty thousand violent crimes solved each year*.[89] Some people no doubt would feel more comfortable without CCTV, but is avoiding that discomfort really worth fifty thousand or more avoidable failures of justice in violent criminal cases every year?

There are numerous high-profile examples of the importance of CCTV in bringing justice. For example, the Boston

Marathon bombers were identified using CCTV cameras.[90] To solve the case, police used a combination of Boston's public surveillance cameras and cameras from private retailers.[91] In 2014, Maryland police shared their CCTV footage with Philadelphia police who used it to locate a man who had abducted a young woman.[92] Police in London pieced various surveillance footage together to finally catch the London Nail Bomber, who let off three bombs around the city in 1999.[93] Also in London, CCTV footage was responsible for identifying the killers who brutally murdered two-year-old James Bulger in 1993.[94] More recently, it was CCTV footage that caught and confirmed the brutal and fatal beating of Tyre Nichols by five Memphis police officers in 2023. The footage from a pole camera gave a clear view of the unjustified beating, which the criminal officers might otherwise have argued was warranted based on the limited perspective provided by body cameras.[95] Nichols's case highlights how CCTV can actually hold police accountable, a benefit likely to be appreciated by those concerned with limiting police abuses and yet another reason to install more CCTV in high-crime areas where police use of force incidents are more common.

In addition to solving crimes, CCTV can deter crime, thus increasing public safety and short-circuiting the possibility of justice failures. A study by the UK College of Policing found that the installation of CCTV may reduce crime generally by 13 percent.[96] The experience from many cities appears to support this. Atlanta, the US city with the highest number of police CCTV cameras per person (60,864 total),[97] has seen crime decrease by as much as 20 to 50 percent in the locations where cameras are operating.[98] Overseas data suggests the same dynamic. For example, in Montevideo, Uruguay, crime decreased by 20 percent in areas of the city where cameras were installed.[99]

There are over fifty million CCTV cameras in the United States,[100] but most are private. Police may or may not be able to get access to this footage, and in any case, any access will be after the fact rather than the real-time coverage police CCTV provides. However, some high-crime cities have worked to integrate these private cameras into the police surveillance system. For example, Newark, Baltimore, San Francisco, and Detroit have public-private CCTV camera agreements that allow increased sharing of video footage with police for crime-solving purposes.[101] To address an increase in crime near gas stations, police in Detroit partnered with gas stations around the city to install CCTV cameras with real-time footage streaming to police departments.[102] The project, known as Project Green Light, now give police direct access to over seven hundred cameras installed at roughly five hundred businesses.[103] Such partnerships between police and privately controlled cameras have even successfully targeted lesser crimes—like "porch piracy" (stealing delivered packages).[104]

These partnerships are important because police in the United States normally need consent or a warrant to access private CCTV footage. In contrast, a police officer in the United Kingdom must be granted access to private CCTV footage if the potential footage "is evidence in relation to an offence which he is investigating or any other offence," according to Section 19 of the Police and Criminal Evidence Act of 1984.[105]

Another notable restriction on CCTV camera installation in the United States is the lack of funding. CCTV installation and maintenance can be expensive, and some in the United Kingdom, which has more CCTV coverage than the United States, are worried that the "CCTV bubble is likely to burst unless extra revenue can be found to maintain public systems."[106] One-time grants are often not enough as the annual cost of maintaining a CCTV network can be 8 to 12 percent of the initial installation cost.[107] Private funding sources are unreliable, and many local governments in the United States choose not to fund potentially politically contentious surveillance technology.

RESTRICTIONS ON AUTOMATIC LICENSE PLATE READERS ALPR are a combination of camera plus software that automatically flags suspect cars by sifting through camera snapshots of passing cars' license plates and flagging those cars with plates police are searching for. As a result, ALPR systems allow police to quickly identify cars likely driven by wanted suspects.[108] Police might receive notification of the license plate of a drunk driver or robbery suspect and immediately input it into the ALPR system to identify the car as soon as it passes an ALPR camera. ALPR technology has been essential in solving crimes such as shootings, hit-and-runs, kidnappings, and homicides.[109] One study found that ALPR technology increased the recovery of stolen vehicles by 68 percent, increased arrests by 55 percent, and increased officer productivity by 50 percent.[110]

While no states ban the use of automated plate reading technology by police,[111] one significant limitation on ALPR technology for crime solving is legal limitations on its long-term storage prompted either by economic or privacy concerns. Scanning the license plates of passing cars produces reams of data, and every state has different provisions dictating how long ALPR data can be stored. For example, Arkansas allows ALPR data to be stored for up to 150 days, but Maine allows for ALPR data to be stored for only twenty-one days, which poses serious risks to criminal investigations that often seek to analyze the movements of suspects weeks or months in the past.[112] Massachusetts is now considering deleting ALPR data after only fourteen days, "except in connection with a specific criminal investigation based on articulable facts linking data to a crime."[113] In New Jersey, on the other hand, ALPR data can be stored for up to five years, and some states store the data indefinitely.[114]

Additionally, many law enforcement agencies in the United States do not share their ALPR data as police do in the United Kingdom. In fact, only 43 percent of US departments are part of a regional ALPR system, and only 40 percent share ALRP data with any other agencies.[115] This lack of information sharing can substantially decrease the ability to solve crimes, as cars often move between police jurisdictions. As ALPR usage in the United States increases,[116] the importance of integrated and shared ALPR systems increases.

As with other police technologies, the United Kingdom offers an example of earlier adoption and a more integrated national system. UK police forces utilize automated number plate recognition (ANPR) technology (the equivalent of American ALPR technology), and there are currently roughly 11,000 to 13,000 ANPR cameras throughout the United Kingdom, submitting around fifty million ANPR records to national ANPR systems every day.[117] Additionally, beginning in 2001, 100 percent of police forces in England and Wales (of which there

are forty-three) were provided with vans equipped with ANPR technology.[118]

Opposition to expanding ALPR technology makes little sense from a privacy perspective as the same data could be gathered by a police officer sitting in a squad car and manually typing in the license plates going past. ALPR technology is not an additional infringement on privacy but simply allows police to be far more efficient at existing license plate monitoring efforts in the public sphere. It seems unlikely that communities would want to recognize a right to inefficient policing, which only benefits criminals.

RESTRICTIONS ON ACCESS TO CELLPHONE TRACKING Tracking a cellphone's location through triangulation is a powerful tool to find criminals and solve crimes. Tracking can either be done with real-time tools that imitate cell towers ("stingrays") or by accessing past triangulation data stored by a cell service provider. Seeing whether a particular phone number was near a crime scene at the time of the crime can allow police to quickly filter or identify suspects. When police have a specific cellphone number under suspicion, they can obtain the phone location history from the cell service provider (though after 2018, a warrant is now required). Police can also scan for the location of all nearby phone numbers, or the presence of a specific phone number, in real time using a portable briefcase-sized device known as the "the stingray," which imitates a cell tower and thus receives location data from nearby phones.[119] In 2015, the US Department of Homeland Security noted that cellphone tracking raises privacy concerns, but also noted that such practices "are invaluable law enforcement tools."[120] In Baltimore alone, investigators used cellphone tracking in solving 176 homicides, 118 shootings, and 47 rapes between 2008 and 2015.[121]

Before 2018, limitations on police access to cellphone location data stored by service providers was a state-by-state issue with some states requiring warrants and others not. However, in 2018, the Supreme Court ruled in *Carpenter v. U.S.* that cellphone location data is protected by the Fourth Amendment despite being held by a third party (cellphone service providers). This built on the Court's 2012 decision in *U.S. v. Jones*, which prevented police from putting GPS location trackers on vehicles without a warrant.[122] Police must now obtain a warrant or show exigent circumstances (such as when pursuing an actively fleeing suspect or when actively trying to recover a kidnapped person) in order to access such third-party cellphone location data.[123] The new restrictions are likely to limit the effectiveness of cellphone location data as an investigative tool because police may not have established the probable cause required for a warrant in the earlier stages of an investigation, which is when cellphone location data can be most useful to sort through a large number of possible suspects. However, the ruling in *Carpenter* left a legal gray zone around the use of real-time tracking via stingrays as it is unclear whether temporarily intercepting signals meant for a cell tower violates a reasonable expectation of privacy.[124] As a result, state regulations and lower court opinions vary as to whether police need a warrant before using a stingray.

However, even with warrant requirements in place, there are still ways for police to exploit geolocation data from phones to find initial suspects. Police can apply for a "geo-fence warrant,"[125] which is a type of reverse search warrant that allows police to "search a database to find all active mobile devices within a particular geo-fence area."[126] This can enable police to request location data from companies like Google or Uber for a list of all users who may have been in the proximity of a crime scene. Such geo-fence warrants do not rely on cell companies' triangulation data but rather the detailed location history many apps store on users.[127] Geo-fence warrants are a promising new way to find suspects, but they raise constitutional issues that have yet to be settled. In fact, some privacy activists argue the entire category of reverse search warrants is unconstitutional as it borders on general warrants by not targeting a specific individual but rather a location where a crime is known to have occurred.[128]

RESTRICTIONS ON ACCESS TO ELECTRONIC PERSONAL DATA In addition to more standard forms of surveillance data, there are an increasing number of online sources of data police may be able to exploit. For example, in one case, a judge ordered Amazon to release data collected from Amazon Echo voice searches that could help in a murder investigation.[129] As long as police have a warrant, searching a suspect's online searches or communications can also yield critical evidence. (Recall chapter 1's discussion of Casey Anthony, who escaped justice for murdering her daughter because investigators neglected to review all her online search data.) People's social media is also a source of data, as police in Chicago have turned to social media to fight gang violence, conducting "network analyses" of known gang members to identify and map their social media connections and determine who is most likely to be killed and who is most likely to be a perpetrator.[130] This activity may even have prevented some killings: after police began utilizing network analyses, seventy-six fewer homicides occurred than in the previous year and shootings decreased by 350.[131] Police have also on occasion used Google Earth to track suspects[132] and have used AI algorithms to analyze Google Earth satellite images to locate murder scenes and solve cold cases.[133] In the case of publicly available data like social media accounts or Google Earth, no privacy issues appear to be raised, and the main restraints on using the technology are a lack of investigator training or imagination.

However, when it comes to utilizing personal electronic data stored on computers or smart devices, police usually face warrant restrictions that limit the usefulness of such data in the early stages of an investigation. For example, the federal Stored Communications Act requires that warrants be obtained before searching computers or data stored on the internet.[134]

In addition to legal restrictions, police sometimes face resistance from private technology companies in cooperating with investigations. Apple, Google, Facebook, and Microsoft received over 114,000 data requests from law enforcement in the first half of 2020 and provided data in 85 percent of those cases.[135] However, the 15 percent of denied cases represent thousands of instances of frustrated justice. For example, in a Mississippi case, a man confessed to his possession of videos and photos of children being raped, but Google refused to grant police access to the man's Gmail account that would have helped the police locate the origins of the child pornography.[136] Such technology companies are able to routinely refuse to provide data requested even with a search warrant because US customer data is often stored overseas, meaning the data is currently beyond US jurisdiction.

Reforms

Many reforms have been undertaken or proposed to authorize or expand the use of modern surveillance technology, where constitutionally permissible. The challenge in many instances is how to overcome suspicions that exaggerate the potential dangers of technology and understate its benefits.

Prevent Possible Abuse by Anonymizing License Plate Readers. Many fears about CCTV and license plate readers center on their possible abuse in targeting innocent individuals. When it comes to license plate reading technology, some have proposed—and some police have already adopted[137]—a reform that makes ALPR cameras initially reveal only vehicle registration information from scanned license plates rather than revealing personal information as well. Then, if the registration provides a match and reveals a "basis for further police action," the officer can request and obtain, perhaps on approval of a senior officer, "'personal information' of the registered owner, including name, address, social security number, and if available, criminal record."[138] This would reduce the chances of abuse by preventing individual officers from using ALPR to target innocent individuals as was done to patrons of a gay club in DC in 1997 by a rogue officer.

Create Guidelines and Oversight for CCTV Usage. As with ALPR systems, some of the resistance to CCTV installation arises from fears that it may be abused. States, municipalities, and individual police departments can combat this fear by creating guidelines for the use of CCTV that will promote strict internal oversight of how police use CCTV footage and prevent public cameras from being used voyeuristically or on the personal whims of investigators.

Recommendation: Fund Increased Use of CCTV Where Community Does Not Object

As is perhaps already apparent, we recommend making greater use of modern surveillance technology that does not expand the public sphere but simply better records what occurs in it. We support expanded and integrated CCTV and ALPR networks and highly recommend greater sharing of surveillance data between law enforcement agencies. In most instances, such sharing is not likely to alter the extent of a privacy intrusion but will significantly increase the investigative benefits of existing data collection. When it comes to other forms of surveillance such as cellphone tracking, where courts currently make the rules, our view is the same one we present in chapter 6: we would prefer legislatures to make these rules democratically based on the balance of interests most supported by the community. However, we recognize it will often be more practical for investigators and policymakers to focus on adopting new technology not currently heavily restricted by courts.

Even when there are few judicial limits on a technology, however, the broader question is how to ensure that communities are satisfied with the balance between justice and privacy that is struck in deciding whether to adopt modern surveillance technologies and how they will be used. Because surveillance involves a specific privacy tradeoff for the locality's residents, it makes the most sense to let individual communities decide (normally through their elected representatives on municipal councils) the extent to which they want the installation of CCTV cameras and other surveillance technologies. Some communities may decide they wish more surveillance than others, and

such democratic variation is the best way to ensure communities are satisfied with the balance of interests. What matters most is that increased CCTV coverage remains a voluntary action undertaken by the community it is intended to protect. While 78 percent of Americans view added street surveillance as a good idea, this support varies widely depending on the community.[139] Any community ought to be free to choose less privacy intrusion and more criminal victimization of its members, as long as that decision truly represents the community and not a minority of vocal activists.[140]

Even when communities wish for more surveillance to advance justice and safety, funds dedicated for surveillance technology are scarce, particularly given chronic inadequate police financing and ideologically motivated budget cuts. The lack of funding for CCTV is especially pertinent given rising violent crime across parts of the United States.[141] This means state and federal funding is likely necessary to permit wider CCTV adoption. States currently spend surprisingly little on policing with police department expenditures constituting a mere 1 percent of states' total budget allocation.[142] Spending more on local technology grants would be a way to increase local funding without creating extra bureaucracy. In providing these state and federal grants, priority should be given to those communities with the highest crime to current CCTV ratio—in other words, those communities most likely to benefit from the increases in justice and safety produced by greater CCTV coverage.

This proposal is not wholly novel. There already exist funds that offer grants for CCTV system implementation. Such funds include the Department of Justice–sponsored "Justice Assistance Grant," the Department of Homeland Security's "Homeland Security Grants," and the Community Oriented Policing Services's (COPS) "Secure our Schools" Program, all three of which offer some funds related to surveillance and CCTV investments.[143] Unfortunately, these grants are typically too small to significantly aid CCTV adoption, and they also fail to take into account community opinion, which should be an essential component of the decision to add more surveillance.[144] Internationally, Germany has made major strides toward increasing CCTV use across the country, with the national parliament granting 180 million euros to install CCTV in high-risk areas.[145] Notably, the national government in Germany left it to more local decision makers as to whether CCTV cameras should be added.[146]

An additional benefit of this proposal is that a community's vote to install more CCTV can aid judges in interpreting whether a police request for surveillance violates a right to privacy because part of the judicial consideration is whether a person's subjective expectation of privacy is recognized by the community.[147] In the case of Nelson Mora, for example, the Massachusetts Supreme Court might not have found the pole cameras a violation of a constitutional privacy right if the community had explicitly voted to install such cameras.

E. RESTRAINTS ON THE USE OF DATA ANALYTICS (INCLUDING FACIAL RECOGNITION SOFTWARE)

In a world where technology allows police to collect enormous quantities of data, analytical tools, like AI algorithms that employ machine learning, are a critical way for police to efficiently find the needles in the haystack.[148] While the future likely holds many useful crime-

solving algorithms, one of the most useful current such algorithm is facial recognition software that allows police to quickly sort through reams of surveillance footage to identify relevant images and find suspects in a wide range of cases, including murders.[149]

Of course, algorithms and data analytic tools are only as good as their input data, and opposition to police algorithms often stems from the fear that such tools may produce biased or inaccurate results due to biased inputs. The result of such fears has sometimes been restrictions or bans on such technology as facial recognition. However, in a world where data analysis is increasingly essential to justice and is constantly improving, algorithms will increasingly become powerful and even essential parts of crime investigation. The only real question is how they should be regulated and adopted.

Case Example: Danueal Drayton

Danueal Drayton is arrested three times in Connecticut for violence against women. While on probation for the most recent assault, he moves to New York, where he begins dating Zynea Barney. Barney quickly tires of his controlling nature and calls off the relationship. This is too much for Drayton, who becomes enraged. In his rage, he attacks her, screaming, "'F***ing b***h, I'm going to kill you. I'm going to kill you. . . . I told you, it's just me and you."[150] Some bystanders intervene, and police are called. Drayton is not arrested. A few days later, he attacks her again and is arrested and released a week later. Two weeks later, Drayton goes on a Tinder date with a nurse from Queens. He beats the woman to death and flees.

New York police use his Tinder photo with facial recognition software to locate his driver's license and thereby identify him. From there, they follow his credit card purchase of an airline ticket to California. The trail stays warm, and when the California authorities arrest him, Drayton is with a woman who is tied up. She tells police she is being held against her will and has been a hostage for two days. The facial recognition software also links him to a second woman who was raped during a Tinder encounter. Drayton eventually confesses to six killings. Without police use of facial recognition technology, Drayton might have escaped justice, and it seems likely that other innocent women would have been killed.

Despite its usefulness, California passed a three-year ban on most police uses of facial recognition over privacy and bias concerns. Fortunately, the ban expired in 2023.[151]

The Nature and Extent of the Problem

The use of computer algorithms in crime investigation has enormous potential to avoid failures of justice in serious cases, but that potential is far from being realized, often because of gross misunderstandings among the public about how algorithms function and their level of accuracy.

RESTRICTIONS ON THE USE OF FACIAL REC-OGNITION TECHNOLOGY Facial recognition technology (FRT) has already proved extremely useful for police. In New York, the use of FRT found potential matches in 1,851 cases and led to arrests in 998 cases in 2018.[152] A significant number of these crimes included rape, assault, or murder. Indiana police officers have noted how essential the technology is to solving cases, especially when traditional leads are limited and all investigators have is an image, which is not an uncommon situation.[153]

While FRT is still not widely used in the United States, where it has proved

useful in successfully identifying suspects.[154] Some European countries have begun using the technology more widely. The United Kingdom, for example, has relied significantly on facial recognition technology since 2018, particularly in London, which is already heavily covered by CCTV. The new technology will enable London's police force to process images from CCTV feeds, social media, and other sources to identify and locate suspects.[155] In Geneva in 2021, the World Economic Forum issued a white paper that examined a variety of situations in which facial recognition technology could be useful and developed policies aimed at maximizing its effective and responsible use. The paper states: "The development of FRT presents considerable opportunities for socially beneficial uses, mostly through enhanced authentication and identification processes, but it also creates unique challenges."[156]

While facial recognition can be extremely useful in the investigation of serious crimes, it also has the potential to create problems when a person is incorrectly identified. Detroit's experience highlights the benefits and potential downsides of FRT. On the one hand, Detroit police have used facial recognition technology to catch and charge a shooter with three counts of first-degree murder, but they also incorrectly arrested and held a man for thirty hours because of a faulty facial recognition match for a shoplifting he did not commit.[157]

It is important to remember though that every crime investigation tool is imperfect, and it is not uncommon that innocent persons will be inconvenienced as investigators pursue leads. Witnesses, for example, commonly misidentify perpetrators, and innocent persons can be detained and questioned as a result.

By contrast, the accuracy rate of good facial recognition technology is 99.97 percent,[158] dramatically higher than the vast majority of criminal investigation methodologies. Thus, if one is concerned about minimizing inconvenience to innocent persons, use of FRT ought to be much preferred over other traditional investigative mechanisms, such as reliance upon witnesses.

Restrictions on police use of FRT have been passed by several states and municipalities as a result of lobbying by privacy advocates and those fearing facial recognition algorithms may be biased or inaccurate. For example, California placed bans on most uses of facial recognition technology by police until the end of 2022.[159] In 2021, Virginia completely banned the use of FRT by police but recently replaced the ban with strict guidelines allowing police to search only for matches on specific individuals they have cause to suspect—a limitation that tends to eviscerate the usefulness of a technology used in identifying suspects in the first place.[160] Some members of Congress in 2021 proposed a similar law that would ban US government agencies or law enforcement agencies from using FRT without a warrant.[161] In seventeen communities across the country—including Sommerville, Massachusetts; San Francisco, Oakland, and Berkeley, California; and Portland, Oregon—municipalities have banned all use of facial recognition technology by government agencies, including police departments.[162]

Moreover, in October 2023, several US Representatives introduced a bill to Congress with the objective to limit or ban the use of FRT by law enforcement authorities. The bill would require police to seek a warrant to use FRT and prohibit law enforcement officials from using a positive facial recognition match

as the sole basis upon which probable cause can be established, thus destroying a primary use of the technology in identifying potential suspects in the first place.[163] In other words, the bill essentially destroys a primary use of the technology in identifying potential suspects in the first place.

Some private companies have also refused to sell facial recognition technology to law enforcement in order to avoid the disapproval of political opponents of the technology. In 2020, Microsoft decided against selling facial recognition technology to law enforcement agencies due to claimed privacy concerns, the current lack of federal regulation of the technology, and concerns that FRT could lead to wrongful arrests and convictions.[164] Around the same time, Amazon and IBM also decided to prohibit the sale of facial recognition technology to police departments, citing the lack of federal regulation.[165]

But opposition to facial recognition technology seems to be based largely on public misconceptions. From a privacy perspective, facial recognition does not record any more of a citizen's life than is already available through CCTV cameras, photographs, or witness observation. Facial recognition simply makes police vastly more efficient at sorting through camera footage, much like automatic license plate readers make the process of searching through license plates vastly easier.

Additionally, fears over accuracy and racial bias in facial recognition are wildly overstated. Advances in accuracy over the past several years have made false positive identifications extremely rare and made the discrepancy between accurately identifying Caucasians and non-Caucasians miniscule. Fears of racial disparity began with a 2012 study showing the accuracy rate for matching faces overall was 94.5 percent but was only 88.7 percent for Blacks and 89.5 percent for women (raising concerns about gender disparity as well).[166] But, as noted earlier, even the lowest accuracy rate of 88.7 percent is dramatically higher than most crime investigation methodologies, such as relying on witness recollection at the beginning of an investigation.

As it turns out, further research revealed that those disparities were caused by the greater prevalence of certain faces in original training set data used to develop the technology, not from a flaw in the technology itself. For example, facial recognition algorithms developed in East Asia have higher accuracy for Asian faces than non-Asian faces.[167] However, as far back as 2018, advances in facial recognition technology had brought the accuracy rate up to *99.97 percent, and false matches were almost never due to race or gender* but due to aging or injury.[168] Studies have repeatedly confirmed that the best available facial recognition algorithms have vanishingly small error rates across all demographics, making any remaining disparities irrelevant in practice.[169]

There is little question that facial recognition technology has greater benefits for solving crime perpetrated by people of all races than the downside of a trivial number of false identifications which, while regrettable, have not led to false convictions and rarely lead to mistaken arrests.[170] But many in the public have been led to oppose FRT based on a faulty understanding of these facts.

Internal police failure to implement is another major limitation on FRT. Even if these misperceptions are corrected and legal and corporate restrictions are removed, it seems that facial recognition technology, as with many modern technologies, is likely to fall far short of its potential to prevent justice failures simply because police departments fail to appreciate its potential or lack the training or funding to take advantage of it.

RESTRICTIONS ON THE USE OF CRIME ALGO-RITHMS Crime algorithms that use crime data to reveal patterns in offenses or potential crime hot spots can also be extremely useful to both solving crimes and preventing them with proactive policing. While there are no legal restrictions on police use of such algorithms, police have often failed to embrace their use for reasons ranging from a lack of knowledge to inertia. This is unfortunate because such algorithms can be enormously useful and will likely become even more effective as AI models advance. For example, some police departments and prosecutors have already used data mapping algorithms on individual crime instances to uncover and prosecute large criminal operations. Some algorithms, such as one created by the Murder Accountability Project in 2015 and used by Atlanta, seek to identify serial killers by comparing victim information, details of the murder, location, and time.[171] Algorithms like these can overcome human "pattern blindness" that occurs when investigators fail to notice subtly connected crimes.[172] Similarly, the Department of Justice has developed two software prototypes to analyze homicide and sexual assault data called CATCH and CATCHRAPE.[173] The software analyzes detailed crime data on murder and sexual assault cases to identify patterns and catch serial murderers and rapists that human data analysts might not otherwise recognize.

Other types of crime algorithms target organized crimes by documenting types of crimes, victim and witness information, and geocoordinates. Once crime information is consistently placed into the database, "the system might flag gang associations or loyalty to a particular housing complex, building, or neighborhood."[174] Using data analysis gives insight into "complex criminal patterns, schemes, relationships, and violations that would otherwise go undetected" to the naked eye and can provide necessary evidence during a prosecution by preventing the defense from describing the police observations as "merely a series of innocent coincidences."[175]

The Manhattan DA's office was the first to establish a Crime Strategies Unit (CSU), which used an "intelligence-driven prosecution model" to predict crime patterns and locate crime hot spots.[176] By discovering patterns of crime, prosecutors can target their efforts toward groups of people or locations. For example, the Manhattan DA's office investigated certain housing complexes with intelligence collection and data modeling to eventually arrest dozens of people associated with violent criminal activity. In six years, the CSU investigative method has been responsible for the indictment of 377 gang members.[177] San Francisco has implemented a CSU based on the New York model to identify hot spots and repeat offenders. In San Francisco, "just 5 percent of offenders are responsible for 25 percent of crime," and "nearly 60 percent of homicides occur in known gun violence hot spots."[178]

Identifying patterns of crime can also be enormously useful for policing strategies as shown by New York City's experience with CompStat, a computer program processing the city's crime data and showing police where to target crime control efforts based on which crimes are rising where. When New York City police began to use CompStat in the 1990s, crime rates fell by 12 percent and declined in all seventy-six police precincts, and homicides decreased by 67 percent between 1993 and 1998.[179] Computer programs of this sort have been shown to be "statistically more likely to predict when and where crime will occur than human crime analysts."[180]

Many police departments don't use new data analysis algorithms because they perceive the technology as unhelpful or time consuming. A study by ProPublica found that police investigators often find VICAP (the FBI's serial offender analysis tool) too "cumbersome" because it takes hours to enter case information. As a result, only "1,400 of the 18,000 law enforcement agencies in the country used the system."[181] This was surely not what the FBI hoped for when it designed its crime-solving technology. Additionally, police complained that "hits," or identifications, are quite rare and "false positives are common."[182] Of course, to improve the accuracy of the system, more data is needed, which police are reluctant to provide given its current relative costs versus effectiveness. To make matters worse, available training for using the program is minimal, so many officers don't even attempt to use it.

In contrast, Canada has implemented a similar system but has "poured funding and staff" into the project and mandates that all crimes are uploaded into the system, whereas reporting is voluntary for US agencies.[183] As one former detective noted, "anytime you ask for voluntary compliance, it won't be a priority. It's not going to happen."[184] As a result, the system has been significantly more effective in Canada than in the United States. One obvious way to broaden the adoption of useful crime algorithms is to require local police to adopt them or make sure the resources and training are available from a state or federal level to help minimize the implementation burden.

Reforms

Several reforms have been proposed or undertaken to further the adoption of crime algorithms, including the use of facial recognition systems.

Ensure Transparency in the Use of Algorithms. In order to allay public concerns over the use of facial recognition technology, a recent law in New York City requires the police department to increase transparency and reveal how the technology is used to surveil the public.[185] If communities are made aware of how FRT is used and how data is protected (and how many cases can benefit from its use), they may become more accepting of it.[186] Similarly, many reforms to crime data mapping programs have involved increasing transparency and information access to communities so people can see the inputs to crime algorithms themselves. For example, the San Diego Police Department incorporated such a project into its efforts to increase community collaborations. The public was concerned that they were not informed often enough about crime in their area. With the help of the Automated Regional Justice Information System (ARJIS), the SDPD created a "near real-time, publicly accessible crime mapping application known as ARJIS Interactive Mapping Application."[187]

Create Best Practice Guidelines/ Regulations for Police Algorithms. One of the main concerns for community members and technology companies is the lack of regulation on the use of facial recognition technologies and other algorithms, which creates a fear that they exist in a black box. Many concerns over

police algorithms could be addressed if states created a set of regulations, or at least guidelines, for the use of algorithms by investigators to ensure accuracy and proper use. For example, the best practice regulations on facial recognition technology could provide that police should only use FRT algorithms that have been tested to a high degree of accuracy across all racial groups.[188] With such best practice guidelines established, it could be easier to obtain funding and community support for the use of such technologies. Some organizations have already drafted guidelines for police use of facial recognition technology.[189]

Recommendation: Fund Use of Facial Recognition Where Community Does Not Object

Facial recognition technology is especially useful as an addition to an existing CCTV system, so it makes sense to incentivize its adoption in a similar manner to our recommendation for CCTV adoption presented in the previous section. As with CCTV, communities should be allowed to decide the extent to which they wish to utilize facial recognition technology. Those communities supportive of increased CCTV adoption are likely to support facial recognition as well once they understand such algorithms merely multiply the effectiveness of existing CCTV cameras and image databases. Once a city council approves the use of FRT, the training and funding necessary to implement the software ought to be supplied in part through state and federal grants, as in our proposal for CCTV adoption. Additionally, these funding grants can specify the accuracy, usage, and transparency standards any proposed facial recognition technology must meet in order to qualify for funding.

Unlike our previous recommendation on CCTV, there are no examples of federal funds solely dedicated to advancing the use of facial recognition technology among local law enforcement. Instead police departments requesting funds to implement FRT within their communities have historically appealed to programs with general funding scopes, such as the Community Development Policing Program sponsored by the Department of Justice's COPS office.[190] While offering over $14 billion intended for various policing initiatives, COPS has granted only insignificant portions toward facial recognition.[191] There are examples of grant funding, but only in small amounts. In 2016, for instance, the Jacksonville Police Department applied for the federal Edward Byrne Memorial Justice Assistance Grant Program (JAG)

in the hope of increasing the use of facial recognition technology, arguing that FRT would prove vital in identifying perpetrators.[192] The Department of Justice ended up granting the Jacksonville Police Department $12,882.[193]

As noted earlier, the United Kingdom has increasingly relied on facial recognition technology since 2018, particularly in London, which is already heavily covered by CCTV.[194] Notably, it was the mayor of London who decided to invest in facial recognition technology after multiple consultations with experts, even though "political support for the use of facial recognition remains contested in the U.K."[195] This reflects the sort of local initiative our proposal calls for in that individual communities should make the balancing judgements inherent in both CCTV and facial recognition usage.

Part III

CRIMINAL JUSTICE ADJUDICATION PROCEDURES

Excluding Reliable and Probative Evidence

OF ALL THE CAUSES OF JUSTICE FAIL- ures, judges excluding reliable and probative evidence from trial is one of the most heavily criticized. Public faith in the justice system is undermined when judges let serious offenders escape justice based on what ordinary people see as a technicality having nothing to do with guilt or innocence. The first part of the chapter examines the judicial suppression of reliable and even compelling evidence through the exclusionary rule, aimed at deterring police and prosecutors from violating legal limitations on criminal investigation. The second half of the chapter discusses the suppression of reliable and probative evidence that, in the judge's opinion, would be "prejudicial" to the defendant if not hidden from the jury. Both these common practices regularly produce justice failures and create a public impression that the criminal justice system simply does not care about finding truth and doing justice.

A. EXCLUDING RELIABLE EVIDENCE TO RESTRAIN POLICE AND PROSECUTORS (THE EXCLUSIONARY RULE)

The exclusionary rule requires judges to exclude from introduction at trial evidence that was obtained in violation of the rules governing police investigation, most notably those rules related to search and seizure or suspect interrogation,

both of which are discussed in chapter 6. The theory behind the exclusionary rule is that police and prosecutors would have no incentive to obey constitutional restrictions if illegally gathered evidence could be used at trial. However, the exclusionary rule does not punish investigators (who suffer little personal cost from lost cases) but rather innocent victims and society through generating a continuing stream of justice failures.

A Brief History of the US Exclusionary Rule

Unlike many US legal rules, the exclusionary rule finds little support in English common law.[1] While the common law excludes evidence obtained by forced self-incrimination, such as a confession obtained by torture, it does not automatically exclude other evidence no matter how intrusively or illegally it was collected. Many scholars observe that the Fourth Amendment, on which the exclusionary rule is based, provides no basis for excluding illegally obtained evidence, an argument strengthened by the lack of common law support for exclusion at the time of the Bill of Rights.[2] On the other hand, proponents of the exclusionary rule have argued that even if exclusion is not itself a constitutional right, it was, at least in the past, the only practical means available to courts to enforce the constitutional prohibition against illegal evidence gathering.

The US Supreme Court initially adopted the common law rule and limited exclusion only to cases of forced self-incrimination. In the 1904 case of *Adams v. People of State of New York*, the Supreme Court explicitly rejected an exclusionary rule for evidence obtained in violation of the Fourth Amendment.[3] However, the court changed direction in the 1914 case of *Weeks v. United States* and excluded improperly obtained evidence in federal criminal cases.[4] The court expanded the exclusionary rule further in the 1920 case of *Silverthorne Lumber Co. v. United States*, which established that secondary information obtained from illegally seized evidence is also impermissible in court—a rule known as the "fruit of the poisonous tree" doctrine—because admitting such evidence might undermine the exclusionary rule's disincentive to violate search and seizure rules. This fruit of the poisonous tree doctrine has become a central feature of the exclusionary rule, and one that is peculiar to the United States.[5]

Some state courts followed the Supreme Court's lead in establishing an exclusionary rule after *Weeks* and *Silverthorne*, but it was not until the 1961 Supreme Court case of *Mapp v. Ohio* that the federal exclusionary rule was extended to the states.[6] Later, in 1966, the Supreme Court held in *Miranda v. Arizona* that the exclusionary rule applies not only to physical evidence obtained in violation of search and seizure rules but also to voluntary self-incriminating statements elicited by law enforcement in violation of custodial interrogation rules.[7] Recall the case of Julius Wideman from chapter 1, who had his murder conviction overturned because the court judged his voluntary confession came too long after he was last read his Miranda rights.

Consider three other case examples of the exclusionary rule at work.

Case Example: Larry Eyler

In 1982, car wash attendant Steven Agan is hitchhiking in Terre Haute, Indiana, when one of his customers, Larry Eyler, stops to pick him up.[8] Once Agan is in his truck, Eyler pulls a knife and drives the man to an abandoned farm. Eyler ties and gags Agan, drags him into a shed, and pulls out a complete torture kit. With the scene lit by flashlights, Eyler selects from his kit a particular knife, leaving the metal-tipped whip and tear gas for other victims. He then slowly slices and stabs Agan to death. Agan is one of at least twenty-one young (mostly gay) men murdered by the sadistic serial torturer-killer. The random nature of Eyler's attacks make it difficult for police to catch him. But more than a dozen

Figure 8.1. Larry Eyler was released from custody despite strong evidence implicating him in more than ten murders, 1983. Photo courtesy of the Indiana State Police.

murders later, his luck runs out. Eyler picks up Steve Haywood while driving on a highway and lures him out of the truck while promising $100 in exchange for a sex act. By chance, a passing state trooper sees the truck parked illegally along the open highway and stops to investigate. The trooper is suspicious of Eyler's attempt to hide something in a bag and his inability to explain what he is doing with Haywood. (Haywood apparently does not realize how close he has come to being tortured and killed.) The trooper radios the situation to his dispatchers, and several other officers recognize that Eyler's behavior matches the serial killer they are looking for. The trooper detains Eyler and Haywood while waiting for backup. The men are given Miranda warnings, Haywood admits that Eyler solicited him for sex, and the two men are taken to the police station. Further

investigation reveals compelling evidence in Eyler's truck and on his person that conclusively tie Eyler to the past killings. Eyler's lawyer moves to have all the evidence excluded because the initial stop and questioning went on too long to be justified under *Terry v. Ohio* (in which the Supreme Court authorized short stops based on reasonable suspicion a person is involved in a crime). A judge agrees, excludes all the evidence, and Eyler is released. He quickly resumes killing. Eventually he is caught "correctly," convicted, and sentenced to death, but only after more young gay men are needlessly slaughtered.

Case Example: William Ellis

On October 4, 2006, in Butte, Montana, Dr. William Ellis gives his thirteen-year-old daughter some extra potent pills to help her sleep.[9] Once the girl

Figure 8.2. The hospital where William Ellis worked as an emergency room physician, 1914. Photo courtesy of Jack Parker.

is asleep, Ellis returns to her room and begins molesting her. The girl wakes up during the assault but feigns sleep. In the morning, she claims to be sick and stays home while her father leaves for work. She then calls the police to report the sexual assault and invites the officers into the house to show them where the assault took place. The police gather evidence such as the girl's sheets, blankets, pajamas, and underwear. A drug test reveals the girl was given fifty grams of Ambien CR (an inappropriate dose of sedative clearly meant to knock the girl out). Subsequent analysis also finds Ellis's semen on his daughter's sheets. With a defense on the facts impossible, Ellis files a motion to exclude all the evidence on the grounds that his daughter was too young to legally consent to a search of the house. The Montana Supreme Court agrees and suppresses almost all the evidence the prosecution would use at trial, making it impossible to prosecute Ellis for sexually assaulting his daughter.

Case Example: Harry Skinner

On June 21, 1975, forty-five-year-old Harry Skinner picks up twenty-year-old Diane Snell at a bar in Amherst, New York.[10] When Snell refuses his sexual advances in the car, Skinner flies into a rage and beats the young woman to death before dumping her body in a ditch by the side of the road. Witnesses at the bar point to Skinner, and police question him repeatedly but get the same story that Skinner dropped Snell off safely in Buffalo. Skinner even passes two polygraph tests. Skinner then hires a lawyer who tells his client not to talk to police without him. The lawyer also tells Amherst police not to question Skinner without him being present. On March 10, 1977, police arrive at Skinner's apart-

ment to deliver a court order to appear in a lineup. Skinner becomes extremely upset, and the officers ask him if he would like to get the truth off his chest. Skinner once again voluntarily tells his previous story, but this time he slips up and makes damaging statements about the crime that reveal he is the murderer. Skinner is convicted of killing Diane Snell but appeals. Even though he was not in custody at the time (and, in any case, had previously been read his Miranda rights), he nonetheless claims that his voluntary statements should be suppressed because his lawyer was not present, even though he ignored his lawyer's advice and voluntarily made the statements. The New York Court of Appeals, which is the highest court in the state, excludes the voluntary statements, finding them a denial of the right to counsel, and overturns the conviction.[11] Skinner walks free.

Competing Interests

The judicial creation of the exclusionary rule was not arbitrary. There are legitimate interests advanced by it but also strong interests opposing it.

INTERESTS SUPPORTING THE CURRENT EXCLUSIONARY RULE

- *Deterring Police Violations of Constitutional Rights.* When formulating and adopting the exclusionary rule, the Supreme Court explicitly made clear it was justified on the basis of deterring police from violating people's constitutional rights. If evidence gathered in contravention of the Fourth or Fifth Amendment was admissible, police might have an incentive to use illegal tactics to close cases, rendering the constitutional protections toothless. Without some form of deterrence, police could break into suspects' houses, ransack their belongings, and wring confessions from unwilling detainees. It was against such a despotic vision of government that the Bill of Rights was drafted in the first place. If the exclusionary rule is the only thing standing between citizens and this nightmare, then it is undoubtedly justified. However, many scholars argue that the exclusionary rule has done little to deter most police violations.[12] In the United States, the majority of violations are committed accidentally or inadvertently because the complicated judicial rules are beyond easy police comprehension. Exclusion does little or nothing to deter such mistakes. Furthermore, exclusion does not deter police from illegal searches and seizures unrelated to gathering evidence (such as seizures aimed at taking guns or drugs off the street). Most importantly, the exclusionary rule fails as a means of controlling police conduct because officers have little personal stake in whether evidence is excluded months or years later in some distant court.

- *Protecting Police Officers.* Some argue that the exclusionary rule protects police officers who violate constitutional rights while still attempting to alleviate the damage caused to individuals whose rights have been violated. If the exclusionary rule did not exist, some other legal remedy would be needed to enforce constitutional protections. Such other proposed remedies usually involve punishing police officers or departments for illegal searches and seizures. The exclusionary rule's protection of police does undermine its deterrence, but it also prevents a widespread discouragement of all searches and seizures that might occur if officers were personally liable for their mistakes.

- *Procedural Justice.* The Supreme Court has held the exclusionary rule is a policy measure and not a personal procedural right guaranteed by the constitution.[13] However, some state courts have determined their own exclusionary rules are rights guaranteed by their state constitutions. These state courts conceptualize the rule's purpose as being broader than merely deterring police misconduct but rather see the rule as safeguarding individual rights and providing an affirmative remedy when violations occur (thus these states decline to adopt a good faith exception).[14] If gathering evidence in violation of constitutional rights is a wrong, then the exclusionary rule serves to promote a form of compensation by letting the offender escape criminal liability and punishment. However, this justification for the rule benefits only guilty offenders and can impose a societal cost grossly disproportionate to the nature of the violation, as in letting serial torturer-murderer Larry Eyler walk free because he was minorly inconvenienced by being held a few hours too long during an investigation.

- *The Integrity of the Justice System.* Some have argued that the exclusionary rule can promote the integrity of the justice system because excluding illegally gathered evidence shows the system is committed to fair treatment of the accused and that law enforcement is not allowed to violate citizens' rights.[15] On the other hand, the exclusionary rule also damages the integrity of the justice system by making justice appear a game where the goal is not to find the truth by determining guilt or innocence but rather to ignore the search for truth in favor of technical rule following.

INTERESTS OPPOSING THE CURRENT EXCLU-
SIONARY RULE

- *Doing Justice.* The exclusionary rule clearly produces significant failures of justice by allowing even the most serious offenders to escape unpunished. As noted earlier, the exclusionary rule does promote a form of procedural justice, but at the expense of substantive justice no matter how serious the crime. Other countries have discretionary exclusionary rules that try to best serve justice in a given case, while the US rule is typically applied in an inflexible fashion that ignores all justice costs.
- *Deterrence and Preventing Crime.* The exclusionary rule helps perpetuate the belief that the legal system is a game by showing that even caught guilty criminals can evade liability entirely through technicalities such as a police deviation from a search warrant or failure to read Miranda rights. When people see more criminals escaping, the credibility of the law is diminished, and crime is encouraged. Additionally, offenders who walk free because of the exclusionary rule commonly go on to commit more crimes (as Larry Eyler did).
- *Efficiency.* Motions to suppress illegally gathered evidence consume a great deal of time and resources, as they are part of the standard defense program, and prosecutors and judges must deal with every such claim for exclusion. For obviously guilty offenders, suppression claims are essentially the entire game for criminal defense (as in the case of William Ellis). One can roughly estimate that more than two million suppression claims must be resolved by courts every year.[16] Even when motions to suppress fail, they cost time and money and delay justice.

No deterring penalty is attached to a defendant filing a meritless motion to suppress, so the system is swamped with baseless motions. Any reform reducing the number of motions to suppress would increase efficiency in the legal system.[17]
- *Punishing the Violation of Constitutional Rights.* The exclusionary rule does not actually punish the violation of constitutional rights, as individual officers who violate those constitutional rights go unpunished. The exclusion of evidence merely punishes society in general by releasing blameworthy offenders without punishment. Furthermore, the rule provides no form of relief to innocent suspects who are never charged with a crime and were never in danger of conviction. The vast majority of violations of constitutional rights (which occur in cases that do not lead to prosecution) are thus not addressed or ameliorated by the exclusionary rule (which only works against conviction), so society's interest in actually vindicating constitutional rights is largely ignored by the rule.

The Nature and Extent of the Problem

The American exclusionary rule as a mechanism for controlling investigators is unique in both its inflexibility and the extent of its damaging societal costs. Both the uniqueness of the rule and its costs are examined here.

THE UNIQUELY MANDATORY NATURE OF THE US RULE
The American exclusionary rule is an international anomaly. While there are some countries, typically European, that have adopted a discretionary exclusionary rule for application in extreme cases of rights violations, none have a rule so broad and inflexible in its application and so devastating in its crime

and reputational costs as the American rule. The United States is the only common law system that mandates applying the rule whenever an individual's constitutional rights have been violated.[18] Other countries, including Canada,[19] the United Kingdom,[20] Australia,[21] Israel,[22] and New Zealand, all permit judicial discretion in the application of the exclusionary rule on a case-by-case basis, wherein considerations of justice play a role in the deliberation. Unlike for many other US rules, there is no discretionary balancing of competing societal interests in the exclusionary rule. This uniquely mandatory nature creates many serious failures of justice that would be avoided in other countries, which, for example, take the seriousness of the crime into account when deciding whether to exclude evidence.[23]

ANOTHER UNUSUAL PART OF THE US EXCLUSIONARY RULE: "FRUIT OF THE POISONOUS TREE" In addition to being mandatory and inflexible, the US exclusionary rule is also unusual in that it extends its reach beyond the evidence obtained improperly. While many other countries sometimes exclude illegally collected evidence, the US rule also excludes evidence properly obtained, as under a judicial warrant, but that is in some way connected with evidence that was improperly obtained previously, as "fruits of the poisonous tree."[24] For example, if a suspected murderer confesses without being read his Miranda rights and tells the police where he has hidden the body, not only is his confession suppressed but also the body, which may have forensic evidence inculpating the defendant. Other countries, like the United Kingdom, reject this doctrine and allow the introduction of such derivative evidence.[25] Even Israel, which is one of the few countries to employ a

version of the "fruits of the poisonous tree" doctrine, applies its exclusionary rule on a discretionary basis and takes into account both the reliability of the evidence in question and the effect the exclusion will have on the credibility of the criminal justice system as a whole.[26] Under this approach, such derivative evidence can be treated differently from primary evidence depending on the case, while the wooden US rule stands entirely indifferent to the gross justice failures it produces. Similarly, Germany allows for "tainted" evidence to be admissible in court depending on the circumstances of the case and the type of crime; and the farther evidence is from the initial violation, the more likely it is to be admitted.[27] Consider an example of how the United Kingdom's refusal to employ the "fruits of the poisonous tree" doctrine ensures justice in cases where it might fail in the United States.

CASE EXAMPLE: ISMAIL ABDURAHMAN In 2008, a terrorist group is placing multiple explosive devices around London.[28] As the police search for the bombers, they come across Ismail Abdurahman and ask him to come in to provide information as a witness. However, during the questioning, his statements begin incriminating him as an accomplice.[29] The statements in themselves are insufficient to establish criminal liability, but they spark further investigation that prompts a second interrogation in which Abdurahman, after being warned of his rights, gives incriminating statements. Those statements from his second interrogation are introduced at trial, and he is convicted and sentenced to ten years in prison. He appeals, claiming his statements given in the second interview should have been excluded from evidence because that second interrogation occurred in part because of his statements during the first interview, where he was not properly warned. His reasoning is analogous to that of the American doctrine of "fruits of the poisonous tree." However, UK courts reject the American doctrine and allow Abdurahman's conviction to stand.

EVEN STRICTER EXCLUSIONARY RULES AMONG US STATES Despite the Supreme Court having applied the federal exclusionary rule to all state cases, some states have gone even further to employ stricter exclusionary rules than the Supreme Court requires. The majority of state courts have adopted the Supreme Court's "good faith" exception to their state exclusionary rule (discussed in the reforms section shortly), which allows for the admission of evidence that was obtained in violation of the Fourth Amendment if police officers were searching in "good-faith reliant on a search warrant that later proves to be defective."[30] However, fourteen state supreme courts, including those of New York and Pennsylvania, have rejected this exception, thus making the already inflexible exclusionary rule harsher and even more likely to produce serious failures of justice.[31] Such extreme exclusionary rules are perplexing. They cannot serve to deter illegal police searches because, if police act on a faulty warrant, it is the issuing judge's fault and not the officers'. Exclusion in such cases commonly amounts to some judges second-guessing other judges on the meaning of probable cause, while clearly guilty criminals escape justice. Recall the case of Trido Rogers, mentioned in chapter 1,[32] where a murderer escaped because one judge disagreed with a previous judge's decision to issue a warrant.

FREQUENCY OF THE EXCLUSIONARY RULE'S APPLICATION IN SUPPRESSING EVIDENCE AT TRIAL Defendants often try to use the ex-

clusionary rule to suppress incriminating evidence even if no constitutional violation was committed—a guilty defendant facing clear evidence of guilt has few other options than to make a false claim for suppression. For example, defendants sometimes claim a consensual search was actually not consented to, forcing courts to weigh the defendant's claim against investigators' claims. The tactic commonly fails, but there is little reason for defendants not to make such claims.[33] Research studies have come to different conclusions about the percentage of cases in which suppression motions are filed, but it likely ranges from 4 to 10 percent of all felony cases.[34] As noted previously, with twenty-one million cases a year, a 10 percent rate would mean something like two million suppression claims being resolved by courts every year (assuming motions to suppress are filed at a similar rate in criminal misdemeanor cases).[35] Even a 4 percent rate would mean something just short of a million claims a year.

Studies have found that when filed, motions to suppress are granted on average around 25 to 27 percent of the time.[36] However, the rate at which these motions are granted differs significantly depending on the jurisdiction. One study, which reviewed nine counties in Illinois, Michigan, and Pennsylvania, found that an average of 16.9 percent of all motions to exclude physical evidence were granted, whereas in Chicago nearly 64 percent of motions to suppress physical evidence were granted.[37] Similarly, whereas an average of 2.5 percent of motions to suppress confessions were granted throughout the nine counties, nearly 6 percent of such motions were granted in Chicago.[38]

When prosecutors decide to continue with a case despite a successful suppression motion, the lack of sufficient evidence can make an acquittal almost inevitable. One study found that only 2.1 percent cases were successfully prosecuted after a suppression motion was granted.[39] In contrast, where the motion to suppress physical evidence was unsuccessful, the conviction rate was 74.9 percent.

FREQUENCY OF THE RULE'S APPLICATION IN PRODUCING DROPPED PROSECUTIONS AND LOST CONVICTIONS The exclusionary rule also commonly produces failures of justice by preventing cases from ever making it to court; prosecutors will simply refuse to invest in the prosecution of a case if there is a likelihood that the exclusionary rule will prevent the presentation of the full evidence necessary for a jury to convict beyond a reasonable doubt.[40] Nationally, one study revealed that almost 5 percent of felony arrests are rejected for prosecution due to worries over the suppression of evidence, though this number has been contested by other researchers who argue the correct figure is closer to 1 percent.[41] In California, an NIJ study found 4.8 percent of felony cases which were rejected for prosecution were rejected solely because of the exclusionary rule.[42] A 1983 study found that up to 2.35 percent of all felony arrests were lost due to the exclusionary rule at all stages of the process (including cases dismissed by prosecutors or lost in court).[43]

Additionally, when a trial judge rules against a suppression motion, it often provides fruitful grounds for appeal, consuming valuable appellate time and resources and sometimes leading to overturned convictions. A study of state courts in 2010 found that in cases where the exclusionary rule was used as grounds for appeal, 8 percent of the convictions were reversed.[44]

Some researchers have claimed that the low percentage of cases lost due to the exclusionary rule means that the rule "exact[s] only marginal social costs."[45] But this focus on percentages misses the true magnitude of the costs.[46] The figure of 5 percent of arrests dropped because of the exclusionary rule would mean almost 25,000 arrests for violent crimes dropped by prosecutors every year.[47] Even adopting a more conservative estimate, one academic estimated that at least "10,000 felons and 55,000 misdemeanants evade punishment" each year due to granted motions to suppress evidence under the exclusionary rule.[48] These figures hardly suggest the exclusionary rule has a "marginal social cost." Rather, the rule constitutes a significant justice-frustrating mechanism, which also produces a series of entirely preventable future crimes.

An even larger justice-frustrating cost of the exclusionary rule is probably its effect on plea bargaining. Whenever a suppression claim is made, even when only as a threat by defense counsel rather than an official court filing, prosecutors must take this threat into account in calculating what plea agreement they should offer or accept. Just the possibility of an exclusion claim introduces an uncertainty into the calculations that will buy guilty defendants a better deal—a deal further from the level of criminal liability and punishment that they actually deserve for their offense.

Overall, the exclusionary rule stacks the deck in favor of guilty offenders at every point in the justice system. The rule has a significant effect on the conviction of serious offenders, either by leading to acquittal at trial, by preventing prosecution altogether, or by generating grossly lenient plea agreements. Given the high volume of defendants in the criminal justice system, the exclusionary rule leads to a high absolute toll of justice failures and preventable future crimes. Furthermore, even when suppression motions are not granted, the fact that up to two million are filed each year in U.S. courts leads to an enormous expenditure of time and resources.[49] Even if most frivolous motions are quickly dismissed, prosecutors still end up battling "tens of thousands of contested suppression motions each year."[50] This expenditure of limited criminal justice resources on often obviously guilty offenders prevents those resources from being used to secure justice elsewhere.[51]

EFFECTS OF THE EXCLUSIONARY RULE: MORE CRIME Unsurprisingly, the exclusionary rule increases crime both by letting criminals walk free and by encouraging potential criminals to think they can get away with it. Studies show that crime has risen as a result of the exclusionary rule.[52] Quantifying the increase in crime requires care, however, because the significant crime rate increases in the years following *Mapp v. Ohio* in 1961 were due to a combination of factors. This task is made somewhat easier by the fact that while some states did not have an exclusionary rule before *Mapp*, for some states the decision simply confirmed their existing state exclusionary rule. One study using this fact to isolate the effects of the Supreme Court's ruling found that robberies increased by 7.7 percent nation-wide and assault increased by 18 percent nation-wide.[53] Additionally, the study found that the exclusionary rule had a far greater impact in suburban areas of the country, where property crimes increased by 20 percent and violent crimes increased by 27 percent (perhaps the typical suburban offender was more likely to be aware of

the legal change and take advantage of it).[54] These crime rate increases suggest a horrific effect even if the exact numbers are off. Such increases have resulted in tens or even hundreds of thousands of preventable serious crimes each year since the Supreme Court's decision in *Mapp*. The effects of the rule measured in absolute terms are staggering. For example, if 10 percent of violent crime is due to exclusion-related decreases in deterrence, investigation effectiveness, and prosecution success, that would translate to an additional unnecessary two hundred thousand violent victimizations a year.[55] If removing the exclusionary rule reduced violent victimizations by even a seemingly trivial 1 percent, this would translate into twenty thousand cases a year where individuals were spared the cost of serious crime. The exclusionary rule undoubtedly made it easier for serious offenders to escape justice, with resulting effects on deterrence and crime rates. The sad truth is that the exclusionary rule is likely responsible for *at least* hundreds of thousands of additional serious violent crimes and justice failures since the Supreme Court imposed it nation-wide in 1961. The true number could be in the millions. That cost is not, as some put it, "only marginal" but rather appalling in human terms.

EFFECTS OF THE EXCLUSIONARY RULE: DETERRING POLICE MISCONDUCT? The Supreme Court's justification for the exclusionary rule explicitly rests on the assumption that it will deter police misconduct. However, there is little to no evidence of the rule having such an effect. Where a rule violation occurs due to mistake or accident by the police officer, the deterrence justification will have limited application: the officer has not made a conscious decision to violate the governing rule. And, of course, the increasing complexity of judicial search rules makes mistakes likelier. Even in the context of conscious violations, the exclusionary rule only prevents use of the evidence in court, but there are numerous other reasons why police might be motivated to improperly seize possessions, especially in cases of guns or illegal drugs. Even if police cannot convict a drug dealer or armed criminal, simply removing drugs or weapons from the street may be enough incentive for officers to engage in illegal searches and seizures. Additionally, as noted previously, individual officers may have little stake in whether the evidence they seize is excluded months or years later in one of the many cases they investigate. The risk of exclusion is thus likely to have at best a limited effect on police conduct far outweighed by more immediate concerns.

Empirical support for the rule's lack of deterrent effect has existed for some time.[56] The most widely respected study on the effects of the exclusionary rule on police behavior, a 1970 study by Dallin Oaks, found that there was no significant deterrent effect created by the rule.[57] The Oaks study has been cited by Supreme Court Justices multiple times to support broadening exceptions to the rule by pointing out how little exclusion of evidence gathered in "good faith" does to deter misconduct.[58]

If it is true that the rule does little to deter police misconduct, the exclusionary rule's justification according to Supreme Court precedent would seem to collapse.[59] In fact, the Supreme Court has all but conceded that the exclusionary rule is ineffective at deterring police misconduct, thus setting up an inevitable challenge to the rule's legitimacy.[60] Perhaps because of the scanty empirical

basis for the exclusionary rule's deterrent effectiveness, some state courts have sought to base the exclusionary rule on a different foundation by justifying its existence as a personal right in order to uphold one's constitutional liberties. The Supreme Court, however, has never accepted the existence of such a right to suppress reliable evidence of criminality.

For the reasons reviewed here, some scholars now believe the exclusionary rule is likely to be further eroded or abolished by the Supreme Court in coming years.[61] In fact, Chief Justice Roberts and at least four other justices have signaled a willingness to end the rule entirely, making the replacement of the exclusionary seem only a matter of time.[62]

Public Complaints About the Exclusionary Rule

The exclusionary rule's justice-frustrating effect has not gone unnoticed. At the time of its nation-wide implementation after *Mapp v. Ohio*, the rule was seen unfavorably by the public—who care a good deal about justice being done[63]—as yet another soft on crime decision by a Court completely indifferent to the community's concerns for justice and safety.[64] While the anger against the rule has faded over time, it remains a point of discontent. A majority of the public believes that trials should seek to expose the truth, while many lawyers and defense activists feel entirely comfortable with the justice-frustrating effects of the rule.[65]

Public sentiment against the rule led President Ronald Reagan to suggest that Congress ease the rule.[66] In 1981, Reagan criticized the rule as relying upon the "absurd proposition that a law enforcement error, no matter how technical, can be used to justify throwing out an entire case."[67] Reagan spent years urging

Congress to try to limit the reach of the rule, and perhaps his calls were ultimately heard by the Supreme Court itself.[68] In the 1984 case of *United States v. Leon*, the Supreme Court created a "good faith" exception to the exclusionary rule (an exception discussed in more depth in the "Reforms" section). The Court had been considering such an exception for years. President Richard Nixon had responded to public hatred of the rule by nominating two anti-exclusionary rule justices in 1971 in order to lay the groundwork for relaxing it.[69] Once the Court created the good faith exception, which was "the most sweeping limitation of the exclusionary rule since the Court first required its use in the Federal courts in 1914,"[70] Reagan and most of the public were pleased, while some "civil rights lawyers bitterly denounced the ruling."[71] The prominence of the rule has since faded from public debate despite the good faith exception only partly mitigating the rule's damaging effects.

The lack of high-quality recent public opinion research on the issue makes it difficult to estimate the current state of public concern, but there is no reason to think it has become more favorable to letting criminals escape justice. What research has shown is that examples of criminals walking free without deserved punishment due to technicalities simply degrade the public's trust in the legal system.[72]

As would be expected, police opinion has been decidedly negative about the exclusionary rule's results. When Chicago narcotics officers were surveyed about the effects of implementing the exclusionary rule, 50 percent believed it did a "moderate amount" of harm to police investigations and 17 percent believed it did a "great deal" of harm.[73] Police resistance to the exclusionary rule takes many forms, including willful perjury about how evidence was collected, known as "testilying," which some police see as morally justifiable given what they see as the immorality of a rule that allows dangerous guilty offenders to revictimize their communities.[74]

Who Should Decide the Balance of Interests in Creating Rules to Govern Investigative Conduct?

The question of who should decide whether the exclusionary rule is the best mechanism for gaining compliance with investigative rules (and if not, what system should replace it) overlaps significantly with the discussion in chapter 6 about the proper decision maker for rules limiting police investigation. The discussion in chapter 6 presented several arguments in favor of returning power now exercised by the judiciary to legislatures. Elected legislators better represent community views than judges on the proper balance of competing interests (as judges are appointed at the federal level for life, and either appointed or elected, often for long terms, at the state level). Legislatures are also able to account for changing circumstances over the years rather than being frozen into a fixed rule by the judicial doctrine of stare decisis. And legislatures can reflect the different balance of interest conclusions of different communities as compared to the federal judiciary that must adopt a single rule for the entire country.[75]

However persuasive one might have found these arguments in chapter 6, there is reason to think they are even more compelling with respect to the exclusionary rule, which actively frees even serious offenders (who are likely to harm the community again). Because the stakes are higher for the community, one might think that the community's role in deciding how to balance the competing interests should be greater. If some form of the exclusionary rule is to be kept, the same consideration weighs in favor of empowering states, rather than the federal government, to determine how the rule should operate. (Remember, the issue here is not in setting the rules for what is proper police investigation but rather determining the *consequences* when those rules are not followed.)

Some people may fear that letting legislatures decide the future of the exclusionary rule would lead to law enforcement overreaches going unpunished and undeterred. But history, especially recent history, suggests that this concern is unfounded. We commonly see the election of legislators and prosecutors who campaign on restricting police and protecting defendants, suggesting that many communities place a high value on preserving or expanding limitations on police. Each community ought to be free in how they strike the balance of interests—and therefore take responsibility for the consequences that follow from their choices. Even before the recent rise of progressive prosecutors, prominent scholars were pushing back against the "conventional wisdom . . . that elected legislators would never adequately protect the interests of criminal suspects and defendants."[76]

Judicially created doctrines like the exclusionary rule restrict communities' ability to balance the competing interests of deterring improper police conduct and promoting justice. The community is also stripped of the opportunity to experiment with different policies based on the evolving empirical evidence that emerges.[77]

None of this is to say that empowering legislators over courts is not without

downsides, but as long as the exclusionary rule is mandated by the Supreme Court, these debates are likely to remain confined to lecture halls and law review articles rather than being profitably tested in the public sphere.

Reforms

The only implemented reforms to the exclusionary rule have been judicially created exceptions, but broader reforms have also been proposed that might better uphold justice while still deterring police violations.

Judicially Created Exceptions. Since the original introduction of the exclusionary rule, various exceptions and clarifications to the rule have been added by the Supreme Court. First, the exclusionary rule only applies to members of law enforcement. Under the "the private search doctrine," evidence that is obtained improperly by private citizens is not subject to the exclusionary rule and is admissible in court. This logically follows from the justification of the rule as a mechanism for controlling police.

Second, *Nix v. Williams* (1984) established the "inevitable discovery doctrine" that allows improperly obtained evidence by investigators to be admitted if the evidence would have inevitably been found legally by law enforcement. Similarly, if police obtain through legal means the same evidence that was previously obtained illegally, that evidence is admissible. The latter case is known as the "independent source" doctrine when multiple methods discover the same evidence.

Third, as noted previously, the "good faith" exception established in *United States v. Leon* (1984) allows for improperly obtained evidence to be permitted in court if officers conducted the search in good faith, relying on a search warrant that was later deemed defective. In other words, if the judge granting the search warrant is responsible for the search being improper, the seized evidence may be admissible in court. (The good faith exception does not cover police mistakes during warrantless searches that may have been made in "good faith.") Again, the holding logically follows from the purpose of the rule as a mechanism to deter police overreach, which the Supreme Court reaffirmed in *Leon*. However, fourteen states do not accept the good faith exception on the basis that their state constitutions offer greater protection than the federal constitution.[78]

Fourth, and somewhat similar to the good faith exception, is the "knock-and-announce exception," created in the 2006 case of *Hudson v. Michigan*, which declares that evidence obtained by police in violation of the requirement that police knock and announce themselves before entering a home is admissible.[79] Another good faith–type exception was established in *Arizona v. Evans* (1995), in which the Supreme Court determined that evidence obtained during an unlawful search is still admissible if the search itself was the result of a clerical error by a court employee.[80]

What is noticeable about all these judicial reforms to the exclusionary rule is that they attempt to make the rule more compatible with doing justice by engaging in something of a balancing test in which society's interest in justice is given some weight through discretely carved exceptions to the rule (as opposed to perhaps a more comprehensive discretionary rule).

The following are some reforms to the rule that have been proposed.

Expand Exceptions to the Exclusionary Rule. Some propose expanding the good faith exception to include all evidence except that obtained through clear and willful police misconduct.[81] Thus, police must have intentionally and knowingly violated constitutional rights in order for the exclusionary rule to apply even in cases of warrantless searches. The unpassed congressional Exclusionary Rule Limitation Act of 1995 would have attempted to legislatively expand the court's good faith exception to include illegally obtained evidence if the investigators genuinely believed that their conduct was in accordance with constitutional requirements. Of course, such an expanded good faith exception would essentially limit the application of the rule to a dramatically smaller number of cases, as the proportion of cases where investigators knowingly and willfully break the law is small.[82]

Adopt a Balancing Test for a Discretionary Exclusionary Rule. One reform takes the approach used in many European countries in which a discretionary exclusionary rule is based on a balancing test to uphold the integrity of the justice system. As previously mentioned,[83] many other countries utilize their exclusionary rules with discretion, based on a balancing test weighing such factors as the severity of the crime, the severity of the constitutional violation, and the damage to the criminal justice system's credibility with the community if a clearly blameworthy serious offender is intentionally released without punishment. For example, a deliberate police violation of rights to seize evidence of drug possession would be excluded, whereas a violation that discovers a serial killer might not be. In 1999, a group of legal scholars laid out a proposed eleven-part balancing test, but the Supreme Court has not moved to adopt it.[84] Balancing tests of one sort or another have sometimes played a role in decisions by state courts to address questions of potentially illegal searches and seizures. For example, in *People v. Scott*, the California Supreme Court dealt with the issue of whether a court-ordered body intrusion to collect seminal fluid violated the Fourth Amendment. The court based its decision on a balancing test including the reliability of the evidence and the seriousness of the crime.[85]

Provide Regular Police Training and Testing on Constitutionality Requirements. One way to reduce the number of cases lost due to the exclusionary rule without directly altering it is to more effectively train police in constitutional law. Police could be required to undergo regular refresher training and pass tests on what constitutes a lawful search or seizure. While police already receive some training in this regard, the proposal would see testing and training as a routine part of keeping a police badge, similar to how doctors must regularly take exams and training to maintain certification. However, given the complexity of search and seizure rules, it seems unlikely that even a yearly examination could prevent officers from making mistakes when even courts quarrel as to what is permitted in the realm of Fourth Amendment law, especially considering that officers commonly must make such decisions under the pressure of time and the ambiguity and complexity of real-world situations.

Provide Monetary Compensation for Constitutional Violations. One possible reform is to replace the exclusionary rule with monetary compensation for all victims of unreasonable searches and seizures, as is the standard form for compensating people for other violations of their civil rights. Such compensation could either be determined judicially (a tort remedy) or by a community oversight or internal police board (an administrative remedy). Such money would be paid by the municipality, and thus would create an incentive for the municipality to do whatever is necessary to educate and control the conduct of its officers. It would be useful to pair this reform with some form of administrative penalty of officers for violations in order to create a deterrent effect, as in the recommendation below.

Recommendation: Replace the Exclusionary Rule with Direct Sanctioning of Officers for Their Violations

Giving criminals the opportunity to escape punishment through means wholly unrelated to their blameworthiness is a failure of justice, even if the offender's rights were violated in the investigation process. Unless the evidence was obtained in a way that makes it unreliable (such as a coerced confession), evidence that has probative value ought to be allowed in criminal adjudication. At the same time, however, society obviously needs some mechanism for ensuring that police abide by constitutional limitations in the exercise of their investigative powers. But as noted earlier, the exclusionary rule has generally failed in this task because individual police officers know little of the law's complexity and have little at stake in whether evidence is excluded. Additionally, the exclusionary rule offers no vindication of the constitutional rights of innocent people who were never in danger of conviction on any crime.

By contrast, a system of directly sanctioning officers for their violations is likely to have a greater effect in controlling their conduct in all cases, even if the sanctions are relatively minor. Our proposal would see the exclusionary rule replaced with a system where officers who violate constitutional rules are subject to departmental disciplinary action. Sanctions would range in severity depending on the nature and intentions of the violation with minor or good faith violations being addressed with warnings, training, or conduct marks. In especially severe, intentional, and repeated violations, individual officers could be demoted, dismissed, or even referred for criminal prosecution. A system of "sentencing guidelines" for such administrative sanctions could be drawn up to ensure uniformity and proportionality. While police unions would likely oppose such a system, the sanctions would not be particularly harsh in the vast majority of cases. (Even the slightest form of punishment is likely to better deter violations than the exclusionary rule does today.) Police unions might be more willing to accept such a system once they realize it could both improve justice and a perception of police accountability among the public. Reliable and probative evidence discovered by such officers would still be admitted at trial. The fact that the officer has erred does not alter the blameworthiness of the offender.

One concern in adopting this approach is that it could provide too much deterrent effect. Given the direct and personal impact of a violation, an officer might simply refuse to undertake the searches needed for a successful investigation. (And police unions might encourage and support such refusals.) On the other hand, an officer interested in an investigative career also has an incentive to do what is required for the investigation, even though they may be inclined to avoid borderline or ambiguous conduct. While the introduction of the new system might initially be challenging, it seems likely that one could find a point of equilibrium where the seriousness of the sanctions and the fairness of the adjudication procedures could be adjusted so as to allow effective investigation.

There will naturally be concerns about whether officers would be sufficiently punished by an internal disciplinary system, and to alleviate these concerns, the investigation of complaints and administration of sanctions by the department should be overseen by a Police-Community Oversight Commission, proposed and explained in detail in chapters 14 and 15, which would include police, community members, and legal experts.[86] This commission could publish an annual report on the number of violations and sanctions taken to show the extent to which civil liberties are upheld. A similar system of oversight by civilian review boards already exists for many forms of police misconduct.[87]

In addition to implementing a system of sanctions against offending officers, states could enact civil damage remedies to compensate the victims of violations of constitutional rights.[88] Citizens already have the legal right to sue over such violations, but it would be useful to make suits against police officer violations easier to bring. Such litigation is not likely to directly contribute to the deterrence of police overreach because the qualified immunity that police officers currently hold means that it would be the municipality rather than the individual officer who would be paying the compensation. With a system of easy access to compensation for constitutional infringement (for both criminals and non-criminals), municipalities would have a clear financial incentive to improve their officer oversight. In this context, it is important to stress that this recommended reform does not entail eliminating the qualified immunity police enjoy today. Eliminating qualified immunity is simply unrealistic and probably unwise: as chapter 15 discusses, municipalities already have a critical problem in hiring and retaining officers.

A system that replaces the exclusionary rule with sanctions on officers and compensation for those whose rights were infringed would avoid the failures of justice that so offend the community and damage the criminal justice system's reputation—as with the release of serial torturer-murderers like Larry Eyler—yet would provide a mechanism much more likely to deter intentional violations by officers.

Replacing the exclusionary rule with a system of officer sanctions and victim compensation would require approval from the Supreme Court as well as from some state supreme courts. However, given that the exclusionary rule was explicitly adopted by the Court as a mechanism for deterring police overreach, and given that the proposed system here would do a better job at this, with dramatically less social cost from justice failures, the proposal might actually be welcomed by the Court as a more effective means of protecting constitutional rights with less societal damage. The proposal presents an alternative solution that was not and is not within the Court's judicial power to create but might well be one they would logically prefer. As noted previously, some scholars already see the Supreme Court as treading an inevitable path to reconsidering the exclusionary rule given the building consensus that it

does not effectively deter police misconduct.[89] Legislatures adopting this proposal might be just the opportunity the Court needs to make that move.

B. EXCLUDING RELIABLE PROBATIVE EVIDENCE TO AVOID "PREJUDICE"

While the exclusionary rule is a judicial doctrine of constitutional criminal procedure, a number of evidentiary rules—on which Congress has the final say at the federal level[90]—also function to exclude reliable and probative evidence from being seen by juries. The most prominent of these rules is Federal Rule of Evidence 403 (hereafter FRE 403 or the Rule),[91] which allows courts to "exclude relevant evidence if its probative value is substantially outweighed by a danger of one or more of the following: unfair prejudice, confusing the issues, misleading the jury, undue delay, wasting time, or needlessly presenting cumulative evidence."[92]

FRE 403 gives judges broad discretion to suppress evidence in a wide variety of contexts. Its most frequent application is excluding evidence to avoid unfair "prejudice" to the defendant. For example, an appellate court reversed a conviction because the trial court judge admitted photographs of a three-year-old murder victim before he was attacked, displayed next to photographs of his body during and after an autopsy.[93] The court found that, while both the preattack photos and the autopsy photos of the child victim may have each carried probative value, displaying them side by side created improper "prejudice" that could arouse the jury's ire against the defendant.

With just a handful of limited exceptions, the balancing test put forward in FRE 403 applies to all evidence, regardless of whether admission of the evidence is also affected by another more specific rule of evidence.[94] The language of FRE 403 is intended to err on the side of allowing otherwise admissible evidence in, as it requires that the evidence's probative value be "substantially outweighed" by a danger of unfair prejudice.[95] However, in practice, trial judges retain enormous discretion, and a decision to suppress is only subject to an "abuse of discretion" standard of appellate review, which is arguably a "virtual shield from reversal,"[96] thus allowing individual judges to prevent juries from hearing probative evidence that even Congress did not intend for FRE 403 to exclude.

The significant discretion of trial judges here is all the more problematic because only one side is subject to review: if the defendant is wrongfully acquitted because the evidence is excluded, there can be no appellate review of the trial court's decision.[97] In other words, when exercising their discretion in whether to exclude evidence, trial judges know they will only be subject to reversal if they *fail* to exclude. As a result, many trial judges err on the side of excluding probative evidence.

FRE 403 was enacted by Congress in 1975, but a related rule existed previously in the common law.[98] Although FRE 403 applies only in federal cases, all fifty states have "identical or nearly identical counterpart[s]" to FRE 403 through case law or their statutory codes of evidence.[99] This section focuses specifically on FRE 403, though the issues discussed apply to other rules allowing suppression of probative evidence in order to avoid prejudice.

Consider two examples of how the rule can be applied to cause justice failures in practice.

Case Example: Christopher Westpoint

Christopher Westpoint pleads guilty to third-degree sexual assault against his eight-year-old daughter.[100] The crime carries a maximum sentence of ten years imprisonment, but he gets far less.[101] Four years later, Westpoint is again charged with sexual assault of his daughter who is now twelve. The case goes to trial and the defendant testifies. As a means of undermining his credibility, the state introduces Westpoint's prior conviction. The jury ultimately convicts him of second-degree rape, sexual abuse of a minor, fourth-degree sexual assault, third-degree sexual assault, and second-degree assault.[102] On appeal, Westpoint's conviction is reversed. The appeals court rules that introduction of Westpoint's prior conviction for sexual assault of his daughter four years earlier was prejudicial. It would have been permissible to introduce evidence of the prior assault, the court rules, but the fact that he was actually convicted of the assault must be hidden from the jury.[103]

Case Example: Artez Thigpen

A female member of the Unknown Vicelords (a local street gang) is on a Chicago street corner delivering drugs to a male fellow gang member.[104] A rival faction drives up, beats the man, and steals the drugs. Artez Thigpen, for whom the robbery victims work, soon arrives. Outraged by the theft, he declares war on the thieves' faction. Thigpen and another man do a drive-by shooting of two members of the rival faction, killing one and wounding the other. Multiple witnesses identify Thigpen and recall a partial license plate. The next day, Thigpen and several other men kidnap two teenage members of the rival faction and announce that they are going to "make the news." He later tells the female member of his faction that he has killed the pair and gives her $50 to tell everyone that the police arrested the two teenagers because they were selling drugs.

The woman later identifies Thigpen to police. The man wounded in the earlier drive-by identifies Thigpen in a lineup and with police permission temporarily leaves the city because he is afraid for his life. Other witnesses also identify Thigpen. He is charged with first-degree murder and aggravated battery for the original drive-by shooting.

By the day of the trial, however, one witness has been killed and two others have recanted their testimony for fear of also being killed. Despite the loss of witnesses, the prosecution proceeds and presents the jury with the full picture of Thigpen's war against the rival faction, including his kidnapping and killing of the teenage dealers. The jury convicts Thigpen of murder, aggravated battery, and other offenses and he is sentenced to seventy-five years in prison.

Thigpen appeals. One of his complaints is that the trial judge allowed too much information to be introduced about the kidnapping and murder of the teen dealers.[105] While the appeals court agrees with the prosecution that the testimony about the murdered teens is relevant to demonstrate the "overarching scheme to eliminate competition,"[106] it also finds that the jury heard too much information about the teens. And as the crime being tried was a drive-by shooting and the teens incident was a kidnapping (and later murder), the crimes are not sufficiently similar, in the view of the court, to justify allowing the jury to hear this much information about the latter.[107] The appellate court reverses Thigpen's conviction.

Competing Interests

There are valid interests for and against the current formulation of fed-eral and state rules governing the exclusion of reliable and probative evidence on the grounds that it is "prejudicial."

INTERESTS SUPPORTING CURRENT RULES SUPPRESSING PROBATIVE EVIDENCE TO AVOID "PREJUDICE"

- *Reducing Emotional Jury Decisions.* If more "prejudicial" evidence is allowed at trial, it is possible more false convictions would occur due to juries making emotional and irrational decisions on the basis of highly inflammatory evidence (such as gruesome pictures or testimony about past crimes).
- *Judicial Experience and Impartiality.* While the argument could be made that juries should be allowed to see all evidence and be warned against emotional decisions, it is also possible that judges, who have far more experience with criminal cases, are better placed to decide what evidence is needlessly emotionally inflammatory.

INTERESTS OPPOSING CURRENT RULES SUPPRESSING PROBATIVE EVIDENCE TO AVOID "PREJUDICE"

- *Justice.* If more reliable probative evidence is admitted, it would lead to the conviction of more guilty offenders who might otherwise escape due to reliable and probative evidence being suppressed.
- *Respect for Trial by Jury.* The US criminal justice system is meant to uphold the right to trial by jury, but judicial suppression of reliable and probative evidence makes it harder to say a case is truly being decided by a jury, as opposed to the judge, when judges are allowed to hide certain facts from the jury. Such a false by omission picture of reality is not really a trial by jury but rather a trial by what judges allow juries to see.
- *Credibility of the Justice System.* When reliable and probative

evidence against a clearly guilty offenders is suppressed due to fears
of "prejudice," the credibility of the
criminal justice system is undermined because it shows the system
is concerned not with doing justice
but rather with upholding a set of
abusable rules.

The Nature and Extent of the Problem

The problem of inappropriate suppression of reliable probative evidence
upon a claim of "prejudice" arises in part
from a distrust of juries by trial judges
and in part from a lack of deference
among some appellate judges toward
trial judges who decline to suppress such
evidence.

**A PATERNALISTIC AND POTENTIALLY UN-
CONSTITUTIONAL VIEW OF JURIES** Evidentiary rules like FRE 403 are grounded in
a distrust of juries. One can intuitively
understand where this distrust comes
from. Juries are composed of humans,
who possess emotions and are susceptible to a host of cognitive biases.[108] By
preventing jurors from hearing evidence that may stoke these emotions or
biases, it is thought that jurors will be
able to produce verdicts that are more
accurate. However, this requires giving
judges more power, not only with deciding the probative value of specific pieces
of evidence (a job meant for juries by
definition because juries decide the verdict based on the probative nature of the
evidence) but also with evaluating the
likelihood that the jury will not be able
to interpret the evidence appropriately.
Some scholars argue this redistribution
of responsibilities is constitutionally
questionable because it so clearly cuts
against the intent of trial by jury.[109] One
scholar, Kenneth Klein, who noted that
Rule 403 is "unambiguously . . . based on
a distrust of juries,"[110] went so far as to ar-

gue that Rule 403 is actually unconstitutional, summarizing the case as follows:

> FRE 403 permits the exclusion of
> "relevant" evidence, which FRE 401
> defines as evidence making a fact "of
> consequence" "more or less probable."
> If constitutionally [under the Sixth and
> Seventh Amendments] a jury is the ex-
> clusive fact finder on a particular issue,
> and if a piece of evidence makes a fact
> of consequence to that issue more or
> less likely, then it would seem there is
> no way constitutionally to keep that
> evidence from the jury, at least not on
> a justification of more efficient trials
> and, in the judge's view, more accurate
> verdicts. The Supreme Court has held
> that neither efficiency nor accuracy is a
> basis for constricting the right to a trial
> by jury. Yet, that is the effect and goal
> of FRE 403.[111]

Allowing judges to suppress allegedly "prejudicial" evidence is also questionable for non-constitutional reasons.
Judges are humans too, and many of the
fears motivating distrust of juries apply
to judges. Indeed, research has found
that "judges are likely to be vulnerable to
many of the ordinary cognitive and social
biases that pervade human cognition,"
even if they may be able to suppress specific biases in some circumstances. When
it comes to exposure to potentially biasing information, research has found that
the effect on judges is similar to that
on jurors.[112] Findings like this raise the
question of whether rules like FRE 403
are actually grounded in sound theory.
There is no doubt that jurors may be susceptible to misinterpreting or misusing
evidence—but is the proper solution to
give more power to isolated judges who
possess the same emotional and cognitive shortcomings? Moreover, judges
may try to compensate for knowledge

of their own shortcomings by excluding more evidence than is necessary—evidence that could have been appropriately interpreted and used by the jury. A system of trial by jury depends on juries competently weighing cases where emotionally charged evidence exists. It is hard to logically or morally square depriving juries of the complete set of facts on the paternalistic notion that judges know the jurors better than the jurors know themselves.[113]

THE PROBLEM OF APPELLATE REVERSALS OVER EVIDENCE CLAIMED "PREJUDICIAL" When a defendant is convicted after a judge has refused to suppress reliable and probative evidence on the defendant's claim that it would be "prejudicial," the denial provides an easy claim to make on appeal, no matter how frivolous it may be. Unfortunately, it is too often the case that appellate judges apply unreasonable standards and grant reversals in many questionable cases. Because there is no ability for prosecutors to appeal a wrongful acquittal based upon improper exclusion under FRE 403, trial judges have every incentive to exclude the evidence and thereby protect themselves from such questionable reversals. In addition to the previous case examples, consider a few more examples, all of which involve an appellate court reversing a trial court's verdict on the basis of claimed "prejudicial" evidence being admitted and thereby somehow perverting the jury's ability to accurately judge the case:[114]

- *Old Chief v. United States*, 519 US 172 (1997): The court reversed the conviction for being a felon in possession of a firearm because the jury heard the details of the defendant's prior felony conviction—assault causing serious bodily injury.[115]

- *State v. Chapple*, 660 P.2d 1208 (Ariz. 1983): The court reversed a murder conviction because the trial court should have excluded photographs of the victim's skull and burned body.[116]
- *United States v. Bland*, 908 F.2d 471, 473 (9th Cir. 1990): The appellate court concluded that the trial court erred under Rule 403 in admitting evidence that the basis of the defendant's arrest warrant was the torture-murder of a seven-year-old girl because it might suggest that acquittal meant "releasing an exceedingly dangerous child molester and killer."[117]

It reflects a troubling distrust of juries to think that any of the evidence cited in these cases as "prejudicial" somehow prevented the jurors from being able to come to reliable conclusions about the defendant's guilt, especially if they received an instruction from the judge that drew their attention to whatever potentially prejudicial effect one might imagine. If juries were really this fickle and irrational—such as convicting an innocent person simply because jury members saw a gruesome photograph—it would seem to call into question the wisdom of having a jury system at all. In fact, a subtle contempt for juries seems to underlie these judicial reversals and the application of FRE 403 in general.

EFFECTS ON CRIMINAL CONVICTIONS OF SUPPRESSING EVIDENCE FOR "PREJUDICE" Unfortunately, there is no collected data available on the number of criminal cases that are affected by the exclusion of reliable probative evidence claimed to be "prejudicial," but the number is likely significant in absolute terms. Defense attorneys will commonly try to exploit FRE 403 to suppress probative evidence against their clients because it is an easy claim to make and, even if denied, provides an issue for appeal. Consider this list of issues frequently litigated under FRE 403: evidence of a defendant's gang membership; evidence of weapons possessed by the defendant at the time of arrest; evidence of drug usage, possession, or arrest; gruesome photographs; sympathetic photographs of victims; mug shots; and results of prior related cases.[118] Even in a run-of-the-mill jury case, it would be surprising if none of these issues emerge. In some portion of these cases, evidence that would have led the jury to convict is suppressed, allowing guilty offenders to go free. Guilty offenders who have their convictions reversed on appeal may also permanently escape justice if the prosecution decides not to go through with the difficulty of a retrial. Unfortunately, no statistics are kept on the rate at which reversed convictions are retried, but a significant number of these likely end with no retrial at all.[119] Even where a retrial is conducted successfully, the justice system's time and resources are taken away from ensuring justice in other cases, leading to other serious offenders receiving overly lenient plea bargains or having their cases dismissed.

Public Complaints About Excluding Reliable Probative Evidence to Avoid "Prejudice"

Perhaps due to its technical legal nature, FRE 403 and other rules that allow for the suppression of reliable probative evidence have not drawn significant public attention. But FRE 403 was considered "controversial" during Congress's consideration of the rule,[120] and as is evident from the previously mentioned concerns about the rule's constitutionality, the rule continues to draw criticism from some scholars.

As an institution, juries are among the most important in America's cultural and legal history—one scholar has commented that the "jury is a cultural icon as revered in the United States as the flag, its contribution to democracy equated to voting."[121] In light of the public value placed on jury decision making, it is reasonable to think that if better understood by the public, rules allowing judges to hide reliable and probative evidence from juries would be likely to attract significant public opposition.

Another glimpse of the public view of the rule may be seen in the nearly three million California voters who passed the Truth-In-Evidence Act in 1982, which was meant to prevent evidence from being kept from juries.[122] While the act's passage clearly reflected public frustration with the fact that relevant evidence was being hidden from jurors, the act did not alter the ability for judges to suppress evidence upon claims of "prejudice."[123]

Reforms

Several reforms have been proposed for FRE 403 and its state equivalents.

Repeal Rule 403's Suppression of Evidence in Favor of Enhanced Jury Instructions. The most sweeping proposed reform, notably championed by the philosopher Larry Laudan, calls for admitting all relevant probative evidence regardless of claims of potential "prejudice" but "accompanied . . . by an explicit reminder from judge to jury to bring their critical faculties to bear in evaluating the . . . evidence . . . and in keeping their emotional reactions . . . firmly in check."[124] This reform would still allow trial judges to apply a version of FRE 403 in deciding what evidence might be unfairly prejudicial, but it would make the remedy a more strongly worded warning to the jury about the dangers of prejudice instead of outright suppressing the evidence. This would allow judges to still exercise their judgment and discretion in choosing when and how to warn the jury against potential prejudice caused by particular pieces of evidence, but it would not undermine juries as finders of fact.

Allow Appellate Review in Cases of Jury Acquittals Based Upon the Suppression of Reliable Probative Evidence upon a Claim of "Prejudice." The practical problems created by FRE 403 may be less a matter of an improper rule than the fact that there is no remedy for judicial abuse of the rule leading to a jury acquittal. When improper suppression leads to a jury acquittal, as noted previously, the decision by the trial judge to suppress the evidence as "prejudicial" can never be reviewed, thus creating every incentive for trial judges to allow suppression and thereby reduce the chance of reversal. Issues of perverse incentives aside, presumably one would want to avoid wrongful acquittals derived from improper suppression, so appellate review of such decisions seems desirable. At very least, such an appellate review possibility would make defense counsel somewhat more reasonable in requesting such suppression.

All major European countries, such as the United Kingdom, Germany, France, and Italy,[125] allow appellate review of wrongful acquittals based upon judicial error. But, of course, to the extent that appellate review of jury acquittals is unconstitutional in the United States (recall chapter 2's discussion of how the double jeopardy clause is currently interpreted to ban appealing acquittals), this reform option is off the table. The best remaining alternative may be the following.

Recommendation: Require Additional Findings for Appellate Reversals Based Upon Claims of "Prejudicial" Evidence

When applied appropriately and consistently, FRE 403 and its state equivalents should lead to relatively few failures of justice because the types of evidence that would be properly excluded under the rule would carry low probative value. If a piece of evidence's probative value is so high as to be necessary for conviction, for example, one would hope that no trial judge would suppress it under FRE 403. However, justice failures under the rule still arise because trial judges abuse their discretion under the rule and suppress evidence despite its probative importance.

As discussed previously, nothing can be done to address this abuse when it results in a wrongful acquittal. However, at the very least the current system can be improved by reducing the cases in which appellate judges create failures of justice by applying inappropriate standards in judging claims of prejudice. Currently, the standard of review is an "abuse of discretion" standard that one would hope would require considerable deference to the trial judge who admitted the evidence now claimed to be prejudicial. But as the sample cases illustrate, some appellate courts are nonetheless happy to substitute their judgment for that of the trial court and to reverse the case because the evidence was not suppressed.

One method of mitigating the problem would be to require specific findings by an appellate court before reversing for a refusal to suppress such evidence. For example, one could provide that a failure to suppress such evidence can be the basis for appellate reversal only if the appellate court finds that suppression of the evidence would have in fact produced some significant possibility of an acquittal. Further, the appellate court might be required to find that any cautionary instruction given by the trial court would have been clearly inadequate to avoid irrational and emotional decision making by an ordinary juror. Such measures would likely reduce the chance of appellate judges reversing a case for a failure to suppress simply because they disagreed with the trial judge's decision and are unwilling to give the trial judge the deference called for under the "abuse of discretion" standard.

It seems clear that this modified standard of appellate review would have prevented the justice failures in the cases of Thigpen and Westpoint mentioned earlier. In the case of Thigpen, there was sufficient evidence for a jury to convict him of his drive-by shooting even if they never heard of his additional murders. Similarly, there was more than enough evidence for any reasonable person to convict Westpoint of sexual assault even

if they had never heard of his prior history of offending. Neither clearly guilty offender should have avoided liability simply because the appellate court disagreed with the trial judge on questions of the potentially prejudicial effect of evidence that was unnecessary to support the conviction.

While this kind of reform would not directly address the largely invisible justice failures caused by trial judges who improperly exclude reliable probative evidence, it would likely make trial judges more willing to allow certain probative evidence because such decisions would be less likely to be reversed on appeal under the new standard. At the very least, the reform would help reduce the justice failures created by improper appellate reversals that are then never retried. The reform would also be more likely to gain legislative support than more ambitious reforms because it does not require a radical revision of the rules of criminal evidence.

CHAPTER 9

Pretrial Procedures

AS PREVIOUS CHAPTERS DEMONSTRATED, violent offenders often get away with their crimes without being caught by police, thereby avoiding a trial altogether. However, even when offenders are caught, various pretrial procedures regularly produce failures of justice. Pretrial release lets defendants leave jail prior to their trial date, traditionally through posting bail. Pretrial release has expanded in recent years, largely due to progressive criminal justice policies that promote release without cash bail. However, when an offender's risk of flight is ignored and incentives to appear at trial are reduced, failure to appear rates usually increase, producing a stream of justice failures as offenders simply skip trial. Pretrial release is an important mechanism to ensure liberty for innocent defendants or those defendants who will follow the law and appear at trial, but poorly designed pretrial release policies often focus on maximizing the number of defendants released without regard to justice or safety.

In addition to increasing failure to appear rates, pretrial release also increases crime as released defendants go on to commit more crimes, often triggering the same catch-and-release cycle all over again. Sometimes the only punishment such offenders receive is the minor inconvenience of a trip to the police station, a fact that significantly decreases the deterrent effect of the law. As a result, poorly designed pretrial release policies can allow crime and justice failures to pile up in a vicious cycle, with increased crime exacerbating justice failures by stretching investigative resources even thinner, thus decreasing clearance rates. The increasing lawlessness produced by such policies also undermines the moral credibility of the law as community members see the same offenders freed and reoffending without any punishment.

Another pretrial procedure that produces failures of justice is the speedy trial rule. Defendants are constitutionally guaranteed a speedy trial, and if they are kept waiting beyond the time limit as defined in speedy trial statutes, their cases may be dismissed. While speedy trial laws are necessary to uphold a defendant's right to due process and prevent indefinite confinement, rigid application of fixed time limits without regard to case circumstances can free dangerous offenders. The first part of this chapter examines pretrial release while the second half discusses speedy trial laws.

A. PRETRIAL RELEASE

Across the United States, defendants can remain out of jail while awaiting trial so long as they meet pretrial release conditions. These conditions generally take one of three forms: monetarily secured release (posting a bail bond that is forfeited should the defendant not appear at trial), non-monetarily secured release (such as wearing a GPS tracker), or unsecured release on recognizance where the defendant is bound by law but no other conditions to reappear at trial. Monetarily secured release is supposed to provide a strong financial incentive to appear at trial, but defendants normally satisfy bail requirements with the help of a third-party bail bondsman, who is then given certain legal authority to bring the defendant to court.[1] About 80 percent of monetarily secured releases involve a commercial bail bond.[2] According to a 2009 study of felony defendants in large urban counties, the median bail amount was $10,000.[3] Bail agents within the commercial bond industry usually charge an average fee of 10 percent of the defendant's bail, often with some additional collateral, in exchange for guaranteeing the defendant's appearance in court or paying the court the full bail amount.[4] This means defendants rarely pay anything near the full amount of their bail to obtain release. While the bail system has many flaws, expanding the use of unsecured release has merely exacerbated the problem of offenders skipping trial.[5]

Defendants have a right to bail under the Constitution's Eighth Amendment, which prohibits "excessive bail." Many state constitutions also provide a right to bail pending trial, as figure 9.1 indicates.[6] As a result of this right, judges consider a defendant's monetary circumstances in setting bail amounts. However, this right is not absolute and not every defendant is allowed to post bail. In all jurisdictions, some defendants may be held without bail. For example, Pennsylvania's bail statute states:

> All prisoners shall be bailable by sufficient sureties, unless: (1) for capital offenses or for offenses for which the maximum sentence is life imprisonment; or (2) no condition or combination of conditions other than imprisonment will reasonably assure

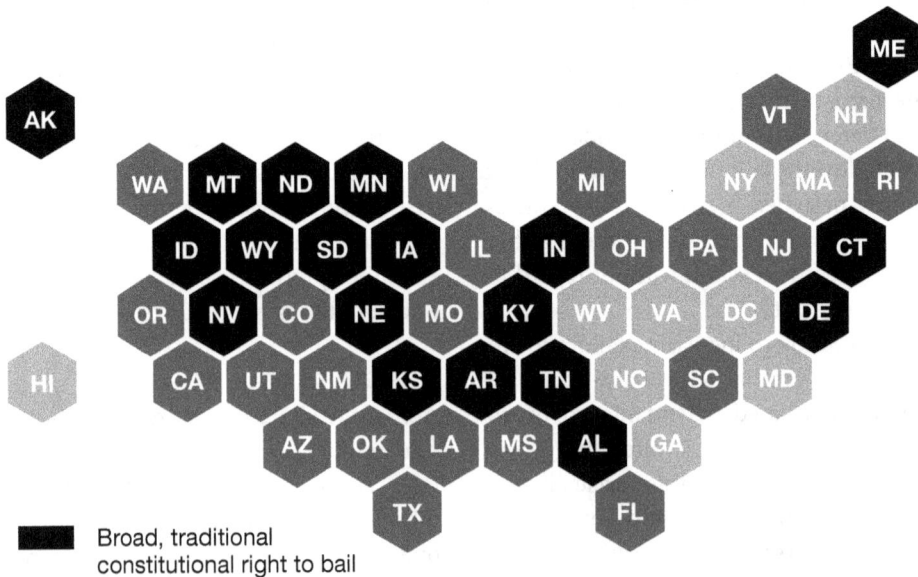

Figure 9.1. Constitutional right to bail provisions, National Council of State Legislators, 2020. Figure from Amber Widgery, *The Statutory Framework of Pretrial Release*, November 2020, National Conference of State Legislatures, https://documents.ncsl.org/wwwncsl/Criminal-Justice/Framework-of -Pretrial-Release_v07_web.pdf.

the safety of any person and the community when the proof is evident or presumption great.[7]

In the federal system and every US state besides New York,[8] pretrial release determinations consider a defendant's dangerousness in addition to their risk of flight. Under this approach, individuals who are deemed a threat to community safety by the judge may be denied pretrial release if there are no conditions that could allow their safe release.[9] However, almost half of states provide statutory guidance for judges creating a presumption of release on recognizance (unsecured release),[10] which essentially mandates judges to release many individuals with dubious prospects of returning to court. Even in states without a presumption of unsecured release, judges are often required to use the least restrictive means necessary to ensure defendants appear in court.

The bar for unsecured release is set so low in most states that a substantial portion of offenders qualify despite being flight risks (not to mention public safety threats). Even those offenders too risky to clear the low bar of unsecured release may still qualify for a relatively minor bail amount. No matter the type of release, the system faces the hard tradeoff that releasing only those likely to return to trial still means a large portion of offenders will fail to appear. For example, if judges only released defendants who were 75 percent likely to appear at trial, that would still mean one out of four such releases would end with the offender skipping trial. In fact, this ratio appears to roughly approximate the threshold used by judges, as historically about a quarter of persons released pretrial fail to appear in court, leading to a bench warrant for their arrest.[11] However, tightening release conditions (for example, to a 90 or 95 percent likelihood of reappearance) would lead to many more defendants spending time in jail who would have been safe to release with or without bail. As a result, most statutory guidelines and individual judges err on the side of release, even for more serious criminals, with most felony defendants being released pretrial. For example, in New York during 2020 and 2021, of the 141,095 felony arraignments, over 90 percent resulted in pretrial release, with only 9 percent of White, 9 percent of Black, and 5 percent of Hispanic defendants being remanded to custody while everyone else was released by one means or another.[12] While New York's felony release rate may be somewhat higher than other states due to its recent bail reform, most felony defendants are released. One national study showed that between 1990 and 2004, 62 percent of state felony defendants were released pretrial, with that rate almost certainly rising in the past two decades due to widespread bail reform.[13] While almost all misdemeanor offenders are released without bail, about 60 percent of felony defendants receive a cash bail assignment[14]—though this rate differs by jurisdiction, with states passing bail reform often releasing more felony defendants without cash bail.

The arguments for reforming bail are not without merit and have attracted bipartisan support in some jurisdictions. Under standard bail laws, the amount of cash bail that a defendant is required to pay is set to be proportionate to the defendant's economic status; a wealthy defendant would be expected to pay more in bail than a poor defendant would for the same crime. However, even with this proportionality, there is still a minimum amount of bail necessary to incentivize reappearance by poor defendants as well as a maximum amount of bail allowable (based on the Eighth Amendment protection against excessive bail). The result is that a wealthier defendant will likely always be able to pay bail, but a sufficiently poor defendant, without assets and nothing to lose, simply cannot afford even the minimum possible bail amount. Nor can this problem be solved by creating "bail funds" for indigent defendants. Bail paid by third-party groups gives defendants no incentive to appear at trial, and the failure to appear rate can be over 50 percent for defendants bailed out by such funds.[15] Proponents of eliminating cash bail point out that defendants charged with the exact same crime may have different pretrial outcomes based solely on their economic status. Some have claimed that keeping indigent defendants in jail is criminalizing poverty, but it should also be noted that new crimes committed by those released without bail are likely to affect the poor the most.[16] Pretrial release policies are a complicated issue, raising important societal interests on all sides, but justice and safety should not be forgotten in the debate. One could argue the justice system ought to exercise more caution in pretrial releases because the system bears a special burden in controlling the actions of those released pretrial because it was the system's decision to release defendants back into the community.

Even when cash bail is required, poorly considered pretrial release requirements can still frustrate justice. Consider the following example.

Case Example: Deon Waynewood

Deon Waynewood is convicted of sexually assaulting a child. During his fourteen-year sentence, he is paroled on four occasions and returned to prison each time for violating his parole terms. He leaves custody as a registered sex offender. Following his release, he collects multiple subsequent convictions for sexual contact with minors. In 2019, he is charged with sexually assaulting a young teenager on multiple occasions in Idaho. After spending another year in jail, his bail is reduced to $150,000, which he posts and is released. After his release on bail, Waynewood begins to stalk the same young woman he was convicted of sexually assaulting. The prosecutor has his release on bail revoked, but Waynewood flees the state. Several months later, he is arrested in Colorado for a new sexual assault offense. Colorado sets the bail for his new sexual assault charge at a mere $10,000, which he posts and then flees the state.[17] Many of Waynewood's crimes and his eluding justice could have been avoided if pretrial release conditions had better considered his past failures to appear and his continuing victimizations.

Competing Interests

One can identify interests in support of increasing pretrial release and interests against such expansion.

INTERESTS SUPPORTING INCREASING PRETRIAL RELEASE

- *Liberty (Especially for the Innocent).* Part of the reason for pretrial release is that those jailed pretrial have not been convicted and could be innocent of the crimes they are charged with. Expanding pretrial release makes it less likely that innocent people will spend time in jail. Moreover, there is a general liberty interest even for guilty defendants—some of whom may be able to live safely and even productively in the community while awaiting trial.

Figure 9.2. Deon Waynewood failed to appear for several court dates; he was eventually taken into custody, 2019. Photo by the Idaho Falls Police Department, from News Team, "UPDATED: Wanted Man Found in Denver, June 2, 2021," LocalNews8.com: NPG of Idaho, Inc., https://localnews8.com/news/breaking-news/2021/06/02/reward-offered-for-information-leading-to-arrest-of-wanted-man/.

- *Fairness.* The mechanics of bail make it easier for rich suspects to go free than poorer ones. Expanding pretrial release, such as by eliminating cash bail, makes it easier for poor suspects to be released. Existing bail systems can also be opaque and dependent on the whims of individual judges who get to decide what exactly counts as evidence of flight risk or dangerousness—a discretion that could lead to biased decisions.
- *Saving Jail Space and Resources.* Expanding pretrial release saves jail space and resources for the state. The cost attached to new crimes committed by suspects out on pretrial release complicates this potential societal benefit, however. New forms of non-monetarily secured pretrial

release, such as GPS tracking, may offer ways of saving incarceration resources while also limiting the risk of additional crime or failures of justice.

INTERESTS AGAINST INCREASING PRETRIAL RELEASE

- *Justice.* Every time a guilty suspect is released before trial, there is a danger they may flee and escape justice for their crimes. As mentioned previously, failure to appear rates are commonly around 25 percent, meaning that as many as one in four charged offenders escape justice, at least temporarily, due to pretrial release.
- *Reducing Crime and Improving Public Safety.* Defendants out on

pretrial release often commit additional crimes, creating more victims and forcing the police and court system to handle even more cases. Suspects who intentionally flee trial clearly do not intend to stay law-abiding citizens, meaning that each such failure of justice caused by pretrial release almost inevitably carries with it additional crime and victimizations. Additionally, if people know they can get out of jail without posting bail, there is less deterrence for crime because even if offenders are caught, they know they can simply skip trial. This is especially damaging to deterrence because some have argued that for many criminals, pretrial detention or the cost of hiring a commercial bail bondsman is the only real punishment associated with crime, given how few end up receiving a prison sentence.[18]

- *Preventing Evidence or Witness Tampering.* Pretrial release provides suspects with more opportunities to tamper with evidence that police may not yet have obtained, as well as to influence or threaten witnesses.[19] Such conduct, while a crime in its own right, reduces the chances for conviction and increases justice failures.

The Nature and Extent of the Problem

Even before recent bail reforms expanded pretrial release, failure to appear rates were disturbingly high. However, instead of working to reduce these existing justice failures, many jurisdictions have expanded pretrial release by eliminating or reducing cash bail, with severe resulting effects on justice and public safety unless coupled with other means of monitoring offenders and assuring their appearance at trial. Unfortunately, many attempts at bail reform have ignored these unintended, yet predictable, consequences. While pretrial release of any kind inevitably leads to some failures to appear, expanding the use of unsecured releases has made a bad situation worse. Typically, the greater the financial incentive to appear, the greater the appearance rate. "Compared to release on recognizance, defendants on financial release were more likely to make all scheduled court appearances. Defendants released on an unsecured bond or as part of an emergency release were most likely to have a bench warrant issued because they failed to appear in court."[20] For example, those released without cash bail in New York are more than three times more likely to fail to appear than those released after posting bail.[21] Failures to appear on unsecured release are also more costly to the state as there is no bail forfeiture money to be gained (money that could presumably be used to fund locating and rearresting the offender). This section examines the costs imposed by increasingly lax pretrial release policies, first through increasing the failure to appear rate and second through increasing crime as released offenders revictimize their communities.

INCREASED FAILURE TO APPEAR RATES DUE TO EXPANDED PRETRIAL RELEASE High failure to appear and reoffending rates suggest the conditions for pretrial release need tightening in many jurisdictions.[22] However, a recent push for progressive criminal justice reform has made pretrial release even looser. Bail reform has been enacted in over twenty states and numerous local jurisdictions across the country.[23] One popular reform is to reduce or eliminate cash bail altogether in favor of unsecured or non-monetarily secured releases.[24] But the results of these reforms have been problematic. In New York, for example, a 2019 reform banned judges from setting bail for individuals arrested for any but the most serious violent offenses. Those who committed "stalking, assault without serious injury, burglary, many drug offenses, and even some kinds of arson and robbery" were all allowed to go free after arrest without posting bail.[25] New York's law means that each year at least 20,000 additional offenders, previously considered too risky to be released without bail, are released with little to no incentive to face trial.[26] In New York during 2020 and 2021, of the 39,467 felony defendants given release after posting cash bail, 5 percent were issued failure to appear warrants. In contrast, of the felony cases where no cash bail was required, 16 percent of those 18,956 persons—3,033 people—were issued failure to appear warrants. This meant the failure to appear rate more than tripled in cases without cash bail.[27] A crime surge exacerbated by such easy releases has led to more justice failures and sparked an outcry over public safety. The result was New York rolling back some of the reforms in 2020, with additional rollback coming into effect in 2022.[28]

Expanding pretrial release has dramatically increased failure to appear rates in many other jurisdictions as well. This should not be surprising, as with nothing to lose in the form of posted bail, defendants often take the chance to escape and never face justice. Police are usually too busy investigating new crimes to bother chasing down those who skip trial, especially for more minor offenses. So unless a defendant is arrested for a new crime, they are likely to get away without punishment for the earlier crime. Even when defendants do have to post bail, serious offenders may decide forfeiting the money is worth it. For

example, Gary Creek, a Baltimore gang founder, was released on bail in 2021 despite being charged with eighteen murders. He (quite predictably) did not like the prospect of life in prison and failed to appear at trial.[29] The incentive to run for many serious offenders is so high that releasing them pretrial seems reckless.

Expanding pretrial release across all categories of offenders has continually been shown to increase failure to appear rates. In 2013, Jefferson County, Colorado, conducted an experiment in ending commercial bail in favor of "robust pretrial services" to check in on defendants. The result was a 42 percent increase in outstanding felony warrants as felons simply skipped trial. Jefferson County leadership chose to end the program and reinstate commercial bail while warning other counties not to try their same mistaken approach.[30] In 2017, New Mexico mostly eliminated financially secured release and replaced it with a new risk assessment tool.[31] The governor of New Mexico later criticized the state's bail reform efforts and urged other states not to take a similar approach due to its increasing of crime and failure to appear rates.[32]

When Harris County, Texas, began releasing defendants on unsecured bonds, they failed to appear in court 50 percent of the time.[33] Similarly, El Paso, Texas, has experienced concerning failure to appear rates. In 2015, El Paso changed from a cash bond system of release to a pure risk assessment model in order to allow more indigent defendants to qualify for personal recognizance bonds. After doing so, their failure to appear rate more than tripled.[34] When Atlanta adopted bail reform in 2018 that allowed poorer defendants to be released without any cash guarantee, the failure to appear rate doubled, with thousands of defendants taking the opportunity to simply skip trial and escape justice.[35] Typically, wherever it has been tried, allowing offenders to leave jail before trial without an incentive to return has led to more failures of justice—hardly a difficult outcome to predict.

INCREASED CRIME DUE TO EXPANDED PRE-TRIAL RELEASE If defendants who skip trial proceeded to live law-abiding lives, the effects on justice would still be serious but less attention grabbing and damaging than is the case. In fact, defendants released prior to trial often take the opportunity to keep breaking the law, often leading to more justice failures and public disillusionment with a system that cannot seem to control even offenders who have been caught. Frustrated police too often scoop up criminals only to have them promptly released on cashless bail and out committing a new offense, again and again. The known reoffending rate for all defendants granted pretrial release varies by jurisdiction but appears to be around 16 percent.[36] Consider some specific examples of troublesome conditions caused by lax pretrial release.[37] In Indianapolis in 2021, 43 percent of those accused of killing people did so while they were on pretrial release or serving postconviction sentences outside of jail:[38] fifteen such killers were awaiting trial and four were serving sentences out of prison.[39] In other words, at least fifteen people died in just one year in Indianapolis because of poorly designed pretrial release policies. In San Francisco, roughly half of people charged with crimes and released from jail before trial fail to show up in court, and a similar share are accused of committing a new crime while free, with many of these being serious crimes. More than one in six defendants released before trial allegedly committed a new violent offense, according to the

findings from May 2016 to December 2019 published by the California Policy Lab, based at UC Berkeley and UCLA.[40]

Eliminating cash bail can make restraining serial offenders difficult. For example, hundreds of looters who smashed and robbed stores across New York City in June 2020 were released on cashless bail to continue to spread chaos and crime.[41] Of all individuals arrested for a felony or serious crime in New York City released under New York's new "non-monetary conditions" for bail, roughly 43 percent were rearrested.[42] With cashless bail, an arrest can be reduced to little more than a trip to the police station and an interruption to a career criminal's busy life of crime. In the first fifty-eight days of 2020 in New York City, "482 people who had been arrested on charges where cash bail was prohibited went on to commit 846 new crimes."[43] Thirty-five percent of these postrelease crimes were for "murder, rape, robbery, felony assault, burglary, grand larceny and grand larceny auto," and overall crime in the city was three times the rate compared to the same time period in 2019.[44] Police, recognizing the familiar faces they were picking up again and again, blamed the rise in crime squarely on policies such as bail reform.[45] In 2019, 20.2 percent of those arrested for violent felonies in New York City already had a previous open case. In 2020, after more bail reform, that number rose to 25.1 percent, reflecting how much serious crime was being driven by offenders out on pretrial release.[46] Tightening pretrial release could have potentially prevented up to 25 percent of the violent crime in New York City—preventing thousands of unnecessary victimizations.

There is a significant and growing amount of research showing that any expansion of pretrial release procedures leads to increased crime caused by those released. In Houston, Texas, after the city eliminated cash bail in 2020, "18,796 defendants were charged with new felonies and misdemeanors while out on bond, a number that has tripled since 2015."[47] More recent data has shown that 156 murders in Texas have been committed by individuals out on bond since 2018.[48]

A study in Cook County, Illinois (Chicago), revealed that after new bail procedures were adopted in 2017, releasing a significantly greater number of defendants awaiting trial, "the number of released defendants charged with committing new crimes increased 45%" and "the number of pretrial releasees charged with committing new violent crimes increased by an estimated 33%."[49] This percentage accounted for at least seventy additional violent crimes due to the expanded pretrial release measures.[50] Particularly unfortunate, the new measures made it easier for "defendants accused of aggravated domestic batteries to obtain pretrial release," providing a perfect opportunity for such abusers to retaliate against their victims.[51]

After Yolo County, California, implemented $0 bail in 2020, 70 percent of the offenders released under the policy were rearrested for new crimes, including 20 percent for violent felonies such as kidnapping, robbery, and murder. Unsurprisingly, the county ended the policy in 2021 once its (predictably) disastrous consequences became clear.[52]

Expanding pretrial release, while often well intentioned, almost always leads to more crime, a fact acknowledged by its more honest proponents. For example, Milwaukee's progressive DA John Chisholm has helped eliminate and reduce bail requirements in his district

since 2007. When asked about his policies, he admitted: "Is there going to be an individual that I divert, or I put into treatment program, who's going to go out and kill somebody? You bet."[53] Chisolm was of course correct. His office let Darrell Brooks out on a trivial $1,000 bond in November 2021 after Brooks ran over the mother of his child with a car. Brooks went on to massacre six people and wound over sixty at a Christmas Parade in Waukesha, Wisconsin, a few days after being released.[54] In another instance, a Wisconsin man was released on a $250 bail for a domestic violence charge and was subsequently charged with beating the same woman to death only a few months later.[55] The tragic reality is that lax pretrial release conditions are responsible for thousands of entirely preventable violent crimes every year, a fact raised by those who accuse bail reformers of having blood on their hands.

Public Complaints

The public often responds with outrage when a defendant with a violent criminal record goes on to commit another crime after being released pretrial.[56] These types of tragedies have been happening more frequently in recent years due to various bail reforms that make pretrial release easier. The public generally disapproves of expanded pretrial release for violent offenders. A 2018 survey found that 94 percent of Americans believed offenders accused of violent crimes should usually or always remain in jail.[57]

In addition to families of crime victims,[58] many prosecutors and police have been particularly vocal in calling for recent expansions in pretrial release to be rolled back. For example, after a South Carolina man with a lengthy criminal record was released without posting bail and later opened fire on police, the Oxford, South Carolina, police chief Bill Partridge publicly complained: "We shouldn't be dealing with this. These [police] men and women shouldn't be out here every day on our streets putting their life on the line because judges and courts allow these individuals to walk out of a door without bond."[59] A Democratic prosecutor in New Hampshire, Michael Conlon, endorsed the same opinion: "While nobody should be incarcerated solely because they are indignant or suffering from addiction, nor should someone be released to the community when there is reasonable risk to public safety."[60]

Lawmakers on both sides of the aisle have pushed back against recent changes in bail—even when those very same officials were part of the initial bail reform effort that increased pretrial release. In New Hampshire, Republican governor Chris Sununu, who signed 2018 legislation allowing for most "low-risk" defendants to be released without cash bail, revised his stance and said the legislation needs to be modified.[61] Many New Hampshire state legislators are similarly changing their opinions and looking to revise the law.[62]

Many public complaints about increased pretrial release have reflected a general discontent with the criminal justice system's failure to adequately punish offenders. For example, Louise Turco, head of the NYPD's Lieutenants Benevolent Association (a police organization), spoke to the *Washington Post* about violence during demonstrations in New York: "This has been put in motion by our politicians that have allowed the criminal element to feel as if there's no consequences for any crime that you do and now you've seen this coming out. Now they go home and tell all their friends, 'Listen, I got out the next day and nothing's going to happen to me.'"[63] Many in New York noted the lack of credibility of a criminal justice system that allowed 2022 gubernatorial candidate Lee Zeldin's attacker to be released without bail—Zeldin had spoken of the need to tighten bail laws and was almost stabbed in the neck by an assailant who was then released without bail under New York's bail reform aimed at "non-violent" offenders.[64] In fact, public concern over lawlessness generated by New York's lax bail policies almost led the deep blue state in 2022 to unseat its incumbent Democratic governor, Kathy Hochul, who was not perceived as taking the problem seriously.[65]

Victims have often spoken of their disillusion with pretrial release. Nortasha Stingley, the mother of a woman who was killed by a man out on bond while awaiting trial, said: "I just really want to ask some of these judges, what if it was your child? What if the shoe was on the other foot?"[66] These kinds of complaints illustrate the fact that increasing pretrial release is dangerous not only because released defendants reoffend or fail to appear but also through a more indirect undermining of the criminal law's credibility with the community.

Reforms

Many current bail reform efforts are still focused on ending cash bail so that pretrial detention does not hinge on the defendant's ability to pay bail. While there are legitimate reasons to reform bail, too often the push is ideological without regard to adverse consequences. The reforms discussed here all attempt to strike some balance between justice, safety, and the concerns driving opposition to cash bail.

Prohibiting Bail for Serious Crimes. Many states already prohibit bail for certain extremely serious crimes (such as first-degree murder) in recognition that society's interests in justice and safety in such cases outweigh the defendant's interest in liberty once probable cause is established for an arrest. Some have suggested expanding the list of crimes for which bail can or must be denied to include all serious felonies. For example, Alabama gives judges discretion to deny bond for suspects charged with "murder, first degree assault, first degree kidnapping, first degree rape, first degree sodomy, sexual torture, first degree domestic violence, first degree human trafficking, first degree burglary, first degree arson, first degree robbery, terrorism and aggravated child abuse."[67]

Use Behavioral Nudges. There is evidence that certain behavioral nudges—such as redesigning summons forms to draw the defendant's attention to actions required of them and sending reminder text messages—can be used to reduce failure to appear rates by reminding defendants of the serious legal consequences that could follow from their failing to appear as promised.[68] This proposed reform has been tested experimentally in New York City and found that for some kinds of defendants reminder text messages decrease the failure to appear rate.[69] Some charitable organizations have also used reminder text messages with success.[70] An improved approach might be to nudge a defendant's close contacts (such as family or friends), in addition to the defendant, to bring additional reminders and social pressure to bear on the defendant to appear in court. While these reforms represent inexpensive ways to improve appearance rates, they only work on those forgetful defen-

dants who do not intentionally wish to skip trial. Less than a majority of states have implemented such text messaging tools, with states such as Massachusetts and California leading the way.[71]

Electronic Monitoring. Many jurisdictions have begun using electronic monitoring (such as GPS ankle bracelets) of defendants as either a substitute for or in addition to bail. There is evidence from both experimental and anecdotal studies that electronic monitoring can effectively reduce pretrial misconduct and decrease failure to appear rates.[72] Electronic monitoring has been shown to reduce failure to appear rates by around 13 percent,[73] and recidivism rates by 31 percent.[74] Such monitoring is more expensive than a traditional bail system but may be worth the investment because it avoids many of the costs incurred by failures to appear and reoffending. Even if a monitored defendant does not voluntarily appear for trial, the tracker allows police to easily rearrest the defendant in a way that could not be done for unsecured releases.

Allow Judges to Detain Without Bail for Current or Previous Violation of Pretrial Release Conditions. When a defendant is released and then violates the conditions of their release or is rearrested for another offense, judges should be allowed to order the defendant detained. All states currently have laws permitting the revocation of bail if a defendant violates the conditions of release, fails to appear, or commits another crime while on bail.[75] But in some states like New York, judges are barred from doing so if the violation by itself would not warrant pretrial detention[76]—indeed, in one month in New York City, "143 individuals committed at least 230 crimes—ranging from robbery, burglary, and felony assault to criminal mischief, grand larceny, and drug offenses—after being released pretrial."[77] One hundred ninety-nine of these new crimes were ineligible for bail under New York law, meaning judges were powerless to hold the offenders who had already violated their release conditions for their previous offense.[78] Empowering judges to detain pretrial release violators not only allows judges to respond to the new information concerning the defendant's likelihood to skip trial or reoffend but also helps deter violations of pretrial release conditions.[79] New Jersey's 2014 bail reform allowed for this and, on prosecutorial motion, New Jersey judges revoked one thousand pretrial releases in 2018 due to a defendant's rearrest or violation of conditions.[80]

Provide Judges Feedback on Pretrial Detention and Misconduct Rates. In light of growing evidence that learning and experience mitigate errors in judicial decision making, some scholars have proposed that judges be provided with systematic feedback on the outcomes of their pretrial detention decisions.[81] A related proposal is for this kind of feedback to be provided to the general public as a kind of pretrial release "public report card," which has been shown to improve outcomes in other contexts by highlighting the best and worst performers in each court and putting pressure on the "bad apples" among judges to modify their decisions.[82] These public report cards could also compare each judge's performance to the decisions that would be made based on purely objective measures, such as through risk-assessment tools. However, such measures would not solve the part of the problem that does not result from judicial discretion in bail decisions but rather from laws mandating laxer pretrial release.

Reimplement Cash Bail or Create Other Incentives to Appear. In light of the evidence that removing cash bail without alternative incentives to appear for trial is unwise, there have been calls to reinstate cash bail or other incentives to reappear. For example, those who fail to reappear might have their sentences increased if later convicted, or the conviction for intentionally failing to appear could carry a sentence equivalent to the crime for which the defendant fled trial (or the conviction for a crime committed on pretrial release might carry a significantly higher penalty). Other incentives might include non-cash monetary inducements such as posting non-cash collateral or requiring defendants to provide employment, bank, or payment details so they could be automatically fined for failing to appear even if they did not have to post a substantial initial sum.

Recommendation: Reduce Failures to Appear Through Flight Risk Assessment But with Preference for Non-Incarcerative Restraints

In order to reduce failures of justice caused by pretrial releases, release decisions should be made according to tested and effective flight risk assessment tools with a scaling range of incentives to appear at trial based on a defendant's risk of flight. Judges are not good at predicting a defendant's risk of flight, as studies show.[83] As a result, legislatures should mandate that courts use flight risk assessment algorithms that are backed by data and testing to prove their effectiveness.[84] Such algorithms would rely on metrics including "charges pending against the defendant at the time of arrest," "number of prior misdemeanor arrests," "number of prior felony arrests," "number of prior failures to appear," "employment status of defendant at the time of arrest, defendant's residency status, defendant's substance abuse problems," "the nature of the primary charge," and "if the primary charge is a misdemeanor or a felony."[85] Such key factors have been used in various algorithms to predict flight, including the Federal Risk Assessment Tool.[86]

If a defendant's flight score is above the cutoff for pretrial release, the defendant would stay in jail. When the flight score is below the cutoff, the defendant would be released pretrial on conditions ranging from electronic monitoring to posting bail with an explicit stipulation that indigent defendants would be granted non-monetary release conditions. In other words, posting bail would be a possible release condition for those who could afford it, but non-monetary conditions (such as electronic monitoring through ankle bracelets) would guarantee that anyone with a flight risk assessment below the cutoff would be released regardless of economic status. The greater the risk of flight, the more demanding the conditions for pretrial release would be. Those who have been rearrested while on pretrial release normally should not be released again as they have shown a high likelihood of violating their terms of release.[87]

Judges would have limited discretion to depart from the decisions of the risk assessment tool, with such departures requiring a written explanation of the factors that were not considered by the algorithm that make the defendant unusually more or less likely to appear at trial. This proposal would replace—or at least supplement—the current emphasis in many states on dangerousness assessments where laws or judicial opinions often provide standards for judges to consider in determining dangerous versus non-dangerous offenders as opposed to considering which offenders are likely to actually return for trial.[88] Focusing on flight risk is preferable because it is not only easier to do, but it also works to minimize justice failures regardless of the perceived future dangerousness of the offender.

What should make this proposal particularly appealing to a wide range of groups is that it shields defendants from judicial biases as a defendant's flight risk assessment would be calculated according to a transparent metric with corresponding release conditions being prescribed by law depending on the defendant's score.[89] Aside from objectivity, the best currently available flight risk assessment tools allow for added reliability, proving to be significantly more accurate than judges' intuitions regarding the likelihood of a defendant's flight.[90] As a result, adopting systematic flight risk assessment tools can optimize and even reduce the use of funds for pretrial detention, which costs an estimated $13.7 billion in the United States each year to jail 443,000 people pretrial on any given day.[91]

Flight risk assessment tools could also be continually refined based on data generated by their use in order to get closer to the goal of allowing all those who would reappear to be released pretrial while confining all those who would attempt to flee. For example, the algorithm could process past data on bail amounts to determine the optimal level to set bail to ensure appearance (for those defendants who can afford bail). Additionally, recidivism would be reduced as those most likely to commit crimes on pretrial release are also at high risk of flight and thus are more likely to be detained. Moreover, states could tune their pretrial release algorithms as needed to reflect the public's view on the balance between justice, safety, and liberty inherent in pretrial release conditions.

Our recommendation takes no position on the extent to which dangerousness assessments beyond those necessary for a flight risk assessment should inform pretrial releases (because our primary focus is avoiding failures of justice rather than maximizing effective crime control), but in any case, it would be easy to supplement a flight risk algorithm with a separate dangerousness algorithm if so desired by the community, though it should be noted that trying to assess dangerousness apart from flight risk has mixed results.[92]

Various jurisdictions have already adopted flight risk assessment tools (although typically not in the systematic and transparent way we recommend). The Virginia Pretrial Risk Assessment Instrument (VPRAI), adopted in 2005, is one of the oldest flight risk assessment tools and has served as a model for other states.[93] States that have later adopted such tools include Kentucky and Colorado, both of which now rely heavily on such tools. As of 2019, it is reported that at least one pretrial tool (including dangerousness assessment tools) is in use in every state except Massachusetts, Arkansas, Wyoming, and Mississippi.[94] Internationally, New Zealand has adopted a flight risk assessment tool called ROC*ROI. In 2020, the New Zealand government made the workings of the algorithm transparent by requiring that variables relied upon to make a judgment and data collected all be made public. Additionally, all explanations for why each variable is included must also be made public and must be written in simple English so that the average citizen can understand.[95]

Looking back at the Waynewood case, given his numerous past crimes and failures to appear, we can assume that any flight risk assessment tool would have yielded a do not release score if it had been used. At the very least, he would have been released with electronic tracking that would have both increased the chance of deterring any subsequent offenses and made rearresting him easier. Our proposal is meant to ensure criminals who would skip trial remain in custody, while thousands of low-risk defendants are allowed to live freely (regardless of their financial status) with incentives in place to ensure their appearance in court.

B. SPEEDY TRIAL RULES

Sometimes, regardless of whether a defendant is granted pretrial release, their prosecution may be barred by speedy trial laws. The Sixth Amendment to the US Constitution states that "in all criminal prosecutions, the accused shall enjoy the right to a speedy trial," and such a right makes perfect sense because the government should not be allowed to delay a defendant's trial indefinitely. The Supreme Court has found that the Due Process Clause of the Fourteenth Amendment imposes speedy trial rights on the states as well,[96] and state constitutions have also generally enshrined the right to speedy trial in provisions that mirror the Sixth Amendment.[97] As a result, if the justice system is unable to process a criminal case speedily enough, serious offenders may end up having their charges dropped.

The federal and state constitutions do not define what constitutes a "speedy" trial, nor do they quantify what delay amounts to a violation of the constitutional right. In determining whether the constitutional right to speedy trial has been violated, both federal and state courts apply a multifactor test, articulated by the Supreme Court in the 1972 case of *Barker v. Wingo*:

> The approach we accept is a balancing test, in which the conduct of both the prosecution and the defendant are weighed. A balancing test necessarily compels courts to approach speedy trial cases on an ad hoc basis. We can do little more than identify some of the factors which courts should assess in determining whether a particular defendant has been deprived of his right. Though some might express them in different ways, we identify four such factors: Length of delay, the reason for the delay, the defendant's assertion of his right, and prejudice to the defendant. The length of the delay is to some extent a triggering mechanism. Until there is some delay which is presumptively prejudicial, there is no necessity for inquiry into the other factors that go into the balance. Nevertheless, because of the imprecision of the right to speedy trial, the length of delay that will provoke such an inquiry is necessarily dependent upon the peculiar circumstances of the case. To take but one example, the delay that can be tolerated for an ordinary street crime is considerably less than for a serious, complex conspiracy charge.[98]

Such a multifactor case-by-case approach, under which the judge weighs the totality of the circumstances in the particular case, would minimize justice failures caused by strict speedy trial time limits. While we support this balancing test, which allows courts to weigh competing interests, the test has widely fallen out of use following the passage of speedy trial laws across states, which create stricter rules and specific fixed timelines for trials.[99] Today, almost every state

has enacted speedy trial statutes, like the federal Speedy Trial Act of 1974, typically setting a fixed maximum amount of time that may pass between arrest, indictment, and trial, where violation of that timeline exempts the defendant from liability no matter how compelling the evidence against them and no matter how serious their offense.

While a four-part balancing test is used to determine if the constitutional right has been denied, usually no such test is used in determining if there has been a violation of statutory speedy trial rights. As one scholar described it, "the mere expiration of the prescribed time limits, absent trial and without justification, violates the defendant's rights, making it unnecessary to inquire into such constitutional factors as prejudice to the defendant or his assertion of the right. Consequently, after the prescribed time period has elapsed, the [statutory] right violation obviates the necessity of determining whether any other speedy trial right . . . has been violated."[100] Thus, deviating from the time cutoffs that the statute dictates leads in many jurisdictions to a dismissal of charges against the offender regardless of the seriousness of the crime or the circumstances surrounding the delay.

For example, in Colorado, if a defendant is not brought to trial within six months after pleading not guilty, "he shall be discharged from custody . . . and the pending charges shall be dismissed, and the defendant shall not again be indicted" based on the same conduct.[101] In Florida, if the defendant is not tried within the time specified in the rules, the court ought to conduct a hearing upon the defendant's request and order that he be brought to trial within ten days. "A defendant not brought to trial within the 10-day period through no fault of the defendant, on motion of the defendant or the court, shall be forever discharged from the crime."[102] In Ohio, "a person charged with an offense shall be discharged if he is not brought to trial within the time" stipulated by the statute, and such dismissal bars "any further criminal proceedings against him based on the same conduct."[103]

Fortunately, speedy trial statutes exclude certain periods from the prescribed time limits. These include continuances (a specified period of delay) that may be granted by the judge for good reason upon request of either the prosecution or the defense: delays caused by unavailability of the offender or his failure to appear, delays caused by the defendant's physical or mental incompetence, natural disasters, and others.[104] Nevertheless, major failures of justice can still regularly occur when a delay is caused by reasons not specified in the statute, of which there are endless possibilities—such as an administrative error in scheduling or formal non-compliance with the statute because the court forgets to record the reasons for a properly granted continuance. Moreover, speedy trial laws often force prosecutors to drop or generously plea bargain other cases to focus on bringing the most important ones to trial within the requisite time period.[105]

Speedy trial laws serve an important purpose within the justice system by acknowledging and protecting the rights of those who have not yet been convicted of a crime, but their inflexible application can produce unnecessary and serious justice failures that would be avoided under the more nuanced constitutional balancing analysis. Consider a few examples.

Case Example: Vance Collins

On November 30, 1992, Vance Collins breaks into and burglarizes the apartment of Brenette Orr in Ohio. Collins is armed with a gun, and when he realizes Orr is home, he overpowers and rapes her. She provides a clear description of her attacker to police, and less than two weeks later, Collins is arrested for burglarizing another house while armed. Orr selects his picture from a photo array. Two days later, a grand jury indicts Collins for the rape, burglary, and various firearm offenses, and the speedy trial time period begins to run, giving authorities 270 days to bring Collins to trial. However, if a defendant is held in jail in lieu of bail, each day in jail counts under the statute as three days for the purposes of the speedy trial clock, so authorities must begin the trial within ninety days of indictment. Two continuances amounting to fifty-eight days are granted by the trial judge. One was requested by the defense, but the record on appeal does not indicate which party requested the other continuance. Collins is convicted at trial and sentenced to ten to twenty-five years for each offense with the sentences to run concurrently. However, the appellate court reverses the convictions, holding that Collins's right to a speedy trial was violated because the trial court had not adequately documented its reason for granting the second continuance.[106] The appellate court stressed that the requirements of the speedy trial statute "are mandatory and must be strictly adhered to by the state."[107] That the evidence is clear beyond a reasonable doubt, that the offenses are serious, and that Collins suffered little or no prejudice to his case could not be taken into account in determining whether this rapist-burglar was to go free because the speedy trial statute prevented the more nuanced constitutional balancing analysis from being used.

Case Example: Michael McFadden

Michael McFadden is heading to trial in Colorado for a long list of sexual offenses against six different children.[108] He has previously been convicted of similar offenses and his defense team asks for and receives two continuances to prepare the defense's case. Prior to the third trial date, all parties have agreed to the jury questionnaire *as drafted by defense counsel* that includes information about McFadden's prior conviction. After jury members are given the questionnaire, the judge notices the mention of the prior offenses. A continuance is declared so that the court can decide if the trial can continue. After studying the problem, it is determined that the problematic

language "did not violate any existing authority or order of the court." McFadden is ultimately found guilty in 2015 and sentenced to 316 years. McFadden appeals his conviction based on a claim of a speedy trial violation. The appeals court finds that the final delay, the third one of the trial, caused the case to go beyond the state's allowable six-month speedy trial statute.[109] It rules that because the "defendant did not agree to or otherwise occasion a necessary continuance, he cannot be charged with the trial delay."[110] His conviction is vacated, and he is released from custody.[111] Again, the beyond a reasonable doubt strength of the evidence, the seriousness of the sexual offenses against children, and the lack of prejudice from the continuance during which the judge reviewed the jury questionnaire drafted by the defense were all held by the speedy trial law to be irrelevant to deciding whether this child molester should go free.

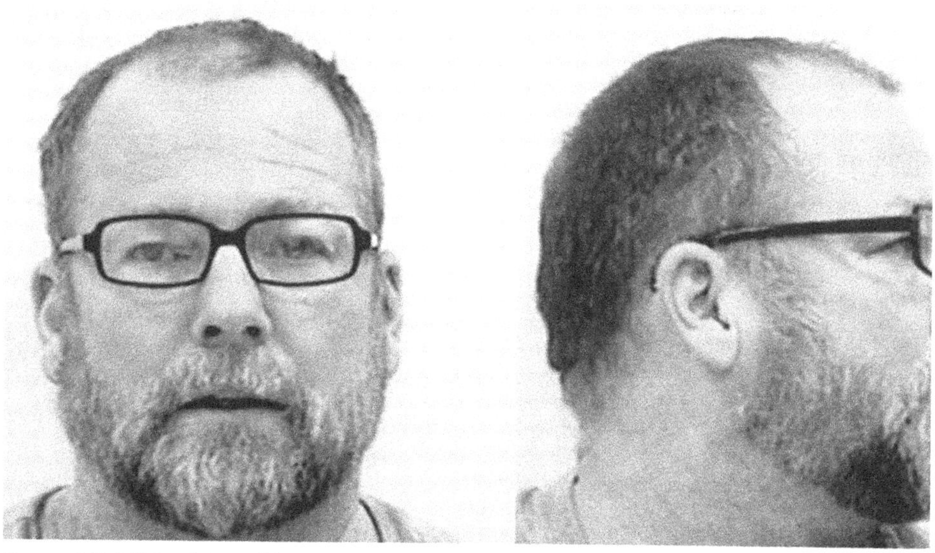

Figure 9.3. Michael McFadden escaped a life sentence when his conviction was overturned, 2015. Photo by Colorado Springs Police Department, from "Trial Set for Sex Offender Michael McFadden, Man Let Out of 316-Year Sentence," KKTV, February 28, 2018, https://www.kktv.com/content/news/Colorado-man-sentenced-to--475480273.html.

Competing Interests

One can identify legitimate interests on each side of the issue.

INTERESTS SUPPORTING CURRENT APPLICATION OF SPEEDY TRIAL RULES

- *Preventing Government Abuse.* The right to a speedy trial is essential to prevent the government from holding suspects indefinitely whether it is due to delays or intentional deprivation. If there is not some mechanism guaranteeing the release of prisoners, then the government would have little incentive to honor the right to a speedy trial. The right to a speedy trial also prevents the government from constantly holding the possibility of a future trial over an arrested person's head as a threat.
- *Efficiency.* Forcing the government to wrap up criminal cases in a timely fashion makes prosecutors allocate resources to the most provable and important crimes while preventing massive backlogs of trials from forming.
- *Fairness.* Delays can make it harder to conduct a fair trial for either the defense or prosecution because with time witnesses may forget, die, or move away. Time also increases the chance that evidence will be lost or mishandled. It would be unfair, for example, if prosecutors waited to conduct a trial until after a crucial defense witness had died. Besides, in the context of fairness, speedy trial laws usually prevent the time an arrestee remains in jail pending trial to exceed the time in prison for which he is eventually sentenced.

INTERESTS OPPOSING THE CURRENT APPLICATION OF SPEEDY TRIAL RULES

- *Greater Justice.* Inflexible speedy trial laws can allow criminals to escape deserved punishment because of administrative scheduling errors or unusual circumstances. It makes little sense from a justice standpoint to let criminals escape because of clerical errors or because the system is temporarily overwhelmed. Justice is also harmed when the pressure to ensure a speedy trial forces prosecutors to let some cases slip through the cracks—allowing some offenders to escape unpunished or with grossly unjust plea bargains.
- *Protecting Society from Criminals.* Criminals who are released due to speedy trial laws, as well as criminals whose arrest or prosecution is delayed to avoid starting the trial clock, go on to commit more crimes. Society would be safer if these criminals were held accountable.
- *Improving Investigations.* Shortening the time police have to finish an investigation following an arrest undermines their ability to conduct a thorough and proper investigation and gather sufficient reliable evidence. This may commonly result in a wrongful acquittal, further increasing justice failures caused by speedy trial statutes.

The Nature and Extent of the Problem

Speedy trial laws differ by jurisdiction, but they all create a time limit for achieving justice that sometimes goes unmet through no fault of the prosecutor. Using the federal system as an example of American speedy trial rules, the federal Speedy Trial Act of 1974 requires that a charge or indictment be filed within thirty days after an arrest, and the trial commenced within seventy days after the charge or indictment. Delays for pretrial motions are excepted, and continuances can still be granted for exceptional circumstances (such as a valid reason why more time is needed to prepare the case for argument) by the trial judge.[112]

There is, however, a great deal of variety among the states on speedy trial time limits. For example, California has a sixty-day window for felonies (thirty to forty-five for misdemeanors),[113] while Pennsylvania allows up to a year,[114] and Delaware uses an overall percentage whereby "at least 90% of all criminal cases shall be adjudicated as to guilt or innocence or otherwise disposed of within 120 days from the date of indictment/information."[115] Individual states have different rules about what can serve as the basis for a discharge. In some states, even a validly granted continuance can serve as the grounds for a claim that speedy trial rights have been violated.[116]

The gravity of the impact of speedy trial laws on justice stems from the fact that the only remedy for violating these statutes in most states is dismissal of the charges with prejudice (that is, with no possibility to prosecute the offender ever again for his crime).[117] It is hard to gauge exactly how many cases are dismissed due to the application of speedy trial laws because many if not most of these justice failures come through prosecution decisions (such as dropping cases) made in order to avoid speedy trial dismissals. For example, a Department of Justice report on the effects of the 1974 Speedy Trial Act found that the number of cases dismissed each year was minimal, but the law compelled prosecutors to decline more cases in order to finish other cases within the fixed speedy trial limits. Provable cases with weaker evidence ended up being dropped to keep stronger cases within the time limit.[118] The law also caused justice officials to strategize about when to arrest criminals, causing the number of preindictment arrests to fall in order to stop the clock from starting. This leads to potentially dangerous offenders being allowed to roam free while the state waits to arrest them for fear of starting the countdown to trial too soon.

Public Complaints

When speedy trial laws let offenders go free, the public usually reacts with confusion and anger at criminals escaping on a "technicality." While the public naturally supports preventing the government from indefinitely detaining people without trial, seemingly unreasonable applications of speedy trial statutes are routinely condemned. The serial child sex offender case of Michael McFadden, discussed earlier, provides a useful example. When McFadden was released in 2018 because of a claimed violation of his speedy trial right, the public and the parents of McFadden's victims were outraged that a dangerous sex offender was allowed to go free for such a reason.[119] The district attorney expressed his horror at the speedy trial law's ability to create such failures of justice: "I find it offensive that our justice system would allow this to happen."[120]

Similar public outrage occurred in the 2019 case of serial killer Tommy Ross, who was allowed to go free in Washington State due to a complicated set of events forty years earlier. Ross had been arrested for strangling a woman to death in Port Angeles, but he was also implicated in other killings, including one in Canada. Police allowed Ross to first be extradited, convicted, and sentenced in Canada. After Ross's release from prison in Canada, Washington prosecutors attempted to bring charges against him for his Port Angeles murder, but speedy trial laws barred prosecution as too much time had elapsed from when he was first arrested. In other words, the speedy trial clock apparently began and continued to run because authorities allowed Canada to prosecute first. The victim's family expressed outrage and grief at the fact they would never get justice and that a dangerous killer would be allowed to walk free.[121]

Reforms

Some reforms and exceptions to speedy trial laws have been proposed or implemented.

Recognize More Exceptions to the Speedy Trial Period. Most state speedy trial laws allow certain time periods to not count against speedy trial time limits. In Colorado, for example, which has a six-month time limit for trials, the prosecution may seek additional delay without the defendant's consent for such reasons as interlocutory appeals or "when the defendant is joined for trial with a co-defendant as to whom the time for trial has not run and there is good cause for not granting a severance." Moreover, the prosecution can ask for an additional six months because of the "unavailability of the evidence," as well as requesting continuances for felony trials due to other exceptional circumstances.[122]

Create Longer Time Periods for More Serious Crimes. Most laws already differentiate between speedy trial time limits for felonies versus misdemeanors, with felonies usually being allowed more time. One way to minimize serious failures of justice would be to extend the time limit still further for serious felonies like rape and murder. This would help incentivize prosecutors not to drop weaker yet potentially provable cases in order to focus on rushing less serious but more prepared ones to trial.[123]

Suspend Speedy Trial Rights During Emergency Situations. The COVID-19 pandemic placed strains on the criminal justice system, and trials were delayed across the country to prevent the spread of the virus. Courts around the country suspended speedy trial rights because "the universal need for social distancing to respond to COVID-19 has hindered the operation of the courts and made it more difficult for the government to comply with [Speedy Trial Act] requirements."[124] For example, the US District Court for the Eastern District of Virginia concluded that the risk of COVID-19 would make it "practically impossible to seat a jury and/or obtain a quorum of grand jurors."[125] The Pennsylvania Supreme Court declared a "Judicial Emergency" and suspended speedy trial rights, ruling that "any postponement due to the coronavirus emergency does not count towards speedy trial rights."[126] Similarly, Illinois suspended the state's speedy trial law due to the pandemic, and while it reinstated the law on October 1, 2021, defendants had to wait three additional months to invoke their right to a speedy trial.[127] However, these emergency suspensions of the right to speedy trial have been criticized, with questions raised over the constitutionality of such suspensions and how long they can and should last.[128] Despite these criticisms, perhaps the suspension of speedy trial rights amid the pandemic will help normalize the practice of suspending speedy trial time limits during other emergency situations that cause unavoidable case backlogs.[129]

Recommendation: Have Statutory Speedy Trial Rules Continue to Control Court Scheduling But Allow Permanent Dismissal Only Upon a Constitutional Violation

Though necessary in preventing governmental abuse of power, speedy trial laws should not be applied inflexibly to allow criminals to escape responsibility, especially when considerations of justice and public safety outweigh the defendant's interest in a speedy trial. Therefore we recommend that statutory speedy trial rules continue to control court scheduling, but permanent case dismissal should only occur upon a constitutional violation, which involves the balancing of factors presented in *Barker*, noted previously: the length of the trial delay, the reason for it, the timing of the defendant's assertion of the right, and the resulting prejudicial effect the delay causes the defendant. Consequently, the court must determine whether the delay is so prejudicial as to warrant dismissing the charges, by considering *Barker* factors. Under this approach, a delay attributed to the defense or to an administrative error would not be treated the same as a delay that the state caused deliberately, a delay of a year beyond the statutory time limit would be taken more seriously than a delay of a week, and a minor delay in a murder case would be seen differently than the same delay in an unarmed robbery. (This approach would not give prosecutors the ability to simply ignore speedy trial statutes without a valid continuance as a deliberate failure to adhere to the statutory time limit would not survive a challenge under *Barker*.)

Such an approach is in line with the view expressed by some courts vis-à-vis the interrelation between the statutory and constitutional speedy trial rights, deeming the former to be supplementing and construing the latter.[130] Additionally, a somewhat similar version of this reform was implemented in Canada. The Canadian Charter of Rights and Freedoms mandates trying any person charged with a crime in a reasonable time. Until 2016, a defendant who wished to raise a claim for speedy trial violation had to establish an unreasonable delay based upon factors similar to *Barker*. In 2016, the Canadian Supreme Court in *R v. Jordan* changed the old framework and set a time limit of thirty months in superior

courts and eighteen months in provincial court—not counting any delay attributed to the defense—beyond which the delay is presumed to be unreasonable and the state has to disprove the unreasonableness by showing exceptional circumstances, such as unforeseen events or the complexity of the case. As in the Canadian system, we propose that there be an initial time limit (the statutory time frame) and that if this limit is exceeded, the prosecution is forced to show the delay was not unconstitutional under the standards set forth in *Barker*.

Our proposal ought to be appealing for both conceptual and practical reasons. First, it provides meaning to both the constitutional and the statutory speedy trial guarantees. The current approach where once the statutory times elapses the charges must be dismissed renders the constitutional balancing test crafted by the Supreme Court in *Barker* largely irrelevant. On the other hand, solely using the *Barker* test would discard legislatures' work in attempting to demark time limits and would lead to less clarity in the normal course of court business. An integrative approach uses the best of both worlds by retaining the clarity and purpose of statutory time frames while also adding the flexibility of *Barker* for exceptional cases. On the practical level, our suggested approach would prevent the dismissal of serious criminal cases in which the delay was not too lengthy, was in good faith, or was induced by the offender. Under this approach, it is hard to imagine offenders accused of homicide or sexual crimes, like Vance Collins and Michael McFadden, walking free because of a technical error in recording a continuance or when a significant share of the delay occurred because of the defendant.

CHAPTER 10

Plea Bargaining

A. INTRODUCTION

People understand the American criminal justice system is supposed to be built around jury trials, and the iconic courtroom showdown is a staple in entertainment. But in practice, trials are rare, with most cases settled by plea bargains, not juries. The prospect of a trial is still important, however, as prosecutors and defense counsel negotiate a plea agreement based on what they believe the strengths and weaknesses of the case would be if it went to trial. All parties are usually anxious to avoid the cost and uncertainty of a trial, and so they almost always reach an agreement. Approximately only 2 percent of federal criminal defendants go to trial. The odds of a case proceeding to trial are even slimmer in state court.[1] As a result, changes to trial rules (such as those relating to the exclusion of evidence discussed in chapter 8), which alter the relative strength of the prosecution's case at trial, have a corresponding effect on plea bargained case dispositions, with prosecutors often being forced to offer extremely lenient bargains in cases where they fear trial rules may undercut their best evidence.

There are two main types of plea bargains: charge bargaining and sentence bargaining. Charge bargaining occurs when the defendant agrees to plead guilty to a lesser charge (which likely carries a lesser punishment) in exchange for the prosecutor agreeing not pursue any other charges. In sentence bargaining, the defendant agrees to plead guilty in exchange for the prosecutor recommending a lighter sentence to the judge. Even in jurisdictions where judges are free to ignore the sentence recommendation, in practice they commonly defer to sentence bargains. Plea bargains can also be a mix of the two types with a defendant pleading guilty to a lesser charge and the prosecutor recommending a lighter sentence for that charge. Less commonly, plea bargains can involve fact bargains that occur when prosecutors cut out certain damning facts (which might result in an increased sentence) from the indictment in exchange for a guilty plea before passing the case on to the judge for sentencing. No matter its form, plea bargaining can significantly benefit serious criminals who routinely bargain down to a lesser felony or even misdemeanor conviction, thus minimizing their punishment and maximizing victims' and society's sense that justice has failed.[2] Such justice failures are made worse by the opaque nature of plea bargaining that often leaves justice up to the whims of individual prosecutors who may be more influenced by a desire to clear caseloads or pursue personal or political ideologies than delivering a just punishment as the community sees it. As a result, similar offenders who commit the same crime may end up with vastly different punishments based on their luck in who sits opposite them at the bargaining table.

Plea bargaining has been widely practiced in the United States since the nineteenth century, with its use accelerating in the early twentieth century. By 1925, 90 percent of convictions were the result of plea agreements.[3] The Supreme Court upheld the constitutionality of plea bargains in the 1970 case of *Brady v. United States*, which established that plea bargains must include a voluntary waiver of the right against self-incrimination, the right to a jury trial, and the ability to confront witnesses, and furthermore, the bargain must not be accepted or denied due to physical coercion.[4] Once struck, a plea bargain is treated like any other legally binding contract where it is the technical language of the contract rather than principles of justice that govern its enforcement. (Recall the case of Jean Packwood from chapter 1, who lied to investigators about his role in a murder but still had his conviction for murder overturned due to the technicalities of his plea bargain for bank robbery.) A judge typically has the right to reject a plea bargain,[5] which forces the parties to reformulate the bargain or go to trial, but judges rarely exercise this right, preferring to defer to the attorneys, who are in the best position to judge the strength and weakness of their case from the point of view of their clients (the defendant and the community). While most plea bargains are struck without judicial input, some states allow judges to take part in the bargaining.[6] Connecticut, for example, allows judges to mediate plea negotiations and weigh in on the merit of various offers.[7]

Prosecutors engage in plea bargaining for several reasons, including the desire to save resources given the costs of trials, a desire to avoid the uncertainty of trial, and a desire to secure a defendant's cooperation in another ongoing investigation or criminal case. The leniency of a plea bargain is generally determined by how motivated prosecutors are to avoid a trial, though some prosecutors simply ignore justice entirely in favor of clearing cases. On a fundamental level, plea bargaining can turn the scales of justice into the scales of commerce where criminals purchase lesser punishments in exchange for sparing the state expensive trials. As one scholar notes, "Pervasive bargaining, without specific guidelines, perpetuates the image that justice is for sale."[8] Plea bargaining allows even caught criminals to escape full justice. As the same scholar notes, "the existence of significant sentencing differentials between guilty pleas and jury trials supports the idea that the defendant 'got away' with something."[9]

Plea bargaining compels society to contemplate whether priority should go to securing any conviction for a criminal or to securing the most accurate conviction and deserved punishment for the crime, as well as how to balance the two goals in a world of expensive trials and limited resources. It would require massively increased financing to bring every case to trial, and bargaining also allows prosecutors to secure convictions without the uncertainty of a trial or the need to traumatize victims through testimony and cross-examination. As a result of these factors, plea bargaining has become a core component of the American justice system, and removing it seems unlikely to succeed.[10]

But it is still worth asking whether plea bargaining can be made less justice frustrating given how often it regularly produces major justice failures in even the most serious cases. Consider two examples.

Case Example: Michael Adkins

In October 2010, twenty-eight-year-old Michael Adkins begins raping his eleven-year-old daughter while the girl's stepmother turns a blind eye. When the child becomes pregnant, her parents arrange for an abortion at a clinic that asks no questions about the young girl's path to pregnancy. The procedure is botched, and the couple must seek further medical care for the child. This time the doctor calls the police. Adkins is charged with sexual assault, sexual battery, incest, child neglect, and more. With Adkins facing life in prison, the prosecution offers him an incredible plea deal allowing him to enter a "no contest" plea to one charge of incest in exchange for five years of probation. The deal seems like a pretext to simply clear a case that has been dragging on for a long time. The presiding judge is so furious about the proposed deal that he refuses to accept the plea agreement, but Adkins's lawyer

gets the judge removed from the case, and a new one accepts the deal. Finally, in 2017, Adkins is sentenced to five years of probation for repeatedly raping his daughter. He later goes on to commit more domestic abuse, this time against his new girlfriend.[11]

Case Example: Sammy Gravano

In the 1970s, the Gambino mafia family in New York City recruits Sammy Gravano, a hard-as-nails fighter dubbed "The Bull" for once fighting off two older boys who tried to steal his bicycle when he was ten. Gravano quickly proves his worth by ruthlessly assassinating his own mafia colleagues when they get out of line, and in 1976, the thirty-one-year-old Gravano becomes a "made man" admitted to an inner circle of trust and responsibility. He kills efficiently and without remorse, the only twinge of discomfort coming when he attends the funerals of friends he murdered. In 1985, Gravano

Figure 10.1. Michael Adkins while in court for the rape of his daughter, 2017. Photo by Courtney Hessler. Permission to reprint by Allison Gerber of HD Media, LLC.

helps lead a coup in the Gambino family by orchestrating the murder of his own boss, Paul Castellano, on a crowded street in the middle of Manhattan. In 1990, he is second-in-command to new boss, John Gotti, when both are arrested by the FBI. Gravano agrees to testify against Gotti and other mafiosos in exchange for leniency. With Gravano's help, prosecutors manage to put Gotti away for life and get prison terms for forty others, essentially taking down organized crime in New York. Despite confessing to nineteen murders, Gravano is charged only with racketeering and receives a five-year sentence in 1994 with credit for time served. He walks free a few months later and ends up using his second chance to become a drug lord in Arizona.[12]

Figure 10.2. Sammy Gravano was a key informant for the FBI, 1990. Photo by FBI, December 11, 1990, https://en.wikipedia.org/wiki/Sammy_Gravano#/media/File:Sammy_Gravano_(arrest_photo_-_1990).jpg.

B. COMPETING INTERESTS

The interests for and against the justice system's current extensive use of plea bargaining might be summarized this way.

Interests Supporting the Current Extensive Use of Plea Bargaining

- *Efficiency and Savings.* Plea bargaining saves time and money by avoiding costly and time-consuming trials. While decreasing the cost of trials could make reducing plea bargaining more feasible, under current trial costs, any decrease in plea bargaining would likely require large increases in funding for prosecutors, judges, and public defenders. Plea bargaining has become so prevalent precisely because it is efficient at saving resources. Quantifying the financial cost of trials is difficult as it varies greatly depending on factors such as length and complexity, but the average cost is likely hundreds of thousands of dollars.[13] Murder trials often cost more than a million, or even several million, dollars.[14] By contrast, a plea bargain can cost the justice system a few thousand dollars.
- *Allowing for Speedy Case Dispositions.* If more cases went to trial instead of being resolved by plea bargains, it would be much harder for prosecutors and courts to meet the requirements of speedy trial laws, which are not easy to meet even currently (recall chapter 9's discussion of speedy trial laws). Any significant reduction in plea bargaining might lead to far more dropped cases to comply with speedy trial requirements.
- *More Convictions and Deterrence.* For the reasons noted earlier, plea bargaining may maximize the number of total convictions given the justice system's current resources.

Plea bargaining also increases the number of convictions by providing an incentive for some criminals to plead guilty who might have been falsely acquitted at trial. Maximizing convictions may also increase deterrence because what deters offenders the most is a higher likelihood of punishment rather than a greater severity of punishment.[15] Of course, overly lenient plea bargains for serious crimes may also reduce deterrence by convincing offenders they will be able to escape serious punishment even if caught.

- *Allowing Local Variations in Justice.* While plea bargaining can create notable discrepancies in punishment between jurisdictions for the same crime, some may see this as desirable because it allows prosecutors to potentially tailor punishments to the views of the local community. For example, in jurisdictions that have a death penalty law but a community that no longer supports its use, plea bargaining allows prosecutors to easily obtain lesser punishments in line with the community's views.
- *Inducement to Cooperate.* Plea bargains are an essential tool for getting criminals to testify against each other, which is especially critical in organized crime cases, many of which could not be prosecuted otherwise (recall the Gravano case earlier). Plea bargains can also secure other types of cooperation such as getting killers or kidnappers to reveal the locations of their victims.
- *Avoiding Traumatic or Dangerous Testimony.* Plea bargaining allows easier convictions in cases that would have required traumatic victim testimony at trial. In cases of rape or child abuse, the victims are often glad to secure a conviction without having to testify and relive the trauma, even if it means less

punishment for their attacker. Plea bargaining also allows prosecutors to avoid exposing witnesses to the danger of testimony in open court where their names and addresses are often revealed, exposing them to possible retaliation. (The problem of witness intimidation is examined in chapter 14.)

Interests Opposing the Current Extensive Use of Plea Bargaining

- *Greater Justice in Convictions and Sentences.* Plea bargaining undermines justice by publicly convicting criminals of less serious crimes than they actually committed and letting them escape the full punishment they deserve. Charge bargaining is especially pernicious to justice because it can cause a gross failure of justice by permanently distorting the official record of an offender's serious crimes.
- *Punishing Defendants for Exercising Their Right to Trial.* Because plea bargains are a business negotiation, it makes sense for prosecutors to start by overcharging as much as possible and threatening the most severe punishments unless defendants accept a deal.[16] If defendants do exercise their right to trial, then the system often exacts a "trial penalty" by imposing more severe punishment. It strikes many as unjust to harshly punish individuals for simply exercising their constitutional right to trial. On the other hand, the current situation could be described not as punishing the exercise of the right to a jury trial but rather as providing a special (perhaps undeserved) discount to those who choose to waive that right.
- *False Convictions.* It is alleged that as a result of the "trial penalty" and the power prosecutors may wield,

some innocent defendants plead guilty and are falsely convicted because they do not wish to risk a false conviction at trial with even greater punishment.[17] For example, there are on average one to two cases per year in the United S where people plead guilty to a murder for which they are later exonerated.[18] Some of these defendants have stated that they pled guilty in order to avoid the risk of harsher punishments.[19] Such false convictions, while admittedly rare, are a terrible injustice and allow the real perpetrators to escape.

• *Undermining the Credibility of the Criminal Justice System.* The economics of plea bargaining makes it advantageous for the government to place overly harsh punishments on the books in order to provide prosecutors with the best starting negotiating position. This undermines the credibility of the justice system in two ways. First, such overly harsh statutory punishments can reduce the law's moral credibility by conflicting with people's intuitions of justice (as is commonly the case with some drug penalties, for example). But more prevalent still, the massive gap between what the law says is a just punishment and what most plea bargains provide makes people question whether the legal system is concerned with justice at all. Plea bargaining also erodes transparency and procedural justice in a system that is ideally built on jury trials in open court. Plea bargaining reduces the criminal justice system to at best a negotiation and at worst a casino. Interestingly, a 1972 study of criminal defendants showed this erosion of moral credibility most starkly. Defendants, regardless of guilt, felt that the practice of plea bargaining proved the "lying" and "deceitfulness" of the criminal justice system,

which seemed to determine sentencing based on the "way the bargaining game is played" as opposed to objective characteristics such as the seriousness of the crime.[20] Overall, the study found that the disapproval of plea bargaining among the defendants contributed to their distrust of the legal system, thus greatly reducing their respect for the system and their willingness to defer to it and its norms in the future.

• *Deterrence and Less Crime.* When people believe they can use plea bargains to escape deserved punishment even when caught, the legal punishments are less likely to deter lawbreakers.[21] Of course, as noted earlier, plea bargaining may also increase deterrence by maximizing the number of convictions. While plea bargaining's net effect on deterrence is hard to determine, the practice does clearly allow dangerous offenders to be released after only a fraction of just punishment, allowing these criminals the freedom to reoffend during the period they would have still been in prison if sentenced without a plea bargain. (Nationally, around 40 percent of offenders will be rearrested within three years; Delaware has the highest rate at 64.5 percent and Virginia has the lowest rate at 23.4 percent.[22] Even worse, studies have found that 70 percent of state prisoners are rearrested within five years,[23] and 83 percent are rearrested at least once nine years after their release.[24])

• *Separation of Powers and Abuse of Prosecutorial Power.* Plea bargaining blurs the line between judge and prosecutor by essentially giving the prosecutor the power to determine the punishment for a crime. Plea bargains can also allow individual prosecutors to abuse their power in determining punishments. For example, a prosecutor might be more inclined to give preferential plea bargains to rich Whites than poor Blacks or might decide that rape shouldn't be punished as harshly as the law demands. Plea bargaining concentrates enormous power in the hands of prosecutors with little oversight. (See chapter 16 for more on the problem of prosecutors making ideological prosecution decisions.)

- *Demoralizing Police.* Plea bargaining can demoralize police when officers know the criminals they catch are likely to negotiate their way out of just punishment. This can demotivate police from working hard enough to investigate cases and gather compelling evidence when they know the actual charges are likely to be less severe than the evidence warrants.

C. THE NATURE AND EXTENT OF THE PROBLEM

The prevalence of plea bargains and their effect on reducing serious offenders' punishments is well documented.

The Prevalence of Plea Bargaining

Plea bargains, rather than trials, resolve the vast majority of criminal cases, including serious cases like rape and murder. Some sample statistics illustrate this widely documented part of the criminal justice system: 90 percent of federal defendants plead guilty (8 percent of cases are dismissed),[25] and the percentage of guilty pleas is often even higher in state cases. In 2006, 94 percent of felony offenders pled guilty in state courts.[26] In 2010, 96.8 percent of all crimes in US district courts resulted in a guilty plea.[27] Though much lower than the overall total, 87.5 percent of sexual assault cases and 68.2 percent of homicide cases resulted in a guilty plea instead

of a trial.[28] The frequency of plea bargaining also varies by local jurisdiction. In 2017, as few as 1.11 percent of criminal cases resulted in a trial in Pennsylvania, and a mere 0.86 percent of criminal cases resulted in a trial in Texas.[29] In a 1976 Philadelphia study of plea bargaining in homicide cases, no defendants in a sample of 118 went to trial, and no defendants pled guilty to first-degree murder.[30] While this was an unusually high rate of plea bargaining in murder cases, jurisdictions overwhelmed with cases still often resort to clearing them through lenient plea bargains.

While there are practically no restrictions or guidelines on plea bargaining in the United States, unrestricted bargaining is not the norm around the world. Some countries limit what cases can be bargained, while other countries limit how much of a bargain can be given. "Japan will limit them to serious crimes where the accused informs on someone else. In Germany, South Africa and Spain defendants are shown all the evidence to be presented against them before they decide whether to accept a deal. In Germany, the discounted sentence cannot be less than the statutory minimum for that crime. In England, sentences can be cut by at most a third."[31]

The Effect of Plea Bargaining on Justice

The vast majority of offenders who accept a plea bargain serve shorter sentences than they would have received at trial and shorter sentences than are recommended by sentencing guidelines. Trials result in an average maximum sentence of 2.68 times that of a plea bargained sentence, and actual time served is more than double for those defendants who go to trial, meaning offenders escape over half their expected punishment through plea bargaining. The "plea discount" is also real in that the chance of receiving an exceptionally harsh sentence is dramatically less with a plea agreement than after a trial.[32] Plea bargains also routinely lead to below-guideline sentences for serious crimes: 38.3 percent of federal murder sentences fall below minimum sentencing guidelines due to plea bargaining, and the average below-guideline sentence for murder is 52.1 percent less than the *minimum* recommended sentence.[33] Thus, plea bargaining often results in killers getting less than half the justice they deserve even if they are convicted of murder.

The evidence is clear: defendants are richly rewarded for pleading guilty. While it makes sense to offer offenders some small reduction in sentence in exchange for a public confession of guilt, reductions of 50 percent or more seem unjustly lenient to most people. There are also the costs to justice caused by charge bargaining whereby serious offenders avoid felony convictions entirely. Studies suggest that about one in five felony arrests that end in a conviction end in a *misdemeanor* conviction, often allowing serious offenders to be convicted for crimes far more minor than the harms experienced by their victims.[34]

It is easy to forget what all these percentage reductions can mean in terms of how lenient plea bargained punishments become, but consider a few examples drawn from historical studies of plea bargaining that show how bargaining can lead to serious crimes being barely punished at all. In New York in 1973, 80 percent of defendants accused of homicide accepted a plea bargain and served reduced sentences of fewer than ten years. Most were eligible for parole after only three years.[35] The same 1976 Philadelphia study mentioned earlier observed that 82 percent of killers served fewer than two years in prison due to plea bargains, and only 3 percent served more than six years in prison.[36] While sentencing guidelines and harsher statutory punishments enacted since the 1970s have somewhat increased punishments (perhaps by giving prosecutors better starting positions in negotiations), plea bargaining still routinely allows murderers and rapists to escape with barely a fraction of the punishment society would consider just.

One reason the reductions in sentences are so large for serious criminals is that a charge bargain reducing the crime severity by one or two degrees can have an enormous impact on sentence range. For example, a prosecutor can usually only obtain a plea in a first-degree murder case by reducing the charge to second-degree murder or even manslaughter, thus making it possible for judges to sentence a killer to only a few years in prison, whereas the law and the society are likely to view a life sentence, or even death, as more appropriate for an offender who actually committed first-degree murder. Similarly, rape is often downgraded to battery, unlawful restraint, or lewd conduct leading to mere months in jail instead of decades in prison. (Our recommended reform seeks to solve this problem by creating many more grading distinctions, including for serious offenses like murder and rape, which would then give prosecutors the ability to offer less dramatic reductions in charges and punishments in exchange for a guilty plea.)

Plea Bargaining to Clear Backlogs: The COVID-19 Example

Prosecutors' offices are frequently overwhelmed and underresourced (recall chapter 5's discussion of inadequate financing in the justice system). As a result, letting offenders off lightly to clear case backlogs may seem an attractive way forward to many prosecutors. For example, plea bargaining became even more common during the COVID-19 pandemic due to case backlogs and the prospect of delayed trials piling up in the future. Instead of rescheduling COVID-canceled trials in order to achieve appropriate justice, prosecutors took to offering more lenient plea bargains in order to clear cases. A survey of defense attorneys found that more than 60 percent said prosecutors were being more generous during the COVID-19 pandemic.[37] Evidence from individual counties also bears this out. For example, Dubuque County in Iowa saw thirty-three trials in the year before the pandemic, but only eight trials in 2020, with only one trial during the pandemic period, with increased plea bargaining picking up much of the slack.[38]

Pandemic plea bargaining was exemplified in the case of an Oregon man who raped and took explicit photographs of a teenage girl. With prosecutors prioritizing clearing cases without a trial, the rapist was given a plea bargain of probation, avoiding a potential conviction on over two dozen felony sex crimes. Meg Garvin, executive director of the National Crime Victim Law Institute, criticized pandemic plea bargaining, stating that "the pandemic should not mean justice delayed equals justice denied" and that prosecutors "seem to be more concerned with moving people through the system than paying attention to victims' interests."[39]

D. PUBLIC COMPLAINTS

It is not just pandemic plea bargaining that has attracted public outrage. Many people would prefer a just sentence for serious criminals even if it meant providing more time and resources for trials. The public, legal scholars, victims, and victims' families have all expressed outrage at the failures of justice brought about by bargaining. Charge bargaining is considered especially unacceptable as it does not even acknowledge the full seriousness of the wrong done. One 1981 study found that 82 percent of respondents from the general public were against charge reductions or plea bargaining.[40] In 1982, California voters attempted to restrict the use of plea bargaining, largely unsuccessfully, with the passage of Proposition 8 (discussed in the reform section).[41] While there have been virtually no recent surveys of public opinion toward plea bargaining, there is little reason to think the public has grown more supportive of the practice. Even the opinion makers continue to have their doubts. As one scholarly assessment in 2019 found, "It is fair to say that among the academy, a subset of judges and practitioners, and some in the popular media, the dominant view of plea bargaining is grim."[42]

Many prominent members of the legal system have expressed concern at the prevalence of plea bargaining and its results. The Supreme Court lamented the negative ways in which plea bargaining has changed the legal system in the 2012 case of *Missouri v. Frye*, where the Court regretfully notes that "ours 'is for the most part a system of pleas, not a system of trials.'"[43] Similarly, in *Lafler v. Cooper*, the Supreme Court lamented that "the system has created a functioning market where defendants do not expect the maximum sentence."[44] The public admission that the criminal justice system now operates in such a way that serious punishments are not taken seriously concerns many legal professionals. Judge Stephanos Bibas, a judge on the US Third Circuit Court of Appeals, complained, "the expected post-trial sentence is . . . like the sticker price for cars: only an ignorant, ill-advised consumer would view full price as the norm and anything less as a bargain."[45] Similarly, many decades ago, Professor Raymond Mosely described the process of plea bargaining as "more akin to a game of poker than to a process of justice."[46] There is a wide recognition and regret among legal experts that plea bargaining has reduced the criminal justice system to a bargaining game but, given its usefulness, relatively few have advocated eliminating the practice.

Examples of criminals winning the bargaining game often outrage the public. Residents of Philadelphia have harshly criticized District Attorney Larry Krasner's use of charge bargaining to get around sentences required by the law. After a charge bargain reduced a murder charge to voluntary manslaughter, protesters gathered outside of Krasner's office. Families and mothers of victims in Philadelphia protested that such plea bargains "victimize [you] a second time," and others claimed that plea bargaining is simply "giving people the green light to go out and kill people because they know that Krasner is not going to give them harsh sentences."[47] Similar outrage occurred after Michigan prosecutor Carol Siemon implemented policies that automatically offer plea deals to nearly all accused first-degree murderers, reducing charges at least to second-degree murder.[48] Families of victims have begged the prosecutor to revoke these plea deals, but Siemon continued with the practice. In other cases, members of the public have argued that "plea deals should not be permitted when a murder is involved" and have expressed general bewilderment toward the practice of plea bargaining for such serious offenses.[49]

In the case of Jacob Anderson, a student who raped a fellow student at Baylor University in Texas, the plea bargain of "unlawful restraint" was so generous as to spark outrage in the community. The deal gave the rapist no jail time, no requirement to register as a sex offender, and instead required him to serve probation and pay a $400 fine. This prompted a widespread online petition signed by ninety thousand people hoping to dissolve the plea deal.[50] Had Anderson gone to trial on the original charges, he would have faced up to twenty years in prison. In another case that provoked community fury, Colorado Judge Michael McHenry received voicemail threats and was assigned a security guard after approving a plea bargain that gave two defendants no prison time despite being convicted of raping a thirteen-year-old girl.[51] Giving an offender some slight sentence reduction for publicly acknowledging their guilt (as the federal sentencing guidelines formally do,[52] for example) makes sense to most people, but providing a lenient plea bargain inevitably produces public resentment and disillusionment. For example, turning a twenty-year sentence into a nineteen-year sentence is unlikely to be seen as a failure of justice by the public, but turning a twenty-year sentence into a $400 fine is.

E. REFORMS

Many reforms have been proposed or undertaken to make plea bargaining less justice frustrating. Those reforms seeking to reduce or eliminate the practice have not met with much lasting success, suggesting that the most workable reforms may be those seeking to change the way plea bargaining works as opposed to changing its frequency.

Increase Transparency in Plea Bargaining. A majority of US jurisdictions have implemented reforms that make plea agreements matters of public record and thus increase the transparency and public knowledge of plea bargaining.[53] Some states have also made the bargaining positions of parties more transparent. Texas and North Carolina have enacted reforms that require the prosecution and defense to share their respective evidence with each other before negotiating plea agreements.[54] Still, unless the facts of the case are extremely shocking, a public record of unjust plea bargains is unlikely to gain much notice or prompt much improvement in avoiding serious failures of justice.

Limit or Ban Plea Bargaining. Some jurisdictions have attempted to limit plea bargaining, while other jurisdictions have gone so far as to temporarily eliminate plea bargaining altogether. In 1973, the National Advisory Commission on Criminal Justice Standards and Goals "called for the abolition of plea bargaining in all states by 1978," but hardly any jurisdictions even attempted such a ban, and the vast majority of scholars, prosecutors, and other members of the legal community were shocked at the notion.[55] However, plea bargaining was at one point entirely in New Orleans, Louisiana; Ventura County, California; and Oakland County, Michigan, though all such bans were eventually repealed.[56]

The State of California attempted to dramatically limit plea bargaining in 1982 with the passage of Proposition 8, which prohibited plea bargaining in "serious felonies, including those committed while in possession of a gun, violent sex crimes," and "driving under the influence of alcohol or drugs."[57] However, the ban only applied to bargains that reduced the offense charged in the formal written indictment, so the ban could easily be circumvented simply by engaging in bargaining before the formal indictment was filed. The result today is that the legal limitations do little to hinder plea bargaining even for serious felonies, and it is still the case that the majority of criminal cases in California are resolved through plea bargaining.[58]

In 1975, the attorney general of Alaska, Avrum Gross, ordered that plea bargaining (both charge and sentence bargaining) be entirely abolished.[59] Gross believed the ban was necessary to do justice and restore the "public confidence in the justice system."[60] If prosecutors can plea bargain, they do plea bargain, so the Alaska ban contained no exceptions. The ban was found to be effective in improving police investigations, case strength for prosecutors, and increased the amount of trials by 30 percent (most defendants still chose to plead guilty even without a bargain, perhaps expecting greater leniency from the sentencing judge).[61] Sentence lengths also increased in the two years following the ban's implementation, doubling sentences for violent and property offenders and increasing sentences "substantially" for those convicted of fraud.[62] Despite ending the ban in 1993, Alaska appears to have been the most successful in abolishing plea bargains for a significant period of time. However, the ban was never widely supported by state prosecutors and other legal authorities and was met with "stiff resistance" when introduced.[63] In fact, some prosecutors continued to surreptitiously plea bargain because the policy was never strictly enforced. Despite the positive benefits in Alaska, convenience ultimately won out and led to the repeal of the ban by executive direction from the attorney general.

Formalize and Legislate the Rules of Plea Bargaining. One oft-proposed reform is to formalize and legislate transparent rules of plea bargaining that would specify the sort of reductions allowed. For example, the law might state that pleading guilty would automatically lead to a sentencing discount of a fixed percentage such as 15 or 20 percent, or perhaps there would be several possible fixed reductions that prosecutors could offer based on the assessed strength of the evidence. However, such formal rules would have difficulty dealing with charge bargaining where prosecutors get to decide what to charge the defendant with in the first place. While detailed plea bargaining guidelines (similar to judicial sentencing guidelines discussed in chapter 11) might add more structure and consistency to charge bargaining, the process of plea bargaining is likely too case dependent to allow for complete formalization. At the same time, more structured guidance could help reduce disparities in plea bargaining practices between prosecutors. Interestingly, the Federal Sentencing Guidelines provide a standard sentencing discount of two offense levels (commonly a 20 to 25 percent reduction of sentence guideline range) for "acceptance of responsibility" for the offense, which typically means pleading guilty.[64]

F. RECOMMENDATION: USE CONSOLIDATED OFFENSE DRAFTING WITH PARTICULARIZED OFFENSE GRADES TO REDUCE THE JUSTICE-FRUSTRATING COSTS OF PLEA BARGAINS

Plea bargaining is so deeply embedded in the legal system due to its efficiency that attempts to end it are unlikely to succeed. However, in order to mitigate the failures of justice arising from plea bargains (especially charge bargains), we recommend prosecutors be given more nuanced criminal codes, with more nuanced offense grading, with which to plea bargain. (Such more nuanced criminal codes have other important benefits that alone would justify their adoption.[65])

Legislatures ought to implement "consolidated offense drafting"—that is, collecting all related offenses within a single offense definition. An unconsolidated criminal code may have degrees of the same type of offense scattered across many different parts of the criminal code as separate offenses, which typically produces irrational differences and inconsistencies between the related offenses.[66] For example, in Delaware there exist eleven statutory offenses scattered across the code criminalizing recklessly causing injury to another person that only differ in their aggravating factors or the circumstances under which the injury is caused, such as the seriousness of the injury, the characteristics of the victim, or the way the injury is caused.[67] Each offense in the present Delaware code is graded separately with different maximum penalties and inconsistent grading distinctions. These eleven statutes could be consolidated into a single offense in which the first subsection defines the prohibited conduct (recklessly causing injury) while the second subsection specifies the proper grading and penalty depending upon the various relevant factors identified in the eleven different provisions. Instead of having eleven different offenses, the code would end up with one offense with many different offense grades. In addition to this consolidation of existing criminalization distinctions ("consolidated offense drafting"), states should also provide a more comprehensive collection of offense and offender characteristics that ought to be taken into account—what has been called "particularized offense grading."[68]

This proposed shift in offense drafting structure gives prosecutors and defense counsel a greater ability to strike a plea agreement that gives some credit for pleading guilty but does not require a plea bargain to be dramatically lenient simply because the only available lesser offense to plead guilty to requires a very substantial discount (as is often the case when pleading guilty to manslaughter from an original charge of second- or first-degree murder, a charge reduction often carrying more than a 50 percent reduction in sentence). Under the consolidated and particularized offense grading system, each offense would have numerous different offense grades, reflecting different levels of seriousness of the offense or culpability of the offender, and thus would allow a variety of lesser discounts as an inducement for a guilty plea. For example, under the more nuanced offense grading we propose, homicide might have quite a few offense grades that would allow a plea that reduced the offender's liability only 15 or 20 percent (for example, charging a second-degree murderer with a newly created third-degree murder charge instead of manslaughter). Such particularized offense grading would allow prosecutors to plea bargain within the category of crime that was actually committed instead of downgrading to a lesser offense that wrongly misrepresents the type of harm done. Of course, in some cases, the parties to a plea bargain may agree that more than a single grade discount is appropriate. Consolidated and particularized offense grading does not require a single grade discount but rather provides the negotiating parties with a full range of possibilities.

Consider another example. Assume, for instance, there are only three grades of assault—aggravated assault punishable by up to ten years, (unaggravated) assault carrying a one-year maximum punishment, and simple assault punishable by a maximum thirty days. Downgrading the offense by one grade in a plea bargain means a dramatic reduction in punishment available, a reduction likely to be seen as a failure of justice by many. However, if assault had more grades, the prosecutor could still bargain the conviction down a grade while only reducing the sentence by 15 to 25 percent.

It might be argued that defendants would refuse to take smaller sentence reductions under a particularized offense grading scheme than what they had become accustomed to under the current system, but clearly guilty offenders are likely to accept any deal that sees the severity of their charge reduced. It might also be argued that while particularized offense grading could help improve charge bargains, it does nothing to address pure sentencing bargains that negotiate recommended sentence, not charge. However, the discounts provided by most sentencing bargains are anchored by the range of recommended or allowable sentences for a given charge provided by statutory punishments or sentencing guidelines, so providing more possible charges within a given offense category would help raise the starting sentencing range for sentence bargains.

This reform would also lead to cleaner, clearer, and crisper legal codes, thus facilitating trials and simplifying jury instructions. For instance, instead of explaining to the jury multiple theft offenses scattered throughout the penal code, where each is defined and classified differently, the judge would only need to instruct the jury regarding a single theft offense, defined clearly in the first subsection, whose grade would depend upon the aggravating factors specified in the second subsection. Additionally, consolidating all variations and aggravating factors under one single offense would likely prompt legislatures to regrade the particular variations of the basic offense into a more rational form and to more easily identify and eliminate the inconsistent and irrational offense grading differences that commonly exist in today's scattered criminal codes.[69] A common irrationality, for instance, arises when conducts of materially different severity are punished as though they were the same. In Delaware, for example, the age of the offender is taken into consideration for rape yet not for sexual assault, and therefore sexually assaulting a child may carry the same maximum punishment regardless of whether the offender is an adult or a minor.[70]

Particularized offense grading has already been implemented in other coun-tries. For example, the Maldives adopted a criminal code predicated upon a combination of particularized offense grading and consolidated offense drafting in 2016.[71] The implementation of these two drafting techniques empowered prosecutors to close smaller cases at a quicker rate while simultaneously guaranteeing justice for victims.[72]

If US states adopted consolidated and particularized offense grading, it is likely many of the justice-frustrating plea bargains discussed in this chapter could have been avoided. For example, in the Adkins case, where the defendant raped his eleven-year-old daughter, prosecutors would likely have been able to secure a plea to rape (of a lesser grade) while offering a sentence reduction that involved at least some prison time. While Adkins might still have escaped the full punishment he deserved, he would have at least received a conviction more in line with his actual crimes. Similarly, particularized offense grading might have allowed mafia hitman Sammy Gravano to at least be officially convicted of murder, even if he received a generous several grade reduction within that murder charge.

CHAPTER 11

Unchecked Judicial Sentencing Discretion

A. INTRODUCTION

THE RULE OF LAW AIMS TO REDUCE THE power of individuals to arbitrarily decide when and how to punish crime. Codified criminal law expresses society's judgments about what conduct is criminal and how seriously it should be punished. However, unchecked judicial sentencing discretion can undermine justice and the goal of equal treatment under the rule of law by leading to dramatically different punishments for similar offenders committing similar offenses under similar circumstances.

While the criminal code typically provides a maximum allowable punishment for a given crime, judges often have broad discretion to decide what punishment should be imposed below that statutory maximum. Providing judges with some discretion in determining sentences is necessary because the special circumstances of a case may change the offender's overall blameworthiness and deserved punishment. But when unjustified leniency and disparities arise from individual judges' idiosyncrasies and subjective biases and preferences, the result can often be severe failures of justice. For example, when a man who repeatedly raped his daughter receives 1,503 years in jail from a judge in California, while the same crime receives only sixty days from a judge in Montana, the disparity suggests that "just" sentencing is often a game of roulette.[1]

Sentencing discretion has always existed in the American legal system, but the range of sentences was less nuanced in the past. Originally, discretion often involved deciding whether to apply a simple fixed sentence (such as corporal punishment or death).[2] However, the expansion of prison as a form of punishment meant a much greater range of sentences became possible, and judges soon came to have wide sentencing discretion with little guidance. Additionally, a lack of appellate review of lenient sentences (an unusual feature of the American sentencing system compared to other common law countries[3]) meant judges in practice had almost completely unchecked discretion in setting punishments. This wide discretion and the disparities in punishment it produced were eventually recognized as a problem in the latter half of the twentieth century, leading to many attempts to solve the problem, including mandatory minimum punishments and a variety of state and federal sentencing guidelines, examined in this chapter. While sentencing disparities have been reduced in some jurisdictions, the problem remains far from solved.

As chapter 3 discussed, desert-based justice calls for punishments to be assigned according to blameworthiness proportionality: proportionate punishment of different offenders should place each offender at their appropriate rank among all other offenders according to their relative blameworthiness. A justice system can easily lose credibility when this ordinal ranking is upset, and murderers or rapists end up being punished less than thieves or drug possessors. Even if all judges had the same exact beliefs about relative crime seriousness (which they do not), the ranking of punishments would still be upset by some judges choosing a lower or higher starting point for their own proportional punishment scale. How is a just ranking of sentences across the entire justice system to be achieved when so many different judges decide sentencing? One temptation in tackling the problem of sentencing disparities is to move to a system of fixed punishments, such as mandatory minimum sentences. However, a system with little or no flexibility in sentencing guarantees a continuous stream of injustices and failures of justice by ignoring the special circumstances of each crime. The challenge is to construct a means by which judicial sentencing discretion can be maintained yet guided according to societal understandings of desert.

To illustrate how unchecked sentencing discretion can produce serious failures of justice, consider three examples.

Case Example: Ronald Ebens

On June 19, 1982, twenty-seven-year-old Vincent Chin is preparing to enjoy his penultimate night of bachelorhood with three friends at a suburban strip club in Detroit.[4] At the club, he runs into forty-one-year-old Ronald Ebens and his stepson Michael Nitz. Ebens has recently been laid off by the local Chrysler plant, and he is angry about the competition posed by Japanese automakers. Mistak-

Figure 11.1. Vincent Chin was beaten to death on the night of his bachelor party, shortly after this photo was taken, 1982. Courtesy of Helen Zia/Estates of Vincent and Lily Chin.

ing Chin's Chinese ancestry as Japanese, Ebens begins hurling racist insults and a bar fight soon erupts, leading to all the men being ejected from the club. Ebens goes to retrieve a baseball bat from his car to finish the fight. Chin and his friends scatter. Ebens and his stepson then cruise around in their car looking for Chin and finally locate him outside a McDonald's. Jumping out of the car, the two men wrestle Chin to the ground and beat him to death with the bat.

The guests who should have attended Chin's wedding attend his funeral instead. The murderers get a generous plea bargain of manslaughter punishable by a maximum of fifteen years in prison. But Judge Charles Kaufman, claiming the men made an understandable mistake, concludes that prison wouldn't do them any good. He sentences the men to three years of probation and a $3,000 fine. Neither killer ever spends a day in prison for the murder of Vincent Chin.

Case Example: Dong Lu Chen

In August 1987, Dong Lu Chen, a Chinese immigrant working at a garment factory in New York City, finds out his wife is having an affair.[5] He restrains his rage, but two weeks later, after she refuses to have sex with him, Chen feels fresh rage surge. He leaves the room to search for a weapon and returns with a claw hammer. He then beats his petite ninety-nine-pound wife to death as she futilely tries to shield herself. When he is done, his wife's head is badly smashed and blood is spattered across the room. Chen meets his teenage son at the door and admits to the murder. Because Chen does not deny his guilt, his lawyer focuses on getting the lightest punishment possible. At a bench trial with a judge, Chen's lawyer presents an innovative cultural defense. The lawyer claims Chen's Chinese culture programmed him to kill his wife, and the absence of fellow villagers to restrain him resulted in the killing. He backs up this claim with the testimony of a college professor who once worked in China. Judge Edward Pincus is impressed with the dubious cultural defense and finds Chen liable for only second-degree involuntary manslaughter and sentences him to five years of probation, noting that Chen's teenage daughter's marriage prospects would suffer if her father was in prison.

Case Example: Drew Clinton

Sixteen-year-old Cameron Vaughan is invited to a 2021 Memorial Day party near her home in Quincy, Illinois.[6] At the party, she drinks alcohol and passes out. When she regains consciousness, a pillow is being pushed into her face, and Drew Clinton is forcibly raping her. She fights to breathe and escape, screaming for him to stop, but he does not. She

reports Clinton to police, and he is tried and convicted of criminal sexual assault at a bench trial. Vaughan's mother reports that her daughter attempts suicide after the assault.

In Illinois, the conviction carries a mandatory minimum sentence of four years in prison. But the judge disapproves of the application of the mandatory minimum sentence because Clinton is only eighteen, so he simply reverses the guilty verdict and Clinton walks free. Vaughan's father reports that his daughter now wishes she didn't report the assault: "It's worse now than it was [before], because not only does she not have her justice, but now she feels like she spoke up for nothing, you know that hurts." The case shows the dangers not only of unchecked judicial power (in this instance the ability to overturn a bench conviction at sentencing for reasons unrelated to guilt or innocence) but also of fixed sentencing laws that can motivate judges or juries to acquit guilty defendants instead of imposing what they see as an unjustly harsh punishment.

B. COMPETING INTERESTS

One can identify reasonable competing interests on each side of the question concerning the breadth of judicial sentencing discretion.

Interests Supporting Broad Judicial Sentencing Discretion

- *Individualized Just Sentences.* A just sentence depends on the individual circumstances of the crime and the offender, so strict limitations on judicial discretion risk creating overly harsh or lenient sentences. Because ordinary people's judgments of justice are highly nuanced and depend upon a wide variety of factors relating to the offense and offender, it is unlikely any rigid set of rules could fully capture these complex community judgments.

- *Promoting Goals Other than Doing Justice.* If society wishes to promote other principles of punishment than desert, such as deterrence or incapacitation, sentencing discretion is essential as those principles require wide flexibility without regard to justice. Of course, leaving it to individual judges to decide what goals to pursue in sentencing will inevitably lead to serious disparity among judges in similar cases.

- *Changing Societal Views of Desert.* Society may consider certain crimes more or less blameworthy as time passes, so sentencing flexibility may allow judges to track society's view of justice within the framework of the law. However, there is little evidence suggesting that judges attempt to track changing societal beliefs as opposed to their own views of justice. And many will argue that the process of altering punishments as societal views change is a task better handled by legislatures than by individual sentencing judges.

- *Avoiding False Findings of Innocence.* Mandatory sentences and inflexible sentencing guidelines sometimes lead to a false finding of innocence to avoid the imposition of what some actors in the justice system believe to be an overly harsh sentence (recall the previous Drew Clinton case example). Prosecutors might refuse to file charges, a jury might wrongly acquit, or a judge might overturn a verdict all in order to avoid imposing a mandatory sentence that they think does not match the crime or the criminal. This is especially an issue with habitual offender laws such as "three strikes" statutes that impose serious statutory punishment for

repeated offenses even if the most recent offense, the one for which the offender is being sentenced, is relatively minor.[7] Sentencing discretion allows prosecutors, juries, and judges to focus on the extent of an offender's actual blameworthiness instead of having to weigh the seriousness of a justice failure from a false acquittal against the injustice of a mandatory sentence.

Interests Supporting Restricting Broad Judicial Sentencing Discretion

- *Greater Desert-Based Justice.* Because many judges prefer to use non-desert distributive principles for criminal sentencing, restricting such sentencing discretion in favor of desert-based guidelines can result in more just sentences. Even when a judge tries to prioritize desert without guidelines, that judge may have an idiosyncratic view of what factors contribute to blameworthiness (recall the judge in Dong Lu Chen's case accepting a cultural defense that Chinese men are programmed to kill their wives in cases of infidelity).

- *Fairness and Equality.* Unchecked sentencing discretion increases the disparity in sentences for the same crime across jurisdictions and even among judges within the same jurisdiction. These disparities make justice seem like a game of chance—with the sentence depending on the luck in the sentencing judge one draws—which in turn seriously undermines the criminal justice system's moral credibility with the community. As discussed in chapter 3, reduced moral credibility means less deference, acquiescence, and internalization of the criminal law's norms. In addition to disparities caused by different sentencing philosophies, sentencing disparities can also emerge due to the conscious or unconscious biases of judges, and stricter sentencing guidelines can help reduce such disparities.[8]

- *Avoiding De Facto Decriminalization.* Sentencing discretion allows judges to go lightly on crimes they personally consider to be less serious than the law and society do, thereby essentially rewriting the criminal code. For example, some judges have chosen to practically decriminalize some drug offenses and others have essentially decriminalized theft.[9] Sentencing discretion in rape cases has also commonly let rapists off with less punishment than what society would consider just.

- *Upholding the Democratic Role of Legislatures.* The criminal justice system is supposed to be built around laws codifying the views of society on unacceptable behavior and its relative seriousness. Criminalization authority must be reserved for legislatures, which are the most representative bodies of government (recall chapter 2's discussion of the legality principle). Sentencing discretion can undermine the role of democratically elected legislatures in favor of the personal preferences of often unaccountable judges. The more statutory guidelines restrict judicial sentencing discretion, the more likely society will see the resulting punishments as matching its democratic judgment of what is just.

- *More Deterrence and Less Crime.* When criminals believe punishments are a game of roulette depending on the whims of the judge, the criminal law's deterrent effect is seriously undercut because the threat of punishment becomes less significant as it becomes less predictable. Increasing predictability in sentencing outcomes makes deterrence more effective.

C. THE NATURE AND EXTENT OF THE PROBLEM

Unchecked judicial sentencing discretion leads to widespread sentencing disparities in similar cases. While mandatory minimums are effective at reducing leniency, they are increasingly unpopular due to their creation of many injustices. Sentencing guidelines can reduce sentencing disparities while preserving some level of limited discretion, but guidelines vary widely in their effectiveness depending on how detailed and binding they are. The problem of sentencing discretion is particularly pronounced at the state level where few effective guidelines exist. It is also worth noting that mandatory minimums and sentencing guidelines are routinely thwarted by prosecutors changing their charging and plea bargaining practices to get around statutorily recommended or required punishments.[10]

The Problem of Sentencing Disparity

Judicial sentencing disparities can arise from many sources, from differing judicial sentencing philosophies to the quality of a judge's day. The resulting disparities can significantly affect the length of a prison sentence or even the chance of getting a prison sentence. Judge Marvin Frankel's 1973 book *Law Without Order* was instrumental in drawing public attention to the problem.[11] Since then, numerous studies have confirmed how disparate, lenient, and random judicial sentencing decisions can be. Supreme Court Justice Stephen Breyer noted one of the more famous studies on the subject:

> In a well-known 1974 Second Circuit "experiment," fifty district court judges each sentenced twenty offenders on the basis of the same set of pre-sentence reports. And the results diverged dramatically. Where one judge sentenced

a defendant to three years, another judge chose twenty years; where one imposed a suspended sentence for an immigration crime, another imposed a three-year prison term. The Department of Justice, later repeating the experiment with 208 federal judges, found them unanimous about whether to impose a prison term in only three of 16 hypothetical cases. It also found serious disparity as to length. For example, while the judges sentencing one particular hypothetical fraud defendant imposed a 1-year prison term on average, one judge gave that same defendant 15 years.[12]

These sentencing disparities were not lessened even by having experienced judges or by having judges confer with other judges on a sentencing council before sentencing.[13]

Mandatory Minimum Sentences

The bluntest way of curbing sentencing discretion and sentencing disparities is the use of mandatory minimum sentences that completely remove judicial discretion in deciding how low a sentence can be. All states, as well as the federal government, have passed mandatory minimum sentences for at least some offenses or categories of offenders.[14] Mandatory minimums are a fairly recent concept, with Congress passing the first mandatory minimum in 1914, setting a five-year sentence for manufacturing opium for smoking.[15] These early federal mandatory minimums were actually repealed, however, and it was only in the 1970s and 1980s that legislatures began to enact currently existing mandatory minimums in response to a widely recognized crisis in sentencing disparities and a rise in violent crime rates.[16] By 1991, the US Congress had created almost one hundred mandatory

minimums across sixty criminal statutes, which accounted for 44 percent of federal criminal cases.[17] Especially popular was the adoption of mandatory minimum sentences for repeat offenders. Mandatory minimum sentencing reached peak adoption around 1994 when forty-one states applied mandatory sentencing for repeat or habitual offenders, as well as for crimes accompanied by the possession of a firearm.[18] A significant majority of states also had mandatory minimums for drug offenses and drunk driving.[19]

In more recent years, mandatory minimums have begun to lose favor as many have highlighted the injustices they can cause. For example, one third-time felon in Texas received a life sentence for the crime of defrauding a customer of $120 after promising but failing to repair an air conditioner (his previous two felonies amounted to stealing just over $100).[20] The general scholarly and legal consensus is that mandatory minimums represent a crude attempt to solve a complex problem, as they cannot consider many important circumstances of each case.[21] It does not advance justice to fix some lenient sentences by guaranteeing other offenders receive unjustly harsh sentences. By 2014, at least twenty-nine states had taken steps to relax mandatory minimums.[22] While the popularity and usage of mandatory minimum sentences is waning, they continue to dictate sentences for some offenses at the federal level and in numerous states. Many states and the federal system use both sentencing guidelines and mandatory minimums.

Federal Sentencing Guidelines

A more nuanced approach to reducing the problems of judicial sentencing discretion takes the form of sentencing guidelines that provide judges with ranges of appropriate sentences as well as factors to consider in choosing a specific sentence. The most comprehensive sentencing guidelines exist at the federal level and were drafted by the United States Federal Sentencing Commission created in 1984.[23] The guidelines take into account the seriousness of the offense and the defendant's criminal history.[24] The guidelines provide a relatively narrow range for each subcategory of offense and "the maximum of the range . . . shall not exceed the minimum of the range by more than the greater of 25% or six months."[25] The federal guidelines were initially mandatory under the Sentencing Reform Act of 1984, and judges could not depart from them except for certain specific reasons such as if the prosecutor requested a lighter sentence due to a plea bargain or if judges provided a written explanation of case circumstances not considered by the guidelines. Additionally, such deviations from the guidelines based on unconsidered circumstances were subject to appellate review under a *de novo* standard allowing the appellate court to consider the sentence without deference to the sentencing judge's opinion. This creation of appellate review, especially under a *de novo* standard (added by Congress in 2003), helped incentivize judges to stay within the guidelines while still allowing flexibility for exceptional case circumstances.

For a while, it seemed that the problem of judicial sentencing discretion had been solved, or at least significantly reduced, at the federal level as all sentences fell within the specified range unless made more lenient by plea bargaining or unusual case circumstances. While there was still a minor problem of inter-judge sentencing disparities within the narrow guideline range, this was not significant as 96.6 percent of federal judges sentenced at the bottom of the recommended range.[26]

But in 2005, the Supreme Court held in *United States v. Booker* that the federal sentencing guidelines violated the Sixth Amendment right to trial by jury because the guidelines allowed judges to enhance punishment beyond the prescribed statutory maximum based on facts not submitted and proved to the jury beyond a reasonable doubt. Such sentence enhancements could be based on facts (such as drug or weapon possession) merely shown to the sentencing judge and proved by a preponderance of evidence.[27] The Court rejected the obvious remedy of engrafting the Sixth Amendment requirement onto the statute by simply requiring prosecutors to prove all relevant sentencing facts to the jury. Instead the Court significantly altered the guidelines by excising two provisions from the Sentencing Reform Act. The first change was removing the mandatory nature of the federal sentencing guidelines, thus rendering them effectively advisory, meaning the act "requires a sentencing court to consider Guidelines ranges . . . but it permits the court to tailor the sentence in light of other statutory concerns as well."[28] The second change was replacing the standard of *de novo* appellate review for sentences falling outside the guideline range with a standard of "reasonableness"[29] that provides greater deference to the sentencing judge and makes it easier for lenient sentences to withstand scrutiny.

While these changes damaged the full effectiveness of the guidelines, the remaining requirements of providing a written justification for departing from the guidelines and the possibility of any appellate review still serve to ensure compliance with the guidelines in most cases. After the Court's decision in *Booker*, the percentage of federal sentences that fell outside the guideline's range increased only modestly. Prior to *Booker*, the out-of-guidelines rate was 27.8 percent, and post-*Booker* the rate grew to 37.8 percent.[30] Most of these departures were due to increased leniency as the percentage of cases where the judge elected to sentence below the guidelines grew from 5.2 to 12.5 percent post-*Booker*.[31] Perhaps more troublingly, a study of federal sentences post-*Booker* showed that interjudge sentencing disparities (a measure of variability in sentences) doubled as judges used the advisory nature of the guidelines as an invitation to give more weight to their personal sentencing choices.[32] Unfortunately, the severity of a criminal's punishment is now more dependent on the individual sentencing judge than it was before the *Booker* decision.

However, while the *Booker* decision reopened the problem of sentencing disparities at the federal level, the federal sentencing guidelines, even in their advisory role, have clearly been effective at taming the problem of wide variations in sentences outside the guideline range.

State Diversity in Adopting Sentencing Guidelines

The problem of unchecked judicial sentencing discretion is greatest at the state level because most states do not have sentencing guidelines, and many state guidelines that do exist are noticeably less specific and binding compared to the federal guidelines (which though advisory still require written justification for sentences outside the recommended range). A 2008 report by the National Center for State Courts found

that twenty-one US states currently have sentencing guidelines that range from vague to specific and purely advisory to presumptive.[33] The report rated the states based on how binding the guidelines were, with only five states implementing guidelines that were described as mandatory in the statute (though deviations were allowed for special circumstances). The scores were calculated based on six criteria with 0, 1, or 2 points given on each issue, with the higher score for greater guidance.[34] The state guidelines ranked as follows: Ohio (1), Wisconsin (1), Missouri (2), Alabama (3), DC (3), Tennessee (3), Arkansas (4), Louisiana (5), Utah (6), Virginia (6), Alaska (7), Maryland (7), Massachusetts (7), Michigan (8), Pennsylvania (9), Washington (10), Kansas (10), Oregon (10), Minnesota (11), and North Carolina (12).[35] The remaining twenty-nine states had no guidelines at the time of the study.

As shown by the preponderance of low scores, even states with sentencing guidelines do not provide nearly as comprehensive or binding guidance as the federal guidelines, with only the highest scoring of these states having guidelines anywhere near as comprehensive as the federal system. For example, North Carolina also requires written justification if judges wish to sentence outside the recommended sentencing range. Also similar to the federal guidelines, North Carolina requires that sentencing judges complete a worksheet that lists the details of the offense, the corresponding guidelines applied, and the sentence granted, with the state sentencing commission regularly reviewing and reporting on judges' decisions.[36] By contrast, many state sentencing guidelines, such as Ohio's, do little but provide suggested sentences or factors to consider. Additionally, in Ohio, judges are permitted to depart from the guidelines and "substantial and compelling reasons" for the departure are not required. [37] Moreover, in states like Ohio with purely advisory guidelines, abuses of judicial discretion can go almost unnoticed given the lack of accountability and data collection. [38]

State guidelines also have varying degrees of precision. Most state guidelines are broad with general crime categories and little consideration of mitigating or aggravating circumstances. See appendix A of this chapter for a typical state sentencing guideline chart (Minnesota's) showing how unspecific state sentencing guidelines usually are. The eleven severity levels actually match the standard number of offense grading categories in most modern American criminal codes, so the guidelines provide no more nuance in assessing offense seriousness than is already contained in the state's criminal code. Compare this to the federal sentencing guidelines in appendix B, which sort offenses into four times that number of offense seriousness categories.

Most problematically, the majority of states (twenty-nine) have no sentencing guidelines of any sort and judges have complete sentencing discretion outside of mandatory minimums, which still exist for some offenses in most states. Additionally, most states do not collect and monitor sentencing data, making it difficult to determine the extent of sentencing disparities, which are presumably quite large.

The Effectiveness of State Sentencing Guidelines

As a result of being significantly less detailed and binding, state sentencing guidelines are commonly less effective than the federal guidelines at reducing sentencing disparities. [39] That said, sentencing guidelines—even when easy to ignore[40]—are better than nothing as they have been shown by a number of studies to decrease interjudge sentencing disparities. [41] The harder it is to depart from the guidelines, the stronger the reduction in disparities. This phenomenon was documented in a recent study of more than 200,000 criminal sentences given by 355 judges in Alabama between 2002 and 2015. [42] Alabama presented a unique natural experiment during this period because from 2002 to 2006, the state had no sentencing guidelines for any crimes. Then in 2006, the state introduced purely voluntary sentencing guidelines for non-violent crimes, which gave judges a starting suggested sentence. In 2013, Alabama made the guidelines presumptive for some non-violent offenses, which meant judges could not depart from the guideline range unless they could cite a specific aggravating or mitigating factor in the case. [43] The study found, among other things, that the adoption of presumptive sentencing guidelines "coincided with around eight-to-twelve-month reductions in race-based sentencing disparities and substantial reductions in inter-judge sentencing disparities across all classes of offenders."[44]

Other studies of state sentencing guidelines have been more pessimistic on their ability to reduce disparities. For example, a study of Pennsylvania sentencing disparities by gender (whereby women received more lenient sentences for the same crimes than men) found that the introduction of voluntary sentencing guidelines did nothing to reduce the disparities. [45] Studies also show that sentencing guidelines are only effective at reducing sentencing disparities among judges willing to accept them. The Alabama study found that advisory sentencing guidelines did little to affect the behavior of judges who had a history of particularly punitive or particularly lenient sentencing, who were willing to make the effort to get around even presumptive guidelines.[46]

Overall, studies suggest that carefully formulated sentencing guidelines can help reduce inappropriate leniency and unjustified disparities, but their current drafting and adoption at the state level is woefully inadequate at stopping the steady flow of justice failures generated by unchecked sentencing discretion. Not only does the US federal system provide a better example of comprehensive sentencing guidelines that states could imitate, but the usefulness of sentencing guidelines is also reflected in many foreign countries including the Netherlands, Canada, the United Kingdom, and Ireland.[47] By failing to adopt comprehensive sentencing guidelines, many US states are stuck in the past and tolerating unnecessary sentencing disparities and justice failures.

D. WHEN JUDICIAL SENTENCING DISCRETION DAMAGES THE CRIMINAL LAW'S MORAL CREDIBILITY: THE EXAMPLE OF RAPE

Judicial sentencing discretion produces failures of justice across all crimes, but it can be particularly harmful to the law's moral credibility when it affects historically underpunished crimes such as rape. Unjustly lenient sentences for rape have outraged victims, reduced crime reporting, emboldened perpetrators, and undermined the criminal law's credibility with many in the community.

Case Example: Stephan Addison and Benjamin Butler

On August 7, 2005, twenty-seven-year-old Stephan Addison and twenty-eight-year-old Benjamin Butler are drunk at a tavern in Ripon, Wisconsin.[48] The two friends have lost their car keys and need a ride home. Luckily, Addison hits it off with twenty-seven-year-old Dawn Paez on the dance floor, and after the two men reveal they are respectable lawyers she agrees to drive the tipsy men home. Once in her car, the two men start propositioning and groping Paez. She stops the car at a public boat dock to let them out, but they pull her out of the driver's seat, rip off her clothes, and take turns raping her on the hood of the car. Paez manages to bolt free after Addison starts forcing her to perform oral sex, but he quickly catches her and throws her

Figure 11.2. Stephan Addison, a local lawyer, was given a very light sentence for his participation in a rape, 2005. Photo by Green Lake County Sheriff's office, from Cary Spivak, "Lawyers' Licenses Suspended by State Supreme Court: Men Were Accused in 2005 Sexual Assault," *Milwaukee Journal Sentinel*, April 4, 2012, https://archive.jsonline.com/news/wisconsin/lawyer-accused-of-rape-has-license-suspended-for-two-months-vd4sarq-146092705.html/.

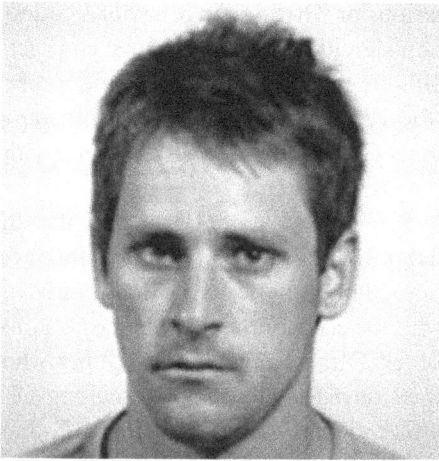

Figure 11.3. Benjamin Butler, also a lawyer, was Addison's codefendant and received an even lighter sentence, 2005. Photo by Green Lake County Sheriff's Office, from Cary Spivak, "Lawyers' Licenses Suspended by State Supreme Court: Men Were Accused in 2005 Sexual Assault," *Milwaukee Journal Sentinel*, April 4, 2012, https://archive.jsonline .com/news/wisconsin/lawyer-accused-of-rape-has-lic ense-suspended-for-two-months-vd4sarq-1460927 05.html/.

back against the hood of the car. Finally, the men let the crying woman go. They are quickly arrested but claim the sex was consensual. After consulting the victim, prosecutors strike a plea agreement in which the men plead guilty to reckless endangerment and sexual gratification in public, carrying a maximum sentence of up to ten years. Judge William Mc-Monigal accepts the deal but views any lengthy prison time as being too harsh. He instead sentences Addison to thirty days of jail with work release and gives Butler only community service.[49]

Justice Failures in Rape Sentencing

Unchecked judicial sentencing discretion has the potential to cause large-scale failures of justice in rape cases by diminishing the seriousness with which such offenses are viewed, discouraging victims from reporting rapes, and un-

dercutting the criminal law's credibility with the community and its deterrent effect. Judges too often participate in a type of de facto "decriminalization" of rape by not taking rape cases seriously and by granting perpetrators exceedingly light sentences. This can happen when a judge allows their personal opinions about what constitutes "true rape" to affect sentences for convicted rapists. For example, in the 1980 case *People v. Guthreau*, the judge sentenced a forcible rape perpetrator to a year in jail (which in fact meant seven months because of the standard early release for "good time" credit).[50] The judge's rationale for the sentence was that "after all, [the victim] wasn't hurt."[51] The judge did not consider lifelong trauma a "hurt" worth considering. Such sentences are not limited to male judges. Female judges have also handed down lenient sentences. In a 1991 Indiana rape case, the female judge suspended a convicted rapist's sentence and stated that she "thought it was obvious it was non-consensual sex, but [she didn't] believe it was a violent act as most people think of rape."[52]

Also problematic in rape cases is the tendency of some judges to discount the seriousness of the offense if they see the victim as promiscuous. A Washington state judge claimed that "the law was never intended to protect a tramp" after granting a rapist the minimum sentence, which the judge believed was much too harsh.[53] The rape survivor was in fact a twelve year old who had been given drugs and alcohol by the rapist to "extort sex."[54] In another case involving the rape of a twelve year old, a Nebraska judge placed the perpetrator on four years of probation because the judge considered the girl the "aggressor" because, in his view, she "made advances."[55] Recall also the case of Stacey Rambold (mentioned in chapter 1), a high school teacher who received only thirty days in jail from a judge who believed Rambold's fourteen-year-old victim was largely to blame.

Such attitudes among judges seriously undermine the law's message regarding the seriousness of rape. Kristen Houser, chief public affairs officer for the National Sexual Violence Resource Center, believes that such light sentences are "interpreted by many people as a value of the claim" and suggest both disbelief of the victim and that rape is not deemed worthy of serious punishment.[56] If rape is treated by judges as a "lighter crime" and rapists are given more lenient sentences, victims can be easily disillusioned and report fewer rapes in the first place, allowing even more failures of justice to occur.[57] John Wilkinson, an attorney advisor for a non-profit focused on prosecuting gender-based violence, believes that lenient rape sentences make victims feel that they are wasting their time by reporting crimes in the first place.[58] This is likely a factor in the non-reporting that explains part of why only twenty-eight out of every one thousand cases (2.8 percent) of sexual assault result in a felony conviction.[59]

While judges may not undersentence rape at a higher rate than other crimes (comparative data is difficult to come by), the undersentencing of rape is likely to be particularly damaging to the law's moral credibility with the community as it casts doubt on victims of a crime that has historically been treated less seriously than it deserves. Even a lenient sentence for murder is unlikely to cause society to view killing as permissible or to decrease homicide reporting, but lenient sentences for rape can raise questions such as whether rape is all that

serious or whether the behavior in question should be seen as criminal conduct. This in turn causes those in the public who care strongly about justice in rape cases to become more disillusioned with the justice system.

Sometimes the public discontent with judicial sentencing can boil over into action. Many Americans were so infuriated with the six-month jail sentence given to Brock Turner, a Stanford swimmer who was convicted of sexually assaulting fellow student Chanel Miller in 2015, that a petition requesting the judge's removal acquired more than 240,000 signatures.[60] The judge was subsequently successfully recalled from office over the lenient decision, which itself was partly due to lenient sentencing guidelines for sexual assault.[61] Still, Turner's sentence seemed positively just when compared to other even more appalling examples. Irate lawmakers and Oklahoma residents called for the removal of a judge who in 2009, in the case of the rape of a four-year-old girl that would normally call for a twenty-year sentence, imposed a sentence of one year.[62]

E. PUBLIC COMPLAINTS ABOUT UNCHECKED JUDICIAL SENTENCING DISCRETION

Even beyond the crime of rape, examples of lenient judicial sentencing are a constant source of public dissatisfaction and cynicism about the criminal justice system. For example, the lack of prison time for Vincent Chin's killers (recall the case example at the start of the chapter) triggered widespread public outcry and protest by Asian Americans, who described the sentence of a fine as a "$3000 license to kill."[63] Historically, many in the legal system have seen sentencing as "the least understood, the most fraught with irrational discrepancies, and the most in need of improvement of any phase in our criminal justice system."[64] The public too has historically expressed deep dissatisfaction with judicial sentencing, and not just in America. In fact, as many as 70 to 80 percent of people in "a variety of Western countries" feel that sentencing is too lenient.[65] In 1989, polls found that 84 percent of American respondents felt that sentences were too lenient.[66] Usually the public places much of the blame for leniency on judges.[67] A 2006 survey by the National Center for State Courts found that 48 percent of American adults believed that sentencing in their state was too lenient.[68] Of this group, 38 percent believed that judges, rather than elected officials, were primarily responsible for this.

Public concern regarding sentencing discretion is greatest when it comes to violent crimes. For example, the same 2006 survey found that while 39 percent of Americans believed that sentencing for non-violent crimes was too lenient, 65 percent believed that sentencing for violent crimes was too lenient.[69] As a result of such opinions, 73 percent of Americans surveyed in 2006 thought that mandatory sentences for violent crimes were "a good idea," though this and other studies reveal that Americans simultaneously believe the punishments for non-violent crimes are too harsh.[70] Public opinion is often far more nuanced than a survey question such as "Is the justice system too tough on crime?" can reveal. Many Americans believe parts of the system (such as punishments for drug offenses) are too harsh while other parts (such as punishments for rape and murder) are too lenient.[71]

Unfortunately, more recent surveys rarely solicit public opinion on the sentencing of violent crime specifically. However, what little there is suggests that past views still prevail. A 2016 study concluded that "even as many voters express support for rehabilitation, they express no less support for 'giving criminals the punishment they deserve.'"[72] Extrapolating from past data, it is likely a majority of the public still views leniency in the sentencing of violent crime as a problem, especially given the recent surge in violence across America since 2020.

While there seems to be a general dissatisfaction with current American sentencing practices, the sophisticated and nuanced nature of ordinary people's intuitions of justice, as discussed in chapter 3, means the solution is not simply to make sentences for a broad category of crimes (such as violent versus non-violent) more or less harsh. The sophisticated intuitions of justice revealed in social science research suggest that community members prefer sentences that weigh a wide variety of specific case circumstances that determine an offender's blameworthiness proportionality. As a result, more detailed sentencing guidelines, informed by societal views of desert, are likely to satisfy the public more in the long term than simply making all punishments more or less severe.

F. REFORMS

Many reforms have been proposed to mitigate the continuing problem of unchecked judicial sentencing discretion.

Expand Mandatory Minimums. While the federal government and at least twenty-nine states have rolled back some mandatory minimum sentencing since 2000,[73] many still believe mandatory minimums are the best way to end sentencing disparities and unjustly lenient sentences.[74] Proponents of this reform point to the clear effect mandatory minimums had on increasing sentences for violent crimes to be more in line with public views of justice.[75] Additionally, many who might otherwise oppose mandatory minimums for most crimes support them for addressing problems in rape sentencing.[76] However, as we argued earlier, mandatory minimums are an undesirable tool because they prevent an individualized blameworthiness analysis for each offender and so guarantee a continuing stream of injustices.[77] Mandatory minimums are avoided by most other Western countries for this reason, and their previous implementation in America reflected valuations of crime deterrence and incapacitation over desert-based justice.[78]

Make Sentencing Guidelines Mandatory Again. As mentioned previously, the original federal sentencing guidelines created in 1984 were mandatory until they were made advisory and presumptive by the Supreme Court in *United States v. Booker* in 2005.[79] However, the federal sentencing guidelines (and any state guidelines) could avoid constitutional infirmity and become truly mandatory again simply by requiring that all facts considered under the sentencing guidelines be proved to the jury beyond a reasonable doubt. Such a reform could require slightly lengthening jury trials as many facts considered in sentencing (such as previous criminal history) usually cannot be shown to the jury before a verdict. Once a jury has already been impaneled and heard the facts of the case, the additional time needed to consider additional specific sentencing guideline facts should be relatively minor. Besides, as discussed in the previous chapter on plea bargaining, only a tiny fraction of cases actually go to trial. As discussed earlier, mandatory sentencing guidelines can allow for departures in specific unusual circumstances, but the presence of *de novo* appellate review of out-of-guideline sentences would likely limit such departures to cases where society would see an out-of-guideline sentence as appropriate.

Decrease Sentencing Disparities Through Judicial Comparisons. If there was inadequate support for the adoption of sentencing guidelines, one could decrease sentencing disparities among judges by providing judges with regular statistics on the sentencing patterns of their colleagues and how their sentencing compared.[80] Such an approach could be useful if sentencing disparities result in part from judicial ignorance of the typical sentence and would bring knowledge and peer pressure to bear in reducing disparity. However, while such a reform might mitigate disparities caused by ignorance, it would not correct for disparities caused by differing judicial philosophies of punishment, which is the cause of many of the most concerning disparities.

Provide Multijudge Panels. One possible way to reduce the impact of a single judge's whims on sentencing would be to have sentences issued by a multijudge panel's consensus or average of individual sentences. This would reduce individual arbitrariness but would be expensive to implement given the already high workloads of judges, and as mentioned previously, sentencing councils have not been found to be very effective at reducing disparity.[81]

Allow for Greater Appellate Review of Sentences. In the American system, except in very narrow circumstances, prosecutors cannot appeal what they see as even a highly inappropriate sentence because defendants are thought to have the right to be free of the threat of additional consequences once the initial sentencing has occurred in the trial court.[82] (Recall chapter 2's discussion of the current interpretation of the double jeopardy clause.) While defendants can appeal sentences they believe are unreasonably excessive, prosecutors generally cannot appeal sentences they believe are unreasonably lenient. (As noted previously, sentences that fall outside federal and some state sentencing guidelines sometimes can be appealed under a reasonableness standard of review.[83]) One way to combat unjustly lenient (and harsh) sentences caused by judicial sentencing discretion would be to allow prosecutors (or defendants) the right to appeal any sentence. If the sentence falls within the guideline range, the standard of review would be one of reasonableness (where deference is given to the lower court), but if the sentence falls outside the guideline range, the standard would be *de novo* review (where no deference to the lower court is given). Recall that before *Booker*, federal sentences outside the guideline range could be appealed under a standard of *de novo* review.

Some variations on expanding appellate review include making appellate review of sentences outside sentencing guidelines mandatory. Interjudge disparities within the guideline range could also potentially be addressed by allowing for appeal or marking for automatic appeal any sentence that is sufficiently disparate from the median sentence given by all judges, though this would require better data collection and review of sentences.

G. RECOMMENDATION: ADOPT COMPREHENSIVE PRESUMPTIVE SENTENCING GUIDELINES (AS IN THE FEDERAL SYSTEM)

Our recommendation for reforming sentencing discretion is the adoption of comprehensive and binding sentencing guidelines similar to those that currently exist in the federal system.[84] This approach would seem to be the best proven way to reduce the problem of unchecked judicial sentencing discretion without generating the injustices that make mandatory minimums so problematic. The relative success of the federal sentencing guidelines at reducing sentencing disparities and unjustified lenient sentencing should be copied by all state legislatures. The creation of such comprehensive guidelines should be undertaken by a state sentencing commission composed of qualified legal experts (similar to the federal sentencing commission), with the legislature retaining the authority to block the new guidelines within ninety days before they go into effect.

If the sentencing guidelines are comprehensive and specific, as are the federal guidelines (including relevant factors such as the criminal history of the offender, the particular variation of the offense, the age of the offender, etc.), then judges can be given a relatively narrow range within which to sentence. The resulting guidelines should not be mandatory but rather presumptive in that judges could still deviate when a case presents unusual circumstances not considered in the guidelines, but judges ought to be obliged to provide a written explanation that justifies the reasons for the departure. Any deviation should be subject to appellate review (which would normally mean by a multijudge panel) employing at least a reasonableness standard (if not a stronger standard such as *de novo*).

This proposal would solve most of the disparities and unjust leniencies caused by unchecked judicial sentencing discretion. Such guidelines strike a reasonable balance between ensuring uniform punishments across similar criminal cases and similar offenders while still allowing variations based on special circumstances that can arise.

It is easy to see how such guidelines would have prevented the unjust sentences in the cases of Vincent Chen and Dong Lu Chen where murderers escaped without prison time. Even if the judges had gone against the guidelines and imposed the same sentences, such highly inappropriate leniency would have fallen below any sentencing guideline range and would have led to appellate review, which would have overturned them under even a reasonableness standard of review. Sentencing guidelines would also have avoided the justice failure in the case of Drew Clinton, who had his sexual assault conviction overturned by a judge who opposed applying the mandatory minimum sentence. If sentencing guidelines had governed the case instead of mandatory minimums, the judge would

merely have issued a lenient sentence, which might have been overturned on appeal in favor of a more just sentence. Sentencing guidelines are not a perfect solution to all problems related to judicial sentencing discretion, but they are proven to significantly reduce the frequency and extent of inappropriate leniency and disparity.

APPENDIX A: MINNESOTA SENTENCING GUIDELINE GRID

Presumptive sentence lengths are in months. Italicized numbers within the grid denote the discretionary range within which a court may sentence without the sentence being deemed a departure. Offenders with stayed felony sentences may be subject to local confinement (see table 11.1 below).

APPENDIX B: UNITED STATES SENTENCING COMMISSION GUIDELINE TABLE[85]

Table 11.1. Minnesota Sentencing Guidelines Grid

Severity Level of Conviction Offense (Example offenses listed in italics)		Criminal History Score						
		0	1	2	3	4	5	6 or more
Murder, 2nd Degree (Intentional; Drive-By Shootings)	11	306 *261–367*	326 *278–391*	346 *295–415*	366 *312–439*	386 *329–463*	406 *346–480[2]*	426 *363–480[2]*
Murder, nd Degree (Unintentional) Murder, 3rd Degree (Depraved Mind)	10	150 *128–180*	165 *141–198*	180 *153–216*	195 *166–234*	210 *179–252*	225 *192–270*	240 *204–288*
Murder, 3rd Degree (Drugs) Assault, 1st Degree (Great Bodily Harm)	9	86 *74–103*	98 *84–117*	110 *94–132*	122 *104–146*	134 *114–160*	146 *125–175*	158 *135–189*
Agg. Robbery, 1st Degree Burglary, 1st (w/ Weapon or Assault)	8	48 *41–57*	58 *50–69*	68 *58–81*	78 *67–93*	88 *75–105*	98 *84–117*	108 *92–129*
Felony DWI Financial Exploitation of a Vulnerable Adult	7	36	42	48	54 *46–64*	60 *51–72*	66 *57–79*	72 *62–84[2,3]*
Assault, 2nd Degree Burglary, 1st Degree (Occupied Dwelling)	6	21	27	33	39 *34–46*	45 *39–54*	51 *44–61*	57 *49–68*
Residential Burglary Simple Robbery	5	18	23	28	33 *29–39*	38 *33–45*	43 *37–51*	48 *41–57*
Nonresidential Burglary	4	12[1]	15	18	21	24 *21–28*	27 *23–32*	30 *26–36*
Theft Crimes (Over $5,000)	3	12[1]	13	15	17	19 *17–22*	21 *18–25*	23 *20–27*
Theft Crimes ($5,000 or less) Check Forgery ($251–$2,500)	2	12[1]	12[1]	13	15	17	19	21 *18–25*
Assault, 4th Degree Fleeing a Peace Officer	1	12[1]	12[1]	12[1]	13	15	17	19 *17–22*

*12[1] = One year and one day

*Unshaded cells = Presumptive commitment to state imprisonment. First-degree murder has a mandatory life sentence and is excluded from the Guidelines under Minn. Stat. § 609.185. See section 2.E, for policies regarding those sentences controlled by law.

*Shaded cells = Presumptive stayed sentence; at the discretion of the court, up to one year of confinement and other non-jail sanctions can be imposed as conditions of probation. However, certain offenses in the shaded are of the Grid always carry a presumptive commitment to state prison. See sections 2.C and 2.E.

Note. Presumptive sentence lengths are in months. Italicized numbers within the grid denote the discretionary range within which a court may sentence without the sentence being deemed a departure. Offenders with stayed felony sentences may be subject to local confinement.

Table 11.2. U.S. Sentencing Table (in months of imprisonment)

	Offense Level	Criminal History Category (Criminal History Points)					
		I (0 or 1)	II (2 or 3)	III (4, 5, 6)	IV (7, 8, 9)	V (10, 11, 12)	VI (13 or more)
Zone A	1	0–6	0–6	0–6	0–6	0–6	0–6
	2	0–6	0–6	0–6	0–6	0–6	1–7
	3	0–6	0–6	0–6	0–6	2–8	3–9
	4	0–6	0–6	0–6	2–8	4–10	6–12
	5	0–6	0–6	1–7	4–10	6–12	9–15
	6	0–6	1–7	2–8	6–12	9–15	12–18
	7	0–6	2–8	4–10	8–14	12–18	15–21
	8	0–6	4–10	6–12	10–16	15–21	18–24
Zone B	9	4–10	6–12	8–14	12–18	18–24	21–27
	10	6–12	8–14	10–16	15–21	21–27	24–30
	11	8–14	10–16	12–18	18–24	24–30	27–33
Zone C	12	10–16	12–18	15–21	21–27	27–33	30–37
	13	12–18	15–21	18–24	24–30	30–37	33–41
Zone D	14	15–21	18–24	21–27	27–33	33–41	37–46
	15	18–24	21–27	24–30	30–37	37–46	41–51
	16	21–27	24–30	27–33	33–41	41–51	46–57
	17	24–30	27–33	30–37	37–46	46–57	51–63
	18	27–33	30–37	33–41	41–51	51–63	57–71
	19	30–37	33–41	37–46	46–57	57–71	63–78
	20	33–41	37–46	41–51	51–63	63–78	70–87
	21	37–46	41–51	46–57	57–71	70–87	77–96
	22	41–51	46–57	51–63	63–78	77–96	84–105
	23	46–57	51–63	57–71	70–87	84–105	92–115
	24	51–63	57–71	63–78	77–96	92–115	100–125
	25	57–71	63–78	70–87	84–105	100–125	110–137
	26	63–78	70–87	78–97	92–115	110–137	120–150
	27	70–87	78–97	87–108	100–125	120–150	130–162
	28	78–97	87–108	97–121	110–137	130–162	140–175
	29	87–108	97–121	108–135	121–151	140–175	151–188
	30	97–121	108–135	121–151	135–168	151–188	168–210
	31	108–135	121–151	135–168	151–188	168–210	188–235
	32	121–151	135–168	151–188	168–210	188–235	210–262
	33	135–168	151–188	168–210	188–235	210–262	235–293
	34	151–188	168–210	188–235	210–262	235–293	262–327
	35	168–210	188–235	210–262	235–293	262–327	292–365
	36	188–235	210–262	235–293	262–327	292–365	324–405
	37	210–262	235–293	262–327	292–365	324–405	360–life
	38	235–293	262–327	292–365	324–405	360–life	360–life
	39	262–327	292–365	324–405	360–life	360–life	360–life
	40	292–365	324–405	360–life	360–life	360–life	360–life
	41	324–405	360–life	360–life	360–life	360–life	360–life
	42	360–life	360–life	360–life	360–life	360–life	360–life
	43	life	life	life	life	life	life

Textbox 11.1. Commentary to Sentencing Table

Application Notes:

1. The offense level (1–43) forms the vertical axis of the sentencing table. The criminal history category (I–VI) forms the horizontal axis of the table. The intersection of the offense level and criminal history category displays the guideline range in months of imprisonment. "Life" means life imprisonment. For example, the guideline range applicable to a defendant with an offense level of 15 and a criminal history category of III is 24–30 months of imprisonment.
2. In rare cases, a total offense level of less than 1 or more than 43 may result from application of the guidelines. A total offense level of less than 1 is to be treated as an offense level of 1. An offense level of more than 43 is to be treated as an offense level of 43.
3. The criminal history category is determined by the total criminal history points from chapter 4, part A, except as provided in §4B1.1 (Career Offender) and 4B1.4 (Armed Career Criminal). The total criminal history points associated with each criminal history category are shown under each criminal history category in the sentencing table.

Early Release on Parole and Compassionate Release

IN AMERICA'S JUSTICE SYSTEM, DOING the crime does not mean doing the time. A prison sentence imposed rarely equals a sentence served. Over 80 percent of offenders serving time in state prisons are released early.[1] Many people might be disturbed to learn that individuals convicted of rape or sexual assault in state court serve only 62 percent of their sentence on average before being released.[2] Further, averaged across all crimes, state prisoners only serve 46 percent of their maximum sentence length.[3] Early release from prison takes several forms including mandatory and discretionary early release on parole (discussed in the first part of this chapter) as well as compassionate release for special circumstances such as ill health (discussed in the second part).

When does early release become a failure of justice? The prevalence of early release is concerning because if offenders' original sentences are just, then early release likely amounts to a failure of justice. If it is not a failure of justice, that suggests the original sentence was significantly unjust. Either way, early release highlights how the "justice" system is commonly distracted from its important task of doing justice in favor of other goals. After all, early release might make sense if the goal in setting a prison sentence is not to do justice but rather to protect society by incapacitating the offender or deterring others. For example, a harsh public sentence might deter other potential offenders, while a quiet early release on parole reduces prison costs. But as chapter 3 demonstrates, these kinds of antijustice distributive principles not only conflict with just punishment but also undermine effective long-term crime control.

However, early release fails even for the utilitarian reasons that might initially seem to favor it. First, attempts to increase deterrence through increased headline sentences at no cost to the state always fail as criminals find out that imposed sentences are not representative of actual time served and members of the public become increasingly suspicious and skeptical when they hear about regular early releases. But perhaps more important from a societal cost perspective, arguments for early release fail to account for the fact that *over 70 percent of released state prisoners are rearrested within five years and almost half are returned to prison.*[4] Less than half of parolees successfully complete their term of supervision, meaning most of those released early reoffend during the time they should have been in prison if they served their original sentences in full.[5] It is difficult for parole boards to predict which offenders are safe for release and which are not. Many killers and rapists have been released early only to later attack other innocents. Early release may seem forgiving and financially attractive, but it is often purchased at the price of justice and safety.

In addition to early release on parole, compassionate release sometimes serves as a justification for allowing an offender to leave prison early regardless of the length of their sentence. While it was meant to be granted only to offenders deemed too sick or elderly to be a threat to society, its recent expansion (in part due to the COVID-19 pandemic) has allowed many offenders even with a sentence of life without parole to go free.[6] Compassionate release raises the question of how to balance mercy and justice in a society that values both.

A. EARLY RELEASE ON PAROLE

Parole refers to the supervised release from prison of an offender before the court-imposed length of their sentence is over. Just as with probation (which may be provided in lieu of a prison sentence), prisoners on parole are required to check in with parole officers and follow certain rules, such as restrictions on travel or association. Violating the conditions of parole (such as by committing a new crime) can result in the parolee being returned to prison for the rest of their original sentence.

Early release on parole can be either discretionary or mandatory. Under mandatory parole, prisoners are released according to a fixed system set by law—usually after serving some fixed portion of their sentence such as one-third or one-half. The higher sentence publicly imposed is thought to be useful because it projects a more serious punishment than the government pays for—a sleight of hand seen as cost effective at increasing general deterrence, at least until the deception is discovered by the public, after which public skepticism tends to discount every publicly imposed sentence.[7]

Under discretionary parole, criminals are released when a parole board considers them sufficiently rehabilitated, or at least not dangerous. Prisoners often must serve some portion of their sentence before becoming eligible for discretionary parole, at which point it is up to the parole board to release them early or keep them in prison. Unfortunately, all such discretionary systems perform poorly at deciding what counts as rehabilitation and in determining whether an offender will reoffend upon release.[8] Perhaps more importantly, the use of a discretionary system of early release on parole represents a commitment to an antijustice distributive principle of incapacitation of the dangerous, which as discussed in chapter 3 holds a criminal should not be punished for their actions or culpability but for the possibility they may commit future crimes. As with mandatory parole, discretionary parole is also designed to serve general deterrence by allowing harsh statutory punishments for crime to be publicly imposed without the state having to pay for the full incarceration time.

Parole should not be confused with good time credits, which allow prisoners to earn a small reduction off their prison sentence if they display good conduct in prison. Good time credits offer a small reduction (for example, up to 15 percent off in the federal system if a prisoner displays maximum good behavior) and are considered a necessary part of keeping order in prisons, as they incentivize following prison rules. Good time credits pose little threat to justice, so long as they remain small and are applied fairly and consistently, because they do not seek to replace desert with a different distributive principle such as incapacitation of the dangerous or general deterrence.

Parole should also be distinguished from postrelease supervision, which is a feature of early release on parole but also occurs when a prisoner is released after serving their full sentence. It makes sense to provide some oversight and conduct rules for recently released prisoners, and such a period of supervision exists even in systems without any early release. In the federal system, for example, the length of supervision after release from prison is set by the judge at the time of sentencing and by statute is typically no longer than three or five years, depending upon the seriousness of the offense.[9] The length of postrelease supervision terms across states varies widely, with maximum allowable terms varying from two to ten years.[10] Some indeterminate sentencing systems will set the unserved remainder of the original sentence as the maximum supervision term.[11]

A desert-based distributive principle of punishment has no need for early release on parole because typically all relevant factors to an offender's just punishment are known at the time of sentencing.[12] A desert-based system would not inflate the judicially imposed sentence only to later reduce it in a less public parole hearing but rather would impose in open court the shorter, deserved sentence. In fact, it is likely that under a desert-based system, many statutory maximum punishments should be substantially reduced because the justification for exaggerating the maximum sentence to better serve deterrence or incapacitation is eliminated. The problems with the deception inherent in early release on parole led to the "truth in sentencing" movement formed in the 1970s, which led to the abolition of federal early release on parole as part of the federal Sentencing Reform Act of 1984.[13] But the problem of antijustice systems of early release on parole remains in many states.

In addition to damaging the credibility of the justice system, early release on parole also gives many criminals the chance to reoffend, thus offsetting the resource savings of early release. As mentioned previously, data shows that only 42 to 49 percent of those on parole successfully complete their term of supervision.[14] Recidivism is especially strong for violent offenders, with studies showing that 62 percent are rearrested within three years and 45 percent are returned to prison.[15] Early release on parole not only allows some guilty offenders to serve drastically less time than they deserve, but it also allows them to commit more crimes during the time they should have been in prison.

Cases of tragic costs imposed by early release on parole are legion. Consider just one example.

Case Example: Arthur Shawcross

On May 7, 1972, twenty-six-year-old Arthur Shawcross lures his ten-year-old neighbor, Jack Blake, into the woods of Watertown, New York, on the pretense of a fishing trip. Once in the woods, he rapes and murders the boy before cutting out the boy's heart and genitals for later consumption.[16] A few months later, Shawcross rapes and murders eight-year-old Karen Hill. He is arrested for Hill's murder, and in exchange for showing investigators the location of Blake's body, he is sentenced to only twenty-five years in prison. Shawcross's application for early release is rejected repeatedly, but in March 1987, with ten years still left on his (already reduced) sentence, he is granted early release by a parole board willing to give the killer-rapist-cannibal a second chance.

Officials attempt to settle him in several towns, but the residents rebel each time at the prospect of having such a criminal in their midst. Finally, Shawcross's parole officer finds him a home in Rochester without informing the local authorities of Shawcross's history. When prostitutes start turning up strangled and with missing body parts, the police have no leads. Due to the brutality of the killings, the authorities feel the offender is not new to the behaviors. They check the local list of sex offenders, but Shawcross is not on it, so they focus on other men.

The parole board's decision to release Shawcross ends with devastating and completely avoidable consequences. Shawcross is eventually caught in January 1989, after murdering twelve women.[17]

Competing Interests

One can identify legitimate interests on each side of the issue of early release.

INTERESTS SUPPORTING EARLY RELEASE ON PAROLE

- *Saving Resources.* Releasing prisoners early on parole saves money and prison space for the state, but this saving is offset by the high rate of recidivism among those released on parole, many of whom soon return to prison with the added costs of new crimes and convictions.[18]
- *Encouraging Rehabilitation and Good Behavior in Prison.* Parole can encourage prisoners to engage in rehabilitation programs, demonstrate good behavior, and attempt to reform in prison in order to increase the likelihood of their being released early. Of course, this often involves simply gaming the system to appear to be on the path of reform, but it is still beneficial to have more offenders engage in rehabilitation programs and attempt good behavior in prison.

Figure 12.1. Arthur Shawcross at his first arrest, circa 1969. Photo by Green Lake County Sheriff's Office, from Cary Spivak, Lawyers' licenses suspended by state Supreme Court: Men were accused in 2005 sexual assault, April 4, 2012, *Miwaukee Journal Sentinel.*

- *Non-Desert Distributive Principles.* Principles of punishment not based on desert should logically have an early release mechanism for when the purpose of the punishment has been achieved, whether that is incapacitation or deterrence. Under these distributive principles, it makes no sense to hold criminals longer than necessary to achieve the non-desert-based aims. However, empirical evidence suggests discretionary parole boards perform poorly in predicting who will reoffend.[19] And as discussed in chapter 3, the antijustice distributive principles ultimately undermine effective crime control rather than furthering it because they undermine the system's moral credibility with the community.

- *Recognizing People's Ability to Change.* Discretionary parole, especially for long sentences, recognizes a criminal's ability to change. After ten, twenty, or forty years, an offender is likely to be a very different person, and some argue it is immoral, and certainly counterproductive, to continue to punish such a changed person for crimes that their past self committed. On the other hand, even a generally "good" person still deserves to be punished if they commit crimes, and becoming a better person does not negate the harms caused in the past. Most people do not believe that personal growth excuses one from consequences for past behavior.

INTERESTS OPPOSING EARLY RELEASE ON PAROLE

- *Doing Justice.* Early release on parole undermines desert-based justice. If the original sentence was just, early release means a criminal is escaping without their full deserved punishment. If releasing the criminal early is just, then the original sentence was unjustly harsh. Either way, the presence of early release seems to guarantee justice is not done at some point in the legal system.

- *Fairness and Equal Treatment.* Discretionary parole decisions are prone to human arbitrariness and biases that undermine fairness and equal treatment of offenders. Discretionary parole raises many of the same concerns that judicial sentencing discretion does (discussed in the previous chapter) because both involve individuals deciding, sometimes arbitrarily, how much punishment an offender should receive.

- *Deterrence and Public Safety.* Because most parolees soon reoffend, early release on parole undoubtedly increases crime compared to a world where all offenders serve their full sentence.[20] Parole may also reduce the deterrent threat of punishment because it makes headline sentences untrustworthy. When criminals know even a harsh decade-long sentence can turn into a few years through early release, the ability to deter serious crime decreases.

- *The Well-Being of Victims and Public Faith in the Justice System.* Early release on parole strikes many victims and their families as a slap in the face from the legal system. The thought of criminals going free without enduring their deserved punishment makes many victims believe the system prioritizes helping criminals over valuing victims and delivering justice. This creates legal cynicism in victims, their families, and their communities. The general public is also commonly outraged when the legal system releases a criminal early, only to have that criminal go on to harm more people.

The Nature of Early Release in the United States

Parole systems (or the lack thereof) vary across the United States, with states employing combinations of discretionary, mandatory, or no early release on parole depending on the crime.

SENTENCING AND PAROLE SYSTEMS ACROSS THE UNITED STATES Systems for early release on parole vary across the United States. Under a determinate sentencing model, an offender is given a fixed length sentence that might include an additional term of postrelease supervision. The time served is primarily determined by the judge based on statutes or sentencing guidelines (minus any minor good time credits earned in prison). Under purely determinate sentencing, early release on parole does not exist. Currently, the federal system, seventeen states, and DC primarily use such a determinate

sentencing model.[21] By contrast, thirty-three states primarily use an indeterminate sentencing model where an offender is given a sentence range, such as five to fifteen years, and they become eligible for parole (either mandatory or discretionary) after some proportion of the sentence is served. For example, an offender might become eligible for parole after 25 percent of the lower bound of the range is served.[22] Under a mandatory parole system, a prisoner would be automatically released after the time-served requirement, while under a discretionary parole system, a prisoner would only be released if such release is approved by the state parole board. While states can be classified as primarily indeterminate or determinate, no state is purely one or the other. For example, even states that are primarily indeterminate in sentencing may have higher time-served re-

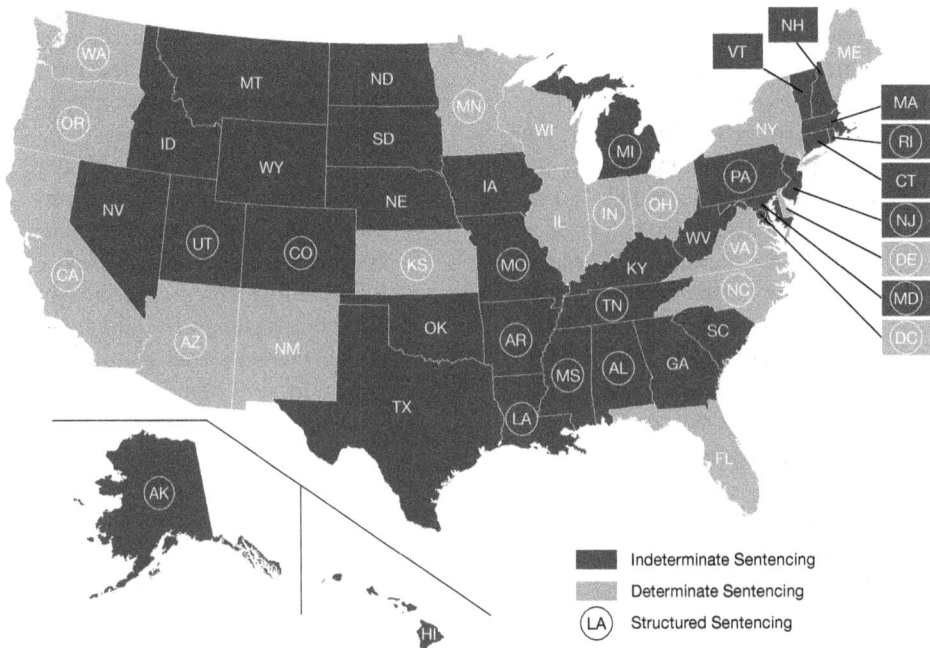

Figure 12.2. Map of the primary sentencing scheme used by each state, 2014. Figure by National Conference of State Legislators, 2014, from Alison Lawrence, *Making Sense of Sentencing: State Systems and Policies*, June 2015, Figure 2, pg. 5, https://documents.ncsl.org/wwwncsl/Criminal-Justice/sentencing.pdf.

quirements for specific crimes (such as requiring select violent offenders to serve 85 percent of their sentence before being eligible for parole). Figure 1.2 classifies states by the primary nature of their sentencing and release system. "Structured sentencing" refers to the use of sentencing guidelines or some other mechanism to reduce unjustified disparity among judges.[23] Of course, there may be limited value in increased uniformity in judicial sentencing if the real sentencing is done later by a parole commission in making early release decisions.)

VARIATIONS ACROSS STATES IN TIME-SERVED REQUIREMENTS The truth in sentencing movement had significant success in increasing time-served requirements regardless of sentencing system. The federal system adopted a determinate system without parole in 1984 and later incentivized states to tighten their parole release requirements with the 1994 Truth in Sentencing Act, which offered prison funding grants to states that adopted a requirement that violent offenders serve at least 85 percent of their *minimum* sentence before being eligible for parole.[24] Since then, some thirty-five states and DC have adopted such an 85 percent time-served requirement for violent offenders, but parole still drastically reduces punishment in those states with indeterminate sentencing ranges where the 85 percent requirement only applies to the lower bound of the sentencing range (for example, five years in a five to twenty year sentence).

The remaining fifteen states that do not adhere to the federal 85 percent time-served model have varying rules on parole eligibility. For example, Colorado's discretionary requirements depend on the offender's record: "violent offenders with two prior violent convictions

serve 75 percent of their sentences and offenders with one prior violent conviction serve 56.25 percent" of their original sentence before becoming eligible for parole.[25] Other discretionary parole states are more lenient, with Texas only requiring violent offenders to serve at least half their original minimum sentence or thirty years, whichever is less.[26] In states with early release on parole, the time-served requirements for non-violent offenders are normally less strict, and the federal government has made no move to incentivize tighter standards as they have for violent offenders. For example, Texas requires non-violent offenders to serve only one-fourth of their sentence or fifteen years before becoming eligible for parole.[27]

In all jurisdictions, those sentenced to life may become eligible for early release so long as the sentence is not life without parole. The time-served requirement for lifers to become eligible for parole differs by state. In Georgia, for example, offenders serving a life sentence for a serious violent felony, such as murder or rape, may be considered for parole after serving fourteen years.[28] In California, the requirement is twenty-five years for most life sentences, although some life sentences only require seven years of time served before eligibility for parole.[29] In Colorado, some life sentences can mean eligibility for early release after just two years.[30]

In the federal system, as noted earlier, early release on parole does not exist and prisoners serve at least 85 percent of their determinate sentence before being eligible for release if they have earned maximum good time credits. However, state prisons, not the federal system, hold most inmates, and state rules are far more generous with parole. Overall, available

state prison data shows that violent offenders serve on average 54 percent of
their original maximum sentence, though
this varies significantly by state.[31] This has
not changed much since 1999 when violent offenders served 55 percent of their
maximum sentences, public order offenders served 51 percent, property offenders
served 46 percent, and drug offenders
served 43 percent. Among violent criminals, according to the 1999 data, rapists served 58 percent of their maximum
sentences while assaulters served 59 percent.[32] A different study using data from
2000 found that murderers serve only 50
percent of their sentences.[33] According to
2016 data, convicted murderers in state
prisons serve an average of roughly 57
percent of their original maximum sentences, and rapists serve 62 percent of
their sentences.[34] According to the same
data, 40 percent of murderers are released
on parole after serving less than ten years,
and 40 percent of rapists are released after
serving less than three years.[35] Overall,
from 1990 to 2000, over 80 percent of
state prisoners were released early on parole, and the majority of those offenders
served less than 50 percent of their original maximum sentence.[36]

Some criminals serve even smaller
fractions of their sentences. For example,
some offenders in California are able to
reduce their original sentence by up to 83
percent through a combination of parole
and good time credit policies.[37] Several
other states—Oklahoma, Alabama, and
Kentucky—allow for discounts in excess of 70 percent of the court-imposed
sentence.[38] Such massive discounts on
the publicly imposed sentence significantly undermine the credibility of the
justice system as any headline sentence
becomes practically meaningless in such
jurisdictions.

Of course, it is worth noting that not
every instance of early release on parole
is a failure of justice. If lawmakers and
judges intentionally oversentence offenders with severe headline sentences only to
release them early, the time served may
actually accord with desert. However,
given the often arbitrary nature of parole
decisions, such justice is only achieved
haphazardly, and the credibility of the
entire system is undermined by either
the unjust starting sentence or the justice
failure of a lenient early release.

**PUBLIC COMPLAINTS ABOUT EARLY RELEASE
ON PAROLE** Many in both the legal community and the broader public reject the
claim that offenders ought to be released
prior to serving their deserved sentence
if they are no longer deemed dangerous. This view has been put simply: "A
criminal's sentence should turn on his
moral fault, not his uncertain propensity
for violence."[39] Even those who in theory
might accept releasing non-dangerous
offenders still have to reckon with the
fact that recidivism rates prove parole
boards do a poor job of predicting who
will reoffend.

Public outcry is especially intense
when a paroled offender commits a murder or rape that would have been avoided
if they had been serving their original
sentence. Recall the case of twelve-year-
old Polly Klass, mentioned in chapter 1,
who was kidnapped and murdered by a
felon who had been repeatedly paroled
for violent crimes in the past. Cases such
as these led to the public turning against
early release on parole and fueled the
truth in sentencing movement in the
1970s and 1980s. A 1974 poll, for example, found that 50 percent of respondents
believed that prisoners "should serve
their full terms" and only 35 percent of
respondents believe prisoners "should

be paroled as soon as possible."[40] While recent public opinion data is scant, this anti-early-release sentiment has likely persisted. According to a 2014 New York poll, 58 percent of the respondents supported abolishing early release on parole for serious violent crimes, while 35 percent opposed.[41] It was the strength of public feeling that led to the abolition of discretionary early release on parole at the federal level in 1984 and in many states in the years leading up to and following the federal reform.

Many citizens have a particular aversion to early release on parole when it is implemented to relieve prison overcrowding. In a survey from 1997, only 20 percent of respondents favored addressing prison overcrowding by "giving parole boards more authority to release offenders early." The public concern appears mainly driven by fears about dangerousness,[42] but a sizable proportion of the public is concerned about justice as well, with victims and their families being especially concerned with the failures of justice produced by early release. Many writers have noted the disillusioning effects of early releases on the public's view of the justice system.[43] As has been argued by many opponents of parole, "Fixed sentences would be preferable to parole for one powerful reason: They would eliminate the damaging public confusion."[44] It is better to sentence a criminal to a shorter prison term served in full than a longer prison term only served partially because in the latter case, the public will blame the justice system if the criminal reoffends, while in the former, the public is more likely to put the blame on the individual offender and not see the system as at fault, so long as the previous sentence was just. One can support ending parole for this reason alone

while at the same time believing actual time served in prison should remain the same or even decrease.

The negative public sentiment regarding early release has sparked a form of what has been called "shadow vigilantism"[45] by inducing some judges around the country to issue longer sentences to try to keep criminals in prison longer before parole becomes possible. Many judges "claim to be responding to public sentiment when they impose harsher sentences than they otherwise might."[46] This can sometimes lead to the worst of both worlds where the imposed sentence is unjustly harsh, but the early release is still overly lenient—a situation maximizing the loss of credibility for the legal system. Frustration with early release can also lead to shadow vigilantism in the form of overly harsh statutory punishments designed to thwart early release, such as three strikes laws passed in the 1980s and 1990s, partly in response to the problem of violent felons being released from prison early and committing more crimes. As a result, even those primarily concerned with overpunishment should be skeptical of early release on parole as it can lead to a punitive overreaction among a frustrated public.

Reforms

In addition to efforts to limit or abolish early release on parole, several other reforms have been proposed or implemented to mitigate the problem.

Use More Non-Incarcerative Punishments. Many supporters of early release on parole argue that some prison sentences, especially longer ones, waste money and make it harder for offenders to reintegrate into the community upon their eventual release. These arguments have merit, as incarceration may well be overused as a sanctioning method. One possibility, explored more in our recommendation in chapter 16 on the topic of decarceration, is for legislatures to make it easier for non-incarcerative punishments to be imposed by sentencing judges under clear guidelines that set reliable punishment equivalencies between non-incarcerative punishments and prison sentences.[47] For example, legislatures could design a system whereby likely non-dangerous offenders, after serving some portion of their sentence in prison, could be released upon the imposition of non-incarcerative punishments equivalent in punitive bite (that is, "units of punishment") to the remaining time on their sentence. For example, a prisoner released after serving two years of a five-year prison sentence might be required to spend the next five years undergoing some non-incarcerative punishments including travel restrictions, fines, community service, alcohol or drug treatment, or training programs. Any activity that intruded upon the offender's liberty ought to be eligible for "punishment credit." The two years in prison plus five years of non-incarcerative punishment might equal the punitive bite of a five-year prison sentence without requiring the additional three years of expensive and counterproductive incarceration. Such a reform would recast early release on parole as a continuation of punishment by a different means as opposed to an escape from deserved punishment. Critically, such a reform would remove the duplicitous nature and arbitrariness of early release by making the true sentence clear at the time of sentencing. It would be a judge—not a parole board—that would impose such a hybrid sentence combining prison and non-incarcerative sanctions.

Recommendation: Abolish Early Release on Parole (as Per the Federal System)

Early release on parole, whether discretionary or mandatory, is fundamentally deceptive and antijustice in its formulation. To ensure honest and transparent sentencing based on just deserts, states should adopt determinate sentencing and abolish early release such that all prisoners must serve their imposed sentence (minus a small percentage credit for good behavior in prison). While we focus on the issue of imprisonment in this recommendation, we support the previously mentioned reform of using more non-incarcerative sanctions at time of sentencing, so long as they provide the total punitive bite required by desert.

This recommendation to abolish early release is not an attempt to provide more incarceration. On the contrary, we believe it is better from a perspective of justice to have shorter honest sentences than longer sentences with wildly varying degrees of enforcement that attempt to deceive the community as to what the actual punishment for crime is. The abolition of early release should be accompanied by an overhaul of statutory punishments and sentencing guidelines to make sure the resulting punishment system provides a just sentence carried out in full.[48] Abolishing early release should actually result in considerably shorter imposed sentences as judges seeking to impose a just sentence realize they no longer need to exaggerate their imposed sentence in anticipation of early release.

Moreover, this proposal is not meant to affect supervision after release from prison. At sentencing, offenders should be assigned a fixed postrelease supervision term. This supervision term would be longer for serious crimes and shorter for less serious ones, and violation of the conditions of postprison probation could result in a fixed additional period of imprisonment. The important point is that all such punishment details should be fixed at sentencing and be part of the desert-based calculus. Abolishing early release on parole and its vagaries will bring clarity, predictability, and transparency to criminal penalties, bolstering the moral credibility of the criminal justice system.

This proposal is modeled after the successful approach taken by the federal Sentencing Reform Act of 1984, which abolished federal early release on parole and capped good time credit at no more than fifty-four days per year (15 percent of the total sentence if the maximum credits are earned).[49] States should adopt this approach to good time credit. Compared to the tangled web of state regulations on parole eligibility and good time credits, the federal system offers admirable simplicity.

It is easy to see how a system without early release on parole would avoid the failures of justice and public safety risks associated with lenient discretionary parole as well as mandatory parole. Recall the case of Arthur Shawcross who was released by the New York State Parole Board on discretionary parole despite Shawcross still having ten years on his already lenient sentence for raping, murdering, and eating two children. If Shawcross had not been released early, his later victims would likely still be alive. Moreover, even if Shawcross had served his full sentence and then continued killing, the criminal justice system would not have suffered the significant loss in credibility that it did when the public

learned that Shawcross had been voluntarily released by the state.

B. COMPASSIONATE RELEASE

Compassionate release refers to the release of prisoners who show "extraordinary and compelling" reasons for why they should be released from prison early on compassionate grounds.[50] Usually, this means the release of prisoners who are elderly and disabled or terminally ill, so long as they are judged to pose little danger to society. However, the previously infrequent practice has recently expanded, and accelerated even more sharply during the COVID-19 pandemic, turning it into a real and increasing threat to justice. This chapter uses the term "compassionate release" broadly to include all releases of prisoners on grounds of compassion and mercy—including medical and geriatric reasons as well as the many irregular releases that occurred during the COVID-19 pandemic.

Competing Interests

One can identify legitimate interests on each side of the issue of compassionate release.

INTERESTS SUPPORTING THE GENEROUS USE OF COMPASSIONATE RELEASE

- *Saving Resources.* The elderly are a growing and expensive component of America's prison population. Expanded compassionate release has the potential to save a significant amount of money and prison space without greatly increasing recidivism due to the small likelihood of recidivism among older releasees.
- *Recognizing Human Dignity and Mercy.* Compassionate release recognizes the human dignity of all individuals, no matter their crimes, and seeks to uphold mercy when the danger to society is insignificant.

While compassionate release certainly treats criminals better than they treated their victims, a humane and merciful society—and even a just society—should not aspire to render an eye for an eye.

- *Ensuring Proportional Sentences in Changing Circumstances.* If the punitive weight of a sentence increases due to the prisoner's changing circumstances, justice might call for a reduction in the sentence. For example, if a thirty-year-old robber receives a five-year sentence but then develops pancreatic cancer and is given two years to live, is it just to make the offender die in prison? The sentencing judge did not expect the sentence to take up the offender's entire remaining lifespan, and an argument can be made that it would be more in accordance with desert-based justice to release the offender early because the punitive weight of each year of the sentence has changed dramatically due to the offender's changed circumstances. Of course, this could not be used to justify the compassionate release of a prisoner with a longer sentence who normally would die in prison. Theoretically, this argument can be generalized beyond terminal illnesses to justify the earlier release of any criminal when the punitive bite of the punishment increases, be it from illness, disability, or even risk of catching an infectious disease in prison, as long as those circumstances did not exist when the offender was sentenced. Some might reject this argument by claiming sentences are not proportional to life expectancy and people's circumstances change all the time for better or worse regardless of whether they are being punished or not. It should also be noted that current compassionate release schemes do

not premise themselves on promoting proportionally just punishment.

INTERESTS OPPOSING THE GENEROUS USE OF COMPASSIONATE RELEASE

- *Doing Justice.* Putting aside the question of ensuring proportionally just sentences in changing circumstances, there are many clear cases where compassionate release simply voids a desert-based sentence. A criminal sentenced to life in prison being released early because they are sick can only be justified on merciful grounds, not on grounds of deserved justice. The fact that compassionate release is usually tied to lack of dangerousness, not seriousness of the crime, also suggests that the calculation does not involve justice considerations.

- *Public Confidence in the Justice System and the Nature of Mercy.* Many victims feel embittered against the justice system when they see their attackers or killers of loved ones being allowed to go free even in the name of mercy. In their view, the criminal justice system ought to be about justice. Mercy may be an admirable trait in an individual or religious setting but is inappropriate in the context of a criminal justice system. In this view, encouraging "mercy" is just a fig leaf for promoting justice failures. Moreover, a compassionate release system that applies mercy to some but not all can be seen as arbitrary and unfair to the vast majority of prisoners who do not receive a compassionate release.

- *More Crime.* Though historically only a small fraction of the offenders who are released on compassionate grounds go on to commit further crimes, one cannot ignore the fact that compassionate release can cause crime that could otherwise have been avoided. This risk became more substantial during the COVID-19 pandemic, which resulted in more expansive compassionate release policies often disconnected from dangerousness judgments.

The Nature and Extent of the Problem

Forty-nine states, the District of Columbia, and the federal prison system have some form of compassionate release, with Iowa being the only state without a defined set of laws regarding the practice.[51]

FEDERAL COMPASSIONATE RELEASE Before 2018, federal law required prisoners to apply for compassionate release through the Bureau of Prisons (BOP) with a detailed application explaining their circumstances. If the BOP approved the application, the bureau could then request a court to order an early release. However, the requirements of the BOP were stringent, and only 6 percent (324) of the 5,400 compassionate release requests were granted between 2013 and 2017.[52]

However, the First Step Act of 2018 substantially altered federal compassionate release policies to allow prisoners to directly petition a judge for compassionate release if they believe they meet the "extraordinary and compelling reasons" laid out in the US Sentencing Commission (USSC) Guidelines.[53] The USSC guidelines are looser than the BOP guidelines and allow courts to consider age, medical considerations, family situation, and other reasons. The 2018 reform resulted in a significant increase in compassionate releases. Between December 2018 and September 2020, approximately 1,700 inmates were released under the new law,[54] a more than 500 percent increase in releases granted in half the number of years, yielding a 1,000 percent increase in the release rate. Allowing judges to directly

decide on compassionate releases has also led to many of the same problems associated with judicial sentencing discretion, as some judges decide to put their own personal non-desert distributive principles ahead of what even the First Step Act intended. For example, Judge Frederic Block, a federal judge in New York, decided in 2022 to let two mafia killers, who had taken part in a bloody mafia war that saw at least a dozen murders, out of prison, despite the men being sentenced to life.[55] While the two killers had applied for compassionate release, Judge Block ultimately based his decision on the fact he believed the original sentences were too harsh—showing how the new rules of compassionate release are sufficiently open to uncontrolled discretion so as to allow lenient judges to simply resentence serious criminals as they personally see fit.

STATE COMPASSIONATE RELEASE At the state level, statistics regarding the beneficiaries of compassionate release are generally unavailable. In fact, "only 13 states are required by state law to keep track of and report compassionate release statistics, with very few of them making that information public."[56] Because most prisoners are under state jurisdiction, it is hard to say how many offenders receive compassionate releases each year, but it is likely in the thousands. The number likely varies significantly by state given that states have varying guidelines on who may qualify for compassionate release and who decides whether compassionate release should be granted. Different states vest the power to grant compassionate release in the sentencing court, the governor, the parole board, or the commissioner of the department of corrections.[57] For example, in Pennsylvania, which has quite strict requirements, the decision is made by the sentencing court, and compassionate release may only be granted if the prisoner can show a terminal illness with a life expectancy of twelve months or less. By contrast, at least nineteen states do not require any life expectancy diagnosis for compassionate release.[58]

COMPASSIONATE RELEASE AND RECIDIVISM The traditional rationale for compassionate release policies was based on the idea that the elderly and terminally ill no longer pose a threat to society and can be released from prison on humanitarian and public safety grounds. Studies have found that there is only a 3 percent recidivism rate among elderly offenders who were granted federal compassionate release (though this was before the laxer release guidelines).[59] Another study found that only 2 percent of released offenders ages fifty to sixty-five are arrested again and that almost no released offenders older than sixty-five are arrested again.[60] However, the low probability of violent recidivism among elderly or ill individu-

als does not void the failure of justice that results from cutting short a desert-based sentence. Additionally, expanded compassionate release (especially for younger and more able prisoners) has increased the danger of recidivism, as shown in the next section on COVID-19 releases.

EXPANDED COMPASSIONATE RELEASE DURING COVID-19 The COVID-19 pandemic prompted a dramatic increase in compassionate release requests and in the granting of such releases, including for the relatively young and non-terminally ill. As COVID-19 spread through prisons across the country, many of those who either contracted the virus or were at risk of contracting it were released. (The category of persons at risk of infection would seem to be particularly large, potentially all inmates not in solitary confinement.) Indeed, some prisons released individuals lacking any special risk from COVID-19 simply to mitigate the spread of the virus. Figure 12.3 shows state-by-state approaches to com-

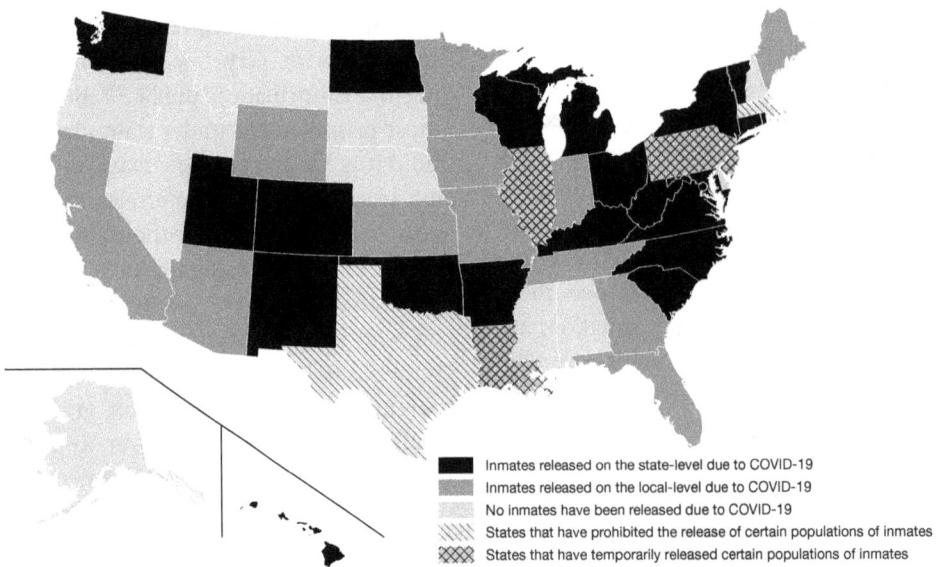

Figure 12.3. **State-by-state prison inmate release in response to COVID-19, 2020.** Figure from "Prison Inmate Release Responses in Response to the Coronavirus (COVID-19) Pandemic, 2020," Ballotpedia, July 1, 2020, https://ballotpedia.org/Prison_inmate_release_responses_in_response_to_the_coronavirus_(COVID-19)_pandemic,_2020. GNU Free Documentation License.

passionate release during the COVID-19 pandemic in 2020.[61] These releases led to many criminals being released after serving only a fraction of their sentence or being released from a sentence of life without parole. During the first year of the pandemic in 2020, state prison populations declined by 15 percent and jail populations declined by 25 percent.[62] Such statewide releases were largely justified on humanitarian grounds even if they did not go through the typical legal channels for compassionate release.

On the federal level, the CARES Act of 2020 authorized a widespread expansion of early release and home confinement for those at risk of COVID-19. As of December 2021, the BOP had granted around 36,000 early releases, with only around 4,500 of those prisoners still serving their sentences under home confinement. Despite a widespread decrease in the risk from COVID-19 due to the availability of vaccines and treatments, the Justice Department declined to return these offenders to prison, preferring to let them serve out the rest of their sentences at home.[63] This suggests that at least part of the motivation behind the releases was simply reducing prison populations generally in line with non-desert distributive principles.

Compassionate release during the pandemic even extended to some of the most violent offenders. In Massachusetts alone, twenty-one convicted murderers, who had been sentenced to life in prison without parole, were released under the state's medical parole compassionate release law.[64] One of these was the publicized story of John Stote, a prisoner who was placed on a ventilator after contracting COVID-19. He was released from his mandatory life sentence for murder because doctors did not think he would

survive. In fact, he recovered, and his brush with death became a get out of jail free card.[65]

In California, while the state prohibited the early release of violent offenders during the pandemic, the state's narrow definition of a violent crime still allowed for the release of dangerous offenders. For instance, the list of violent offenses ineligible for compassionate release excluded "a lot of weapons offenses, elder abuse, and rape by drugging a victim."[66] Hate crimes, sex offenders, and domestic violence also were also were eligible for early release on compassionate grounds.[67] One such California releasee, David Nelson, was convicted on seventeen counts of arson but qualified for early release as a non-violent offender.[68] While prepandemic compassionate releases rarely endangered communities, expanded use of the practice after the start of the pandemic has worried many about potentially increased recidivism.[69] Moreover, the precedent set by dubious compassionate releases during the pandemic is likely to make such releases more widespread in the future.

Consider another dubious compassionate release during the pandemic that illustrates its dangers.

Case Example: Eric Reinbold

In 2015, thirty-eight-year-old Eric Reinbold quarrels with his wife and ends up ramming her car with his pickup truck when she attempts to go shopping with two of their six children.[70] Reinbold then engages in a bizarre armed standoff with responding police officers before surrendering two days later. Despite pleading guilty to assault and child endangerment, Reinbold avoids jail when his wife requests that he be allowed to return home. Reinbold soon turns to plotting revolutionary terrorism and writes a thirty-two-page commando handbook on how "to start the second American Revolution and win." He begins building elaborate and effective pipe bombs while plotting to become a serial killer targeting police, teachers, and the IRS. His activities are discovered, and Reinbold is sentenced to five years in prison in 2018 for his bomb making.

During the COVID-19 pandemic, Reinbold files for compassionate release in district court, claiming his own medical conditions make him vulnerable to COVID-19 and his wife needs help taking care of their children. Despite prosecutors warning that he is a dangerous man,

a judge releases Reinbold on March 18, 2021, with less than half his sentence served.

Less than four months later, Reinbold stabs his wife to death. He then takes off into the woods and avoids a massive manhunt for the next month before finally being captured.

Public Complaints About Compassionate Release

Compassionate release's main objectors have traditionally been victims and their families. Victims' relatives have been extremely outspoken against the policy, feeling that early release, regardless of the reason, is a failure of justice for the vic-

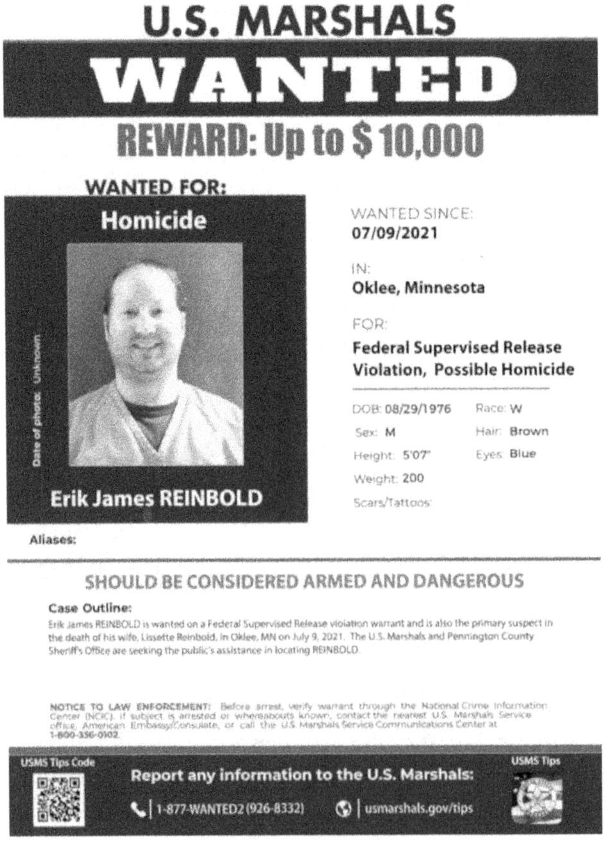

Figure 12.4. Eric Reinbold was released during COVID-19 and soon killed his wife, 2021. Graphic by US Marshals Service, July 9, 2021, from Joe Nelson, "Reward to Help Locate MN Man Wanted for Murder of His Wife," Bring Me the News LLC, July 11, 2021, https://bringmethenews.com/minnesota-news/reward-to-help -locate-mn-man-wanted-for-murder-of-his-wife.

tim.[71] After a terminally ill murderer from Philadelphia was released, the children of his victim complained that the act was a "miscarriage of justice."[72] If their murdered father had not been allowed to die with dignity, why should his murderer?

In a New York City case, a victim's family was never informed about the killer's release during the pandemic and were outraged when they found out. LaTor Scott, the victim's sister, explained that "to let him get out even extra early, that's just a double slap in our faces . . . it goes to show you that the justice system is flawed, its real flawed."[73] Many argue that early releases can revictimize victims' families and interfere with their ability to heal. While compassionate release shows compassion to offenders, it can deeply wound victims and their families and undermine their trust in the legal system. It is just one more example, in their minds, of a system little concerned with delivering justice.

The surge in compassionate releases due to COVID-19 also angered many in the public who believed politicians were prioritizing the well-being of criminals over justice and public safety. In response to the compassionate release of over twenty convicted murderers in Massachusetts, Norfolk District Attorney Michael Morrissey stated that the compassionate release policies "set up a conflict in the law: a first-degree murderer is not eligible for parole, yet we're allowing them to be released."[74] Similarly, Fresno County District Attorney Lisa Smittcamp criticized California's claim that it was excluding "violent crime" offenders from the new, expanded compassionate release rules, while defining that category narrowly to exclude many forms of clearly violent offenses: "Now they're using that term, 'violent crime,' to try to sugarcoat what they are doing, which is releasing violent and dangerous criminals into our counties every single day."[75] Orange County District Attorney Todd Spitzer criticized California's attempts to cut the Orange County jail population in half, arguing that "nothing, not even a pandemic suspends the rule of law."[76]

Many California district attorneys have expressed concern over the new rules' increase in the "amount of good-conduct credits that thousands of inmates could earn toward release," a policy enacted "on an emergency basis" due the pandemic.[77] These district attorneys were concerned that the new rules could "have the effect of significantly shortening the length of sentence for 76,000 violent and serious offenders" throughout the state.[78]

Reforms

Several reforms have been suggested to make compassionate release policies less justice frustrating.

Limit Eligibility for Compassionate Release. Prompted by the pandemic-inspired early release of twenty-one murderers who were supposed to serve life sentences, Massachusetts State representative Bruce Ayers cosponsored a bill that would make first-degree murderers ineligible for medical parole unless they were younger than eighteen years old when they committed their offense.[79] The bill would attempt to eliminate the "unintended consequence" of the state's current compassionate release laws in cases where the medical condition used to support the compassionate release request improves but there is no mechanism for the person to be returned to custody. Other proposals for limiting eligibility would make it so that only truly terminally ill offenders would be eligible for release, and perhaps only if their crimes were not the most serious violent felonies.

Involve Victims and Their Families in Compassionate Release. One possible way to balance the interests of compassion and justice while respecting victims and their families would be to require the victim's (or their family's) input before making compassionate release decisions to avoid revictimizing those who see compassionate release as a slap in the face. It could be argued that because compassionate release is not so much a right as a mercy granted by society, it is appropriate only where it would not significantly harm innocents. On the other hand, allowing a victim or their family a veto would raise concerns about unequal treatment of similar cases. Should an offender's punishment depend upon their good or bad luck in how merciful their victim is? While we do not believe victims or their families should be given decision-making power due to their inability to approach the situation objectively, any compassionate release system should at least take care to inform and demonstrate concern and respect for victims and their families when making compassionate release decisions.

Abolish Compassionate Release. One possible reform is to simply abolish compassionate release altogether and allow for mercy only through the use of executive clemency, an issue discussed in chapter 13.

Recommendation: Substitute Administrative Transfers in Place of Compassionate Release from Criminal Justice Control

Justice and mercy are always hard to balance, but there are better options for creating a humane justice system than simply releasing serious criminals because they have become old or ill or are at risk of becoming ill. We propose that administrative transfers should replace compassionate release in the criminal justice system. Such transfers would allow non-dangerous prisoners who are old, ill, or have other special mitigating circumstances to be moved to different prisons or other facilities (such as hospitals or old age homes under state control). Such transfers would not result in a sentence reduction or a relinquishing of criminal justice control of the prisoner, but they would be a compassionate move to allow some offenders to live out their sentences more safely and comfortably with the opportunity for easier visitation from family and friends.

This reform would mean that courts and parole commissions would no longer have the power to cut down sentences and release prisoners from justice system control simply on compassionate grounds. We see no reason that the criminal justice system should give up control over an offender simply because their circumstances have changed. However, this proposal would allow any change in a prisoner's circumstances to be considered in changing their custody situation, probably allowing nearly any custody situation analogous to that now available under compassionate release. What the proposal would change is the correctional system relinquishing control over the offender's custody situation. If the prisoner's health improves or other reasons behind the transfer change, then correctional officials are free to adjust the location and conditions of confinement or control accordingly.

Perhaps most importantly, because the offender is never released from correctional authority control, there is less likely to be a public perception that they are escaping deserved punishment. Like all other offenders, they remain under correctional control and, like all other offenders, the exact nature of their custody circumstances will be dictated by the correctional authority's assessment of their dangerousness, their health, their vulnerability, and a host of other factors.

Justice can be done in a merciful way, and the administrative control scheme that we suggest would likely increase the availability and use of compassionate remedies for prisoners' ill health by creating an easier mechanism for administrative transfers with the goal of easing unnecessary suffering. The sort of facilities ill prisoners could be transferred to already exist. For example, the Minnesota Correctional Facility at Fairbault is a medium-security facility with a special unit of over one hundred beds devoted to the care of old, disabled, or ailing prisoners in a more comfortable environment.[80] Some clearly non-dangerous prisoners could even be transferred outside of prison facilities so long as they continued to be supervised by the justice system and serve their sentences with restrictions on leaving their new non-prison facilities.

Indeed, the ability of administrative transfers to take account of compassionate circumstances is quite high. It would even allow transfers out of state, closer to a location where family could have greater opportunity to visit and provide support or, in extreme cases, take supervised control over a prisoner. Administrative transfers of a prisoner from one prison to another already exist within the United States. Transfers can occur both within state and out of state. The Interstate Corrections Compact (ICC) consisting of thirty-seven states, the federal government, and the District of Columbia allows correctional officials to make agreements "coordinating care, treatment, and rehabilitation for offenders."[81] Among the most frequent causes for

transfers are facility overcrowding or when inmates need protection, special programs, or have compelling familial reasons.[82] State Departments of Corrections already possess the power to implement many of our proposed administrative transfers, and a fairly comprehensive system could likely be created solely by executive direction, although such a system would have to operate parallel to current legislatively enacted compassionate release laws. However, in some jurisdictions it may require a legislative enactment to grant additional power, especially for transfers to non-prison facilities. Regardless, our proposal would be best served through legislation creating a comprehensive framework for administrative transfers on compassionate grounds (including specifying which grounds should qualify for what transfers), thus replacing existing faulty compassionate release schemes.

It is easy to see how such a reform would end much of the controversy and abuse surrounding current compassionate releases. Victims and their families would no longer feel revictimized by having killers released from the justice system. People would no longer need to fear that dubious releases would lead to more crime. Replacing releases with administrative transfers would have prevented Eric Reinbold, mentioned in the previous case example, from killing his wife and leading police on a month-long manhunt. If Reinbold could have shown a legitimate medical vulnerability to COVID-19, he could have been moved to a secure medical facility better able to prevent him from getting COVID-19 and better able to treat him if he did. What should not have occurred was releasing a convicted violent felon back into the community before his sentence was served.

CHAPTER 13

Executive Clemency

A. INTRODUCTION

WHEN DOES AN ACT OF MERCY BECOME A failure of justice? The power of executive clemency to pardon or commute a criminal's sentence is nearly absolute at the state and federal levels. The authority is a holdover from monarchical power at a time when all justice was the king's justice.[1] Article II, Section 2 of the US Constitution provides that the president "shall have Power to grant Reprieves and Pardons for Offenses against the United States, except in Cases of Impeachment."[2] While this only applies to federal criminal cases, a similar power is held by all state governors, though sometimes through the appointing of an independent pardon commission or with the advice and consent of an independent advisory board.[3]

While the number of clemency cases is small compared to the scale of the justice system, executive clemency is not so rare as some might imagine. There have been over twenty thousand acts of federal presidential clemency since 1900, and many of these have been acts of political favoritism, not commendable mercy.[4] The cumulative number of state-level acts of clemency is much greater still, with around ten thousand such grants of clemency being issued each year.[5]

Forms of Clemency at the Federal and State Level

Executive clemency takes several different forms. At the federal level, all clemency power is vested in the president, who can use any of five different clemency types. First, a *general pardon* can make "it as though the conviction never happened,"[6] thus absolving the pardoned individual of all liability and punishment and restoring all rights and privileges.[7] Such pardons can even be issued preemptively before a conviction. Second, a president may grant *amnesty*, which grants a (often preemptive) pardon to a class of persons who have committed a crime "that might later be looked at as having been beneficial to public welfare or at least that is not viewed as treasonous or criminal behavior."[8] For example, President Andrew Johnson issued an amnesty for all former Confederate soldiers in 1868.[9] Third, a president can grant a *commutation*, which does not absolve the offender of guilt or reverse the conviction but can decrease the punishment.[10] For example, some offenders have been granted a commutation to life imprisonment as opposed to receiving the death penalty.[11] Fourth, presidents may offer *remission*, which "forgiv[es] fines and costs imposed as a result of conviction."[12] Fifth, a president can offer a *reprieve*, which delays the start of the punishment but does not pardon an offender or absolve them of guilt.[13] The president can use these five kinds of alleviations on federal prisoners, but not to pardon or commute state offenses.[14]

However, most pardons and commutations occur at the state level where the benefits bestowed by clemency vary by state. For example, in Ohio, a pardon "forgives the conviction, but does not entitle [the] recipient to have court records sealed,"[15] while in Louisiana, there is a special "First Offender Pardon" that restores full rights and allows for expungement, after sentence completion. In Minnesota, a pardon "restores civil rights and removes employment disabilities, gun restrictions, [and] obligations to register" but offers no expungement.[16]

Every state's constitution creates a power of executive clemency, but in some states, this power is less expansive than that held by US presidents. In twenty states, governors do not have unilateral pardoning power, which is either held by an appointed board (six states) or shared between the governor and the board (fourteen states).[17] For example, in Pennsylvania, the governor may not issue a pardon "without affirmative recommendation of [the] pardon board chaired by [the] lieutenant governor."[18] In Florida, the governor sits on the pardon board but cannot act without its concurrence.[19] And in Georgia, the governor appoints an independent board that exercises full pardoning authority.[20] Another eight states require the governor to consult with an advisory board on all potential clemency, but the governor can ignore the board's recommendation.[21] The remaining twenty-two states grant unilateral pardoning power to the governor, though some of these states do require the governor to ask (but not necessarily follow) the advice of an advisory board in select cases.[22] For example, in California, the governor may or may not consult with the board in most cases but must consult with

the board when granting clemency to recidivists.[23]

Even in the twenty-two states where the governor has unilateral authority, pardon boards often exist to advise the governor in a non-binding way. Only three states (Maine, Oregon, and Wisconsin) have no advisory board.[24] Typically, advisory boards are appointed by the governor and include the attorney general, members of the state parole board (if one exists), and citizens of the state. In North Dakota, the role of the board is to provide the governor with critical case information to aid in pardon decision making.[25] In many instances, the governor will leave politically unimportant pardons to the pardon board and simply rubber stamp their decisions. For example, in North Dakota, the "Pardon Advisory Board" can research and prepare executive clemency recommendations that the governor can choose to simply sign off on, but the governor retains the ability to independently decide to issue any clemency.[26]

As noted, even if a governor does have authority to override the recommendation of an advisory board, they may still be legally required to consult with such a board in some or all cases. In Ohio, the governor decides which pardons to grant but must consult with the parole board, "which investigates and advises on each case."[27] The governor can still go against the advice of the board in these jurisdictions, but making consultations mandatory increases the political price a governor must pay to issue a pardon of which the board disapproves.

Some states such as Connecticut require a public hearing on an act of clemency and other states such as Florida require a notification to all the victims of the offender being considered for clemency.[28] Requiring some form of legal notice to the public, victims, or other legal officials is common. As of the beginning of the twenty-first century, "thirty-nine states require advance notice that a pardon is being considered; twenty-five states demand that pardons be accompanied by the reasons for their issuance; and thirty-seven states prohibit pre-conviction pardons."[29] Yet other states still allow governors to unilaterally issue pardons, without consultation or even public announcement, similar to how a president may.[30]

The Process of Requesting Clemency

While executives sometimes grant unrequested pardons and commutations, a process does exist for individuals to request clemency. Each jurisdiction has a different process and different eligibility rules. At the federal level, Department of Justice rules provide that an offender is only allowed to request a pardon five years after their "sentence or release from confinement,"[31] and a person is likely ineligible if on parole.[32] To be considered for a presidential pardon through this process, one must write a letter explaining why one is requesting the pardon, display a clean record since the conviction, and provide three supporting recommendations from non-family members.[33] Officials in the Office of the Pardon Attorney (a part of the Department of Justice) will then review the application across several stages, including requesting the offender's pre-sentencing report used by the sentencing judge, as well as requesting a possible FBI investigation into the applicant's recent behavior, before writing a recommendation for the president on whether to grant the request.[34] Of course, a president can choose to forego these require-

ments and pardon an individual who does not follow the procedures.

The process of applying for clemency at the state level is similar in many respects, but specific requirements for eligibility differ among the states.[35] For example, in Arizona any felon may apply for clemency after serving two years of a sentence that is at least three years in length,[36] but in California, absent exceptional circumstances such as a claim of factual innocence,[37] the offender must wait ten years after their sentence is complete to apply.[38] Other states, such as Rhode Island, have no specified process for requesting clemency, and many states have no eligibility requirements whatsoever.[39] Often the clearest path to clemency is having a powerful connection, someone capable of convincing the executive to grant clemency without regard to request processes or eligibility requirements.

The Debate over Executive Clemency

There are strong arguments that can be made in favor of the continuing existence of some form of clemency power. An offender's situation could change significantly after being sentenced, possibly through suffering some injury or disease that makes their incarceration dramatically more punitive in its effect than initially intended. In that case, justice might logically call for reducing the length of the sentence via a commutation. (An alternative mechanism might be compassionate early release by judicial or prison authorities examined in the previous chapter.) After conviction, an offender might also show enormous genuine remorse and work to atone for their offense so earnestly that most people would see the offender as deserving a reduction in punishment.[40] One could also view the clemency power as an additional check on the criminal justice system, a final failsafe to avoid injustices in individual cases.

On the other hand, there are strong reasons to think the current system of largely unguided and unaccountable executive clemency is open to profound justice-frustrating abuse. Unrepentant murderers, child molesters, corrupt politicians, and war criminals have all benefited from well-placed friends who take advantage of clemency powers. Also troubling from a separation of powers perspective is the executive's ability to use commutations to resentence whole classes of offenders, as several state governors have done with those sentenced to death or as President Obama did in his 2014 clemency initiative, thus nullifying the previous democratically enacted legislative criminalization and punishment standards.[41] Executive clemency is a largely unaccountable way for powerful individuals to decide which select criminals escape justice.

Consider several examples of the kinds of questionable clemency cases that are all too common.

Case Example: FALN Terrorists

On January 24, 1975, a bomb explodes on the second floor of the historic Fraunces Tavern in New York City. The explosion is so powerful it is felt on the sixtieth floors of nearby buildings. When firefighters arrive, they find the street covered in debris and dismembered bodies. Amazingly, only four people die, but over sixty are injured. The FALN, a Puerto Rican communist paramilitary organization devoted to securing Puerto Rican independence and the downfall of capitalism, immediately takes responsibility. From the mid-1970s through the mid-1980s, the FALN are responsible for over 130 bombings, killing six people, injuring and maiming many others, and causing the loss of millions of dollars in property damage. Most of the terrorists are eventually caught and given sentences between thirty-five and ninety years.

On August 11, 1999, President Bill Clinton announces his intention to commute the sentences of sixteen convicted FALN terrorists if they will renounce violence. The commutations are meant to curry favor for the Democrats with Puerto Rican voters who might be sympathetic to the FALN. Clinton believes this will help his wife Hillary Clinton's bid for the Senate in New York where Puerto Rican voters are a key constituency. Most of the terrorists do not want to renounce violence, but after frantic pressure from the White House, fourteen of the sixteen agree to sign the statement and are released. The political gambit fails as the public is outraged, and Congress overwhelmingly votes to condemn the clemency, with Hillary Clinton being forced to join in condemning her husband's decision.

Case Example: Haley Barbour

When Haley Barbour is first elected governor of Mississippi in 2004, he claims to disapprove of executive clemency, which he sees as undermining justice. His view starts to change when he gets to know the governor's mansion's staff. Like all Mississippi governors, Barbour is assigned a detail of five prison "trusties" as personal manservants. All five are serving life sentences, four of them for murder. Joseph Ozment callously shot a store clerk pleading for his life during a robbery in 1992. David Gatlin calmly shot his wife while she was holding their six-

Figure 13.1. Joseph Ozment, in prison for killing a man, was pardoned by Governor Haley Barbour, 2012. Police handout photo by Mississippi Department of Corrections, from Rich Phillops, "Lawyer: Pardoned Murderer 'Not Going' Back to Mississippi for Hearing," CNN, February 7, 2012, https://www.cnn.com/2012/02/06/us/mississippi-pardons-ozment/index.html.

week-old son in 1993. Charles Hooker is a middle school teacher who murdered his school's principal in 1993. Anthony McCray murdered his wife to settle an argument in 2001. All received life sentences, but Barbour gives them a farewell gift when he leaves office in January 2012. Calling them together, he announces they are all getting full pardons. Barbour also pardons an additional 193 people, including nearly thirty murderers. (Nine of the murderers who receive pardons had killed their domestic partner.[42]) The Mississippi public is outraged by Barbour's last-minute methods and his show of personal favoritism, but an attempt to overturn the pardons in court fails.

Case Example: Matt Bevin

Matt Bevin has only a few hours left in his position as governor of Kentucky in December 2019. He uses the time to issue 657 pardons.[43] Nearly half of the pardons, 300, are for drug-related offences. The other pardons include offenders who committed murder, sexual assault, and child rape. For example, Micah Schoettle

was recently convicted of raping children between the ages of nine and twelve. He has served just over one year of his twenty-five-year sentence. While the jury was convinced of his guilt beyond a reasonable doubt, Bevin argues that the evidence was shoddy and that the physical damage to the child, in his opinion, did not support the charges. Perhaps more importantly, Schoettle is the son of a wealthy northern Kentucky businesswoman with political influence.

Another case that attracts Bevin's attention is a group of four men who were convicted of sodomizing a drunk fifteen-year-old boy with a sex toy so brutally that it perforated his bowel and nearly killed him. Dayton Jones, a member of a wealthy old-money family, is among the group. According to court records, while

Figure 13.2. Dayton Jones, a member of an influential family, was pardoned by Governor Matt Bevin, circa 2018. Photo by Christian County Sheriff's Office, from Melissa Pettitt, "Teen Sex Assault Case: Jones Blames Attorney, Seeks Relief from Sentence," *Kentucky New Era*, February 13, 2018, https://www.kentuckynewera.com/news/article_9d912f7a-1113-11e8-b59f-e784c5afc2b0.html.

the case was pending, Jones's family offered the victim $500,000 if he would support a plea deal that would allow Jones not to register as a sex offender. Beyond the sodomy, Jones also pled guilty to making and posting a video of the attack. He was sentenced to fifteen years, of which he has served only three. Jones is pardoned by Bevin, while the other men who acted with Jones to assault the boy receive no sentence reduction.[44]

Other Notable Cases of Controversial Pardons or Mass Commutations

President Bill Clinton indulged in an infamous and widely condemned midnight pardon session just before he left office in January 2001, granting over 140 pardons to well-connected family members, arms dealers, and child molesters, among other dubious recipients. For example, March Rich was indicted along with his partner in 1983 on more than sixty criminal counts, including income tax evasion, wire fraud, racketeering, and trading with Iran during the oil embargo. These charges could have yielded a punishment of more than three hundred years in prison. Rich fled the country in 1987 and was on the FBI's Most-Wanted Fugitives List. Through his wife, Rich made a remarkable donation of more than a million dollars to President Clinton's reelection campaign and was among those who received a pardon from him as he left office.[45] The midnight pardon party as an executive leaves office has become a tradition where executives are free to indulge in venal decision making with no accountability.

Not all controversial clemency decisions are corrupt, but they can still pose separation of powers problems.

Mass clemency being used to resentence a class of offenders irrespective of individual case details is an example. While amnesty is a form of mass clemency preemptively pardoning a group of technical offenders whom society does not believe should be punished by the criminal justice system (often because their motivations were non-criminal), mass commutations are concerning as they allow the executive to perform the legislative and judicial function of deciding what punishment a class of undoubtedly criminal offenders should receive.[46] From a constitutional perspective, such mass executive clemency is a loophole that enables an executive veto on any legislative criminalization or punishment decision, even though an executive's veto on the actual law in question can be overridden by sufficient legislative majorities. For example, a governor opposed to the death penalty might veto a state's death penalty law only for the democratically elected state legislature to override that veto with a supermajority. But if a governor simply commutes all death penalties to prison terms, the executive can foil the democratic decision of the legislature in a way not intended by the constitutional separation of powers. Former Illinois governor George Ryan declared the mass commutation of 164 death row inmates in 2003, putting his personal opposition to the death penalty above the law.[47] Many governors now do this routinely.[48] No matter how much one agrees with the goals advanced, one should still recognize the severe constitutional problems such policy-based group commutations pose. A constitutional system aims to ensure the means used are appropriate even for worthy ends in contrast to authoritarian systems where the ends justify the means.

The federal system has also seen several recent actual and threatened uses of mass clemency that illustrate the problem. President Obama used commutations to effectively resentence 1,696 federal prisoners he argued should have received lower sentences because he disagreed with the drug sentencing policy that existed at the time of their offense.[49] More recently, President Biden announced on October 6, 2022, "a full, complete, and unconditional pardon" to all offenders who committed the federal crime of marijuana possession.[50] This applied to 6,500 federal offenders,[51] plus thousands more District of Columbia offenders.[52] Biden made no pretense that the pardons were based upon any specific factors relating to the individual offenders but simply chose to short-circuit the criminalization decision enacted by Congress. Even more troubling, this mass pardon came immediately following a recent congressional rejection of marijuana decriminalization.[53] It is a strange notion of separation of powers if legislation rejected by the Congress can simply be enacted by the executive.

Many may be tempted to overlook the problem of such mass clemency because they are sympathetic (perhaps rightly) to decriminalizing or reducing the punishment of drug offenses or to abolishing the death penalty. Few are likely to feel so sympathetic to former President Donald Trump's serious consideration of issuing mass clemency to rioters who stormed the Capitol on January 6, 2021, attempting to overturn election results. While he was restrained from doing so in his last days in office by worried advisors, Trump has since declared his willingness, should he be reelected in the future, to pardon some or all of the around seven hundred charged rioters.[54]

The problem of mass clemency remains a troubling constitutional anomaly that should not be overlooked simply because one agrees with the views of the executive exercising it. Executive clemency was created to take account of the special circumstances of individual cases, not to allow the executive to nullify the role of the legislative and judicial branches of government.

B. COMPETING INTERESTS

One can identify legitimate interests supporting and opposing the use of executive clemency power.

Interests Supporting the Use of Executive Clemency

- *Absolving the Innocent and Rectifying Injustice.* While executive clemency has the potential to produce failures of justice, it also has the potential to restore justice and correct previous wrongful convictions and inappropriate sentences. For example, executive clemency can absolve a wrongful conviction when all other options within the justice system are exhausted.[55] Executive clemency is a final safety valve for the system's mistakes. However, there is little evidence that executive clemency serves this role in practice as most pardons are granted to undeniably guilty offenders, and courts are generally able to overturn provably false convictions. It is also hard to see why a single executive would be in a better position to judge the truth of a case than juries or judges.
- *Exercise of Mercy as Providing a Societal Value.* The exercise of mercy can produce an important societal value. For example, there is general consensus that President Gerald Ford's pardoning of an undoubtedly

guilty Richard Nixon ultimately benefited the country by heading off years of retributive political strife. Similarly, Presidents Ford's and Carter's amnesty for Vietnam War draft dodgers was likely beneficial at promoting national healing in the long run.[56] Historian Samuel Morison argued that mercy, along with justice, plays an essential role in a society's social contract. Theoretically, individuals behind a "veil of ignorance," to use the terms of Rawls's social contract theory, might choose to create a society with a form of legal clemency in case any citizen found themselves in a position where they would desire clemency. Clemency given under special circumstances that the public would see as a legitimate basis for mercy can actually strengthen the criminal justice system's reputation instead of harming it.

- *Saving Resources and Promoting Non-Desert Distributive Principles of Punishment.* Other rationales for executive clemency may be based more on practical and financial considerations. Some supporters of executive clemency argue that desert-based justice should not be the only function of the justice system and therefore support the early release of non-violent, rehabilitated, or older offenders who no longer pose a threat to society. Such releases have the potential to save taxpayer dollars and prevent the overcrowding of prisons.[57] However, there is little evidence to suggest executives use their clemency powers in such a utilitarian fashion. And, as discussed in chapter 3, reliance upon non-desert distributive principles is likely to undermine the system's moral credibility with the community and thereby its long-term crime control effectiveness.

Interests Opposing the Use of Executive Clemency

- *Desert-Based Justice.* Many opponents of executive clemency believe that it normally represents a harmful divergence from desert-based justice and allows offenders to escape a punishment proportional to the seriousness of their offense and their blameworthiness in committing it. While commutations and many pardons serve to directly reduce an offender's punishment, it is worth noting that some pardons are granted after an offender has already served their prison sentence. Such postrelease pardons may still represent a justice failure by absolving an unworthy individual of their publicly proclaimed guilt and removing any lingering consequences of a conviction (such as by restoring rights previously lost). However, even a desert-based system of justice is one that might support a grant of clemency in special cases where desert demands it.

- *Increased Corruption and Loss of Legal System Credibility.* Opponents of executive clemency argue that the clemency process is opaque and ideologically or personally driven rather than driven by mercy or justice. Placing such power in the hands of one executive allows for political agendas and personal connections to guide pardons, which hardly brings mercy to worthy individuals or upholds the moral credibility of the system. Given the common practice of the midnight pardon spree as an executive leaves office, it appears that many acts of clemency are largely political affairs rewarding those with the right connections. Executive clemency certainly facilitates political corruption.[58] More frighteningly, executives have only abused their pardon power on a smallish scale so far. The fact that it is entirely legal for an executive to pardon large numbers of his cronies or a politically favored category of offenders, and even potentially himself, should disturb any supporter of the rule of law.

- *Fairness and Equality.* Alongside the concern over desert-based punishments being voided by executive clemency is the concern that clemency is exercised in a deeply unfair or unequal fashion. Even when corruption is not intended, an executive's personal biases may shape their clemency decisions in a manner that undermines equal treatment under the law. Even if clemency judgments are made in an unbiased way, the use of such power for some small subset of offenders inevitably creates unjustified disparity in the allocation of punishment. Only a system-wide process that gives similar attention to all cases could avoid the unjustified disparity problem.

- *Less Deterrence and More Crime.* When offenders know they can be pardoned or granted clemency for political reasons or personal connections, the deterrent effect of the law declines, especially among the privileged and powerful in society. The decreased moral credibility of the legal system caused by corrupt executive clemency also contributes to spurring more crime. Individual offenders released early due to clemency have also gone on to commit more crimes, including murder sprees.[59]

C. THE NATURE AND EXTENT OF THE PROBLEM

While there is no difficulty in finding hundreds of examples of corrupt acts of clemency at both the state and federal levels producing clear failures of justice, it is harder to determine what proportion of pardons or commutations amount to failures of justice in the eyes of society. Oftentimes even dubious pardons receive little public scrutiny due to a lack of transparency. One problem at the state level is that clemency decisions are extremely opaque and data is commonly not collected or reported. This has led the United Nations High Commissioner for Human Rights to conclude that a majority of states in the United States lack the adequate transparency in their clemency systems needed for guaranteeing due process under international standards and protocols.[60]

It is possible, however, to sketch a general picture of the frequency with which executive clemency is given at the federal and state levels. It is also possible to examine the potential structural separation of powers problems posed by the existence of executive clemency in any system.

The Frequency of Federal Executive Clemency

Presidents and governors have employed clemency at widely varying rates depending on the time period and individual executive. In the case of US presidents, the percentage of pardon requests granted has gone down substantially over time.[61] For example, all presidents between President McKinley (in office 1897–1901) and President Carter (in office 1977–1981) granted between 20 and 41 percent of all requests for pardons.[62] However, these percentages began to change with President Reagan, who granted only 12 percent of requests (only 393 total pardons in his two-term presidency).[63] All presidents following Reagan have granted a maximum of 6 percent of pardon requests.[64] (Of course, some of these percentages may reflect in part an increase in the number of requests in recent times.[65]) Some presidents have been even more sparing. President G. W. Bush and President Trump granted a mere 2 percent of clemency requests (200 and 237, respectively). Other presidents have granted low percentages of clemency requests, but high absolute numbers such as President Obama who granted only 5 percent of clemency requests, but still gave clemency in 1,927 cases (including commutations)—more than ten times the number of President G. W. Bush or President Trump.[66] The low percentage rate in Obama's case was due to his administration encouraging federal prisoners to apply for clemency under a program called the Clemency Initiative.[67] In terms of overall numbers, US presidents collectively have granted clemency (including pardons and commutations) to over twenty thousand people since 1900, which averages to a little over nine hundred grants of clemency per president.[68] It is impossible to say how many of these would be perceived as justice failures, but as mentioned in the section on public complaints, the public appears to view most high-profile presidential pardons extremely negatively.

The Frequency of State Executive Clemency

There is no comprehensive study of state executive clemency frequency to date, but available evidence and research suggests that perhaps ten thousand or more acts of clemency occur at the state level every year.[69] There appears to be significant diversity in the frequency of clemency grants among the states. For example, more than five hundred full pardons are granted in Alabama each year.[70] In contrast, not a single pardon was granted in Alaska between 2006 and 2018.[71] Consider the following facts and statistics that seem to suggest a trend toward the increasing use of clemency across states.

- Between 1991 and 2005, governors in California granted a total of sixteen pardons.[72] After only two years in office since 2018, California governor Gavin Newsom had granted seventy-two pardons, seventy-nine commutations, and twenty medical reprieves, which amounted to a massive increase in the rate of pardoning.[73]
- In the entire twentieth century, Ohio governors granted a total of 2,634 pardons and 2,815 commutations.[74] Ohio governor Mike DeWine has stated his belief that "there are thousands of Ohioans, maybe tens of thousands of Ohioans" deserving of a pardon right now.[75] As a result, Ohio has set up a new pardoning initiative meant to greatly increase the use of clemency.[76]
- In 2016, New York governor Andrew Cuomo granted 101 conditional pardons, five full pardons, and twelve other clemencies.[77] Before the term of Cuomo's predecessor, Governor David Paterson, it had been many years since a New York governor had used the pardon power on anything approaching a regular basis.[78]
- In Colorado, Governor Bill Owens granted only thirteen pardons during his eight years in office (1999–2007). His successor, Bill Ritter (2007–2011), granted forty-two pardons and ten commutations. Governor John Hickenlooper (2011–2019) granted 156 pardons in addition to several commutations.[79]

- In Connecticut, the number of pardon applications has increased drastically. In 2006, 393 people underwent the process, while 1,857 applied in 2018. Approximately half of applicants are deemed eligible for relief. The state acted in 2015 to make the process simpler, and by 2019, 511 applications were granted full pardon; in 2020, that number was even higher with 936 Connecticut applicants being granted full pardons.[80]
- In 1988, the governor of Delaware granted twenty-eight pardons. In 2018, that number was 512.[81]
- In just over a decade, the frequency of pardon grants in Virginia increased more than tenfold. From 2010 to 2014, Governor Bob McDonnell granted only fifty-two simple pardons, the vast majority of which were in his final year. From 2018 to the end of his term in 2022, Governor Ralph Northam granted more than 1,200 pardons.[82]

While there has yet to be a comprehensive study measuring the change in state clemency practices, this cursory evidence suggests that state executives are increasingly making use of their clemency powers on a scale never seen before, perhaps out of a desire to reduce prison populations (the issue of decarceration is discussed in chapter 16). The fact that this significant expansion is occurring with little oversight makes it problematic.

Using Executive Clemency to Short-Circuit Legislative Criminalization Authority

In addition to allowing individual criminals to escape just punishment on the basis of corruption and personal favoritism, executive clemency poses a broader threat to the structure of a constitutional system.

First, executive clemency often gives executives broad powers to frustrate any attempt to hold them and their administrations accountable for illegal actions. The fact that pardons can be issued preemptively before conviction to head off a criminal investigation is disturbing to anyone with an imagination of what a corrupt executive could do with such power. While such preemptive pardons are rare (likely not exceeding five per year at both federal and state level),[83] they are an avenue for profound future abuse. Such concerns also apply to the possibility (not yet used) of the power to self-pardon, which is disputed, but may be legally possible by the president and some state governors.

A second structural concern with executive clemency is that it allows the executive to usurp legislative and judicial functions in criminalization and punishment decisions, as discussed previously. While executives have been somewhat restrained in their usurpations to date, the power that clemency gives executives to break the system is frightening. For example, given the policy-based group pardons that have gone without challenge to date, it apparently would be possible for the president to simply pardon all individuals charged or convicted of certain federal crimes of which the president disapproved, thereby de facto decriminalizing them. Even more extreme, but apparently still equally legal, an executive devoted to prison abolition (see chapter 16 for a discussion of the prison abolition movement) could simply announce a policy of pardoning or commuting all (or at least certain groups of) criminals sentenced to prison, thereby forcing sentencing judges to use nonincarcerative sanctions for the defined groups or have the prison sentences executively overturned. Executives could also change legislatively mandated punishments by systematically resentencing offenders through commutations to reduce sentences by the desired amount. As noted earlier, this power of resentencing was used by President Obama to reduce the sentences of drug offenders and has been used by governors to clear their states' death rows by eliminating the legislatively enacted death penalty. Even if one supports reducing the punishment for drug offenses and abolishing the death penalty, it is still concerning that executive clemency allows executives to usurp legislative and judicial roles to reach these goals. If the criminalization or punishment reforms make sense and have public support, the executive should press for changes through the normal legitimate legislative change process instead of exercising almost dictatorial powers unintentionally allowed by the clemency system. While some may argue that executive action is justified due to legislative gridlock, the answer to a partially broken system is not to break it further.

D. PUBLIC COMPLAINTS

Executive clemency has often sparked public controversy and complaint. Criticisms of the practice have been voiced by victims and their families, prosecutors, politicians, and by the public generally. In a case noted earlier, the sister of the man murdered by Joseph Ozment, who was pardoned by Mississippi governor Barbour in 2012, was outraged by the pardon and "angry" that Ozment will now live freely while her murdered brother is dead.[84] Typical of such anger among victims' families, the daughter of the woman kidnapped and raped by Reginald McFadden, a Pennsylvania

murderer who had his sentence commuted in 1994 only to go on a rape and murder spree, has expressed her anger to lawmakers and advocated reforms to the pardon process.[85]

Scholars have also raised concerns with how the pardon process is increasingly being used of late. Harvard Law professor Jack Goldsmith deemed eighty-six of Donald Trump's ninety-four executive pardons to be "aberrant," alerting the public to what he believes is a dire need for clemency reform to prevent future large-scale failures of justice.[86] Government officials have also often complained about the use of executive clemency. In response to Illinois governor George Ryan's commutation of 164 death sentences in 2003, US senator William Haine claimed that "[Ryan] may have irreparably injured the law itself . . . he has profoundly insulted his subordinates in the system—the state's attorneys, the police officers, the jurors and judges."[87] When President Trump commuted the sentence of political ally Roger Stone in 2020, in what was widely perceived as a politically motivated decision, many commentators and politicians similarly called for reform.[88] Many in the public are also concerned about potential future abuses of the pardon power, especially the potential for self-pardons, given that Donald Trump faces possible conviction on federal charges while running for president in 2024.[89]

The general public usually disapproves of high-profile pardons. For example, Gerald Ford's decision to pardon Richard Nixon was disapproved of by a majority of the public at the time and arguably caused Ford to lose the 1976 presidential election.[90] Polls taken after controversial presidential pardons such as those by George H. W. Bush and Bill

Clinton have also shown public disapproval of the pardoning power with opposition ranging as high as 75 percent.[91] More recently, 76 percent of the public opposed Donald Trump pardoning any of his former political aides.[92] The public abhors clemency decisions that smack of corruption or favoritism, but a clemency system sheltered from political or personal considerations, that fairly sought out offenders whom society considers worthy of mercy, might command public support.

E. REFORMS

Some possible reforms to executive clemency have been proposed or implemented at the federal and state level. Reforms involving a restriction of clemency power often require a constitutional amendment, which is far easier at a state level than in the federal system.

More Stringent Conditions in the State Clemency Review Process. Some reforms to the pardoning process at the state level have originated from outraged victims, who argue that pardons should be conditional on the completion of numerous hurdles meant to exclude offenders who do not deserve clemency. Samantha Broun, the daughter of the woman murdered by Reginald McFadden, has become a fierce advocate of clemency reform since her mother's killer was granted clemency in Pennsylvania. Her proposed reforms would require criminals to attend a commutation hearing or meet personally for an interview with a member of the Board of Pardons.[93] Her suggested reforms in Pennsylvania were largely adopted in 1995.[94]

Expanding the Review Process in the Office of Pardon Attorney. Congress cannot restrict the president's pardon power with legislation, a fact affirmed in multiple Supreme Court cases.[95] However, Congress can and has made changes to the review process used by the Office of Pardon Attorney (OPA) in the Department of Justice. Most presidential pardons involve an OPA investigation that can be initiated by a petition from the offender or by presidential request. Congress passed the Pardon Attorney Reform and Integrity Act in 2000, which states that investigations by the pardon attorney should involve obtaining any victim statements regarding the potential pardon, determine the opinion of law enforcement and judicial figures involved in the conviction, determine "whether the person involved may have information relevant to an ongoing investigation or prosecution or effort to apprehend a fugitive," or if the individual would pose a "threat of terrorism or ongoing or future criminal activity" if they were granted clemency.[96] The act also requires that all victims be notified of an investigation into a possible grant of clemency as well as if the clemency is granted and the offender is released. While such reforms improve the review process, presidents remain free to ignore the OPA or refuse to follow its recommendation.

More recently, there have been proposals in Congress to move the OPA review process to a separate panel of criminal justice experts, but this has not been implemented.[97]

Prevent Abuses of the Clemency Power Through Constitutional Amendment. Reforming the clemency power through constitutional amendment would be useful but seems impractical given the enormous difficulty in passing constitutional amendments, especially in the federal system. If a constitutional amendment were to be undertaken, one can imagine numerous forms it might take. For example, it might include bans on self-pardons, pardons of relatives or associates, pardons issued during a president's final months in office, as well as pre-conviction pardons.[98] Other possibilities involve diversifying the pardon power by resting it jointly in the president and the Speaker of the House, though this might do little if both are from the same political party.[99]

Some reformers advocate sweeping and unlikely changes to the very notion of executive clemency such as the following.

Utilize Executive Clemency Only for Wrongful Convictions. Executive clemency could be limited to granting clemency only in those cases where a wrongful conviction is believed to have occurred. Such a reform would require executives to provide proof that the recipient of clemency should not have been convicted and that all other legal remedies have been exhausted. The proposers claim that "American executives primarily utilize the clemency power for political expedience rather than to remedy wrongful convictions" and argue that the limiting of pardon grants to the wrongfully convicted would actually return the power of executive clemency to its original, intended purpose.[100]

End Executive Clemency in Favor of Legislative or Judicial Remedies. Some have gone further to suggest that executive clemency is a relic of the monarchical past that should simply be abolished. Overturning wrongful convictions or reducing unjust sentences could be handled through creating a more robust judicial process of reviewing past sentences based on new legislative guidelines as well as making it easier to challenge potentially wrongful convictions.

F. RECOMMENDATION: ADOPT MODEL PARDON BOARD TO REDUCE CLEMENCY ABUSE AND PROMOTE TRANSPARENCY

There are legitimate arguments in support of maintaining a clemency power both to correct injustices as well as to provide mercy to offenders where society believes they deserve it. However, resting that power in a single executive without outside inspection or review prevents transparency and consistency while allowing corruption to flourish. We recommend that jurisdictions adopt a pardon board that would implement a transparent and consistent set of guidelines in reviewing all clemency requests before providing a recommendation for the executive to grant or deny.

Such a pardon board would have at least five members appointed by the executive (either governor or president) and confirmed by the Senate (or state legislature). Commissioners would serve staggered terms to increase the chance that each executive will appoint only a portion of the members of the board. The pardon board would review all clemency requests according to a detailed set of clemency guidelines approved by the legislature. These guidelines would list important factors to consider in the decision to grant clemency and might include such things as the seriousness of the crime and blameworthiness of the offender, the offender's conduct post-conviction, the views of the victim(s), whether the law or public opinion has changed regarding the crime in question, an evaluation of the offender's ability to reintegrate into society, and other relevant considerations. The guidelines would make clear that clemency should be utilized in a manner consistent with societal understandings of justice, as any other acts of clemency are likely to be interpreted as justice failures undermining the credibility of the justice system. The current process of granting executive clemency, even when it involves state pardon boards, often violates this key criterion.[101] The guidelines could be drafted and updated by the pardon board itself subject to approval by the legislature, or they could be drafted by a separate commission of experts and enacted by the legislature.

The guidelines would be applied in each case in a transparent fashion with a public hearing in all considerations of clemency where the offender, victims, other concerned parties, and the public could voice their views and provide evidence in support or opposition to any grant of clemency. A record of such proceedings should be publicly available along with the pardon board's final written recommendation and the reasoning behind it applying the clemency guidelines. The executive would then decide whether to grant the recommended clemency or not.

This pardon board could be implemented by the legislature regardless of their constitutional ability to restrict the executive's clemency power. For example, Congress could create such a pardon board (similar to its reforms to the Office of Pardon Attorney) that would process all requests for federal clemency and be available to investigate any individuals suggested by the president. Of course, given the current constitutional grant of authority, the president could ignore the pardon board and grant clemency outside its review and recommendation process, but the board would still conduct an investigation and recommendation on any clemency issued by the president. This would create a measure of accountability

as a president who routinely granted pardons against the recommendation of the pardon board would more likely be seen as engaging in abuse of power by a measurable metric, thus incurring a political cost. Yet the reform would not challenge the constitutional power currently vested in the president and so would be constitutionally permissible.

However, where constitutionally permitted, we recommend legislatures require the prior affirmative recommendation of the pardon board before the governor can grant executive clemency, as is already the case in fourteen states.[102] For example, Pennsylvania added a Board of Pardons to the state's constitution in 1872 specifically to "prevent . . . shenanigans by [the] governor."[103] Now the Pennsylvania governor must receive the approval of the Board of Pardons before issuing any executive clemency. Clemency is too important and too powerful to be left to the whims of a single individual. Requiring both the approval of the board and the executive would seem to minimize the possibility of abusing the power while retaining the power for those special cases where it is appropriate.

This proposal of a model pardon board operating under clear and transparent clemency guidelines is by no means unprecedented. Some state pardon boards already operate under guidelines of a sort (though they are not legislatively enacted nor are they very detailed).[104] Internationally, other countries have adopted similar clemency-granting processes. In Australia, the pardoning process is conducted by a pardon board appointed by the attorney general. Petitions are almost always made public and hearing minutes are recorded and published. The royal governor only issues clemency upon the explicit recommendation of the board. The board's decisions are based upon publicly available criteria such as the offender's assistance to law enforcement, their rehabilitation, the seriousness of their crime, and the effect of clemency on any victims, public safety, and deterrence.[105]

A pardon board along the lines of our model would likely have prevented, or at least decreased the likelihood of, most, if not all, of the serious justice failures caused by individual executives abusing their pardoning power discussed previously. The personal and political favoritism shown by governors Matt Bevin and Haley Barbour, as well as President Clinton, would not have been supported by the recommendations of a pardon board acting according to clear clemency guidelines. Moreover, even if such executives defied the pardon board in issuing clemency, they would have suffered the increased political and reputational cost of engaging in an officially recognized abuse of power. Additionally, vesting clemency power in the joint decision of a pardon board and executive (as is ideal where constitutionally permissible) would go far toward addressing structural concerns raised by the ability of a single rogue executive to abuse the clemency power and violate the separation of powers.

Part IV

SOCIAL AND POLITICAL INFLUENCES

Citizen Non-Cooperation

A. INTRODUCTION

WITHOUT COOPERATION AND ASSIS-tance from citizens, police and prose-cutors are often powerless to solve or prosecute crimes. Studies show that wit-nesses are investigators' most useful asset in solving criminal cases, even more so than physical evidence.[1] As one study concluded, "Without individual and community cooperation, very few crimes would come to the attention of the po-lice and very few crimes would ever be solved."[2] Citizen non-cooperation with law enforcement authorities is thus a se-rious and often overlooked cause of jus-tice failures. In terms of magnitude, it is easily one of the greatest causes covered in this book. Citizen non-cooperation stems from a variety of causes, includ-ing witness intimidation, the psychologi-cal pressure and fear of public shaming that arises because of the stop snitching movement, cynicism over the legal sys-tem's ability to do justice, and fear or distrust of police over real or perceived police misconduct and use of excessive force. This chapter examines each issue in turn.

The issues examined in the chapter il-lustrate the problems that arise from the justice system's loss of moral credibility with the community (a topic discussed in chapter 3). When the legal system loses credibility, citizens do not believe the system will deliver justice, and so they are less likely to cooperate with police—

making their view of the system a self-ful-filling prophecy as more justice failures result from the non-cooperation. An-other disturbing feature of the problem is that citizen non-cooperation particularly affects poor and minority communities, where many residents feel abandoned by the system and resentful of police, espe-cially given a tragic history of police rac-ism. Finding ways to break this vicious cycle and replace it with a virtuous cycle of more citizen cooperation leading to more justice, and thus more cooperation, should be of paramount importance to those concerned with doing justice of all kinds, whether racial, social, or criminal.

The problems discussed in this chapter present a somewhat more difficult chal-lenge than those of previous chapters. Typically, the reforms to most previous problems discussed lay in altering the conduct of judges, prosecutors, police, or other official actors involved in the criminal justice system. Those reforms might plausibly be achieved simply by altering a rule or practice through a case decision, statutory enactment, or regu-latory revision. But in this chapter the goal inevitably ends up being to change the perspective of community members, which is more difficult. While policy changes can influence public percep-tions, messaging is often equally if not more important. While media outlets, politicians, and special interest groups have the tools and experience to shift public opinion, the criminal justice system has little experience in this role, instead relying on others to communicate its performance and goals. Unfortunately, outside actors may have their own reasons for portraying the criminal justice system negatively. Thus, some of the reform possibilities suggested in this chapter may require the criminal justice system to take on a more formal role in public communication than it used to or for which it is currently prepared.

Competing Interests

The following discussion of competing interests applies to all the causes of citizen non-cooperation covered in this chapter.

INTERESTS SUPPORTING THE STATUS QUO OF CITIZEN NON-COOPERATION Unlike for other causes of justice failures, there are no societal interests upheld by any form of citizen non-cooperation discussed in this chapter. Community refusal to work with police and prosecutors has only negative effects on society. This makes the problem especially ripe for reform, as there are no societal interests sacrificed by fostering better community cooperation with the justice system.

INTERESTS OPPOSING THE STATUS QUO OF CITIZEN NON-COOPERATION

- *Greater Justice.* More citizen cooperation with the justice system leads to greater justice due to more crime reporting, more witness cooperation with investigations and thus higher clearance rates, and a greater internalization of the law's norms as respect for the legal system increases.
- *Greater Deterrence and Less Crime.* Increased citizen cooperation leads to greater deterrence as criminals fear communities will work with police to catch them. The perception that criminals will eventually be caught

has the greatest effect on discouraging criminal activity.[3] Moreover, criminals who are apprehended will be unable to immediately commit new crimes. Police-community cooperation is a key element in making neighborhoods safer.

- *Public Faith in the Justice System and Vigilantism.* The current epidemic of citizen non-cooperation severely damages the public's faith in the justice system in affected communities. The knowledge that even if a crime is witnessed no justice will result makes many people not even bother reporting crimes. Less faith in the justice system in turn causes more crime and more vigilantism, as people turn to street justice instead of involving police.
- *Breaking the Power of Criminal Gangs.* Gangs depend on intimidating citizens from cooperating with the justice system for much of their power. Increased citizen cooperation in gang-related cases would secure more gang convictions and help break the power of gangs in neighborhoods as well as the fear and crime they spawn. This would yield a host of positive benefits by reducing crime, increasing public trust in the justice system, and allowing children to focus on their education and future instead of worrying about joining the right gangs to ensure survival.

B. WITNESS INTIMIDATION

People often imagine criminals get away with murder thanks to careful planning and avoiding being witnessed in the act. In reality, killers can brazenly shoot their victims in front of crowds of people and still walk away uncaught due to America's epidemic of witness intimidation. Police and prosecutors depend on witnesses to help solve crimes and secure convictions, but witnesses are often too scared to co-operate lest they become the next victim.

Witness intimidation is widespread across America, although when success-ful, it defies efforts at measurement. But available evidence points to a catastro-phe of silence. One study suggests 23 percent of reported serious crimes are not prosecuted because of witness non-cooperation,[4] and prosecutors in Balti-more and Boston, for example, report witness intimidation in up to 80 per-cent of cases.[5] A National Youth Gang Survey found that 83 percent of police departments in larger areas reported that witness intimidation was common.[6] Another study found 36 percent of wit-nesses who testified in criminal courts in Bronx County, New York, received direct threats.[7] Perhaps the single great-est contributor to failures of justice in murder cases is the lack of witnesses will-ing to testify or cooperate with police. In many if not most of the tens of thousands of unsolved murder cases across Amer-ica, police suspect who the likely killer is but are unable to proceed due to a lack of witness cooperation.[8] Witness intimi-dation is also widespread in rape cases and in any criminal case involving gang members. In a country where witnesses are routinely silent or silenced before, during, and after investigations, it is no wonder so many crimes go unsolved and so many serious offenders walk free.

Types of Witness Intimidation

Witness intimidation takes many forms. One report, which surveyed three hundred law enforcement agen-cies, examined the frequency of various types of threats in silencing witnesses. Eighty percent of respondents cited im-plicit threats as causing witness silence, 63 percent cited explicit threats of vio-lence, 53 percent cited actual violence, and 45 percent cited property damage.[9] The internet has also allowed for more effective and widespread intimidation both by targeting specific witnesses and by threatening whole communities that speaking out will result in retaliation.[10] Gang members have used social media to "put the word out that individuals who cooperated with law enforcement or testified against gang members would be targeted for violence or murder."[11] The silencing effect of threatened versus actual violence is similar because intimi-dators regularly carry out their threats.

Case Example: Latasha Shaw

On September 29, 2007, thirty-six-year-old Latasha Shaw and her sister are walking in Rochester, New York, when they observe a crowd at a busy inter-section.[12] Shaw is horrified to see her twelve-year-old daughter is at the center

Figure 14.1. Latasha Shaw was killed while trying to protect her daughter, 2007. Photo courtesy of Charnette Grayson and the Grayson family.

of a mob of mostly teenagers who are tormenting the girl for fun. The mother rushes to intervene and manages to free her daughter, who takes off running with her aunt. The mob, angry at having their fun interrupted, viciously attacks Shaw with anything that comes to hand including bottles, sticks, and knives. As a crowd of observers forms to watch the mob attack, Shaw is thrown to the ground, and the mob jumps on her and kicks her until she dies. The killers make no attempt to conceal themselves, and police hope the case will be easy to solve given the fifty or so witnesses to the murder. For months the police canvass the area trying to get witnesses to come forward, but Rochester is held in the grip of intimidation. The fear is such that no one talks to the police, and Shaw's murderers are never brought to justice.

The Nature and Extent of the Problem

Witness intimidation leads to reduced crime reporting, stunted investigations, and unsuccessful prosecutions. Despite being such a serious contributor to justice failures, witness intimidation is rarely punished. The impact of witness intimidation is especially severe in gang-dominated neighborhoods where intimidation prevents almost any successful legal action against gang members.

WITNESS INTIMIDATION'S PREVALENCE AND EFFECTS Measuring the effects of witness intimidation across all crimes (including unsolved crime) is difficult, as most successful intimidation does not leave traces for researchers to quantify because the cases are never cleared. Indeed, witness intimidation can lead to there being no official case to begin with when the victim is intimidated into not reporting the crime. A fear of reporting crimes is understandable. For example, the Rape

Prosecution Unit in Philadelphia reports that 50 percent of rapists threaten their victims with violence or death if they report the crime.[13] To get a rough sense of what a dramatic effect non-reporting due to intimidation can have in rape cases, consider this: of the 463,000 rapes and sexual assaults annually,[14] 69 percent are not reported,[15] and 20 percent of those non-reporting victims explain they failed to report specifically out of fear of retaliation.[16] That is over 63,000 sexual assaults a year never reported due to intimidation.

For many crimes where police identify the likely suspect, and even technically "clear" the case, conviction is not possible due to widespread intimidation. A study of 1,547 cleared murder, rape, assault, and burglary cases found that 23 percent were not prosecuted due to witness non-cooperation, and 28 percent of all witnesses interviewed expressed a fear of retaliation if they cooperated.[17] In other words, intimidation prevented prosecution of a quarter of *solved* serious crimes.

However, witness intimidation occurs in far more than a quarter of cases in many jurisdictions. Research indicates that, in some gang-dominated areas, the level of witness intimidation is 75 to 100 percent for violent crimes.[18] Two-thirds of law enforcement agencies around the country have described witness intimidation as "common."[19] Though witness intimidation occurs everywhere, it is a somewhat greater problem for prosecutors in large jurisdictions.[20] Fifty-one percent of prosecutors reported it as a significant problem in large jurisdictions compared to 43 percent of prosecutors in small jurisdictions.[21] The problem is especially acute in urban areas where 88 percent of prosecutors reported witness intimidation as a serious problem.[22] Witness intimidation often causes or exacerbates cities' poor clearance rates. For example, in Indianapolis, which has seen would-be witnesses murdered, witness non-cooperation heavily contributed to the city's 35 percent homicide clearance rate in 2017.[23] With roughly 150 criminal homicides per year, at least twenty *cleared* cases in a single year had to be dismissed between 2015 and 2017 due to witness intimidation.[24]

THE FAILURE TO PROSECUTE WITNESS INTIMIDATION Witness intimidation is a crime itself, but efforts to prosecute it almost always fail. Even those few arrested on charges of witness intimidation are often never convicted, sometimes due to more intimidation. In 2014, only 136 federal arrests were made for "threatening communication" in violent crimes.[25] At the state and local level, the prosecution of witness intimidation differs greatly depending on the discretion of prosecutors, with many not even bothering to try to bring charges because they are doomed to fail.[26] Domestic and international comparisons suggest witness intimidation is extremely difficult to prosecute even in that small percentage of cases where charges are brought.[27] While many prosecutors recognize the need to combat witness intimidation,[28] it is hard to generate any deterrent effect given how few instances of witness intimidation lead to an arrest or conviction. Deterrence is also difficult because many intimidators have already committed serious crimes that carry lengthy punishments, so they have little to lose by engaging in intimidation to avoid an upcoming prosecution.

THE SPECIAL PROBLEM OF GANG-RELATED WITNESS INTIMIDATION Some of the main culprits behind witness intimidation are gangs. Gangs foster a culture of fear to suppress any witnesses from interfering with their criminal activities, and witness intimidation occurs in nearly all gang-related cases. In 2004, the DA of Suffolk County testified to the Massachusetts Legislature that witness intimidation occurred in 90 percent of cases involving gangs and gun violence.[29] Other prosecutors estimate that witness intimidation occurs in 75 to 100 percent of violent crimes in gang-dominated neighborhoods.[30] No sane person would choose to testify against gang members who literally hold the power of life and death on their community's streets, and this is one reason why securing convictions is so difficult in gang-infested neighborhoods. As a National Institute of Justice study found, "victim and witness intimidation is *endemic* in neighborhoods infested with gang activity and drug sales and virtually *invisible* to people outside those neighborhoods."[31]

While police are usually criticized for not solving serious crimes, the lack of arrests and subsequent charges and convictions are often due to a lack of cooperating witnesses.[32] For example, officials pointed to gangs and intimidation as the reason why a suspect was only identified or arrested in less than 30 percent of Boston's homicides in 2005.[33] Despite the fact that there are typically more witnesses to gang-related murders than there are to non-gang-related murders, those witnesses are less likely to cooperate with law enforcement, resulting in gang and drug related murders being cleared 69 percent less often than other murders.[34] Even worse, the generalized fear and intimidation the presence of a gang produces is not even an identifiable crime, but it can be far more potent than a direct threat of violence.

Public Complaints

Despite witness intimidation being a leading cause of justice failures, the public often overlooks it because it rarely makes headlines when done successfully. Much of the public concern expressed over intimidation comes directly from victims and their families seeking justice. Tosha Braswell, the mother of a slain fifteen-year-old high school football star in Newark, expressed her grief and anger that prosecutors would not move forward on her son's case because of witness intimidation. "How can they leave him out there?" she said of her son's killer.[35] Prosecutors often have no choice, however, due to witnesses' justifiable fear. Luis Morales, a resident of Allentown, Pennsylvania, summed up the fear of many city residents who keep silent: "From the young to the old, they know." He explained, "You have someone here that is so bold and brazen to shoot at someone in front of people. . . . If they would go to that extent, this is a person that really doesn't care. If they found out that you opened your mouth, they will get you."[36] But while victims' families, police, and prosecutors routinely lament the effects of witness intimidation, the issue does not receive the attention it deserves from policymakers or the news media. There is something tragically appropriate about a problem of silence going unaddressed due to public silence on the issue, and more needs to be done to call attention to the witness intimidation crisis.

Reforms

Witness intimidation is an extremely challenging problem to solve given its prevalence, severity, and diffuseness. It does not make sense for many, if not most, witnesses to testify against violent offenders given the enormous personal risk of retaliation. Choosing to testify often requires tremendous personal courage to willingly risk one's life for justice. However, many reforms have been proposed or implemented to attempt to mitigate the problem.

Anonymous and Secure Crime Reporting. Many police departments have moved to create anonymous and secure crime reporting systems. Some jurisdictions have also introduced anonymous text a tip programs to allow reporting any information, including about ongoing investigations.[37] Boston's anonymous text messaging crime tip program showed promising results, including a "five fold increase in tips" from 2006 to 2007.[38] Some departments even provide incentives, with Palm Beach's "Crime Stoppers" program[39] and Philadelphia's Live Operator Tip Line Service compensating witnesses who provide anonymous information to police.[40] In total, roughly 80 percent of police departments around the country have implemented methods to allow crime victims or witnesses to anonymously report crimes to the police.[41] However, while this can help police identify suspects, it does little to help in situations where court testimony is required to secure convictions. Police often know who committed a crime, sometimes because of anonymous reporting, but presenting enough evidence and proving it in court is impossible when witnesses are scared to publicly testify.

Improve the Availability and Effectiveness of Witness Protection. Many reforms have involved establishing witness protection programs that aim to ensure that threats do not turn into actual physical violence.[42] Witness protection on a federal level was established with the Organized Crime Control Act of 1970, which established the US Marshals Service's Witness Security Program. This program, which has protected nineteen thousand participants since it was established, "provides for the security, health and safety of government witnesses, and their immediate dependents, whose lives are in danger as a result of their testimony against drug traffickers, terrorists, organized crime members and other major criminals."[43] The Victim Witness Assistance Unit in Washington, DC, helps roughly four hundred to five hundred witnesses each year with security concerns, including changing door locks, implementing home alarm systems, paying for moving expenses, and funding deposits at new apartments.[44] Furthermore, the Federal Victim and Witness Protection Act of 1982 and the Federal Victims of Crime Act of 1984 (VOCA) provided assistance to state and local programs assisting victims and witnesses with protection services.[45]

When witness protection programs have been implemented, convictions have significantly increased. A study in 1994 concluded that among witness protection cases there was a trial conviction rate of 100 percent and an overall conviction rate of 95 percent.[46] However, only 47 percent of police departments have some protective measures for witnesses, and only 34 percent have programs to relocate witnesses.[47] A common proposal is simply to increase funding for existing programs to scale up their effects. However, witness protection is normally extremely intensive, expensive, and an enormous burden on witnesses themselves who must sacrifice their normal life in the hopes of helping secure justice. While its expansion can help those witnesses willing to sacrifice their personal interests to help justice, and is essential in

many organized crime cases, it is unlikely to be an effective means of combating the broader plague of witness intimidation where most witnesses would not be willing to bear such life-changing costs even if the state could pay for it.

Promote Community Policing. Other efforts have aimed to decrease witness intimidation by building trust between the community and local law enforcement and promoting a culture of crime reporting. The hope is that witnesses will trust that police and others in their community will keep them safe if they come forward with information. PhillyRising, for example, hopes for police to adopt a form of community policing, where neighborhood associations, clergy members, community groups and activists, and local leaders collaborate to increase trust between police and community members.[48] Rochester, New York's "You Bet I Told" campaign aims to encourage citizens' cooperation with law enforcement by reassuring the community that individuals who come forward with information about a crime will be protected and will not suffer retaliation.[49] Currently, 59 percent of police departments have some kind of partnerships with community groups, 54 percent have partnerships with schools (which seek safer neighborhoods for their children), 43 percent are partnered with religious organizations (which speak about the moral obligation to report crime), 32 percent are partnered with public housing authorities, and 30 percent are partnered with news media outlets.[50] However, without other reforms, such public messaging attempts are largely hollow because they provide no actual security to witnesses.

Ideally, well-designed community policing initiatives can allow neighborhoods to provide their own witness protection by looking out for the safety of witnesses, keeping in contact with police about threats, and ensuring that potential intimidators know they will have to escape the detection and wrath of the community. This requires tackling no-snitch codes (an issue discussed in section C).

Punish Witness Intimidation More Severely. Some states, such as Maryland, have increased penalties for witness intimidation. In 2004, a bill proposed by Baltimore state's attorney Patricia Jessamy was passed, which increased punishment for acts of witness intimidation from a maximum of five years to twenty years in prison. However, such reforms have barely any effect on intimidation rates as state legislator Jill P. Carter of Baltimore explained: they are "just addressing witnesses at the point where they're unavailable for trial, which means they have already been intimidated or maybe even hurt or killed. That's not witness protection."[51] Other proposals have focused on increasing prosecution under existing laws, but the difficulty of prosecuting the crime (and the fact that the intimidation has already occurred) makes it unlikely to have a wide effect.[52]

Greater Federal Assistance in Combatting Witness Intimidation. At the national level, former US senator from Pennsylvania Arlen Specter proposed legislation to make witness intimidation in state court proceedings a federal offense.[53] This would have allowed federal resources to directly combat the problem of witness intimidation at the state level. However, the law did not pass. In 2021, legislation was proposed in Congress that would require the US Attorney General to grant $150 million to local governments seeking to develop short-term witness protection programs.[54] So far, it has yet to be adopted.

Guarantee Non-Prosecution for Witnesses. While it is already common for witnesses who have engaged in criminal conduct to be offered plea deals in order to secure evidence against other criminals, states could consider providing legislative commitments to not prosecute witnesses who are willing to report a crime and testify, even if they were involved in some lesser criminal conduct at the time. However, this would likely do little to solve the problem as retaliation is a greater threat than prosecution to most criminal witnesses.

Adopting Anti-Gang Strategies. Because witness intimidation often stems from gangs, one way to combat the problem is focusing on breaking a gang's power over a neighborhood. Gang-suppression strategies are numerous with varying results.[55] For example, some jurisdictions have established drug loitering ordinances that have helped "disperse gangs and drug dealers in gang-dominated areas."[56] Another common anti-gang policy is to add a gang enhancement penalty to the sentence of any proven gang member. For example, the California Street Terrorism Enforcement and Prevention Act increases the punishment for crimes associated with gang activity.[57] In Nevada, prosecutors can combine the state's intimidation statute with the state's gang membership statute to double the punishment for witness intimidation.[58] With this method, gang-related witness intimidation can face a sentence of up to twelve years in prison, six more years than the maximum sentence for non-gang-associated witness intimidation. Of course, increasing penalties for intimidation by gangs will have little or no effect if the possibility of conviction remains negligible.

Other strategies have targeted gangs by establishing and funding special anti-gang enforcement units. For example, in 1994 and 1995, Arizona granted a total of $15 million to the Department of Public Safety to establish a Gang Intelligence Team Enforcement Mission (GITEM) to address the rise in gang activity throughout the state. The program focused on both urban and rural areas and "established a core group of trained gang investigators, deployed from two locations in the State, that responds to calls for service from any law enforcement agency in the State with both planned responses and crisis intervention."[59]

In terms of prosecution strategies, the federal Racketeer Influenced and Corrupt Organizations Act (RICO) statute makes it easier to prosecute those engaged in illegal activities on behalf of a criminal organization such as organized crime or gangs. Thirty-three states have similar RICO laws. While such laws were initially used mainly to fight the mafia, federal prosecutors have begun using RICO to more aggressively prosecute gang members and their leaders.[60]

Expand Forfeiture by Wrongdoing Exception. Currently, statements made by witnesses before trial generally cannot be admitted at trial under hearsay rules if the witness is killed, intimidated, or otherwise prevented from appearing at the trial (such evidence is inadmissible because the defendant will not have an opportunity for confrontation and cross-examination). The "forfeiture by wrongdoing" exception in the federal rules of evidence allows such statements to be admitted if the defendant took action in order to prevent the witness from appearing at trial. Some have proposed expanding the forfeiture by wrongdoing exception to allow such statements

at trial if the witness does not appear at trial due to criminal action (including witness intimidation) engaged in by any party (not just the defendant). Such a broader exception aimed at allowing intimidated witnesses' prior statements at trial already exists in other countries such as Israel.[61] However, such a reform in the United States would likely require the Supreme Court to overturn its precedent in the 2008 ruling of *Giles v. California*, which strictly limited the forfeiture by wrongdoing exception to apply only if *the defendant* took action that prevented the witness from testifying and took the action for that explicit purpose.[62] In other words, the exception does not currently apply if the gang itself undertakes the intimidation, with no participation by the defendant, which is a common situation.

Recommendation: Protect Witness Identities in Cases of Likely Intimidation

There is no silver bullet solution to the problem of witness intimidation. To a large extent, it presents a chicken and egg problem: intimidation cannot be effectively controlled until police can reduce the perceived threat of intimidation by offenders, but such progress is only possible with witness cooperation. In the absence of an obvious broader solution, we can only recommend what seems like the best of the more modest feasible reforms.

The single most effective means of fighting witness intimidation may be to allow anonymous testimony from witnesses in cases where intimidation is likely. Allowing witnesses to provide court testimony anonymously through prerecorded statements would reduce intimidation risks without imposing the extreme personal costs of witness protection programs. Currently, out-of-court statements by witnesses are generally considered hearsay, and therefore are inadmissible as evidence, but our proposal would create a hearsay exception for instances where there is a demonstrated risk to the physical safety of the witness that cannot be addressed by other means. (Moreover, a form of cross examination would still be available to the defendant, as described shortly.) The risk does not have to be posed by the defendant himself as long as there is reason to believe that the witness' fear of intimidation is likely due to the nature of the crime or the defendant. For example, a witness to a gang murder who lives in a neighborhood with active gang members would clearly be at risk even if there was no evidence of a specific direct threat such as a menacing note or a broken window.

For this proposal to be effective, a witness who fears intimidation should be anonymous to all except police, prosecution, and judge during the investigation and trial. Once the witness has been interviewed by investigators and their prerecorded statements taken, the prosecution would file a motion for an *ex parte* hearing to convince the judge that the witness is at risk of likely intimidation. If the judge is satisfied that the risk exists and cannot otherwise be protected against, they can approve the witness remaining anonymous. If the judge considers the testimony likely reliable and of probative value, the statement would be admitted at trial for consideration by the jury. All non-identifying information and testimony would be shared with the defense. During trial, the defense can (and almost certainly will) raise the anonymous nature of the testimony as reducing its credibility, but the prosecution can (to the extent possible without compromising anonymity) explain the risk posed

to the witness if they had their identity revealed in court. The defendant's constitutional right to cross examination could also still be honored by allowing defense counsel to cross-examine the witness using a video link that distorts the witness' voice and image (with the prosecution being able to object to any questions designed to identify the witness).

For our proposal to work, it is essential that the witness remains anonymous and that as few people as possible know their identity. While some have proposed restricting video recording of trials or closing them to the public to create more anonymity for a witness, this will inevitably fail as even in a closed trial the defendant will still learn the witness' identity. Some have suggested an alternative proposal under which a prerecorded statement by witnesses could be admitted if the witness is later intimidated or killed. But such a system, which provides no anonymity, is unlikely to encourage witnesses to risk their lives by testifying. The fact that their prerecorded statement can be admitted at trial will provide no comfort to them if they are dead. And gangs and other criminals associated with the defendant have every reason to kill witnesses even after they have testified as a means of taking revenge and promoting the credibility of their threats to future witnesses. Only anonymizing the witness to the defendant will protect witnesses and encourage their testimony where a realistic fear of intimidation exists.

Many may worry that allowing anonymous witnesses would damage the fairness and reputation of the American justice system. However, other Western countries, such as the United Kingdom, already allow similar anonymous testimony.[63] Anonymous witnesses were first used in the United Kingdom in 2005 in a case of the murder of two teenage girls; in the end, four men were convicted for the crime. The killers appealed claiming they had not received a fair trial, but the appeal was dismissed due to the rigorous requirements set for cases of witness anonymity being met.[64] For an anonymous witness to be allowed in the United Kingdom, the following is required: (1) a full evidential statement from the witness giving their true identity; (2) a redacted version of the witness' full evidential statement with all elements that could identify the witness removed; (3) a statement from the witness setting out their fear about giving evidence if their identity is made known to the defendant, and, where appropriate, whether the witness will not give evidence without anonymity; and (4) a report that includes a full risk assessment undertaken by the police of the reasonableness of the witness' fears and explaining why other protection measures are not adequate.[65] When the use of witness anonymity at trial is granted by a British court, the prosecution is obliged to provide as much information as possible to the defense.[66] Our proposal is essentially a version of the British system that has proven to work without damaging the right to a fair trial.

The US Supreme Court has not yet addressed the constitutionality of anonymous testimony, but a host of cases by federal courts have reviewed the issue and concluded that such testimony, under certain circumstances, does not violate the defendant's constitutional rights. In *Smith v. Illinois*, the Court, while highlighting the right of an accused person to confront witnesses under the Sixth Amendment, emphasized the duty to protect witnesses from "questions which go beyond the bounds of proper cross-examination merely to harass, annoy

or humiliate him."[67] Justice White remarked, in his concurring opinion, that he would place in that same category "inquiries which tend to endanger the personal safety of the witness,"[68] and many federal courts have followed that interpretation.[69] Several courts have explicitly upheld the constitutionality of anonymous testimony where the government establishes an actual threat to a witness (not necessarily by the defendant) and where the anonymous testimony does not deprive the defendant of an opportunity for effective cross-examination.[70]

It is easy to see how such a reform would make it easier to bring justice in cases where witness intimidation is likely. Recall the case of Latasha Shaw who was viciously attacked and murdered by a mob after she attempted to free her daughter from their physical harassment. Any one of the dozens of witnesses to the very public brutal killing could have identified at least some of the killers, but the pervasive fear of retaliation prevented them from speaking out. A system of anonymous testimony would likely have led to at least one person among the bystanders being willing to help police and provide testimony.

C. THE STOP SNITCHING MOVEMENT

In addition to witness intimidation by criminals and gangs, many urban communities are experiencing a troubling and destructive surge in social pressure to "stop snitching." The "stop snitching" movement refers to social pressure to stay silent about crimes and refuse to cooperate with police. While similar codes of silence existed before the phrase "stop snitching" emerged, the "stop snitching" phenomenon gained prominence in 2004 with the release of a popular Baltimore rapper's *Stop Snitchin*[71] DVD and the widespread sale of "stop snitchin'" t-shirts and other clothing.[72]

What differentiates the stop snitching movement from more direct forms of intimidation is that it operates through a powerful self-enforcing social norm. Adherents to no-snitch codes are not necessarily safer due to their silence—because supporting the alternative of street justice can also be dangerous—but they are silent out of principle. The "code of the street" demands no cooperation with police, and disputes are settled outside the law—often violently.[73] While it is somewhat understandable why those directly involved in crime might not cooperate with police, the wider effects of the "stop snitching" movement have portrayed police as the enemy and made more citizens who might otherwise have cooperated with law enforcement choose not to. One study of the phenomenon concluded:

> But stop snitching broadly writ is more than just witness intimidation: it is an exhortation for the whole community to keep quiet, to not trust in, talk to, or cooperate with law enforcement. In these terms the citizen who calls police because people are dealing drugs on her doorstep may be as much of a snitch as the dealer who coughs up names in exchange for a favorable plea agreement.[74]

While there have been many efforts to curb the movement, it has shown little sign of stopping and has spread online through websites and social media pages devoted to exposing "rats" and "snitches." These codes of silence are particularly popular among the youth, with 89 percent of police departments in one survey reporting young people in crime-ridden communities are especially

unwilling to report crimes and to cooperate with police investigations.[75] Codes of silence are also particularly prevalent in poor and minority communities, which often have a troubled history with law enforcement, high levels of legal cynicism, and are worst affected by serious crime.

These highly destructive norms are epitomized in the last words of a murder victim who told police as he lay dying, "If I knew who shot me, I would not tell you. That's the way the street works."[76] "The way the street works" can be so deeply ingrained in some people that cooperating with the police is seen as betraying one's community. One study interviewing residents in communities with no-snitching codes found that "being labeled a snitch carries a price, not just of potential violence, but of ostracism by neighbors and peers."[77] When "snitches get stitches," even if only metaphorically, there are fewer snitches and more failures of justice.

Case Example: Israel Ramirez

On February 5, 2006, bodyguard Israel Ramirez is providing security for rapper Busta Rhymes at a Brooklyn studio while the rapper films a music video featuring the appearances of other rappers such as 50 Cent, DMX, and Mary J. Blige.[78] Some of 50 Cent's entourage grow increasingly rowdy and are ordered to leave the studio. Rhymes, who wants to soothe ruffled feathers, follows them out. An angry confrontation ensues, and one of the expelled group draws a gun to shoot Rhymes. Ramirez grabs at the gun to protect Rhymes and is shot in the chest. He dies at Rhymes's feet as the killer flees. Despite Rhymes and dozens of others seeing the killer up close, all refuse to cooperate with the police due to

Figure 14.2. Israel Ramirez was killed while working as a security guard for Busta Rhymes, 2002. Photo by Mikael "Mika" Väisänen, 2002, Hamburg, Germany, https://en.m.wikipedia.org/wiki/File:Busta_rhymes-06-mika.jpg.

the "no-snitching" code prevalent in the rap community.[79] After Ramirez's family expresses outrage, Rhymes promises them he will work to bring justice for the man who died protecting him, but in fact Rhymes sticks to the code of silence and does not tell investigators what he knows. The killer is never caught.

The Nature and Extent of the Problem

Most people even in high-crime communities are law abiding with no desire to protect criminality.[80] However, no-snitch codes have gained widespread traction among the youth and criminal subcultures (such as gangs). For example, studies show young people are much less likely to report crimes to police (53 percent) than seniors (87 percent).[81]

One reason for the adoption of no-snitch codes even by innocent civilians who are likely to be victims of criminality is a belief that police will not truly help (an issue discussed more in section D on legal cynicism). In minority neighborhoods especially, many residents have a deep-rooted distrust in law enforcement that makes them more likely to adopt no-snitch codes. This has occurred due to a disheartening combination of perceived police bias, a tragic history of police racism, instances of police misconduct, a belief that violent crime in minority neighborhoods will not be taken seriously, harsh drug laws that are seen as unjust, and the exceedingly low conviction rates for crimes.[82] In other words, the credibility of the law and law enforcement is already so low that many non-criminals have embraced no-snitch codes out of a belief that talking to police can do little good and can bring nothing but trouble.

The effect of no-snitch codes is damaging and widespread. According to a survey of law enforcement, 86 percent of communities have some type of code of silence that deters individuals from cooperating with law enforcement, and 47 percent of respondents specifically identified the stop snitching movement as the motivation.[83] Forty-five percent of respondents also reported stop snitching had reduced crime clearance rates, and 78 percent said it had made witnesses less likely to testify.[84] In Baltimore, for example, police claim that the stop snitching movement and mindset is "still one of the biggest problems their officers encounter."[85] The effects of no-snitch codes are especially evident in the high number and low clearance rate of street shootings where the victims and perpetrators are likely to come from adherents to a code of silence that calls for settling disputes outside the law. Such reliance on street justice in turn drives up homicide rates, often overwhelming limited investigative resources.

Public Complaints

In addition to vocal concerns expressed by police and prosecutors over the existence of codes of silence, activists have also urged their communities to reject the culture of stop snitching. For example, a man who works with children in Harlem lamented how damaging the movement has been to Black communities. He claimed, "It's like you can't be a [B]lack person if you have a set of values that say, 'I will not watch crime happen in my community without getting involved to stop it.'"[86] Many law-abiding residents are furious or saddened at codes of silence that encourage more crime and lead to failures of justice every day.

But perhaps the most determined players in the struggle to end the stop snitching movement and restore community cooperation with law enforcement are the mothers who have lost their sons to homicide and have been left without answers due to the lack of witness cooperation. Monique Irvis, whose son Eric Woods was shot, felt that Eric's best friends knew what happened yet refused to come forward with information out of respect for the code of the street. Monique asked her son's friend, "I mean that light's so bright where my son was shot at, and you right here, and you don't see nothing? . . . So you can't tell me you don't know who did it."[87] Despite being an obvious witness, Eric's friend never helped police.

On her death bed with cancer after the murder of her son, another mother urged the public to prioritize justice over the stop snitching movement. She pleaded, "I'm sick myself. I got cancer. I wasn't expecting to bury my son, I was expecting my son to bury me. I need some justice before I lay my head down. I want him caught."[88] Her grieving daughter echoed her sentiments, begging her community, "Don't be afraid to speak up because it could be your son, it could be your brother, it could be your sister. . . . You would want somebody to help you. You would want somebody to say something. So do the same for others that you would want done for you."[89]

Many such mothers of murder victims are protesting stop snitching and working to end codes of silence in their communities.[90] In Nashville, Clemmie Greenlee, another mother of a murdered son, is working with local organizations, including Nashville Peacemakers and Mothers Over Murder, to start community-wide conversations about stop snitching. But such efforts have yet to bear significant fruit as around North Nashville there are still signs reading, "it still ain't kool 2 snitch."[91]

Reforms

Because abiding by no-snitch codes is not itself a crime, combating their influence can only be done through cultural messaging. Cultural changes are often the hardest to achieve, and despite many recognizing how destructive codes of silence are, such codes remain firmly entrenched across the country. Some attempts at reform have been made or proposed.

Police Counter-Messaging. Police have tried to address stop snitching by launching their own counter-messaging encouraging youth to report crimes. For example, Maryland police responded to the original *Stop Snitchin'* DVD in 2004 with a rebuttal video titled "Keep

Talking."[92] But police often lack the required credibility with those who are vulnerable to joining or being influenced by the stop snitching movement.[93]

Boycotts of Stop Snitching Promoters. Some activists and city officials have responded to the stop snitching movement by urging boycotts of stop snitching merchandise and promoters. Short of boycotts, others have taken to persuading propagators of the message to stop. Reverend William "Rocky" Brown, in Chester, Pennsylvania, organized one such effort by persuading individual stores to stop selling "stop snitching" merchandise. He proposed a different slogan: "Take a stand. Stand up. Speak up. Make a difference."[94]

Community/Celebrity Messaging. Some have proposed enlisting high-profile figures widely admired in affected communities such as rap artists, sports stars, pastors, popular politicians, and others to publicly advocate for cooperation with police. When "snitching" on serious criminals is rebranded as community protection or even personal heroism, the decision to turn in or testify against criminals could start being viewed as right or even cool. But public personalities often depend upon public support and admiration for their success, so criticizing the no-snitch code risks alienating that significant part of the community that supports the code.

Our Recommendation. Unfortunately, there is no simple and effective way to reverse the power of the stop snitching movement. Our recommendation for addressing the problem of no-snitch codes is a combination of two other reforms proposed in this chapter. The first is the previously mentioned anonymous testimony proposal that would allow some witnesses to testify without fearing violent reprisal, which would also have the effect of protecting them from the social ostracism that violating no-snitch codes can bring.[95] The other reform is the recommendation we present in part E of this chapter for a police-community oversight commission to improve the relationship between police and community—thereby building police credibility and increasing the likelihood of cooperation from citizens who might otherwise see going to police as pointless or even a betrayal.

D. CYNICISM ABOUT CRIMINAL JUSTICE EFFECTIVENESS

As mentioned in the previous section on codes of silence, some community members have stopped cooperating with police from a belief that the legal system will not help. Researchers have termed such perceptions "legal cynicism," which one study defines as "a cultural frame in which the law and the agents of its enforcement are viewed as *illegitimate*, *unresponsive*, and *ill equipped* to ensure public safety."[96] Those who report a lower view of police legitimacy report higher levels of legal cynicism.[97] At its core, legal cynicism is a loss of faith in the police and justice system caused by the belief that the system cannot or will not keep communities safe. A primary driver of such legal cynicism is high crime and low clearance rates that seem to prove the claim that the system is failing. Such legal cynicism is especially widespread in poor and minority neighborhoods that are often worst affected by crime and have some of the lowest clearance rates. Regular justice failures breed legal cynicism, which is one reason why it is so important for society to place value on doing justice, as argued in chapter 3. Legal cynicism leads to less crime reporting, less cooperation with police, and therefore more failures of justice, thus causing more legal cynicism in a vicious cycle. In addition to affecting specific communities, legal cynicism can also occur around specific crimes, such as rape, where the system seems unable to deliver the justice the public demands.

Case Example: Alec Cook

In 2015, Alec Cook, a University of Wisconsin–Madison student, is stalking a female classmate. Because he won't stop, she finally goes to campus police. They tell him to stop but he simply ignores them, and the police do nothing about it.[98] In fact, Cook is much more sinister than a mere stalker. Between his business classes, he is a serial rapist. In his final year at the university, he rapes a fellow student who goes to authorities. She tells investigators that Cook had her in a "death grip" and assaulted her repeatedly.[99]

Public reports of her assault have an immediate effect. Ten other women come forward to report that they too were raped by Cook. They did not report the attacks because they did not think they would be believed and, even if they were, they thought that nothing would be done, so the public exposure and investigation was not worth the cost.[100] However, seeing another person report Cook inspired them to come forward.[101]

Cook is facing a prison sentence of over forty years. Defense attorneys seek probation to "allow Cook to receive counseling for sexual sadism proclivities and treatment for narcissistic personality disorder."[102] The prosecutor allows Cook to plead guilty to three counts of third-degree sexual assault, one count of strangulation, and one count of stalking—all felonies—and the judge imposes a sentence of three years.

Outrage at the leniency of the sentence quickly follows. A group of state and local officials join to condemn it:

> We are dismayed and outraged by Judge Ehlke's lenient sentencing of Alec Cook. In just three or fewer years, this predator will be back on the streets, sending a clear message that men like Alec Cook—men with privilege—are above the law.[103]

Many argue that the lack of justice for Cook's victims discourages women who experience sexual assault, violence, or harassment from reporting the crimes. If the eleventh victim had not come forward, Cook's unpunished rapes would have continued indefinitely due to the legal cynicism of his previous victims.

The Nature and Extent of the Problem

Legal cynicism leads to decreased crime reporting and lower clearance rates and particularly affects low-income minority communities and specific crimes such as sexual assault.

DECREASED CRIME REPORTING AND LOWER CLEARANCE RATES Legal cynicism's cost manifests itself in America's dismal crime reporting rates. In 2016, only 42 percent of violent crimes were reported to police.[104] Many victims simply never bothered to involve police out of a belief that it could only make the situation worse. Less crime reporting directly leads to fewer arrests. The more cynical a neighborhood is toward police, the fewer arrests will be made, resulting in higher rates of unsolved violent crime.[105] Legal cynicism is a self-fulfilling prophecy as non-cooperation further ensures no justice will be delivered. Studies have shown that when public faith in law enforcement drops, fewer 911 calls are placed for police help,[106] and fewer arrests are made in violent crimes.[107] As several scholars note, "when residents perceive that the police are unresponsive and that calling the police will do little or nothing to resolve the crime problem endemic to their neighborhood, proportionally more crimes will go unreported and unsanctioned than in neighborhoods where the law and the police are viewed more favorably."[108] The problem of resulting lower clearance rates includes even homicide offenses.[109]

Distrust in police can also increase crime rates. There is evidence that "neighborhoods where the law and the police are seen as illegitimate and unresponsive have significantly higher homicide rates."[110] Of young people in Chicago neighborhoods with strikingly high homicide rates, only 14 percent believe that a shooter or murderer is likely to "get caught" and only 13 percent believe that police were effective at reducing crime.[111] The self-fulfilling prophecy occurs not only from the resulting failures to report but also from the reduced deterrent effect that comes when police are viewed as ineffective. Unsurprisingly, studies have found a correlation in individuals between higher levels of legal cynicism and greater rates of criminality, even when controlling for potential confounding variables.[112]

MINORITY DISTRUST OF POLICE In addition to affecting specific neighborhoods, legal cynicism can disproportionately affect whole racial groups. Black Americans are especially prone to legal cynicism. As noted previously, this often results from a tragic history of police racism, as well as a perception—largely correct—that the system presently fails to control crime and do justice in minority neighborhoods. Studies across many decades show that Black Americans

have less favorable views of police than other racial groups. Sixty-eight percent of White Americans, 59 percent of Hispanic Americans, and only 40 percent of African Americans have favorable views of police.[113] This means African Americans experience the highest levels of legal cynicism and so suffer its consequences at disproportionately high rates. Unsurprisingly, research has found African Americans are 20 percent less likely than White Americans "to say they definitely would report a crime."[114] In fact, 55 percent of Black respondents agreed that calling the police often does more harm than good, a perception shared by just 25 percent of White Americans.[115]

Part of the reason for this legal cynicism among Black Americans is that they are more likely to live in high-crime, low-clearance rate neighborhoods. Another reason for their pervasive legal cynicism is that they are far more likely to believe police are not held accountable for misconduct or unjustified shootings (an issue discussed more in the next section on police use of force).[116] The rise of technology and citizen video journalism, by which citizens can record and upload instances of alleged police misconduct, have only fueled legal cynicism among all racial groups by drawing attention to instances of apparent police wrongdoing.[117] Studies also show that such videos increase cynicism among African American viewers the most, thus further exacerbating the racial gap in legal cynicism.[118] While section E discusses how false narratives around police use of force make this problem worse, it is unreasonable to expect minority communities to simply drop the collective weight of decades—even centuries—of negative police interactions without real effort on the part of police to make the community feel served and protected instead of disliked and controlled. The presence of disrespectful policing practices in some communities (such as unnecessarily roughing up suspects) must be addressed, especially when the community sees them as motivated by racial bias.

LEGAL CYNICISM AND THE NON-REPORTING OF SEXUAL ASSAULT One of the most striking examples of the effects of legal cynicism, highlighted in the previous case example, is the massive underreporting of sexual assault in the United States caused by victims not believing justice will be done. There is a general belief that rapists almost always get away with it, and many view reporting rape as a pointless additional trauma.[119] Sexual assault is the most underreported major crime in the United States. While over 60 percent of robberies and assaults are reported to police, only about one-third of rape victims report the crime.[120] Furthermore, evidence suggests that rape reporting may be declining. In 2018, according to Bureau of Justice data, only 25 percent of rapes were reported to police compared to 40 percent in the year before.[121]

Public Complaints

Policymakers, police, and prosecutors are often concerned by legal cynicism and the poor police-community relations that inspire it and result from it. Police often point toward a lack of community cooperation as the reason they cannot solve many violent crimes, but many communities wonder why they should trust police to do their jobs when they appear to be failing at preventing and solving serious crimes. Communities, especially minority communities, can also be distrustful of police due to the common failure of officers to report other officers' misconduct. In other words, the code of silence among police has contributed to the creation of codes of silence among the community, as discussed in the previous section, and to legal cynicism in the community.

A survey by the Police Foundation found that the majority of American police "felt that it was not unusual for police officers to turn a 'blind eye' to improper conduct by other officers."[122] Consequently, that same report warned that if "communities don't trust the police and are afraid of the police, then they will not and cannot work with police . . . around issues in their own community."[123] Many worry that this lack of cooperation will, in turn, create even more violence and loss of credibility for the police and justice system. To combat these issues, some prosecutors have spoken of the need to "make . . . investments in the community where the community is willing to trust us and come forward with that information."[124] However, reducing legal cynicism is a difficult undertaking given how deep-rooted the causes are on both the side of the community and police. The topic of policing has generated enormous national concern at the present time (an issue discussed further in part E of this chapter), and while much of that concern is specifically focused on faulty police practices, much of it also encompasses how the breakdown in police-community relations is leading to more crime. The police, public, and policymakers are all aware that more trust needs to exist between police and the communities they serve, but the difficulty lies in how to establish that trust.

Reforms

Reforms to reduce legal cynicism usually take the form of attempting to improve the justice system's reputation with the community. Of course, one of the best ways to do this is simply to deliver more justice and safety by better investigations and policing. All reforms discussed in previous (and subsequent) chapters aimed at reducing failures of justice would, to some extent, also help reduce legal cynicism.

Reducing Legal Cynicism through Local Community Outreach Programs. Many reforms have focused on community outreach to reduce legal cynicism. For example, the North Charleston, South Carolina, police department first surveyed residents about their satisfaction with the local police force and subsequently established an outreach program to improve relations. Going forward, the program's success will be evaluated on the metrics of "bringing down crime" and ensuring that "the people [the police] protect trust [them] to do the right thing."[125] The program will follow up with crime victims and individuals who report crimes to see how satisfied they are with the police response. The program will also involve closer monitoring of how officers handle cases and better utilization of citizen feedback.

A similar program was launched in 2000 in Chicago, where the police department met with community representatives every five weeks to discuss how the department could improve its community relations, especially with "the city's various racial, ethnic and religious communities."[126] This initiative helped "the police [forge] relationships with citizens they could turn to for help in solving crimes."[127]

Other jurisdictions have implemented forms of "community policing" (discussed previously in part B of this chapter on witness intimidation) that relies on creating police-community part-

nerships. A Police Executive Research Forum (PERF) national survey of 282 police agencies that implemented community policing strategies found that over 90 percent of such departments reported improved community-police relations and cooperation.[128]

Some community outreach programs can be highly successful, especially when paired with other reforms to increase the effectiveness of police investigations. Camden, New Jersey, dissolved and recreated its police department in 2013 with more of a focus on community relations. Following the reform, clearance rates rose, homicides decreased by 52 percent, and excessive force complaints declined by 42 percent over three years, revealing how committing to improve police reputation with the community can bear fruit.[129]

Similarly, after local partnerships with faith leaders and grassroots organizations encouraged the Oakland, California, police department to adopt more community-sensitive policing strategies, gun homicides decreased by 44 percent and homicide clearance rates increased from 29 percent in 2011 to over 70 percent in 2017.[130]

Another example is the Richmond, California, police department, which undertook to train officers to engage in community policing and "build relationships with people in the areas they patrol."[131] The results were significantly better investigations and increased crime deterrence. From 2004 to 2014, homicides decreased from thirty-eight to eleven per year and violent crimes decreased from 1,078 to 833 per year.[132] The department's emphasis on strengthening the "human connection" with members of the neighborhood clearly was a success.[133] Residents report no longer having their calls ignored and instead praise the fact that officers now "give out their cellphone numbers."[134] Sometimes such good relationships can even help get criminals to cooperate with police, as occurred when a man engaged in an armed standoff with a SWAT team was willing to talk to an officer he was previously acquainted with. The result was the armed man's surrender because of his personal connection with the officer.[135]

Community outreach can also be highly effective when directed at specific groups. For example, some police departments have reached out to the local LGBTQ community to encourage the reporting of hate crimes and harassment, which often go unreported.[136] When Seattle implemented this outreach program, reports of hate crimes and harassment rose by 200 percent, proving that police outreach and communication with underserved communities can build trust and decrease legal cynicism.[137]

Over 80 percent of the public is served by a police department that has some form of community policing strategy in place.[138] While the effectiveness of community outreach programs depends on the specifics of their implementation, empirical evidence has demonstrated that these examples of local improved community-police relations are not simply an anomaly. In fact, evidence shows that "positive intergroup contact" and "positive non-enforcement police-public interactions" have powerful impacts on community-police relations.[139] Overall, increased partnership and relationship building between communities and police has a proven potential to reduce legal cynicism.

National and State Policing Best Practice Suggestions or Mandates. Many federal and state efforts have focused on

identifying and suggesting strategies (such as the community policing reforms mentioned earlier) to improve police-community relations and reduce legal cynicism. At the federal level, President Barack Obama established the Task Force on Twenty-First Century Policing via executive order in an effort to identify best practices of policing that would improve community-police relations and reduce crime.[140] The Task Force consisted of members of law enforcement, academics, and civil rights activists. Similarly, the US Attorney's Office for the District of Connecticut partnered with the FBI and the Department of Justice's Community Relations Service (CRS) in 2014. Together the organizations hosted a symposium "for law enforcement officials to discuss issues surrounding rebuilding police organizations through effective constitutional policing and self-monitoring departments from state and federal perspectives."[141] The symposiums identified strategies to improve community trust and confidence in law enforcement.

At the state level, in 2015, the Illinois Legislature passed the Police and Community Relations Improvement Act (PCRIA), which created a database to track officer misconduct, an oversight board to reduce racial profiling, and use of officer body cameras.[142] Other states have passed similar reforms aimed at improving the reputation of the justice system with the community by signaling that police will be held accountable for any wrongdoing.

Building Rape Victim Trust in Police. As discussed in the reform section of chapter 4,[143] there are several proposals for how to better handle rape investigations in particular. These proposals center on better training and more trauma-sensitive investigative procedures.

Promoting Respectful, Unbiased Policing. As detailed in the next section, there are many false narratives around police use of force, particularly lethal force, and such false narratives contribute to the problem of legal cynicism. That said, there are many legitimate concerns about how policing is conducted, especially in minority neighborhoods, that give rise to distrust of police and legal cynicism in general. Policing, for understandable reasons, can easily slip into a military model that sees the community as an enemy. Additionally, as in any large organization, there are problematic individuals in police forces who may enjoy abusing power or hold biased—including racist—attitudes that affect their decisions in interacting with community members. While the percentage of such individuals is small, they can easily shape a community's perception of the police. While data is poor and research is scarce, there is some evidence to suggest that, at least in some police forces, the presence of such problem officers means Blacks are more likely to experience a higher level of non-lethal force than Whites in a similar encounter. A study conducted by Roland Fryer suggested that after accounting for contextual factors, Blacks were "21.2 percent more likely to endure some form of force in an interaction" with police than Whites (with data mainly being drawn from New York City's "stop, question, and frisk" program).[144] The study confirmed that in absolute terms, force was not used very often and the level of force was generally minor, but none of that negates the disturbing disparity or the effect it has on community members. While caution is necessary in generalizing that specific study to all police forces, disrespectful policing—such as unnecessary pushing, handcuffing, or the needless

drawing of a weapon—is almost certain to lead to higher levels of legal cynicism in the population, regardless of race. Better police training, more frequent police reporting of fellow officers' misconduct, stronger disciplinary procedures, and better rules for identifying and firing bad apple officers can all help promote respectful, unbiased policing (see section E's "Reforms" section for more details). At the same time, as the next section discusses, false narratives surrounding police use of force must be addressed to even allow for better policing practices to make a difference in community perceptions and levels of legal cynicism.

Our Recommendation. A properly implemented police-community oversight commission to provide police accountability and encourage community cooperation would go far toward reducing legal cynicism. Such a commission can help formulate effective community policing strategies and ensure the community is policed respectfully. The proposal is discussed in detail in the recommendation section at the end of this chapter.

E. COMMUNITY UPSET OVER POLICE USE OF FORCE: THE FALSE NARRATIVE PROBLEM

The legal cynicism and codes of silence discussed previously in this chapter are often caused in part by false narratives around policing and the criminal justice system that paint the law and its agents as racist or enforcers of racial oppression. There is a widespread perception, especially among Black communities, that there is an epidemic of racially motivated police killings in America today, a view that naturally leads to police being viewed as dangerous and illegitimate. Intense media coverage of individual police killings and the rise of social media makes it easier to highlight and exaggerate perceived problems with police behavior. Instead of looking to root out bad actors from police forces, the prevailing narrative among many activists, policymakers, and community members is that American policing is systemically racist and, hence, obviously illegitimate. This has led to many efforts to reform police procedures, with a particular focus on changing use of force policies.[145] While making policing more respectful and less violent is a worthy and important goal, this section demonstrates that the disproportionately intense criticism of police killings hurts justice more than it helps.

Available evidence makes clear that most popular perceptions of police use of force are simply wrong. As discussed shortly, police shootings are rare, not racially motivated, and almost always justified. When police do commit an unjustified killing (as in the case of George Floyd), they are prosecuted as civilians would be. There is no epidemic of unjustified police shootings, but there is an epidemic of misinformation that has needlessly and tragically inflamed legal cynicism and undermined citizen cooperation with police. This diminished cooperation has in turn led to more crime and failures of justice. Unfortunately, the false perceptions have been politicized and entrenched to the point that changing them will be extremely difficult.

To be clear, disrespectful police practices have and do contribute to legal cynicism and must be addressed, a point made in the previous section. No officer should abuse their power, and no individual should be targeted because of their race. It is also true that American policing has historically enforced racial oppression (such as Jim Crow), leading to lingering wounds in the psyches of many minority communities, making them prone to confirmation bias where any instance of police misconduct is seen as racially motivated. Nor do we deny that some individual police officers may hold racial animus or act on racist beliefs. Moreover, individual officers have and do, on rare occasions, murder civilians. Nothing in this chapter is meant to minimize the pain or injustice caused by real instances of police misconduct or murder. However, the real epidemic of unjustified violence, sadly ignored by the narrative of racist policing, is the unsolved murder epidemic in America that affects mainly minorities. Young Black men are at high risk of being shot on America's streets—but not by police.[146] While society's attention is drawn to a handful of unjustified police killings, thousands of young Black men are murdered each year with no justice being done. Even worse, no real effort is made on the part of policymakers to close the racial disparities in crime and clearance rates. All people who truly care about justice—be it racial, social, or otherwise—should recognize the false narrative problem around police use of force if they wish to make America a safer and more just place for all. It does not benefit communities—particularly minority communities—to perpetuate lies about policing that lead to higher legal cynicism, unsolved crime, and increased violent victimizations. If the same attention that is now focused on past police oppression or current infrequent unjustified police killings was instead spent on trying to improve crime and clearance rates in minority communities, thousands of Black lives really could be saved each year. Tragically, many activists, policymakers, and media commentators seem content to feed a false narrative on police killings that only further hurts the historically marginalized communities they proport to champion.

Case Example: The Shooting of Michael Brown in Ferguson, Missouri

The shooting of Michael Brown is a tragic story, not least because it is the subject of so many lies and misrepresentations. This case study is longer than usual because it is necessary to provide a detailed and precise account of what actually occurred and how it exemplifies the problem of false narratives.

Just before noon on August 9, 2014, Michael Brown and Dorian Johnson walk into a convenience store in Ferguson, Missouri. Brown robs the store of some cigarillos and roughs up the shop clerk who tries to prevent the theft. Moments later, the pair are walking the yellow line in the middle of a relatively busy street when Officer Darren Wilson pulls up next to the pair and asks, "What's wrong with the sidewalk?"[147] Wilson notices that Brown has a handful of cigarillos in his hands and that Johnson matches the description of a robbery suspect that has just been circulated.[148] Wilson calls for backup and parks to block the pair from walking further. Wilson opens his door, but Brown, who is 6'5" tall and weighs 289 pounds, uses his large size to close the door and prevent Wilson from exiting.[149]

Wilson demands that Brown step back, but instead Brown "lean[s] into the driver's window, so that his arms and upper torso [are] inside the SUV."[150] Brown assaults Wilson with repeated punches. With the assault ongoing, the only defensive weapon that Wilson can reach is his gun. He unholsters the gun and tells

Brown to stop or he will shoot. Brown says, "You are too much of a pussy to shoot."[151] Brown puts his hand over Wilson's and due to his larger size, and superior mobility, given Wilson is sitting, Brown briefly gains control of the gun.[152]

Wilson regains enough leverage to push the gun away from himself and pulls the trigger. A bullet goes through the car door, glass shatters, and Brown steps back. Wilson witnesses a transformation in Brown who becomes enraged and comes at the seated officer looking "like a demon."[153] Brown reaches back into the car and resumes his assault. Wilson fires again. Brown breaks off the assault and turns to leave.

Brown's erratic and violent conduct leaves Wilson in no doubt that Brown is a danger to the public. Leaving the car to pursue Brown, Wilson repeatedly tells Brown to get on the ground. When the two men are separated by about twenty-five feet, Brown turns and comes at Wilson. To Wilson, Brown was "appearing 'psychotic,' 'hostile,' and 'crazy,' as though he was 'looking through' Wilson."[154] (It is later determined that Brown is under the effect of a hallucinogen at the time of the encounter, making his violent and erratic actions more understandable.[155]) When the distance between the two men is down to fifteen feet, Wilson fires multiple rounds. Brown pauses, Wilson again tells him to get on the ground, but instead, as an eyewitness recounts, Brown again "charge[s] at Wilson."[156] When Brown is no more than ten feet away, Wilson again fires his weapon. Now less than a body's length away, "Brown lean[s] forward as though he [is] getting ready to 'tackle' Wilson."[157] Wilson fires again, hitting Brown's head, finally stopping and killing him. A total of six separate bullets are known to have hit Brown.

Wilson uses his shoulder mic and radios, "Send me every car we got and a supervisor."[158] As backup was already on its way, a sergeant arrives within seconds, and Wilson relates the events. The statements given by Wilson at that time, moments after Brown's death, and repeated over the numerous investigations and intense scrutiny that follow are all consistent with the physical evidence recovered. Most eyewitness accounts corroborate Wilson's version of events. All video recordings done by bystanders are consistent with Wilson's account.[159] In the many local and state investigations that follow, as well as in a federal investigation by the Obama Justice Department, Wilson's initial account is found to be accurate and his conduct appropriate under the circumstances.[160]

A wide range of witness statements are gathered by the Ferguson Police Department, the St. Louis County Police Department, and the FBI, all of whom conducted separate investigations. Witness 102 left the scene within five minutes of the shooting and called 911 the following day. He came forward because "he felt bad about the situation . . . he wanted to 'bring closure to [Brown's] family,' so they would not think that the officer 'got away with murdering their son.'"[161] He told investigators that community pressure would make it hard for them to get to the truth. Another man, Witness 103, a man whose own son had been shot by police during a robbery, stated that he feared for his safety if he told the truth.[162] He nonetheless testified that Brown assaulted Wilson and was running at Wilson when he was shot. Witness after witness confirmed the same basic narrative.

But in the immediate aftermath of Brown's death, a false narrative begins.

A person coming on the scene after the shooting claims Brown was shot while he was on the ground, but an actual witness immediately corrects him and explains that Brown was attacking the officer. He says he thought the officer must have been missing with his shots because Brown kept coming at him.[163] But the false rumors gain speed.

The situation is exacerbated when Johnson, who was with Brown during the robbery and the shooting, tells people that "Mike Brown had his hands up."[164] When Al Sharpton addresses a crowd in Clayton, Missouri, he uses the hands-up gesture, and the image becomes part of the narrative.[165]

Investigators insist that the crime scene be handled with extreme care, so Brown's body is not moved for several hours as all aspects of the scene are recorded and all evidence collected. While the body is covered from public view, the delay in moving the body is seen as disrespectful.[166] When it is time for the body to be moved, gunshots ring out, causing further delay.

By the following night, stores are looted, windows smashed, and fires set. Two nights after Brown's death, the unrest has grown beyond the ability of the local authorities, and the state police are called in.[167] On August 16, Missouri is placed in a state of emergency and a curfew is declared.[168]

The media plays a particularly polarizing role during the chaos, misrepresenting facts and providing clear misinformation. In a CNN article issued a few days after the incident, reporters claim that "one thing is sure, though: What police say was self-defense by [Wilson] doesn't jibe with the accounts of those who say they saw the encounter,"[169] which later reports by

Figure 14.3. Michael Brown was killed by police, and soon after the violence began in Ferguson, as shown here, 2014. Photo by Jim Young, from "Ferguson Reacts to Grand Jury Decision," Thomas Reuters, November 25, 2014, https://www.reuters.com/news/picture/ferguson-reacts-to-grand-jury-decision-idUSRTR4FC5R/.

the Department of Justice show to be untrue—in truth, most witnesses corroborate Wilson's account.[170] An article by ABC News claimed that "a gunshot wound to [Brown's] arm could show either that he was hit while walking away from the shooter with his back to the officer, or that he was facing the shooter with his arm up, either in a surrender position, defensive position, or other motion,"[171] completely disregarding the possibility that Brown was instead charging head on toward Wilson with his arms raised in attack, which later eyewitness testimonies and CCTV footage prove to be the case. That same article claimed that the autopsy results were not immediately released as they contained information incriminating Wilson,[172] inciting public outrage and fueling a narrative of conspiracy between the government and police officers. In truth, the autopsy and toxicology reports supported Wilson's account and led the grand jury to exonerate him.[173]

On August 20, at the direction of President Obama, Attorney General Holder visits Ferguson. A Missouri grand jury is empaneled. After three months of investigation and deliberation, on November 24, a recommendation of "no charges" is made by the state grand jury.[174] Civil unrest quickly follows; a dozen buildings are burned and officers are hit with flying objects.[175] On March 4, the Justice Department similarly announces that no federal charges will be brought against Wilson. The next day, in front of the Ferguson police station, two police officers are shot.[176]

In August 2018, Wesley Bell wins the job of Saint Louis County prosecutor, largely based on a promise to pursue new charges against Wilson. Bell makes good on the promise and opens a new investigation, which again fails to bring charges. But the third failure to bring charges does not settle the issue for Prosecutor Bell. Although his office is unable to bring charges against Wilson, he nonetheless attempts to defame Wilson by claiming that he has not been exonerated.[177] While he has in fact been exonerated by three separate investigations, Wilson is concerned that his "continued employment may put the residents and police officers of the City of Ferguson at risk."[178] He resigns, giving up his pension. To this day, the lie that Michael Brown was murdered while surrendering is believed by millions and considered ideological orthodoxy to many.

The Nature and Extent of the Problem

The widespread false public perception of an epidemic of racist police killings has poisoned police-community relations and increased legal cynicism and justice failures, which disproportionately affect minority communities. Setting the facts straight and focusing on solving the real epidemic of violence in minority communities is essential to doing justice.

THE PERCEPTION: WIDESPREAD BELIEF IN REGULAR RACIALLY MOTIVATED POLICE KILLINGS The American public increasingly believes there is a major problem with police use of force, and extensive media coverage of police killing Black suspects has created a perception that police are gunning down Black men for racist reasons with impunity. The perception began with the swift growth of the Black Lives Matter movement after the killing of Michael Brown in Ferguson, Missouri (discussed earlier), and gained majority support after the murder of George Floyd by police in 2020. Floyd's murder, and the belief it reflected widespread police practice, sparked large protests.[179] An estimated fifteen to twenty-six million Americans took part in protests in the weeks following the murder of Floyd.[180] There have been vocal calls to defund and even disband police departments in the wake of police shootings, and although these calls do not reflect a broader public desire to end police, public dissatisfaction with police shootings is at an historic high.[181]

Much of this dissatisfaction is driven by wildly inaccurate perceptions of the facts, not just of the Ferguson case described earlier but of police use of force generally. A nation-wide poll in 2021 revealed how shocking these misperceptions are. When asked to estimate how many unarmed Black men were killed by the police in 2019, 77.5 percent of self-identified liberals (and 84.3 percent of self-identified very liberals) estimated the number as between one hundred and ten thousand or more (53.6 percent of self-identified conservatives and 54 percent of self-identified very conservatives gave this estimate).[182] In reality, in 2021, ten unarmed Black men were killed by police according to a definition of "unarmed" that includes suspects who posed a serious danger to the police or public.[183] More restrictive counting puts the number at just six.[184] Regardless, only around 20 percent of self-identified liberal respondents (and 45 percent of the conservative ones) guessed anywhere close to the right answer. Similarly, the average survey participant guessed that 50 percent of those killed by police are Black, while the actual percentage is 24 percent.

These false perceptions have contributed to a drop in public confidence in police performance. A Pew survey taken after Floyd's murder found declines in public perception of police performance in many categories, a testament to the power of high-profile cases to shift public opinion significantly.[185] The data shows the public, though sharply polarized on the issue, widely believes the police to be doing a poor job tackling issues such as use of force, punishing police misconduct, and treating suspects in an equal manner.

This perception of the police being violent and unreliable is especially prevalent among Black Americans where distrust of the police is high. A poll of Black Americans taken in May 2021 found that 57 percent of respondents viewed police unfavorably, 68 percent believed police treatment of Black people had worsened, and 55 percent of respondents agreed that calling the police often does more harm than good (a perception shared by only 25 percent of White and Asian Americans).[186] The belief that police shootings are racially biased is also widespread. An April 2021 poll found that 90 percent of Black people believe police are more likely to use deadly force against a Black person than a White person (56 percent of all respondents agreed), and 77 percent of Black people believe police violence is a very serious problem (compared to 45 percent of the general public).[187] One study found that "eight in 10 African-Americans . . . said that they thought that young black men were more likely to be shot to death by police than to die in a car accident," when in reality, Black men are more than fifteen times likelier to die in a car accident than be killed by police.[188]

This perception of unjustified racist police killings translates to fear and bitterness at police among community members. As one Black Baltimore resident put it, "Police shoot [B]lack people for nothing. . . . They only kill us because of our skin color and our race. Black people never get to have peace."[189]

Contrast these widely held perceptions with the reality.

THE REALITY: FEW UNJUSTIFIED POLICE KILLINGS, NOT RACIALLY MOTIVATED   In fact, the perception of an epidemic of unjustified racist police killings is simply inconsistent with the facts. Between January 2000 and July 2021, there were 18,368 recorded uses of deadly force by police, and 1,726 recorded uses of non-lethal force that resulted in a death.[190] This amounts to 20,094 total killings by police of people of all races,[191] or about a thousand deaths per year. This number has remained steady over the past two decades.[192] By comparison, fifteen thousand to twenty thousand people are murdered by other civilians each year across the United States.[193]

Furthermore, the vast majority of the one thousand or so police killings each year are clearly justified. The *Washington Post* has tracked the number of individuals killed by law enforcement since 2015.[194] Just 6 percent of suspects killed by police were determined to be unarmed and of these many still presented an immediate danger to others (as in the case of Michael Brown discussed earlier).[195]

In addition to the fact that the vast majority of police killings are of armed individuals, there is no evidence that racial bias accounts for disparities in police shootings. In fact, studies have routinely shown just the opposite: White officers are not more likely to kill Black people and, if anything, are *less* likely to do so, perhaps out of an abundance of caution at sparking a divisive incident.[196] Studies have established that Black people are "23.5 percent less likely to be shot by police, relative to Whites, in an interaction."[197] No scientific study has ever found that Black people are more likely than Whites to be killed by police in a given police-suspect interaction.[198] Yet the well-accepted current narrative pressed by the media, activists, and many politicians is just the opposite.

While it is true that Black people comprise 24 percent of police shooting victims compared to being only 13.6 percent of the population, this disparity results from the fact that Black communities have significantly higher crime rates and thus are more likely to generate police confrontations.[199] Black people comprised over 50 percent of homicide victims in 2019 compared to comprising just 13 percent of the population, a horrifying disparity that is even worse for Black people between the ages of fifteen and thirty-four who are ten times more likely to be murdered than Whites.[200]

In other words, a tragic racial disparity is to be found in crime victimization, which is predominantly intraracial, not in the police response to it.[201] The idea that Black men should be most afraid of being killed by police is simply not supported by the facts. Of the 14,554 homicides of Black individuals in 2021,[202] 233 were killed by police[203]—just 1.6 percent.[204]

The idea that police primarily kill unarmed Black men is also false. Two percent of killings by police in the past six years have been killings of Black men who are "unarmed" based on a very generous definition of the term.[205] In fact, statistics show "a police officer was 400 times as likely to be killed by a [B]lack criminal in 2021 as an unarmed black American was to be killed by a police officer."[206]

When these numbers are put in perspective, it is obvious that there is no epidemic of racially motivated police shootings of Blacks but rather a tragic racial disparity in crime victimization. Politicians and activists who accuse the police of being systemically racist in shootings are either ignorant of the facts or intentionally misrepresenting the facts for their political or ideological purposes.

To claim that racist police shootings is one of the major problems facing Black communities is to distract and mislead, making it less likely that real crime problems in such communities will be solved. Crime in Black communities is the serious problem, and police shootings are an inevitable tragic consequence of that problem. Placing the blame on police is blaming a symptom and missing the disease. Fixating on police shootings prevents progress in reducing crime that would in turn reduce police killings. Additionally, far from being a growing problem, police shootings have dropped over time. While nation-wide historical data is unavailable, jurisdictions that have kept records show a clear decline in police killings since the twentieth century. For example, in 1971, police killed around ninety people in New York City.[207] In 2017, they killed around ten.[208]

None of this is to say that police do not, on rare occasions, unjustifiably kill or murder suspects. George Floyd is a tragic example of a murder of an unarmed Black man by police. But in such cases, the killers are often tried and convicted, as was Floyd's killer, Derek Chauvin.[209] Additionally, such murders are almost never racially motivated. Despite assertions, there is no evidence Chauvin considered Floyd's race. Minnesota's progressive attorney general Keith Ellison "has said he would not call George Floyd's death a hate crime because there was no evidence that Derek Chauvin factored in race."[210]

While of course some unjustifiable police killings do go unpunished (just like normal murders), there is also no reason to believe police killings are underprosecuted based on legal definitions of murder and manslaughter. If anything, the evidence suggests prosecutors prosecute cases against police even when they know they are unlikely to win, simply as a means of publicly demonstrating that they invest proportionally more resources in prosecuting police homicides than they do other homicides.[211] The low conviction rate of police officers has more to do with the circumstances of most police killings, where the chaos of a confrontation invites reasonable mistakes in split-second judgments, than with prosecutorial indifference to "killer cops."

It is difficult to overstate the falsity of the view that there is an ongoing epidemic of police violence in America. Even beyond shootings, police use of force against suspects occurs in only about 0.78 percent of arrests, and in 98 percent of those cases where force is used, the arrested person, even suspects actively resisting arrest, sustains no injuries or only minor ones.[212] Given that police routinely have to confront the most dangerous members of a highly armed society, the fact that in making ten million arrests a year only about one thousand people are killed by police—0.0001 percent—could be considered significantly low.[213]

In fact, more police officers are murdered each year by suspects than even a generous estimate of the number of unarmed suspects murdered by police. Eighty-four police officers were killed in 2021 from a felonious assault while on duty,[214] compared to an average of only around sixty unarmed people killed by police each year, many of whom were dangerous despite being unarmed.[215] However, public perception is quite the opposite. After twenty-two-year-old NYPD detective Jason Rivera was murdered by a suspect in January 2022 and given a funeral that involved closing several streets, one New York resident, actress Jacqueline Guzman, posted online:

We do not need to shut down most of Lower Manhattan because one cop died for probably doing his job incorrectly. They kill people who are under 22 every single day for no good reason and we don't shut down the city for them.[216]

While the callous ignorance of such a comment is unfortunate, the true tragedy is that it captures a perception of police shootings held by many. It is no wonder that many police officers have come to feel demoralized and embittered when faced with such routine false beliefs portraying them as killers when police are exposing themselves to a greater risk of being murdered in order to protect communities that often demonize them. (See chapter 15 for more on police demoralization.)

How did so many Americans come to have such a false view of police shootings? The main reason may be the disproportionate media coverage of unjustified killings as well as the increasing exploitation of police shootings for political purposes. When the media covers police killings, it is almost entirely to focus on the potentially unjustified nature of the killing, and this causes the fallacious generalization on the part of the public that most police killings are unjustified and that the problem is much larger than it is. Much of the news media and activists also rush to pronounce judgment on a killing before the relevant facts are known. For example, the national outrage over Michael Brown's killing, discussed earlier, was in large part created by inaccurate reporting by journalists and activists. Even when the facts in multiple official reports later showed the killing was justified, most protest leaders and media figures were simply unwilling to admit their mistake and continued to press what was then a clearly false narrative. Indeed, it has become a litmus test of ideological purity among some to affirm Michael Brown was murdered. This embrace of false "alternative facts" is highly damaging to police-community relations. Studies have found that exposure to negative media coverage of police has as negative an effect on people as an actual negative interaction with police.[217] As another study concluded, "The current data suggest that, at least on the issue of fatal police shootings, actual events are not a primary driving force [in public perceptions]."[218]

Public Complaints Against Community Misperceptions Regarding Police Use of Force

While overshadowed by the enormous public attention paid to claims of unjustified police killings and calls for police reform, there have also been public complaints about the misperceptions the public holds about police use of force. Numerous contrarian journalists and researchers, such as Heather Mac Donald[219] and Roland Fryer, have noted the falseness of the prevailing narrative on police killings. Daring to speak the truth can exact a high price. Professor Fryer, a well-respected economics scholar at Harvard, who happens to be Black, published empirical research that pushed back against the notion that police are racist killers, specifically finding that police officers were 23.5 percent less likely to kill a Black person than a White person in a given confrontation.[220] Fryer's ideological opponents within the university administration took the next available opportunity (an accusation of workplace harassment with a recommended penalty of additional training) to shut down his research lab and suspend him from teaching.[221] Another ex-

ample of the costs of daring to speak out against the false narrative, particularly in news organizations, is Zac Kriegman, a data science director at Thomson Reuters, whose research into police killings quickly made him realize the problem had been blown massively out of proportion and was preventing potentially life-saving coverage of the murder epidemic in America's Black communities.[222] As Kriegman recalls:

> But when I shared the story with my coworkers, my boss chastised me, telling me expressing this opinion could limit my ability to take on leadership roles within the company. Then I was maligned by my colleagues. And then I was fired.[223]

Honest academic researchers have wondered how focusing on police violence and ignoring the much greater problem of serious crime benefits minority communities. For example, Brandon del Pozo, a former police chief and current professor at Brown University, has publicly "questioned criminology's prevailing focus on the problem of police brutality in minority communities, given their exposure to endemic levels of lethal gang violence."[224] Del Pozo has pointed out that "deploying to Afghanistan as a combat soldier would have been safer, in terms of gun homicide, for young American men living in the most violent zip codes of Chicago or Philadelphia,"[225] but academics, journalists, and policymakers refuse to pay serious attention to the war zone–level violence unfolding in many of America's inner cities, choosing instead to highlight the much smaller problem of police violence.

Ordinary citizens have also complained about the lopsided attention paid to police killings compared to the problem of crime, especially in Black communities. After Minneapolis police in July 2022 killed an armed Black man who had attempted to kill a mother in front of her two children, protestors and activists quickly began scrutinizing the killing and criticizing police. The mother who had been saved by police, Arabella Foss-Yarbrough, responded by begging protestors to consider the facts: "This is not a George Floyd situation. George Floyd was unarmed. This is not OK. . . . He [the man police killed] tried to kill me in front of my kids." Foss-Yarbrough also questioned whether demonstrators would have cared if she had been killed. "I have Black children. I am a woman of color," she said. "If I would have lost my life, would you guys do this for me?"[226]

Another Misleading Narrative that Reduces Community Cooperation: "Systemic Racism" in the Justice System and Black Incarceration Rates

Misperceptions surrounding police use of force are not the only misleading narratives to affect people's view of the justice system. It is often claimed by prominent politicians, academics, and activists that the criminal justice system is "systemically racist" with various examples being cited, usually focusing on police use of force and Black incarceration rates. One effect of such claims, as shown earlier, is to make many community members less cooperative with the justice system because why would one wish to assist a hostile, oppressive force? While it is true that racial disparities exist in the sense that minorities are imprisoned at higher rates than their share of the population, labeling the criminal justice system as "systemically racist" suggests this is somehow caused by the justice system and that

reforms meant to root out racism in the justice system could fix these disparities. But the evidence shows these racial disparities in incarceration are largely or entirely caused by differences in crime rates, which in turn are caused by numerous complex factors including disparities in social circumstances such as wealth and education (often rooted in historic inequity) over which the justice system has no control. It is certainly not our claim that no racial disparities exist or that they are not indicative of large underlying systemic problems in society and governmental policy. If "systemic racism" simply means that current societal structures, aided and abetted by government policy spanning decades, serve to disadvantage certain minority communities, there is no question it is a very real problem. The fact Black communities suffer serious criminal victimization at a higher rate than the rest of the population clearly indicates large underlying systemic problems. But it is equally true that attributing racial disparities in incarceration rates to the specific functioning of the justice system is a false narrative whose major effect is to take attention away from the real problems as well as making those disparities worse by decreasing community cooperation with the justice system.

Claims that the justice system is behind disparities in incarceration are commonplace and made by credible high-profile figures. Former President Obama claimed that Blacks and Whites "are arrested at very different rates, are convicted at very different rates, [and] receive very different sentences . . . for the same crime."[227] Such claims led him to label the justice system an "injustice system."[228] Similarly, former senator and presidential candidate Hillary Clinton decried the "disgrace of a criminal-justice system that incarcerates so many more African-Americans proportionately than whites."[229] Senator Elizabeth Warren slammed the justice system as "racist . . . front to back" and pointed to disparate incarceration rates as proof.[230] These are serious claims guaranteed to damage the credibility of the justice system and reduce community cooperation, and like the false narrative on police shootings, they have little basis in fact.

Studies have repeatedly found that Black imprisonment rates reflect crime rates.[231] For example, in 2018, Black offenders made up 33 percent of America's sentenced prison population,[232] while Black offenders made up 33 percent of arrests for non-fatal violent crime in 2018.[233] Nor do arrest rates for Black offenders reflect discrimination as 34.9 percent of non-fatal violent victimizations reported to police involved a Black offender in 2018.[234] While all these rates are significantly higher than the 13.6 percent Black share of America's population, they paint a picture of tragically disparate crime rates, not a justice system more likely to incarcerate a Black offender than a White offender for the same crime.[235] Once arrested, Black offenders are also not convicted at higher rates than White offenders.[236] If anything, they are more likely to have their cases dismissed.[237] There may be isolated individuals in the justice system who make racially biased decisions, but this does not appear to manifest in systemic discrimination, as one could take the same criminal offender data and predict—assuming a race-neutral system—very similar rates of arrest, conviction, and imprisonment for Black offenders as the actual rates in the supposedly "systemically racist" justice system.

It is worth asking what would result if the justice system implemented policies to ensure incarceration rates reflected societal demographics instead of crime rates. If the criminal justice system artificially prevented Blacks from making up more than 13 percent of the prison population, this would mean a massive increase in failures of justice affecting Black victims since most crime is intraracial.[238] For example, in 2020, Blacks were more likely to be violently victimized than members of other races, and two-thirds of these victimizations were committed by Black offenders.[239] The stark truth is that any policy reducing Black incarceration rates, without reducing Black crime rates, will disproportionately harm Black communities who are already starved for justice.

Some acknowledge these facts for serious crime but argue the criminal justice system is systemically racist in its imprisonment rates for drug offenses. While drug offenders make up a small percentage of the prison population (about 15 percent and mostly for drug trafficking),[240] it is alleged that Blacks are more likely to be arrested and imprisoned for drug offenses than Whites despite both races appearing to use illegal drugs at the same rates. Such claims usually do not take into account race-neutral explanatory factors such as the fact that drug enforcement is targeted for logistical reasons at large metropolitan areas (where Blacks happen to be overrepresented).[241] However, even if such claims are accepted at face value, there is a simple explanation in that law enforcement is more concentrated toward high-crime neighborhoods and so is more likely to catch drug crimes in such neighborhoods than in low-crime neighborhoods. Those who argue this is unjust are really arguing that underlying drug laws are unjust because if current punishments for drug offenses are just, then the outrage should manifest in calls to raise the arrest and imprisonment rate of White drug offenders instead of letting guilty Black drug offenders go free. It may be that many drug laws are unjust in the eyes of the community, in which case the laws should be changed to avoid the law losing credibility with the community (as discussed in chapter 3). But in either case, it is not evidence that the justice system systemically discriminates against Blacks, as in an ideal world, all offenders of any race would be caught and incarcerated if appropriate.[242]

In a way, it is easy to understand how false narratives around systemic racism in police use of force and incarceration rates gain adherents. People intuitively and correctly feel something is wrong about the fact that Blacks are incarcerated and killed by police at higher rates than their percentage of the population. But all too often, people fail to understand why this is the case and so accept a false narrative that the cause lies in institutional racism in the justice system as opposed to differing crime rates caused by deeper societal problems. It would be so much simpler if this problem could be fixed by rooting out racism in the justice system, but the hard truth is that solving these disparities requires much broader societal reforms targeting the causes of high crime rates in Black communities—including the current lack of justice for crimes in such communities. In fact, the only serious accusation of systemic racism that can be made against the justice system is that local and state governments tolerate a status quo that systematically provides less justice for high-crime minority communi-

ties. Even if this governmental failure to provide justice is not for racist reasons, its effect is to entrench racial disparities. But of course, fixing this truly unjust underlying disparity would require a large investment of additional resources that policymakers of all political persuasions are loathe to provide. It is far easier to ignore the problem or blame it on the specific functioning of the justice system, as if it were the individual decisions made by police, prosecutors, and judges that create racial disparities in arrests and imprisonment. Attempting to change Black arrest, conviction, and incarceration rates through targeting supposedly racist decision making in the justice system will achieve little.[243] Tragically, simplistic and misleading narratives of systemic racism in the justice system hurt Black communities the most by reducing citizen cooperation with the justice system and increasing justice failures and crime. Bizarrely, activists who push such narratives seem to view the provision of justice as a threat to minority communities—as if the interests of such communities are represented by criminals as opposed to the vast majority of law-abiding citizens victimized with relative impunity.[244]

Reforms

If there did exist an epidemic of unjustified police shootings, then the reforms discussed shortly dealing with police practices would be critical to stopping police violence. Of course, because unjustified police shootings are not the major problem, such reforms will have little or no effect on improving police-community relations. As shown by the killing of Michael Brown, it does not even require an actual police murder to fuel the false narrative of rampant racist-inspired police killings, and it seems unlikely that the political and ideological actors who have pressed that false narrative would have any reason to end their current campaign, which brings them social influence and political power. Some police shootings are inevitable (and necessary) in a highly armed country that experiences high rates of violent crime. As long as influential figures continue to promote an overblown narrative of police racism, there will always be opportunities to portray police shootings as unjustified and racist.

Having said all that, it makes perfect sense that every effort should be made to closely monitor and control police use of force. While improvements of current practices may not be acknowledged or affect public perceptions, they are still worth pursuing. As mentioned in the previous section, disrespectful policing contributes to community distrust and must be tackled along with other causes of legal cynicism. Unjustified police violence is a problem when it occurs, and we have no desire to minimize the existence of that problem—only put it in proper perspective. We strongly support reforms that make policing more respectful and less violent. One reason why we focus on the problem of false narratives is because until those false narratives are addressed, it will be impossible for the public to even recognize the beneficial effect of police reform. Here are some examples of the kinds of reforms that could improve current police use of force practices.

Reform Policing Procedures. The most common response by policymakers to public discontent with police use of force is to make a show of reforming police procedures to try to restore public confidence. In the wake of the murder of George Floyd and massive protests, po-

lice departments across the nation responded by adopting new use of force rules and policing procedures to make it less likely suspects would be killed like Floyd. At the federal level, President Trump issued the Executive Order on Safe Policing for Safe Communities in June 2020, which instructed the Department of Justice to "create an independent credentialing body that would develop a set of criteria for state and local law enforcement agencies to meet in order to be awarded federal grants. The order stated that the criteria should address excessive use of force, include de-escalation training, and ban the use of chokeholds, except when the use of deadly force is lawful."[245]

Many of these types of reforms were put in place in state and local jurisdictions. In Washington state, for example, two significant bills that changed police operations in 2021 were the Police Tactics Bill and the Use of Force Bill.[246] The Police Tactics Bill limits what equipment and techniques can be used by police and restricts vehicle pursuits. It bans chokeholds, prohibits no-knock warrants, limits tear gas usage, restricts firing at a moving vehicle, and "requires uniformed officers to be identifiable by name tag or something similar."[247] Perhaps more significant, the Use of Force Bill "changes the legal threshold that must be met for officers to use any amount of physical force. There now has to be probable cause for arrest or the person has to pose an immediate threat to the officer, someone else, or themselves."[248] Similar laws regarding police tactics and use of force have been adopted across the country. In fact, all fifty states and DC have "introduced legislation addressing some aspect of policing policy, largely focused on accountability and oversight."[249]

However, predictably, such reforms have had almost no impact on public perceptions because some incidents of unjustified police use of force have still occurred, and the number of police killings since these procedure changes has remained largely steady (as most such killings are justified and so would not be impacted by the procedural reforms).[250] Moreover, polls show these attempts at reform have failed to restore public confidence in police.[251] If anything, they reinforce the false notion that the problem of police use of force largely lies with police instead of crime. With ten million arrests a year, it is essentially guaranteed that, no matter what police procedures are in place, some officers somewhere will either intentionally or unintentionally use unjustified force.

Make It Easier to Fire Bad Actors. Bad actors do exist in police forces. Some research estimates that 50 percent of police misconduct is attributable to 2 percent of officers,[252] and it is a fact that most unjustifiable use of force is committed by only a small, and potentially predictable, pool of officers. Removing bad actors may make the sort of high-profile killings like George Floyd's less likely as well as reducing negative community interactions by expelling disrespectful officers. Dating back to 2015, Floyd's killer, Derek Chauvin, had effected at least six arrests that may have involved use of excessive force.[253] Despite two of those arrests resulting in formal complaints lodged against Chauvin, the Minneapolis Police Department never formally reprimanded Chauvin for any misconduct.[254] The Minneapolis Department's failure to discipline or terminate Chauvin despite his seeming history of problematic conduct legitimized criticisms of police instead of focusing on Chauvin as a bad actor.

Tracking complaints against officers to catch problematic patterns and fostering a culture where police speak up about fellow officers' misconduct is important to weeding out those officers who routinely abuse their power.

Reduce Access to Guns for the Mentally Ill and for Criminals. Reducing the number of guns police face would make police killings decline as most killings are a result of a situation in which a suspect pulls a gun. Such reforms, however, face a legal difficulty with Second Amendment rights and a practical difficulty with getting guns off the street. Additionally, it is not the number of police shootings that causes public misperceptions around them but rather the disproportionate coverage of such shootings.

Create Better Treatments for the Mentally Ill. Mentally ill people are sixteen times more likely to be killed by police both because they are more likely to disobey police instructions and because police are often poorly trained in handling mentally ill suspects.[255] Creating better treatments for the mentally ill in society might reduce the number of police shootings.

Replace Guns with Tasers. One possibility for reducing police killings, and perhaps some of the misperceptions associated with them, is to replace most police officers' guns with high-quality tasers. Because police almost always use their handguns in close confrontations, tasers could theoretically do the job of incapacitation.[256] The main problem is that tasers are currently not reliable enough for police in life-and-death situations. Most tasers have only two shots and sometimes fail to incapacitate their targets due to the taser barbs not penetrating some types of clothing to deliver the electric charge. There is also the potential issue of police using tasers more often and aggressively in less dangerous situations because they know tasers are normally non-fatal. But tasers are not perfectly non-lethal. One older study from the Department of Justice put their risk of causing death at one in four hundred.[257] The solution of replacing handguns with tasers may become increasingly feasible as technology improves their reliability in incapacitating a suspect. Some industry experts predict that by 2030 taser technology will be as reliable as handguns at ensuring incapacitation,[258] so this reform should be monitored closely and explored by police departments.

Establish Rules Around Media Reporting on Police Killings. Just as there is an unstated rule requiring the media not to publish exit poll results in elections until after the polls have closed (to avoid influencing the results), responsible media organizations could agree to some basic rules governing the coverage of police shootings. Such rules might include, for example, not reporting the details of police shootings until the basic facts of the encounter are known. Of course, any reforms directly targeting media coverage will raise free speech concerns unless they are entirely voluntary, which, given the current politically charged environment, seems highly unlikely.

Require Officials to Publish Regular Reports on Homicides in Their Jurisdiction. One way to help stop the false perception of a supposed epidemic of police violence is to require police departments, mayors, state governors, or other prominent officials to release and publicize statistics, broken down demographically, on how many people have been killed in their jurisdiction, how many killed by police, and what percentage of those

killed by police were armed. Such regular reports would both bolster transparency and make it difficult to maintain the false claim that racially motivated police killings is a vast epidemic. Such publicized reports would also make it clear that the real murder epidemic is not by police but by criminals.

F. RECOMMENDATION: CREATE A POLICE-COMMUNITY OVERSIGHT COMMISSION THAT WILL HELP POLICE EARN CREDIBILITY WITH THE COMMUNITY AND PROMOTE COMMUNITY COOPERATION WITH POLICE

Our recommendation for improving police-community relations—and thereby combatting the problems of no-snitch codes, legal cynicism, and public concerns relating to police use of force discussed earlier—is for the local legislature to create a police-community oversight commission (PCOC) with a diverse membership that will build police credibility with the community by promoting two main objectives: first, ensuring that police deal fairly and respectfully in their interactions with citizens and, second, ensuring that police meet their obligation to the community to prevent crime and promote justice.[259] At the same time, the commission should also earn credibility with police (an issue discussed more in chapter 15). By building police-community trust, the PCOC will also promote community cooperation with police.

Purely civilian oversight boards exist, but in addition to lacking diverse membership, such existing boards tend to focus only on the first obligation of ensuring respectful policing and ignore the second of promoting safety and justice. But the duty of police to the community includes both, and loss of public support for the police can come from abusive police interactions or a failure to control crime and justice failures. What is needed is a commission that is charged and empowered to monitor, analyze, strategize, and publicly comment on both police interactions with citizens and police performance in reducing crime and promoting justice.

One way to promote these two objectives—monitoring both police interaction with citizens and police performance in promoting safety and justice—would be to have a commission made up of persons representing a wide range of perspectives, expertise, and influence within the community. For example, one can imagine a commission with the following or similar diverse makeup:

- Community Residents: three citizen members, including one or more resident from a high-crime area. Election by the community would be ideal (to make them independent of existing political officials) but probably impractical, so perhaps appointment by joint agreement of the mayor and the police chief would be best. The larger goal here is to get members of the community that will be well respected and are sufficiently articulate and open to effectively engage with the community about the commission's work.
- Community Institutions: three members drawn from community institutions, such as the head of a victim's organization, a major religious leader in the community (or the head of an organization representing the community's religious groups), the head of the Chamber of Commerce or other such business organization, a representative of (nonreligious) charitable organi-

zations in the community, or the head of a community mental health organization. The larger goal here is to get the most respected and influential members of the community, whatever institutional group they may be leading.
- Police Leadership: three members drawn from the police department leadership, such as the chief of police, the head of criminal investigations, and the head of community patrols. Another possibility is the head of the department's internal affairs department. One can also think of advantages and disadvantages of having the head of the local police union on the commission.
- Government Institutions: three members drawn from governmental authorities in the jurisdiction, such as the mayor, the head of the city council, and the district attorney.

The chairperson of the commission should be elected by the full membership from among the six community members.

There is precedent for such diversity in the membership of an oversight group for police and criminal justice matters, but purely civilian boards are more common.[260] This kind of diverse membership is preferable to a purely civilian oversight board because it is more likely to minimize the us-versus-them dynamic of civilian boards, which can be a destructive rather than a constructive force because the relationship between a purely civilian board and the police inevitably has the potential to turn antagonistic. It is natural for police to see a civilian oversight board as a permanently critical master and for a purely civilian board to see the police as a perpetual problem to be fixed. Thus, it is not uncommon for civilians in the oversight business to have negative views of police. Consider this illustrative remark: "Police, police unions and various interest groups that don't have an interest in accountability, have successfully blocked any type of real civilian oversight from being enacted in almost every turn, in almost every single one of the 18,000 police jurisdictions in the country."[261] Similarly, it is not uncommon for many police to have negative attitudes about civilian oversight: "It would be akin to putting a plumber in charge of the investigation of airplane crashes. It doesn't matter how good a plumber that he or she is. It gives no level of expertise in terms of evaluating the cause of a plane crash."[262] The police-community oversight commission proposed here is one where all the diverse players are colleagues charged with shared goals that they together will be held responsible for meeting. The next chapter's recommendation elaborates on this proposal with an emphasis on how the commission can gain credibility with the police who might otherwise do everything in their power to block the work of a purely civilian oversight board they fear will be controlled by anti-police activists.

Another advantage of this kind of diverse membership is that it provides the differing perspectives and expertise that is important in resolving important issues. For example, should the PCOC approve or disapprove a move to reduce the use of "stop, question, and frisk" below its normal constitutional limits? The answer to that should not depend on the number of activists screaming at a civilian oversight board during a public meeting but rather on a series of discussions among the diverse membership of the PCOC, who are likely to consider what tradeoffs make sense for the community. Reduced stop, question, and frisk may reduce

police-community daily tensions but may end up increasing gun carrying and ultimately gun violence, violence of a sort that is both difficult to prosecute and extremely destructive to the community's sense of safety. The diverse membership on the PCOC can sort through the tradeoffs and give its public recommendation on the subject. The citizen and the police patrol members may have ideas on how to minimize the negative effect of stops, while the district attorney and the police investigation members may have ideas on how to get more successful prosecutions in gun violence cases, which may include getting more community help in ways that the community members might suggest. One can imagine a long list of policing issues that could benefit from discussions among the diverse colleagues on the PCOC.

Of course, the PCOC's duties would include overseeing and criticizing police whenever appropriate. Police cannot earn the respect, and thereby the cooperation, of the community unless the department shows itself fully devoted to identifying and firing (and not hiring) persons who are unsuitable for effective and respectful police work. The PCOC could help with identifying problems with police conduct and ensuring appropriate resolution of inappropriate use of force incidents.

At the same time, the PCOC ought to be equally devoted to the task of educating the public about what the police do right and, especially importantly, authoritatively correcting mistaken or misguided criticisms of the police. For example, if a PCOC had existed in Ferguson, Missouri, it could have quickly and authoritatively set the record straight on the shooting of Michael Brown. In other words, as noted earlier, the PCOC's reason for being is both to improve the quality of policing and to take positive steps to make these policing improvements known to the public—a necessary step in reducing legal cynicism. Additionally, the commission should publish statistics on police use of force to show how relatively rare serious misconduct incidents are—some states have already passed laws requiring the publication of such statistics in order to make the (small) size of the problem more apparent.[263]

Charging the commission with improving police-community relations through minimizing police misconduct and maximizing safety and justice means the PCOC would need to engage in a wide range of activities. For example, it ought to regularly hear from citizens in public meetings about their interactions with police and regularly review the citizen complaints filed against police and the police handling of those complaints. While the commission would not replace a police internal affairs department, it would act like a kind of appellate court where citizens could take a complaint they did not feel was adequately resolved by police, in which case the commission would review the police handling of the complaint and make a judgment on it (either stating the police handled the complaint appropriately or recommending the police reopen the complaint for reasons stated by the commission). Similarly, the commission ought to regularly review police performance in reducing crime as well as police performance in promoting the successful prosecution of offenders. To this end, the commission ought to have the power to demand regular reports from police about their performance in the areas in which the commission has an interest. The commission also should regularly report to

the public its assessment of police performance in areas that it thinks important, as well as issuing special reports on relevant subjects as needed. These public reports ought to describe the current situation, the efforts that the police have made to improve their performance, and the efforts that the commission itself has made to promote better police performance. Importantly, the commission reports should also critique the conduct of the media, activists, social institutions, and the community generally and the extent to which they have helped or hurt improvements in police performance. Too many citizen review boards limit their focus to the police when many of the most influential factors in improving police-community relations are controlled by non-police actors.

Some may argue that a police-community oversight commission like the one described here will not solve the systemic underlying problems plaguing communities facing high crime and high legal cynicism. This is, of course, largely true. Such a commission cannot undo historical inequities or provide better education, healthcare, or economic opportunities (though it might be able to make clear the need for greater justice system resources). However, by providing a forum for the police and community to come together as allies with common goals to solve common problems, it can work to replace the vicious cycle of high crime, low clearance rates, legal cynicism, and citizen non-cooperation with a virtuous cycle of increased cooperation, higher clearance rates, lower crime, and less legal cynicism. This in turn will not only save lives and increase justice, but it will also allow community members and policymakers to spend more time tackling the deeper issues that must be contended with. Even incremental gains in police-community cooperation are worth pursuing, as incremental deterioration in police-community relations starting in 2020 surely contributed to a violent crime surge costing thousands of lives that could have been saved if better cooperation had existed. Our proposed commission is a pragmatic solution that, while not solving everything, can at least begin to solve something.

CHAPTER 15

Police Non-Intervention

THE PREVIOUS CHAPTER EXAMINED CITI-zen non-cooperation with police as a cause of justice failures. This chapter examines a similar and mirrored dynamic of police non-intervention, in which police pull back from engaging in proactive policing or investigation, thus allowing criminals to escape justice and incentivizing more crime. Just as community members or witnesses may be reluctant to participate in crime investigations due to distrusting police, police can similarly be reluctant to effectively respond to crime due to negative attitudes from the public or government policies. Police non-intervention can be driven by demoralization and voluntary pullback or by orders to depolice (as was the case during much of 2020 when police budgets were slashed, police-free zones were created, and police were ordered to stand down in the face of often violent protests).

This chapter examines four main facets of the problem of police non-intervention, considering both causes and effects. First are anti-police rhetoric and physical attacks, which make policing more difficult. Second is depolicing caused by anti-police policies such as defunding or no-go zones. Third is the issue of police demoralization and problems with hiring and retaining officers. Fourth is the so-called Ferguson Effect where police voluntarily pull back from policing in order to avoid confrontations (such as the one that ended with

the justified shooting of Michael Brown in 2014, examined in the previous chapter). These four factors of police non-intervention are closely interrelated and thus we present only one set of competing interests at the beginning of the chapter and only one reform section at the end of it. As this chapter shows, less police intervention in communities almost always leads to more crime and more failures of justice. While there are many valid criticisms of modern American policing, creating a hostile anti-police climate that causes police non-intervention is deeply counterproductive and hurts poor and minority communities the most. Given the unfortunately politicized nature of the discourse around American policing, it is worth clarifying up front that this chapter is not in any way an attempt to excuse police misconduct or shield police from legitimate criticism. However, it is impossible to understand the causes of poor police-community relations without recognizing that hostility flowing in either direction is a serious contributor. Much has been written on how hostile policing affects the community, a point touched upon in the previous chapter's discussion of legal cynicism, but less has been written on how hostility from the community affects policing. This chapter attempts to shed light on that less recognized side of the problem, not deny the two-way nature of police-community relations.

Citizen non-cooperation and police non-intervention are closely interrelated as a hostile community may cause police to pull back, which only further contributes to the community's sense of abandonment by police and distrust of the justice system. The relatedness of the problems is why this chapter's recommendation is an elaboration on the previous chapter's suggested police-community oversight commission aimed at restoring mutual cooperation, respect, and trust. A well-designed police-community commission can ideally work to restore the trust of the community while also earning credibility with the police and creating an environment where officers can best perform their duties to serve and protect.

A. COMPETING INTERESTS

It is not in society's interests to have a police force that does not engage effectively with the community. And there are no interests supporting police demoralization or attacks on police. However, policies of depolicing or voluntary police pullback are sometimes viewed as the least-bad option by policymakers or police officers confronting terrible police-community relations. In such cases, the competing interests include the following.

Interests Supporting Police Non-Intervention

- *Reducing Hostile Police-Community Interactions.* Police non-intervention may reduce the likelihood of negative police-community interactions by decreasing the number of those interactions. This could arguably help mitigate public criticism over police practices, at least in the short term. In fact, this is one reason why

police voluntarily pull back and governments adopt depolicing policies. However, in the long run, such non-intervention will likely lead to further community hostility as police are viewed as doing nothing to stop violence and deliver justice.
- *Saving Resources.* Less active policing can be a way to conserve police resources, especially when, as commonly happens, police departments are understaffed or underfunded (recall chapter 4's discussion of inadequate financing).

Interests Opposing Police Non-Intervention

- *Doing Justice.* Police non-intervention increases crime while decreasing clearance rates, allowing more criminals to escape justice. More active police intervention increases the chances of catching offenders and preventing crime. Although there is a risk of more negative interactions with the community, the effect of those interactions is likely outweighed by the benefits of proactive policing in the long term.
- *Deterrence and Less Crime.* More active policing discourages offenders and deters crime as potential criminals perceive an increased likelihood of being caught.
- *Reducing Legal Cynicism.* When police do not respond to calls for help or pull back and let crime flourish, the public loses faith in the justice system. This legal cynicism in turn leads to more crime, less crime reporting, and fewer arrests as discussed in chapter 14. By contrast, active policing may restore public faith in the law by showing that crime will be punished and innocent people will be protected.

B. ANTI-POLICE RHETORIC AND ATTACKS ON POLICE

In the wake of high-profile police use of force incidents, public figures frequently use their platforms to harshly criticize police. While there are certainly legitimate criticisms that can be made, there is also a disturbing trend of politicians and activists stirring anti-police hatred for personal or political gain. Such anti-police rhetoric is often absurdly false and unfounded, as with the Michael Brown shooting (discussed in the previous chapter), but such falsehoods are then repeated and amplified enough to seem legitimate. For example, after George Floyd's murder in 2020, perhaps seeking to take advantage of the social unrest to rise in prominence, Congressman Bobby Rush accused Chicago police of "stand[ing] shoulder to shoulder with the Ku Klux Klan."[1] Allegations that the Chicago police are a force of hooded racists slaughtering Black men are demonstrably false, but they might seem credible when coming from a US congressman. Rhetoric accusing police of being racist killers is widely used to rile up the public, with resulting donations, votes, and fame for those willing to engage in such conduct. While individual actors may benefit from using this hateful rhetoric, it harms ordinary citizens by increasing legal cynicism and police demoralization, thus producing more crime and justice failures—the negative consequences of which fall disproportionately on the high-crime minority neighborhoods that the demagogues are hoping to rile. Even worse, the opportunity for principled reform often gets quashed by the highly political anti-police sentiments that are neither principled nor based in fact.

Some argue that anti-police rhetoric is an understandable reaction to emotionally charged police killings, some of which, like the murder of George Floyd, are indeed outrageous and criminal. However, because rhetorical attacks on police have practical real-world consequences in reducing the moral credibility of the justice system and increasing legal cynicism, politicians and activists ought to fit their rhetoric to the facts. This is not a matter of going easy on police wrongdoing but rather a recognition that disseminating disinformation and voicing false claims undermines law enforcement and inevitably lead to more crime and lower clearance rates, thus damaging the lives of millions of innocent Americans, particularly in poor and minority neighborhoods. Many police officials and commentators have pointed to wildly irresponsible anti-police rhetoric for helping to incite the orgy of murder and lawlessness that swept across American cities in the wake of George Floyd's murder.[2] Anti-police rhetoric has also made citizens less willing to cooperate with police out of fear, sometimes provoking unnecessary confrontations in a self-fulfilling prophecy.[3]

Anti-police rhetoric has also almost certainly increased physical attacks on police. According to FBI data, the number of felonious police deaths increased by 58.7 percent from 2020 to 2021 and represents the highest number of such killings in the past decade.[4] Part of this increase in killings is due to anti-police hatred as unprovoked attacks accounted for 32.9 percent of killings of police in 2021 compared to 4.3 percent of killings of police in 2020, indicating a rise in targeted assassinations of police. Police Benevolent Association president Patrick Lynch responded to the unprovoked stabbing of an officer in June 2020 by commenting, "Are we surprised? . . . Did we doubt because of the rhetoric we're hearing, the anti-police rhetoric that's storming our streets, are we surprised that we got this call? I'm not. We said it's going to happen."[5]

Anti-police rhetoric, coupled with the community hostility and anti-police violence it generates, is a major cause of police demoralization and voluntary pullback discussed later in this chapter. Recognizing anti-police rhetoric as a serious contributing cause of poor police-community relations should not be a partisan issue, and indeed, there have been bipartisan calls for more responsible rhetoric.[6]

Case Example: Al Sharpton

In 1987, Tawana Brawley, a Black teenager, falsely accuses a group of White men, some of whom are New York police officers, of committing horrible crimes against her, including rape.[7] Activist Al Sharpton capitalizes on the hoax to rise in relevance by leading protests, flinging accusations of racism at the police, and defaming the men (who successfully sue Sharpton for defamation after a grand jury finds the accusations are a hoax).[8] Far from being deterred from stirring up lies and hatred, Sharpton doubles down on his strategy of hate and division, even extending beyond the police to attack New York's Jewish community after a Black child is killed in an ordinary car accident where the vehicle is driven by a Hasidic Jew. Sharpton threatens violence against Jews and leads a protest where one banner reads, "Hitler did not do the job."[9]

Sharpton's divisive rhetoric carries him to political fame, and he makes an

Figure 15.1. Al Sharpton meets with the president in the Oval Office, 2009. Photo from Obama White House Archives, flickr, May 7, 2009, https://www.flickr.com/photos/obamawhitehouse/3532376638.

unsuccessful bid for the Democratic presidential nomination in 2004. Sharpton returns to prominence with his old tactic of attacking police when Michael Brown is killed in Ferguson in 2014. Although a dozen witnesses, Black and White, confirm that Brown attacked the police officer, as discussed in the previous chapter, Sharpton "reimagines" the story as the teenaged gentle giant Brown being gunned down by police as he had his hands raised in surrender. Sharpton organizes protests and helps lead the Black Lives Matter movement, spreading false information about an epidemic of racist police killings in the process. Even though a grand jury, which includes Blacks and Whites, finds no grounds to indict the officer who killed Brown, Sharpton is undeterred and continues to spread false information about the case. Sharpton also latches on to the death of

Eric Garner at the hands of New York City police to lead protests where some chant, "What do we want? Dead cops."[10]

Ismaaiyl Brinsley, a mentally unstable man, attends a protest and is inspired by this anti-police rhetoric to give his life some purpose.[11] On December 20, 2014, Brinsley posts online, "I'm Putting Wings on Pigs Today," and walks up to a parked NYPD police car and shoots two officers dead through the open window.[12] Even during the funerals of the officers murdered as a direct result of unrelenting anti-police rhetoric, Sharpton refuses to hold off on arranging anti-police protests, and he continues to spread false information.[13]

Reverend Jesse Lee Peterson, a prominent member of New York's Black religious community, makes his views clear on Sharpton's culpability for the deaths of the two officers:

Figure 15.2. Officers line along the funeral route of Officer Wenjian Liu, one of Ismaaiyl Brinsley's victims, 2014. Photo by Phillycop, flickr, January 4, 2015, https://www.flickr.com/photos/philly _police/. Courtesy of Phillycop.

My prayers and thoughts go out to the families who lost their family members in the shooting. I have to tell you I blame Mayor de Blasio, I blame Al Sharpton, and I blame the so-called civil rights leaders because they have been encouraging this type of hatred toward police officers for years now.... Sharpton, since the Tawana Brawley situation ... has been encouraging anger and racism from Black Americans toward white cops and White people at large. So now they have blood on their hands.[14]

Sharpton has continued his anti-police rhetoric to this day without regard for the facts or consequences.[15] Stunningly, many powerful politicians such as former Presidents Obama and Clinton, former New York City mayor Bill de Blasio, and former Attorney General Eric Holder have praised and associated themselves with Sharpton, lending his divisive lies credibility.[16]

The Nature and Extent of the Problem
While Sharpton remains a preeminent example of a professional anti-police agitator, his rhetoric is hardly unique.[17] A cynical campaign of anti-police hatred, relying upon false information about particular incidents as well as claims of systemic police racism generally, has advanced the political and economic fortunes of many politicians and activists at the cost of creating elevated levels of cynicism and anti-police hatred that simply increases criminal victimizations and failures of justice within minority communities.

PERSISTENT AND PERVASIVE ANTI-POLICE RHETORIC Not all criticism of the police is necessarily destructive to the credibility of the justice system. Criticisms that are measured, fact based, and reform

oriented can enhance the credibility of the system by publicly acknowledging and condemning police abuses and ultimately leading to better policing. We ourselves leveled such criticism in chapter 4 discussing the problem of investigative errors. However, anti-police rhetoric has become an ideological and political staple for many activists and politicians regardless of the actual facts. False anti-police rhetoric is always destructive to justice as it causes people to hold seriously inaccurate views of the justice system with damaging results on their compliance with the law and cooperation with enforcement agencies. Recall the previous chapter's discussion of the public's massive overestimate of the number of police shootings, with many Americans guessing thousands of unarmed Black men are killed by police every year. In reality, *ten* unarmed black men were killed by police in 2021, under a definition of "unarmed" that could include "suspects grabbing an officer's gun or fleeing in a stolen car with a loaded pistol on the car seat."[18]

How did so many in the public come to hold such distorted views of reality? The answer is that activists, commentators, and politicians have consistently pushed a false anti-police narrative according to which American policing is deeply, perhaps irreparably, marked with patterns of racist killings. While the evidence disproves such a view, advocating it can be politically useful as it allows individuals to ride a wave of misplaced ire to fame, fortune, or power.

For example, the founders of the Black Lives Matter organization took in a windfall of $90 million in donations in 2020 while promoting numerous inaccuracies and fabrications about American policing.[19] (A large portion of this money went into buying private real estate and paying the lavish salaries of family or friends of the founders.)[20] From Al Sharpton forward, it is clear that anti-police rhetoric pays handsomely. Politically, candidates espousing anti-police messages gained significant prominence in the Democratic Party first in 2014 in the wake of the Black Lives Matter movement going mainstream and later more broadly in 2020 after the murder of George Floyd. In the 2020 Democratic primary, candidates competed for the anti-police vote by making numerous false statements on policing, with candidates Kamala Harris, Tom Steyer, and Elizabeth Warren falsely affirming that Michael Brown was "murdered"[21] and Joe Biden calling for redirecting funds from policing to other services.[22] Biden also affirmed that there was "absolutely" a problem of systemic racism in policing, a claim often repeated but—at least as popularly understood—clearly inconsistent with available data.[23] Other figures in the Democratic Party have gone further, with prominent progressive Congresswoman Ilhan Omar calling police "beyond reform" and Congresswoman Ayanna Pressley comparing police to "slave patrols."[24] When Tyre Nichols, a Black man, was beaten to death by five Black officers in Memphis in 2023, Democratic representative Jamaal Bowman bizarrely claimed Nichols was killed by "white supremacy."[25] Coincidentally, the claim was made in a fundraising pitch, perhaps supplying a motive for the false rhetoric portraying even crimes by Black officers as a sign of the brutal racism supposedly common in American policing.

On a local level, some activists have inflamed anti-police hatred to win elections, such as Indira Sheumaker, a twenty-seven-year-old Black Lives Mat-

ter activist who successfully ousted a moderate incumbent for a Des Moines City Council seat in 2021 on a defund the police platform.[26]

In academia, the anti-police narrative has become so entrenched that attempts to disprove the rhetoric with empirical evidence are met with harsh backlash. The authors of a study showing that White police officers were less likely to shoot Black suspects were forced to withdraw their study after intense criticism despite nothing being wrong with the data or methodology.[27] As mentioned in the previous chapter, Roland Fryer, a leading Black economist at Harvard, published a study showing police are actually less likely to shoot Blacks than Whites in any given confrontation, winning him the ire of anti-police academics at Harvard who subsequently took the next opportunity to strip his funding and suspend him from teaching.[28]

In popular culture, anti-police rhetoric has become an accepted and normalized response to any police use of force. For example, after police fatally shot Ma'Khia Bryant, a Black teenager, in April 2021, LeBron James tweeted an image of one of the responding police officers to his millions of followers with the caption "YOU'RE NEXT #ACCOUNTABILITY."[29] The tweet was widely seen as inviting violence against the officer for the shooting, which was later proven to be justified as Bryant was shot while wielding a knife and charging another woman.[30] The fact that James and millions of others would so quicky leap to anti-police conclusions about the case and feel comfortable sharing threats against police shows how pervasive anti-police rhetoric has become.

Despite the claims of many activists that they are merely speaking up for oppressed communities, most anti-police rhetoric has not served to enhance racial justice, as the communities most severely impacted by the resulting legal cynicism and police pullback are minority communities, as shown in the previous chapter. The result is more crime and more failures of justice disproportionately and negatively affecting African Americans.

PHYSICAL ATTACKS ON POLICE Anti-police rhetoric has also inspired an increasing number of violent attacks on police, exacerbating the problems of police demoralization and voluntary pullback. Some of those who have been led to believe police are a systemically racist killing machine are likely to retaliate with violence. For example, a 2016 protest against police in Dallas turned into a massacre when a Black Army veteran seeking "payback" for supposedly racist police killings murdered five White police officers and wounded seven others.[31] The intensification of anti-police rhetoric after the murder of George Floyd has predictably led to an increase in attacks on police. According to FBI data, from January 1, 2021, to September 30, 2021, fifty-nine police officers were killed in the line of duty. That number represents a 51 percent increase in the number of police officers killed when compared to the same period in 2020.[32] According to a report from the National Fraternal Order of Police (NFOP), 346 officers were shot while performing their duties in 2021, marking a 10 percent increase from 2020 and an 18 percent increase from 2019.[33] This increase in attacks continued into 2022, with police shootings as of April 2022 jumping an additional 43 percent compared to the same period in 2021.[34] While some of these increases are simply a result of increased violent crime,

the NFOP report documented that 103 "ambush style and other calculated attacks on law enforcement" occurred in 2021, up 115 percent (more than double) such targeted attacks in 2020.[35] This increase in premeditated attacks on police strongly suggests that anti-police sentiment, and not just increased crime, is responsible for the increasingly dangerous conditions police face. Many experts have pointed specifically to anti-police rhetoric as a cause behind the increased attacks.[36] For example, Maria "Maki" Haberfeld, a professor of police science at John Jay College of Criminal Justice in New York, concludes, "There was a history of anti-police sentiment over the years that was correlated to deaths in the line of duty but it was more local. Right now, we are seeing it all over the country, total disrespect of police officers."[37]

Further evidence pointing to anti-police rhetoric as a major reason behind the attacks is that many of the attacks have occurred in the context of protests or riots against police.[38] For example, in St. Louis in 2020, four officers standing in a police line were shot and injured after someone opened fire at a protest.[39] In Louisville, two police officers were shot during protests in the aftermath of the announcement that only one of the three officers involved in Breonna Taylor's death would be prosecuted.[40] In Seattle, more than fifty police officers were injured in riots where protesters were calling for the abolition of the police.[41] In New York, more than 350 officers were injured in the two weeks of protests and rioting that followed George Floyd's murder, with rioters using weapons such as Molotov cocktails.[42] In Los Angeles, two police officers were shot in their car in what appeared to be a targeted ambush, with protestors shouting anti-police slogans and blocking the entrance to the emergency room where the officers were taken.[43] Anti-police violence is sometimes disturbingly organized. In March 2023, a group of anti-police radicals conducted a "coordinated attack" on a police training center in Atlanta with a variety of explosives including Molotov cocktails and commercial fireworks. The siege ended with twenty-three of the attackers being charged with domestic terrorism.[44]

Policing has always been a dangerous job, fraught with risks and challenges, and too often thankless. But irresponsible anti-police rhetoric has only made it more dangerous and less appreciated, leading to police hiring shortages and voluntary pullback, as discussed later in this chapter.

Public Complaints About Anti-Police Rhetoric and Attacks on Police

There is a deafening silence in the news media about the problem of anti-police rhetoric and violence. Even though killings of police officers were up over 50 percent in 2021 compared to 2020,[45] these police killings received little to no media coverage, especially in comparison to the mass media coverage of the comparatively less frequent police killings of unarmed civilians. For example, during an eleven-month period in 2021, 9.6 police officers per 100,000 were feloniously killed.[46] Over the same period, only four unarmed Black people (including violently resisting suspects) were killed by police officers, which represents less than 0.01 persons killed by police per 100,000 Black people.[47] In 2021, a police officer was about four hundred times more likely to be killed by a Black civilian than an unarmed Black civilian was to be killed by a police officer.[48] If one

simply noted media coverage, however, one would be justified in thinking it was the opposite.

Citizens who do speak out about anti-police rhetoric are regularly silenced by more vocal anti-police protestors. One of many examples of media and public silence about police killings was the 2021 assassination of Baltimore police officer Keona Holley by a felon awaiting trial.[49] A bystander recording the aftermath of the shooting urged his followers to not report the incident.[50] As he had hoped, major news outlets like the *New York Times* failed to run a single story on the shooting despite publishing several articles on shootings by police officers in the meantime.[51] Another example is found in the *Washington Post* practice of tracking every person shot and killed by police, including those that are justified, yet the paper has no such interest in police officers killed by civilians.[52]

As police killings continue to rise, this lack of media attention is increasingly inexcusable and has been called out by some government officials. FBI Director Christopher Wray warned in 2022 that the problem of police killings "doesn't get enough attention" given that a police officer is murdered nearly once every five days in the United States.[53]

C. DEPOLICING: DEFUNDING POLICE AND POLICE EXCLUSION ZONES

Distorted anti-police narratives sometimes lead politicians and activists to pursue policies of depolicing such as cutting police budgets or creating police exclusion zones, areas where police are not allowed to enter even when they receive 911 calls. Such forcible depolicing was a common response from politicians and activists after the murder of George Floyd. Such policies proved disastrous and have since largely been abandoned, with an increasing bipartisan recognition that expanding policing, rather than decreasing it, is necessary to combat crime and secure justice.

Of course, cutting back on some aspects of policing is not always a mistake. It may make sense to recognize that "mission creep" has led many city administrators to dump an increasing number of non-criminal law enforcement responsibilities on police (such as the handling of mentally ill persons), responsibilities that are better served by social service or psychological counseling personnel.[54] Police administrators would likely be pleased to have officers relieved of non-criminal justice responsibilities.[55] But shrinking the role of police is difficult because other services are generally not equipped to quickly deal with potential violence. For example, initial police contact with the mentally ill is often because citizens have reported violence or threats, and it is police, not psychotherapists, who are immediately available and have the training and means to deal with ongoing violence or threats.

While the term "depolicing" has been used by some commentators to refer to a variety of police non-intervention forms, from voluntary pullback to budget cuts, this chapter uses the term to refer only to external pressures on the police that prevent them from doing their job effectively. Depolicing is a cautionary tale of how false rhetoric and ideological decision making can lead to catastrophic policies hurting most the very communities they were supposed to help.

Case Example: Police-Free Zone in Minneapolis

On May 25, 2020, George Floyd, a Black man, is murdered by Derek Chauvin, a White police officer, in Minneapolis. A video of Floyd's slow suffocation under Chauvin's knee is posted online and sparks massive protests across the country. Perhaps taking a page from the Occupy Wall Street playbook, protesters in Minneapolis quickly create a four-block-wide police-free zone around the site where Floyd died.[56] Checkpoints are erected around "the Free State of George Floyd" to keep police out, and Minneapolis mayor Jacob Frey orders police to stand down, even when rioters spread looting and arson throughout the city and burn down a police precinct.[57] As police stand down, the murder rate doubles while the clearance rate dives. Within the police-free zone, an expectant mother and her unborn child are gunned down, a teenager is murdered, and another young man is

Figure 15.3. "Defund the police rallies" often became violent, Minneapolis, 2020. Photo courtesy of Matt Garceau/Camelot Photography.

killed. Even with the rampant criminality, city officials intercede to prevent the police from removing the occupiers. Police are unable to answer 911 calls within the area. Crime victims must find their way out of the zone to get help. People who are unable to make their way out to the police do not receive help, including children who are threatened by domestic violence. Reported violent crime increases by 122 percent in the Minneapolis Ward containing the zone, compared to 34 percent city-wide.[58] Unreported increases in crime are likely much higher, as reporting crime is practically useless when police are not allowed to enter the zone. On March 6, 2021, one of the zone's leaders is shot to death.[59] True to the zone's principles, occupiers lug the bodies outside the zone for police to pick up and refuse to allow them to enter to investigate.[60] After a disastrous thirteen months, in June 2021, Mayor Frey finally allows the zone cleared and repoliced.[61]

Case Example: Depolicing in Portland

In 2018, Portland, Oregon, was the big city with the lowest murder count, with only twenty-seven murders.[62] On May 29, 2020, over a thousand protesters take to the streets in Portland to protest against racism and police brutality in the wake of George Floyd's murder four days earlier. The protest turns into a five-hour riot with looters robbing malls and arsonists burning banks. The city removes $27 million dollars from the police budget and at the same time enacts legislation limiting the powers of police to intervene to stop looting and violence.[63] The Portland police department is already understaffed (having fewer officers than it did when the city was half its current size), but the budget cuts and

increased restrictions prevent Portland's police from effectively securing law and order.[64] The result is a disaster.

As the daily protests and nightly riots continue through July, they cause millions of dollars in damage.[65] Portland quickly becomes "one of the most violent cities in America."[66] By 2021, the homicide count is ninety-two—a 240 percent increase in three years—with an additional nine-hundred-plus non-fatal shootings.[67] The year 2022 continued the upward trend to set a new record, with 101 homicides.[68] As could be expected, these killings disproportionately harm Portland's small Black community. Despite making up less than 6 percent of Portland's population, Black residents make up about half of all homicide victims, with the number of Black murder victims rising by 250 percent between 2019 and mid-2021.[69] Other crimes also surge, with robberies increasing 50 percent in 2022, and vehicle thefts reaching historic highs.[70] Something particular to Portland's policing policies is clearly to blame for the increased lawlessness as crime across Oregon declines between 2019 and 2021 even while Portland suffers a devastating crime wave.[71]

Unrest in Portland not only leads to increased violence but also economic devastation. Businesses struggle to survive. As shop owner Saadi Nikoo explains, "Our windows got broken seven times, and our merchandise was damaged and thrown on the street. We've been dealing with this, no protection. We're on our own. . . . It's a dilemma, no one is doing anything."[72] One progressive business owner, Loretta Guzman, tries to start a "Coffee with a Cop" event for citizens to bring their complaints directly to a police officer. Her shop is quickly attacked and vandalized.[73] She sums up the feelings of law-abiding Portland residents simply: "Some are scared. Some are mad or sad, some feel helpless. . . . There's no consequences. Those who do go to jail, they get right back out."[74]

On a regular basis, large groups take over neighborhoods for street-racing events.[75] When people are shot near these events, emergency crews are unable to respond due to the antagonistic crowds.[76] People far from the action of street racing also have grown fearful. There is a "'substantial increase in fear of violence and crime' due to aggressive people lingering in the area. Over 700 tent cities spring up across the city.[77] Police say open-air drug sales, threats, acts of violence and property crimes are all part of the problem."[78] Portland's shattering decline from a leading example of lawfulness to a violent disaster zone seems to many a predictable result of the city's ideologically motivated depolicing policies. Residents eventually come to understand the problem and its causes. Eighty-five percent of Portland residents in 2022 agree "that the quality of life is worsening," and 82 percent want more police.[79] In the 2022 municipal elections, Portland residents express their outrage by removing city counselor Jo Ann Hardesty—a prominent advocate of Portland's defund the police movement. Her replacement, Democrat Rene Gonzalez, sums up Portland's experience, including its depolicing, simply: "City hall's ineffective, ideologically driven policies are ruining the city we used to proudly call home."[80]

The Nature and Extent of the Problem

Depolicing has most commonly been achieved through the creation of police exclusion zones and through defunding police departments to reduce the number of officers that can be put on the street.

"NO-GO ZONES" AND "POLICE-FREE ZONES" and visible examples of depolicing have been the temporary establishment of "police-free zones" or "no-go zones," as in the Minneapolis example discussed earlier. In 2020, such "autonomous zones" or "police-free zones" were established in cities across the country, where the founders claimed citizens could create "self-governing utopia[s]" and inspire a 'summer of love' within their communities.[81] After all, if police are the problem, as some reasoned, no police might be the solution. Police were often ordered to stand down by local officials eager to appease protesters or to avoid confrontation with armed patrols of anti-police militants. This "summer of love" soon turned into a "summer of blood" as shootings surged in affected cities with the epicenters of violence often being the police-free zones. Such no-go zones also prevented proper police investigations from bringing many of the perpetrators to justice.

In Seattle, a six-block radius in the city named the Capitol Hill Autonomous Zone (CHAZ) soon turned deadly. In a ten-day period in June 2020, a total of four shootings left two people in the police-free zone dead.[82] Victims as young as fourteen and sixteen years old were shot and injured, and sexual assault allegations and mental health problems swept through the area, quickly disheartening the zone's earliest supporters, including Seattle mayor Jenny Durkan.[83] A murder victim's mother filed a lawsuit against the city over her son's death in the autonomous zone, arguing that the medics and Seattle Fire Department were unable to safely enter the zone to save her son.[84] The Seattle Fire Department claimed that the crime scene was too risky to "commit [their] crews to respond in without a police escort."[85] With police excluded from the zone, no medical response to the life-threatening violence was possible. The police were also unable to investigate the crime scene, as they were unable to "collect evidence, map out the location, take photos or videos, or talk" with witnesses.[86] Ms. Sinclair, the victim's mother, expressed her distress over the no-go zone: "I know my son needed the police at that time, and my son needed the paramedics. Why [would we] ever have an event where there was no police available? That's lawless."[87] Having been "undermined by violence,"[88] CHAZ proved a fatal and dangerous failed experiment, and police were finally allowed to dismantle the zone on July 1, 2020.[89] Seattle's experience was not unique.[90] In addition to Minneapolis, discussed earlier, police-free zones sprang up in many major cities across the United States, including Washington, DC; Portland; and Philadelphia.[91]

Without question, police exclusion zones are an inexcusable failure on the part of a city government that has a moral and legal obligation to provide public safety and justice. Such zones justifiably foster legal cynicism among residents who are literally abandoned by law enforcement on the orders of city officials. Fortunately, the disastrous examples provided by such zones in 2020 have shifted public and governmental opinion against their future creation. However, they remain an example of just how destructive false anti-police rhetoric and narratives can be when they play out unchecked in practical policy.

DEFUNDING THE POLICE Another predictably disastrous depolicing policy implemented in many jurisdictions after the murder of George Floyd was defunding police departments, often through diverting police department funds to social programs. In fact, twenty-four of the largest fifty cities in America either cut their police budgets for 2021 (compared to 2020) or refused to approve regular yearly increases (thus amounting to an effective cut given inflation and increased demands from increased crime).[92] By one count, anti-police activists secured almost a billion dollars in direct cuts from police budgets in 2020 budget votes (not counting cutting regular increases).[93] Major cities where cuts occurred included Philadelphia, New York, and Los Angeles. Such cuts had almost universally negative effects, especially in poor and minority neighborhoods. After Milwaukee reduced its law enforcement staff by 120 officers, murders increased by 98 percent.[94] When the city of Portland reduced the Portland Police Bureau's budget, as discussed in the case example earlier, shootings more than doubled.[95] Late in 2021, the Portland City Council added $5.2 million back into the police budget, a tacit acknowledgment of its mistake.[96]

Inadequately funding police naturally leads to failures of justice through reducing the amount of time police can spend on each criminal investigation as well as reducing budgets for training and implementing best practices, as discussed in chapter 4. While some activists support defunding patrol officers more than detectives, it is important to understand that defunding a police department will affect criminal investigations both directly through resources being cut from investigative budgets as well as indirectly through the increased crime overwhelming even uncut investigative capabilities. Ironically, such budget cuts likely make it even harder to hold police accountable for unjustified shootings or killings as those too are expensive criminal investigations that might be sacrificed due to a lack of resources.

And as will be discussed more in section D concerning police hiring difficulties, defunding inevitably produces not only fewer officers but also substandard officers. As the attractiveness of a police job diminishes, be it from lower salaries, stress from understaffing, or anti-police rhetoric, fewer people who would make good police officers are attracted to the job, and departments are increasingly compelled to hire people who they normally would reject as unsuitable. Of course, this simply condemns the community to a downward spiral of increasingly unsuitable police recruits producing an increasing number of instances of improper conduct further sparking anti-police sentiment. (Note, for example, that the five Black officers who beat Black motorist Tyre Nichols to death in Memphis in 2023 were all hired in the past three to six years.[97]) A lack of officers also means police are overworked and spread thin. For example, Chicago police have traditionally followed a common model of assigning officers four days of active work followed by two off days. However, a lack of funding and officers forced over one thousand Chicago police officers to work eleven consecutive days or more in April and May 2022, a situation guaranteed to fray nerves, cause burnout, and increase the likelihood of mistakes.[98]

Fortunately, as with the creation of police-free zones, aggressively defunding police departments has largely fallen out of favor after its disastrous results materialized,[99] although it remains common that police departments are woefully understaffed, as discussed in section D.[100]

Public Complaints About Depolicing Policies

Many activists, politicians, and community members have spoken out against depolicing policies due to their predictably disastrous outcomes. Even many of those advocating for police or criminal justice reform have expressed a desire for continued or expanded law enforcement. For example, Sybrina Fulton, the mother of Trayvon Martin, a Black teenager who was killed by a neighborhood watchman in 2012, has spoken about her disapproval of "defunding" police departments and instead advocates for better police standards and training.[101] Other advocates for police reform point to the fact that defunding police leads to a rise in crime, especially in minority communities, making such policies indefensible from a racial justice perspective.[102] For example, Rev. Harriet Walden of Seattle said that she "supported reforms that made it easier to fire officers who violate policies or brutalize people, but that she didn't want fewer police overall."[103] Others claim that involving police in community-wide development is essential and that excluding police from responses to community violence is "unfair and unrealistic."[104]

The general public clearly does not support defunding police. A poll published in 2021 found that only 18 percent of Americans support the "defund the police" movement (still a shockingly high number given its obvious disastrous consequences), and 58 percent said that they affirmatively oppose the movement.[105] Sixty-seven percent of White Americans actively oppose the movement and 84 percent of Republicans oppose it. But while people's views are influenced to some extent by political affiliation, only 28 percent of Black Americans and 34 percent of Democrats support the movement, proving that along racial and party lines, support for defunding the police is a decidedly minority view.[106] In fact, the supporters of defunding are often a minority of more affluent progressives far removed from the violent victimizations common in poorer minority neighborhoods.[107] Support for defunding the police can be a way to virtue signal behind the safety of well-funded suburban police departments or private security.

In November 2021, the majority of Minneapolis voters demonstrated their opposition to the defund the police movement by rejecting a ballot initiative seeking to replace the police department with a "Department of Public Safety."[108] Many are now realizing in the midst of soaring violence that strong police forces are a necessity. For example, a poll in July 2020 found that 63 percent of Portland residents supported cutting funding for the police department. Less than a year later, in April 2021, a poll conducted by the same company found that close to half of Portland residents wanted to *increase* police presence.[109] Similarly, a poll conducted in June 2020 found that only 38 percent of Democrats have "a little" trust in law enforcement; by March 2021, that number was up to 56 percent as many realized police are necessary to fight crime and deliver justice.[110] While Black Americans may be more mistrusting of police than White Americans (as discussed in the previous chapter), "one primary grievance African Americans have with the criminal justice systems is that black neighborhoods are paradoxically under policed."[111] The lack of effective police intervention in poor and minority neighborhoods contributes to much of the legal cynicism and citizen non-cooperation discussed in the previous chapter. In a national study, increased

policing finds wide support among Black and Latino communities, with 60 percent of African Americans, 65 percent of Latinos, as well as 74 percent of Whites supporting a proposal to increase police presence in high crime areas.[112]

The public has also opposed depolicing in other contexts. When, in 2021, school districts across California drastically reduced school police forces to make the learning environments "safer" under the theory that police are the problem, parents and teachers strongly opposed such policy changes. A recent study found that only 7 percent of teachers agreed that defunding school police officers would make schools safer.[113] Another study found a similar result, demonstrating that only 20 percent of "teachers, principals, and district leaders completely or partly agreed that armed police officers should be eliminated from public schools."[114] Parents share similar feelings. A survey among parents in Los Angeles, a city that has significantly reduced police presence in schools only to see an uptick in school violence, found that 72 percent of Asian American or Pacific Islander parents, 67 percent of Hispanic parents, 54 percent of White parents, and 50 percent of Black parents thought that schools were safer due to the presence of police.[115] Efforts to defund the police no longer reflect the concerns of constituents, even in progressive or left-leaning jurisdictions.

Ideology, Politics, and
Changing Views on Depolicing

The effects of depolicing seem obvious and predictable to many people, as a matter of common sense. Reducing the presence of law enforcement does not make for a safer community, a fact that is readily apparent to residents of crime-ravaged neighborhoods but apparently less clear to those living in gated communities. Studies show that the most serious offenses ("index crimes") are reduced with each new officer added to a police force.[116] In addition to solving more crimes, larger police forces deter potential criminals, leading to fewer index crimes even without necessarily arresting and incapacitating additional offenders.[117]

While a broad consensus has formed against depolicing policies such as defunding or creating exclusion zones, many political and social leaders refused to stand up to the depolicing movement at its beginning and even encouraged depolicing before its disastrous effects became so undeniable. While radical progressives such as the "squad" in Congress quickly and loudly aligned themselves with defunding, many top Democratic officials and Congress members similarly supported efforts to reduce police funding in favor of funding other community programs.[118] Prominent Democratic mayors such as Los Angeles's Eric Garcetti and New York City's Bill de Blasio proposed slashing their police department budgets to political applause from much of their party's leadership.[119]

Once the effects of defunding police became undeniable, however, Democratic leaders largely dropped the issue and reversed course. While she once called for a decrease in the police budget after the murder of George Floyd, San Francisco mayor London Breed has since reversed her position. In December 2021, she called for an end to the "reign of criminals who are destroying [the] city" by arguing the city should be "more aggressive with law enforcement" and by increasing funding for the city's police.[120]

Mayors around the country have made similar policy reversals due to increased crime. In 2021, Chicago mayor Lori Lightfoot pledged to increase police funding to "recruit the next generation of police officers" and respond to the city's 60 percent rise in murders since 2019.[121] Lightfoot had previously ordered the Chicago Police Department to leave vacant positions unfilled and reduced the department's budget by millions of dollars. Similarly, Mayor Ted Wheeler of Portland addressed the need to hire additional police officers to combat rising crime, reversing his attitudes toward the department just one year prior.[122] In Seattle, Mayor Jenny Durkan requested that the city council unfreeze $7.5 million that had previously been unavailable to the police department.[123] While such reversals are desirable, the initial defunding policies were so obviously wrong that it is hard to avoid the conclusion that support for them was guided primarily by expedient political interests and blind ideology rather than a genuine belief that such policies would improve the lives of citizens.

Opposition to defunding the police is now a bipartisan position. Democratic House Speaker Nancy Pelosi explicitly stated, in February 2022, that the movement to defund the police is "not the position of the Democratic Party."[124] President Biden worked to squash the "defund the police" slogan at his March 2022 State of the Union address by saying to bipartisan applause, "We should all agree the answer is not to defund the police; it's to fund the police."[125]

The tragic lesson of the depolicing policies pushed in 2020 is that ideology and political pandering often prevent politicians from either recognizing or speaking the obvious truth on issues as simple as valuing enforcing the law and doing justice. Neither leaders nor commentators should have seriously considered supporting or even tolerating proposals to defund police or to create police-free zones, but when it seemed politically expedient, they did so. The price of that political expediency was an enormous cost in human lives and suffering.

D. POLICE DEMORALIZATION: EARLY RETIREMENTS AND HIRING DIFFICULTIES

Anti-police rhetoric, violent attacks, and anti-police policies have taken a significant toll on America's police forces. The resulting widespread demoralization has made it difficult to staff police departments and motivated much of the voluntary pullback from proactive policing (discussed in the next section on the "Ferguson Effect"). Police officers are already under stress from engaging in daily confrontations with often violent suspects. But normally, police receive support for keeping the public safe and serving justice. When that support turns to widespread criticism and demonization, rife with accusations of racism and murder, police are predictably disheartened. Such demoralization has resulted in almost 90 percent of America's police departments facing a wave of retirements and difficulties in officer hiring, which results in understaffing and requires departments to lower their hiring standards. Of course, this only makes the job less appealing, triggering a downward spiral of more stress and demoralization, resulting in more crime and less justice.[126]

Case Example: Minneapolis Police Shortages and Demoralization

In 2011, Minneapolis has 860 uniformed police and thirty-two murders.[127]

In the next decade, the population of the city increases by approximately fifty thousand (about 15 percent), but the city government keeps the size of the police force unchanged, partly due to an anti-police ideology that views police as the enemy.[128]

By 2014, the city knows that it has a desperate problem of police understaffing. Officers are furious at city leadership for "dangerously" low staffing levels. Many officers see the staffing levels as "well beyond dangerous" and "near catastrophic."[129] One officer writes: "We're holding the street together with spit and duct tape."[130] The city government ignores the warnings and lets staffing levels continue to decline. The shortage of officers has become so acute by 2019 that the city is unable to respond to 6,776 priority one 911 calls,[131] which typically include reports of shootings, stabbings, and sexual assaults. Some priority zero calls, such as "baby not breathing," also get a delayed response.

At the start of 2020, the Minneapolis police force is staffed with approximately 825 police officers.[132] With a city government clearly hostile to them, police are exhausted and demoralized well before the 2020 murder of George Floyd by a Minneapolis police officer. Derek Chauvin, the officer who killed Floyd, has a record as a problem officer with at least twenty-two complaints or internal investigations against him in his nineteen years of service, including excessive force complaints, with one resulting in disciplinary action.[133] But in a department desperate for officers, it is no surprise that Chauvin is not dismissed. Keeping only fully reliable officers is a luxury that the understaffed department cannot afford.

During the violent protests that follow Floyd's murder, city officials order police to abandon much of the city, including a police precinct station, to the rioters. The depolicing orders have a serious effect in further degrading police morale. As one officer explains, "I got a pit in my stomach at that point . . . I had zero confidence in our upper echelon of leadership."[134]

The rhetorical attacks on police continue, and two weeks after the Floyd killing, nine of the thirteen city council members stand on stage before a large crowd. Arrayed at their feet in large block letters is the sign: DEFUND THE POLICE.[135] There are calls for reducing the funding of the police department by $45 million.[136] Some members of the council seek to shut down the department entirely.[137] A group of residents sue the city for illegally diverting funds from the police and failing to meet the police staffing level required by the charter.[138]

In the following two months, two hundred Minneapolis officers (almost a quarter of the force) file the paperwork to leave the force, some retiring and some simply quitting.[139] In exit interviews, "an overwhelming number [of departing officers] cited a lack of support, and felt left to fend for themselves during the riots."[140] As one officer explains, "All of a sudden it was 'The Minneapolis Police Department is rotten to the root. Everybody with that uniform is a killer and a racist.'"[141] Academic research finds that across the board "key factors driving police turnover include loss of trust and confidence in leadership . . . and sustained negative attention."[142]

As discussed previously, the lack of police takes a devastating toll as crime surges. In 2021, the city sees more than six hundred people treated for gunshot wounds[143] and ninety-six murders, sixty-four more than in 2011.[144] Most victims are Black.[145] In addition to the shootings,

in 2021 there are more than 4,600 violent crimes,[146] as compared to 3,722 a decade earlier.[147] Some rich communities in Minneapolis take to hiring private security to protect themselves, but poor communities cannot do the same as safety and justice become a luxury good.[148]

As the city council debates hiring more officers, crime continues to surge and many of the residents in the most hard-hit areas see little to debate. George Saad, a Minneapolis resident complains:

Since the unjustified and unfortunate death of George Floyd, the city council has engaged in rhetoric that has emboldened criminals, the proof of which is in the unprecedented spike in crime. You guys have had years to address any culture problems within the Minneapolis Police Department. You have failed to do so. Instead, you embark on a campaign against your own police department, fighting and demonizing an entire internal city organization instead of making it better.[149]

On May 15, 2021, nine-year-old Trinity Ottoson-Smith is jumping on the trampoline in her grandfather's yard when she is shot in the head and killed instantly by a stray bullet. The grieving grandfather thinks about the next victim: "We need more police officers. There is no doubt in my mind. I'm praying for all of these families [who had family members killed] but, you know what, I'm praying for the next people too."[150]

By this time, the need for more police is so obvious that the city council drops its opposition to hiring. But hiring and even retaining current officers is now difficult. Before the hostilities against police, the city had their pick of seventy applications for every opening. The ability to hire only officers with a suitable background and temperament typically requires just such a large selection pool. But applications plunge everywhere amid the hostile climate, with one nearby county averaging 3.8 applicants per position.[151] That lack of choice does not bode well for a future force of suitable officers.

The officer quoted previously takes his family and moves to a police force in Iowa: "Down here they appreciate you, you get a lot of support from the community."[152] As a former New York City police commissioner explains, "Nobody wants to work in a place where they're not wanted."[153]

The Nature and Extent of the Problem

Anti-police rhetoric, attacks, and policies have had a severe impact on the morale of America's police forces. The result is significant staffing shortages across the country as police departments, especially in cities, are hit by a wave of early retirements and difficulty in finding suitable new officers to fill increasingly thankless and criticized jobs.

Police demoralization's most obvious effect is creating staff shortages. The reduction in the number of available officers intensifies the lack of proactive policing, makes it more likely low-level offenses will be ignored, and lengthens police response times even to serious crimes while hampering investigations that take time and personnel resources. One recent analysis summarized the "spiraling decline" that such shortages create:

> This all has many law-enforcement leaders and academics concerned that the profession could be pushed into a spiraling decline: As more police officers flee their departments and crime increases, the officers who remain face burnout, have less time to engage with

the community, and are more prone to making mistakes, leaving department leaders desperate to fill positions. Some may relax hiring standards and bring in more unqualified cops who get into trouble, creating the next viral encounter, ratcheting up the anti-police climate, leading to more laws that make policing harder, prompting more officers to flee the profession, and on and on.[154]

These effects of demoralization occurred most strikingly in the wake of protests against police after George Floyd's murder in May 2020. Between April 2020 and April 2021, police retirements nation-wide increased by 45 percent and resignations increased by 18 percent compared to the previous year.[155] In New York City, where politicians like councilwoman Kristin Jordan have referred to the police as the "thugs in blue" and a "racist, rogue military force,"[156] police retirements nearly doubled in the first ten months of 2020, compared to the same period in 2019.[157] Many police departments have experienced even more dramatic effects. For example, the Portland Police Bureau "lost more officers to retirement in August 2020 alone than in all of 2019" and an Illinois department received the "lowest turnout in 42 years" for police exam applications.[158]

Meanwhile, "the Asheville, NC, police have stopped responding to low-level crimes because they have lost about a third of their staff to resignations and retirement."[159] It is often hard to replace these retiring officers. The Nashville Police Department, for example, which received 4,700 applications in 2010, received only 1,900 in 2019.[160] Similarly, the Seattle Police Department experienced a 40 to 50 percent decrease in applications, and in other counties, applications have dropped by as much as 70 percent.[161] Eighty-six percent of police chiefs around the country have reported officer shortages, most of which have worsened in recent years.[162] Fewer applicants mean fewer choices which is likely to translate into poorer quality officers.

Even before the increased hiring difficulties of the past few years, a report by the Bureau of Justice Statistics found that the number of police officers nationally was not keeping pace with the growing US population. While the number of sworn officers increased by about fifty-two thousand from 1997 until 2016, the rate of officers per one thousand citizens decreased by 11 percent.[163] And between 2008 and 2019, per-capita police officer rates have decreased by 8 percent, and the rates are likely to continue to drop.[164] Between 2013 and 2018, the population of the United States grew by eleven million[165] while the number of sworn police officers around the country actually *decreased* by about twenty-three thousand.[166]

The lack of police due to high retirement rates and low application numbers has led to a diminished ability to respond to crime. Studies have consistently shown that having more police officers decreases crime and increases clearance rates.[167] For example, the Niskanen Center conducted a retrospective study of 242 large cities over nearly four decades, finding that for every eleven to eighteen officers added to a community,[168] one additional homicide and twenty serious crimes were avoided, and that "the decline in homicide is twice as large for Black victims in per capita terms" than for White victims.[169] That means cities with police shortages of more than one hundred officers in recent years have each likely suffered at least an additional six to nine homicides per year that would not otherwise have occurred.[170] Across the country, it is likely that hundreds of victims are dying each year as a result of police shortages. And, of course, the staff shortages also impair the ability of police to solve crimes and bring offenders to justice.

In Baltimore, for example, where the police department now has five hundred fewer officers than it did a decade ago, arrests have decreased by 48 percent over the past five years, suggesting thousands more criminals are escaping justice in the city each year due to police being unable to solve crimes.[171] In Las Vegas, police from the Violent Crime Initiative team were diverted from their normal duties in order to patrol anti-police protests in June 2020. Subsequently, officer-initiated activity decreased and murder rates increased.[172] In New Orleans in 2022, the police department had less than one thousand officers "for the first time in modern history, down from more than 1,300 a few years ago. The city is losing about 100 officers a year to retirement and resignation."[173] The New Orleans police force, which should be at least 1,400 strong, was unable to deal effectively with crime, and the city became the murder capital of America in the first half of 2022, recording a homicide rate of 41 per 100,000.[174] By the end of the year, that already horrific rate had risen to 70 per 100,000.[175] By contrast, El Salvador, a country with often the highest murder rate in the world, has a murder rate just over 60 per 100,000 people.[176]

While police shortages primarily affect the poorest neighborhoods that experience the most violent crime, shortages affect response times across all neighborhoods. In Portland, for example, increases in crime have contributed to a 25 to 40 percent increase in 911 calls across the city compared to the previous year.[177] But with more than a dozen 911 dispatch staff authorized positions remaining vacant, the average 911 caller wait time has significantly increased.[178] With police resignations expected to continue in high numbers,[179] the effects of police shortages in cities across the country are only likely to worsen.

Complaints About
Police Demoralization

Demoralization is a major source of complaints from police officers and law enforcement officials. One officer who abruptly retired from the NYPD in 2020, Richard Brea, explained his decision as follows: "Everyone has turned their backs on us. From the media, to politicians, to some of our own. Sad to see decades of hard work and many sacrifices (many were officers' lives) be washed away. The media hasn't helped. They irresponsibly portray a department that's out of control. We know that's not true."[180]

However, just as with attacks on police, the crisis of police demoralization and understaffing receives only limited media and public attention. While public support for police officers is not as high as it used to be, most Americans are still concerned at the prospect of a demoralized police force, especially as violent crime surges. The case example of Minneapolis shows how concerned citizens banded together to sue the city for not hiring enough police officers.[181] These citizens won their suit, forcing the hiring of more officers. In an October 2021 survey, researchers found that 47 percent of Americans viewed police funding as a major issue facing the United States, including 21 percent of Americans who say funding must be increased by "a lot" in

order to support police forces.[182] This rise in support for expanding police department funding is shared across political affiliations and racial groups and has been fueled by a rise in violent crime.[183] In June 2020, 41 percent of Americans expressed concerns about violent crime, stating that it was a "very big problem" in the United States.[184] One year later, 61 percent of Americans believed violent crime was a major concern.[185] The public predictably begins to care more about policing as crime and justice failures increase.

E. VOLUNTARY POLICE NON-INTERVENTION: THE FERGUSON EFFECT

In the wake of Michael Brown's shooting by a police officer in Ferguson, Missouri, in 2014, the term the "Ferguson Effect" was coined.[186] Over time, the term has been used most notably by researcher Heather Mac Donald[187] and has come to refer to the observation that increased hostility toward and criticism of police officers by the community tends to lead to reduced engagement by police.[188] In other words, the Ferguson Effect is a natural and predictable result of police demonization and demoralization.[189] Many like Mac Donald have argued that the effect has intensified since George Floyd's killing in May 2020.[190]

Consistent with the Ferguson Effect, many police officers have significantly reduced their proactive policing as they argue it would "be easier to do nothing" than to risk an incident that would result in public retaliation, personal and professional risks for the officer, and greater support for depolicing policies such as defunding.[191] Such voluntary police pullback has a high cost to the community, as studies show less active policing leads to higher crime rates and lower clearance rates—claims borne out by recent statistics showing a massive spike in homicides and fall in clearance rates after the 2020 anti-police protests.[192]

Case Example: The Ferguson Effect in Baltimore

In 2010, the new mayor of Baltimore cuts police salaries and increases the amount police must contribute to their pensions. In reaction, retirements increase and vacancies go unfilled. The number of uniformed officers drops by three hundred, and the murder rate increases by 20 percent by 2013. As one insider puts it, "you can only beat down your horses for so long before they give up."[193] Then in 2014 and 2015, Michael Brown is killed in Ferguson, Missouri, and Freddie Gray dies in police custody in Baltimore. Both deaths prompt rioting. The city announces that it will seek criminal charges against the Baltimore officers involved in Gray's death.[194] (It is later determined there was no criminal conduct by the officers.)

Police respond by voluntarily pulling back to avoid further incidents. Arrests in Baltimore fall by 33 percent. The average citizen notices that more criminals than ever remain free. As one Baltimore community organizer reports: "We saw a pullback in this community for over a month where it was up to the community to police the community. And quite frankly, we were outgunned."[195] The voluntary pullback is driven in large part by police demoralization, caused by the anti-police rhetoric and policies. A police officer working during the riots explains, "It's demoralizing. After 20 years, it's soul-crushing. I know I do good in the community. That's what I do, at great sacrifice to my family and my health. The collateral damage of dealing with horrible, depressing stuff day after day, it adds up. . . . To have them screaming 'All cops are bad; you're a murderer' is soul-crushing. I know better, but it just is."[196] Carl Stokes, a former Democratic city councilor, put it this way: "The police stopped doing their jobs, and let people fuck up other people."[197] Between 2011, a year after defunding the Baltimore police began, and 2021, nearly three thousand Baltimore residents (three hundred a year) are murdered—in a city of 609,000 (that is, one out of every two thousand citizens is killed every year over the decade).[198] By 2021, things have only gotten worse: a record 726 shootings result in the deaths of 337 citizens.[199]

Case Example: Police Disengagement in Atlanta

On June 12, 2020, Rayshard Brooks, a Black man attempting to flee arrest, is shot and killed outside a Wendy's by two White police officers in Atlanta.[200] (A two-year investigation by a special state prosecutor subsequently determined that there was no criminal conduct by the officers.) With protests against police shootings already occurring after the murder of George Floyd, the reaction is swift. Protesters march to the Wendy's and burn it before occupying the site and declaring it a police-free autonomous zone known as the "Rayshard Brooks Peace Center." The "peace center" is maintained as a police-free zone by individuals armed with AR-15s and shotguns. The Atlanta mayor responds by condemning the police, and the county DA criminally charges the two officers before any investigation. Police officers respond by engaging in massive withdrawal and non-intervention, with many officers calling out sick. Arrests fall by 71 percent and crime surges. The evening of July 4 is a dark day for Atlanta with twenty-eight shootings, including the murder of eight-year-old Secoriea Turner, who is shot and killed by four armed militants in the police-free "peace center." Three of the killers are never caught. Secoriea's family blames the de-policing and non-intervention for her death.

The Nature and Extent of the Problem

When police are demonized and de-moralized, they pull back from actively trying to catch criminals, and crime flourishes and justice fails. The existence of this dynamic, the Ferguson Effect, is simply common sense: Why would officers feeling demonized and attacked risk their reputations and physical and economic safety by actively involving themselves in potentially controversial situations if they could avoid it? But there is also plenty of empirical evidence documenting this predictable connection between anti-police protests and rhetoric and the resulting police pullback and increase in crime and justice failures.

While the police non-intervention effect was first noted in Ferguson, it is now recognized as affecting police departments and crime rates in cities of all sizes across the country. Numerous studies and analyses have found that high-profile incidents involving police use of force, especially against Black suspects, have coincided with both decreases in policing activities and increases in homicides. For example, in the wake of Michael Brown's death in 2014, data from most of the country's sixty largest cities showed a decrease in active policing,[201] and an average increase in homicides of 19.8 percent.[202] Another study suggests the Ferguson Effect accounts for more than a 16 percent increase in the homi-

cide rate across fifty-six large cities in 2015.[203] And, as expected, clearance rates fell as crime increased.[204]

Surveys of police officers from departments of all sizes also confirm the influence of the Ferguson Effect triggered by demoralization, a highly critical environment, and concerns for officer safety. Overall, 86 percent of police officers reported that high-profile incidents between officers and Blacks have made their jobs harder.[205] The results were high even among officers in small departments with fewer than three hundred sworn officers (84 percent) and among Black officers (81 percent).[206] Similarly, 93 percent of officers say colleagues in their departments had become more concerned about their safety, even before the 2016 ambush killing of five Dallas police officers.[207] As a result, police are choosing to be more cautious in their interventions. A 2016 survey found that 72 percent of police were less willing to engage in proactive policing because of highly publicized encounters with Black suspects.[208]

A former NYPD official reported that in 2020, police are "shying away from enforcement that could lead to steep consequences for individual officers in an environment often hostile toward the police."[209] The decrease in proactive policing, decrease in arrests, and increase in serious crimes have coalesced into dismal clearance rates. Typically, the NYPD has a clearance rate of around 33 percent for shooting crimes, but in the summer of 2020, only 20 percent of shootings resulted in an arrest, and the clearance rate for shootings was as low as 15 percent in some parts of the city.[210] From June to December 2020, amid protests over George Floyd's murder, New York City experienced a 58 percent increase in homicides and a 38 percent decrease in all arrests, as the NYPD logged forty-five thousand fewer arrests during this period—meaning tens of thousands of crimes went unsolved as a result of decreased policing.[211] Along with those changes, the NYPD's homicide clearance rate in 2020 dropped by 24 percent from the previous year.[212]

A similar situation occurred in Louisville, Kentucky, which experienced an 87 percent increase in homicides and a 42 percent decline in arrest rates during the summer of protests compared to the previous year.[213] A similar trend has been seen in Chicago, where homicide clearance rates dropped for the first time after they had been improving since their last sharp decline in 2015. From June 2020 to February 2021, Chicago murders increased by 65 percent while arrests decreased by 53 percent.[214] Experts have cited poor police-community relations on both ends as a major contributor to these recent disastrous trends.[215] Similar trends have been demonstrated in St. Louis, Los Angeles, Houston, and New Orleans.[216]

The Ferguson Effect as a cause of rising crime and justice failures can be distinguished from the increased crime caused by general chaos accompanying protests. A study by Harvard economists in 2020 examined crime rates before and after a police shooting that led to a "pattern-or-practice" investigation into local police departments by state or federal authorities.[217] Such investigations are designed to determine whether the department has a systematically unlawful pattern or policy regarding use of force. Researchers found that the effect of such an investigation was a reduction in police engagement as police moved to reduce the opportunity for any violent confrontations that the state or federal investi-

gators might disapprove of. The cities experiencing only a viral police incident could be distinguished from the cities experiencing such an incident that also had a pattern-or-practice investigation ongoing. The study found that the latter case (the combination of a viral incident of police violence and a pattern-or-practice investigation) occurred in five studied cities—Chicago, Baltimore, Cincinnati, Riverside, and Ferguson—and led to sharp increases in crime in each city even when controlling for the expected level of increased violence caused by a viral incident and protests. The study calculated that the Ferguson Effect, triggered by the pattern-or-practice investigations, could have caused almost nine hundred excess homicides and thirty-four thousand excess felonies in the five cities over the two years after the viral incidents. And, of course, most of that crime went unsolved. In other words, these justice failures were apparently caused by voluntary police non-intervention, not simply increased rioting.

Public Complaints About the Ferguson Effect

The public responds with the same concern and anger whether the police pull back due to external factors (such as depolicing policies imposed by local government) or voluntary non-intervention (the Ferguson Effect). Citizens rarely distinguish between the two sources of police non-intervention as they only see the same effects of higher crime and less justice. As noted earlier in this chapter, the majority of the public wants more police intervention, not less.

However, some in law enforcement have distinguished the Ferguson Effect from external depolicing policies. Depolicing orders can be quickly and easily reversed, as many have been. But a police force feeling demonized and demoralized is not so easy to fix. Then FBI Director James Comey worried in a 2015 speech that murder was being fueled by police too afraid to do their jobs. "Part of the explanation [for higher violent crime] is a chill wind that has blown through law enforcement over the last year and that wind is surely changing behavior," Comey said. "In today's YouTube world, are officers reluctant to get out of their cars and do the work that controls violent crime?"[218] The answer is a clear yes. As mentioned previously, 72 percent of police in 2016 said they were less willing to engage in proactive policing.[219] That percentage has likely only grown after the murder of George Floyd and the resulting increased attacks on police.

F. REFORMS TO REDUCE POLICE NON-INTERVENTION

As this chapter illustrated, police non-intervention results from a variety of sources, including anti-police rhetoric and attacks, defunding movements, police demoralization driving retirements and hiring difficulties, as well as voluntary police non-intervention due to the Ferguson Effect. Part of the non-intervention problem can be alleviated by refunding police and increasing police staffing, which can reduce the stress and exhaustion that comes with short-staffed departments. But these kinds of reforms will not solve the larger long-term problem of poor police-community relations, which encourages and legitimizes anti-police demonization and hatred. Having more money to hire officers can provide limited benefit if the persons who would make the best officers find the job increasingly unattractive because of its demonization. Our recommendation at the

end of this chapter, which is an elaboration on the previous chapter's proposed police-community oversight commission, hopes to contribute to a solution for that larger and more important problem of police-community relations.

Provide More Funding to Hire More Police Officers. Many policymakers and members of the public have realized the need for more police officers, and this has led to greater funding. Historically, throwing money at the problem has had an effect. The Community Oriented Policing Services (COPS) hiring grant program, founded in the 1990s, expanded in 2009 to send $1 billion to local departments. Cities that received such hiring grants had forces 3.2 percent larger and crime levels 3.5 percent lower than the cities that did not receive grants.[220] In fact, as one large historical survey shows, for every dollar spent on additional policing, there is a $1.63 return in "social benefits, primarily through fewer murders."[221]

More recently, President Biden supported localities in hiring additional police officers, including with funds from the $1.9 trillion COVID-19 relief package.[222] Biden has stated that one of his top priorities is reducing gun violence, and increasing police forces is an effective way to do so. Many cities have increased funding to hire more officers. In 2021, the DC Council approved $5 million to hire roughly sixty more police officers over two years and $6.1 million for safety and training programs.[223] While this is less than half of the $11 million that Mayor Muriel Bowser requested to hire 170 new police officers, it is still a substantial increase in police funding needed amid surging homicides.[224] Similarly, Seattle mayor Jenny Durkan has asked the city council "to remove a $7.5 million restriction on the Seattle Police Department's current budget to help address its current hiring process" and its severe lack of staff after 250 officers left in 2020 and 2021.[225] She also supports a bill that would financially incentivize new hires and transfers to the Seattle Police Department.[226] Expanding budgets seems to be the simplest way to encourage increasing police recruitment and hiring. There is no question that such additional hiring will help reduce crime and subsequent failures of justice. As one study put it:

> Social science literature provides overwhelming evidence that bolstering police forces reduces crime. Hiring more police officers allows departments to engage in community policing and proactive policing strategies, such as concentrating more police officers in areas where crime is high—programs that a report from the National Academy of Sciences notes have been shown in high-quality experimental research to reduce crime.[227]

The same study focused on policing around the University of Pennsylvania's campus to demonstrate this point. The following summary from the study makes clear what is a virtually undisputed fact among researchers:

> We examined the difference in policing between the areas of West Philadelphia with extra University of Pennsylvania (Penn) police patrols and the surrounding neighborhoods that don't receive these extra police services. Penn employs more than twice the number of police in its surrounding neighborhoods compared with the rest of West Philadelphia. We found that property crimes and aggravated assaults increase by more than 50 percent outside the Penn patrol zone, despite the two

areas being otherwise indistinguishable. A study conducted on the extra police provided by the University of Chicago found comparable results.[228]

More police are a cost-effective decision in the long run. Studies have shown that investing in more police can save an additional life for a cost of between $1.6 and $2.7 million, much less than the typical statistical economic value of a life, which exceeds $7 million.[229]

One reason some politicians and activists oppose hiring more police is a belief that it would lead to more "quality of life" crime arrests that they believe disproportionately affect Black civilians. These crimes include disorderly conduct, vagrancy, loitering, and other low-level offenses. One study suggests that hiring an extra police officer leads to seven to twenty-two new arrests for such "quality of life" crimes. "These increases are driven by an increase in arrests for liquor violation and drug possession, with effects that imply that increases in these types of arrests are 2.5-3 times larger for Black civilians."[230]

The problem with this reasoning is that what these activists see as a benefit for minority residents—fewer arrests for low-level offenses—is purchased at the price of more serious crimes against minority residents, as the previous studies have documented. It is hard to see this as a good tradeoff for minority neighborhoods and easier to see the opposition to police hiring as an ideologically driven blind spot to the actual interests of minority communities. Further, for those who support effectively decriminalizing low-level offenses, the appropriate reform should be changing the law around such conduct. Insisting on reduced police staffing seems a perverted way to achieve this objective. Moreover, as the analysis in the next chapter makes clear, the decriminalization of low-level offenses via non-enforcement has a catastrophic effect on crime generally. Not only does it habituate an increasing number of residents to lawbreaking generally, but it also increases violent confrontations between citizens, such as when minor thefts are effectively decriminalized and property owners predictably resist the thievery instead of calling police.

When it comes to serious crimes, more police officers actually lead to fewer arrests in the long term as the additional officers deter crime.[231] In other words, investing in more police officers reduces serious crime, saves lives, and is a financially wise decision for cities to make in the long run.

Provide Better Benefits for Policing. Similar to hiring more officers, governments could raise officer pay or provide additional benefits to attract a larger pool of more qualified candidates for police jobs. Such greater benefits would likely solve some of the problem of early retirements and lack of recruitment, but they would not by themselves address the perception of community hostility that is so demoralizing to many police officers.

Narrow the Role of Police. As mentioned in section C on depolicing, police departments have experienced a form of "mission creep" over the past few decades by becoming the primary governmental response to the mentally ill, the addicted, and the homeless.[232] Additionally, police have many other responsibilities that distract them from the business of preventing and investigating serious crimes—duties such as mundane traffic control and enforcement, routine warrant service, and accident investigation. Some have argued that cities should transfer many of these duties to a vastly

expanded network of non-police administrative and social workers while police are reserved for dealing with serious crimes or situations that present a threat of violence. Such a shift, if successfully implemented, might mean there would finally be enough officers to address serious crimes while other responsibilities were handled more capably by alternative responders less likely to create viral incidents. At the same time, however, there is admittedly a limit to how much divestment of police responsibility is feasible, because many situations have the potential for violence. Nonetheless, applying a principle that reserves police involvement strictly to situations of potential violence would go a long way toward saving trained officers for tasks that require police skills in particular.

Foster Greater Appreciation of Police. One of the best ways to combat police non-intervention is to make police feel valued and appreciated by their communities. Local leaders could organize more events to highlight the good police do every day in communities and provide opportunities for citizens to express gratitude. News media could be encouraged to devote more coverage to stories of police heroism and sacrifice—a far more common occurrence than police misconduct. More awards and official recognition for police contributions to the community could be founded by private organizations or local governments.

G. RECOMMENDATION: CREATE A POLICE-COMMUNITY OVERSIGHT COMMISSION THAT WILL EARN CREDIBILITY WITH THE POLICE

As discussed in chapter 14, improving communication between the community and police is essential to combat legal cynicism, reduce hostility, and improve public trust in law enforcement. The police-community oversight commission proposed in the last chapter could also be an effective way to combat police non-intervention by both reducing the underlying causes of such non-intervention and providing a mechanism for the community and police to come together and strategize on how to most effectively utilize police presence in the community. A hostile community that demonizes and demoralizes the police guarantees less police intervention and thus more crime and failures of justice. Our proposed commission promotes cooperation, communication, and constructive criticism between the police and the community; when citizens can trust that their opinions are being heard, anti-police rhetoric and behavior will become less frequent, thus giving officers more freedom to do their job to the best of their ability. A commission fulfilling its role in speaking out fairly on police-citizen encounters would also give officers the safety of knowing that an out-of-context video of an arrest will not lead to their demonization and dismissal. In turn, the commission can help encourage police to improve their ability to intervene in communities respectfully and effectively. Police appear to be open to learning from even the many current oversight commissions that typically have no police representation. Seventy-eight percent of oversight agencies reported that police executives listened carefully to the recommendations made by oversight staff.[233]

However, it is key to our proposal that any community-police commission has credibility with both police and civilians. This is why we recommended in the previous chapter that any commission include representatives from the police department. Police often view purely civilian oversight commissions as contributing to the problem of exaggerating police use of force instead of also directing attention to pressing problems of depolicing and officer shortages.[234] An oversight commission representing all stakeholders in a community (including police and civilians) and tasked with improving police-community relations (instead of simply investigating police) could establish credibility with both police and civilians, thus helping to solve citizen non-cooperation and police non-intervention.

In addition to having police representation, our proposed commission would not have direct police administrative responsibilities—a feature of some oversight commissions that generates police hostility. When police perceive that a civilian oversight commission has too much decision-making or investigative power uninformed by the reality of real-world policing, they lose trust in the commission and are more likely to see the commission as simply a hostile watchdog.

The practice of allowing a civilian oversight commission to actually take on police administrative duties, as in directly imposing discipline on officers, is usually counterproductive, especially when the commission is purely run by civilians. The dynamic proved problematic in the first attempted civilian oversight commission in Fruita, Colorado, which failed because it was initially given too much power over police. Unsurprisingly, the police feared the commission would be little more than a hostile HR department. After city charter revisions, the commission was "limited to recommending policies, standards, procedures, and limitations for the police department, upon the direction of city council and receiving public comment on the operations and management of the agency."[235] This new commission has since been instrumental in weighing in on several important decisions for the community and the police.[236] However, giving civilian oversight commissions police administrative power continues to be tried, with backlash from police departments whenever it is implemented. For example, a 2022 St. Louis law gave its civilian oversight commission the responsibilities of a police internal affairs department, provoking resistance and a lawsuit from the police.[237] We believe it is a mistake to combine an oversight commission with a police internal affairs department as it is almost guaranteed to create hostility between police and the commission, thus preventing it from effectively improving police-community relations. Further, by remaining as an oversight commission rather than taking on police administrative responsibilities, the commission leaves the police leadership with full responsibility for the department's performance, which keeps the commission in a position to independently judge that performance, as opposed to a situation where all the members of the commission are essentially engaged in police administration. While, as chapter 14 noted, the commission could serve as a kind of "appellate review" of how police internally deal with complaints, it would not have the power to punish officers and would be limited to publicly commenting on the police investigation, including issuing a recommendation that the investigation into a complaint should be reopened if the commission found a citizen's complaint had not been adequately reviewed. But there would never be a situation where the commission's decision directly led to the punishing of any officers.

Ultimately, the best way to combat police non-intervention is by reducing the widespread anti-police hostility driven by false beliefs or misperceptions among many activists, community members, and policymakers. A police-community oversight commission that is seen as fairly representing both the concerns of police and community members is best positioned to correct distorted narratives and suggest substantive policy changes (such as some of the previous reforms suggested) to improve policing, safety, and justice.

CHAPTER 16

Anti-Justice Ideological Movements

IDEOLOGY CAN BE A POWERFUL AND DE-structive force, overriding common sense and basic human intuitions of justice and causing policymakers to make predictably damaging decisions. For example, as discussed in chapter 14, ideological beliefs about the role of racism in society fueled many of the factually false narratives about police being racist killers. These narratives in turn drove many activists and politicians to implement depolicing policies (discussed in chapter 15) with predictably disastrous results, hurting minority communities the most. This chapter examines anti-justice ideological movements more broadly and highlights the justice-frustrating policies produced by ideologies that oppose punishment on principle or at least seek to minimize punishment for criminal wrongdoing, even in cases of violent crime, in order to achieve some other social or political goal (such as "racial equity"). Most ordinary people across all groups have an intuitive commitment to the importance of doing justice (that is, giving offenders the punishment they deserve for serious wrongdoing).[1] While this commitment to justice is part of being human, and will likely always remain so, the power of ideology can temporarily warp or override this part of human nature. Antipunishment efforts also sometimes gain public support for promising to solve real injustices (such as overly punitive sentences for particu-

lar crimes) but then go further than the public supports in reducing punishment for all offenders.

This chapter is split into two parts. The first examines ideological efforts to loosen or abolish criminal punishment, either for its own sake or in service of another social goal. For example, the movement to abolish incarceration, and indeed punishment, is a real one, at least among ideological intellectuals and activists (and history shows what starts in academia often ends in policy). While less extreme, the decarceration and decriminalization movements have had significant success in reducing the punishment for many offenses, often by downgrading many common offenses from felonies to misdemeanors.

The second part of the chapter examines ideological policies of non-enforcement, which are a localized or administrative version of decriminalization in that they involve simply not prosecuting certain offenses contained in the criminal code. For example, "sanctuary" cities and states refuse to follow or aid in the enforcement of certain state or federal criminal laws.[2] Anti-justice ideologies can also affect prosecution decisions. A recent wave of progressive prosecutors have used their charging and plea bargaining powers to circumvent the legislature's criminalization decisions. In addition to raising justice concerns, such local subversion of state and federal criminal codes creates serious punishment disparities under the same law and raise important separation of powers and federalism concerns.

To be clear, seeking reforms to the criminal code or statutory punishments is not anti-justice, as long as it reflects societal views on what is criminally condemnable behavior. Indeed, criminal codes must track changing societal views if they are to maintain credibility with the community, as discussed in chapter 3. To the extent decarceration and decriminalization advocates push the law closer to societal views of justice, they are doing a valuable service. However, when ideological movements attempt to achieve their own social or political goals without regard to democratically enacted judgments about condemnable conduct and deserved punishment, they become fundamentally anti-justice. The political movements discussed in this chapter are causes of justice failures insofar as they prioritize achieving other social or ideological goals over delivering desert-based justice as the broader community sees it. For example, seeking to reduce or abolish certain long sentences that no longer reflect community views of desert is not anti-justice. It may also serve the laudable goal of reducing racial disparities in prison populations. However, seeking to reduce sentences *regardless* of community views on deserved punishment in order to reduce racial disparities in prison is anti-justice because it ignores desert entirely. There are many laudable social goals and many ways to achieve them, but, as chapter 3 discusses, the criminal justice system should devote itself above all to doing desert-based justice in each individual case. Subverting this mission to serve a specific ideology may seem appropriate to some ideological partisans, but it will ultimately end in the system losing credibility and effectiveness.

It is worth noting that we sympathize with some readers who may take issue with the fact the movements critiqued here are largely (though not exclusively) on the political left. This chapter is not a political statement. Anti-justice movements can certainly flourish on the political right, and were this book written in the 1990s, we would devote more space to critiquing a "tough on crime" utilitarian ideology that subordinates desert-based justice to the goal of incapacitating criminals. However, chapter 3 already extensively criticized such ideologies, and their power has significantly receded in academia and the public sphere. Those on the political left who care about avoiding unjustly punitive sentences should be particularly vigilant to avoid left-wing anti-justice ideologies that not only foster justice failures but also invite backlash in the form of anti-justice ideologies from the political right. Upholding the value of desert-based justice, and defending it from ideological threats on all sides, should not be a polarizing stance. The fact that it might be construed as such speaks to our current political climate, not our intent.

A. DECARCERATION, DECRIMINALIZATION, AND PRISON ABOLITION MOVEMENTS

For good or ill, prison sentences are the modern world's most common method of punishing serious criminals. While prison replaced the brutality of corporal punishments, many now believe it is overused in America. The belief that prison is overused and that America suffers from "mass incarceration" has led to the decarceration and abolition movements, which respectively call for greatly reducing and completely abandoning the use of prison.[3] Concerns over high prison populations have also contributed to decriminalization efforts in order to reduce the punishment for certain crimes or legalize previously criminalized behaviors. These movements often claim that reducing the use of prison is essential for fixing racial or economic disparities in society as poor and minority offenders make up a larger proportion of the prison population than their share of the broader population.

While there is nothing anti-justice about desiring to use more non-incarcerative punishments to do justice and reduce prison populations (a reform that we support), the decarceration and prison abolition movements usually elevate the social and ideological goal of reducing prison populations above any desert-based justice considerations. Similarly, while decriminalization in response to shifting societal views of what behavior ought to be criminal is not anti-justice, too often decriminalization is promoted as a means toward the social and ideological goal of reducing prison populations or ending racial disparities regardless of society's views of the criminality of the conduct. Instead of advocating a thoughtful reevaluation of criminalization, sentencing, and punishment procedures to achieve desert without imprisonment, the decarceration, prison abolition, and decriminalization movements broadly prioritize slashing prison populations at the expense of justice by simply letting offenders go, without regard to the resulting failures of justice. These movements aim to achieve a form of "social justice" but jeopardize criminal justice by ignoring the paramount importance of actually doing desert-based justice as society sees

it. Tragically, the additional crime and justice failures created by the anti-justice elements of such movements fall heavily on poor and minority neighborhoods, deeply damaging any attempts to promote equity. While such movements may have temporary success at frustrating justice, fostering crime in the process, in the long run they are likely to lead to a punitive backlash from a public that still deeply cares about criminal justice.

Case Example: Austin, Texas— "Freedom City"

Austin, Texas, has an admirably low violent crime rate in 2018, with only 3,720 incidents of violent crime reported that year,[4] and a violent crime rate of 382 per 100,000,[5] including 32 cases of murder and non-negligent manslaughter.[6] In June 2018, the Austin City Council establishes Austin as "the state's first 'freedom city.'" The council forbids police from enforcing immigration laws and requires them to "avoid arrests" for a variety of lower-level offenses, such as driving without a license and low-level theft.[7] The goal is decarceration. Within three months, "Class C misdemeanor arrests in Austin drop by 63%."[8] At the same time, however, violent crime increases to 518 per 100,000 in 2021—a 34 percent increase.[9] The number of homicides that year rises to 89, a 178 percent increase.[10] A citizens group that monitors police statistics reports in 2021 a 38 percent increase in aggravated assaults, an 87 percent increase in burglaries, and a 124 percent increase in auto thefts since 2019.[11] Most of this increased crime goes unpunished. And even these dramatic increases probably underestimate the extent of the crime surge. Many frustrated crime victims give up reporting crime because the police no longer come to crime scenes.[12]

Business owners are instructed to put on gloves and gather the shells left over from shootings because the police will not respond.[13] Despite these crime increases, the city council is apparently happy to further pursue its ideological agenda of reducing arrests. The city had previously invested in automatic plate reading technology (see chapter 7 for the justice benefits of such technology), but in 2021, the council ends use of the program.[14] Unsurprisingly, vehicle theft increases by 40 percent, with parts of the city seeing an increase of 85 percent.[15] Many law-abiding residents are left wondering who exactly benefits from Austin's ideological push to reduce punishment—criminals certainly, but not the vulnerable neighborhoods they victimize.

Competing Interests

One can identify legitimate interests for and against anti-incarceration movements.

INTERESTS SUPPORTING DECARCERATION, DECRIMINALIZATION, OR PRISON ABOLITION

- *Saving Resources.* Incarcerating millions of people is extremely expensive and finding ways to reduce prison populations (without sparking significantly more crime) could save the federal and state governments billions of dollars.
- *Equity.* Many supporters of decarceration, decriminalization, or prison abolition do so because of the racial and economic disparities in America's prison populations. The poor and racial minorities are over-represented in America's prisons compared to their percentage of the population. And while much of this is due to crime impacting the poor and minorities the most, this is still a disturbing disparity.
- *Reducing Recidivism.* Prison often serves as a criminal bootcamp increasing the chance that prisoners will reoffend upon release. The difficulties of reintegrating into society after prison are noticeable, so less use of prison could lead to less recidivism. Of course, the recidivist effect of prison exists only if prison administrators and the legislatures that fund them allow it to exist by failing to reform the prison environment to provide sufficiently successful training and treatment programs.

Figure 16.1. Austin police erected a billboard to express their frustrations, 2020. Photo from Ginger Scutt, Facebook, September 9, 2020, https://www.facebook.com/photo.php?fbid=10213360432323814&set=p.1 0213360432323814&type=3.

INTERESTS OPPOSING DECARCERATION, DECRIMINALIZATION, OR PRISON ABOLITION

- *Desert-Based Justice.* Unless replaced with alternative punishments, reducing the use of prison to further other social or political goals ensures failures of justice as offenders are allowed to go free without undergoing the punishment society believes they deserve. Of course, some supporters of anti-incarceration actually oppose punishment more generally, believing it is always a form of oppression. Such a view—that criminal justice is inherently immoral—is antithetical to society's view of justice.
- *Crime and Public Safety.* Efforts at decarceration and decriminalization can yield disastrous effects on crime, as without the deterrence of prison, many potential offenders turn to crime with impunity. Locking up criminals is also an effective way to incapacitate them and prevent them from revictimizing their communities for the length of their prison sentence. In fact, the main benefit of prison as a form of punishment is the protection it offers to the community.
- *Equity.* The cost of increased crime is made worse by the fact that increased victimizations typically occur disproportionately in poor and minority neighborhoods. It does disadvantaged communities no service to unjustly release disadvantaged offenders to repeat their crimes. A tragic irony is that while anti-incarceration movements often proclaim a commitment to equity, the effects of such movements are usually destructive to it. Wealthy elites making policy are unlikely to feel the negative effects of emptying prisons, but poor communities already facing high crime and low clearance rates are.
- *Rehabilitation.* Some argue that prison provides an opportunity for convicted offenders to undergo rehabilitation programs, including job training and drug treatment, which they might not if they were given non-prison sentences. Of course, this can be a benefit only if correctional officials have the desire and funding to provide such programs.

The Nature and Extent of the Problem

While there are many legitimate reasons to reduce the use of prison, the decarceration, decriminalization, and prison abolition movements are often based on misperceptions of the facts, as shown by (false) claims that most prisoners are non-violent drug offenders or that the justice system rarely gives second chances. In reality, most prisoners are dangerous repeat offenders who have already received many second chances and have nonetheless continued to victimize their communities.[16] Additionally, despite claims that the prison system is systemically racist, the reality is that Black Americans make up a share of the prison population proportional to the percentage of serious crime committed by Black offenders. While racial disparities do exist in crime rates—a problem at least partly rooted in persistent and disturbing socioeconomic disparities—focusing purely on reducing prison populations will do little to solve racial disparities in crime and in fact may increase the racial disparities in higher Black victimization rates. This section examines the decarceration, decriminalization, and prison abolition movements more closely to see how they are often based on faulty understandings of the facts and can become anti-justice ideologies.

THE DECARCERATION MOVEMENT Decarceration is defined as the "practice or policy of reducing the number of people subject to imprisonment."[17] Decarceration policies are not a purely partisan issue, and they have attracted the support of progressives and conservatives (particularly libertarians) for different reasons.[18] For progressives, decarceration is attractive for reducing the prison population of poor and minority offenders. For conservatives,[19] decarceration represents an opportunity to limit government spending on prisons and promote individual liberty.[20] The movement has gained significant bipartisan support to the point that some believe "the question is no longer whether we should decarcerate American prisons but how."[21] Indeed, many decarceration policies have already been put in place in the form of lowering some sentences (particularly for drug crimes) and providing more non-prison alternative punishments.[22] Many of these reforms have been laudable, and some in the decarceration movement do still care about achieving a just punishment as the community sees it.

Unfortunately, that said, calls for decarceration too often ignore desert-based justice and do not seem to care about replacing prisons with non-incarcerative methods that would still assign offenders punishments the community believes are deserved. Proponents claim that slashing prison populations is itself a matter of justice as it is necessary to solve the problems of racial inequity in prison populations or free the mass of non-violent drug offenders supposedly fueling "mass incarceration."[23] However, claims of unjust mass incarceration and racial inequity are often overblown, and there is no reason to think that reducing prison populations should take priority over doing desert-based justice.

First, despite popular rhetoric, prison populations have actually been falling in America for over a decade. According to the Bureau of Justice Statistics, America's prison population (including those in penitentiaries and local jails) steadily climbed from an estimated half-million people in 1980 to a peak of 2.3 million people in 2008.[24] In the following decade, it has steadily fallen to 2.1 million people in 2019. The COVID-19 pandemic dropped the prison population sharply to 1.8 million in the spring of 2021 before the number rebounded slightly.[25] These trends show the problem of "mass incarceration" is not a growing one.

Second, despite the popular narrative that America's "war on drugs" starting in the 1970s is behind mass incarceration,[26] the fact is that only 3.7 percent of state prisoners have drug possession as their most serious offense, and only another 10.4 percent have another drug charge (such as manufacturing or trafficking) as their most serious charge.[27] Between 2009 and 2019, the numbers of people admitted to and held in state prisons for drug offenses both fell by about a third.[28] Moreover, the vast majority of these drug offenders are not non-violent users but rather have engaged in more serious crimes such as drug trafficking, which involves knowingly victimizing others (often in relation to other crimes as well). For example, in 2012, 99.5 percent of drug offenders in federal prison were serving sentences for trafficking—not possession.[29] Additionally, many of those incarcerated for drug crimes have plea bargained their conviction down from other more serious offenses such as assault or robbery.[30]

More broadly, most people would likely view the vast majority of those incarcerated today as deserving prison sentences. In state prisons—which house about 90 percent of America's prison population[31]—55 percent of inmates in 2018 were serving sentences in which a violent crime was their most serious convicted offense.[32] Of that 55 percent, roughly half were serving sentences for murder or rape/sexual assault.[33] Property crimes and public order offenses such as weapons possession and DUIs accounted for another 28 percent of prisoners under state jurisdiction (and many of these offenders may have plea bargained down from a more serious offense).[34] Figure 16.2 shows the most recent data on state and federal prisoners.[35] Note again that a mere 3.7 percent of prisoners are in state prison for drug possession. Nor are prisons filled with first-time offenders being locked up for large parts of their life. Just 40 percent of state felony convictions result in a prison sentence, and the median violent offender serves less than two and a half years.[36] "Based on a scientific sample representing 711,000 imprisoned felons, Lawrence Greenfeld of the US Bureau of Justice Statistics has shown conclusively that fully 94 percent of state prisoners had either committed one or more violent crimes (62 percent) or been convicted more than once in the past for nonviolent crimes (32 percent)."[37] Almost no one goes to prison for a first offense.

The data shows that many of the claims made by decarceration advocates are based on a faulty understanding of who is in prison. While the public may continue to support reducing the relatively small prison population of drug offenders, it is less likely they wish to support an end to "mass incarceration" if it means letting more serious criminals go.

Finally, as noted in chapter 14, claims of systemic racism in the composition of America's prison populations are popular but largely unfounded. In 2018, Black offenders made up 33 percent of America's sentenced prison population, while Black offenders made up 33 percent of

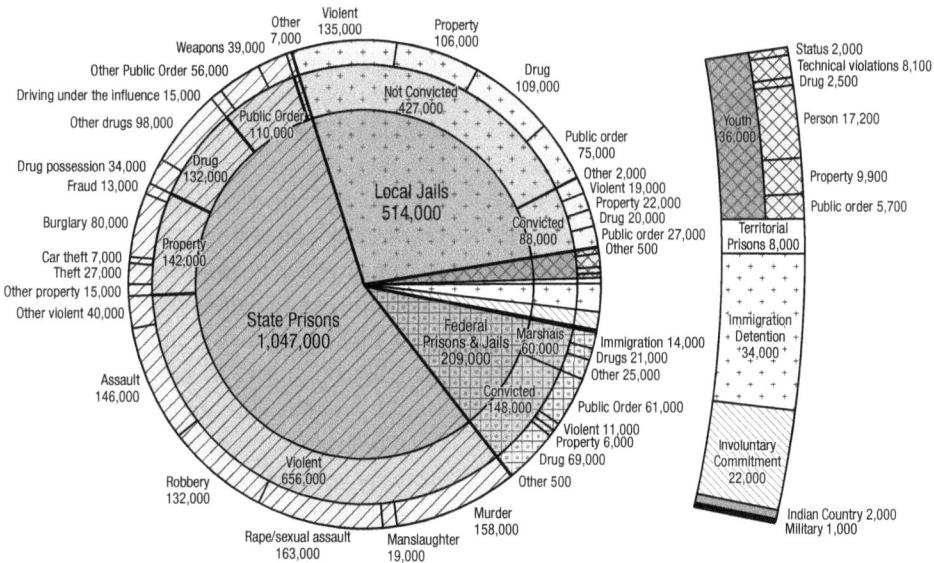

Figure 16.2. This graphic details the segments of the current American prison population, 2022. Figure from Wendy Sawyer and Peter Wagner, "Mass Incarceration: The Whole Pie 2023," Prison Policy Initiative, March 14, 2023, Slideshow 1 www.prisonpolicy.org/reports/pie2023.html.

arrests for violent crime in 2018.[38] While both rates are significantly higher than the 13 percent Black share of America's population, they paint a picture of tragically disparate crime rates, not a criminal justice system more likely to incarcerate Black offenders for a given crime because of their skin color. The solution to the problem does not lie with simply releasing more offenders and letting more serious crimes in Black communities go unpunished but rather with addressing the societal circumstances that lead to these disparate crime rates in the first place. It is unconscionably ignorant for activists and policymakers to congratulate themselves on improving equity for minority communities by ensuring their greater victimization.

THE DECRIMINALIZATION MOVEMENT Decriminalization broadly refers to efforts to change the criminal code to make certain behaviors less criminally liable (such as downgrading an offense from a felony to misdemeanor) or decriminalizing a behavior that was previously criminal. Efforts at decriminalization are not antijustice if they are undertaken to ensure the criminal law corresponds to the community's prevailing views of condemnable conduct. For example, if the public no longer views marijuana possession as criminal behavior, the criminal law *must* change accordingly to reflect community views. As discussed in chapter 3, the criminal law should track public views of desert to increase its moral credibility, and hence maximize compliance, cooperation, and internalization of its norms. To the extent that decriminalization advocates wish to make sure the law is doing justice as the community sees it, their efforts should be applauded.

However, the decriminalization movement often aims to change the criminal code not for the sake of doing justice as the community sees it but rather to achieve social and political goals such as reducing prison populations or reducing racial disparities in criminal convictions. For example, California's Proposition 47, passed in 2014, reclassifying many felonies as misdemeanors did not reflect a public view that these crimes—such as theft of property of less than $950, auto theft, and firearm theft[39]—were not as blameworthy as before. The change in the law was driven by an effort to reduce California's prison population—a policy objective that could have been pursued through changing sentencing rules. The reduction of many felonies to misdemeanor status (as well as non-prosecution policies discussed in section C) were designed not to uphold desert but to achieve other social and political goals even though they conflicted with desert. The unintended consequence of changing the criminal code in this fashion was essentially to signal that these behaviors ($950 theft, auto theft, and firearm theft) were more acceptable and would not be punished, even though the public very much did not hold that view.[40] Progressive voters who passed Proposition 47 wished to reduce prison populations, but they did not understand the effects that the decriminalization would have on criminality and law enforcement.[41]

The carelessness toward justice of some decriminalization efforts was exemplified by a 2020 proposal from Seattle's city council to create a "poverty defense" that would prohibit "prosecution for misdemeanor crimes for any citizen who suffers from poverty, homelessness, addiction, or mental illness."[42] The law would "effectively legalize an entire spectrum of misdemeanor crimes, including theft, assault, harassment, drug possession, property destruction, and indecent exposure. Criminals must simply establish that they have an addiction, mental-health disorder, or are low income in order to evade justice."[43] Such a proposal, even though it was not implemented due to understandable outcry, illustrates the thinking that allows social and ideological goals to undermine community notions of justice.[44] The criminal code is too important to be used as a mere means toward an ideological end—a fact too often ignored by the decriminalization movement.

THE PRISON ABOLITION MOVEMENT Decarceration and decriminalization efforts usually focus on less serious crimes, but some movements are even more radical. The prison abolition movement is based upon a self-described "radical" belief that prisons should be abolished for all offenders.[45] Reasons given for total abolition include the claims that prisons are systemically racist, inhumane, or ineffective. While the abolition movement is backed mainly by radical academics and activists, it should be noted that today's politically vogue ideas are often yesterday's obscure views in academia (consider the popularization of critical race theory). Prison abolitionists demonstrate a disturbing anti-justice attitude by showing no concern for punishing crime and delivering justice (including for the minority victims disproportionately affected by crime). Prison abolitionists claim, "we can imagine and build a more humane and democratic society that no longer relies on caging people to meet human needs and solve social problems,"[46] but such rhetoric falls appallingly short of a responsible policy proposal that would provide for public safety and desert-based justice. One is only left with the hope that the rapists and murderers of this imaginative society would kindly cage themselves.

In fact, several antipunishment societies without prisons have been attempted by free-thinking individuals on small scales. Each time, a familiar pattern occurred: "After an initial period of delight runs into the realities of life and human nature, the cooperative action fails and the group either disbands or adopts rules and sanctions (commonly using the threat of exclusion as the ultimate sanction)."[47] As long as humans commit violent crimes, prison will remain a necessity for modern societies.

Despite the obvious absurdity of ending prisons without any feasible alternative, prison abolitionism has become a trendy way to signal support for social and racial justice while ignoring its catastrophic effects on crime and criminal justice if implemented. The success of bestselling books like prison abolitionist Michelle Alexander's *The New Jim Crow* has led to serious coverage of the movement in outlets including the *New York Times*, *The Guardian*, *GQ*, and *The New Yorker*.[48] Prison abolitionism is a textbook example of an anti-justice political movement that ignores the harms caused by the resulting increases in serious crime, suffered disproportionately by poor and minority neighborhoods, and the resulting decreases in the criminal justice system's credibility with the community. Even those sympathetic to the ambitions of prison abolition have noted that attention devoted to it may prevent a more useful focus on improving prison conditions and designing successful prison rehabilitation programs.[49] There are many things wrong with America's prison system, but its existence is not one of them.

- Public Complaints About Decarceration, Decriminalization, and Prison Abolition

The majority of the public understands that a complete abolition of prison would be dangerous to society.[50] On decarceration, the public is supportive of non-prison alternative punishments so long as they still satisfy desert and provide for public safety. In practice, polls show this means the public does not support reduction in the incarceration of violent offenders.[51] As for decriminalization, opinions vary widely based on the specific offense in question and how the question is asked. According to one 2016 survey, 59 percent of voters supported the legalization of marijuana, but no majority supported the legalization of any other illicit drug, though later surveys have shown different results.[52] Beyond drug laws, there is little evidence that the public supports decriminalizing other types of crime.

AN EXAMPLE OF NEGATIVE IMPACT AND PUBLIC COMPLAINTS: DECRIMINALIZING RETAIL THEFT IS CREATING FOOD DESERTS IN MINORITY NEIGHBORHOODS Indeed, there is growing frustration over the decriminalization of low-level theft, especially because it often forces the closure of vital stores for underserved neighborhoods. Grocery stores operate on thin financial margins, and increased retail theft, euphemistically called "shrinkage" in the industry, is a make-or-break aspect of keeping stores open. As retail theft is decriminalized and theft increases, stores predictably close. Recall California's Proposition 47 that essentially decriminalized theft of property valued at less than $950. Because of that decriminalization (and accompanying nonenforcement policies for misdemeanors), twenty-two Walgreens stores have closed in the city of San Francisco.[53] "Theft in Walgreens' San Francisco stores is four times the average for stores elsewhere in the country, and the chain spends 35 times more on security guards in the city than elsewhere."[54]

Rising retail theft challenges not only fiscal survivability but also employee (and customer) safety. The supermarket chain Aldi closed several of its stores in one Chicago neighborhood without notice, simply leaving a sign that said the store is "permanently closed." Four other food stores in that same area also closed.[55] A spokesperson for Aldi said in a statement: "We do not take the closing of this location lightly. . . . Out of concern for our employees and customers, keeping this store open was no longer a sustainable option."[56]

Tragically, the decriminalization of low-level theft hurts minority communities more than anyone else. As Ruth Jones Nichols, president and CEO of a regional food bank in Virginia, explains on the impact of food deserts, "Black people will be disproportionately impacted by having this new food desert in our community, and we can't ignore that reality. . . . This isn't just a food access or social justice issue. It really is a racial justice issue."[57] *Food desert* is a governmentally defined term that refers to the inability of poor communities to access local, reasonably priced wholesome food.[58] It is estimated that 6.2 percent of the US population lives in a food desert.[59] And that number is growing. Johns Hopkins University researchers found that "Black communities had the fewest supermarkets, white communities had the most."[60] As retail stores close because of increasing retail theft, it is the poor who pay the price of decriminalizing petty theft. Even stores that don't close may need to raise prices to offset the increased theft of merchandise. Meanwhile, most of the policymakers who championed decriminalization are far removed from the fallout of their decision to let thieves steal with impunity.

Reforms

While the prison abolition, decarceration, and decriminalization movements often place little value on doing justice, reforms that seek to end instances of overpunishment and reduce the size of prison populations can be undertaken in a justice-valuing way.

Modifying sentencing and criminalization practices that are inconsistent with current community judgments of justice. Overly punitive prison sentences can occur when social norms and judgments of justice change, rendering sentences inappropriate that once felt warranted. For example, in California, a "three strikes" law was passed in 1994 that imposed a life sentence for almost any crime if the defendant had two prior crimes defined as serious or violent. Almost two decades later, California voters enacted the Three Strikes Reform Act in order to eliminate life sentences for non-violent, non-serious offenses, and allow three strikes prisoners serving life sentences for minor third-strike crimes to obtain a reduced sentence if they were found to no longer pose an unreasonable threat to public safety. Regular reviews of punishment practices can help end overly harsh punishments, thus helping to reduce prison populations and doing justice. Similarly, some part of the prison population may also be incarcerated for behavior that the public is increasingly unsure should be criminal. For example, a survey from 2021 showed that more than 83 percent of Americans believe the War on Drugs has failed, and 66 percent support some legalization of drugs.[61] While drug possessors are not a large share of America's prison population, it is possible that le-

galizing many drugs would reduce the prison population (by ending the incarceration of drug dealers), which could be in line with desert-based justice if it truly reflects a change in community views about what behavior should be criminal.

Improving prison programs and conditions. Decarceration and prison abolition advocates often claim prison is inhumane, but this should be a spur to improving prison conditions rather than letting offenders go free.[62] Overcrowded, understaffed prisons create increased risks of violence among inmates, which endangers inmates as well as guards and reduces any potential for rehabilitation. A majority of states have increased funding for prisons to attract more staff and fund facilities.[63] Another way that governments have addressed prison overcrowding is by contracting with privately run institutions. However, private prisons are susceptible to pressures on their bottom line that can come at the expense of prisoners' safety and rehabilitation.[64] While improving prison conditions would come at a financial cost to taxpayers, multiple studies have found that improved prison conditions reduce recidivism, so bettering prison conditions may represent a sound public investment.[65]

Recommendation: Make Greater Use of Non-Incarcerative Sanctions While Keeping the Total Punitive Effect Proportionate to the Offender's Blameworthiness

The reform that best serves justice while recognizing the serious downsides of prison is using more non-incarcerative punishments where such punishments still uphold desert-based justice as the community sees it. This recommendation should attract the support of policymakers across the ideological spectrum (including proponents of decarceration, decriminalization, and prison abolition). In fact, non-prison sentences may actually better uphold desert in some cases as prison sentences are often used to support non-desert goals such as incapacitation or general deterrence, as discussed in chapter 3. Such overly punitive prison sentences suffer from the same flaw as many decarceration policies as they seek to advance a social goal (less crime) at the expense of desert-based justice.

Prison is not the only form of punishment, nor is it necessarily an ideal one. Incarceration is extremely costly and there is little evidence to suggest it deters future crimes better than other forms of punishment.[66] The Bureau of Justice Statistics estimates that it costs the US state and federal governments $80 billion in taxpayer funds every year to incarcerate two million inmates in prisons and jails,[67] with overcrowding remaining a major issue.[68] While prison is effective at keeping dangerous offenders out of the community (at least for the length of their sentence), there is still substantial room for the use of more non-incarcerative sanctions on less violent offenders, especially with appropriate monitoring to secure public safety.

Non-incarcerative sanctions can retain a proportional punitive severity to fit the offender's blameworthiness. Some non-incarcerative sanctions include home confinement, intensive supervision programs (ISPs), weekends in local jail, community service, restrictions on travel, and day fines. While there is no agreed-upon measure for severity, the range of available punishments allows for constructing a sliding scale of severity. Studies of lay people show that there is an intuitive agreement that the right combination of non-incarcerative

sanctions can equal the punitive "bite" of many prison sentences.[69] For example, one study found that respondents perceived a (2023 inflation adjusted) $50,000 fine as being more punitive than a one-year prison sentence (for certain offenders). Meanwhile, weekends in jail, ISPs, or home confinement for two years were seen as more punitive than six months in prison. These findings show it is possible to construct scalable non-incarcerative punishments that would still be seen by the community as doing justice.[70] Implementing such reforms would allow devoting greater resources to prosecuting and punishing more serious crimes, such as murder or rape, while allowing other offenders the chance for non-incarcerative punishments, including rehabilitation away from costly prison cells.

Consider the range of possibilities in the following list of non-incarcerative sanctions already used (including use in other countries):

1. Verbal sanctions, such as public admonitions, reprimands, warnings, or unconditional discharges accompanied by a formal or informal verbal sanction.
2. Conditional discharges (that set out a series of restrictions on the offender postrelease, enforced by the threat of reincarceration upon a violation).
3. Status penalties that deny the offender specified rights in the community. Such a penalty might, for example, prevent someone convicted of fraud from holding a position of trust as a lawyer or director of a company.
4. Fines are among the most common and effective alternatives to keeping offenders out of prison.
5. Asset forfeiture in cases where the court has evidence showing that money found in the possession of

the offender is the product of the crime.

6. Restitution to the victim.
7. Community service, which can involve a wide range of required activities.
8. Government work requirements, which would require offenders to engage in certain work for the government for a certain period of time, such as work on state park maintenance crews or the like, but without incarceration.
9. Participation in a treatment or training program.
10. Referral to an attendance center, a facility where the offender spends the day, returning home in the evenings. Attendance centers, also known as day reporting centers, may provide a centralized location for a host of therapeutic interventions, training programs, or drug treatment.
11. House arrest.
12. Location monitoring through GPS tracking, sometimes combined with travel restrictions, such as allowing an offender to be only at a list of locations or traveling between them.
13. Location monitoring (without location restriction) and contact availability requirements, which means the offender's location would be tracked and recorded at all times and the offender would be obliged to answer his government-issued phone at any time.[71]

One can imagine a variety of other possibilities as well. Many of these non-incarcerative sanctions would be best offered to an offender as an alternative to incarceration where the offer could be accepted or rejected. Some possibilities, such as GPS monitoring, have also been shown to reduce recidivism among likely reof-

fenders, showing that some non-incarcerative punishments may also preserve public safety even for moderately risky offenders.[72] In fact, non-incarcerative sanctions could be imposed in the context of an "electronic prison" sentence where a combination of location monitoring, audio/visual surveillance (via body camera), device monitoring software, and physiological monitoring (e.g., wearable drug patches) would allow authorities to carefully monitor and restrict an offender's behavior at all times.[73] Such control could preserve public safety equivalent to a prison sentence for most offenders while saving resources and giving prisoners a better chance of reintegrating into the community. Given the possibility of altering the length and intrusiveness of each of these sanctions and monitoring conditions, such a rich selection of possibilities makes it possible to construct a nonincarcerative sentence that matches the punitive bite of many incarcerative sentences.

Some countries, such a Japan, are well ahead of the United States in their reliance on non-incarcerative sanctions; Japan has an incarceration rate seventeen times smaller than the United States (though much of this is due to Japan's lower crime rates).[74] Japan codified its use of non-incarcerative sanctions in what is now called the Tokyo Rules.[75] The rules state that "the selection of non-custodial measures shall be based on an assessment of established criteria in respect of both the nature and gravity of the offence and the personality, the background of the offender, the purposes of sentencing and the rights of victims."[76] Such guidelines are meant to restrict the use of non-incarcerative punishments to those cases in which the public finds such sanctions appropriate and satisfactory to justice.

State legislatures in the United States should adopt a system of ratios that reflect agreed-upon equivalencies between non-incarcerative and incarcerative sentences, based on research of the public's view of the relative punitive bite of different sanctioning methods. Legislatures should also lay out guidelines on which classes of criminals would be eligible for non-incarcerative sentences under the equivalency ratios (nonviolent offenders as well as perhaps some less serious violent offenders). Sentencing judges could then choose to impose (or at least offer) such sentences to convicted offenders. Under such a reform, anti-prison prosecutors should seek the imposition of equally punitive non-incarcerative sentences instead of simply letting offenders escape justice. Relying more on legislatively enacted non-incarcerative sanctions instead of crude decriminalization would have been one way to fix the problems associated with California's Proposition 47 because it would have allowed a reduction in prison populations without harming justice or safety.

B. IDEOLOGICALLY MOTIVATED NONENFORCEMENT POLICIES

Criminal penalties must be enforced when offenders are caught to uphold the moral credibility of the law. However, there are increasing examples of prosecutors and lawmakers adopting policies of nonenforcement of the jurisdiction's existing criminal law for ideological and political reasons. This section examines the two most prominent examples of such nonenforcement: sanctuary cities and prosecutorial policies of non-prosecution.

A sanctuary city is a municipality that refuses to enforce or to assist others in enforcing a law democratically adopted by the state or federal legislature. Entire states can proclaim sanctuary status by refusing to allow the enforcement of existing federal crimes. The most common example involves federal immigration laws, with many cities and states adopting sanctuary laws that prevent local officials from cooperating with federal authorities in enforcing immigration laws. Less common sanctuary laws include the creation of city and county gun sanctuaries that bypass state gun control laws and public health sanctuaries designed to bypass state or federal health mandates. All sanctuary laws stem from political or ideological disagreements with the state or federal law and raise important questions about justice, democracy, and federalism.

Another related phenomenon is individual prosecutors choosing not to enforce certain laws for political or ideological reasons. Such policies of non-prosecution (of theft under $1,000, for example) are generally implemented by "progressive prosecutors" to achieve their social or political goals like decarceration or decriminalization (discussed in the previous section).[77] Regardless of the reason, a stated policy of not enforcing some aspect of the existing criminal law is likely to decrease the moral credibility of the law as a whole, as people may wonder why they should respect the law if the agents tasked with enforcing it do not. All such nonenforcement policies are anti-justice to the extent they elevate political or ideological goals above doing justice.

Non-Prosecution Case Example:
San Francisco Shoplifting

On November 4, 2014, California voters pass Proposition 47, a ballot initiative reclassifying many felonies as misdemeanors, including thefts less than $950.

The proposition is a win for the decarceration and decriminalization movements, which seek to reduce California's prison population. However, as a result of the new policy, shoplifting surges by 15 to 50 percent across major retail stores in California, but decarceration advocates push for even less enforcement in order to keep offenders out of jail. In 2019, San Francisco elects progressive prosecutor Chesa Boudin, a decarceration and decriminalization advocate, who announces a policy of non-prosecution of minor crimes, even those that remain criminal under Proposition 47, in order to keep more offenders out of jail. The consequences are a predictable rise in lawlessness as would-be offenders realize justice will not be done. While burglaries fall nation-wide in 2020, they surge by almost 50 percent in San Francisco. Walgreens is forced to close twenty-two stores in the city due to squads of shoplifters cycling in and out, making sure to take just under $950 worth of goods each time.[78] When store owners try to protect their wares, thieves turn violent, as if they have a right to take the goods. On June 2, 2021, seventy-two-year-old Peter Yohannes is nearly stabbed to death and loses an eye when he tries to remove a would-be thief from his store. The moral credibility of the law plunges in San Francisco, and residents are furious that keeping criminals out of jail is being prioritized over doing justice and public safety. In June 2022, San Francisco voters, probably the most progressive in the United States, vote to recall Boudin, who is replaced by a new prosecutor willing to prosecute and jail offenders.[79]

Sanctuary Law Case Example: Gustavo Garcia

On January 1, 2018, California becomes a sanctuary state for illegal immigrants as progressive lawmakers promise to put a "kink" in the federal administration's immigration enforcement. The law bans local police from honoring immigration detainers issued by ICE, which ask police to hold alien criminals until

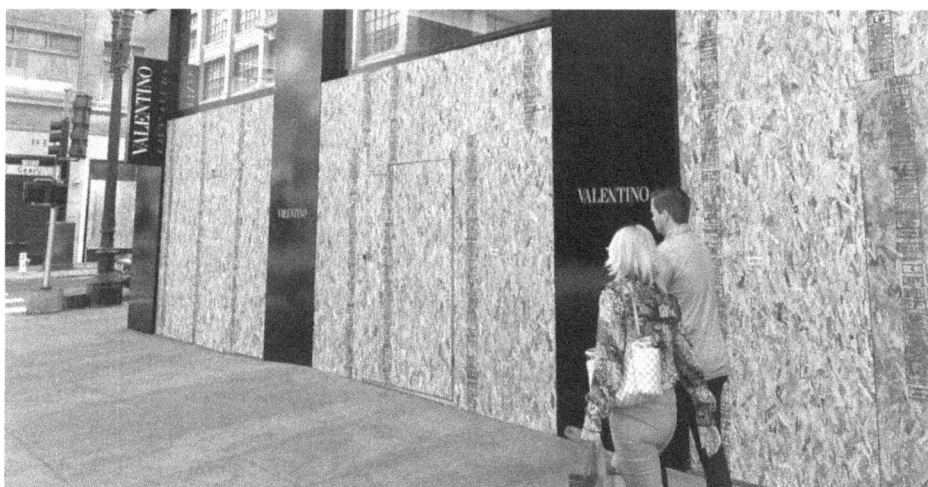

Figure 16.3. In San Francisco shoplifting has gotten severe enough that many stores are no longer able to operate, 2020. Photo by Julian Mark, "Apocalypse Chic: Valencia Street Businesses Board Up Their Windows," Mission Local, March 19, 2020, https://missionlocal.org/2020/03/apocalypse-chic-valencia -street-business-board-up-their-windows/. Courtesy of Julian Mark of Mission Local.

they can be picked up by federal agents for deportation. On December 13, 2018, thirty-six-year-old Gustavo Garcia, an offender with a serious criminal record who has been caught and deported twice previously, is arrested for driving under the influence in Tulare, California. ICE again issues a detainer, which the local sheriff wants to honor because Garcia's past record shows he is dangerous, but the sheriff is obliged under the sanctuary law to refuse the ICE detainer and release Garcia. The next day, Garcia goes on a rampage of robbery, shooting, and murder, killing two people and seriously injuring at least four others. The local sheriff is outraged that the sanctuary law prevented him from holding Garcia and saving lives. The incident highlights how

Figure 16.4. Gustavo Garcia had a long criminal record prior to crashing his truck while fleeing from police, 2018. Photo by Tulare County Sheriff's Office, from John Binder, "California: Illegal Alien Who Killed American Shielded from Deportation," Breitbart, December 23, 2018, https://www.breitbart.com/politics/2018/12/23/california-illegal-alien-killed-american-shielded-deportation/.

California's law, designed for the ideological purpose of foiling federal immigration policy, was willing to disregard the community's interest in justice and public safety. Many wonder how ideologically driven policies shielding criminal aliens serve any just purpose or even protect the undocumented communities that sanctuary laws ostensibly aim to help.

Competing Interests

One can identify legitimate interests on each side of the question of whether nonenforcement policies should be tolerated.

INTERESTS SUPPORTING NONENFORCEMENT POLICIES

- *Local Democratic Representation.* Nonenforcement policies sometimes reflect the views of a smaller jurisdiction within a larger legal system that holds different views. For example, policies of non-prosecution may uphold democracy because many prosecutors are locally elected, and local non-prosecution policies may serve as a democratic check on state legislatures less attuned to local standards of justice and crime conditions.[80] Progressive prosecutors generally openly campaign on the policies they implement, so their policies reflect the will of the people in their communities, at least to some extent.[81] Similarly, state or local governments passing sanctuary laws often represent democratic disagreement with federal policy. Of course, the structurally appropriate way to deal with such federal-state-local disagreement in a democracy is for states to convince the federal legislature to transfer the criminalization authority to the state, or for local authorities to convince the state legislature to transfer criminalization authority to the locality. The practice of "sanctuary" jurisdictions is simply a device to short-circuit those normal democratic requirements.

- *Shifting Societal Standards of Justice.* Some crimes, especially drug-related ones, may be punished under older laws, which are unjust from society's current perspective on desert. The same may also go for older immigration or gun laws that today seem unjust to local communities. Deciding not to enforce such laws, which no longer reflect societal views, may seem an effective way to minimize injustice. Of course, the most appropriate way to deal with shifting judgments of justice is to update the law. And, indeed, if that is politically impossible, it suggests that the shifting judgments may not exist in a large enough segment of the population.

- *Efficiency and Saving Resources.* Nonenforcement policies may save money and time for the government by allowing police and prosecutors to focus on crimes more concerning to their jurisdictions. For example, many progressive prosecutors and their supporters argue that non-prosecution policies are more efficient and allow a greater focus on combating serious crimes, though statistics on conviction rates for serious crimes under non-prosecution policies do not bear this out.[82] Additionally, sanctuary laws do not do much to free up local police resources as the burden of holding criminal aliens for a few days or enforcing gun laws is not significant.

- *Increased Cooperation with Local Police.* Policies of nonenforcement, particularly sanctuary laws, may make the police more trusted when it is known they will not attempt to enforce unpopular laws. For example, when illegal immigrant communities know local police are banned from assisting in federal immigra-

tion enforcement, they are more likely to report crimes and cooperate with police investigations. This may increase trust and cooperation and produce benefits such as deterring crime and bringing justice. The same might be true for illegal gun owners or petty criminals, who could be more likely to cooperate with law enforcement if they know they will not be prosecuted for their crimes.

INTERESTS OPPOSING NONENFORCEMENT POLICIES

- *Doing Justice According to the Law.* Policies of nonenforcement allow people to evade liability and go unpunished even when they engage in behaviors the law declares criminal, such as illegal immigration or gun possession. Non-prosecution of lesser offenses encourages those crimes and can fuel a general atmosphere of lawlessness. Once an offender engages in a minor crime, they are more likely to commit a serious one.[83]

- *Upholding the Rule of Law.* When parts of the government, be it prosecutors or local municipalities, refuse to enforce the law for ideological reasons, the principle of the rule of law is threatened. If the law as a whole is to maintain its credibility and effectiveness, people have to believe it will be enforced even by officials who may disagree with it politically or ideologically.

- *Equal Treatment of Offenders.* Local nonenforcement policies mean similar offenders committing similar actions receive vastly different treatment under the same jurisdiction's law. For example, when a burglar receives a prison sentence in one county but walks free in a different county under the same state law, due to a non-prosecution policy, the result is an arbitrariness that further erodes the moral credibility of the law. Additionally, prosecutors who make individual prosecution decisions driven by ideology instead of law can introduce the same punishment disparities that sentencing judges using different personal philosophies can (recall chapter 11's discussion of sentencing discretion and the problem of disparities).

- *Separation of Powers and Federalism.* Policies of nonenforcement undermine the constitutional separation of powers between branches of government and levels of government. Prosecutors who refuse to enforce certain laws subvert the constitutional role of the legislature as the sole authority to determine what does and does not constitute criminal conduct. Local or state legislatures that pass sanctuary laws subvert the federal system where the laws of the central government should prevail when local governments enact conflicting statutes.

- *Preventing Crimes.* Policies of nonenforcement encourage more crime by reducing deterrence and weakening people's respect for the law. Non-prosecution or sanctuary laws may also let dangerous criminals walk free. For example, the inflexibility of many sanctuary laws prevents local police from using their discretion when it comes to handing over potentially dangerous criminals to ICE. It would also be reasonable to expect nonenforcement of gun control laws to lead to increased gun violence (and perhaps even other forms of violent crime), given the correlation between firearm availability and violent crime.[84]

The Nature and Extent of the Problem

It is probably a sign of increased political polarization (and resulting difficulty in changing laws at the proper democratic level) that policies of nonenforcement are on the rise as local officials decide to act on their own political and ideological preferences even at the expense of justice and the rule of law.

SANCTUARY LAWS The most common sanctuary laws seek to frustrate federal immigration enforcement and usually involve two parts. One part is prohibiting local law enforcement from ever asking any person about immigration status, and such policies make a certain amount of sense as they encourage cooperation and crime reporting from illegal immigrants. The second part of sanctuary laws is less justifiable as it involves requiring local police to refuse to follow federal detainer requests for criminal illegal aliens (arrested for a non-immigration offense). There are sometimes exceptions allowing authorities to hold illegal aliens who were previously convicted of a serious non-immigration crime, but shielding aliens arrested for any serious crime does not appear in the best interests of anyone except the criminals in question.[85] However, concerns about justice and public safety are often ignored in order to score ideological points by frustrating federal immigration enforcement wherever possible. The opinions on immigration sanctuaries generally reflect partisan divides, as Republicans accuse sanctuary cities of enabling crime, while Democrats laud them for frustrating immigration enforcement.[86]

Currently, eleven US states have statewide immigration sanctuary policies (including, most significantly, California), and other jurisdictions around the country have county or city-wide sanctuary policies (including large cities like Baltimore and New York City).[87] As of 2015, roughly three hundred jurisdictions in the United States had some form of sanctuary policies intended to limit enforcement of immigration laws.[88] During the presidency of Donald Trump, who made enforcing immigration law a rallying point of his campaign, progressives reacted by advocating sanctuary cities as a form of "resistance." While the specific policies in each of these sanctuary jurisdictions differ, they all have "laws, ordinances, regulations, resolutions, policies, or other practices that obstruct immigration enforcement and shield criminals from ICE—either by refusing to or prohibiting agencies from complying with ICE detainers, imposing unreasonable conditions on detainer acceptance, denying ICE access to interview incarcerated aliens, or otherwise impeding communication or information exchanges between their personnel and federal immigration officers."[89] The result is that sanctuary cities release "noncitizens with serious criminal records . . . in spite of detainer requests."[90]

However, sanctuary laws are not used solely by progressives as they have become a general ideological tool for subverting law. Despite their relatively recent advent in 2018,[91] "Second Amendment Sanctuaries" have rapidly sprouted up across the country as those on the political right seek to shield illegal gun possession from state gun control laws. According to one count, these sanctuaries can be found in forty-two states.[92] In Virginia, eight-six of the state's ninety-five counties have passed gun control sanctuary measures.[93] According to one analysis, 61 percent of all US counties were designated as Second Amendment Sanctuaries, as of June 2021.[94] While such laws are sometimes little more than non-binding resolutions, some penalize or forbid local police from enforcing gun laws, and all make it more likely that local police will turn a blind eye

to non-violent gun offenses.[95] A number of states such as North Dakota, Texas, and Missouri have also passed statewide measures meant to curb local gun control enforcement and send a message that they will not support any tightening of federal gun policy.[96] At least one state—Missouri—has passed a law that penalizes state and local officials who enforce any federal gun law that is not also a state law. Iowa, Ohio, and others are considering nearly identical bills.[97]

Beyond gun control, some jurisdictions have also declared themselves sanctuaries from public health mandates. For example, in 2021 the town of Oroville, California, declared itself a sanctuary and sought to frustrate the enforcement of state COVID-19 vaccine mandates.[98] Sanctuary jurisdictions are also becoming a weapon in the fight over abortion access following the Supreme Court's overturning of *Roe v. Wade* in June 2022, with some localities attempting to protect abortion access despite state bans.[99] The city of Austin is attempting to shield its residents from prosecution under a Texas law that criminalizes most abortions. In "the first push by a major city in a red state to try to circumvent state abortion policy," the city council is considering a resolution that, among other things, "restrict[s] city funds and city staff from being used to investigate, catalogue or report suspected abortions."[100]

HOW SANCTUARY LAWS AFFECT JUSTICE
From a purely legal perspective, sanctuary laws foster failures of justice by shielding certain offenders. However, many proponents of sanctuary laws seek to pass them because they view federal or state laws as unjust. This raises an interesting question from the perspective of desert-based justice: Should a local jurisdiction where a majority of the

population disapproves of a particular state or federal criminal law refuse to enforce it? Of course, the minority of residents in that jurisdiction, who agree with the majority of voters in the state or country approving the criminalization, will have grounds to object. And one can imagine that criminal justice in a state could become relatively chaotic if the state criminal code is ignored in favor of local criminalization decisions. There is a reason criminal codes generally exist at the state rather than local level—completely localized criminal codes would invite fragmentation, disparity, and confusion among residents.

However, even if one believes in local criminalization trumping state criminalization, many sanctuary laws are still undoubtedly anti-justice in their specific formulation as they are willing to ignore even local views on desert-based justice in favor of advancing some ideological goal. For example, few in California (even among illegal immigrants) are likely to support shielding from deportation illegal aliens who have committed non-immigration crimes while in the United States, yet that is exactly what California's sanctuary law does out of an ideological desire to maximally thwart federal immigration policy. Sanctuary laws like California's remove reasonable discretion in how to best deal with dangerous offenders. In San Diego County, the sheriff's department was unable to notify immigration authorities when illegal immigrants were released on bond following arrests for possession of methamphetamine, drunken driving, and carrying a concealed weapon. The local US Attorney complained, "We have an excellent relationship with our local law enforcement partners, but, dangerously, this law ties their hands. Sanctuary laws

jeopardize public safety by preventing the federal government from locating, arresting, and prosecuting removable aliens inside the United States."[101] While studies have found no evidence that immigration sanctuary laws increase crime overall, this may be because any crime increases caused by refusing to honor ICE detainers for dangerous criminals are offset by the community cooperation fostered by forbidding local police from asking about residents' immigration status.[102] However, these two common parts of sanctuary laws do not need to go together because undocumented immigrant communities would actually be safer if dangerous illegal immigrant offenders were held for possible deportation instead of being released to revictimize their communities. Sanctuary laws are often needlessly justice frustrating when passed as a means of political posturing or point scoring because they do not then reflect a careful consideration of local beliefs on justice but only an ideological desire to "resist" one's political opponents on the left or right.

PROGRESSIVE PROSECUTORS AND NON-PROSECUTION POLICIES The criminal justice system could not function without the over 2,300 local prosecutors who are tasked with upholding the law by charging offenders and seeking their conviction. The vast majority of these local prosecutors are elected at the county level.[103] So what happens to justice when prosecutors decline to enforce the law due to their political or ideological views? Since 2016, a wave of "progressive prosecutors" promising to reduce incarceration and adopt more lenient approaches to crime have taken power in many of America's largest cities and begun altering the operation of the criminal law through sweeping policies of non-prosecution.[104] At least half of America's largest prosecutorial districts, covering some seventy-two million Americans, are run by progressive prosecutors.[105] While some of these have won elections based on grassroots efforts, many others have been boosted to power by enormous campaign contributions from progressive megadonors like George Soros.[106] Many have little prosecutorial experience, but all share a commitment to instituting non-prosecution policies. Such blanket declination policies (BDPs) effectively legalize crimes that were democratically criminalized by the legislature.[107] While such policies increase crime and decrease clearance rates, as discussed shortly, they also raise a serious structural separation of powers concern as well. Recall chapter 13's discussion of the problematic nature of using executive clemency to decriminalize or resentence whole classes of crimes. BDPs raise the same democracy concern in that they involve an executive actor (a prosecutor) overriding the will of the legislature. Even assuming prosecutors always make wise decriminalization decisions (which they do not), the very fact that prosecutors are using their powers to dictate what the law is as opposed to enforcing the existing law should be deeply troubling to all who care about the rule of law.

While progressives may be sympathetic to prosecutorial decriminalization of theft, vagrancy, or drug dealing, they should consider the fact that the same power could be used by conservative prosecutors to decriminalize parts of the criminal code those on the political right disapprove of. Moreover, the idiosyncrasies of individual progressive prosecutors have led to non-prosecution policies even many staunch progressives would disapprove of. For example, Virginia Commonwealth Attorney Buta

Biberaj chose to dismiss two-thirds of domestic violence cases due to her belief that most domestic abuse victims should seek help through social services as opposed to pursuing justice under the law. She states of her non-prosecution policy for domestic violence cases, "We're very fortunate in Loudoun County. We don't have the significant harm ones."[108] Such a view has infuriated many victims in Loudoun County. When in 2022 a woman was beaten to death by her husband, who had previously assaulted her and been released, many blamed the county's lax attitude toward domestic violence.[109] Perhaps unsurprisingly, Buta Biberaj was ousted by Loudon County voters in 2023, in what was otherwise a favorable election cycle for Virginia Democrats.[110] It should not take much imagination to see how supporting individual prosecutors' ability to override legislatures is a bad precedent in a democratic system.

HOW PROGRESSIVE PROSECUTORS AFFECT CRIME, CLEARANCE RATES, AND JUSTICE Progressive prosecutors have shown a reckless disregard for safety and justice through their non-prosecution policies which have increased crime and reduced clearance rates, thus multiplying justice failures. Progressive prosecutors routinely extend leniency to serious criminals by refusing to prosecute, by reducing felony charges to misdemeanors, and by offering outrageously lenient plea bargains to serious offenders. This has led to a significant decline in the rates of guilty pleas and verdicts for felony offenses in the jurisdictions of such prosecutors, thus increasing the number of felons who escape justice. Prosecutors have also decided not to pursue charges against some criminals because of ideological agreement with their cause, as shown by the refusal to prosecute many rioters in the wake of George Floyd's murder.

One study estimates that deprosecution was associated with a statistically significant increase of 74.79 homicides per year in Philadelphia from 2015 to 2019. This accelerated to more than an additional one hundred homicides per year by 2018 and 2019 as the deprosecution policy was used more robustly. Homicide victims were overwhelmingly people of color living in the poorest sections of the city.[111] Another study observed trends in felony convictions in six large districts with progressive prosecutors, including Dallas, Chicago, Philadelphia, San Antonio, St. Louis, and Baltimore. In Dallas, guilty verdicts for felonies decreased dramatically by 30 percent, and in Chicago, dropped or lost felony cases increased

by 40 percent after a progressive prosecutor took over and implemented non-prosecution policies.[112] Chicago's progressive DA Kim Foxx has "dismissed all charges against nearly 30% of all felony suspects,"[113] which, not surprisingly, has contributed to a 50 percent increase in homicides in 2020,[114] followed in 2021 by a further increase. In 2021, Chicago suffered 3,561 shootings, 1,417 more than in 2019.[115] Across the country, progressive prosecutors follow the same justice-frustrating pattern of decreasing felony prosecutions even as serious crime rises.

Figure 16.5 and the case study that follows show the experience of Philadelphia in the years since progressive prosecutor Larry Krasner assumed office in 2017. The downward sloping blue and red lines show the dramatic reduction in cases

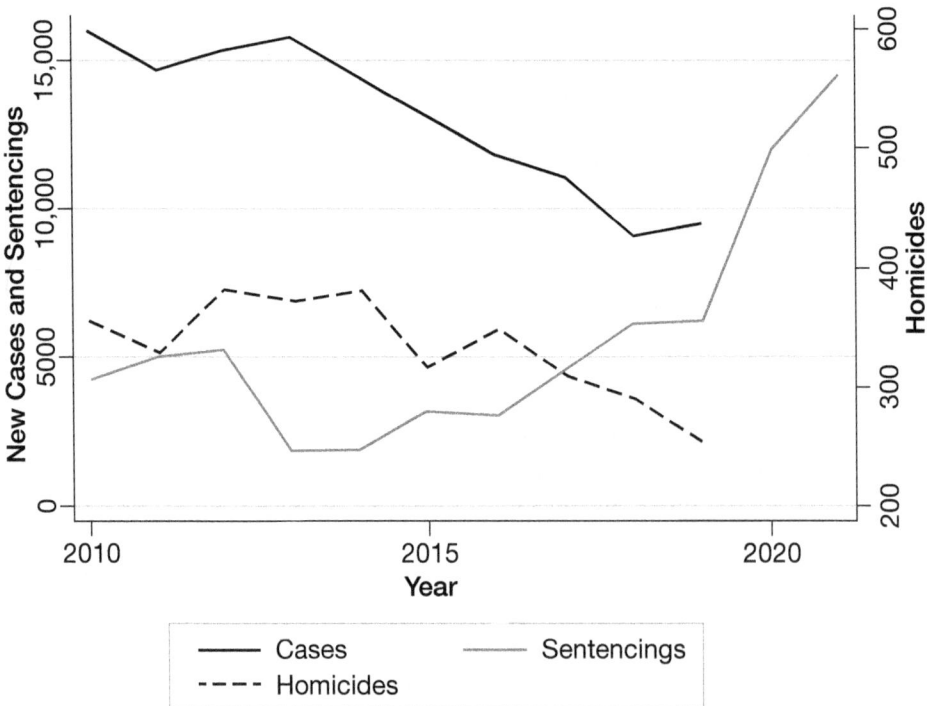

Figure 16.5. New cases filed versus homicide rate in Philadelphia, 2022. Graph by Thomas P. Hogan, "De-Prosecution and Death: A Synthetic Control Analysis of the Impact of De-Prosecution on Homicides," Criminology & Public Policy 21, no. 3 (July 2022), 489–534, Wiley Online Library, https://doi.org/10.1111/1745 -9133.12597. Data sources: Philadelphia Police Department and Pennsylvania Sentencing Commission.

filed and sentenced, while the upward slanting green line shows the dramatic increase in homicides.[116]

THE EXAMPLE OF PHILADELPHIA Philadelphia's District Attorney, Larry Krasner, is one of the most famous progressive prosecutors, and Philadelphia represents a classic case of non-prosecution policies leading to more crime and failures of justice. Since his election in 2017, where he was boosted in the Democratic primary by millions in donations from progressive megadonor George Soros, homicides in Philadelphia have spiked to their highest level in roughly thirty years. In 2020, murders increased by 40 percent, totaling 499—a higher number of homicides than in New York City, which has a population five times the size of Philadelphia.[117] This dramatic increase in homicides coincided with the clearance rate dropping from 52.4 percent in the previous year to 42.3 percent.[118] Much of this is due to Krasner's "deprosecution" policy where he uses his discretion to not prosecute criminals guilty of certain crimes—including felonies. Criminals rarely escalate from nothing to murder, and non-prosecution of lesser crimes, such as illegal gun possession, ensures offenders are allowed free rein until they commit the most serious crimes. For example, "The Krasner office has withdrawn or dismissed 65 percent of gun charges this year [2021], up from 17 percent in 2015."[119] It appears that "under Krasner, Philadelphia is on track to set two city records: the lowest number of felony prosecutions in modern history and the highest number of homicides."[120]

Critics allege that Krasner's non-prosecution policies fail to bring justice or protect the most vulnerable members of crime-plagued communities.[121] In 2020 alone, 195 children were shot, often caught in the crossfire of criminals who have benefited from Krasner's deprosecution policies.[122] One way to stop such tragic deaths is to punish illegal gun possession assiduously to get potential killers and guns off the street. With more guns on the street, the number of arrests for gun crimes in Philadelphia has tripled, but the prosecution rate has dropped by 85 percent.[123] Even more disturbing is the fact that only 21 percent of shootings have prompted criminal charges, and a mere one out of ten of these shootings led to convictions.[124]

Sadly, the violence and lawlessness in Philadelphia reached historic highs under Krasner. Philadelphia suffered 559 homicides in 2021, the highest number since officials began tracking killings in 1960.[125] Through the early months of 2022, the homicide rate remained at high levels, forcing the US Attorney's Office in Philadelphia to "step-up its focused effort to deter violent crime in Philadelphia"[126]—violent crime that is typically the focus of local prosecutors rather than federal ones.

Krasner's non-prosecution policies are so clearly damaging that he has drawn sharp criticism from his own party. After Krasner stated that Philadelphia did not have a "crisis of crime" or a "crisis of violence"—statements that he ultimately walked back due to their outrageous falsehood—former Philadelphia mayor Michael Nutter, who is Black, wrote that if Krasner "actually cared about [Black and Latino communities], he'd understand that the homicide crisis is what is plaguing us the most."[127] The crisis of violence has escalated to the point where the head of the Philadelphia City Council has suggested reinstating stop and frisk policies to deter illegal gun carrying as Krasner is failing to do so.[128] Meanwhile,

Krasner shows no signs of wishing to increase prosecutions of gun felonies and continues to prioritize ideological goals like reducing prison populations over actually doing justice and ensuring public safety. Krasner's non-prosecution policies led to a drop in new criminal cases filed in Philadelphia County from 16,000 in 2013 to 4,000 in 2020, even while crime remained steady or increased.[129] Literally tens of thousands of guilty criminals have escaped justice under Krasner's watch. And Philadelphia is just one city among dozens controlled by progressive prosecutors implementing such destructive non-prosecution policies.

Krasner has also attracted criticism from judges for pursuing an even more extreme form of nonenforcement through seeking dubious exonerations of serious criminals in order to further reduce prison populations. Krasner has supported the exoneration of multiple murderers not based on the availability of new evidence but simply by stating police or prosecutors mishandled the case—without clear evidence that they did.[130] Similar dubious exoneration strategies have also been utilized by other progressive prosecutors, such as Chesa Boudin in San Francisco and Kim Gardener in St. Louis.[131] Krasner's refusal to take enforcing the law seriously led to his unprecedented impeachment by the Pennsylvania House of Representatives in 2022, but he is unlikely to ever face trial in the state senate.[132] Krasner's policies also contributed to the victory of Cherelle Parker in the Philadelphia democratic mayoral primary in May 2023, who promised to hire hundreds of extra police officers and crack down on the crime Krasner has let flourish.[133] Crime was the top concern among democratic voters, with the progressive Krasner-

aligned candidate, Helen Gym, finishing third with only 21.5 percent of the primary vote.[134]

Public Complaints About Sanctuary Cities and Prosecutorial Nonenforcement Policies

Unsurprisingly, many in the public have complained about criminal laws going unenforced. While many people have spoken out about the inherently problematic nature of sanctuary laws, victims and their families have been the most outspoken. In San Francisco, family members of men murdered by a noncitizen claimed that "the city's sanctuary policy was the legal cause of the deaths" because the murderer was a known gang member and drug trafficker who had previously been arrested and allowed to stay in the city due to the sanctuary policies.[135] In another example, a Houston police officer was killed by a previously deported illegal immigrant, and the officer's family sued the city because the sanctuary laws protected the killer but not the officer.[136]

Conservative politicians and media commentators have vocally attacked immigration sanctuaries, but they are notably—and perhaps hypocritically—silent on gun sanctuaries.[137] Liberal politicians have also attacked gun sanctuaries, either not noticing or choosing to ignore the dissonance of tolerating one type of sanctuary law but not others. For example, when a wave of counties in her state began passing "Second Amendment Sanctuary" resolutions, the Democratic governor of New Mexico, Michelle Lujan Grisham, tweeted that she would continue to support gun control reforms despite "rogue sheriffs throwing a childish pity party or bad-faith critics."[138] She also implied that law enforcement officials who refused to enforce gun control laws would be violating their oath of office.[139] Such criticism is somewhat ironic given New Mexico's status as an immigration sanctuary attempting to foil federal immigration law.[140]

However, far more public outrage has been directed at prosecutorial non-prosecution policies because of their greater effects on justice and safety. For example, a large segment of Philadelphians are outraged by their progressive prosecutor, Larry Krasner, because of what they believe is his responsibility for increased crime and justice failures under his watch. Some families in Philadelphia have staged protests against Krasner's non-prosecution policies.[141] A mother of a girl murdered in 2009 and a cofounder of Moms Bonded by Grief explains, "I just want [Krasner] to listen to us, to hear us, and consider that we are actually sentenced to life when we lose our children."[142] Some have called the progressive prosecutor movement a "failed experiment"[143] and have accused Krasner of "doubling-down on ideology or incompetence (or some combination of the two)."[144]

San Francisco's progressive prosecutor, Chesa Boudin, was also despised by many of his city's residents who accused him of tolerating lawlessness. Videos of shoplifting in the city went viral on Twitter. One poll found that 70 percent of San Francisco residents believed that the "quality of life in the city was deteriorating," and 40 percent stated they planned to leave the city.[145] As a result of this public discontent, in June 2022, in a rare occurrence given the difficulty of the recall process, Chesa Boudin was successfully recalled from office. Over 80,000 San Francisco residents signed the recall petition despite only 53,000 being needed and despite the fact the

city of 876,000[146] has only 33,000 registered Republicans.[147] In a similar vein, many jurisdictions have recently rejected would-be progressive prosecutors in favor of keeping more moderate incumbents.[148] In May 2023, Kim Gardner, St. Louis's progressive chief prosecutor, resigned from office after a firestorm of criticism over her failures to effectively prosecute crime led the Missouri state legislature to consider legislation that would have brought the local prosecutor's office more directly under state control.[149] Gardner's prosecution policies had included a stunning blanket refusal to prosecute *any* criminal cases referred by a sizable list of police officers she personally considered unreliable.

Reforms

There have been many reform proposals addressing policies of nonenforcement. The most obvious reform is simply electing officials who will change such policies either by ending or modifying sanctuary laws or resuming the normal prosecution of crimes. However, even if nonenforcement policies remain in place in local jurisdictions, there are possible reforms at the state or federal level that can mitigate their justice-frustrating effect and incentivize their reversal.

Defunding Sanctuary Jurisdictions. A common proposal for dealing with sanctuary jurisdictions is making federal or state funds contingent on cooperation with state or federal law. For example, conservative lawmakers have advocated denying federal funding to jurisdictions that refuse to cooperate with federal immigration authorities.[150] Similarly, one could imagine state governments cutting off funds to municipalities defying state law on issues such as gun control or public health mandates. However, such defunding proposals are problematic because they would both negatively impact innocent residents of sanctuary jurisdictions and might raise constitutional concerns over federal coercion of state governments on issues reserved in the Constitution for state determination. Attempts to cut off funding to sanctuary jurisdictions have so far failed.[151]

Altering Sanctuary Laws to Exclude Arrested Criminals. Perhaps the most sensible reform on the specific issue of immigration sanctuaries is to alter the law in a way that provides police with the discretion to honor immigration detainers of illegal aliens arrested for serious crimes (such as felonies). Local police would still not be in the business of immigration enforcement, and undocumented communities would likely benefit from having serious criminals quickly removed. This reform would stem the worst failures of justice caused by immigration sanctuaries without sacrificing the interests underlying such laws.

Limiting Prosecutorial Discretion. Some have suggested combatting non-prosecution policies by creating legislative oversight committees or independent boards to limit prosecutorial discretion. The problem with such proposals is that prosecutors are often elected with their own independent authority and attempts to bring them under the legislature's control or oversight could raise separation of powers and state constitutional issues. One possible way to control prosecutors is for legislatures to withhold funding of prosecutor offices unless they sign cooperation agreements agreeing to enforce certain laws.[152]

Using Executive Authority to Fire Local Prosecutors. Some states allow the governor to dismiss even elected local prosecutors for misconduct or failure to fulfill their duties. Some have argued that non-prosecution policies amount to a legal failure to fulfill a prosecutor's duties as opposed to an allowable exercise of prosecutorial discretion. Republicans unsuccessfully called for New York governor Kathy Hochul to remove Manhattan DA Alvin Bragg from his post over his non-prosecution policies that were seen as fueling crime in New York City and allowing thousands of criminals to escape justice.[153] Florida governor Ron DeSantis suspended elected state attorney Andrew Warren in 2022 over Warren's signed pledge that he would not enforce the state's abortion laws or laws on transgender healthcare.[154] Warren has sued, so far unsuccessfully, to be reinstated, alleging the firing was politically motivated. Governors should proceed cautiously in any potential dismissals of elected local prosecutors, however, as the power to dismiss was not meant to be used politically or anti-democratically and risks setting a precedent that could easily be abused.

Recommendation: Facilitate State AG Prosecution Where Local DA Rejects State Legislative Rules

Solving the problem of prosecutors who refuse to enforce the law is difficult, but the best way to work within existing constitutional structures is to legislatively empower state attorneys general to prosecute those crimes under state law that a local district attorney refuses to punish for ideological or political reasons. Such a proposal requires two parts. First, state attorneys general must be provided with the authority to prosecute cases involving the breaking of state criminal laws typically handled by the local prosecutor without the requirement of special permission from the governor, legislature, or local DA. Second, additional state funding and prosecutorial personnel may be needed to handle those local cases arising from local non-prosecution policies.

Currently, a minority of states—twenty-one of them (including three state where there are no local prosecutors)—already provide such independent authority to their state attorney general when the law is not being enforced by the local prosecutors.[155] In the rest of the states, attorneys general have either not been provided with such an independent authority,[156] or their ability to prosecute is contingent upon a request or an authorization from the governor, the legislature, or the courts.[157] Even in those states where AGs have independent prosecution power, it is possible that many do not fully appreciate their existing legal authority.[158]

This proposed reform would allow state AGs to step in to uphold state law when individual local prosecutors are failing to do so for reasons ranging from ideology to incompetence. It would encourage state AGs to monitor local DAs and provide accountability for justice-frustrating non-prosecution policies by publicly stepping in to enforce the law and highlighting the criminal cases where the local prosecutor would have let justice fail. Additionally, granting more resources to state AGs to independently prosecute local crimes could also help when DAs face unexpectedly high caseloads and would normally be forced to drop some cases that they could instead hand off to the AG.

Some states have recently undertaken a related reform. Tennessee, for example, recently changed its law to create such

local prosecution authority for the state AG. "If a district attorney 'peremptorily and categorically' refuses to prosecute charges under a certain criminal offense regardless of the facts, the new bill would allow the attorney general to ask the court to install [a] temporary prosecutor to handle all cases charged under that offense."[159]

Other countries have adopted similar policies to allow for more centralized correction of local prosecutors. The United Kingdom's Parliament has provided the attorney general a broad mandate in overseeing cases handled at a local level. In particular, the UK attorney general may look at any case they find has been mishandled, any complaints about local prosecutors not enforcing the law, or any other case they deem fit, and appoint a prosecutor from their office to handle the case.[160] Additionally, the attorney general in the United Kingdom may also receive additional funding from Parliament when they do not have the necessary resources to undertake such prosecutions.[161]

It is easy to see how granting state attorneys general the legal authority and funding to pursue local cases would correct some of the worst abuses of non-prosecution policies. For example, California's AG could have stepped in to stop failures of justice caused by Chesa Boudin's unpopular policies, or Pennsylvania's AG could intervene to prosecute the dangerous gun crimes Larry Krasner refuses to. States have a duty to ensure citizens receive the protection of state laws no matter their locality, and expanding the reach of state attorneys general will make sure state laws are upheld statewide.

CHAPTER 17

Insights, Patterns, and Reform Priorities

EVEN A CURSORY STUDY OF THE EXTENT of justice failures in America's legal system leads to a disturbing conclusion: the justice system regularly and unnecessarily fails to do justice. More than half of all murderers escape conviction. More than nine out of ten rapists, robbers, and assaulters go free. The costs of these justice failures are enormous both in personal and societal terms, yet relatively little attention is paid to the problem by academics, the media, or policymakers. As a society, we can and must do better at ensuring our justice system actually punishes serious offenders and delivers the justice millions of innocent victims are denied. Other problems traditionally highlighted—such as the rights of criminal defendants or false convictions—are worthy of attention, but they must not be used as an excuse to ignore the basic and overwhelming problem of justice failures. Too often academic scholarship on the justice system is concerned with mowing the unruly front lawn while the house burns in the background.

This concluding chapter draws on the previous sixteen to highlight important themes that emerge from studying justice failures and their causes. These include the criminogenic effect of justice failures (which should convince even those unconcerned with moral notions of desert that the issue of justice is important), the racial inequities inherent in a justice system that fails to punish serious crime, and the problem of false claims in academia, the media, and government that serve to exacerbate the problem of justice failures.

The chapter also pulls together many of the previous discussions in the volume about the important concept of interest balancing, and how all aspects of justice system policymaking should take account of the competing societal interests at stake in both the status quo and possible reforms. Special interest groups—be they criminal or victim rights advocacy groups—are unlikely to advocate for the proper balance. The answer to present unrelenting failures of justice is not a blind reaction in the opposite direction, because many justice-frustrating rules and practices promote legitimate and even important interests. It also seems clear that those who decide the societal balance of interests in the justice system should represent society as a whole, which is why we argue for more legislative decision making in the justice system. There are certainly potential difficulties that arise from relying upon legislative balancing, but the dangers of relying instead upon judicial or executive balancing seem greater.

Finally, we survey the wide range of reform recommendations that we have made throughout the volume and try to reason out which reforms ought to be given highest priority by policymakers.

A. WHY WE SHOULD CARE ABOUT JUSTICE FAILURES AND WHY SOME DON'T

The Criminogenic Effects of Failures of Justice

A theme throughout this book has been the connection between justice failures and crime.[1] While we, and most of society, believe it is important to do justice for its own sake, justice failures also create more crime, making the problem one that should concern even those who believe the legal system's only job is ensuring public safety. Most obviously, failing to punish offenders allows them to revictimize society. Every time a serious offender escapes justice through any of the means described in previous chapters, that failure commonly guarantees additional victimizations. Offenders are not typically one-time rapists, robbers, or assaulters.

Further, just punishment is needed from a utilitarian perspective because failing to deliver desert erodes the moral credibility of the law and thereby promotes crime, as documented in chapter 3. The implications of this are important and observable throughout this book. First, failing to impose the amount of punishment deserved, even when an offender is caught and receives some punishment, is damaging to the credibility of the law. The failures of justice caused by plea bargaining, sentencing discretion, early release, and executive clemency rarely lead to an offender receiving no punishment at all, but they can make a mockery of justice, causing victims and the public to lose faith in the justice system while emboldening would-be offenders. For example, even if a rapist is caught, a lenient plea bargain or judicial sentence may simply reinforce the notion that rape is an easy crime to get away with, thus making future victims less likely to report crimes and potential offenders more likely to commit them. Therefore, the crime control utilitarian must recognize that the justice system is not simply about catching the maximum number of offenders but also about punishing them justly in the eyes of society.

A second and related point is the importance of doing justice even for lesser crimes because the moral credibility of the law—and its crime control effectiveness in harnessing the powerful forces of social influence—can still be eroded when the community sees any regularized failures of justice. Recall the example in chapter 3 of how a failure to enforce Prohibition laws led to a surge of criminality even for crimes that had nothing to do with alcohol. Many well-intentioned non-enforcement policies (addressed in chapter 16) are aimed at not punishing minor crimes, but regularly refusing to enforce the law at any level calls into question the credibility of the criminal law generally. If a law is considered unjust by the community, then it should be changed, and we support continual efforts to update the criminal code to track changing societal views of what constitutes criminal behavior and just punishment. The law should not simply be ignored, however, and policymakers would do well to remember that allowing some kinds of crime to go unpunished may soon lead to all kinds of crime flourishing. Increasing crime of any kind is also dangerous to justice because as crime increases, the justice system's limited resources are stretched thinner and thinner, allowing more serious and minor cases to slip through the cracks. Increasing crime will inevitably increase justice failures, and allowing justice failures will inevitably increase crime. Innocent victims bear the cost of both, and the solution to this devastating circle lies in doing desert-based justice in every individual case.

Failures of Justice and
Promoting Racial Equity
in the Criminal Justice System

It would be impossible to address the topic of failures of justice without noting its intersection with racial justice, an issue that we have touched on in several previous chapters.[2] Many scholars, politicians, and activists have highlighted real or perceived racial disparities and inequities in the criminal justice system, but few have addressed the most grievous disparity: the fact that unsolved serious crime is an epidemic in minority, particularly Black, neighborhoods. Over half of all homicide victims are Black, despite Blacks making up just 13 percent of the population.[3] In America's cities, this disparity is even worse. Ninety-seven percent of shooting victims in New York City in 2021 were Black or Hispanic.[4] A *Washington Post* report examining nine cities with some of the highest homicide rates found that "Black people made up more than 80 percent of the total homicide victims in 2020 and 2021."[5] As noted in chapter 1, police typically make an arrest in the homicide of White victims 63 percent of the time compared to just 47 percent of the time for Black victims across America's largest cities.[6] The disparity is even more striking in cities such as Chicago, where the murders of White victims are solved at a rate more than double that of Black victims.[7] Every year, thousands of Black men die, not at the hands of police but at the hands of violent criminals who are allowed to continue victimizing America's most vulnerable communities. If there is "systemic racism" in the criminal justice

system, it lies in the fact that policymakers of all parties have routinely neglected the desperate calls for justice from those who need the justice system most. This book has not. While we have argued it is essential to reject false narratives that cast the specific mechanisms of the criminal justice system as racially prejudiced (see chapters 14, 15, and 16), it is equally essential to recognize that failures to ensure justice affect minorities the most. Legal cynicism is rampant among America's Black communities not simply because of false narratives about police violence but because, more often than not, the system fails to deliver justice when Black lives are taken by criminals.

Solving the problem of failures of justice should be an imperative for any honest academic, politician, or activist rightly concerned with ensuring racial justice. The solution does not lie in unfounded rhetorical attacks on a "racist" criminal justice system, as if racial differences in police shootings or imprisonment rates are caused by racial prejudice in the justice system rather than differing racial crime rates. But differing crime rates should not be an excuse for policymakers to claim nothing can be done. In addition to combating the underlying causes of differing crime rates, policymakers must actively reflect on the reasons justice fails in so many serious cases—reasons this book has examined and suggested possible solutions for. Whether it is ensuring the criminal code reflects community views of justice, investing in more and better-quality criminal investigation in crime-afflicted neighborhoods, rebuilding trust between police and the community, tackling the scourge of witness intimidation, changing bail policies, or adopting new technologies, there are many ways to solve more serious crimes and bring greater justice for all victims and communities. The evidence shows the best way to fight for racial equity in the criminal justice system is to make it a priority to solve all serious crimes so that Black victims receive the justice they deserve—and have so far been denied.

The Problem of False Claims and Unreliable Studies

An unfortunate theme that emerges from studying justice failures is that public discourse on the justice system and crime is riddled with false claims, half-truths, and deliberate obfuscation, often motivated by ideological biases. For example, as mentioned in chapter 1, the popular claim that concerns over crime and justice are rhetorically overblown because crime is decreasing and historically low is based on deceptive comparisons. While crime is much lower than it was in the 1970s, 1980s, or 1990s (though the recent violent crime surge has undone some of that progress in places), all crime in America is still higher than it was in the 1950s or early 1960s, and more worryingly, serious violent crime has risen over the past two decades. Problems of serious crime and justice failures will not solve themselves, contrary to many "expert" opinions.[8]

There is a disturbing amount of deliberate obfuscation or even outright fabrication in crime reporting at all levels of government, thus distorting crime statistics. Recall chapter 4's discussion of how some police departments have systematically underreported crimes such as rape. Another example is a 2001 scandal that revealed the Detroit Police Department had inflated rape and homicide arrest numbers to appear to be doing a better job at solving crime. As one criminologist has warned, "[Crime data] is a tool that politicians and police leaders use, yet the system is so incentivized to cast a favorable light and there [are] very little checks and balances to make sure it's accurate."[9]

Even when deliberate fabrication does not occur, cities can reclassify crimes to make it seem like crime rates are low and crime solving high. In Milwaukee, for example, Mayor Torn Barrett and Police Chief Edward Flynn touted four straight years of declining crime numbers before the *Journal-Sentinel* reported in May 2012 that five hundred "serious assaults" had been misclassified as minor offenses by police officials from 2009 to 2012.[10] Other parts of crime data that might prove uncomfortable to government officials—such as statistics on the race of offenders or victims—are also often scrubbed from official reports.[11] Data does not lie, but those in charge of the data can and do for political or ideological gain.

Even if data is not strategically edited, it is often never released. The Bureau of Justice Statistics has grown increasingly tardy at publishing up-to-date information, most likely due to some combination of funding inadequacies and political expediency. As an open letter published by the American Statistical Association complains, "In recent years, numerous regularly released publications—as well as some special projects—have fallen substantially behind schedule or not been published at all."[12] Consider a few data collection programs the Bureau of Justice Statistics has abandoned or delayed indefinitely: Survey of Inmates in Local Jails (last data available in 2002), Justice Assistance Data Survey (last data available in 2010), and the National Judicial Reporting Program (last data available in 2006). The full list is far longer, but the point is clear: there is a chronic problem with a lack of data disclosure in the criminal justice system.

The ideological bias of most academic discourse on crime and justice cannot be ignored either. Unfortunately, promoting ideological claims has taken precedence over seeking the truth. A 2017 study of fifty-one of the top-ranked liberal arts colleges in the United States found that 39 percent had not a single registered Republican professor on faculty, and 78 percent "have either zero Republicans, or so few as to make no difference."[13] In the academic fields most important to crime and justice, the ratio of Democrats to Republican faculty is overwhelming. The ratio in sociology departments is greater than 40:1.[14] In criminology departments, the ratio is 30:1 for liberals to conservatives.[15] Other social sciences have similar ideological compositions.[16] A plurality of scholars in criminology self-identify as "radical" or "critical" and are devoted to advancing narratives of racism and systemic oppression that always cast the justice system as the problem and offenders as largely victims of forces beyond their control.[17] This mainstream academic narrative often sees desert-based punishment as a tool of oppression and elevates concepts of "group justice" above doing what society sees as just in individual cases. These voices should be heard, but academia should not simply accept such ideological premises as absolute truths. One does not have to be a conservative to see the dangers of the lack of ideological diversity in academic discourse. Jonathan Haidt and other self-identified liberal scholars have pointed out the dangers of groupthink and ideological drift that occur in academia when scholarly claims are only ever challenged when they appear "conservative" while claims

that appear "progressive" are lauded regardless of their professional merits.[18] For example, while there is strong evidence to believe that protests against police in the wake of police shootings lead to voluntary police pullback and an increase in crime (the Ferguson Effect), many academics have attempted to cast doubt on these findings. By contrast, there has been no widespread academic attempt to debunk obviously false claims about police shootings.[19] Despite its labeling, there is nothing "progressive" about an ideological echo chamber that stifles the ability to conduct dissenting research and forces faculty to self-police within the safe confines of presumed ideological truth.

To search for truth effectively, academic discourse and scientific studies must include voices from across the political and ideological spectrum. Studies must be scrutinized regardless of the claims they advance. However, the current academic environment is far from this ideal. Personal ideological agreement with the accepted academic narrative of criminal justice keeps most researchers from asking inconvenient questions. Perfectly honest and reputable researchers who do valuable work contribute to this problem by only undertaking research that is likely to confirm the official progressive narrative. Those who might wish to undertake studies that could combat the mainstream face enormous pressures not to, with funding and publishing obstacles at every turn.[20] Those few studies that do challenge the orthodoxy are sure to be attacked from every possible angle if they cannot simply be ignored. Recall chapter 14's mention of a 2019 study on police shootings whose authors were forced to retract it, not due to flaws in the methodology or data but over fears that it was being "misused" in a way to undermine a false narrative about racism in police shootings.[21]

Unfortunately, the ideological lock on criminal justice disciplines is unlikely to be broken anytime soon. As a result, researchers, policymakers, and the public broadly should consider academic research and recommendation with significant caution and considerable skepticism.

B. BALANCING COMPETING INTERESTS

The Importance of Balancing Competing Interests

As shown by each chapter's competing interests section, this book acknowledges the tradeoffs that policymakers must necessarily face. There are almost always some legitimate interests that can be identified in support of justice-frustrating rules or practices. Thus, rational policymaking cannot simply demand exclusive focus on doing justice but rather must balance competing societal interests. That said, the analyses in previous chapters suggest that the balance of societal interests in current rules and practices is commonly skewed and much in need of rational and thoughtful rebalancing. Even the interpretation of constitutional rules represents a balancing of interests—by judges—that is sometimes explicit and sometimes implicit. A proper balancing of interests is likely to produce more compromise policies than the partisans of a particular issue might like. On the issue of privacy, for example, a proper balancing of interests reflecting society's preferences would likely satisfy neither extreme privacy advocates nor extreme justice proponents.

The importance of interest balancing is often ignored by those who might be called "rights absolutists" who believe that any attempt at accommodating a competing interest fatally undermines the other interests at stake. For example, a privacy rights absolutist would see no room for creating less justice-frustrating search rules as it would start policymakers and judges down a slippery slope to a totalitarian world with no privacy rights. Such absolutist thinking creates false dichotomies in policymaking where policymakers and the public are confronted with an either/or fallacy and asked to choose between two extreme versions of the world. Such absolutism can occur on all sides, of course. In constructing our proposed reforms, we have tried to adhere to a nuanced balancing of interests that can be grounded in overall societal good.

The three subsections that follow explore three questions related to interest balancing: Who should decide the proper balance of interests? What role should victims play in formulating criminal justice rules and punishments? And should crime severity be routinely taken into account in setting criminal law rules and practices that have a justice-frustrating effect?

Who Should Decide the Proper Balance of Interests When Formulating Criminal Law Rules and Practices?

As noted, the rules and practices of the justice system ought to reflect a balance between competing societal interests. This raises the question of who should determine the appropriate balance of interests when making criminal justice rules. This book has showcased the variety of actors who currently decide the balance of interests.[22] Legislatures are the primary determiner over matters such as funding, statutes of limitation, pretrial procedures, rules of evidence, sentencing guidelines, and early release laws. Courts hold primary determining power over constitutional rules such as double jeopardy, search and seizure restrictions, interrogation rules, and the exclusionary rule, as well exercising sentencing discretion. Prosecutors hold determining power in matters of plea bargains and prosecution policies, while executives hold power in matters of clemency. Some practices, such as which distributive principle of punishment to apply (for example, desert, deterrence, or incapacitation), are decided by multiple actors such as courts and legislatures who sometimes work against one another.

However, because the rules of the justice system should reflect the balance of interests most in society support, it is commonly the case that legislatures are best placed to make fundamental balancing decisions. In a democratic society, it is elected legislatures that are designed to speak most directly to society's values. As noted in chapter 6, judges are too removed from the public to be properly responsive to changes in public preferences, and the doctrine of *stare decisis* means old judicial decisions may continue to dictate a balance of interests no longer supported by society. Claims that courts are better placed to make rules because of their lack of political partisanship also ring increasingly hollow as accusations of judicial partisanship and threats of court packing are made with ever greater regularity. There is also no reason to believe that judges—who are generalists by the necessity of their wide-ranging caseloads—possess more relevant expertise in specific criminal law policymaking than legislative committees and subcommittees. Judges were never meant to be makers of law in America's constitutional system, and

it is unfortunate that the latter half of the twentieth century saw courts strip legislatures of their ability to weigh the balance of interests in matters such as search and seizure, interrogation, and the question of excluding improperly obtained evidence.

Those who argue against an interest-balancing approach to criminal law, such as the "rights absolutists," often prefer judges as decision makers because judicial decisions are harder to change than democratically passed laws and because they see judges as commonly enforcing "rights" without regard to societal consequences, an approach they feel comfortable with. However, such an absolutist perspective mischaracterizes the situation by seeing judges as somehow immune to personal or political preferences. Judges engage in lawmaking when they turn a dozen constitutional words into a book-length set of constitutionally mandated—and usually very complex— rules, and this lawmaking is often done through application of judges' idiosyncrasies in balancing the competing interests. There is no greater sanctity in the resulting judicially created book of rules than there is in a legislatively created book of rules, except that the judicially enacted rules are less democratic in their balance of interests and harder to change. Many "rights absolutist" legal scholars felt comfortable with less democratic judicial decision making in the past when they tended to agree with the results of judicial lawmaking, but as the recent shift in the ideology of Supreme Court decision making shows, such a view was based on convenience— not something inherent in the judiciary. In fact, a critical step toward depoliticizing the judiciary is returning more interest-balancing power to democratically elected legislatures who are more constitutionally suited for settling political questions.

Perhaps a wiser and more democratic system of decision-making responsibility can be seen in the United Kingdom's parliament, which possesses ultimate power to set criminal law rules and practices. For example, when public sentiment in the United Kingdom turned in favor of allowing a new and compelling evidence exception to the double jeopardy rule, all that was required was an act of Parliament instead of a battle over judicial interpretation or clearing the almost impossible bar of passing a constitutional amendment. A better approach for the United States might be for courts to more frequently decline opportunities to become lawmakers and to more regularly signal the legislative branch that a balancing debate needs legislative resolution or even that a particular reform is needed. Even if the legislative branch refuses to act on such judicial advice, any judicial remedy should be limited and open to revision by later legislative enactment. Judges should not simply make new laws if we are to take seriously the constitutional separation of powers.

What Role, If Any, Should Victims Have in Formulating Criminal Justice Rules and Punishments?

As this book has shown, the criminal justice system is often indifferent to actually doing desert-based justice. The previous chapters have offered a wide variety of case examples of the justice system letting justice fail and the resulting public outrage from such failures—an outrage commonly spearheaded by victims and their families.[23] Understandably, the victims' rights movement has argued for more victim participation in the workings of the justice system in order to ensure the system actually does justice. While we are sympathetic to victims' concerns and support the justice system reevaluating the balance of interests to give greater weight to the value of doing justice, we do not support granting victims decision-making power in matters of criminal liability and punishment. Several chapters have noted reforms proposed by others that would give individual victims more influence over punishment decisions through the ability to guide or veto plea bargains, judicial sentences, and clemency grants.[24] People have proposed such reforms because it might be argued that if victims are given the power to play a direct role in deciding their offender's punishment, a failure of justice is less likely.

However, requiring decision-making input from individual victims would cause far more problems than it would solve because it would tend to destroy the system's impartiality and introduce unjust disparities.[25] Judges and prosecutors are not allowed to participate in cases where they have a vested personal interest lest their impartiality be undermined and the justice system be reduced to a system of personal grievance and favoritism. Victims have been severely wronged, and it is unrealistic to think that they can be entirely impartial any more than the offender could be.

Furthermore, if criminal punishment depended on the views of the victim, similar crimes with similarly blameworthy offenders would be punished vastly differently depending on the vindictive or forgiving nature of the victim. As discussed in chapter 3, the proper purpose of the criminal justice system is enforcing justice as society sees it—not as the individual offender or victim sees it. The justice system should not be reduced to a state-funded tool of a victim's anger or mercy.

None of this is to say that victims' input is not important to the formulation of criminal justice rules and punishments. Victim testimony provides an essential avenue for prosecutors and judges to understand the harms inflicted by a crime, a key element in determining an offender's overall blameworthiness. On a broader level, victim advocacy groups can bring policymakers' attention to flagrant failures of justice and push for policy changes to rectify them. And of course, the justice system should strive to be respectful of victims whether it is through providing notifications of case developments, providing opportunities for victims to express their opinions, or expanding access to victims' services. However, we believe it is inappropriate to grant individual victims or victim groups institutional power at any point in the justice adjudication system—just as it would be wrong to allow offenders or their advocates formal power to decide on criminal sentences or the rules under which offenders would be tried.[26] Lawmakers and justice officials should strive to strike a balance of interests in all criminal rules and punishment decisions that best reflects society's views of justice—not the views of any single individual or group. Victims can already seek individualized remedies from their offenders through civil lawsuits, and civil litigation provides an avenue to exclusively pursue individual interests, unlike criminal proceedings in which wider societal interests must take precedence.

Should Doctrines and Practices that Produce Failures of Justice Be Formulated in a Way that Takes Account of the Seriousness of the Offense?

As reflected in its title, this book has primarily focused on the justice system's failure to punish serious crimes. Sometimes justice fails in serious criminal cases because of a rule that makes no distinction between serious and less serious crimes. Often the status quo rule reflects an appropriate balance of interests in less serious criminal cases but not in more serious ones. This is a common problem in judicial rule making as judges must focus on the case before them rather than on creating a system-wide rule that logically would apply differently to offenses of different seriousness. For example, the American double jeopardy rule applies equally to criminal cases of all severity despite the fact that society clearly has a much greater interest in convicting a wrongly acquitted murderer and rapist than a wrongly acquitted thief. Similarly, American search, seizure, and interrogation rules do not consider the seriousness of the crime, but it seems likely ordinary citizens would be far more willing to sanction privacy intrusions to bring killers or rapists to justice than illegal drug users or fraudsters. New technologies such as DNA analysis, CCTV cameras, and facial recognition might have an easier time being accepted if their use depended on the seriousness of the offense under investigation. In fact, it is often the insensitivity of criminal law rules to offense seriousness that outrages the public. Few get angry if a drug possessor goes free because of the exclusionary rule, but most are outraged when a murderer or rapist walks free because police made a minor mistake.

The preceding chapters have shown that the criminal justice system misses many opportunities to take crime seriousness into account.[27] Misdemeanors are not the same as felonies. Crimes of violence are different from non-violent offenses. In a few places, the justice system does make use of seriousness in formulating its rules, but often in a very blunt manner. For example, statutes of limitation have never been applied to murder due to its special seriousness, but as argued in chapter 2, taking crime seriousness into account would suggest eliminating statutes of limitation for many other serious crimes, not just murder. The more serious the crime, the greater society's interest in bringing the perpetrator to justice—a fact that should be reflected in more criminal law rules and doctrines. Rectifying this oversight would go a long way toward solving many of the failures of justice catalogued in this book.

C. REFORM PRIORITIES

We have offered several dozen reform recommendations in this volume, all worthy of consideration by policymakers, that we hope will be supported and pursued. However, it seems useful to identify those we think deserve the most attention. Making that assessment requires considering a variety of factors: For which current rules and practices are the competing societal interests in greatest imbalance? Which cause justice failures with the greatest frequency? Which justice-frustrating rules and practices would be the easiest to change, and which the hardest? This section considers these factors before concluding with our "top ten list" of reforms that we think are most important to pursue.

The Most Justifiable Doctrines and Practices that Generate Failures of Justice

It is worth reiterating a point noted in chapter 1, that not all doctrines producing failures of justice are unjustified or even in need of change. And even those that need reform may only require a small adjustment to a fundamentally sound principle. In fact, some justice-frustrating doctrines are so completely justified as to not even warrant scrutiny in this book. The presumption of innocence clearly causes many wrongful acquittals, but no one would seriously argue it should be replaced by a different standard. Even some of the rules mentioned in this book are eminently justified. The best example is the legality principle that upholds the entire legal framework by guaranteeing no punishment except in accordance with existing law. Without a doubt, the legality principle does cause failures of justice in the sense that society will see some offenders escaping their "just deserts" as a result of poorly written laws. Recall the chapter 2 cases of Ray Marsh, who badly mistreated hundreds of corpses entrusted to him for cremation by leaving them to rot in the woods behind his crematorium,[28] or the case of Lee Curtis Davis who sexually abused his thirteen-year-old and wheelchair-bound daughter.[29] But such failures do not mean the legality principle should be waived in favor of a "principle of analogy," where any action could be punished if it is generally analogous to a codified offense, or in favor of a principle allowing criminal liability for any conduct odious enough in the eyes of society or individual judges to warrant punishment.

The societal interest in having a clearly written law applying equally to all regardless of the perceived morality of their actions is such that the inevitable failures of justice from the legality principle are worth accepting. However, while the legality principle is obviously justified, there are elements around its edges that can be reformed without doing damage to it—such as the Model Penal Code Reform, which we support, of replacing the rule of strict construction with the rule of fair import, where ambiguities in criminal codes are read with more of an eye toward their intended meaning rather than a wooden rule that adopts any interpretation, no matter how unsound, that benefits the defendant.

A similar dynamic applies to other rules causing failures of justice in the sense that the overall rule is clearly justified, but there are modifications that can be made around its edges to reduce the frequency of justice failures caused by it (for example, double jeopardy or speedy trial rules). Another example of a clearly justifiable cause of justice failures might be diplomatic immunity, which does not appear to have any good alternative that could preserve easy diplomatic functioning. However, as with the legality principle, diplomatic immunity can be modified around its edges (such as by introducing non-criminal sanctions) to reduce the frequency with which it causes justice failures.

The Least Justifiable: The Doctrines and Practices of Greatest Imbalance

While the justice system is admittedly a system of tradeoffs, some doctrines and practices are so poorly balanced in terms of societal interest—or reflect such outdated balances—that they deserve the special attention of policymakers. In fact, several chapters have raised situations in the justice system that promote no existing societal interest. Two obvious ones

are citizen non-cooperation (chapter 14) and police non-intervention (chapter 15). Society does not benefit from witness intimidation, codes of silence, legal cynicism, or community misperceptions fueled by misinformation. Similarly, no one except criminals benefits when police pull back from enforcing the law, whatever the cause. Reforms aimed at addressing America's troubled police-community relations and restoring trust and cooperation do not risk sacrificing any interest upheld by the status quo because there are none. Other issues for which the balance of interests points entirely toward reform would include addressing investigative errors (chapter 4) and writing clearer, MPC-based law codes (chapter 2). No societal interests are upheld by shoddy investigations or unclear laws.

In addition to the previous issues where no societal interest would be threatened by reform, this book has explored several topics where the competing societal interests seem wildly out of balance. While the status quo for these issues does seek to benefit society, we argue it has clearly failed and better alternatives exist. An obvious example is the exclusionary rule (chapter 8), which was designed to protect constitutional rights but has only protected criminals while offering no recourse for innocent victims of crime or police violations. Similarly, the status quo on interrogation rules (chapter 6) has bizarrely encouraged silence and allowed ambush defenses for the sake of preventing coerced confessions—something that the current system of Miranda warnings has not been shown to do, either theoretically or practically.

Some rules may once have reflected a clearly appropriate balance of interests but today do little for society. Statutes of limitation for serious crimes (chapter 2) are almost indefensible given the rise of new forms of evidence and better legal systems. Double jeopardy (chapter 2), while an important rule to protect against governmental harassment, unnecessarily protects previously acquitted serious criminals whose guilt is now certain beyond the slightest shadow of a doubt. While judges must have some discretion in sentencing (chapter 11) to uphold societal interests in making the punishment fit the unique circumstances of each offense and offender, it makes little sense not to provide sentencing guidelines so long as judges are not rigidly bound to them. While there are legitimate societal interests in upholding a clemency power (chapter 13), its unchecked and venal application is hard to justify when almost all its benefits could be retained by adding more oversight.

This book has also explored doctrines and practices that, though we think worthy of reform, we concede reflect a more contentious balance of interests and their reform depends to a greater degree on differing values. Examples include issues relating to upholding desert as a distributive principle as opposed to deterrence or incapacitation (chapter 3). While we have argued "empirical desert" should take precedence over deterrence and incapacitation even on purely utilitarian grounds (because adhering to desert is the most effective way to prevent crime in the long run), society does have a clear interest in deterring crime and incapacitating criminals. The status quo of plea bargaining (chapter 10) and early release on parole (chapter 12) makes some sense from the perspective of deterrence and incapacitation, which do not care if an offender is punished according to what society would see as just. Our proposed

reforms of replacing some incarcerative sanctions with non-incarcerative sanctions (chapter 16) and making pretrial release decisions based on flight risk scores (chapter 9) may uphold desert but could be seen as acting counter to deterrence or incapacitation. Another clash of values is manifested in compassionate release (chapter 12), where more frequent compassionate release is more justifiable to the degree one supports the value of mercy in the justice system as opposed to desert.

Another set of contentious issues with a thorny balance of interests relates to privacy. This book has covered search and seizure rules (chapter 6) and limitations on new technology (chapter 7), which both invoke the tension between preserving individual privacy and the need to ensure justice and safety. While we have suggested reforms that could advance justice and safety without significant infringement upon privacy, we acknowledge the subjective weight many people may place on keeping as much of their lives out of the government's purview as possible. The differing weight people give to privacy is one reason why we suggest in several places that laws dictating the balance between privacy and investigation be struck democratically at the state and local levels. Our prioritization of local, democratic decision making also makes us acknowledge that some proposed reforms, such as checking the power of local prosecutors to enforce non-prosecution policies (chapter 16), raise strong conflicting interests.

The Failure of Justice Causes that Occur with the Greatest Frequency

Every failure of justice is a problem in its own right, but in order to balance societal interests appropriately, it is necessary to have some idea about the frequency with which the underlying doctrines or practices cause justice failures. This book has covered doctrines that only cause a small absolute number of justice failures (for example, double jeopardy or diplomatic immunity) as well as doctrines that have the potential to undermine justice in almost all criminal cases (for example, plea bargaining or poor investigative procedures). The causes of justice failures covered in the previous chapters can be divided into three broad categories based on how many cases they affect in the justice system each year.

The first category is majority frequency, meaning that the doctrine or practice affects, or at least has the possibility to affect, the majority of criminal cases. The doctrines and practices in this category include investigative errors, inadequate financing, citizen non-cooperation, police non-intervention, unchecked sentencing discretion, plea bargaining, interrogation rules, search and seizure restrictions, early release on parole, restrictions on the use of new technology (for example, CCTV and DNA analysis), pretrial release, and the problem of criminal codes that do not prioritize desert.

The second category are those doctrines and practices that affect a significant absolute number of criminal cases each year but are not as impactful as the first category. The topics in this category are statutes of limitation, the exclusionary rule, compassionate release, executive clemency, speedy trial laws, and prosecutorial non-enforcement policies.

The third category are those doctrines and practices that, while capable of causing serious failures of justice in individual cases, do not seem to affect justice in a large number of criminal cases. Issues

in this category include diplomatic immunity, the rule of strict construction, double jeopardy, and rules around prejudicial evidence.

Of course, the frequency at which a doctrine or practice causes justice failures is not the only, or even the most important, factor to consider when setting a reform agenda. The imbalance of interests associated with the status quo on the issue (see the previous section) is perhaps even more relevant. Another relevant factor to consider (see the next section) is the ease with which potential reforms could be adopted for a given issue.

Which Proposed Reforms Would Be the Easiest to Adopt, and Which the Hardest?

In judging which reforms should be given priority on a reform agenda, practical necessity suggests that one ought to take account of how realistic it is to actually get the reform adopted. We have sought to limit our recommendations to reforms that we think are feasible, but certainly some will be much easier to implement than others. For example, to the extent that a reform requires a judicial shift in constitutional interpretation, no matter how worthwhile that shift is and no matter how constitutionally supportable, the ultimate decision is one that is out of the hands of a legislative reform committee and therefore may not be a particularly good investment for a priority reform agenda.

On the other hand, some factors may suggest that the possibility of reform for some rules or practices is particularly good. For example, to the extent that other jurisdictions, especially other American states, have adopted the reform already, one would expect this demonstration of feasibility would make it easier for another jurisdiction to follow the same path. For example, as we noted in chapter 2, a majority of states have followed the Model Penal Code's lead and adopted the rule of fair import. So while the rule of strict construction lives on in many jurisdictions, the path to replacing it is clear.[30] Similarly, as we noted in chapter 7, thirty-four states have enacted laws allowing DNA collection from at least some arrestees, with a smaller number allowing for the collection of DNA from any arrestees. This kind of existing adoption of a recommendation would seem to significantly increase the chances that other jurisdictions will seriously consider the reform.[31]

Other factors that affect the ease of adoption include public opinion and the existence of organized lobbying groups either in favor of or opposed to the reform. For example, reforms that involve changing search rules or using new technologies may run into fierce opposition from organized privacy rights advocates even if the reforms in question are supported by the wider public.

With all these factors in mind, we rank our proposed reforms into three categories: less difficult, more difficult, and most difficult (the choice of "difficult" instead of "ease" being an intentional recognition of the challenges inherent in changing the status quo). We recognize that the difficulty of adoption may vary somewhat by jurisdiction as the previous factors vary by jurisdiction as well, but the following is a best guess at the situation most policymakers will face.

Less difficult reforms include adopting the rule of fair import with modern penal code drafting, creating a police-community oversight commission, abolishing statutes of limitation for serious felonies, enlarging DNA databases but

limiting their use to serious offenses, and facilitating state attorney general prosecution of offenses when local DAs refuse to enforce the law.

More difficult reforms include adopting comprehensive sentencing guidelines, using particularized offense grading to reduce the cost of justice-frustrating plea bargains, adopting the Model Penal Code distributive principle of punishment based on desert, maximizing the use of non-incarcerative sanctions consonant with desert, abolishing early release as per the federal system, substituting administrative transfers for compassionate release, adopting pre-trial release conditions based on risk of flight scores, creating a national body of experts to set best practice guidelines for criminal investigations and help secure funding, adopting a pardon board to reduce executive abuse of clemency, codifying search and seizure rules, and expanding and funding the use of CCTV and facial recognition technology where the community approves.

Most difficult reforms include replacing the exclusionary rule with direct sanctioning of police officers, creating a new and compelling evidence exception to double jeopardy in cases of serious crimes, changing interrogation rules to impeach ambush defenses and adopt a UK version of arrest warnings, imposing collateral sanctions on diplomats whose governments do not waive immunity, tightening standards of appeal on cases involving supposedly "prejudicial" evidence, withholding witness identities at trial in cases of likely witness intimidation, and changing speedy trial rules to only force dismissal where a constitutional, as opposed to statutory, violation is found. As may be apparent, many of these reforms are in this category because they depend upon judicial rather than legislative action.

Highest-Priority Reforms: Our Top Ten List

In creating our list of recommendations that we believe ought to have the highest priority on a reform agenda, we considered the factors discussed in each of the three previous sections, and we would recommend policymakers do so as well when coming up with their own reform priority lists. One would obviously want to give greatest attention to those doctrines and practices in which the balance of competing interests is most dramatically unjustifiable. At the same time, however, if a doctrine or practice affects fewer instances, its reform has less practical urgency. The doctrines that most frequently generate failures of justice ought to have highest priority. But it also makes sense to consider whether a reform effort is likely to be successful. These considerations rely in part upon some quite subjective evaluations. Reasonable minds could easily come to different conclusions, especially if special circumstances exist in one's jurisdiction. Policymakers aiming to improve their jurisdiction's justice system will want to come up with their own specific list of priorities. Overall, however, we think these ten reforms ought to get highest priority. They are presented in the order in which they appear in the volume, as we do not attempt to rank within these top ten.

1. Abolish the Statutes of Limitation for Serious Felonies, and for Other Felonies Restart the Limitation Clock after Any New Felony (chapter 2). As discussed in chapter 2, while statutes of limitation might have had more justification when introduced centuries ago, the reasons for

their continued use are lacking, especially when they regularly produces failures of justice for serious offenses. The strong trend among US states is clearly to abolish statutes of limitation for an increasing number of serious offenses and to lengthen them where retained. Thus, our abolition proposal simply reinforces the current trend, but the clock-restart twist makes perfect logical sense wherever a statute of limitation is retained. What could possibly be the justification for providing a limitation defense to a career burglar who has never stopped?

2. Adopt a Fair Import Test in Place of a Strict Construction Test, After Adopting a Modern Criminal Code Format (chapter 2). As with statutes of limitation, the rule of strict construction might have made sense back when it was first adopted, but the advent of modern criminal codes with their careful drafting and defined terms have left it with little continuing justification. Today, its application is typically seen by the public as one more of those mindless "legal technicalities" that tend to make the community think the criminal justice system has little interest in doing justice. Again, adopting the rule of fair import is the existing modern trend.

3. Adopt a Desert-Based Distributive Principle, as Per the Model Penal Code (chapter 3). Half a century ago, when the Model Penal Code was first drafted by the American Law Institute, the state of criminal law theory left it unsettled as to whether criminal law ought to be primarily aimed at doing justice—giving offenders the punishment they deserve, proportionate to the seriousness of the offense and the blameworthiness of the offender—or in the business of avoiding future crime through general deterrence or incapacitation of the dangerous, even if doing so meant violating principles of deserved punishment. But as the 2007 amendment of the Model Code illustrates, it has now become clear that abandoning desert as the guiding principle for criminal liability and punishment creates its own enormous costs to effective crime control. Over the past half-century, social science has exposed not only the inherent weaknesses in and limitations of general deterrence and incapacitation of the dangerous as mechanisms of crime control but has also demonstrated the crime control effectiveness of a criminal justice system singularly devoted to doing justice and avoiding injustice. It is now clear that the most effective mechanism for fighting crime is to do justice, and states should clarify the purpose of their criminal codes accordingly to guide future reforms.

4. Establish a National Experts Group to Set Best Investigative Practices and to Help Gain Funding to Meet Them (chapters 4 and 5). Chapters 4 and 5 made clear the frequent failures of justice that come from investigative errors, poor training, and inadequate financing. Given the importance of doing justice in the community's eyes, these problems, which can easily be fixed with greater investment, ought to be high on the reform list. This proposed reform could have an enormous practical effect in reducing failures of justice in a wide range of cases without requiring more complicated legal changes.

5. Enlarge Investigative Databases and Capabilities but Establish Limitations on Their Use (chapter 7). There is understandable reluctance to allow governments to be too intrusive in our private lives, but at the same time, there seems to be strong support for the idea that minor intrusions in our collective privacy are worth the enormous benefits to justice and safety that can be obtained by allowing investigators to have greater access to modern technology. Greater access can dramatically alter the level of serious criminality in a society with only minor intrusions on our privacy, as in the collection of a genetic fingerprint from all arrestees to only be used when investigating serious offenses. Additionally, expanding the use of CCTV and automatic license plate readers in public spaces, where the community approves, improves justice at little cost to privacy. A key to adopting modern investigative technology is making sure sufficient limitations and safeguards are put in place to prevent its abuse and assuage public concerns.

6. Replace the Exclusionary Rule with Direct Sanctioning of Offending Officers (chapter 8). For many people, the exclusionary rule will stand as one of the most offensive doctrines disregarding the importance of doing justice. Should a serial torturer and murderer like Larry Eyler go free (to kill again) because he was held too long during a *Terry* stop? Such applications of the exclusionary rule bring into disrepute the entire criminal justice system. What kind of society would think that the cost of detaining the serial torture-murderer an extra hour is worth more than the lives and suffering of so many innocents? The existence of the rule is even more offensive because it commonly fails in its stated justification of deterring police overreach. The overreaching police have little or nothing to personally lose by violating citizens' rights. Any direct sanctioning of overreaching officers, no matter how minor it might be, is likely to provide more deterrent effect than the current justice-frustrating exclusionary rule.

7. Use Consolidated Offense Drafting with Particularized Offense Grading to Reduce the Justice-Frustrating Costs of Plea Bargaining (chapter 10). Plea bargaining may be the most common source of justice failures in the current system among caught criminals. Nearly every "bargain" is a case in which the offender is getting less criminal liability than they deserve, with the prosecution trading that deserved punishment for the efficiency and certainty of a guilty plea. While it may be impractical to stop offering plea bargains, there is no reason to have a system that offers any greater reduction in justice than is needed to induce a plea. If the criminal code provides only the options of murder, with a sentence of thirty years, or manslaughter, with a sentence of twelve years, then that code grading structure gives prosecutors little choice but to tolerate a large failure of justice. A homicide offense that distinguishes nine grades of homicide rather than three provides the opportunity to induce a plea for a considerably smaller deviation from deserved punishment. The same problem exists in lesser form for most felony offenses because most criminal codes provide few offense grades within any given offense. Prosecutors can try to work around the problem in a variety of ways, but the most obvious and cleanest solution is simply to draft criminal codes in a way that consolidates all related offenses into a single offense provision (for homicide, theft, assault, sexual assault, fraud, etc.) and provides many offense grades within each consolidated offense, as some modern and proposed codes already do.

8. Adopt Comprehensive Sentencing Guidelines, as Per the Federal System (chapter 11). A common source of justice failures is the exercise of sentenc-

ing discretion by judges who have their own idiosyncratic view of what justice requires. To make things worse, these failures of justice also introduce unacceptable punishment disparities among similar cases. The promulgation of comprehensive sentencing guidelines by the United States Sentencing Commission, and their effectiveness at reducing disparities and unjustly lenient sentences, demonstrates that it is indeed feasible to provide guidance in the exercise of discretion that will still allow judges to give special treatment to special cases.[32]

9. Abolish Early Release on Parole, as Per the Federal System (chapter 12). The federal Sentencing Reform Act of 1984 demonstrates the value of abolishing early release on parole. The federal system retains postrelease supervision for all offenders upon release but requires offenders serve at least 85 percent of the sentence publicly imposed. The federal system provides transparency with the public about how offenders are dealt with: the sentence publicly imposed in court really is the sentence served. Compare such honesty with the shell game played currently in many states where the sentence publicly imposed means little or nothing. The actual sentence served will be determined later out of public view by a parole commission. This systemic deception simply contributes to the lack of confidence that so many communities have in their criminal justice system. The shift to "truth in sentencing," where the sentence publicly imposed really does mean something, logically calls for much shorter sentences to be originally imposed, but such honesty will likely improve the law's credibility with the community. Additionally, the predictability and consistency of the new system protects some offenders from being the unfortunate prisoner whom the parole board chooses to make an example of and have serve their full (unjustly long) term.

10. Create a Police-Community Oversight Commission Designed to Build Trust with Both the Community and the Police (chapters 14 and 15). Chapters 14 and 15 documented the existence and resulting problems from poor police-community relations, which stem from a variety of factors. Whatever their cause, such poor relations have an enormous negative effect by producing a regular stream of serious justice failures and increasing crime. The solution to the problem cannot be found simply in "fixing" the police, as some political activists seem to think, but rather in building a police-community relationship that changes community views as well as police practices. Thus, our recommendation is a joint police-community oversight commission that has broad jurisdiction to oversee police-community interactions and to actively promote better policing and public recognition of such.

CONCLUSION

The tragic irony of the American justice system is that so little justice is done by it. Change begins with awareness, however, and this book has attempted to investigate the reasons why justice fails so frequently and suggest ways to make it succeed more often. This volume is not a work of one-sided activism but acknowledges and confronts the serious tradeoffs faced in creating criminal justice policy. As such, it is our hope that it can be useful to everyone—from academics to policymakers to concerned voters—of whatever political persuasion who wish to make the American justice system a more just system for all. Our ultimate goal is simple: a system that punishes the guilty in proportion to their blameworthiness, protects the innocent from liability and crime, and upholds the moral credibility of the law in the eyes of the community. We hope this work will help further that end.

Appendix
Discussion Issues

CHAPTER 2: LEGAL BARS TO PROSECUTION

Statute of Limitation

Q1: Why do jurisdictions typically have statutes of limitation? Are the justifications offered for such statutes accurately reflected in the statutory requirements for the defense? Explain.

Q2: Do you support the recommended reform to the statute of limitation? Explain why or why not. If not, what reform would you support that would reduce the failures of justice? In other words, if you were chair of a state legislative criminal code drafting commission, what kind of statute of limitation would you draft?

Double Jeopardy

Q3: Why does the Constitution have a double jeopardy prohibition? How should that statutory language be interpreted? As you know, the Fifth Amendment provides: "No person shall be subject for the same offense to be twice put in jeopardy of life or limb." But it is left to the courts to determine what meaning to give to those nineteen words. If you were the Supreme Court, what meaning would you give?

Q4: Do you support the recommended reform to the double jeopardy rule? Explain why or why not. If not, what reform would you support that would reduce the failures of justice? Explain.

Diplomatic Immunity

Q5: Would you support any kind of reform of the grant of diplomatic immunity from criminal prosecution? If so, what reform would you propose? Obviously, we need some kind of grant of diplomatic immunity. So the real question is: What kind of exceptions or limitation, if any, would you want to recognize? Understand that whatever exceptions that you grant will be applied to your own diplomats in other countries.

Q6: Do you support the recommended reform relating to diplomatic immunity? Explain why or why not. If not, what reform would you support that would reduce the failures of justice? Explain.

Legality Principle and the Rule of Strict Construction

Q7: Would you support a narrowing of the operation of the legality principle? If so, how would you modify the rule? Would you have adhered to the legality principle at Nuremberg so as to provide a defense to aggressive warmaking? If so, where would you draw the line for the exception that you have recognized?

Q8: Would you support the rule of strict construction? Or would you prefer the Model Penal Code's rule of "fair import"? Explain why you are taking the position that you are.

CHAPTER 3: ANTI-JUSTICE DISTRIBUTIVE PRINCIPLES

Q1: Are you persuaded that the criminal law's reputation—its "moral credibility"—with the community affects its crime control effectiveness? Why or why not? Explain your answer.

Q2: Are you persuaded that the operation of criminal justice rules and procedures that produce regular failures of justice undermine criminal law's moral credibility? Why or why not? Explain your answer.

Q3: If you were a crime control utilitarian, would you find general deterrence a more attractive distributive principle than maximizing criminal law's moral credibility with the community? Why or why not? Explain your answer.

Q4: If you were a crime control utilitarian, would you find incapacitation of the dangerous a more attractive distributive principle than maximizing criminal law's moral credibility with the community? Why or why not? Explain your answer.

Q5: The original and the revised versions of the Model Penal Code's distributive principles section are reproduced in the text. Do you approve or disapprove of the Model Code's change? Explain.

Q6: If you were in charge of constructing a criminal justice system, what distributive principle or hybrid distributive principle would you propose? Write out the statutory text of your proposed principle (that is, in a form analogous to the MPC distributive principles section, which defines the distributive principle or principles to be used and their interrelation

with one another) and be prepared to explain and defend it.

CHAPTER 4: INVESTIGATIVE ERRORS

Q1: It would seem difficult to imagine any opposition to the suggestion that investigators should get more and better training and should be carefully selected, so there seems little to debate about the appropriate goals here. One might ask, however: If there are limited resources (which is always the case), what reforms ought to be given priority? Which are the most important? And which are the most cost-effective?

Q2: What branch of government ought to make such decisions? (The next chapter [chapter 5] takes up this issue in more detail.)

Q3: Do you support the recommended reform? Explain why or why not. If not, what reform would you support that would reduce the failures of justice? Explain.

CHAPTER 5: INADEQUATE FINANCING

Q1: Given people's different views on societal values, especially those relating to policing, is it even possible to come to a rationally calculated decision about the proper allocation of society's financial resources? Different people will have different perspectives on what values are most important. Are there rational ways of sorting through the issue?

Q2: Of the many systemic shortcomings in the investigation and prosecution of serious offenses, which do you think are the most troubling, and why? In your view, if you had the ability to direct significant new financing to the investigative and prosecuted elements of the system, what investment do you think would have the highest payoff in reducing failures of justice?

Q3: Do you support the recommended reform? Explain why or why not. If not, what reform would you support that would reduce the failures of justice? Explain.

CHAPTER 6: LEGAL LIMITATIONS ON POLICE INVESTIGATION

Search Issues—Warrant Requirement
Q1: Do you agree or disagree with the current balance of interests struck in the current US formulation of search and seizure rules? Explain.

Q2: Do you support the recommended reform? Explain why or why not. If not, what reform would you support that would reduce the failures of justice? Explain.

Interrogation Issues—Miranda
Q3: Do you agree or disagree with the current balance of interests struck in the current US interrogation rules? Explain.

Q4: Do you support the recommended reform? Explain why or why not. If not, what reform would you support that would reduce the failures of justice? Explain.

Universal Issue
Q5: Who in the society should be deciding how to balance the societal interests in these and other similar criminal justice policy decisions? Explain.

CHAPTER 7: RESTRAINTS ON USE OF TECHNOLOGY

Q1: What factors should be taken into account in assessing the importance of privacy as against more effective crime control? The nature of what is being kept private? For example, a person's sexual conduct and toileting behavior versus a person's physical location at a particular time? The seriousness of the suspected offense? A suspected rape versus a $500 theft? (Notice that most privacy-founded rules apply without regard to the seriousness of the offense. Is that a mistake?)

The primary challenge in assessing the proper balance between effective crime control and privacy may be the common occurrence during a search of collateral intrusion on the privacy of innocent non-suspects. But if this is the major problem,(**is somethingmissing here or the next question is sort of a continuance to this paragraph?**) [AQ2]

Q2: Is the balance between effective crime control and privacy best struck by democratic action where the community can express their views about the appropriate balance? If democratic action is the appropriate mechanism for striking the balance in these situations, why is it not the appropriate mechanism in setting the search and seizure rules, for example, where the same problem exists of potentially intruding upon the privacy of innocent citizens? Is there a justification for having search and seizure rules created by judges rather than by democratic action?

Q3: Should the balance of privacy versus effective prosecution depend in some part upon the current state of one's society? To put it another way, is promoting privacy at the expense of effective prosecution a luxury that only some societies can afford? Consider, as an extreme example, Colombia under the increasing control of drug cartel kingpin Pablo Escobar who through corruption and violence was able to seriously influence the exercise of governmental powers. Ineffective prosecution in Colombia meant the loss of all liberal democratic values—including privacy. In judging the proper balance between privacy and effective prosecution, do we need to take into account the existing risks caused by ineffective prosecution? Those risks might be dramatically higher for most countries in the world who are in greater danger from political corruption, organized crime, or terrorist activities than is the United States. Would that suggest, then, that the privacy balancing might well come out quite differently in different societies? (This question is a challenge of sorts to the absolutists who want to think about privacy rights—and many other sorts of rights—as absolute inalienable rights that can never be compromised. In some situations, that kind of absolutist thinking could lead to not only complete obliteration of the right but of much of the rest of democratic society as well.)

Q4: Do you support the recommended reforms concerning DNA? Concerning CCTV? Concerning facial recognition? Explain why or why not. If not, what reforms would you support that would reduce the failures of justice? Explain.

CHAPTER 8: EXCLUDING RELIABLE AND PROBATIVE EVIDENCE

Exclusionary Rule

Q1: If the exclusionary rule did not exist, what mechanisms would you use to compel police and prosecutors to comply with judicially created rules relating to searches and seizure or interrogation? Is the exclusionary rule more effective than these alternative mechanisms in gaining compliance? Given its justice-frustrating nature, why should a society prefer reliance upon the exclusionary rule?

Q2: Do you support the recommended reform? Explain why or why not. If not, what reform would you support that would reduce the failures of justice? Explain.

Excluding "Prejudicial" Evidence

Q3: In your view, what would be an example of a case in which the introduction of reliable and probative evidence that was fully relevant to proving legal liability ought to be hidden from the jury because it would "prejudice" them, even if such exclusion meant that a serious offender would go free? What does such an exclusion rule say about the system's view of juries?

Q4: When reliable and relevant evidence is excluded from trial, the jury is being presented an account of the case that is false (by reason of the omission). What arguments can you make in support of such official deception by omission? Is such official deception, once exposed, likely to have an effect on the criminal justice system's credibility with the community?

Q5: Do you support the recommended reform? Explain why or why not. If not, what reform would you support that would reduce the failures of justice? Explain.

CHAPTER 9: PRETRIAL PROCEDURES

Pretrial Release

Q1: If an arrestee has previously failed to appear for court proceedings without a good reason, what argument can you make that when they finally do appear before the court they should be released again (pretrial)?

Q2: If the offense charged carries a serious penalty and there exists good evidence of the defendant's guilt, what kind of conditions for release would you provide that would assure the defendant will appear for trial?

Q3: Do you support the recommended reform? Explain why or why not. If not, what reform would you support that would reduce the failures of justice? Explain.

Speedy Trial

Q4: If the prosecution exceeds the authorized trial preparation period, what different kinds of sanctions other than granting the defendant immunity from prosecution can one imagine?

Q5: Do you support the recommended reform? Explain why or why not. If not, what reform would you support that would reduce the failures of justice? Explain.

CHAPTER 10: PLEA BARGAINING

Q1: Do you think the current plea bargaining system needs reform, and if so, why?

Q2: If yes, what specific reforms would you propose? For each of the reforms that you propose, how feasible would it be to actually implement it? Who needs to do what to make it happen? (Remember that some prosecutors are independently elected; others are appointed by an elected person or body.)

Q3: Do you support the recommended reform? Explain why or why not. If not, what reform would you support that would reduce the failures of justice? Explain.

CHAPTER 11: UNCHECKED JUDICIAL SENTENCING DISCRETION

Q1: Would you support the use of mandatory minimum sentences? If so, can you offer a principled defense of such a practice?

Q2: Would you support the use of sentencing guidelines? And if so, how would you structure them? (For example, would they be mandatory or just advisory? Or something in between—that is, if mandatory, would you have some mechanism that allows the sentencing judge under some circumstances to go outside the guideline recommendation, and if so, under what circumstances? What factors would you take into account in setting the guideline sentences? Presumably you would take into account the seriousness of the offense and the culpability of the actor. What else? Presumably you would exclude some factors from the guideline, such as race, religion, gender. What else?)

Q3: Can you imagine other ways of dealing with judicial sentencing discretion other than through mandatory minimums or sentencing guidelines? What kinds of mechanisms can you imagine? (For example, would you support a system without mandatory sentences or sentencing guidelines but where sentencing judges within a jurisdiction are given detailed information about how cases like the case in front of them were dealt with in the past by the other judges in the jurisdiction, perhaps leaving it to the judges as a group to discuss and establish sentencing norms enforced only by judicial peer pressure? Would you support a system in which jurors were involved in the sentencing decision?)

Q4: Do you support the recommended reform? Explain why or why not. If not, what reform would you support that would reduce the failures of justice due to inappropriate judicial leniency? Explain.

CHAPTER 12: EARLY RELEASE ON PAROLE AND COMPASSIONATE RELEASE

Early Release on Parole
Q1: What, if anything, justifies having parole boards with discretionary authority to order early release? What are the costs or dangers of having such discretionary early release on parole? What arguments can you make that the early release authority should and can be simply eliminated?

Q2: With which distributive principles (recall chapter 3) is discretionary early release consistent and with which distributive principles is it inconsistent?

Q3: Do you support the recommended reform? Explain why or why not. If not, what reform would you support that would reduce the failures of justice? Explain.

Compassionate Release
Q4: What, if anything, justifies having discretionary authority to provide compassionate early release? What, if anything, would be lost if it were completely abolished? Isn't it inevitable that discretionary early release authority will create unjustified disparity in the application of criminal punishment?

Q5: If a change in a prisoner's health makes their imprisonment appreciably more burdensome, shouldn't this change in health logically shorten the length of the offender's imprisonment by an amount that would keep their total punishment equal to that to which they were sentenced? Should compassionate release authority be limited to this kind of sentence adjustment? (**I found it hard to understand the question, perhaps we should rephrase it**). [AQ2]

Q6: Do you support the recommended reform for compassionate release? Explain why or why not. If not, what reform would you support that would reduce the failures of justice? Explain.

CHAPTER 13: EXECUTIVE CLEMENCY

Q1: What is the justification for having executive clemency at all? Why should the executive have any say as to the punishment imposed upon an offender? We already have a system of appellate review and rereview, as well as a system of habeas corpus review on top of those. Why would we need something more? If something more was needed, why would the executive be the appropriate source of that additional review? Even if one assumes that there is some purpose to be served by having an executive clemency power, is the potential for abuse a sufficient danger so as to outweigh any benefit?

Q2: Is the provision for an executive clemency power unjust and anti-democratic? That is, shouldn't all defendants be judged by the same law and isn't that law properly for the determination of the legislative branch? Is allowing the executive unfettered discretion to alter the results of the criminal justice process an invitation to the creation of unjustifiable disparity in the treatment of similar offenders and to undermining the legislative branch's criminal lawmaking authority? Do you support or oppose the use of clemency as a mechanism for the executive to decriminalize conduct made criminal by the legislature? Explain.

Q3: Do you support the proposed recommendation for clemency reform? If not, what reform to the executive clemency power, if any, would you support?

CHAPTER 14: CITIZEN NON-COOPERATION

Q1: What would you recommend as a means to most effectively reduce witness intimidation? To most effectively counter the stop snitching movement? To most effectively eliminate or reduce people's legal cynicism?

Our discussions in chapter 3 examined the connection between the criminal law's moral credibility with the community and people's willingness to defer, support, acquiesce, and internalize its norms. The studies in that chapter also suggest that criminal law's moral credibility depends in large part upon the extent to which the community sees the criminal justice system as devoted to doing justice—avoiding both injustice and failures of justice. (It also suggests the importance of community perceptions of fair adjudication procedures and respectful and professional policing.) Thus, improving the system's reputation with the community by reform that promotes fairness and justice are an obvious way to proceed.

On the other hand, it seems natural for the news media to focus on the criminal justice system's failures. Regularly doing justice and avoiding injustice are not likely to be seen as big news. Further, many politicians have as their central political theme the failures of the criminal justice system, both in allowing spiraling crime and in doing injustice. Without criminal justice system failures, they have no political vehicle. Thus, they have every incentive to highlight and exaggerate the system's failures rather than its successes. Given these dynamics, how realistic is it to think that the criminal justice system can ever earn a good reputation with the community? It will always be the case that it can do better—every human institution can—and thus whatever its current failings, there will always be something to use as a basis to trash its reputation. With this background, then:

Q2: What procedures, practices, or reforms would you recommend to most effectively improve the criminal justice system's reputation for doing justice, despite the inevitable headwinds from media coverage and political maneuvering? If you were the chief law enforcement officer of a large city, what would be at the top of your reform list?

Q3: Do you support the recommended reform? Explain why or why not.

CHAPTER 15: POLICE NON-INTERVENTION

Q1: Do you agree that there is a problem with police non-intervention? If so, does it have practical negative consequences? If so, what are those exactly? Do they disproportionately affect minority neighborhoods?

Q2: What can be done realistically and specifically to solve the problem of police non-intervention that increases the rate of failures of justice as a result of each of these four circumstances?

   a. Insufficient officers due to defunding the police.
   b. Insufficient officers due to early retirements and hiring difficulties (police demoralization).
   c. Police "no-go" zones.
   d. Voluntary police disengagement (Ferguson Effect).

Q3: Do you support the recommended reform? Explain why or why not.

Q4: Is it possible that the police-community relations problem simply cannot be solved? For example, if the criminal justice system, including police, and indeed if the entire society is hopelessly racist, perhaps the problem simply can't be solved? Further, much of the media and many politicians regularly portray

police shootings of Black citizens as something uniquely cataclysmic that it ought to generate public outrage (and perhaps justify public lawlessness). But if there will necessarily always be police shootings of Black (and White) citizens (including some justified and some unjustified but due to reasonable mistakes), is it realistic to think that the problem of police-community relations can ever really be fixed?

Q5: What does the American experience as a case study tell other societies, if anything? Which of the US reforms that you find attractive for the United States would be useful for other societies, if any? What aspects of the American situation, if any, might be of limited use as an example for other countries?

CHAPTER 16: ANTIJUSTICE IDEOLOGICAL MOVEMENTS

Focusing on three examples of ideologically inspired justice failures:

Q1: Decriminalizing lower-level offenses (such as theft under $1000).

Q2: Sanctuary cities.

Q3: Non-prosecution of offenders who are motivated by an ideology that the prosecutor shares.

For each of these three progressive policies or practices, address these three issues:

   A. For and Against?—Do you support or oppose the policy or practice? Explain. If you are critical of the policy or practice, is there nonetheless perhaps some underlying problem with the current system, which has motivated progressives, for which you have some sympathy?

B. Alternatives?—Focusing on the concerns that have motivated progressives to undertake the policy or practice, can you recommend an alternative mechanism that would address their concerns but do so in a way that is less justice frustrating?

C. Prevention?—If you assume for the sake of argument that the progressive policy or practice is wrong, what could be done, if anything, to prevent progressive prosecutors or progressive city councils from undertaking such a policy or practice?

Q4: Do you support the first recommended reform (make greater use of non-incarcerative sanctions while keeping the total punitive effect of the sentence consistent with the offender's relative blameworthiness)? Explain why or why not. If not, what reform would you support that would reduce the failures of justice? Explain.

Q5: Do you support the second recommended reform (facilitate state AG prosecution where local DA rejects state legislative rules)? Explain why or why not. If not, what reform would you support that would reduce the failures of justice? Explain.

Notes

CHAPTER 1

1. Criminal justice statistics are notoriously difficult to pin down precisely. For example, there are several possible homicide numbers for 2020. The CDC reported 24,567 homicides for 2020, but this makes no distinction between justifiable and criminal homicides. See Centers for Disease Control and Prevention Wonder, "About Underlying Cause of Death, 1999–2000 Results: Deaths Occurring Through 2020," https://wonder.cdc.gov/controller /datarequest/D76;jsessionid=F40BCB177 B9B04859F3B1983F725. FBI UCR data (the most comprehensive national data for criminal homicides) reports 21,570. However, this number is derived from incomplete local police agency reports, making it necessary to estimate. Other estimates from the UCR data include 20,250 and 22,000. The latter appears to be the FBI's best estimate for criminal homicides in 2020 based on NIBRS reports—a more detailed crime reporting method within the UCR program. See "The Transition to the National Incident-Based Reporting System (NIBRS): A Comparison of 2020 and 2021 NIBRS Estimates," FBI, table 1, chrome-extension://efaidnbmnnnib pca jpcglclefindmkaj/https://kfor.com/wp -content/uploads/sites/3/2022/10/NIBRS- Trend-Analysis-Report.pdf. It is similarly difficult to determine how many homicides police actually solved, but 10,115 is one number given by FBI UCR data. See Weihua Li and Jamiles Lartey, "As Murders Spiked, Police Solved About Half in 2020," Marshall Project, January 12, 2022, https://www.themarshallproject .org/2022/01/12/as-murders-spiked -police-solved-about-half-in-2020. Other sources offer slightly different estimates. See, for example, "America's Declining Homicide Clearance Rates 1965–2020," Murderdata.org, https://www.murderdata .org/p/reported-homicide-clearance-rate -1980.html (suggesting 21,570 homicides in 2020 with a clearance rate of 54.4 percent). The exact number may be higher or lower, but the picture is clear regardless: around 50 percent or fewer homicides were even declared solved by police, and of course, many of these officially solved cases did not end in an arrest or conviction. Similar problems of varying numbers for crimes and clearance rates exist throughout this book. We have used our best judgment in presenting what appears to us to be the numbers most reflective of reality, but we will sometimes mention alternative numbers in the notes. No significant arguments or claims depend on a disputed number, however, as all available numbers paint the same general picture. More recent homicide data from 2022 confirms 2020's dismal picture of homicide and clearance has not changed: there were over 21,000 murders with a clearance rate around 50 percent. See "America's Declining Homicide Clearance Rates 1965–2022." We present the 2020 data because it represents the start of the current elevated murder trend and has had more time for correction of initial reporting inaccuracies.

2. The government stopped publishing data on state murder conviction rates in 2006. The last year for which public statistics are

available is 2006. At that time, there were 17,309 murders, of which 10,507 were officially cleared ("America's Declining Homicide Rates 1965-2022," https://www.murderdata.org/p/reported-homicide-clearance-rate-1980.html), and of those cleared, 6,240 resulted in a homicide conviction. See Sean Rosenmerkel, Matthew Durose, and Donald Farole Jr., "Felony Sentences in State Courts, 2006—Statistical Tables," NCJ 226846, US Department of Justice, Bureau of Justice Statistics, 2006, at 2.

3. This average is calculated by taking a five-year average (2015–2019) of the number of aggravated assault victimizations reported by the Bureau of Justice. See Rachel Morgan and Jennifer Truman, "Criminal Victimization, 2019," US Department of Justice, September 2020, table 1, chrome-extension://efaidnbmnnnibpcajpcglcle findmkaj/https://bjs.ojp.gov/content/pub/pdf/cv19.pdf. The conviction rate is calculated based on the last available state conviction numbers for aggravated assault released in 2006. Rosenmerkel, Durose, and Farole, "Felony Sentences in State Courts, 2006—Statistical Tables," Table 1.1.

4. This number is also produced by taking a five-year average. "The Criminal Justice System: Statistics," RAINN, https://www.rainn.org/statistics/criminal-justice-system; "Victims of Sexual Violence: Statistics," RAINN, https://www.rainn.org/statistics/victims-sexual-violence#:~:text=Sexual%20Violence%20Affects%20Millions%20of,year%20in%20the%20United%20States.

5. This book uses "justice failures" and "failures of justice" interchangeably to refer to a guilty person escaping deserved punishment. "Injustices" refer to those cases where an innocent person is punished or a guilty person is punished overly harshly.

"Justice" is used in its common language sense of deserved punishment, as ordinary people would use the term, rather than in its broader sense of "social jus-

tice" or "distributive justice" as some academics might use the term.

6. Paul H. Robinson, *Intuitions of Justice and the Utility of Desert* (Oxford University Press, 2013), 184.

7. Rod Brunson and Brain Wade, "Oh Hell No, We Don't Talk to Police: Insights on the Lack of Cooperation in Police Investigations of Urban Gun Violence," *Criminology and Public Policy* 18, no. 2 (July 2019): 624, https://doi.org/10.1111/1745-9133.12448.

8. "The Crisis of Cold Cases," US Department of Justice, July 10, 2019, https://www.ojp.gov/archives/ojp-blogs/2019/crisis-cold-cases. Note, this does not account for the recent murder spike starting in 2020, which has seen far more than six thousand cold cases added each year.

9. Project: Cold Case, "Uniform Crime Report for Homicides: 1965–2021," https://projectcoldcase.org/cold-case-homicide-stats/.

10. "The Crisis of Cold Cases."

11. "America's Declining Homicide Clearance Rates 1965–2020."

12. Centers for Disease Control and Prevention Wonder, "About Underlying Cause of Death, 1999–2000 Results: Deaths Occurring Through 2020."

13. According to the FBI definition, a case is cleared when an arrest is made or by exceptional means. Exceptional means is intended to capture unusual cases. Arrest rates tend to closely track standard clearance rates, but when cases that are exceptionally cleared are factored in, the clearance rate becomes significantly higher than the arrest rates. See Shima Baughman, "How Effective Are Police? The Problem of Clearance Rates and Criminal Accountability," *Alabama Law Review* 72 (April 2020): 89; see text infra at notes 17–26.

14. Datalytics, "Uniform Crime Report," https://www.ahdatalytics.com/dashboards/ucr/.

15. Rebecca Rhynhart, "Data Release: Gun Violence Clearance Rates and Case Outcomes, Office of the Controller," January 15, 2022, https://controller.phila.gov /philadelphia-audits/data-release-gun -violence-trends/.

16. Datalytics, "Uniform Crime Report."

17. Annie Sweeney and Jeremy Gorner, "Chicago Police's Homicide Clearance Rate Dips in 2020 After Improvement in Recent Years," *Chicago Tribune*, December 14, 2020, https://www.chicagotribune.com /news/criminal-justice/ct-chicago-police -2020-clearance-rates-20201215-2evyu aybxbcvxex7s4wlvrx62q-story.html; Aamer Madhani, "Chicago Police Solved Fewer than One in Six Homicides in the First Half of 2018," *USA Today*, September 21, 2018, https://www.usatoday .com/story/news/2018/09/21/chicago -police-homicide-clearance-rate-killing -murder-shooting/1368099002/.

18. Claudia Vargas, "As Gun Violence Surges in Philly, Police and DA Are Losing the Arrest Battle," NBC Philadelphia, November 13, 2020, https://www.nbc philadelphia.com/investigators/as-gun -violence-surges-in-philly-police-and -da-are-losing-the-arrest-battle/259 3744/.

19. Andy Grimm, "Half of Murder Cases Considered 'Solved' by CPD in 2021 Did Not Lead to Charges," *Chicago Sun Times*, March 31, 2022, https://chicago.suntimes .com/crime/2022/3/31/22996487/cpd -police-department-clearance-murder -solved-rate-david-brown-kim-foxx -prosecutor-charges.

20. Aki Roberts, "Explaining Differences in Homicide Clearance Rates Between Japan and the United States," *Sage Journals* 12, no. 1 (February 2018), https://doi.org /10.1177/108876790731086.

21. Virkram Dodd, "Sharp Fall in Met's Conviction Rate for Rape and Murder," *The Guardian*, May 17, 2018, https:// www.theguardian.com/uk-news/2018 /may/17/metropolitan-police-london -rape-murder-conviction-fall.

22. "The Criminal Justice System: Statistics, Rape, Abuse, & Incest National Network," RAINN, https://www.rainn.org/statistics /criminal-justice-system.

23. Andeew Van Dam, "Less than 1% of Rapes Lead to Felony Convictions," *Washington Post*, October 6, 2018, https://www.wash ingtonpost.com/business/2018/10/06 /less-than-percent-rapes-lead-felony -convictions-least-percent-victims-face -emotional-physical-consequences/.

24. Rachel Morgan and Jennifer Truman, "Criminal Victimization: 2019," US Department of Justice, September 2020, table 1.

25. See "Data Collection: National Judicial Reporting Program (NJRP)," Bureau of Justice Statistics, 2006, https://www.bjs .gov/index.cfm?ty=dcdetail&iid=241; Baughman, "How Effective Are Police?" 47, at fn 229 at 92.

26. Rosenmerkel, Durose, and Farole, "Felony Sentences in State Courts, 2006—Statistical Tables."

27. Ibid. The low rate of convictions for aggravated assault may be due to fewer resources being devoted to non-homicide cases, as the difficulty of solving the two are commonly similar. In the case of shootings, for example, non-fatal shootings are cleared five times less often than fatal shootings. Brunson and Wade, "Oh Hell No, We Don't Talk to Police," 623: "Furthermore, in an examination of fatal and nonfatal shootings in Durham, NC, researchers found that an arrest was made in half of all gun homicides; less than 10% of nonfatal shootings, however, resulted in arrest (Cook, Ho, & Shilling, 2017). Similarly, in a study of fatal and nonfatal shootings in New Orleans, LA, researchers revealed that 53% of homicides were cleared compared with approximately one in ten nonfatal shootings (Schirmer, 2017). Differences in clearance rates are noteworthy considering that the underlying dynamics (e.g., victim–offender relationship) of fatal and nonfatal shootings are in-

credibly similar (Braga & Cook, 2018; Zimring, 1972). For instance, Queally & Friedman (2012, para. 9) aptly noted that, 'the only difference between a non-fatal shooting and a homicide might be a combination of aim, luck and a good hospital trauma ward.'"

28. The data submitted to the FBI by the state of Minnesota (https://dps.mn.gov /divisions/ooc/news-releases/Pages /BCA-Releases-2021-Uniform-Crime -Report.aspx) shows 10,967 aggravated assaults in the state in 2021. This number is a count of the crimes reported to the authorities. Victimization surveys have calculated that only 46 percent of assault victims report their victimization (https://bjs.ojp.gov/library/publica tions/criminal-victimization-2021 #:~:text=From%201993%20to%202021 %2C%20the,higher%20than%202020 %20(40%25). 46 percent of 23,841 is 10,967.

29. See the state's conviction data at "District Court Criminal Charges Data," Minnesota Judicial Branch, https://www .mncourts.gov/Help-Topics/Court-Sta tistics/District-Court-Criminal-Charges -Data.aspx, showing that 1,400 individuals were convicted of felony assault (under one of the following statutes: 609.2242.4 [528 convictions], 609.222.1 [298 convictions], 609.223.1 [271 convictions], 609.2247.2 [187 convictions], 609.221.1 [64 convictions], 609.222.2 [46 convictions], 609.221.2(a) [6 convictions]).

30. See Pamela K. Lattimore et al., "Homicide in Eight U.S. Cities: Trends, Context, and Policy Implications," US Department of Justice, December 1997, 131–33, https:// www.ojp.gov/sites/g/files/xyckuh241 /files/media/document/homicide _trends.pdf.

31. "Recidivism Among Federal Offenders: A Comprehensive Overview," United States Sentencing Commission, March 2016, 5.

32. Ibid.

33. Lattimore et al., "Homicide in Eight U.S. Cities," 133.

34. Cheryl Corley, "Massive 1-Year Rise in Homicide Rates Collided with the Pandemic in 2020," NPR News, January 6, 2021, https://www.npr.org/2021 /01/06/953254623/massive-1-year-rise -in-homicide-rates-collided-with-the -pandemic-in-2020.

35. Crime and Justice News, "Clearance Rate Drops as Homicides Rise in Big Cities," The Crime Report, December 28, 2020, https://thecrimereport.org/2020/12/28 /clearance-rate-drops-as-homicides -rise-in-big-cities/.

36. Ibid.; Mario Diaz, "Houston Homicide Numbers Continue to Skyrocket in 2022," Click2Houston, February 8, 2022, https://www.click2houston.com/news /investigates/2022/02/08/houston-homi cide-numbers-continue-to-skyrocket -in-2022/.

37. "America's Declining Homicide Clearance Rates 1965–2020."

38. Li and Lartey, "As Murders Spiked, Police Solved About Half in 2020."

39. Frank Main, "Chicago's Murder-Clearance Rate Rose Sharply in 2019, Police Say," Chicago Sun Times, December 31, 2019, https://chicago.suntimes.com /politics/2019/12/31/21044720/murder -clearance-rate-chicago-police-depart ment.

40. Joshua Vaughn, "Philly Cops Are Solving Fewer Homicide. The City Keeps Paying Them Millions," The Appeal, March 1, 2021, https://theappeal.org/philly-cops -are-solving-fewer-homicides-the-city -keeps-paying-them-millions/.

41. For example, when President Trump said in 2021 crime was increasing significantly, CNN's Facts First column announced the statement to be "misleading." "Has Crime in NYC Increased by 100% to 200%?" CNN, https://www.cnn.com /factsfirst/politics/factcheck_32e9be35 -6a60-4440-b068-0b668329cca3. In the same vein, NPR posted a headline a week

before the 2022 election that read, "Many midterm races focus on rising crime. Here's what the data does and doesn't show," with the article going on to quote their crime data expert Jeff Asher claiming that the increases in crime are really about poor data collection: "Absent that, we get a lot of politicians that are saying a lot of things that frequently are based on anecdote or sort of the vibes of the moment." Rachel Treisman, "Many Midterm Races Focus on Rising Crime. Here's What the Data Does and Doesn't Show," NPR, October 28, 2022, https://www.npr.org/2022/10/27/1131825858/us-crime-data-midterm-elections. This kind of minimization in the face of crime increases was not new with the recent election. See, for example, Matt Ford, "What Caused the Great Crime Decline in the U.S.?" *The Atlantic*, April 15, 2016, https://www.theatlantic.com/politics/archive/2016/04/what-caused-the-crime-decline/477408/. See generally Nicole Gelinas, "See No Evil: Your Guide to Minimizing the Crime Crisis," *New York Post*, December 12, 2021, https://nypost.com/2021/12/12/your-guide-to-minimizing-the-crime-crisis/.

42. Jeffrey Anderson, "Criminal Neglect," *City Journal*, October 4, 2022, https://www.city-journal.org/violent-crime-in-cities-on-the-rise. See also note 50 for a distinction between rising serious violent crime and falling violent crime.

43. Since 1960 the overall crime rate, based on FBI data, was reported through the Disaster Center of the Library of Congress, the Center ceased reporting this data after 2019. "United States Crime Rates 1960–2019," Disaster Center, https://www.disastercenter.com/crime/uscrime.htm.

44. Ibid.

45. Ryan Lucas, "FBI Data Shows an Unprecedented Spike in Murders Nationwide in 2020," NPR, September 27, 2021.

46. Gary Fields and Cameron McWhirter, "In Medical Triumph, Homicides Fall Despite Soaring Gun Violence," *The Wall Street Journal*, December 9, 2012, https://www.wsj.com/articles/SB10001424127887324712504578131360684277812.

47. Roger Dobson, "Medical Advances Mask Epidemic of Violence by Cutting Murder Rate," National Library of Medicine, September 21, 2002.

48. Centers for Disease Control and Prevention Wonder, "About Underlying Cause of Death, 1999–2000 Results: Deaths Occurring Through 2020," Center for Disease Control, https://wonder.cdc.gov/controller/datarequest/D76;jsessionid=F40BCB177B9B04859F3B1983F725.

49. Dobson, "Medical Advances Mask Epidemic of Violence by Cutting Murder Rate."

50. Moreover, the decline in overall crime rates for the past several decades conceals stagnation or reversal for several of the most severe crime categories. Declines in the violent crime rate have largely been driven by the decline in robbery. The past decade (2010–2019) saw stagnation in forcible rape rates and aggravated assaults (252.8 out of every 100,000 in 2010 compared to 250.2 in 2019). Even worse, murder rates have reversed from their recent low in 2014 (4.4) and steadily risen to 5.0 in 2019 before exploding in 2020. The United States saw the largest year-on-year increase in the murder rate ever recorded in 2020 with an increase of almost 30 percent, erasing all gains since the 1990s. Even worse, the murder rate continued to rise in 2021 (Jeff Asher, "Murder Rose by Almost 30% in 2020. It's Rising at a Slower Rate in 2021," *New York Times*, September 22, 2021). While crimes of stealing (whether robbery, burglary, or theft) seem set to continue to decline, it appears that America is not on course to return to the actual historic low of the 1940s–1960s for severe violent

crime but may be stuck with a violent crime rate more than double what it was sixty years ago. People across the country are less likely to have their homes burgled than they were a few years ago, but they are more likely to be shot and killed (David A. Graham, "America Is Having a Violence Wave, Not a Crime Wave," *The Atlantic*, September 29, 2021). In an era of steady or rising severe violent crime, the problem of failures of justice could not be more salient.

51. Brandon L. Garrett and Gregory Mitchell, "Error Aversions and Due Process," January 12, 2022, 2.

52. See, for example, Paul H. Robinson and Sarah Robinson, *Crimes that Changed Our World: Tragedy, Outrage and Reform* (Rowman & Littlefield, 2018), 183.

53. See, for example, Mark Lungariello, "Angry Mob Beats Man to Death for Allegedly Hitting Pregnant Girlfriend: Report," *New York Post*, June 15, 2021, https://nypost.com/2021/06/15/angry-mob-beats-utah-man-to-death-for-allegedly-hitting-pregnant-girlfriend/; Jeff Tavss, "Details Released After Man Beaten to Death by Group in Magna," Fox 13, June 15, 2021, https://www.fox13now.com/news/crime/details-released-after-man-beaten-by-group-in-magna; Jax Miller, "Group Chases Down and Fatally Beats Man After He's Accused of Assaulting His Pregnant Girlfriend, Police Say," Yahoo, June 16, 2021, https://www.yahoo.com/now/group-chases-down-fatally-beats-154000296.html; Jack Longstaff, "Mob Beat Domestic Abuser to Death After He Gave His Pregnant Girlfriend a Black Eye," Metro, June 18, 2021, https://metro.co.uk/2021/06/17/mob-beat-domestic-abuser-to-death-after-he-gave-his-girlfriend-a-black-eye-14789365/.

54. See, for example, "This Is the Best Chance for Justice," *Grand Rapids Press*, December 15, 2011, A4; "Father Continues Search for Answer," *Grand Rapids Press*, December 19, 2011, A4; "Body of 1989 Murder Victim to Be Exhumed by Cold-Case Task Force," *The Muskegon Chronicle*, July 26, 2012; Heather Peters, "Slaying Victim Was Never Forgotten," *Muskegon Chronicle*, June 26, 2014; John Hausman, "Expert: Victim in '89 Murder Case Was Brutally Beaten," *The Muskegon Chronicle*, September 19, 2014.

55. Robinson and Robinson, *Crimes that Changed Our World*, 265.

56. See, for example, "Lasting Effects of Child Molestation," Oprah.com, November 5, 2010; "Molestation Victims Back Defendant's Killer," *Fort Worth Star Telegram*, April 6, 1993, 3; Mareva Brown and Nancy Vogel McClatchy, "Mother Shoots Accused Molester in Court," *Daily News of Los Angeles*, April 3, 1993; Rick Bentley, "Truth and Justice Christine Lahti Portrays Ellie Nesler, the Woman Convicted of Killing a Man Accused of Molesting Her Son," *The Fresno Bee*, June 20, 1999, J1.

57. See, for example, "Casey Anthony Found Not Guilty of First-Degree Murder," AP, July 5, 2011; "Caylee Anthony: The Untold Story," CBS News, October 17, 2009, https://www.cbsnews.com/news/caylee-anthony-the-untold-story/; Mikaela Conley, "Public Irate over Casey Anthony Verdict; Social Media Sites Explode with Opinions," ABC News, July 5, 2011, https://abcnews.go.com/Health/casey-anthony-verdict-outrage-spills-online/story?id=14002257; Katie Escherich and Lee Ferran, "Timeline: Caylee Anthony Case," ABC News, December 12, 2008, https://abcnews.go.com/GMA/TheLaw/caylee-anthony-case-timeline-autopsy-released/story?id=10909865.

58. Yung Hyeock Lee, "How Police Policies and Practices Impact Successful Crime Investigations: Factors that Enable Police Departments to 'Clear' Crimes," *Justice System Journal* 41, no. 1 (2020): 38.

59. Chapter 3 looks more carefully at how different distributive principles might have different views on the significance of failures of justice.

60. See page [6].

61. "Effects of Sexual Violence," RAINN; Van Dam, "Less than 1% of Rapes lead to Felony Convictions."

62. Dean G. Kilpatrick, "The Mental Health Impact of Rape," National Violence Against Women Prevention Research Center.

63. "Victims of Sexual Violence: Statistics," RAINN.

64. Christine Englebrecht, Derek T. Mason, and Margaret J. Adams, "The Experiences of Homicide Victims' Families with the Criminal Justice System," *Violence and Victims* 29, no. 3 (January 2014), http://dx.doi.org/10.1891/0886-6708.VV-D-12-00151.

65. Katherine Lorenz, Anne Kirkner, and Sarah E. Ullman, "Qualitative Study of Sexual Assault Survivors' Post Assault Legal System Experiences," *Trauma Dissociation* 20, no. 3 (2019): 263–87.

66. Myra Marx Ferree and Patricia Yancey Martin, *Feminist Organizations: Harvest of the New Women's Movement* (Temple University Press, 1995), 230.

67. Kaelyn Forde, "Why More Women Don't Report Sexual Assaults: A Survivor Speaks Out," ABC News, September 27, 2018, https://abcnews.go.com/US/women-report-sexual-assaults-survivor-speaks/story?id=57985818.

68. Center for Victim Research, "Losing a Loved One to Homicide: What We Know about Homicide Co-Victims from Research and Practice Evidence," Office for Victims of Crime, NCJ 253107, July 2019, 1.

69. Marilyn Peterson Armour, "Experiences of Covictims of Homicide: Implications for Research and Practice," *Trauma, Violence & Abuse* 3, no. 2 (April 2002): 109–24; Center for Victim Research, "Losing a Loved One to Homicide," 4.

70. Englebrecht, Mason, and Adams, "The Experiences of Homicide Victims' Families with the Criminal Justice System"; Forde, "Why More Women Don't Report Sexual Assaults"; Center for Victim Research, "Losing a Loved One to Homicide," 1; Armour, "Experiences of Covictims of Homicide."

71. Julia C. Martinez, "Sick and Grieving: The Toll of Unsolved Murders," *The Colorado Trust*, May 21, 2019, https://collective.coloradotrust.org/stories/sick-and-grieving-the-toll-of-unsolved-murders/.

72. Roxanna Altholz, "Living with Impunity: Unsolved Murders in Oakland and the Human Rights Impact on Victims' Family Members," International Human Rights Law Clinic & UC Berkeley School of Law, January 2020, 32.

73. Daniella Harth da Costa, Kathie Njaine, and Miriam Schenker, "Repercussions of Homicide on Victims' Families: A Literature Review," *Cien Saude Colet* 22, no. 9 (September 2017): 3092.

74. Ibid., 3091.

75. Altholz, "Living with Impunity," 12.

76. Ibid.

77. Englebrecht, "The Experiences of Homicide Victims' Families."

78. Englebrecht, "The Experiences of Homicide Victims' Families"; Da Costa et al., "Repercussions of Homicide on Victims' Families," 3088; BrenShavia Jordan, "Justin Bibles Family Fighting for Justice Three Years After Murder," KWKT FOX 44, May 3, 2021, https://www.fox44news.com/news/local-news/local/justin-bibles-family-fighting-for-justice-three-years-after-murder/.

79. Center for Victim Research, "Losing a Loved One to Homicide," 12.

80. Anton van Wijk, Henk Ferwerda, and Ilse van Leiden, "Murder and the Long-Term Impact on Co-Victims: A Qualitative, Longitudinal Study," *International Review of Victimology* 23, no. 2 (May 2017): 1–13, https://doi.org/10.1177/0269758016684.

81. Sarah Kopelovich, *Psychosocial Sequelae of Homicide Among Murder Victims' Family Members: An Appraisal of Depression, Grief, and Posttraumatic Stress* (CUNY Academic Works, 2015), 5.

82. Carroll Ann Ellis and Janice Lord, "Chapter 12: Homicide | Supplement," in *2000 National Victim Assistance Academy*, ed. Anne Seymour et al.; Center for Victim Research, "Losing a Loved One to Homicide," 12.

83. Marilyn Peterson Armour, "Journey of Family Members of Homicide Victims: A Qualitative Study of Their Posthomicide Experience," *American Journal of Orthopsychiatry* 72, no. 3 (July 2002): 372–82, https://doi.org/10.1037/0002-9432.72.3.372.

84. Englebrecht et al., "The Experiences of Homicide Victims' Families."

85. Despite the disproportionately high amount of suffering associated with failures of justice in African American communities, the available research on the effects of homicide on covictims has largely ignored this population. Altholz, "Living with Impunity," 12. It is essential that this area of research seek to better understand the severe trauma inflicted on Black communities by the failings of the criminal justice system to do justice.

86. Martinez, "Sick and Grieving: The Toll of Unsolved Murders."

87. Ibid.

88. Ibid.

89. Ibid.

90. Shima Baradaran Baughman, "Crime and the Mythology of Police," *Washington University Law Review* 99 (May 2021): 65. Shawn Blue, "A History of Injustice—Coping with Racial Trauma," Thomas Jefferson University, June 18, 2020, nexus.jefferson.edu/health/a-history-of-injustice-coping-with-racial-trauma.

91. This issue is explored in greater depth in chapter 14 on the topic of legal cynicism.

92. "New Research Examines the Cost of Crime in the U.S., Estimated to Be $2.6 Trillion in a Single Year," *VanderbiltNews*, February 5, 2021, https://news.vanderbilt.edu/2021/02/05/new-research-examines-the-cost-of-crime-in-the-u-s-estimated-to-be-2-6-trillion-in-a-single-year/#:~:text=Cohen%2C%20along%20with%20research%20team,financial%20impact%20of%20%242.6%20trillion. One NCBI estimate of the societal cost of specific crimes on average placed murder at 8,982,907 USD; rape: 240,776 USD; assault: 107,020 USD; and robbery: 42,310 USD. See Kathryn E. McCollister, "The Cost of Crime to Society: New Crime-Specific Estimates for Policy and Program Evaluation," The National Center for Biotechnology Information, 2011.

93. Paul H. Robinson, "The Moral Vigilante and Her Cousin in the Shadows," *University of Illinois Law Review* (2015): 401.

94. Thomas Hogan, "A Deadly Team," *City Journal*, November 29, 2021, https://www.city-journal.org/article/a-deadly-team.

95. Paul H. Robinson and Sarah M. Robinson, *Pirates, Prisoners, and Lepers: Lessons from Life Outside the Law* (University of Nebraska Press, 2015), 141–48.

96. Robinson, "The Moral Vigilante and Her Cousin in the Shadows," 404.

97. Paul H. Robinson and Sarah Robinson, *Shadow Vigilantes: How Distrust in the Justice System Breeds a New Kind of Lawlessness* (Prometheus Books, 2018), 133.

98. Robinson, "The Moral Vigilante and Her Cousin in the Shadows."

99. Ibid., 54.

100. Ibid., 2.

101. Chase Sackett, "Neighborhoods and Violent Crime," Office of Policy Development and Research, Summer 2016, https://www.huduser.gov/portal/periodicals/em/summer16/highlight2.html.

102. Erika Harrell et al., "Household Poverty and Nonfatal Violent Victimization, 2008–2012," US Department of Justice, https://bjs.ojp.gov/content/pub/pdf/hpnvv0812.pdf: Office of Justice Programs: Bureau of Justice Statistics, November 2014, figure 3. See also Melissa S. Kearney and Benjamin H. Harris, "The Unequal Burden of Crime and

Incarceration on America's Poor," The Hamilton Project.

103. GianCarlo Canapro and Abby Kassal, "Who Suffers the Most from Crime Wave," The Heritage Foundation, April 12, 2022, https://www.heritage.org /crime-and-justice/commentary/who -suffers-the-most-crime-wave.

104. Zolan Kanno-Youngs and Coulter Joines, "New York City Murders Drop, but Most Go Unsolved in Poor Neighborhoods," *The Wall Street Journal*, January 31, 2019, https://www.wsj.com /articles/new-york-city-has-record-low -crime-but-in-some-neighborhoods -most-murders-go-unsolved-1154 8936000.

105. "Black Murders Accounted for all of America's Clearance Decline," Murder Accountability Project, February 18, 2019.

106. Robert VanBruggen, "An Update on America's Homicide Search," *City Journal*, January 25, 2023, https://www.city -journal.org/update-on-americas-ho micide-surge.

107. "Number of Murder Victims in the United States in 2022, by Race," Statista, October 20, 2023, https://www.statista .com/statistics/251877/murder-victims -in-the-us-by-race-ethnicity-and -gender/.

108. "These Are Nine Stories from America's Homicide Crisis," *Washington Post*, November 27, 2022, https://www-wash ingtonpost-com.proxy.library.upenn .edu/nation/interactive/2022/america -homicide-victim-stories/n/interac tive/2022/america-homicide-victim -stories/; James Freeman, "Bloody Blue Cities," *The Wall Street Journal*, November 28, 2022, https://www.wsj.com/ar ticles/bloody-blue-cities-11669674866.

109. German Lopez, "There's a Nearly 40 Percent Chance You'll Get Away with Murder in America," Vox, September 24, 2018, https://www.vox.com/2018 /9/24/17896034/murder-crime-clear ance-fbi-report.

110. Conor Friedersdorf, "Criminal Justice Reformers Chose the Wrong Slogan," *The Atlantic*, August 8, 2021, https:// www.theatlantic.com/ideas/archive /2021/08/instead-of-defund-the-police -solve-all-murders/619672/.

111. Josiah Bates, "LaTanya Gordon Lost Two Sons to Gun Violence in Three Months," *Time*, July 16, 2021, https:// time.com/5944949/gun-crime-shoot ings-police-unsolved-cases/.

112. "Black Murders Accounted for All of America's Clearance Decline," Murder Accountability Project.

113. Douglas J. Gagnon and Marybeth J. Mattingly, "Most U.S. School Districts Have Low Access to School Counselors," University of New Hampshire Carsey Research, Fall 2016.

114. "Poor Health: Poverty and Scarce Medical Resources in US Cities," *Pittsburgh Post-Gazette*, June 14, 2014, https://www.post-gazette.com/news /health/2014/06/15/Poor-Health-Pov erty-and-scarce-medical-resource-in -U-S-cities/stories/201406150218.

115. Jennifer Tolbert, Kendal Orgera, and Anthony Damico, "Key Facts about the Uninsured Population," Kaiser Family Foundation, November 6, 2020.

116. Part of the problem, as discussed further in parts II and III of this volume, is an obsession with procedural correctness. The criminal justice system seems devoted primarily to preventing false convictions even if it means letting criminals go free, a view epitomized by William Blackstone's famous ratio, "It is better that ten guilty persons escape than that one innocent suffer." The concern is admirable, but when it moves to the level of obsession, where it ignores all costs, including significant and dramatic failures of justice in serious cases, it becomes unwise and threatens serious long-term consequences, including lost moral credibility, and will do more societal damage than good. As noted earlier (see note 57), Blackstone's fa-

mous ratio does not reflect the view of most people in society, who view false acquittals and false convictions as errors of similar magnitude. The legal system's extraordinary focus on avoiding injustice while ignoring justice failures needs rethinking.

117. See, for example, Robinson and Robinson, *Shadow Vigilantes*, 254–55.
118. Ibid., 265–66.
119. Ibid., 259–60.
120. See, for example, "3 Men Charged in Fatal Beating on North Side," *Columbus Dispatch*, September 16, 2003; "A Deadly Year In Columbus—Part 4 Of 4," *Columbus Dispatch*, January 4, 2004; Bruce Cadwallader, "Evidence Excluded in Murder Trial of Trio—Judge Rules Police Used Faulty Warrant to Find Bloody Jeans," *Columbus Dispatch*, June 15, 2004; Bruce Cadwallader, "Trio Acquitted of Murder Charges in Beating Death," *Columbus Dispatch*, June 19, 2004.
121. Cadwallader, "Trio Acquitted of Murder Charges."
122. See, for example, John Bacon, "Judge Apologizes for Teen Rape Remarks, Not Sentence," *USA Today*, August 28, 2013, https://www.usatoday.com/story/news/nation/2013/08/28/teacher-rape-montana/2722817/; Christina Ng and Anthony Castellano, "Montana Rapist Freed After 30 Days," ABC News, September 26, 2013, https://abcnews.go.com/US/montana-rapist-freed-30-days/story?id=20379760; State of Montana, Plaintiff and Appellant, v. Stacey Dean Rambold, Defendant and Appellee.
123. Bacon, "Judge Apologizes for Teen Rape Remarks."
124. Ibid.
125. Ibid.
126. See, for example, Robinson and Robinson, *Shadow Vigilantes*, 253–54.
127. See, for example, Malinda Seymore, "Appellate Reversal for Insufficient Evidence in Criminal Cases: The Interaction of the Proof and the Jury Charge," *American Journal of Criminal Law* 16, no. 2 (Winter 1989): 161; Joyce Lee Lewis Garrett v. State Texas, 656 S.W.2d 97 (1983).
128. Other such cases include:

• Arthur Huey. In the early 1990s, Arthur Huey is a major marijuana distributor in Louisiana, but the law catches up with him. During the jury screening phase prior to the trial, Huey's counsel seeks to exclude six prospective jurors from the pool because they are African American or Hispanic, and some of the phone calls that will be used as evidence record Huey using racial slurs. When the prospective jurors are asked about the issue, all respond they will not be prejudiced by the racial epithets, and so none are excluded from the jury pool. Huey's counsel then uses his peremptory challenges to remove five of the jurors solely because of their race. When Huey is convicted on all charges, he files an appeal complaining that the jury selection process was improper because African American jurors were excluded solely due to their race. Even though this was entirely Huey's own doing and could not have prejudiced the trial against him, the US Court of Appeals for the Fifth Circuit disregards Huey's obvious guilt and overturns all convictions against him on the basis that he did not get a fair trial. (United States v. Huey, 76 F.3d 638 (5th Cir. 1996).)
• Alonzo King. On April 10, 2009, Alonzo King is arrested in Wicomico County, Maryland, on assault charges. In accordance with state law, his DNA is taken with a cheek swab and uploaded to the state database. King is convicted on the assault charge, and police later realize his DNA matches that from an unsolved rape in 2003. King is tried for the rape, convicted, and sentenced to life in prison. An appeals court overturns his conviction on the basis that taking his DNA upon his arrest but before his conviction was an illegal seizure. With no other evidence tying him to the crime, King goes free. (King v. State Court of Appeals of Maryland,

April 24, 2012, Filed No. 68, September Term, 2011.)

- Freeman and Metz. In 1999, Charles Freeman and Joseph Metz are drug dealers in West Virginia when Metz's mother and grandmother accidentally discover their illegal operation. Metz and Freeman kill the two women and hide their bodies. In 2013, the men are finally arrested for the murders, but the special magistrate issuing the arrest warrants once worked as a police officer on the same murder investigation in 1999. To avoid the appearance of impropriety, prosecutors dismiss the charges, and the murderers walk free. (See, for example, Robinson and Robinson, *Shadow Vigilantes*.)
- Howard Chisvin. On July 21, 2011, Ontario Judge Howard Chisvin returns unexpectedly from a recess to a courtroom of criminals waiting to plead guilty or be sentenced. The only person missing is the prosecutor, Brian McCallion, who is delayed reading a presentencing report. Chisvin is stressed today and in no mood to wait. He barks at the clerk to page the prosecutor and tell him he has thirty seconds to show up. After 127 seconds pass, Chisvin angrily dismisses the charges against the entire docket of criminals. When McCallion shows up a few minutes later, he apologizes for not hearing his pager, but Chisvin will have none of it. "Court comes when court is back," he growls. "They're dismissed for want of prosecution." The entire docket of grateful criminals, including domestic abusers, robbers, and fraudsters, walk free because one judge wishes to punish a prosecutor's minor tardiness. (See, for example, Kirk Makin, "Ontario Judge Blasted for Freeing Defendants Over Tardy Prosecutor," *The Globe and Mail*, March 19, 2012; Curtis Rush, "Judge Faces Disciplinary Hearing for Throwing Out Tardy Crown's Cases," *Toronto Star*, October 18, 2012; Christie Blatchford, "Ontario Judge Lets Perps Walk," *National Post*, July 21, 2011; Christie Blatchford, "Personal Stresses No Excuse for Tossing Guilty Pleas Over Late Prosecutor: Panel Reprimands Ontario Judge," November 26, 2016; Curtis Rush, "Judge Faces Disciplinary Hearing

for Throwing Out Tardy Crown's Cases" *Toronto Star*, October 18, 2012.)
- Lee Curtis Davis. In 1985, Florida resident Lee Curtis Davis rapes a wheelchair-bound thirteen-year-old girl with muscular dystrophy. Despite being unable to stop her attacker, the girl screams and feebly uses her arms to try to push him away, but he easily rapes her twice. Davis is charged with rape against a physically helpless victim, convicted, and sentenced to life in prison. Davis appeals based on the fact that Florida law defines a physically helpless victim "as asleep, unconscious, or physically unable to communicate her unwillingness to the act." Davis argues his victim was able to communicate her unwillingness, and so his conviction was technically incorrect. An appeals court agrees and overturns Davis's conviction despite the judges acknowledging Davis's obvious guilt and knowing double jeopardy will bar him from being retried for rape. Davis walks free. (See, for example, Bob Greene, "System of Justice Is Helpless, Too," *Chicago Tribune*, May 10, 1989; Chuck Murphy, Bruce Vielmetti, et al., "It Probably Makes for Better Law Enforcement," *St. Petersburg Times*, December 6, 1991.)

CHAPTER 2

1. Paul H. Robinson and Michael T. Cahill, *Criminal Law* (Wolters Kluwer Law & Business, 2012), 406.
2. See, for example, Andrew Tobias, "Ohio Senators Hear Testimony on Bill that Would Eliminate Statute of Limitation on Rape," *Ohio Politics*, February 19, 2020, https://www.cleveland.com/open /2020/02/ohio-senators-hear-testimony -on-bill-that-would-eliminate-statute-of -limitations-on-rape.html; "RAINN's Recommendations for Effective Sex Crime Statutes of Limitation," Rape Abuse & Incest National Network.
3. See Ruth Padawer, "Should Statutes of Limitation for Rape Be Abolished?" *New York Times*, June 19, 2018, https://www .nytimes.com/2018/06/19/magazine /should-statutes-of-limitation-for-rape

-be-abolished.html; "Woman Hopes to Revive Bill Eliminating Time Limits for Sex Crimes," *The News Times*, June 11, 2007, https://www.newstimes.com/news/article/Woman-hopes-to-revive-bill-eliminating-time-63749.php; John Murray, "To Catch a Monster," *The Waterbury Observer*, November 1, 2004, https://www.waterburyobserver.org/wod7/node/2243.

4. The case is derived from the following references: "Cook County Sheriff's Police Department Report," Cook Country Sheriff's Office, March 17, 1978; Paul H. Robinson and Michael T. Cahill, *Law Without Justice: Why Criminal Law Doesn't Give People What They Deserve* (Oxford University Press, 2006), 53.

5. Matt DeLisi, Mark Ruelas, and James E. Kruse, "Who Will Kill Again? The Forensic Value of 1st Degree Murder Convictions," *Forensic Science International: Synergy* 1, no. 1 (2019): 11–17. "In conclusion, the United States is in the midst of an emerging justice paradigm where cold cases—often decades old—are being solved with the proliferation of genetic data that are publicly available (cf., [71,72]. A non-trivial number of these offenders had 1st degree murder arrests or convictions in their offending history."

6. Science has changed statutory bars to prosecution in the past such as with the repeal of the "year and a day rule," which prevented a murder conviction if the victim died over a year after the violent act. Due to modern science, determining the cause of death is easier today and all states besides Alabama have either abolished or amended the rule to prevent failures of justice caused by it. See, for example, California Penal Code § 194, California Office of Legislative Counsel, January 1, 1997.

7. Paul H. Robinson and Tyler S. Williams, *Mapping American Criminal Law: Variations Across the 50 States*, first edition (Praeger Publishing, 2018), 183.

8. Ibid.

9. "Five Things that Make an Effective Statute of Limitations," Rape, Abuse & Incest National Network, https://www.rainn.org/articles/five-things-make-effective-statute-limitations.

10. See "RAINN's Recommendations for Effective Sex Crime Statutes of Limitation."

11. Padawer, "Should Statutes of Limitation for Rape Be Abolished?" Washington State has a ten-year statute of limitations for rape, but if the victim does report within a year of the crime occurring, the time a prosecutor has to bring charges is reduced to three years. Ten states—California, Delaware, Illinois, Kentucky, Maryland, North Carolina, South Carolina, Virginia, West Virginia, and Wyoming—have no time limit for filing charges for all or nearly all felony sexual assaults, no matter the victim's age at the time of the crime.

12. Charles Doyle, Cong. Rsch. Serv., RL31253, Statue of Limitation in Federal Criminal Cases: An Overview, 2017.

13. "State by State Guide on Statutes of Limitation," Rape, Abuse & Incest National Network, https://www.rainn.org/statutes-limitations.

14. Ibid.

15. Padawer, "Should Statutes of Limitation for Rape Be Abolished?" Brandon Smith, "Bill to Eliminate Statute of Limitations for All Sex Crimes Significantly Scaled Back," WFYI, Jan. 20, 2024, https://www.wfyi.org/news/articles/bill-to-eliminate-statute-of-limitations-for-all-sex-crimes-significantly-scaled-back.

16. See, for example, Model Penal Code 1.06(3)(a)-(b); Fla. Stat. Ann. 775.15(4); Robinson and Cahill, *Criminal Law*.

17. A. J. Vicens and Jordan Michael Smith, "Map: How Long Does Your State Give Rape Survivors to Pursue Justice?" *Mother Jones*, November 24, 2014, https://www.motherjones.com/politics/2014/11/rape-statutes-of-limitation-maps-table/.

18. Conn. CT Gen Stat § 54-193b (2018).

19. Findlaw Staff, "Time Limits for Charges: State Criminal Statutes of Limitation," FindLaw, last modified November 16,

2022, https://www.findlaw.com/criminal/criminal-law-basics/time-limits-for-charges-state-criminal-statutes-of-limitations.html.

20. "Increasing Victims' Access to Justice: The Statute of Limitations and the Prosecution of Sexual Assault Cases," The National Center for Victims of Crime, https://evawintl.org/wp-content/uploads/exceptions-to-sol.pdf.

21. TN Code § 40-2-103 (2021).

22. "Criminal Statutes of Limitations Maine," Rape, Abuse & Incest National Network, April 2023, https://apps.rainn.org/policy/policy-crime-definitions.cfm?state=Maine&group=7&ga=2.103291072.1396645413.1692963405-1807829930.1690212196.

23. "Criminal Statutes of Limitations: Time Limits for State Charges," LawInfo.com, January 3, 2023, https://www.lawinfo.com/resources/criminal-defense/criminal-statute-limitations-time-limits.html#colorado.

24. "Increasing Victims' Access to Justice."

25. See, for example, Andrew J. Tobias, "Ohio Senators Hear Testimony on Bill that Would Eliminate Statute of Limitations On Rape," Cleveland.com, February 19, 2020, https://www.cleveland.com/open/2020/02/ohio-senators-hear-testimony-on-bill-that-would-eliminate-statute-of-limitations-on-rape.html.

26. Sarah Buduson and Mark Ackerman, "Despite DNA Evidence, Statute of Limitation Prevents Prosecution of Ohio Rape Cases," ABC News 5 Cleveland, January 15, 2020, https://www.news5cleveland.com/news/local-news/investigations/despite-dna-evidence-statute-of-limitations-prevents-prosecution-of-ohio-rape-cases.

27. Hannah Giorgis, "The Biggest Deterrent to Reporting Child Sexual Abuse," *The Atlantic*, June 26, 2019, https://www.theatlantic.com/entertainment/archive/2019/06/fixing-statute-limitation-laws-child-sexual-abuse/592627/.

28. Michael Dolce, "Congress Should Expunge Statutes of Limitations on Child Sexual Assault—Nationwide," Newsweek, July 20, 2020, https://www.newsweek.com/statutes-limitation-child-sexual-assault-repeal-nationwide-1519179.

29. Nora G. Hertel, "Is This the Year Minnesota Gets Rid of the Statute of Limitation on Sexual Assault?" *St. Cloud Times*, March 31, 2021, https://www.sctimes.com/story/news/2021/03/31/year-minnesota-gets-rid-statute-limitation-sexual-assault-rape-time-limit/7053878002/.

30. Padawer, "Should Statutes of Limitation for Rape Be Abolished?"

31. Robin Abcarian, "Bill Cosby Is Out of Prison. What Does that Mean for His Dozens of Accusers?" *Los Angeles Times*, July 4, 2021, https://www.latimes.com/opinion/story/2021-07-04/column-bill-cosby-is-out-of-prison-what-does-that-mean-for-his-dozens-of-accusers.

32. Padawer, "Should Statutes of Limitation for Rape Be Abolished?"

33. Ibid.

34. Courtney Spinelli, "Illinois Removes Statute of Limitation for Sex Crimes," KWQC, July 29, 2019, https://www.kwqc.com/content/news/Illinois-lifts-statutes-of-limitation-for-sex-crimes-513365041.html#:~:text=Original%207%2F29%2F19%20at%207%3A22%20p.m.&text=1%2C%202020%2C%20will%20eliminate%20a,as%20well%20as%20public%20safety.

35. Padawer, "Should Statutes of Limitation for Rape Be Abolished?"

36. US Congress Senate, No Time Limit for Justice Act. S. 3107. 117th Cong., 1st sess., October 28, 2021, https://www.govinfo.gov/app/details/BILLS-117s3107is.

37. "Increasing Victims' Access to Justice."

38. Ibid.

39. Ibid.

40. Emily Clarke, "Tolling Time: How John Doe DNA Indictments Are Skirting Statutes of Limitation and Crippling the

Criminal Justice System," Georgetown University Law Center, 2019.

41. See "RAINN's Recommendations for Effective Sex Crime Statutes of Limitation," Rape Abuse & Incest National Network (describing the various state statutes of limitations).

42. Court of Justice of the European Union, Limitation Rules in Criminal Matters, May 2017, Research Note, https://curia.europa.eu/jcms/upload/docs/application/pdf/2019-12/ndr-2017-005_synthese_en_neutralisee_finale.pdf.

43. Paul H. Robinson, "The Moral Vigilante and Her Cousins in the Shadows," *University of Illinois L. Review* (2015): 443.

44. Ibid.; US Const. amend. V.

45. Interestingly, where the defendant has previously been charged with the crime but ultimately convicted only for a lesser offense, the jury's rejection of the more serious offense is treated as an acquittal. Robinson, "The Moral Vigilante and Her Cousins in the Shadows," 443. On the other hand, conviction for an assault does not prohibit subsequent conviction for homicide when the victim later dies. See US v. Peel 595 F.3d 763, 167 (7th Cir. 2010).

46. Kenneth G. Coffin, "Double Take: Evaluating Double Jeopardy Reform," *Notre Dame Law Review* 85 (2010): 772 (see note 11).

47. Robinson, "The Moral Vigilante and Her Cousins in the Shadows," 443; Evans v. Michigan, 568 US 313, (2013) (holding that a midtrial directed verdict and dismissal, based on a trial court's erroneous requirement of an extra element for the charged offense, was an acquittal for double jeopardy purposes).

48. National Institute of Justice, NCJ 200005 Advancing Justice Through DNA Technology (2003); Paul H. Roberts, "Double Jeopardy Law Reform: A Criminal Justice Commentary," *The Modern Law Review* 65, no. 3 (2002): 393–420.

49. Kyden Creekpaum, "What's Wrong with a Little More Double Jeopardy? A 21st Century Recalibration of an Ancient Individual Right," *American Criminal Law Review* 44 (2007): 1180.

50. Susan Craighead, "Attorney's Slip of the Tongue Led to Break in Schaefer Case," *Courier-Journal*, March 1, 1990, 1A; Susan Craighead, "Family Urge Bond Be Set at Affordable Level," *Courier-Journal*, February 1, 1990; Bob Hill, *Double Jeopardy: Obsession, Murder, and Justice Denied*, first edition (William Morrow & Co. 1995., 1995).

51. Pat Reavy, "Acquitted Man Says He's Guilty," *Desert News*, January 19, 2006, https://www.deseret.com/2006/1/19/19933580/acquitted-man-says-he-s-guilty; Ted Rowlands, "Mom: I Let My Son's Killer Go Free," CNN.com, January 18, 2006, http://www.cnn.com/2006/LAW/01/17/btsc.rowlands/; Pat Reavy, "Coroner Sad Boy's Death Is Unpunished," *Desert News*, January 20, 2006, https://www.deseret.com/2006/1/20/19933768/coroner-sad-boy-s-death-is-unpunished.

52. Defendants are allowed to petition for a new trial in several states: see Texas Statutes & Codes Title 1 Code of Criminal Procedure of 1965 (Arts. 1.01–67.305), Proceedings After Verdict Chapter 40 New Trials (Arts. 40.001–40.11), New Trial on Material Evidence, "A new trial shall be granted an accused where material evidence favorable to the accused has been discovered since trial."

53. Creekpaum, "What's Wrong with a Little More Double Jeopardy?" 1189.

54. Ibid.

55. Ibid.

56. Ibid.

57. Brian Reaves, "State Court Processing Statistics: Felony Defendants in Large Urban Counties, 2009—Statistical Tables," US Department of Justice: Office of Justice Programs.

58. Ibid., table 21.

59. This precedent was recently reestablished in 2019 with *Gamble v. United States*, which allowed the defendant Terance

Martez Gamble to be charged with possession of a firearm in both Alabama court and federal court. This exception has been argued in appellate court dozens of times in the last century alone. See Gamble v. United States, 587 US (2019).

60. On appeal to the US Supreme Court, it was held that where the evidence has met the test of legal sufficiency as established in *Jackson v. Virginia*, but the court reviewing the jury's verdict finds it against the weight of the evidence, a new trial is not barred by the double jeopardy clause. Tibbs v. Florida, 102 S. Ct. 2211 (1982); Covert James Geary, "Double Jeopardy—Retrial After Reversal of a Conviction on Evidentiary Grounds," *Louisiana Law Review* 43, no. 4 (March 1983), https://digitalcommons.law.lsu.edu/lalrev/vol43/iss4/11.

61. Robinson, "The Moral Vigilante and Her Cousins in the Shadows," 443.

62. Ann Marie Dorning, "Double Jeopardy: Getting Away with Murder," ABC News, August 4, 2011, https://abcnews.go.com/US/double-jeopardy-murder/story?id=14230469.

63. Mark White, "How Scrapping Double Jeopardy Has Brought Killers to Justice," *Sky News*, February 24, 2019, https://news.sky.com/story/how-scrapping-double-jeopardy-has-brought-killers-to-justice-11646468.

64. Shemir Wiles, "Column: Till's Murderers Shouldn't Have Gone Free," *The Oracle*, April 5, 2007, https://www.usforacle.com/2007/04/05/tills-murderers-shouldnt-have-gone-free/.

65. Dorning, "Double Jeopardy."

66. Ibid.

67. White, "How Scrapping Double Jeopardy Has Brought Killers to Justice."

68. Ibid.

69. Justin W. Curtis, "Allen Chair Symposium: The Role of the Death Penalty in America: Reflections, Perceptions, and Reform: Comment: The Meaning of Life (or Limb): An Originalist Proposal for Double Jeopardy Reform," *University of*

Richmond Law Review 41, no. 4 (May 2007): 991.

70. "Retrial of Serious Offenses," The Crown Prosecution Service, 2017, https://www.cps.gov.uk/legal-guidance/retrial-serious-offences.

71. Curtis, "Allen Chair Symposium."

72. Caroline Derry, "What Is Double Jeopardy?" The Open University, August 30, 2019, https://www.open.edu/openlearn/society-politics-law/law/what-double-jeopardy.

73. Mark Williams-Thomas, "Cold Case Killer," *The People*, April 19, 2020, 8.

74. Paul Roberts, "Double Jeopardy Law Reform: A Criminal Justice Commentary," *The Modern Law Review* 65, no. 3 (May 2002): 393–424; "Can I Be Tried Twice for the Same Crime in Canada?" *Alberta Legal*, March 22, 2021.

75. Criminal Justice Act 2003, UK Public General Acts, https://www.legislation.gov.uk/ukpga/2003/44/contents.

76. Curtis, "Allen Chair Symposium."

77. Robinson and Cahill, *Law Without Justice*.

78. Paul H. Robinson and Sarah Robinson, *Shadow Vigilantes: How Distrust in the Justice System Breeds a New Kind of Lawlessness* (Prometheus Books, 2018), 86.

79. Robert Ferrigno, "There's Also a Short Arm of the Law," *Chicago Tribune*, September 27, 1987, 1C; Jo-Ann Moriarty, *States News Service*, June 25, 1987; Interview by Lynn Sherr of 20/20 with Chuck Ashman.

80. Joshua E. Keating, "Can You Get Away with Any Crime If You Have Diplomatic Immunity?" *Foreign Policy*, February 15, 2011, https://foreignpolicy.com/2011/02/15/can-you-get-away-with-any-crime-if-you-have-diplomatic-immunity/.

81. Robinson and Cahill, *Law Without Justice*, 200.

82. Ibid.

83. Tisha Thompson, "Secret Crimes: How the Dept. of State Is Classifying and Covering Up Violent Crimes Committed in the US," NBC4 Washington, March 16, 2016.

https://www.nbcwashington.com/news /local/secret-crimes-how-department-of -state-is-classifying-covering-up-violent -crimes-committed-in-the-us/657% E2%80%A6.

84. Ibid.

85. S. R. Subramanian, "Abuse of Diplomatic Privileges and the Balance between Immunities and the Duty to Respect the Local Laws and Regulations under the Vienna Conventions: The Recent Indian Experience," *The Chinese Journal of Global Governance* 3 (2017): 182–233.

86. Nathaniel Reed, "A Call for the Reform of Diplomatic Immunity," *The Prindle Post*, March 5, 2018, https://www.prindle post.org/2018/03/call-reform-diplo matic-immunity/.

87. Rina Goldenberg, "Abuse of Diplomatic Immunity: Is the Government Doing Enough?" *ILSA Journal of International & Comparative Law* 1, no. 1 (1995).

88. Robert Longley, "Is Diplomatic Immunity a 'License to Kill?'" ThoughtCo, October 14, 2019.

89. Melissa Chan, "A Teen's Death Has Put Diplomatic Immunity Under a Spotlight," *TIME*, October 9, 2019, https:// time.com/5696300/diplomatic-immu nity-harry-dunn/.

90. Alison Pert, "Diplomatic Immunity: Time to Change the Rules," *The Interpreter*, October 15, 2019, https://www .lowyinstitute.org/the-interpreter/diplo matic-immunity-time-change-rules.

91. Jennifer Hassan, "Boris Johnson Says He and Biden Are 'Working Together' on Case of Harry Dunn," *Washington Post*, June 11, 2021, https://www.washington post.com/world/2021/06/11/harry-dunn -case-biden-johnson/.

92. Chan, "A Teen's Death Has Put Diplomatic Immunity Under a Spotlight."

93. Ibid.

94. Agence France-Presse, "Belgium Ambassador's Wife Invokes Immunity Over Seoul Assault Claims," *The Guardian*, May 17, 2021, https://www.theguardian .com/world/2021/may/17/belgium-am bassadors-wife-invokes-immunity -over-seoul-assault-claims.

95. Mitchell S. Ross, "Rethinking Diplomatic Immunity: A Review of Remedial Approaches to Address the Abuses of Diplomatic Privileges and Immunities," *American University International Law Review* 4, no. 1 (1989): 173–205.

96. Thompson, "Secret Crimes."

97. "Q&A: The International Criminal Court and the United States," Human Rights Watch, https://www.hrw.or /news/2020/09/02/qa-international -criminal-court-and-united-states#2.

98. Goldenberg, "Abuse of Diplomatic Immunity."

99. Ibid.

100. Ibid.

101. Karen Brettell, "Analysis: As Sanctions 'Weaponize' U.S. Dollar, Some Treasury Buyers Could Fall Back," Reuters, March 29, 2022, https://www.reuters.com /business/finance/sanctions-weaponize -us-dollar-some-treasury-buyers-could -fall-back-2022-03-29/.

102. "Denied Persons & Specially Designated Nationals," Federal Register, https:// www.federalregister.gov/denied-per sons-specially-designated-nationals.

103. Under our proposal, sanctioning diplomats would not require special approval from Congress but would be statutorily vested with the executive who would be tasked with implementing such sanctions in accordance with the guidelines mentioned earlier.

104. Tom Ruys, "Sanctions, Retorsions and Countermeasures: Concepts and International Legal Framework," Research Handbook on UN Sanctions and International Law, April 2016.

105. Nullum crimen sine lege, Cornell Law School, last accessed February 2, 2023, https://www.law.cornell.edu/wex/nul lum_crimen_sine_lege.

106. Robinson and Cahill, *Law Without Justice*, 64.

107. Ibid.

108. Paul H. Robinson, "Criminal Law's Core Principles," *Washington University Jurisprudence Review* 14 (2021): 155, 157.

109. Paul H. Robinson, "Fair Notice and Adjudication: Two Kinds of Legality," *University of Pennsylvania Law Review* 154, no. 2 (December 2005): 335–98.

110. Erin McClam, "The Living Remain Strangers in a Town of Uncremated Dead; Georgia's Community Is Really a Strip of Road," *Record*, March 23, 2002; Sara Rimer, "Dazed by Crematory Scandal, Undertakers' Trust Is Shaken," *New York Times*, February 21, 2002, https://www.nytimes.com/2002/02/21/us/dazed-by-crematory-scandal-undertakers-trust-is-shaken.html; David Firestone and Michael Moss, "More Corpses Are Discovered Near Crematory," *New York Times*, February 18, 2002, https://www.nytimes.com/2002/02/18/us/more-corpses-are-discovered-nearcrematory.html?mtrref=www.google.com&gwh=297566A6849BD8585226E16DEF802601&gwt; Sara Rimer, "Crematory Owners' Family Asks Why," *New York Times*, February 24, 2002, https://www.nytimes.com/2002/02/24/us/crematory-owners-family-asks-why.html?mtrref=www.google.com&gwh=84BB61970DE61E20209B25FF6F6D91A4&gwt.

111. United States Holocaust Memorial Museum, "Holocaust Encyclopedia: Polish Victims," June 13, 2019, https://www.ushmm.org/wlc/en/article.php?ModuleId=10005473; *Historical Review of Developments Relating to Aggression*, UN Doc. E.03.V.10 (2003); G. M. Gilbert, *Nuremberg Diary* (Da Capo Press, 1995); "World War II in Europe," The History Place, 1997, http://www.historyplace.com/worldwar2/timeline/nurem.htm; Douglas O. Linder, "The Nuremberg Trials: An Account," Famous Trials, 2007, http://www.famous-trials.com/nuremberg/1901-home.

112. Robinson and Cahill, *Criminal Law*, 64. Some American states have statutes that authorize the prosecution of uncodified common law offenses. Robinson and Cahill, *Law Without Justice*, 64. The codification requirement is a statutory one, not a constitutional one.

113. Art. 1, § 9 prohibits Congress from passing any laws that apply *ex post facto*. Art. 1 § 10 prohibits states from passing any laws that apply *ex post facto*; see "Ex Post Facto," Cornell Legal Information Institute, https://www.law.cornell.edu/wex/ex_post_facto.

114. Robinson and Cahill, *Criminal Law*, 64.

115. The Fifth Amendment says that no one shall be "deprived of life, liberty or property without due process of law," and the amendment applies to the federal government. The Fourteenth Amendment uses the same language, called the Due Process Clause, to describe a legal obligation of all states; "Due Process," Cornell Legal Information Institute, https://www.law.cornell.edu/wex/due_process#:~:text=The%20Fifth%20Amendment%20says%20to,legal%20obligation%20of%20all%20states.

116. Philip A. Dynia, "Vagueness," The First Amendment Encyclopedia, 2009, https://www.mtsu.edu/first-amendment/article/1027/vagueness.

117. 162 Cal. App. 3d 280 (1984).

118. Ibid., 283.

119. Ibid. 284.

120. Susan Barbosa, "Wheelchair Rapist's Release Expected Today," *Lakeland (FL) Ledger*, September 17, 1991.

121. Paul H. Robinson and Marcus Duber, "The American Model Penal Code: A Brief Overview," *New Criminal Law Review* 10 (2007): 319.

122. American Law Institute, "Model Penal Code: Official Draft and Explanatory Notes, Complete Text of Model Penal Code as Adopted at the 1962 Annual Meeting of the American Law Institute at Washington, D.C., Section 1.02(3)," May 24, 1962.

123. It is hard to know just how frequently the rule of strict construction is applied to frustrate justice, as in the Davis and Marsh examples earlier. Legislatures often move quickly in the aftermath of court cases to rewrite laws to more clearly criminalize conduct that has been held under the rule of strict construction as not adequately criminalized.

124. Bob Greene, "System of Justice Is Helpless, Too," *Chicago Tribune*, May 10, 1989, https://www.chicagotribune.com /news/ct-xpm-1989-05-10-8904110347 -story.html.

125. See generally Robinson and Cahill, *Criminal Law*, section 2.7, 84–85.

126. United States v. Wiltberger, 5 Wheat. 76, 95 (US 1820).

127. United States v. Brown, 333 US 18, 25-26 (1948).

128. State v. Carter, 570 P.2d 1218, 1221 (Wash. 1977).

129. See Callanan v. United States, 364 US 587, 596 (1961) ("The rule comes into operation at the end of the process of construing what Congress has expressed, not at the beginning as an overriding consideration of being lenient to wrongdoers").

130. Paul H. Robinson, Matthew Kussmaul, and Ilya Rudyak, "Report of the Delaware Criminal Law Recodification Project," Delaware Recodification Project Working Group 1, 24 (July 2017).

131. Fleming v. State, 523 S.E.2d 315 (Ga. 1999); Glover v. State, 533 S.E.2d 374 (Ga. 2000).

132. Moreover, if the Model Penal Code had been adopted, section 213.1 on rape and other offenses could have been invoked in order to convict Davis of a first-degree felony (Model Penal Code §213.1 Rape and Other Offenses).

133. Zachary Price, "The Rule of Lenity as a Rule of Structure," *Fordham Law Review* 72, no. 4 (2004): 885, 902–3, and nn.111–18.

CHAPTER 3

1. Mihailis E. Diamantis, "Invisible Victims," *Wisconsin Law Review* 2022, no. 1 (2022): 1–56.

2. Paul H. Robinson and Lindsay Holcomb, "The Criminogenic Effects of Damaging Criminal Law's Moral Credibility," *Southern California Interdisciplinary Law Journal* 31 (2022): 277, https://scholarship.law .upenn.edu/faculty_scholarship/2249.

3. Chapter 1, [pp. 11–12.]

4. Robinson and Holcomb, "The Criminogenic Effects of Damaging Criminal Law's Moral Credibility."

5. Paul H. Robinson and Markus D. Duber, "The American Model Penal Code: A Brief Overview," *Faculty Scholarship at Penn Law* (2007): 131, https://scholarship.law .upenn.edu/faculty_scholarship/131.

6. To illustrate the problem of operationalizing deontological desert, consider, for example, the issue of ranking the blameworthiness of criminal attempts. Should an unsuccessful attempt to commit a crime be graded the same as the completed substantive offense or graded as less severe because the contemplated offense harm or evil did not come about? The empirical studies make clear that nearly all ordinary people would grade the completed offense as more serious than the failed attempt because the harm or evil of the offenses actually comes about and, in their minds, this fact increases the offender's blameworthiness and deserved punishment. Nevertheless, the deontologists are split on the issue. Some agree with the community view, but many disagree, correctly pointing out that the conduct and intention of the offender are exactly the same in both cases, and it is only a matter of moral luck as to whether, say, a shooting victim is missed or killed. How is the criminal code or sentencing commission drafter to decide which of these conflicting camps to follow when they decide how to grade criminal attempts? What is the mecha-

nism that they are to use in evaluating which of these camps is "correct"?

The larger point is that any mechanism the code drafters use for endorsing one philosophical camp over another would simply illustrate the impossibility of operationalizing such a principle. If they take a vote among the moral philosophers to see which position is the majority view or if they look to see which group is made up of scholars with better reputations within the moral philosophy community, they are no longer operating under the reasoned analysis that is the draw of deontological desert.

One must conclude that deontological desert simply cannot provide the "correct" deontological desert answer. It is not in fact a workable distributive principle but rather an aspirational expression of the value of reasoned analysis and of thinking critically about criminal liability and punishment rules. While academics may cherish reasoned debate and can provide useful insights by doing so, that is something quite different from providing a distributive principle for criminal liability and punishment upon which the real world can draft a criminal code or sentencing guidelines and policy statements.

Moreover, deontological desert would not have the crime control effectiveness that empirical desert does. Unless deontological desert by chance comes out to exactly match empirical desert in its distribution of criminal liability and punishment, it will in places conflict with community-shared views and thereby undermine the criminal law's moral credibility. This would be the case, for example, if criminal code drafters adopted the deontological desert arguments in favor of punishing attempts the same as the substantive offense.

As a practical matter, empirical desert is probably the best approximation of deontological desert rules. In discussing the issue of grading attempts earlier, we saw that the deontologists are split on the

issue, while ordinary people are not. However, while the attempt grading issue is a useful example to illustrate the potential conflict between empirical and deontological desert, it is also true that on most issues the majority of moral philosophers are likely to support the community's empirical desert position. That should be no surprise, really, given that deontologists are human beings that probably share the community's intuitions of justice, even if their reasoned theoretical work may in some instances lead them to different conclusions. In our experience, most moral philosophers reviewing the results of the empirical studies on community intuitions of justice are likely to feel comfortable with most if not all of those results. Paul H. Robinson, *Distributive Principles of Criminal Law: Who Should Be Punished How Much?* (Oxford, 2008), chap. 7.

7. See Paul H. Robinson, *Intuitions of Justice and the Utility of Desert* (Oxford, 2013); Robinson, *Distributive Principles of Criminal Law*; Paul Robinson and Josh Bowers, "Perceptions of Fairness & Justice: The Shared Aims and Occasional Conflicts of Legitimacy and Moral Credibility," *Wake Forest Law Review* 47 (2012): 211; Paul Robinson, Geoff Goodwin, and Michael Reisig, "The Disutility of Injustice," *New York University Law Review* 85 (2010): 1940; Paul Robinson, "Empirical Desert," in *Criminal Law Conversations*, ed. Paul H. Robinson, Stephen Garvey, and Kimberly Kessler Ferzan (Oxford University Press, 2009), 29–39, 61–66; Paul Robinson, "Competing Conceptions of Modern Desert: Vengeful, Deontological, and Empirical," *Cambridge Law Journal* 67 (2008): 145–75; Paul Robinson and John Darley, "Intuitions of Justice: Implications for Criminal Law and Justice Policy," *Southern California Law Review* 81 (2007): 1–67; Paul Robinson and John Darley, "The Utility of Desert," *Northwestern University Law Review* 93 (1998): 453; Paul Robinson, "Why Does the Criminal Law Care What the Layperson Thinks Is

Just? Coercive vs. Normative Crime Control," *University of Virginia Law Review* 86 (2000): 1839–69.

8. Joshua Klienfeld and Hadar Dancig-Rosenberg, "Social Trust in Criminal Justice: A Metric," Northwestern Public Law Research Paper No. 22-16, February 22, 2022.

9. Kevin Carlsmith, John Darley, and Paul Robinson, "Why Do We Punish? Deterrence and Just Deserts as Motives for Punishment," *Journal of Personality and Social Psychology* 83, no. 2 (2002): 284–89, https://doi.org/10.1037/0022-3514.83.2.284.

10. Carlsmith, Darley, and Robinson, "Why Do We Punish?," 288–89.

11. Ibid., 285.

12. Ibid., 289–95.

13. Ibid., 289.

14. John Darley, Kevin Carlsmith, and Paul Robinson, "Incapacitation and Just Deserts as Motives for Punishment," *Law and Human Behavior* 24 (2000): 659.

15. Ibid., 661, 663.

16. Ibid., 661–62.

17. Ibid.

18. Ibid., 671.

19. Ibid.

20. Ibid., 672.

21. Ibid., 673.

22. Ibid., table 2.

23. Kevin M. Carlsmith, "The Roles of Retribution and Utility in Determining Punishment," *Journal of Experimental Social Psychology* 42, no. 4 (July 2006): 437. In one study from 2006, researchers found that people are intuitively drawn to desert ("retributive")-related information. In that study, subjects were given vignettes of crime and were presented with different categories of information about that crime—some with a desert bent, some with a deterrence bent, and some with an incapacitation bent. A whopping 97 percent of subjects chose to consult desert-related information rather deterrence-related information or incapacitation-related information.

When, on a second survey, the same subjects were asked to sentence the offender and rate the confidence of their choices, those who had consulted desert materials were substantially more confident in their sentencing decisions, while those who consulted general deterrence or incapacitation materials exhibited far less confidence, indicating that they believed they had made poor choices. Thus, desert instincts prevailed as the strongest and most comfortably intuitive for the subjects.

24. Dena Gromet and John Darley, "Restoration and Retribution: How Including Retributive Components Affects the Acceptability of Justice Procedures," *Social Justice Research* 19 (2006): 395. In another study from 2006, a narrower examination of people's desert impulses found that people are unlikely to endorse a system of restorative justice that lacks retributive features. The study asked subjects to read vignettes of crimes and assign the offenders to one of three courts. The first court was purely restorative, with no punitive elements; the second court was mixed; and the third was desert-based only. The authors of the study found that people generally ascribed punishment according to desert principles. For higher levels of offending such as attempted rape or murder, none of the respondents accepted a purely restorative system. As the authors explained, "These findings suggest that in order for citizens to view a restorative justice procedure as an acceptable alternative to the traditional court system for serious crimes, the procedure must allow for the option of some retributive measures."

25. Kevin Carlsmith, "On Justifying Punishment: The Discrepancy Between Words and Actions," *Social Justice Research* 21 (2008): 119. In a 2008 study, researchers found that self-reported justifications for punishment bear little relation to actual punishment-related behavior, underlying most people's subconscious incli-

nation to punish along desert grounds. Participants completed an anonymous online experimental survey in which they were asked to sentence offenders based on varying vignettes and give reasons for their sentences. Some scenarios were manipulated to encourage the participant to think about desert, while others were manipulated to encourage the participant to think about deterrence. Participants then completed two further surveys that assessed each participant's endorsement of desert, deterrence, incapacitation, and rehabilitation. The results showed that people's self-reported punishment justifications did not at all align with their actual punishment-related decisions. Even though people expressed support for deterrence-related or incapacitation policies, they abandoned these policies as soon as they realized that such policies failed to track blameworthiness proportionality.

26. Robinson, *Intuitions of Justice and the Utility of Desert*, 23–24; in-text citation of Alfred Blumestein and Jacqueline Cohen, "Sentencing of Convicted Offenders: An Analysis of the Public's View," *Law & Society Review* 14, no. 2 (Winter 1980): 223, https://doi.org/10.2307/3053313.

27. Peter H. Rossi et al., "The Seriousness of Crimes: Normative Structure and Individual Differences," *American Sociological Review* 39 (April 1974): 224; Robinson, *Intuitions of Justice and the Utility of Desert*, 24–25.

28. Charles Thomas, Robin Cage, and Samuel Foster, "Public Opinion on Criminal Law and Legal Sanctions: An Examination of Two Conceptual Models," *J. Crim. L. & Criminology* 67 (1976): 110, 112; Robinson, *Intuitions of Justice and the Utility of Desert*, 24–25.

29. Mathias Twardawski et al., "What Drives Second- and Third-Party Punishment?" *Zeitschrift für Psychologie* 230, no. 2 (April 1, 2022): 77–83, https://econtent .hogrefe.com/doi/10.1027/2151-2604 /a000454.

30. Ibid.

31. Yasuhiro Kanatogi et al., "Third-Party Punishment by Preverbal Infants," *Nature Human Behavior*, 2022, https://www .nature.com/articles/s41562-022-013 54-2.

32. Katherine McAuliffe, Jillian J. Jordan, and Felix Warneken, "Costly Third-Party Punishment in Young Children," *Cognition* 134 (2015): 1–10.

33. In addition to the studies discussed in section C.2., see, for example, the studies presented in Robinson, *Intuitions of Justice and the Utility of Desert*, chap. 9.

34. See section C.2.

35. Johnathan Casper, Tom Tyler, and Bonnie Fisher, "Procedural Justice in Felony Cases," *Law & Society Review* 22, no. 3 (1988): 487–88. In a similar 1988 study, researchers interviewed hundreds of male defendants charged with felonies shortly after their arrest and after the disposition of their case in order to determine what factors most strongly influenced their perceptions of their satisfaction with the outcome of their case. The sentences received by the men ranged from time served to a prison term. The men were asked about the severity of their sentence, which was measured by the researchers in terms of three factors: months incarcerated, sentence type, and deviation from expected sentence. This estimation of severity was compared with the results of questions regarding distributive justice—focusing on the defendant's evaluation of how his sentence compared with those of similar defendants convicted of the same crime—as well as procedural justice—focusing on the defendant's perceptions of the fairness of the process by which he was treated. The study found that the defendants had more confidence in the outcome of their case and trust in the criminal justice system where they felt that their sentence was fair.

36. Jonathan Casper, *American Criminal Justice: The Defendant's Perspective*

(Prentice Hall, 1972). In a 1972 study, dozens of defendants were interviewed by researchers about their perceptions of fairness of the sentences they received. The study found that the defendants focused most intently on the process of plea bargaining, specifically making the best possible bargain and arranging a quick release. The defendants felt that the plea bargain exemplified the "lying" and "deceitfulness" of the system writ large because sentencing depended not on deterrence, rehabilitation, or retribution but rather on the "way the bargaining game is played." They told researchers that using the plea bargain made them feel that the justice system was just "a game to be played" or a "ritual" to be performed where the smart defendants were able to totally evade punishment. Plea bargaining made the men distrustful of the system because it reminded them of the criminal environments where many of the men came from. The author of the study concluded that the effect of plea bargaining was to undercut the moral authority of the criminal justice system and contribute to defendant cynicism.

37. Two potential weaknesses in the proposed distributive principle of empirical desert are worth mentioning. First, the proposed distributive principle puts limits on the extent to which criminal law can be used to change existing norms. Second, the proposed principle requires one to be ever vigilant in testing existing norms for whether they might deserve special reform attention. See Paul H. Robinson and Lindsay Holcomb, "The Criminogenic Effect of Damaging Criminal Law's Moral Credibility," *Southern California Interdisciplinary Law Journal* 31 (2021).

38. Brandon L. Garrett and Gregory Mitchell, "Error Aversions and Due Process," *Mich. L. Rev.* 121, nos. 707, 730 (2022), https://repository.law.umich.edu/cgi/viewcontent.cgi?article=11374&context=mlr.

39. Jennifer Arlen and Lewis A. Kornhauser, "Battle for Our Souls: A Psychological Justification for Corporate and Individual Liability for Organizational Misconduct," *University of Illinois Law Review* (forthcoming): 5.

40. Paul H. Robinson, Geoffrey Goodwin, and Michael Reisig, "The Disutility of Desert," *New York University Law Review* 85 (2010): 1940.

41. Paul H. Robinson and Sarah M. Robinson, *Pirates, Prisoners, and Lepers: Lessons from Outside the Law* (Potomac Books, 2015), 139–63.

42. Steven Pinker, "Decivilization in the 1960s," *Human Figurations* 2, no. 2 (July 2013): 2, https://quod.lib.umich.edu/h/humfig/11217607.0002.206/-decivilization-in-the-1960s?rgn=main;view=fulltext. An analogous dynamic is seen in widespread resistance to the draft during the Vietnam War, which was enforced by criminal statutes requiring service. Starting in 1964, many young men fled the country or feigned injuries or illnesses in order to avoid service. Many who did not resist were nonetheless highly critical in their view of not only this particular crime—failure to report—but the criminal justice system and the government generally. This view was supported by a significant portion of the public. Polls showed a society-wide dramatic drop in trust in government. With this widespread disillusionment, crime rose significantly; crime statistics showed an enormous spike for both crimes of violence and property crimes. The Vietnam War was seen by many as exposing a moral stain on American institutions that had long been widely trusted and revered. In response to this disillusionment, many people felt free to abandon self-regulating behaviors and to commit crimes.

43. James Rolph, "Proclamation of Mayor Asks Masks for All," *San Fransisco Chronicle*, October 22, 1918, https://quod.lib.umich.edu/f/flu/1620flu.0009.261/1

/--proclamation-of-mayor-asks-masks -for-all?rgn=full+text;view=image;q1 =conscience%2C+patriotism+and+self -protection+demand+immediate+and +rigid+compliance. (San Francisco mayor James Rolph told citizens, "Conscience, patriotism and self-protection demand immediate and rigid compliance.") John Davie, "Wear Mask, Says Law, or Face Arrest," *Oakland Tribune*, October 25, 1918, https://quod.lib.umich .edu/f/flu/8540flu.0007.458/1/--wear -mask-says-law-or-face-arrest?rgn=full +text;view=image;q1=Face+Arrest. (Oakland mayor John Davie explained to his constituents: "It is sensible and patriotic, no matter what our personal beliefs may be, to safeguard our fellow citizens by joining in this practice.")

44. J. Alexander Navarro, "Mask Resistance During a Pandemic Isn't New—In 1918 Many Americans Were 'Slackers,'" *Michigan Health*, October 29, 2020, https://healthblog.uofmhealth .org/wellness-prevention/mask-resis tance-during-a-pandemic-isnt-new -1918-many-americans-were-slackers.

45. In Denver, one local newspaper reported that the order to wear a mask was "almost totally ignored by the people; in fact, the order was a cause of mirth." See "New Orders Are Issued by Officials in Flu Fight," Rocky Mountain News 1, November 26, 1918, 5, https://quod.lib.umich.edu/f/flu /2290flu.0003.922/3/--new-orders-are -issued?page=root;rgn=full+text;size =200;view=image;q1=New+Orders+are +issued. In San Francisco, two thousand members of the Anti-Mask League held a rally to denounce the mask ordinance, and in Tucson, despite widespread arrests and incarceration, the mask ordinance was intentionally disregarded. In Tucson, the local paper declared that the mask ordinance "was incapable of enforcement. No matter how many citizens the city authorities might have taken to the lock-up nor how many fines they imposed,

they never could have brought about the general observance of masking."

46. "New Orders Are Issued by Officials in Flu Fight," Rocky Mountain News.

47. David Blanke, *The 1910s* (Bloomsbury Academic, 2002).

48. See James Queally, "Watts Riot: Traffic Stop Was the Spark that Ignited Days of Destruction in L.A.," *Los Angeles Times*, July 29, 2015, https://www.latimes.com /local/lanow/la-me-ln-watts-riots-ex plainer-20150715-htmlstory.html (explaining that "anger and distrust between Watts' residents, the police, and city officials had been simmering for years" and that many Watts residents suggested that the "riot had been triggered by long-smoldering resentment against alleged police brutality"); see also Elizabeth Hinton, *From the War on Poverty to the War on Crime* (Harvard University Press, 2017), 108 (arguing that "haphazard, undisciplined, and aggressive police response only spawned an ever-more-violent reaction" and police warned that aggressive policing had backfired by "starting guerilla war in the streets").

49. "Watts Riot," Civil Rights Digital Library, last modified January 7, 2021, http://crdl .usg.edu/events/watts_riots/?Welcome.

50. Lincoln Steffens, *The Shame of the Cities* (McClure, 1904). Lincoln Steffens's essays on corruption in *McClure's Magazine* painted a dismal picture of a political system hanging on to credibility by a thread. Discussing the rampant rent-seeking practices to get legislation passed, Steffens wrote, "As there was a scale for favorable legislation, so there was one for defeating bills. It made a difference whether the privilege asked was legitimate or not. But nothing was passed free of charge."

51. Charles Ellwood, "Has Crime Increased in the United States Since 1880?" *Journal of Criminal Law & Criminology* 1, no. 3 (1910): 378.

52. Daniel Czitron, *New York Exposed: The Gilded Age Police Scandal that Launched*

the Progressive Era (Oxford University Press, 2016), 246–47; Elizabeth Garner Mazerick, "Selling Sex: 19th Century New York City Prostitution and Brothels," *The Dig*, September 3, 2017, https://digpodcast.org/2017/09/03/19th-century-new-york-city-brothels/; Margaret R. Laster and Chelsea Bruner, eds., *New York: Art and Cultural Capital of the Gilded Age* (Routledge, 2019) (explaining that despite the strenuous efforts of social reformers, "pornography constituted an insistent part of Gilded Age visual culture").

53. Dan Herbeck, "Crime Was Rampant and Routine in 19th Century New York City," *The Buffalo News*, February 10, 1991, https://buffalonews.com/news/crime-was-rampant-and-routine-in-19th-century-new-york-city/article_bee1c130-9005-5c8e-9443-a3188c1bb889.html; Herbert Asbury, "The Gangs of New York," *Vintage* 64 (2008): 232; Elaine Abelson, *When Ladies Go A-Thieving: Middle Class Shoplifters in the Victorian Department Store* (Oxford University Press, 1989).

54. Paul Steege, *Black Market, Cold War: Everyday Life in Berlin, 1946–1949* (Cambridge University Press, 2007); Katie Lange, "The Berlin Airlift: What It Was, Its Importance in the Cold War," US Department of Defense, June 25, 2018, https://www.defense.gov/Explore/Inside-DOD/Blog/Article/2062719/the-berlin-airlift-what-it-was-its-importance-in-the-cold-war/.

55. Malte Zierenberg, *Berlin's Black Market 1939–1950* (Palgrave Macmillan, 2015), 127–86; Mark Fenemore, *Fighting the Cold War in Post-Blockade, Post-Wall Berlin* (Routledge, 2019).

56. Alice Autumn Weinreb, "Matters of Taste: The Politics of Food and Hunger in Divided Germany 1945–1971," University of Michigan Department of History, 2009, 100–101 ("The remarkable scale of bartering, stealing, and gathering food stuffs throughout all four zones, and especially the almost universal participation in the black market, make clear that the rationing calories allotted German civilians were not the population's only source of sustenance").

57. Andrie Cherny, *The Candy Bombers: The Untold Story of the Berlin Airlift and America's Finest Hour* (Dutton Caliber, 2008), 434; Steege, *Black Market, Cold War*, 185.

58. Leslie Colitt, "Escape From East Berlin," *The Guardian*, August 16, 2011, https://www.theguardian.com/world/2011/aug/16/escape-from-east-berlin.

59. Cherny, *The Candy Bombers*, 475; Steege, *Black Market, Cold War*, 233; Mary Fulbrook, "The State and the Transformation of Political Legitimacy in East and West Germany Since 1945," *Comparative Studies in Society & History* 29 (1987): 214–30.

60. Robinson and Holcomb, "The Criminogenic Effects of Damaging Criminal Law's Moral Credibility"; Paul Robinson, Geoff Goodwin, and Michael Reisig, "The Disutility of Injustice," *New York University Law Review* 85 (2010): 1940.

61. Robinson, Goodwin, and Reisig, "The Disutility of Injustice."

62. Ibid.

63. Ibid.

64. Janice Nadler, "Flouting the Law: Does Perceived Injustice Provoke General Non-Compliance?" Northwestern Law and Economics Research Paper Series, No. 02-09, 2002, 3, https://papers.ssrn.com/sol3/papers.cfm?abstract_id=353745.

65. Ibid., 9.

66. Ibid., 11.

67. Ibid., 9.

68. Ibid., 12.

69. Ibid., 9.

70. Ibid., 14.

71. Ibid., 28.

72. Lode Vereeck and Klara Vrolix, "The Social Willingness to Comply with the Law: The Effect of Social Attitudes on Traffic Fatalities," *International Review of Law*

& Economics 27 (2007): 385. A study using data from the European Union found that social willingness to comply with the law has significant positive effects on controlling traffic fatalities, outweighing even the influence of traffic exposure, speed, and alcohol consumption. The authors examined road safety data from fifteen European countries and modeled the number of fatalities in terms of social willingness to comply, controlling for factors such as traffic exposure, vehicle fleet characteristics, road infrastructure and economic conditions, population characteristics, and road user behavior. The authors found that social legitimacy is "a sine qua non for effective road safety policy because lack of public support will lead to insufficient willingness to comply and, in turn, more traffic fatalities." Regardless of the specific content of the country's traffic laws, the law-abiding behavior of drivers was found to have a positive, measured effect on traffic fatalities. "The core idea of our paper is that social norms prevail over laws," the authors explained. That is, the public's allegiance to the law writ large—evidenced by their willingness or unwillingness to comply with the law—was simply more important than the effectiveness or ineffectiveness of specific traffic laws at theoretically improving safety.

73. Johanna Ahnquist, "Institutional Trust and Alcohol Consumption in Sweden: The Swedish National Public Health Survey 2006," *BMC Public Health* 8 (August 2008): 283, https://doi.org/10.1186/1471-2458-8-283. A Swedish study assessed whether there was a correlation between low institutional trust and illegal alcohol consumption. Alcohol consumption is a hotly contested topic in Sweden, and the Swedish national parliament has passed several laws intended to limit alcohol consumption. Sweden also has a state monopoly over alcohol sales. The authors of the study hypothesized that lower institutional trust "may be associated with high alcohol consumption" because "public institutions in Sweden are consistent and coherent in the way they view aspects such as high alcohol consumption." The researchers asked respondents about their drinking habits and probed their trust in various societal institutions. The results showed that lack of trust was associated with increased likelihood of harmful alcohol consumption. High trust in institutions, on the other hand, was correlated with a greater inclination to follow the advice of public officials, to trust in experts, and with steps to limit their own alcohol consumption. Ultimately, the study showed that those who do not doubt a particular institution's legitimacy are more likely to heed that institution's rules and recommendations.

74. Benno Torgler, "Tax Morale, Rule Governed Behavior and Trust," *Constitutional Political Economy* 14 (2003): 119. A study on the reasons why taxpayers obey rather than simply evade taxes found that trust in the legal system had a strong effect on compliance. Based on survey data from Europe, the study's authors asked respondents to rank whether they thought that cheating on taxes was "always justified," "never justified," or one of several options in the middle. They were also asked to rank how much confidence they had in the legal system on a scale of "a great deal of confidence," "no confidence," or somewhere in between. The study's authors found that a perception of legitimacy in the legal system had a highly significant effect on so-called tax morale. In fact, an increase in the trust scale of just one unit increased the subjects' likelihood to find cheating on taxes to be unjustified by 3.5 percentage points. "Trust in the legal system leads to acceptance of governments' decisions and produces the incentive to obey the rules," the authors found. Furthermore, where the public believed that officials were honest and competent—measured

by their ranking of agreement with the statement "public officials can usually be trusted to do what's right"—willingness to comply with tax payments increased further. Ultimately, the study suggested that rather than focusing on enforcement, governments concerned with cultivating "tax morale" should try to create confidence in the legal system and in the trustworthiness and capacity of tax officials.

75. Margaret Levi, Audrey Sacks, and Tom Tyler, "Conceptualizing Legitimacy, Measuring Legitimating Beliefs," *American Behavioral Scientist* 53, no. 3 (2009): 354, https://doi.org/10.1177/000276420933879. A study using survey data from a number of African countries to model the relationship between perceptions that a government was fair and trustworthy and beliefs that such a government deserves deference to its rules. The authors focused on those factors that they believed would induce "voluntary deference to the directives of authorities and rules precisely because they are believed legitimate." The data used in the study was collected through a survey of more than twenty-three thousand respondents across eighteen countries modeled in an effort to capture citizens' legitimating beliefs in terms of their willingness to obey the police, courts, and the tax department. The survey asked respondents the degrees to which they believed administrators were corrupt, authorities were capable of detecting and punishing crime, and the government treated citizens fairly. Standard sociodemographic variables that can affect citizens' acceptance of government authority were controlled for, including age and household income. The authors found considerable evidence of a link between the perceived trustworthiness of government and criminal justice mechanisms and citizens' willingness to defer to these institutions. The results indicated that "the more trustworthy and

fair the government, the more likely its population will develop legitimating beliefs that lead them to accept the government's right to make people obey its laws and regulations."

76. Robinson, *Intuitions of Justice and the Utility of Desert*, 179.

77. Tom R. Tyler, "Procedural Justice, Legitimacy, and the Effective Rule of Law," *Crime and Justice* 30 (2003): 283–357; Tom R. Tyler, "Legitimacy and the Maintenance of Public Order," *Yale Law Review* (2012); Tom R. Tyler and David Markell, "The Public Regulation of Land-Use Decisions: Criteria for Evaluating Alternative Procedures," *Journal of Empirical Legal Studies* 7, no. 3 (2010): 538–73.

78. See Tom Tyler, *Why People Obey the Law* (Princeton University Press, 2006), 57; Tom Tyler, "Enhancing Police Legitimacy," *Annals of the American Academy of Political and Social Science* 593 (May 2004): 95; Tom R. Tyler and Yuen J. Huo, *Trust in the Law: Encouraging Public Cooperation with the Police and Courts* (Russell Sage Foundation, 2002), 101.

79. For a discussion of how Tom Tyler's legitimacy and Robinson's moral credibility compare and interact, see Joshua Bowers and Paul Robinson, "Perceptions of Fairness and Justice: The Shared Aims and Occasional Conflicts of Legitimacy and Moral Credibility," *Wake Forest Law Review* 47 (2012): 211.

80. Tom R. Tyler, "Procedural Justice and the Courts," *Court Review: The Journal of the American Judges Association* 44, no. 1/2 (2007), 217, https://digitalcommons.unl.edu/ajacourtreview/217.

81. Ibid.

82. Ibid.

83. Ibid. What may be most interesting about the Tom Tyler's studies for our present purposes is that Tyler finds that the effect in gaining compliance from increased moral credibility in getting the results right is nearly three times more powerful than gaining compliance from increased

legitimacy from having fair procedures. See Tyler, "Procedural Justice and the Courts," 101 (conceding that moral credibility has a greater effect in shaping compliance than does legitimacy; Tyler reports that the relative weight of the factors shaping compliance with the law are: morality 0.33, legitimacy 0.11, and deterrence 0.02).

84. Youngki Woo et al., "Direct and Indirect Effects of Procedural Justice on Cooperation and Compliance: Evidence from South Korea," *Police Practice and Research* 19, no. 2 (February 2018): 168, https://www.tandfonline.com/doi/full/10.1080/15614263.2018.1418147. In a study of South Korean adults, researchers found that a perceived just distribution of punishment was one of the strongest predictors of compliance with the law. The study used data from surveys questioning citizens' attitudes and opinions toward the police and comparing it to their willingness to cooperate with law enforcement. The justness of police decisions was measured by asking whether pedestrian stops, traffic stops, and arrests were allocated in a just and unbiased manner. The survey found that respondents who perceived the police as allocating outcomes fairly were more likely to comply than those who view the police as unjust in their dealings. Lyn Hinds and Kristina Murphy, "Public Satisfaction with Police: Using Procedural Justice to Improve Police Legitimacy," *Australia and New Zealand Journal of Criminology* 40 (2007): 27, https://doi.org/10.1375/acri.40.1.27. An Australian study came to a similar conclusion, finding that people who viewed the police as delivering fair outcomes were more compliant toward law enforcement than those who did not.

85. "Everyone's in on the Game: Corruption and Human Rights Abuses by the Nigeria Police," Human Rights Watch, August 17, 2010, https://www.hrw.org/report/2010/08/17/everyones-game/corruption-and-human-rights-abuses-nigeria-police-force#. The relationship between the police and the public in Nigeria presents something of an extreme case of unprofessional policing leading to diminished compliance. The police in Nigeria have been notoriously corrupt since the turn of the twenty-first century. According to several reports, the Nigerian police often extort money from the public at taxi stands, marketplaces, and roadblocks. When citizens fail to pay the bribes, they are sometimes beaten, sexually assaulted, or shot. Further, the police often neglect to perform their basic duties unless they are bribed. Crimes are not investigated unless the victim is able to persuade the police to act. Officers at the upper echelons of the police force are widely known to siphon off significant portions of public funds for their personal uses. A survey of Nigerian public opinion regarding police legitimacy found that a plurality of Nigerians expressed having "no confidence" in the police. Another found that Nigeria is plagued by "low levels of citizen cooperation with the police" and "a loss of confidence of the common man in the criminal justice system." Interviews reflected widespread distrust of the Nigerian police. One woman reported, "Any witness or crime victim who approaches the police without bearing in mind their lack of integrity and possible complicity in crime may end up becoming the criminal. The police doubt everything about you." As a result of this distrust, crime throughout Nigeria has increased. Analyses of crime data between 1999 and 2013 show that murder, armed robbery, and assault have increased dramatically during this period even as the Nigerian police have received more and more resources from the state. In fact, some members of the Nigerian public have taken the law into their own hands by lynching suspects of crimes or by flouting the law altogether with shoplifting, car thefts, fraud schemes, and

computer crimes. Ultimately, crime has only become more widespread and more diverse in Nigeria as the police have become more corrupt, unprofessional, and ineffective in their practices.

86. After the shooting of Michael Brown in Ferguson, Missouri, an investigation found that Ferguson's policing practices led to distrust and resentment among many in the Ferguson community, which is 67 percent African American. The report explained, "African Americans' views of FPD are shaped not just by what FPD officers do, but how they do it." Dozens of Ferguson residents told of officers cursing at them, verbally harassing them, and randomly brandishing their weapons in threatening ways. Crime rates in Ferguson rose precipitously after the shooting. While some of this may have been due to reduced police intervention, the so-called Ferguson Effect, one study suggests that a major contributor was the dramatic loss in police legitimacy crystallized by the Michael Brown killing and the protests that followed it.

87. In 2003, then Mexico City mayor Manuel Lopez Obrador and billionaire Carlos Slim combined efforts to reduce crime in one of Mexico City's most notoriously lawless neighborhoods called Tepito. The pair invested millions in surveillance technology and increased policing in order to curb the violence, drug trafficking, and sale of stolen or counterfeit goods. Most notably, they relied on the help of a former New York City mayor whose private security firm provided high-definition "hawkeye" surveillance cameras to monitor the goings on of the neighborhood and employed former New York City Police Department officers to train their Mexican counterparts. Residents of the neighborhood, including those who were not involved in any sort of criminal group, resisted. Feeling as though they were being policed by Americans, as opposed to their own countrymen, they viewed the neighborhood's security

system as wholly illegitimate. In 2004, crime in the area increased by 25 percent. Tepitans took part in a variety of activities that actively interfered with the new police procedures. Eventually, the Mexican government realized that the perceived illegitimacy of their new enforcement mechanisms was doing more harm than good and decided to sever ties with the American security personnel.

88. Similarly, consider the experiences of various Native American tribes whose tribal justice systems conflicted with the federal criminal justice system. The federal government had previously allowed tribes to have criminal justice jurisdiction on their reservations, but in 1953 Congress passed Public Law 280 allowing states to decide whether to assume complete or partial jurisdiction over crimes by or against Native Americans on reservations. The law was viewed as an affront to tribal sovereignty, failing to recognize Native Americans' status as members of domestic sovereign nations and stifling the effectiveness of tribal courts. Over the following decades, Native Americans developed increasingly negative views of the non–Native American criminal justice system, stemming from widespread distrust of the instruments of justice implemented by the federal government. As views became more negative, crime soared.

89. The situation of Northern Ireland in the 1970s provides another example of the connection between perceived legitimacy and increased crime. As tensions rose between Catholics who wanted a united Ireland and Protestants who claimed allegiance to the United Kingdom, violence escalated. In 1972, the British government suspended the Northern Ireland parliament and instituted direct rule from the United Kingdom, replacing Irish criminal justice policies with their own. Law enforcement powers were expanded enormously, allowing for the indefinite detention of suspects

without trial, juryless courts in cases of alleged terrorism, and increased police and army powers. The British police force, the Royal Ulster Constabulary, was widely perceived as unfairly partial to Protestant Loyalists and unaccountable to, and discriminatory against, Catholic Unionists. As two criminologists observed, "the costs in terms of negative effects on public trust in British institutions have been incalculable." Politically motivated crimes increased with the rise in political tensions, but so did crimes unrelated to political action. As a result of this perceived illegitimacy, throughout the 1970s, the levels of recorded crime increased nearly sixfold. Murders rose rapidly, but property crime increased at an even higher rate during this period. The burglary rate increased by a factor of fifteen, and drug dealing rose exponentially. As the Irish populace became more disaffected and distrusting of the influence of the Royal Ulster Constabulary, they expressed their disillusionment by—among other things—committing more crime.

90. See Daniel Zizumbo-Colunga, "Crime, Corruption and Societal Support for Vigilante Justice: Ten Years of Evidence in Review," Americas Barometer Insights: 2015, Number 120; Rashid Gabdulhakov, "Citizen-Led Justice in Post-Communist Russia: From Comrades' Courts to Dotcomrade Vigilantism," *Surveillance & Society* 16, no. 3 (2018): 314–31, https://ojs.library.queensu.ca/index.php/surveillance-and-society/index 2018.

91. German Lopez, "A Continuing Drop in Murders," *New York Times*, December 30, 2022, https://www.nytimes.com/2022/12/30/briefing/crime-murders-us-decline.html.

92. Rod K. Brunson and Brian Wade, "Oh Hell No, We Don't Talk to Police," *Criminology and Public Policy* 18 (2019): 623.

93. For another example, consider the case of Danny Palm. John Harper is an auto mechanic who devotes his attentions to cars and methamphetamines. Paul H. Robinson and Sarah Robinson, *Shadow Vigilantes: How Distrust in the Justice System Breeds a New Kind of Lawlessness* (Prometheus Books, 2018), 24–31. He has recently moved in with his parents in a quiet residential neighborhood, where he begins to threaten random neighbors. A typical encounter has Harper tailgating a car, yelling obscenities, and declaring, "Don't fuck with me, I know where you live." The police say they are unable to do anything. The community starts compiling a record—150 incidents against 42 different neighbors soon fills their list. When a case finally makes it to court, the fear of retaliation leaves few people brave enough to testify. One neighbor, Danny Palm, a retired Navy commander, feels he is honor bound to testify. At the end of the hearing, Harper is sentenced to only probation and a $500 fine. Later that morning Harper drives his El Camino into Palm's driveway and sits there for a while to send a threatening message. When he leaves, Palm, hoping to dissuade Harper from further threats to the neighborhood, follows him and shows Harper that he has a gun. Seeing the weapon, Harper yells, "You and your family are as good as dead." Ron Donoho, "Law and Disorder," *San Diego Magazine*, March 1997. In response, Palm shoots and kills Harper. The criminal justice system that ignored Harper's threats and harassment convicts Palm of second-degree murder. A judge later reduced Palm's second-degree murder conviction to manslaughter because of his sympathy for the vigilante, showing that even officials in the justice system can see disillusionment and have sympathy for vigilante action. The Associated Press, "Judge Reduces Term for Man Who Killed Bully," *New York Times*, April 19, 1997, https://www.nytimes.com/1997/04/19/us/judge-reduces-term-for-man-who-killed-bully.html.

94. Robinson and Robinson, *Shadow Vigilantes*, 151–54.
95. Ibid., 151–54.
96. Paul H. Robinson, "The Moral Vigilante and Her Cousins in the Shadows," *University of Illinois Law Review* (2015): 453.
97. A female victim, now grown, expresses disbelief: "The judge says he is not going to get a fair trial because of his history, but surely it's that history which proves what a dangerous man he is." Ibid.
98. Brunson and Wade, "Oh Hell No, We Don't Talk to Police."
99. Robinson, "The Moral Vigilante and Her Cousin in the Shadows," 404.
100. See, for example, Jason Knobler, "Desperate Parents: San Francisco Couple Accused of Killing Their Daughter's Pimp," NBC Bay Area, June 14, 2012, https://www.nbcbayarea.com/news/local/cops-sf-couple-killed-daughters-pimp/1918345/.
101. See, for example, Robinson and Robinson, *Shadow Vigilantes*, 105–6.
102. For example, Project Perverted Justice members trick would-be pedophiles into aggressive confrontations that the group films and circulates. Michael Mullen, a member of the group, poses as an FBI agent and arranges to "interview" three convicted offenders who share an apartment. He shoots and kills two of the men to ensure they receive his idea of justice. The existence of a vigilante group can inspire and appear to legitimize conduct that would seem otherwise clearly inappropriate. See, for example, Robinson and Robinson, *Shadow Vigilantes*, 133. In another milder instance, a group of students at Paschal High School in Fort Worth, Texas, believe that they know who is responsible for a rash of petty thefts and recent drug use at school. They go to the administration, who do not act to the group's satisfaction. The group starts bringing guns to school to intimidate the supposed offenders. When that

does not work, they vandalize some cars and construct a pipe bomb. After a cat is killed and the bloody remains left on a student's car, the authorities step in. The group saw themselves as defending their school. Once a vigilante group takes action, it is easy for it to escalate to increasingly inappropriate conduct. See, for example, Robinson and Robinson, *Shadow Vigilantes*.
103. Ibid., 147–200.
104. Robinson, *Distributive Principles of Criminal Law*, 107–8.
105. Daniel S. Nagin, "Deterrence in the Twenty-First Century," *Crime and Justice* 42, no. 1 (2013): 199–263.
106. United States of America, Plaintiff, v. John Eugene Walker, Defendant. Case No. 2:13–cr–379, signed May 18, 2017.
107. The court increases his probation to ten years but agrees to a review in five years as to whether probation should continue. United States v. Walker, 252 F.Supp.3d 1269 (2017).
108. Nina Golgowski, "Murderer Deemed Unlikely to Hurt Again Because of Age Is Convicted in 2nd Killing," *The Huffington Post*, July 21, 2019, https://www.huffpost.com/entry/albert-flick-convicted-kim-dobbie-murder_n_5d3496ace4b0419fd32e6bc6.
109. Golgowski, "Murderer Deemed Unlikely to Hurt Again Because of Age Is Convicted in 2nd Killing."
110. Dennis MacDougal, *Angels of Darkness: The True Story of Randy Kraft and the Most Heinous Murder Spree of the Century* (Warner Books, 1991), 146.
111. Bonin is convicted on ten counts of murder in 1982 and executed in 1996.
112. MacDougal, *Angels of Darkness*, 21–95.
113. This is a particular problem in the United States where there are fifty-one American criminal codes.
114. Robinson, *Distributive Principles of Criminal Law*.
115. Ibid.
116. Ibid.

117. See Part II (A)(3), Part II(A)(5); Paul Robinson and John Darley, "Intuitions of Justice: Implications for Criminal Law and Justice," *Southern California Law Review* 81, no. 1 (2007): 39 (explaining that several studies have "examined the issue of what criteria people rely on when they make intuitive judgments of justice and found that it is desert, not deterrence or incapacitation, that drive people's intuitive assignments of punishment"). One might argue that it is unfair to offer this criticism because empirical desert has a similar education challenge. Its compliance mechanism depends upon the community having an opinion about the system's justness. One critic, for example, explains, "A wide range of survey research indicates that the public lacks knowledge about crime, crime rates, offender characteristics, and legal reforms. In turn, these misconceptions could influence the 'ordinary' person's perceptions of certain legal doctrines." Robinson and Holcomb, "The Criminogenic Effects of Damaging Criminal Law's Moral Credibility," 765. But the effective communication hurdle that is so problematic for general deterrence does not apply to empirical desert. The message that general deterrence must send is one that identifies a particular kind of situation as one in which there is some exaggerated criminal liability and punishment threatened, more than that which the ordinary person would think was deserved. That is a specific non-intuitive fact that the general deterrence system must get into the minds of its target audience and to get them to use in evaluating the cost-benefit analysis when they make their conduct decision. In the case of empirical desert, in contrast, all that is required is for the person to have some general opinion about the moral credibility of the criminal justice system, an opinion that every ordinary person will necessarily have simply by being exposed to the endless stream of information that they take in from news media, governmental statements, friends, acquaintances, and others. Their having an opinion on the criminal law's general justness does not require that they have a particular fact, as general deterrence's educational challenge requires. It is certainly true that the criminal justice system ought to make an effort to improve its reputation because that improvement can bring greater compliance, but even if the system has no public relations campaign to improve its image, the moral credibility-compliance dynamic will be at work. It will still be the case that regular conflicts with community views will reduce its credibility and reduction in conflicts will increase it.

118. Robinson and Robinson, *Shadow Vigilantes*, 99–107 (examining rehabilitation as a distributive principle).

119. United States v. Salerno, 481 US 739 (1987).

120. Robinson and Holcomb, "The Criminogenic Effects of Damaging Criminal Law's Moral Credibility." For an argument that the use of incapacitation as a distributive principle is unconstitutional, see Lee Pershan, "Selective Incapacitation and the Justifications for Imprisonment," *NYU Review of Law & Social Change* 12 (1983–1984): 385.

121. Paul H. Robinson, "Punishing Dangerousness: Cloaking Preventive Detention as Criminal Justice," *Harvard Law Review* 114 (2001): fn. 39 and 40.

122. See supra note 7, 112. [AQ1]

123. Michele Cotton, "Back with a Vengeance: The Resilience of Retribution as an Articulated Purpose of Criminal Punishment," *American Criminal Law Review* 37 (2000): 1313:

Indeed, the activist state courts seem to have been following a general trend toward reducing the role of utilitarian purposes and reinstating retribution. States that adopted or amended their statutory statement of purposes, or adopted sentencing guidelines with stated purposes, during the late 1970s and afterward, were much more likely to adopt retributive purposes for punishment than previously. California endorsed retribution as "the" purpose for its punishment in 1977 and Pennsylvania identified it as the "primary" purpose in 1982, while states such as Arizona (1978), North Dakota (1973), and Tennessee (1989) adopted language evocative of the "just deserts" of traditional retributive punishment. Still other states—Hawaii (1972), North Carolina (1981), New York (1982), Montana (1991), and Arkansas (1993)—enacted various other kinds of retributive statements of purpose. The states that had adopted laws on purposes in the 1960s and early 1970s were much more likely to have adopted utilitarian, nonretributive statutes.

Ibid., 1355–56. California changed its code in 1977 to endorse desert as the sole purpose of punishment. Cotton, *Back with a Vengeance*, 1355–56. The California Penal Code section 1170(a) (1) states that "the Legislature finds and declares that the purpose of imprisonment for crime is punishment. This purpose is best served by terms proportionate to the seriousness of the offense with provision for uniformity in the sentences of offenders committing the same offense under similar circumstances." California Penal Code 1170: Determinate sentencing; Sentence recall; medical release, 2004, Originally from Statutory Appendix, Model Penal Code: Sentencing Preliminary Draft No. 3, §1.02(2), American Law Institute, 2004.

124. Alaska, California, Kentucky, Connecticut, and Rhode Island. Paul H. Robinson and Tyler Scot Williams, *Mapping American Criminal Law: Variations Across the 50 States* (Praeger Publishing, 2018), 3.

125. Weems v. United States, 217 US 367 (1910).

126. J. S. Bainbridge Jr., "The Return of Retribution," *A.B.A. J.* 71 (1985): 60.

127. Williams v. New York, 337 US 241, 248 (1949).

128. Ibid., 343.

129. Ibid., 345.

130. Furman v. Georgia, 408 US 308 (1972).

131. Ibid., 34950.

132. Ibid.

133. Bainbridge, "The Return of Retribution."

134. 433 US 584 (1977).

135. Enmund v. Florida, 458 US 798 (1982).

136. Harmelin v. Michigan, 501 US 998-999 (1991).

137. Ibid., 999.

138. Ibid., 1001.

139. See Graham v. Florida, 560 US 48, 71 (2010). The Supreme Court in *Graham v. Florida* applied the principles articulated in Harmelin in determining whether the constitution permits a juvenile offender to be sentenced to life in prison without parole in a non-homicide case. The Court echoed that four goals of criminal punishment have been recognized as legitimate—retribution, deterrence, incapacitation, and rehabilitation—and emphasized that criminal punishment may have different goals—and it is within the legislature's discretion to choose among them. The Court added that "a sentence lacking any legitimate penological justification is by its nature disproportionate to the offense." Regarding the sentence in *Graham*, the Court held that none of the four recognized distributive principles provides an adequate justification for imposing life in prison without parole on a juvenile in non-homicide cases, rendering it unconstitutional.

140. "Assemblyman Urges a Refocus on Public Safety and Victims' Rights," *Journal and Republican*, July 31, 2019, https:// infoweb-newsbank-com.proxy.library .upenn.edu/apps/news/document-view ?p=AWNB&docref=news/175285C85 D378DA0. Criticism of the handling of Albert Flick's case by State Assembly-

man Kenneth D. Blankenbush, R-Black River, who represents the 117th District for the New York State Assembly: "In a society that truly valued victims' rights, [Albert Flick] should've been incarcerated for life. . . . The judge, citing his age, ordered a much shorter sentence. . . . It is an insult to the families who grieve. It is an insult to the basic precept of public safety, and it really makes you wonder where the justice is in so many ongoing efforts by progressives to undermine victims' rights. . . .This session, [Democrats] pushed a bill that would make all inmates eligible for parole at age 55. The most serious offenders who present the most serious risk to society belong in only one place—prison."

141. "Recent Election Sexual Assault Law—Judicial Recall—California Judge Recalled for Sentence in Sexual Assault Case," *Harvard Law Review* 132, no. 4 (February 2019): 1369.

142. Alison Siegler, "End Mandatory Minimums," Brennan Center for Justice, October 18, 2021, 8.

143. See Paul H. Robinson, "Report on Offense Grading in New Jersey," Penn Carey Law School Scholarship, 2011; Paul H. Robinson, "Report on Offense Grading in Pennsylvania," Penn Carey Law School Scholarship, 2009.

144. Nancy J. King and Rosevelt L. Noble, "Felony Jury Sentencing in Practice: A Three-State Study," *Vanderbilt Law Review* 57 (2004): 886 ("Today, in six states, felons convicted by juries are routinely sentenced by juries. These states form a sizeable segment of the United States, beginning with Virginia at the eastern end, and proceeding west, through Kentucky, Missouri, Arkansas, Texas, and Oklahoma Weary had this in 134").

145. Model Penal Code section 1.02 (1962):

Section 1.02(2). Purposes; Principles of Construction.

(2) The general purposes of the provisions governing the sentencing and treatment of offenders are:

(a) to prevent the commission of offenses;

(b) to promote the correction and rehabilitation of offenders;

(c) to safeguard offenders against excessive, disproportionate or arbitrary punishment;

(d) to give fair warning of the nature of the sentences that may be imposed on conviction of an offense;

(e) to differentiate among offenders with a view to a just individualization in their treatment;

(f) to define, coordinate and harmonize the powers, duties and functions of the courts and of administrative officers and agencies responsible for dealing with offenders;

(g) to advance the use of generally accepted scientific methods and knowledge in the sentencing and treatment of offenders;

(h) to integrate responsibility for the administration of the correctional system in a State Department of Correction [or other single department or agency].

146. Model Penal Code, section 1.02, American Law Institute, 2007.

CHAPTER 4

1. See, for example, Emily Shapiro, "27 Years Ago, Nicole Brown Simpson and Ron Goldman Were Killed: Timeline of OJ Simpson's Life," ABC News, June 12, 2021; Christopher Bucktin, "Forensics at the OJ Simpson Trial, Crime Museum; Diana Aizman, Lessons Learned from Evidence Gathering Mistakes in Simpson Case," Aizman Law Firm, June 16, 2014, https://aizmanlaw.com/lessons-learned-evidence-gathering-mistakes-simpson-case/; "O. J. Simpson Trial: 26 Years Later," Crime Traveller, May 25, 2020, https://www.crimetraveller.org/2020/05/oj-simpson-trial-26-years-later/; Dave Schilling, "OJ Simpson and the 24-hour Cable Show with No End in Sight—The Public's Obsession with OJ Simpson

Means There Is Always Work for Those Who Feed Our Fascination," *The Guardian*, March 5, 2016, https://www.theguardian.com/us-news/2016/mar/04/oj-simpson-knife-discovery-24-hour-news.

2. Jim Hane et al., "Cases Crumble, Killers Go Free," *Baltimore Sun*, September 29, 2002, https://www.baltimoresun.com/balte.murder29sep29-story.html.

3. Ibid.

4. Jennifer Doleac and Anna Harvey, "Policing and Public Safety: What Do the Experts Think," Niskanen Center, May 26, 2021, https://www.niskanencenter.org/policing-and-public-safety-what-do-the-experts-think/; Anthony A. Braga et al., "The Influence of Investigative Resources on Homicide Clearances," *Journal of Quantitative Criminology* 35 (2018): 337–64.

5. Vernon J. Geberth, "10 Most Common Errors in Death Investigations," *Law and Order* 56, no. 1 (2008): parts 1 and 2.

6. Barbara Boland and Elizabeth Brady, "The Prosecution of Felony Arrests, 1980," Bureau of Justice Statics NCJ-97684, September 1985.

7. "The Prosecution of Felony Arrests," US Department of Justice, September 1985, 12.

8. "Crime in the United Stats: 2019 Arrest Data," FBI, https://ucr.fbi.gov/crime-in-the-u.s/2019/crime-in-the-u.s.-2019/tables/table-29. Eighteen percent of 500,000 is 90,000. While the FBI data is not entirely complete, it is the best source available for this data.

9. Corey Rayburn Yung, "Rape Law Gatekeeping," *Boston College Law Review* 58, no. 1 (2017): 219.

10. Ibid., 224.

11. Ibid., 225.

12. Nina J. Westera et al., "Want a Better Criminal Justice Response to Rape? Improve Police Interviews with Complainants and Suspects," *Violence Against Women* 22, no. 14 (2016): 1750, https://doi.org/10.1177/1077801216631439.

13. Karen Rich and Patrick Seffrin, "Police Interviews of Sexual Assault Reporters: Do Attitudes Matter?" *Violence and Victims* 27, no. 2 (2012): 276.

14. End the Backlog, "Why the Backlog Exists," last visited March 3, 2023, https://www.endthebacklog.org/what-is-the-backlog/why-the-backlog-exists/.

15. Yung, "Rape Law Gatekeeping," 249.

16. Amy D. Page, "Judging Women and Defining Crime: Police Officers' Attitudes Toward Women and Rape," *Sociological Spectrum* 28, no. 4 (2008): 391.

17. Ibid.

18. Rich and Seffrin, "Police Interviews of Sexual Assault Reporters," 274.

19. Ibid., 271–72.

20. For an explanation of how the four hundred thousand estimate for untested rape kits was derived, see Caitlin Dickson, "How the U.S. Ended up with 400,000 Untested Rape Kits," *Daily Beast*, April 14, 2017, https://www.thedailybeast.com/how-the-us-ended-up-with-400000-untested-rape-kits.

21. Kevin J. Strom and Matthew J. Hickman, "Unanalyzed Evidence in Law Enforcement Agencies: A National Examination of Forensic Processing in Police Departments," *Criminology & Public Policy* 9, no. 2 (April 2010): 386.

22. Ibid., 394.

23. Kevin J. Strom et al., "The 2007 Survey of Law Enforcement Forensic Evidence Processing," US Department of Justice, NCJRS 228415, October 2009, Exhibit E-1. The study estimated that 18 percent of unsolved rape cases "contained forensic evidence that was not submitted by law enforcement agencies to a crime laboratory for analysis" (vii). Additionally, 14 percent of unsolved homicide cases contained evidence that had never been submitted for testing (vii). Of all of these unsolved rapes and homicides, 40 percent of the available evidence contained DNA evidence, which may have been valuable in identifying suspects (xi).

24. Ibid., xi.

25. Ibid., xii.
26. Ibid., xii, xv, and xiii.
27. Yung, "Rape Law Gatekeeping," 207.
28. Catherine Rentz, "Testing Rape Kits Can Deliver Exonerations, Closure and Cost Savings. Why Does It Still take So Long?" ProPublica, December 16, 2021, https://www.propublica.org/article/testing-rape-kits-can-deliver-exonerations-closure-and-cost-savings-why-does-it-still-take-so-long-to-do; End the Backlog, Joyful Heart Foundation.
29. End the Backlog, "Why the Backlog Exists."
30. End the Backlog, "Where the Backlog Exists and What's Happening to End It."
31. End the Backlog, "Why the Backlog Exists."
32. Tommaso D'Anna, Maria Puntarello, Giovanni Cannella, et al., "The Chain of Custody in the Era of Modern Forensics: From the Classic Procedures for Gathering Evidence to the New Challenges Related to Digital Data," *Healthcare* (Basel) 11, no. 5 (February 2023).
33. Paul C. Giannelli, "Chain of Custody and the Handling of Real Evidence," *American Criminal Law Review* 20, no. 4 (Spring 1983): 567.
34. Brandon L. Garrett, "The Costs and Benefits of Forensics," *Houston Law Review* 57, no. 3 (2020): 600; Tina Daunt, "LAPD Blames Faulty Training in DNA Snafu," *Los Angeles Times*, July 31, 2002, https://www.latimes.com/archives/la-xpm-2002-jul-31-me-dna31-story.html.
35. Catherine Rentz and Alison Knezevich, "A Flawed, Inconsistent Police Response to Sexual Assault in Maryland," *The Baltimore Sun*, December 3, 2016, https://www.baltimoresun.com/news/investigations/bs-md-rape-investigations-20161203-story.html.
36. David Collins, "AG Report Finds Some Police Departments Destroying Rape Kits Despite State Law," WBAL TV 11, January 10, 2020, https://www.wbaltv.com/article/ag-report-police-departments-destroy-rape-kits-state-law-maryland/30472713.
37. Rentz and Knezevich, "A Flawed, Inconsistent Police Response to Sexual Assault in Maryland."
38. Ashley Fantz et al., "Destroyed: How the Trashing of Rape Kits Failed Victims and Jeopardizes Public Safety," CNN, November 29, 2018, https://www.cnn.com/interactive/2018/11/investigates/police-destroyed-rapekits/index.html.
39. Ibid.
40. Ibid.
41. Brandon Stahl, "KARE 11 Investigates: Police in Minnesota Destroyed Hundreds of Rape Kits, Putting Cases in Peril," Kare 11, February 6, 2020, https://www.kare11.com/article/news/investigations/kare-11-investigates-police-in-minnesota-destroyed-hundreds-of-rape-kits-putting-cases-in-peril/89-1ff69998-cabe-49ce-998c-771e5f0f61dc.
42. Daunt, "LAPD Blames Faulty Training in DNA Snafu."
43. Stahl, "KARE 11 Investigates."
44. "The Importance of Chain of Custody for Legal Proceedings," Superior Bag, November 14, 2017, https://superiorbag.com/evidence-bags/importance-chain-custody-legal-proceedings/.
45. "Evidence Management—Chain of Custody and a Rogue Police Officer," Tracker Products, September 18, 2019, https://trackerproducts.com/evidence-tracking-chain-of-custody-and-a-rogue-police-officer/.
46. Charles F. Lehman, "America's Shrinking Police Forces Could Spell Trouble for Our Safety," *New York Post*, February 8, 2020, https://nypost.com/2020/02/08/americas-shrinking-police-forces-could-spell-trouble-for-our-safety/.
47. Police Executive Research Forum, "Promising Strategies for Strengthening Homicide Investigations, Findings and Recommendations from the Bureau of Justice Assistance's Homicide Investigations Enhancement Training and Technical Assistance Project," October 2018, 42 and 12.

48. Don Babwin, "Researchers: Chicago Must Overhaul Homicide Investigations," Associated Press, October 30, 2019, https://apnews.com/article/4c12e3 15c3a049e495d31405585842c0.

49. Haner, et al., "Cases Crumble, Killers Go Free."

50. Police Executive Research Forum, "Promising Strategies for Strengthening Homicide Investigations," 132.

51. Evidenced by instances of failures to give Miranda warnings and their consequences. See, for example, United States v. Kim, 292 F.3d 969, 970 (9th Cir. 2002) (holding that the defendant was "in custody" for Miranda purposes while being interrogated at her store during the execution of a search warrant and affirming a motion to suppress evidence).

52. Aqsa Hussain, "Shortage of Detectives Leave Inexperienced Police Officers Investigating Serious Crime," The Justice Gap, May 9, 2019, https://www .thejusticegap.com/under-qualified -police-investigating-serious-crime-due -to-shortage-of-detectives/.

53. Barbara B. Hagerty, "An Epidemic of Disbelief," The Atlantic, July 22, 2019, https://www.theatlantic.com/magazine /archive/2019/08/an-epidemic-of-dis belief/592807/?; Evie Taylor, "Untested Rape Kits Are Sitting in Laboratories," The Boar, August 5, 2020, https://the boar.org/2020/08/untested-rape-kits -are-sitting-in-laboratories/; "Detroit Free Press, Detroit Rape Kit Testing Backlog Lingers," USA Today, April 21, 2014, https://www.usatoday.com/story/news /nation/2014/04/21/detroit-rape-kits -backlog/7954957/; Violet Ikonomova, "The Last of Detroit's Neglected Rape Kits Are Being Tested," Detroit Metro Times, March 13, 2018, https://www .metrotimes.com/news/the-last-of-de troits-neglected-rape-kits-are-being -tested-10104983; Anna Clark, "11,341 Rape Kits Were Collected and Forgotten in Detroit. This Is the Story of One of Them," ELLE, June 23, 2016, https://

www.elle.com/culture/a37255/forgot ten-rape-kits-detroit/; Nancy Kaffer, "Rape Kit Backlog Is Over. Here's Why They Say It Can't Happen Again," Detroit Free Press, August 18, 2019, https://www .freep.com/story/opinion/columnists /nancy-kaffer/2019/08/18/detroit-rape -kit-backlog-wayne-county/2013234001/.

54. Matt Agorist, "Women Across the US Suing Police for Refusing to Investigate Their Rape Kits," Activist Post, October 14, 2019, https://www.focusforhealth.org /women-across-the-us-suing-police-for -refusing-to-investigate-their-rape-kits/.

55. Marci A. Hamilton and Steve Berkowitz, "Why Would Police Ever Destroy a Rape Kit Belonging to a Child or Teenager?" CNN, December 1, 2018, https://www .cnn.com/2018/12/01/opinions/ham ilton-berkowitz-op-ed-on-rape-kits/in dex.html.

56. Tami Abdollah, "OJ Simpson Case Taught Police What Not to Do at a Crime Scene," Associated Press, June 8, 2014, https://apnews.com/article/658b9110e3f 2448490b3c2a5db9d61ef.

57. Ibid.

58. Ibid.

59. Bob Giles, "The Times They Are A-Changing: Up-Grading Storage Facilities," The Evidence Log 2010, no. 3 (2010), 16, https://home.iape.org/images/pdf/evi dence-log-archive/2010-EL/Evidence _Log_2010_3.pdf.

60. Ibid.

61. Ibid.

62. Ibid.

63. Vernon J. Geberth, "The Homicide Crime Scene," Law and Order 51, no. 11 (November 2003).

64. The following is an excerpt from an SOP for homicide written by former Maryland investigator John M. Howell in 1999 that shows some of the specific details police should keep in mind. John M. Howell, "Homicide Investigation Standard Operating Procedures," last revised March 1, 1999.

- Policy: The initial responding officer should proceed to the scene quickly but cautiously, park in a way that does not disturb the scene, take time to absorb all details of the scene, and document all observations (what the officer sees, hears, smells, etc.). The officer should proceed cautiously so as not to contaminate or destroy possible evidence.
- Policy: A law enforcement officer will take into custody any person who has committed a crime against the laws of the jurisdiction. The officer will ensure that the suspect is afforded all rights accorded to him or her by the applicable laws of the jurisdiction and the Constitution of the United States.
- Policy: The initial responding officer must secure the crime scene, identify those persons present, and limit access to the scene to authorized personnel only.
- Policy: The initial responding officer shall request additional personnel to assist in crowd control, maintaining the perimeter, gathering witness information, transporting witnesses or suspects, processing the scene, searching the scene, canvassing the area, and other tasks.
- Policy: The investigator will document preliminary information, evaluate the complexity and scope of the scene, and plan the course of the investigation.
- Policy: The investigator will make preliminary assignments, document observations, and work with patrol to establish a command post outside the crime scene.
- Policy: The investigator will conduct a walk-through of the scene, being careful not to disturb items of evidentiary value. A permanent record of the scene, as found, will be made.
- One person should be responsible for collecting and packaging all evidentiary items seized at the scene. If the crime scene is too large for that to be practical, assign areas of responsibility. The chain of custody must be maintained for all items of evidence recovered. Whenever an item of evidence is transferred from one person's control to another person's control, that transfer must be documented. The chain of custody begins at the crime scene.

A report from the Bureau of Justice Assistance recommends the following policies to strengthen homicide investigations:

- Police agencies should ensure that all written standard operating policies and procedures (SOPs) that govern homicide investigations are updated to provide clear and comprehensive guidance on the duties and responsibilities of homicide unit personnel.
- All current homicide unit personnel should be given a copy of the Homicide Unit Manual, and new personnel should be given a copy of the manual upon their arrival to the unit.
- All written general orders, policies, SOPs, and other guidance governing the homicide unit should reflect current best practices for homicide investigations. When developing policies, police departments should look to research-based practice guides and consult with police agencies that have demonstrated successful investigative practices.
- Police agencies should establish a rigorous, formal process for selecting detectives into a homicide unit. The process should be based on a set of established qualification criteria that are stated in written policy and consistently applied to all candidates.
- Police agencies should implement a formal process for selecting homicide unit supervisors (sergeants, lieutenants, and commanders). The process should be stated in written policy and consistently applied for all candidates.
- All newly-assigned homicide detectives should be required to receive formal training on topics related to homicide investigations. Training should be mandatory, consistent for all detectives, and focused on establishing skills and techniques needed to conduct effective homicide investigations. Training should be offered shortly after a detective is first assigned to the homicide unit. The topics that training for newly-assigned homicide detectives should cover include:
  ○ Advanced interview and interrogation techniques

- Updates on legal requirements for searches and seizures
- Advanced forensics and evidence collection
- Advanced computer and cell phone forensics
- How to prepare homicide cases for court
- Steps that detectives can take to prevent the potential for wrongful convictions, such as how to properly record witness statements and assess and utilize eyewitness testimony and other evidence
- Investigating specific types of cases handled by homicide detectives, such as officer-involved shootings, child deaths, in-custody deaths, mass casualty scenes, infant deaths, arson deaths, etc.
- Best practices for conducting homicide investigations.
- Advanced training for new homicide unit detectives should take place within the detectives' first year in the unit. For example, according to the BJA best practices guide, the San Diego Police Department requires new homicide detectives to complete five weeks of advanced training within a year of joining the homicide unit.
- A homicide unit ideally should be staffed so that each detective is the lead on an average of four to six new homicide cases per year. This recommendation is based on best practices and on concerns that an increase in detectives' caseloads can be related to a decline in clearance rates.
- When possible, police agencies should seek to maximize the amount of time that homicide detectives spend investigating homicide cases by limiting the time they spend performing other duties, such as investigating non-homicide cases, performing administrative work, and serving on departmental details.
- Police agencies should explore creating a specialized unit whose full-time function is to locate witnesses and other persons of interest in violent crime investigations, including homicides. Having a specialized unit to serve this function is considered an effective use of personnel and a good practice for homicide investigations.
65. Rentz and Knezevich, "A Flawed, Inconsistent Police Response to Sexual Assault in Maryland"; End the Backlog, Joyful Heart Foundation.
66. Garrett, "The Costs and Benefits of Forensics," 605.
67. Ibid.
68. Allen Slater, "NYU School of Law Policing Project, Five-Minute Primers: Rapid DNA," Policing Projects, January 24, 2020, https://www.policingproject.org/news-main/2020/1/23/policing-project-five-minute-primers-rapid-dna.
69. National Institute of Justice, NCJ 220336, "Increasing Efficiency in Crime Laboratories," January 2008, 1.
70. Ibid., 2.
71. Ibid.
72. Ibid.
73. National Institute of Justice, "Status and Needs of Forensic Science Service Providers: A Report to Congress," NCJ 213420, March 2006, 4.
74. Paul C. Giannelli, "Crime Labs Need Improvement," *Science and Technology* 20, no. 1 (Fall 2003).
75. National Science and Technology Council Committee on Science Subcommittee on Forensic Science, Strengthening the Forensic Sciences, Executive Office of the President, May 1, 2017, 5.
76. *Id.* at 6.
77. Michael Kusluski, "An Easy Win for Criminal Justice Reform: Independent Crime Labs," *The Hill*, June 3, 2022, https://thehill.com/opinion/criminal-justice/3511295-an-easy-win-for-criminal-justice-reform-independent-crime-labs/.
78. Ibid.
79. Anthony A. Braga and Desiree Desseault, NCJ 252529, "Can Homicide Detectives Improve Homicide Clearance Rates?" Department of Justice, *Crime & Delinquency* 64, no. 3 (November 2016): 291, https://doi.org/10.1177/0011128716677916.
80. Ibid., 302–03.
81. Committee on Identifying the Needs of the Forensic Sciences Community, NCJRS 228091, "Strengthening Forensic

Science in the United States: A Path Forward," August 2009, 2.

82. Ibid.

83. See description of each OJP office on the
"About Us" page on the US Department
of Justice, Office of Justice Programs
website.

CHAPTER 5

1. Department of Justice Oversight, Funding
Forensic Science—DNA and Beyond Before the Subcommittee on Administrative
Oversight and the Courts and Committee on the Judiciary United States Senate,
108th Congress, 1, 2003 (Opening Statement of Jeff Sessions, Senator from the
State of Alabama).

2. Stephen Rushin and Roger Michalski,
"Police Funding," *Florida Law Review* 72,
no. 2 (2020): 277.

3. "Criminal Justice Expenditures: Police,
Corrections, and Courts," The Urban
Institute, 2020, https://www.urban.org
/policy-centers/cross-center-initiatives
/state-and-local-finance-initiative
/state-and-local-backgrounders/criminal
-justice-police-corrections-courts-expen
ditures.

4. Daniel T. Mollenkamp, "How Police
Departments Are Funded," Investopedia, April 15, 2022, https://www.investo
pedia.com/how-are-police-departments
-funded-5115578.

5. "Criminal Justice Expenditures: Police,
Corrections and Courts," Urban Institute,
https://www.urban.org/policy-centers
/cross-center-initiatives/state-and-local
-finance-initiative/state-and-local-back
grounders/criminal-justice-police
-corrections-courts-expenditures
#Question1Police.

6. Barbara B. Hagerty, "An Epidemic of
Disbelief," *The Atlantic*, July 22, 2019,
https://www.theatlantic.com/magazine
/archive/2019/08/an-epidemic-of-dis
belief/592807/?; Evie Taylor, "Untested
Rape Kits Are Sitting in Laboratories,"
The Boar, August 5, 2020, https://theboar
.org/2020/08/untested-rape-kits-are-sit

ting-in-laboratories/; Detroit Free Press,
"Detroit Rape Kit Testing Backlog Lingers," *USA Today*, April 21, 2014, https://
www.usatoday.com/story/news/nation
/2014/04/21/detroit-rape-kits-backlog
/7954957/; Violet Ikonomova, "The Last of
Detroit's Neglected Rape Kits Are Being
Tested," *Detroit Metro Times*, March 13,
2018, https://www.metrotimes.com/news
/the-last-of-detroits-neglected-rape-kits
-are-being-tested-10104983; Anna Clark,
"11,341 Rape Kits Were Collected and
Forgotten in Detroit. This Is the Story of
One of Them," *ELLE*, June 23, 2016, 6,
https://www.elle.com/culture/a37255/for
gotten-rape-kits-detroit/; Nancy Kaffer,
"Rape Kit Backlog Is Over. Here's Why
They Say It Can't Happen Again," *Detroit
Free Press*, August 18, 2019, https://www
.freep.com/story/opinion/columnists
/nancy-kaffer/2019/08/18/detroit-rape
-kit-backlog-wayne-county/2013234001/.

7. Bruce Vielmetti, "A Suspect in a Domestic Homicide Posted $250 Bail Af-
ter a Previous Violence Case. Here's
How Wisconsin Lawmakers Plan to
Prevent Repeats," *Milwaukee Journal Sentinel*, January 4, 2022, https://
www.jsonline.com/story/news
/crime/2022/01/04/dennis-kurasz
-charged-killing-girlfriend-milwaukee
-business/9095156002/.

8. John Rudolf, "Stockton's Poor Mired in
Violence After Police Cuts, Recession,"
Huffington Post, April 3, 2012, https://
www.huffpost.com/entry/stockton-poor
-poverty-crime-california_n_1346096.

9. Kimbriell Kelly et al., "Buried under
Bodies," *Washington Post*, September 13,
2018, https://www.washingtonpost.com
/news/national/wp/2018/09/13/feature
/even-with-murder-
rates-falling-big-city
-detectives-face-daunting-caseloads/.

10. Rudolf, "Stockton's Poor Mired in Violence After Police Cuts, Recession."

11. Kelly et al., "Buried under Bodies."

12. Ben Duronio, "Stockton Goes Bankrupt
and Already the Murder Rate Is Soaring,"

Business Insider, June 27, 2012, https://www.businessinsider.com/while-stockton-heads-for-largest-city-bankruptcy-ever-murder-surges-2012-6.

13. Kelly et al., "Buried under Bodies."
14. Duronio, "Stockton Goes Bankrupt and Already the Murder Rate Is Soaring."
15. Samuel Stebbins, "Stockton, CA Is Among the Most Dangerous US Metro Areas," 24/7 Wall St., last accessed March 4, 2023, https://247wallst.com/city/stockton-ca-is-among-the-most-dangerous-us-metro-areas/.
16. Michael Fitzgerald, "Stockton Police Force Still Shrinking," *Stocktontonia*, February 8, 2023, https://stocktonia.org/2023/02/08/stockton-police-force-still-shrinking/.
17. Barry Latzer, "Poverty and Violent Crime Don't Go Hand in Hand," *City Journal*, May 25, 2022, https://www.city-journal.org/article/poverty-and-violent-crime-dont-go-hand-in-hand.
18. For SPM measures, see Chad Stone et al., "A Guide to Statistics on Historical Trends in Income Inequality, Center for Budget and Policy Priorities," last modified January 13, 2020, https://www.cbpp.org/research/poverty-and-inequality/a-guide-to-statistics-on-historical-trends-in-income-inequality; John Creamer, "Supplemental Poverty Measure that Accounts for Additional Government Benefits Lowest on Record at 7.8%," US Census Bureau, September 13, 2022, https://www.census.gov/library/stories/2022/09/government-assistance-lifts-millions-out-of-poverty.html. For the 1967 crime rate, see "United States Crime Rates 1960–2019: United States Population and Rate of Crime per 100,000 People 1960–2019," Disaster Center, https://www.disastercenter.com/crime/uscrime.htm; for the 2021 rate, see "Reported Violent Crime Rate in the United States from 1990 to 2021," Statista, https://www.statista.com/statistics/191219/reported-violent-crime-rate-in-the-usa-since-1990/.

19. Estimates of the cost of crime in the United States range from over $300 billion to over $1 trillion annually. The cost of justice failures contributes to this crime cost (by generating more crime) and adds to it through hard-to-quantify personal costs to victims and society of seeing justice failing. See Aaron Chalfin, "The Economic Cost of Crime," December 16, 2013, 13, http://www.antoniocasella.eu/nume/Chalfin_2013_b.pdf.
20. "Criminal Justice Expenditures: Police, Corrections, and Courts," The Urban Institute; Richard C. Auxier, "What Police Spending Data Can (and Cannot) Explain Amid Calls to Defund the Police," *Urban Wire*, June 9, 2020, https://www.urban.org/urban-wire/what-police-spending-data-can-and-cannot-explain-amid-calls-defund-police. This in-depth analysis of police spending in New York adds additional insight into funding over time: Nicole Gelinas, "Defund the Police? New York City Already Did," Manhattan Institute, March 21, 2023.
21. "Criminal Justice Expenditures: Police, Corrections, and Courts," The Urban Institute.
22. Catherine Jacquet, "Domestic Violence in the 1970's," National Library of Medicine, October 15, 2015, https://circulatingnow.nlm.nih.gov/2015/10/15/domestic-violence-in-the-1970s/ https://circulatingnow.nlm.nih.gov/2015/10/15/domestic-violence-in-the-1970s/.
23. National Library of Medicine, "Appendix B: The History of Homelessness in the United States," https://www.ncbi.nlm.nih.gov/books/NBK519584/.
24. Counsel of State Governments, Eastern Kentucky University, NCJRS 216642, "The Impact of Terrorism on State Law Enforcement: Adjusting to New Roles and Changing Conditions," June 2006, 7.
25. Joel F. Shults, "Mission Creep in Policing," National Police Association, https://nationalpolice.org/mission-creep-in-policing/; David McElreath, Daniel Doss, et

al., "Modern Law Enforcement, Defunding, Mission Creep and the Next Generation of Policing," June 2020.

26. Shults, "Mission Creep in Policing"; McElreath et al., "Modern Law Enforcement, Defunding, Mission Creep and the Next Generation of Policing."

27. David Gambacorta, "More Murders, Fewer Cases Solved; Now Philly Police Are Fighting About Overtime," *The Philadelphia Inquirer*, December 6, 2018, https://www.inquirer.com/philly/news/murders-solved-homicides-philadelphia-police-overtime-20181205.html.

28. Ibid.

29. Ibid.

30. Ibid.

31. "Crime without Punishment: Homicide Clearance Rates Are Dropping in Philadelphia as Murder Rates Skyrocket," CBS Philadelphia, June 29, 2022, https://www.cbsnews.com/philadelphia/news/crime-without-punishment-homicide-clearance-rates-are-dropping-in-philadelphia-as-murder-rates-skyrocket/.

32. Ibid.

33. Ibid.

34. Ibid.

35. Mike D'Onofrio, "Philadelphia Homicides Hit Historic Level in 2021," Axios Philadelphia, January 10, 2022, https://www.axios.com/local/philadelphia/2022/01/10/philadelphia-record-homicides-2021-police.

36. Campbell Robertson, "'Everybody Is Armed': As Shootings Soar, Philadelphia: City Awash in Guns," *New York Times*, August 11, 2022, https://www.nytimes.com/2022/08/11/us/philadelphia-gun-violence-shootings.html.

37. Kelly et al., "Buried under Bodies."

38. Police Executive Research Forum, "Promising Strategies for Strengthening Homicide Investigations, Findings and Recommendations from the Bureau of Justice Assistance's Homicide Investigations Enhancement Training and Technical Assistance Project," October 2018, 42 and 12.

39. Lynda Cohen, "Atlantic County Has the Worst 2010 Homicide Solve Rate in New Jersey," *The Press of Atlantic City*, January 16, 2011, https://pressofatlanticcity.com/news/local/atlantic-county-has-the-worst-2010-homicide-solve-rate-in-new-jersey/article_00775d7c-2106-11e0b2c7001cc4c03286.html.

40. Charles Kuffner, "We Need More Context to the HPD No-Investigations Issue," Off the Kuff, June 23, 2014, http://www.offthekuff.com/wp/?p=61246.

41. John Lott, "Discussion of Chicago's Crime Problems Ignore What Rahm Emanuel Has Done to the Police Department," Crime Prevention Research Center, July 9, 2014.

42. Ibid.

43. Ibid.

44. Joseph Ferrandino, "Getting Away with Murder: Homicide Clearance by Arrest in Chicago and Its Community Areas," *Sage Journals* 25, no. 2 (May 2021): 163–88, https://doi.org/10.1177/1088767920941563.

45. Wale Aliyu, "State Report Finds Local Police Officers Aren't Getting Enough Training," Boston 25 News, November 19, 2019, https://www.boston25news.com/news/report-finds-local-police-officers-don-t-undergo-enough-training/1010040817/.

46. Ibid.

47. Fola Akinnibi et al., "Cities Say They Want to Defund the Police. Their Budgets Say Otherwise," Bloomberg, January 12, 2021, https://www.bloomberg.com/graphics/2021-city-budget-police-funding/.

48. Rod Brunson, "Protests Focus on Overpolicing. But Under-policing Is Also Deadly," *Washington Post*, June 6, 2020, https://www.washingtonpost.com/outlook/underpolicing-cities-violent-crime/2020/06/12/b5d1fd26-ac0c-11ea-9063-e69bd6520940_story.html.

49. Samir Ferdowsi, "Inside the Now 'Cop-Free' Zone Where George Floyd Was Killed," *Vice News*, March 12, 2021.

50. Jess Hardiman, "There's A No-Go Zone in US City that 'Police Won't Enter at Night,'" LAD Bible, July 3, 2021, https://www.ladbible.com/news/news-theres-a-no-go-zone-in-us-city-that-police-wont-even-enter-at-night-20210703.

51. Ibid.

52. Jeri D. Ropero-Miller and Nicole Jones, NCJ 304929, "Forensic Science State Commission and Oversight Bodies—A 2022 Update," US Department of Justice Office of Justice Programs, June 2022.

53. Department of Justice Oversight, Funding Forensic Science, 2.

54. Ibid.

55. Ibid.

56. National Institute of Justice, NCJ 213420, "Status and Needs of Forensic Science Service Providers: A Report to Congress," March 2006.

57. Ibid. In 2002, the report estimated that just to bring the turnaround time for evidence testing down to thirty days in those fifty largest laboratories would cost an additional $54 million.

58. Alan Neuhauser, "DNA Evidence Backlog Has Soared by 85 Percent," *US News*, March 22, 2019, https://www.usnews.com/news/national-news/articles/2019-03-22/dna-evidence-backlog-has-soared-by-85-percent. And this is despite the federal government spending a billion dollars since 2004 to combat the problem.

59. Mark Nelson, "Making Sense of DNA Backlogs: Myths vs. Reality," *NIJ Journal*, no. 266 (June 2010): 20–25, https://www.ojp.gov/sites/g/files/xyckuh241/files/media/document/230415.pdf.

60. Illinois State Police, "Reduction in State Forensic Backlog," *Chicago Daily Herald*, July 3, 2020.

61. Department of Justice Oversight, Funding Forensic Science, 2.

62. Staff Reports, "Funding for State Crime Lab a Disaster," *The Natchez Democrat*, February 4, 2021, https://www.natchezdemocrat.com/2021/02/04/funding-for-state-crime-lab-a-disaster/.

63. National Institute of Justice, "Status and Needs of Forensic Science Service Providers: A Report to Congress," 4.

64. Radley Balko, "Opinion—Mississippi Continues to Underfund Its Death Investigation System," *Washington Post*, February 20, 2018, https://www.washingtonpost.com/news/the-watch/wp/2018/02/20/mississippi-continues-to-underfund-its-death-investigation-system/.

65. Brandon L. Garrett, "The Costs and Benefits of Forensics," *Houston Law Review* 57, no. 3 (April 2020): 593–616.

66. Department of Justice Oversight, Funding Forensic Science, 2.

67. Kate Mather and Richard Winton, "LAPD Fingerprint Backlog More than Doubled in the Last Two Years," *Los Angeles Times*, September 9, 2014, https://www.latimes.com/local/crime/la-me-fingerprints-backlog-20140910-story.html.

68. "Acoma Pueblo Becomes the First Native American Tribe to Use the AB Kiosk System for Alcohol Monitoring," *Business Wire*, September 24, 2020, https://www.businesswire.com/news/home/20200924005009/en/Acoma-Pueblo-Becomes-the-First-Native-American-Tribe-to-Use-the-AB-Kiosk-System-for-Alcohol-Monitoring.

69. Kimmy Gustafson, "Modern Forensic Science Technologies," Forensic Colleges, last modified February 1, 2023, https://www.forensicscolleges.com/blog/resources/10-modern-forensic-science-technologies.

70. Department of Criminal Justice Services, "Review of Applicability of Transdermal Continuous Alcohol Monitoring Devices for First-Time DUI Convictions," October 2013, table 2.

71. Disha Raychaudhuri and Karen Sloan, "Prosecutors Wanted: District Attorneys Struggle to Recruit and Retain Lawyers,"

Reuters, April 13, 2022, https://www
.reuters.com/legal/transactional/prose
cutors-wanted-district-attorneys-strug
gle-recruit-retain-lawyers-2022-04-12/.

72. Ibid.

73. Ibid.

74. Raúl Torrez, "Underfunding of DA's Office Must Be fixed," *Albuquerque Journal*,
February 8, 2017, https://www.abqjour
nal.com/944875/underfunding-of-das
-office-must-be-fixed.html.

75. National Legal Aid & Defender Association, "National Advisory Commission
on Criminal Justice Standards and Goals,
The Defense (1973), Standard 13.12
Workload of Public Defenders," last accessed March 9, 2023, https://www.nlada
.org/defender-standards/national-advi
sory-commission.

76. Adam M. Gershowitz and Laura R. Kill-
inger, "The State (Never) Rests: How
Excessive Prosecutorial Caseloads Harm
Criminal Defendants," *Northwestern
Law Review* 105, no. 1 (2011): 272.

77. Ibid., 263.

78. Oren Bar-Gill and Omri Ben-Shahar,
"The Prisoners' (Plea Bargain) Dilemma," University of Michigan, Law
& Economics Working Papers Archive:
2003–2009, Art. 71 [2007], 11; see Jessica
Savage, "Jury trials Declining in Angelina
County," *The Lufkin Daily News*, September 26, 2009, https://lufkindailynews
.com/news/article_e086621f-3822-571a
-8e4c-60d7d3010dc5.html.

79. See Steven Perry and Durn Banks,
"Prosecutors in State Courts, 2007—
Statistical Tables," Bureau of Justice Statistics, December 2011, https://bjs.ojp
.gov/content/pub/pdf/psc07st.pdf.

80. "2007 State & Local Government Finance
Historical Datasets and Tables," US Census Bureau, 2007, table 1, https://www
.census.gov/data/datasets/2007/econ
/local/public-use-datasets.html.

81. Eric Westervelt, "'Where's the Anger?':
Oakland Family Reels from Death of
Beloved Teen Amid Rise in Gun Vio-
lence," NPR, December 7, 2021, https://

www.kqed.org/news/11898323/wheres
-the-anger-oakland-family-reels-from
-death-of-beloved-teen-amid-rise-in
-gun-violence.

82. Ibid.

83. Kim Parker and Kiley Hurst, "Growing Share of Americans Say They Want
More Spending on Police in Their Area,"
Pew Research Center, October 26,
2021, https://www.pewresearch.org/fact
-tank/2021/10/26/growing-share-of
-americans-say-they-want-more-spend
ing-on-police-in-their-area/.

84. Gathered from an analysis of data from
the US Census Bureau from 2018 and
2019. See "Datasets," US Census Bureau,
October 8, 2021.

85. Camille Squires, "US Cities Are Increasing Funding for Police, with Biden's Bless-
ing," Quartz, January 25, 2022, https://
qz.com/2116614/biden-calls-for-more
-funding-for-police-in-us-cities.

86. Don Babwin, "Report: Chicago Must
Overhaul Homicide Investigations,"
Associated Press, October 31, 2019,
https://www.police1.com/investigations
/articles/report-chicago-must-overhaul
-homicide-investigations-FJZKe7Flx
EYEdEMm/.

87. Jessica Lussenhop, "Clinton Crime Bill:
Why Is It So Controversial?" *BBC News
Magazine*, April 18, 2016, 6, https://
www.bbc.com/news/world-us-canada
-36020717.

88. Jonathan Klick and John M. MacDonald,
"Hire More Cops," *City Journal*, August
4, 2020, https://www.city-journal.org
/bolstering-police-forces-reduces-crime.

89. Weihua Li and Ilcha Mahajan, "American Police Say Officers Are Quitting in
Droves. Federal Data Says Otherwise,"
Time Magazine, September 4, 2021,
https://time.com/6093684/police-quit
ting-federal-data/.

90. "Test Rape Kits. Stop Serial Rapists," End
the Backlog, https://www.endthebacklog
.org/what-is-the-backlog/why-test-all-
kits/test-rape-kits-stop-serial-rapists/;
Tribune wire reporters, "Memphis

Police: 12,000 Backlogged Rape Kits Tested, Suspects ID'd," *Chicago Tribune*, March 9, 2015, https://www.chicagotribune.com/nation-world/chi-memphis-rape-kits-20150309-story.html.

91. Jessica Hamzelou, "US Rape Test Backlog Down to Mindset, Not Just Money," *New Scientist*, March 11, 2015, https://www.newscientist.com/article/mg22530125-200-us-rape-test-backlog-down-to-mindset-not-just-money/; "Hamm Consulting Client City of Memphis Secures $1.9 Million in Federal Funds," HAMM Consulting Group, September 10, 2015, https://www.hammconsulting.com/2015/09/hamm-consulting-client-city-of-memphis-secures-1-9-million-in-federal-funds/; Office of Manhattan District Attorney Cyrus R. Vance Jr., Results from the Manhattan District Attorney's Office, Sexual Assault Kit Backlog Elimination Grant Program 1, 14, March 2019.

92. Ryan Poe, "Memphis Wins Federal Grant to Process Rape Kits," Memphis Commercial Appeal, October 2, 2017, https://www.commercialappeal.com/story/news/government/city/2017/10/01/memphis-wins-federal-grant-process-rape-kits/721077001/.

93. "Test Rape Kits. Stop Serial Rapists."

94. Rachel Dissell, "Cleveland Police Expect All Untested Rape Kits to Be Cleared Out by Late Spring," *The Plain Dealer*, December 3, 2013, https://www.cleveland.com/court-justice/2013/12/cleveland_police_expect_all_un.html; "Cuyahoga Sexual Assault Kit Task Force," Cuyahoga County Office of the Prosecutor, http://prosecutor.cuyahogacounty.us/en-US/DNA-cold-case-task-force.aspx

95. "Test Rape Kits. Stop Serial Rapists"; Avery Williams, "Cuyahoga County Sexual Assault Task Force Brings over 800 Predators to Justice," 19 News, September 9, 2020, https://www.cleveland19.com/2020/09/09/cuyahoga-county-sexual-assault-kit-task-force-indictments

-survivors-conviction-rate-serial-offenders/.

96. United States Attorney's Office, "Eastern District of Michigan, Press Release: United States Department of Justice Announces Grants for the Eastern District of Michigan to Address Backlog of Untested Sexual Assault Kits," September 10, 2015.

97. "Test Rape Kits. Stop Serial Rapists: Detroit Michigan," End the Backlog, https://www.endthebacklog.org/what-is-the-backlog/why-test-all-kits/test-rape-kits-stop-serial-rapists/ .

98. Department of Justice Oversight, Funding Forensic Science, 2.

99. Ibid.

100. Garrett, "The Costs and Benefits of Forensics," 599.

101. Ibid.

102. Rachel Tillman, "Justice Dept. Announces $210M for Forensic Testing Aimed to Clear DNA Backlog," Spectrum News NY1, December 23, 2021, https://www.ny1.com/nyc/all-boroughs/news/2021/12/23/doj-grant-funds-dna-test-backlog-forensic-science.

103. Washington Courts, "Cost Fee Codes," last accessed March 9, 2023, https://www.courts.wa.gov/jislink/public/codes/clj/costfee.htm.

104. Patrick Marley, "Lawsuit Alleges Wisconsin Officials Knew Fee for DNA Database Was Unconstitutional but Imposed It Anyway," *Milwaukee Journal Sentinel*, March 7, 2018, https://www.jsonline.com/story/news/politics/2018/03/07/lawsuit-alleges-state-officials-knew-fee-dna-database-illegalviolated-constitution-fee-fund-dna-data/400796002/.

105. Office of the Executive Secretary, "Virginia Fees—Appendix B—Criminal & Traffic Fines and Fees, General District Court Manual," Department of Judicial Services, July 2021, B-1.

106. Sarah J. Berger, "New York Should Re-Examine Mandatory Court Fees Imposed on Individuals Convicted of

Criminal Offenses and Violations," New Yok City Bar, May 2019.

107. Joseph Shapiro, "As Court Fees Rise, the Poor Are Paying the Price," NPR, May 19, 2014, https://www.npr.org /2014/05/19/312158516/increasing -court-fees-punish-the-poor.

108. Garrett, "The Costs and Benefits of Forensics," 599.

109. See Kari Paul, "How Target, Google, Bank of America and Microsoft Quietly Fund Police through Private Donations," *The Guardian*, June 18, 2020,https://www.theguardian.com/us -news/2020/jun/18/police-foundations -nonprofits-amazon-target-microsoft; Daniel Fridman and Alex Luscomb, "Gift-Giving, Disreputable Exchange, and the Management of Donations in a Police Department," *Social Forces* 96, no. 2 (December 2017): 507–28.

110. Rushin and Michalski, "Police Funding," 325.

111. Ibid., 285.

CHAPTER 6

1. US Constitution amend. 4.

2. S. J. Wasserstrom, "Fourth Amendment's Two Clauses," *American Criminal Law Review* 26, no. 4 (1989): 1396, https:// www.ojp.gov/ncjrs/virtual-library/ab stracts/fourth-amendments-two-clauses.

3. "Fourth Amendment Search and Seizure," S. Doc. No. 103-6, 1203–5, https://www .govinfo.gov/content/pkg/GPO-CONAN -1992/pdf/GPO-CONAN-1992-10-5.pdf.

4. Ibid., 1217.

5. 367 US 643 (1961).

6. Ibid., 559–660.

7. Raymond A. Atkins and Paul H. Rubin, "Effects of Criminal Procedure on Crime Rates: Mapping Out the Consequences of the Exclusionary Rule," *The Journal of Law & Economics* 46, no. 1 (April 2003): 174.

8. Alan Judd, "Prestige Protects Even the Worst Abusers," *Dayton Daily News*, December 14, 2016, https://doctors.ajc.com /why_abusive_doctors_not_caught/.

9. Bradley v. State, 2011 WL 145177, at 1 (Del. April 13, 2011).

10. Ibid., 3.

11. Daniel Sandford, "US Airmen Terror Attack: Junead Khan Found Guilty," BBC News, April 1, 2016, https://www.bbc .com/news/uk-35944661.

12. Police and Criminal Evidence Act, 1984, c. 60 §§ 18(4-5), 32(2)(b) (Eng.); Christopher Slobogin, "An Empirically Based Comparison of American and European Regulatory Approaches to Police Investigation," *Michigan Journal of International Law* 22, no. 3 (2001): 442.

13. Ibid., 424.

14. 9/11 Commission Report, Final Report of the National Commission on Terrorist Attacks Upon the United States, July 22, 2004, 273.

15. Brinegar v. United States, 338 US 160, 164 (1949).

16. Ornelas v. United States, 517 US 690, 695 (1996).

17. Brinegar v. United States, 175–76.

18. Police and Criminal Evidence Act; Slobogin, "An Empirically Based Comparison of American and European Regulatory Approaches to Police Investigation," 426.

19. "Exceptions to the Warrant Requirement, Cornell Law School Legal Information Institute, last accessed February 3, 2023, https://www.law.cornell.edu/con stitution-conan/amendment-4/excep tions-to-the-warrant-requirement.

20. Kentucky v. King, 563 US 452, 460 (2011).

21. Slobogin, "An Empirically Based Comparison of American and European Regulatory Approaches to Police Investigation," 424.

22. Ibid., 426; Christopher Slobogin, "Comparative Empiricism and Police Investigative Practices," *North Carolina Journal of International Law* 37, no. 2 (2011): 348.

23. Ibid., 323–24.

24. Craig M. Bradley, "Germany Exclusionary Rule," *Harvard Law Review* 96, no. 5 (March 1983): 1039.

25. Ibid., 1038.
26. The German homicide clearance rate is above 90 percent. "Murder Case Clearance Rates of the Police in Germany from 2010 to 2021," Statista, 2023, https://www-statista-com.proxy.library.upenn.edu/statistics/1101828/police-murder-case-clearance-rate/. France has an 80 percent clearance rate. Marieke Liem et al., "Homicide Clearance in Western Europe," *European Journal of Criminology* 16, no. 1 (2019): 96, https://doi.org/10.1177/1477370818766484.
27. Slobogin, "Comparative Empiricism and Police Investigative Practices," 434.
28. Ibid., 434.
29. See the 1984 case of United States v. Leon 464 US 889; Megan McGlynn, "Competing Exclusionary Rules in Multistate Investigations: Resolving Conflicts of State Search and Seizure Law," *Yale Law Journal* 127, no. 2 (November 2018): 406, 410.
30. Yale Kamisar, *Mapp v. Ohio: The First Shot Fired in the Warren Court's Criminal Procedure "Revolution"* (Foundation Press, 2006).
31. Paul G. Cassell, "The Mysterious Creation of Search and Seizure Exclusionary Rules under State Constitutions," *Utah Law Review* (1993): 759.
32. 338 US 25, 28 (1949).
33. Elkins v. United States, 364 US 206 (1960).
34. Stone v. Powell, 428 US 465, 500 (1976) (Burger, C. J., concurring); Yale Kamisar, "In Defense of the Search and Seizure Exclusionary Rule (Law and Truth—The Twenty-First Annual National Student Federalist Society Symposium on Law and Public Policy—2002)," *Harvard Journal of Law & Public Policy* 26, no. 1 (2003): 112.
35. See "Fourth Amendment: State Criminal Procedure Statutes," Legal Information Institute, Cornell, https://www.law.cornell.edu/wex/fourth_amendment; Sydney Goldstein, "Search and Seizure Laws by State," FindLaw, March 4, 2021, https://www.lawinfo.com/resources/criminal-defense/search-seizure-laws-by-state.html.
36. Donald Dripps, "The Warren Court Criminal Justice Revolution: Reflections a Generation Later," *Ohio State Journal of Criminal Law* 3 (1983): 140.
37. Ibid., 140.
38. Sydney Goldstein, "Search and Seizure Laws by State," Lawinfo.com, last modified March 4, 2021, https://www.lawinfo.com/resources/criminal-defense/search-seizure-laws-by-state.html#new-hampshire.
39. Thomas K. Clancy, "Independent State Grounds: Should State Courts Depart from the Fourth Amendment in Construing their Own Constitutions, and If So, on What Basis Beyond Simple Disagreement with the United States Supreme Court Result?" *Mississippi Law Journal* 77 (2007).
40. Slobogin, "Comparative Empiricism and Police Investigative Practices," 431.
41. Ibid., 430.
42. Oren Bar-Gill and Barry Friedman, "Taking Warrants Seriously," *Northwestern University Law Review* 106, no. 4 (2012): 1666.
43. Ibid., 1667.
44. The violent crime rate in Pittsburgh is reported as having been 899/100,000 in 2010, while Los Angeles's rate was 559/100,000. "Los Angeles CA Crime Rate 1999–2018," Macrotrends, https://www.macrotrends.net/cities/us/ca/los-angeles/crime-rate-statistics.
45. Atkins and Rubin, "Effects of Criminal Procedure on Crime Rates," 157.
46. The rate of violent crime increased by nearly fivefold between 1960 and 1992. In 1960, an individual had a 1 in 622 chance of being a victim of a violent crime, and by 1992 the odds were 1 in 132. In a study by MIT, it was determined that a boy born in 1974 had a greater chance of being a homicide victim than a World War II soldier had of dying in battle. Office of

Justice Program, NCJ 152752, "Report Card on Crime and Punishment," 1994.

47. Pamela K. Lattimore, James Trudeau, K. Jack Riley, Jordan Leiter, and Steven Edwards, "Homicide in Eight U.S. Cities: Trends, Context, and Policy Implications," US Department of Justice, December 1997, 131–33, https://www.ojp.gov/sites/g/files/xyckuh241/files/media/document/homicide_trends.pdf.

48. David W. Moore, "Public Little Concerned About Patriot Act," Gallup News Service, September 9, 2003, https://news.gallup.com/poll/9205/public-little-concerned-about-patriot-act.aspx.

49. Ibid. Moore explains that Americans largely supported the PATRIOT Act's efforts to thwart terrorism despite the act raising some privacy concerns. In other words, fear of terrorism may have overpowered concerns about privacy in this instance. When the fear of terrorism began to fade, however, support for the PATRIOT Act faded as well, and some of its provisions lapsed in 2020. India Mckinney, "Section 215 Expired: Year in Review 2020," Electronic Frontier Foundation, December 29, 2020, https://www.eff.org/deeplinks/2020/12/section-215-expired-year-review-2020.

50. In 1967, 52 percent of people polled felt that the criminal law system was "too easy" on criminals. Post-Warren, in 1981, that number had grown to 83 percent. See Office of Legal Policy, "Report to the Attorney General on the Search and Seizure Exclusionary Rule," US Department Of Justice, 1986, reprinted in *Michigan J. L.* 22 Ref. (1989): 630.

51. See chapter 8, Section A, Reforms.

52. Ibid.

53. Leslie R. Caldwell, "Rule 41 Changes Ensure a Judge May Consider Warrants for Certain Remote Searches," Office of Public Affairs, US Department of Justice, June 20, 2016, https://www.justice.gov/archives/opa/blog/rule-41-changes-ensure-judge-may-consider-warrants-certain-remote-searches.

54. Elizabeth Groff and Tom McEwen, "Identifying and Measuring the Effects of Information Technologies on Law Enforcement Agencies: The Making Officer Redeployment Effective Program—A Guide for Law Enforcement," US Department of Justice, Office of Community Oriented Policing Services, 2008, 25.

55. Elaine Borakove and Rey Banks, "A Guide to Implementing Electronic Warrants," The Justice Management Institute, 2.

56. Jessica Miller and Aubrey Wieber, "Warrants Approved in Just Minutes: Are Utah Judges Really Reading Them Before Signing Off?" *The Salt Lake Tribune*, January 16, 2018, https://www.sltrib.com/news/2018/01/14/warrants-approved-in-just-minutes-are-utah-judges-really-reading-them-before-signing-off/.

57. Borakove and Banks, "A Guide to Implementing Electronic Warrants."

58. Jeffrey Bellin, "Crime-Severity Distinctions and the Fourth Amendment: Reassessing Reasonableness in a Changing World," *Iowa Law* 97 (2011): 6.

59. Bruce D. Hausknecht, "The Homicide Scene Exception to the Fourth Amendment Warrant Requirement: A Dead Issue," *Journal of Criminal Law & Criminology* 71, no. 3 (1980): 289, at 29.

60. Leslie G. Scarman, "Codification and Judge-Made Law: A Problem of Coexistence," *Indiana Law Journal* 42, no. 3 (1967): 365–66.

61. Ibid., 355.

62. Proceeds of Crime Act 2002, §47 Search, Seizure, and Detention of Property (Eng. & Wales, 2015).

63. Scarman, "Codification and Judge-Made Law," 355.

64. A comprehensive list of the most important Police Acts can be found at "Police Legislation," Police-Information.Co.UK, https://www.police-information.co.uk/Docs/legislation/index.html.

65. Sydney Goldstein, "Search and Seizure Laws By State," LawInfo, https://www.lawinfo.com/resources/criminal-de

fense/search-seizure-laws-by-state.html #alabama.

66. In Texas, the power given to officers to search a phone without a warrant is codified. See Texas Code of CRIM P Art. 18.0215; Riley v. California, 573 US 373 (2014).

67. Dickerson v. United States, 530 US 428 (2000) (explaining that voluntariness is only one inquiry in the Miranda warning procedure and declining to overturn the precedent case); Bram v. United States, 168 US 531, 1898, at 540–41.

68. Scott W. Howe, "Moving Beyond Miranda: Concessions for Confessions," *Northwestern University Law Review* 110, no. 4 (2016): 906.

69. Approximately 90 percent of juveniles waive their Miranda rights. Barry C. Feld, "Real Interrogation: What Actually Happens When Cops Question Kids," *Law & Society Review* 47, no. 1 (March 2013): 11.

70. Paul G. Cassell, "Miranda's Social Costs: An Empirical Reassessment," *Northwestern University Law Review* 90, no. 2 (Winter 1996): 437–38.

71. Miranda v. Arizona, 384 US 436, 542 (1966) (White, J., dissenting).

72. Paul G. Cassell and Bret S. Hayman, "Police Interrogation in the 1990s: An Empirical Study of the Effects of Miranda," *UCLA Law Review* 43 (1996): 848.

73. Paul G. Cassell and Richard Fowles, "Keynote Address: Still Handcuffing the Cops? A Review of Fifty Years of Empirical Evidence of Miranda's Harmful Effects on Law Enforcement," *Boston University Law Review* 97 (2017): 687.

74. Tommy Simmons, "Miranda Rights Error Undercuts Evidence in Kuna Rape Case," *Bingham County Chronicle*, September 29, 2019.

75. R. v. Argent, EWCA Crim J1216-2, 1996, https://www.casemine.com/judgement/uk/5a938b3e60d03e5f6b82baf5.

76. *Brown v. Mississippi* established the basis for the Fourteenth Amendment "voluntariness" doctrine as the due process test for assessing the admissibility of confessions in state cases. Brown v. Mississippi, 297 US 278 (1936), https://supreme.justia.com/cases/federal/us/297/278/.

77. Vanguard Court Watch Interns, "Death Penalty Abolition Group Charges Wrongful Conviction Rate Means Death Penalty Should Be Abolished," The People's Vanguard of Davis, January 22, 2022.

78. "Beneath the Statistics: The Structural and Systemic Causes of Our Wrongful Conviction Problem," Georgia Innocence Project, February 2022, https://www.georgiainnocenceproject.org/2022/02/01/beneath-the-statistics-the-structural-and-systemic-causes-of-our-wrongful-conviction-problem/.

79. Andriana Moskovska, "33 Startling Wrongful Convictions Statistics [2021 Update]," The High Court, October 13, 2021, https://thehighcourt.co/wrongful-convictions-statistics/#:~:text=1.-,Between%202%25%20and%2010%25%20of%20convicted%20individuals,in%20US%20prisons%20are%20innocent.&text=According%20to%20the%202019%20annual,between%202%25%20and%2010%25.

80. "Combining empirically based estimates for each of these three factors, a reasonable (and possibly overstated) calculation of the wrongful conviction rate appears, tentatively, to be somewhere in the range of 0.016%–0.062%." Paul Cassell, "How Often Are Innocent People Convicted," Volokh Conspiracy, November 1, 2018.

81. Ibid.

82. Cassell, "Miranda's Social Costs," 439.

83. Paul G. Cassell and Bret S. Hayman, "Police Interrogation in the 1990s: An Empirical Study of the Effects of Miranda," *UCLA Law Review* 43 (1996): 589.

84. Ibid., 871.

85. Cassell, "Miranda's Social Costs," 471.

86. Ibid., 419.

87. Slobogin, "Comparative Empiricism and Police Investigative Practices," 448.

88. Cassell and Hayman, "Police Interrogation in the 1990s," 850–54 (Salt Lake City data was used, there were 219 suspects in the study, which was conducted in 1994; Pittsburgh was used in a study with 157 suspects in 1966).

89. FBI, "Crime in the United Stats: 2019 Arrest Data," https://ucr.fbi.gov/crime-in -the-u.s/2019/crime-in-the-u.s.-2019 /tables/table-29. One-third of 500,000 is 167,000. While the FBI data is not entirely complete, it is the best source available for this data.

90. Because if 167,000 violent crime confessions occur each year after Miranda, and Miranda reduced confession rates by 10 percent, then the unreduced number of confessions would have been about 185,000.

91. Cassell, "Miranda's Social Costs," 395.

92. Ibid., 395–437.

93. Stephen J. Schulhofer, "Miranda's Practical Effect: Substantial Benefits and Vanishingly Small Social Costs," *Northwestern University Law Review* 90, no. 2 (1995–1996): 545.

94. Paul G. Cassell and Richard Fowles, "Handcuffing the Cops? A Thirty-Year Perspective on Miranda's Harmful Effects on Law Enforcement," *Stanford Law Review* 50, no. 4 (1998): 1126. ("Our regression equations and accompanying causal analysis suggest that, without Miranda, the number of crimes cleared would be substantially higher—by as much as 5.5–29.7% for robbery, 6.2–29.8% for burglary, 0.4–11.0% for larceny, and 12.8–45.4% for vehicle theft.")

95. Cassell and Fowles, "Keynote Address," 731–32.

96. Schulhofer, "Miranda's Practical Effect," 546.

97. 4,700 lost violent criminal convictions times 56 years (1966 to 2022) = 263,200. If the true number of lost violent criminal clearances each year is 28,000, the number becomes 1,568,000, which even accounting for the lag between clearance

and conviction rates would still be well over a million.

98. Griffin v. California, 380 US 609, 615 (1965) (holding that the Fifth Amendment privilege against self-incrimination "forbids either comment by the prosecution on the accused's silence or instructions by the court that such silence is evidence of guilt").

99. See the "Public Concerns" subsection.

100. Ibid.

101. Darryl K. Brown, "Permitting Post-Miranda Questioning in Exchange for Regulating Interrogation Tactics," *Texas Tech Law Review* 54 (Fall 2021): 18.

102. See, for example, Erwin Chemerinsky, "Why Have Miranda Rights Failed," *Democracy a Journal of Ideas*, June 27, 2016, https://democracyjournal.org/argu ments/why-have-miranda-rights -failed/; Cassell, "Miranda's Social Cost," 478.

103. Feld, "Real Interrogation," 11.

104. Chemerinsky, "Why Have Miranda Rights Failed."

105. Steven B. Duke, "Does Miranda Protect the Innocent or the Guilty?" *Chapman Law Review* 10, no. 3 (2007): 552.

106. Jerold H. Israel, "Criminal Procedure, the Burger Court, and the Legacy of the Warren Court," in *Neither Conservative nor Liberal: The Burger Court in Civil Rights and Liberties* (R. E. Krieger Pub. Co., 1983), 81.

107. Lackland H. Bloom, "Miranda v. Arizona, in Do Great Cases Make Bad Law?" *Oxford Academic*, April 2014.

108. Ibid.

109. Dickerson v. United States, 530 US 428 (2000).

110. "Supreme Court's Miranda Decision—The Public's Opinion," Gallup News Service, June 27, 2000, https://news .gallup.com/poll/2779/supreme-courts -miranda-decision.aspx.

111. New York v. Quarles, 467 US 649 (1984).

112. People v. Doll, 21 N.Y.3d 665, 668 (2013).
113. Slobogin, "Comparative Empiricism and Police Investigative Practices," 450.
114. Roman Battaglia, "Bill Filed to Require Recording of Police Interrogations," Delaware Public Media, May 28, 2021, https://www.delawarepublic.org/politics-government/2021-05-28/bill-filed-to-require-recording-of-police-interrogations.
115. Yvonne Daly et al., "Human Rights Protections in Drawing Inferences from Criminal Suspects' Silence," *Human Rights Law Review* 21, no. 3 (September 2021): 697.
116. Israel: The Criminal Procedure Law (Enforcement Powers—Arrests), 5766-1996, Courts and legal procedures—criminal procedure—enforcement powers—arrests, Section 28, https://www.nevo.co.il/law_html/law01/055_103.htm#Seif17 (in Hebrew).
117. William Pizzi, *Trials Without Truth: Why Our System of Criminal Trials Has Become an Expensive Failure and What We Need to Do to Rebuild It*, first edition (New York University Press, 1998) (see chapter 3).
118. Slobogin, "Comparative Empiricism and Police Investigative Practices."
119. Steven Aftergood, "The Right to Remain Silent Around the World," The Federation of American Scientists, June 30, 2016, https://fas.org/blogs/secrecy/2016/06/miranda/.
120. David Dixon and Nicholas Cowdery, "Silence Rights," *Australian Indigenous Law Review* 17, no. 1 (2013): 23–37.
121. "American Civil Liberties Union, FAQ: The Covenant on Civil & Political Rights (ICCPR)," ACLU, https://www.aclu.org/other/faq-covenant-civil-political-rights-iccpr.
122. Scott W. Howe, "Moving Beyond Miranda: Concessions for Confessions," *Northwestern University Law Review* 110, no. 4 (2016): 906.
123. United States Sentencing Committee, §3E1.1—Acceptance of Responsibility, https://guidelines.ussc.gov/gl/§3E1.1.
124. Vega V. Tekoh, 597 US (2022) (holding that a defendant who is not read their Miranda rights cannot sue the officer civilly).
125. Pizzi, *Trials Without Truth*.
126. Criminal Justice and Public Order Act 1994, c. 33, https://www.legislation.gov.uk/ukpga/1994/33/contents.
127. Ibid.
128. See, for example, United States v. Goldman, 563 F.2d 501 (1st Cir. 1977).

CHAPTER 7

1. Paul R. Brewer and Barbara Ley, "Media Use and Public Perceptions of DNA Evidence," *Science Communication* 32, no. 1 (2010): 94, https://doi.org/10.1177/1075547009340343.
2. Andrew Perrin, "About Half of Americans Are OK with DNA Testing Companies Sharing User Data with Law Enforcement," Pew Research Center, February 4, 2020, https://www.pewresearch.org/fact-tank/2020/02/04/about-half-of-americans-are-ok-with-dna-testing-companies-sharing-user-data-with-law-enforcement/.
3. Ann Coulter, "Why Is Ancestry.com Protecting Serial Killers?" *Waterloo-Cedar Falls Courier* (online), June 6, 2021.
4. Brooke Auxier and Lee Rainie, "Key Takeaways on Americans' Views About Privacy," Pew Research Center, November 15, 2019, https://www.pewresearch.org/fact-tank/2019/11/15/key-takeaways-on-americans-views-about-privacy-surveillance-and-data-sharing/.
5. Eric Tucket and Hannah Fingerhut, "Americans Warier of U.S. Government Surveillance: AP-NORC Poll," AP News, September 7, 2021, https://apnews.com/article/technology-afghanistan-race-and-ethnicity-racial-injustice-government-surveillance-d365f3a818bb9d096e8e3b5713f9f856 .

6. Mark Landler and Dalia Sussman, "Poll Finds Strong Acceptance for Public Surveillance," *New York Times*, April 30, 2013, https://www.nytimes.com/2013/05/01/us/poll-finds-strong-acceptance-for-public-surveillance.html.

7. "What's Wrong with Public Video Surveillance?" American Civil Liberties Union, March 2002, https://www.aclu.org/other/whats-wrong-public-video-surveillance.

8. Ibid.

9. Ibid.

10. Tanvi Misra, "Who's Tracking Your License Plate," Bloomberg News, December 6, 2018, https://www.bloomberg.com/news/articles/2018-12-06/why-privacy-advocates-fear-license-plate-readers.

11. Michael McLaughlin and Daniel Castro, "The Critics Were Wrong: NIST Data Shows the Best Facial Recognition Algorithms Are Neither Racist Nor Sexist," Information Technology & Innovation Foundation, January 27, 2020, https://itif.org/publications/2020/01/27/critics-were-wrong-nist-data-shows-best-facial-recognition-algorithms.

12. Open Technology Institute, "Civil Rights Concerns Regarding Law Enforcement Use of Face Recognition Technology," June 3, 2021, https://www.newamerica.org/oti/briefs/civil-rights-concerns-regarding-law-enforcement-use-of-face-recognition-technology/.

13. Christopher Reddick, "Public Opinion on National Security Agency Surveillance Programs: A Multi-Method Approach," *Government Information Quarterly* 32, no. 2 (April 2015): 129–41.

14. "What's Wrong with Public Video Surveillance?"

15. Lee Rainie and Mary Madden, "Americans' Views on Government Surveillance Programs," Pew Research Center, March 16, 2015, https://www.pewresearch.org/internet/2015/03/16/americans-views-on-government-surveillance-programs/.

16. Sam Sabin, "States Are Moving on Privacy Bills. Over 4 in 5 Voters Want Congress to Prioritize Protection of Online Data," Morning Consultant, April 27, 2021, https://morningconsult.com/2021/04/27/state-privacy-congress-priority-poll/.

17. David Cuthbertson, "Privacy Impact Assessment Integrated Automated Fingerprint Identification System National Security Enhancements," Department of Justice, June 2021.

18. Thales Group, "Automated Fingerprint Identification System (AFIS) Overview—A Short History," last modified January 27, 2022, https://www.thalesgroup.com/en/markets/digital-identity-and-security/government/biometrics/afis-history.

19. See, for example, "The FBI Story: 2011," Federal Bureau of Investigation, December 1, 2011, 98.

20. Federal Bureau of Investigation National Press Office, "The FBI's Combined DNA Index System (CODIS) Hits Major Milestone," May 21, 2021.

21. Ibid.

22. "DNA Arrestee Laws," National Conference of State Legislatures, 2013, https://leg.mt.gov/content/Committees/Interim/2015-2016/Law-and-Justice/Meetings/Apr-2016/Exhibits/ncsl-arrestee-dna-laws-april-2016.pdf.

23. For example, Maryland House Bill 30 sought to ban law enforcement from accessing DNA databases entirely. However, this ban ultimately failed. Lindsey Van Ness, "DNA Databases Are Boon to Police but Menace to Privacy, Critics Say," Stateline, February 2020, https://www.pewtrusts.org/en/research-and-analysis/blogs/stateline/2020/02/20/dna-databases-are-boon-to-police-but-menace-to-privacy-critics-say.

24. Shelby Kail, "The Unintended Consequences of California Proposition 47: Reducing Law Enforcement's Ability to Solve Serious, Violent Crimes," *Pepperdine Law Review* 44, no. 5 (2017): 1059–60 .

25. "Frequently Asked Questions on CODIS and NDIS," Federal Bureau of Investigations, https://www.fbi.gov/how-we-can -help-you/dna-fingerprint-act-of-2005 -expungement-policy/codis-and-ndis -fact-sheet.

26. Andrea Marks, "DNA Search Method that Caught Golden State Killer No Longer Available," *Rolling Stone*, May 23, 2019, https://www.rollingstone.com /culture/culture-news/dna-search -method-that-caught-the-golden-state -killer-no-longer-available-839315/; Emily Shapiro, "'Golden State Killer' Survivor Confronts Rapist: 'Remember what I have to say,'" ABC News, August 19, 2020, https://abcnews.go.com/US /golden-state-killer-survivor-confronts -rapist-remember/story?id=72451348; Brandi Cummings, "Stockton Couple 'Lucky' to Have Lived through Serial Killer's Attack," KCRA 3 NBC, April 26, 2018; Peter Crooks, "Chasing Evil," *Diablo Magazine*, January 29, 2018, https:// www.diablomag.com/people-style /people/chasing-evil/article_9efb68ea -3e74-5401-9ece-af7529a92c12.html; Tim Arango et al., "To Catch a Killer: A Fake Profile on a DNA Site and a Pristine Sample," *New York Times*, April 27, 2018, https://www.nytimes.com/2018/04/27 /us/golden-state-killer-case-joseph-de angelo.html; Justin Jouvenal, "To Find Alleged Golden State Killer, Investigators First Found His Great-Great-Great-Grandparents," *Washington Post*, April 30, 2018, https://www.washingtonpost .com/local/public-safety/to-find-alleged -golden-state-killer-investigators -first-found-his-great-great-great -grandparents/2018/04/30/3c865fe7 -dfcc-4a0e-b6b2-0bec548d501f_story .html.

27. DeAngelo is also sometimes referred to as the "Original Night Stalker" because the label "Night Stalker" would later be applied to Richard Ramirez, a different serial killer.

28. Jennifer L. Doleac, "The Effect of DNA Databases on Crime," August 1, 2016, https://papers.ssrn.com/sol3/papers.cfm ?abstract_id=2556948). While correlation is not causation, the rise of DNA databases across the United States in the first decade of the twenty-first century coincided with a decrease in both violent and property crimes, with violent crime falling by 17 percent in that period, leading some to suggest a partial causal connection.

29. National Institute of Justice, NCJ 207203, "DNA in 'Minor' Crimes Yields Major Benefits in Public Safety," November 2004.

30. "Perpetrators of Sexual Violence: Statistics," Rape, Abuse & Incest National Network, https://www.rainn.org/statistics /perpetrators-sexual-violence.

31. Philip J. Cook et al., "Criminal Records of Homicide Offenders," National Library of Medicine, August 3, 2005, https:// pubmed.ncbi.nlm.nih.gov/16077054/.

32. What used to be a 370 number of matches in a year increased to over 700 following the implementation of the policy. See Julie E. Samuels et al., "Collecting DNA at Arrest: Policies, Practices, and Implications, Final Technical Report," The Urban Institute Doc. No. 242812, 2013.

33. See People v. Buza, 129 Cal. Rptr.3d 753 (2011).

34. California Department of Justice, Impacts of Buza Decision on CAL-DNA Submissions and Hits June 2011–March 2012 (4/30/12); see People v. Buza, 4 Cal.5th 658 (Cal. 2018).

35. Kail, "The Unintended Consequences of California Proposition 47," 1058.

36. Ibid.

37. 28 CFR § 28.12—Collection of DNA Samples.

38. The 2013 decision in *Maryland v. King* compared taking DNA to taking an arrestee's photographs or fingerprints. Maryland v. King 569 US 435 (2013). The Court specifically approved the taking of DNA from anyone arrested on a

"serious offense," the issue in the case, but as the dissent notes, the logic of the decision means that DNA also could be taken from a misdemeanor arrestee. Ibid., 480; See Samuels, "Collecting DNA at Arrest," 33.

39. The federal government has jurisdiction to criminalize and punish only those criminal offenses that touch upon a federal interest, such as damaging federal property, or involve multiple states, as in multistate drug conspiracies. The Tenth Amendment of the US Constitution reserved to the states all powers not specifically granted to the federal government.

40. Thea Denean Hall, "Public Perception and Privacy Issues with DNA Regulations and Database in Alabama," *Walden Dissertations and Doctoral Studies Collection* (2016): 25; Richard Wolf, "Supreme Court OKs DNA Swab of People under Arrest," *USA Today*, June 3, 2013, https://www.usatoday.com/story/news/politics/2013/06/03/supreme-court-dna-cheek-swab-rape-unsolved-crimes/2116453/.

41. "DNA Arrestee Laws."

42. Charlotte Spencer, "What Is the Arrestee DNA Collection Law in Your State?" Biometrica, May 27, 2021, https://www.biometrica.com/what-is-the-arrestee-dna-collection-law-in-your-state/.

43. Ibid.

44. Sarah B. Berson, "Debating DNA Collection," *NIJ Journal* 264 (November 2009): 10; Hall, "Public Perception and Privacy Issues with DNA Regulations and Database in Alabama," 24.

45. Ibid.

46. Ibid., 11.

47. See Jason Kreag, "Going Local: The Fragmentation of Genetic Surveillance," *B. U. Law Review* 95, no. 5 (October 2015): 1554.

48. "Currently, nearly 6 million samples are stored, although one in seven of these are estimated to be duplicates, but that is still approaching 10% of the population." Peter D. Turnpenny, "Forensic Science and DNA Databases," Emery's Elements of Medical Genetics and Genomics, 2022, https://www.sciencedirect.com/topics/medicine-and-dentistry/dna-database.

49. Duncan Carling, "Less Privacy Please, We're British: Investigating Crime with DNA in the U.K. and the U.S.," *Hastings International and Comparative Law Review* 31, no. 1 (2008): 496. Though the DNA of arrested, but not convicted, persons is eventually deleted if they are not implicated in any new crimes. Ibid.

50. Ibid., 496.

51. Virginia Hughes, "Two New Laws Restrict Police Use of DNA Search Method," *New York Times*, May 31, 2021, https://www.nytimes.com/2021/05/31/science/dna-police-laws.html.

52. Ibid.

53. Van Ness, "DNA Databases Are Boon to Police but Menace to Privacy, Critics Say"; "HB 340: Legitimizing Law Enforcement's Access to DNA," Libertas Institute, 2022, https://libertas.org/bill/hb-340-legitimizing-law-enforcement-access-to-dna/; Jessica Miller, "Utahns, Lawmaker Disagree on Police Use of DNA Databases," *The Salt Lake Tribune*, February 17, 2020, https://www.sltrib.com/news/2020/02/17/utah-lawmaker-wants-stop/.

54. Van Ness, "DNA Databases Are Boon to Police but Menace to Privacy, Critics Say."

55. Jon Schuppe, "Police Were Cracking Cold Cases with a DNA Website. Then the Fine Print Changed," NBC News, October 23, 2019, https://www.nbcnews.com/news/us-news/police-were-cracking-cold-cases-dna-website-then-fine-print-n1070901.

56. Van Ness, "DNA Databases Are Boon to Police but Menace to Privacy, Critics Say."

57. Schuppe, "Police Were Cracking Cold Cases with a DNA Website."

58. Perrin, "About Half of Americans Are OK with DNA Testing Companies Sharing User Data with Law Enforcement."

59. Terry Spencer, "Use of Online DNA Databases by Law Enforcement Leads to Backlash and Website Changes," PBS News Hour, June 7, 2019, https://www.pbs.org/newshour/nation/use-of-online-dna-databases-by-law-enforcement-leads-to-backlash-and-website-changes.

60. Spencer, "What Is the Arrestee DNA Collection Law In Your State?" Also see "DNA Arrestee Laws."

61. Michele Hanisee, "New DNA Tools Helps to Identify Murder Victims and Rapists," Association of Deputy District Attorneys, August 28, 2019, https://www.laadda.com/2019/08/28/new-dna-tool-helps-identify-murder-victims-and-elusive-killers-and-rapists/.

62. US Department of Justice, Global Justice Information Sharing Initiative, "An Introduction to Familial DNA Searching for State, Local, and Tribal Justice Agencies," August 2016.

63. For example, children with criminal parents are 2.4 times more likely to engage in criminality themselves. See Sytske Besemer, Shaikh Ahmad, Stephen Hinshaw, and David Farrington, "A Systematic Review and Meta-Analysis of the Intergenerational Transmission of Criminal Behavior," *Aggression and Violent Behavior* 37 (2017): 161–78, https://doi.org/10.1016/j.avb.2017.10.004.

64. Protection of Freedoms Act 2012, 2012 UK, https://www.legislation.gov.uk/ukpga/2012/9/contents/enacted. The legislation also added a further limitation that the DNA of those arrested—but not charged or convicted—would be deleted from the database after a set period of time if no new arrests take place.

65. While it is not expected that the individuals who voluntarily submit their DNA for addition to the database are the individuals at high risk of committing the serious offenses discussed earlier, it remains beneficial to have their DNA in the database in case they do commit such felonies later or in case their relatives do.

66. House of Lords, Select Committee on the Constitution, "Surveillance and Citizens of the State," February 6, 2009, 43.

67. Eric L. Piza et al., "CCTV Surveillance for Crime Prevention, A 40-Year Systemic Review with Meta-Analysis," *Criminology & Public Policy* 18, no. 1 (2019): 159.

68. Dale Weidman, "Does DNA and Video Surveillance Assist in Solving Homicides?" Master of Arts Dissertation, University of the Fraser Valley, 2017 (on file with the author).

69. Thomas D. Albright, "Why Eyewitnesses Fail, National Center for Biotechnology Information," July 24, 2017, https://www.ncbi.nlm.nih.gov/pmc/articles/PMC5544328/.

70. Kyle Cheromcha, "Florida Uber Driver in Stolen $250,000 Ferrari Busted by Cop's License Plate Reader," The Drive, January 2, 2018; Trey Couvillion, "License Plate Reader Spots Stolen Car, Man Arrested After Brief Pursuit," WBRZ2 ABC, March 24, 2018; Bay City News, "License Plate Cams Lead Sausalito Police to Vehicle Stolen from San Jose," ABC7 News, April 28, 2018; James W. Jakobs, "License Plate Reader Helps Fresno Police Catch Stolen Car Suspect," ABC30 Action News, July 24, 2018.

71. Alina Haines, "The Role of Automatic Number Plate Recognition Surveillance Within Policing and Public Reassurance," Doctoral Thesis submitted to the University of Huddersfield, December 2009, 61.

72. Brad Heath, "Police Secretly Track Cellphones to Solve Routine Crimes," *USA Today*, August 23, 2015, https://www.usatoday.com/story/news/2015/08/23/baltimore-police-stingray-cell-surveillance/31994181/.

73. Ibid.

74. Commonwealth v. Henley, No. SJC-12951 (Mass. August 5, 2021); Commonwealth v. Zachery 488 Mass. 95; Peter Schworm, "2 Arraigned in Snow-Crew

Fatal Shooting; Victim had Belonged to Rival Boston Gang," *The Boston Globe*, May 5, 2015; Associated Press, "18-Year-Old Boston Man, Josiah Zachery, Faces Murder Charge," Mass Live, March 24, 2019; Laura Crimaldi, "Calls, Texts Linked to Shooting: Boston Man Held in Shoveler's Death," *The Boston Globe*, February 28, 2015; Antonio Planas, "Cops: Slay Suspect Story a Snow Job," *Boston Herald*, February 13, 2015; Electronic Privacy Information Center, Commonwealth v. Zachery; David Ertischek, "Life Terms with Possible Parole for Two Convicted in Jamaica Plain Murder," *Jamaica Plain News*, December 4, 2017; Evan Allen, "Second Suspect Held in Death of Worker Who Shoveled Snow: Victim's Kin Laud Police for Arrest," *The Boston Globe*, February 27, 2015; Adam Vaccaro, "Use of CharlieCard Data by Police Raises Concerns," *The Boston Globe*, July 23, 2020.

75. See, for example, Commonwealth v. Mora 150 N.E.3d 297 (Mass. 2020); Paul Leighton, "Wiretaps, Undercover Buys Led to Big Drug Bust," *Salem News*, May 24, 2018; Julie Manganis, "SJC: Police Will Need Warrants for Remote Surveillance," *Gloucester Times*, August 6, 2020; Douglas Ankney, "Massachusetts Supreme Judicial Court Announces Use of Pole Cameras for Extended Surveillance of Residence Constitutes Search Under State Law," *Criminal Legal News*, December 15, 2020.

76. Commonwealth v. Mora, 486 Mass 360 (Mass. 2020).

77. See Gary C. Robb, "Police Use of CCTV Surveillance: Constitutional Implications and Proposed Regulations," *University of Michigan Journal of Law Reform* 13, no. 3 (1980): 602.

78. The Fourth Amendment seems to be the primary potential restraint, but some have argued that even the First Amendment provides a barrier to surveillance camera usage as well. See Nancy G. La Vigne et al., "Evaluating the Use of Public Surveillance Systems for Crime Control and Prevention," Urban Institute Justice Policy Center, September 2011; Jennifer M. Granholm, "Video Surveillance on Public Streets: The Constitutionality of Invisible Citizens Searches," *University of Detroit Law Review* 64, no. 4 (Summer 1987); Gillian Vernick, "Supreme Court Asked to Consider Whether Long-Term Pole Camera Surveillance Constitutes Search under Fourth Amendment," Reporters Committee for Freedom of the Press, October 18, 2021, https://www.rcfp.org/scotus-pole-camera-surveillance/.

79. See Joseph Lanuti, "Caught Holding the Bag, Constitutional Limits on Live Video Surveillance," *American Criminal Law Review* 55, no. 1 (2018): 1; also see Commonwealth v. Mora, 486 Mass 360 (Mass. 2020).

80. Lanuti, "Caught Holding the Bag, Constitutional Limits on Live Video Surveillance," 3–4.

81. La Vigne et al., "Evaluating the Use of Public Surveillance Systems for Crime Control and Prevention," 11.

82. Ibid.

83. Paul Bischoff, "Surveillance Camera Statistics: Which Cities Have the Most CCTV Cameras?" Comparitech, July 11, 2022, https://www.comparitech.com/vpn-privacy/the-worlds-most-surveilled-cities/#:~:text=London%2C%20England%20(UK)**%20%E2%80%94,13.35%20cameras%20per%201%2C000%20people; see also Jurgita Lapientye, "This Is the Most Heavily Surveilled City in the U.S.: 50 CCTV Cameras per 1,000 citizens," Cyber News, September 28, 2021, https://cybernews.com/editorial/this-is-the-most-heavily-surveilled-city-in-the-us-50-cctv-cameras-per-1000-citizens.

84. This is one camera for every thirteen people. Bischoff, "Surveillance Camera Statistics."

85. Fiona Brookman et al., "The Use of CCTV During Homicide Investigations:

Contributions, Challenges, and Risks," Briefing Paper for Homicide Investigation and Forensic Science Protect at the University of South Wales.

86. Lily Robin et al., "Public Surveillance Cameras and Crime: The Impact of Different Camera Types on Crimes and Clearance," Urban Institute, February 8, 2020, 8, https://www.urban.org/sites/default/files/publication/101649/public_surveillance_cameras_and_crime.pdf.

87. Natalie Delgadillo, "Amid Spiking Homicide Rate, D.C. Will Spend $5 Million to Install New Security Cameras Around the City," dcist.com, November 24, 2019, https://dcist.com/story/19/11/25/amid-spiking-homicide-rate-d-c-will-spend-5-million-to-install-new-security-cameras-around-the-city/.

88. Weidman, "Does DNA and Video Surveillance Assist in Solving Homicides?" 29; Similarly, an Australian study found that the use of CCTV cameras on rail networks increased crime clearance rates by 18 percent. Anthony Morgan and Christopher Dowling, "Does CCTV Help Police Solve Crime?" *Trends and Issues in Crime and Criminal Justice* 576 (April 2019): 15.

89. FBI UCR data for 2019 showed 1.2 million violent crimes reported to police. While violent victimizations were much higher, increasing the clearance rate affects only reported crimes. While CCTV might allow police to catch some unreported crimes, the effect is not likely to be large. "UCR FBI: 2019," Department of Justice, https://ucr.fbi.gov/crime-in-the-u.s/2019/crime-in-the-u.s.-2019/topic-pages/violent-crime.

90. Kate Dailey, "The Rise of CCTV Surveillance in the US," BBC, April 29, 2013, https://www.bbc.com/news/magazine-22274770.

91. Elizabeth Kennedy, "Boston Marathon Leverages Surveillance for Security," Security 101, April 14, 2016, https://www.security101.com/blog/boston-marathon-leverages-surveillance-for-security.

92. Greg Botelho, "Trail of Videos, Receipts, Tips Lead Police to Philadelphia Woman, Alleged Abductor," CNN, November 6, 2014, https://www.cnn.com/2014/11/06/justice/philadelphia-abduction/index.html.

93. Marco Margaritoff, "The Neo-Nazi Terrorist Behind the London Nail Bombings," All That's Interesting, May 27, 2021, https://allthatsinteresting.com/david-copeland.

94. Daniel Rennie, "How James Bulger Was Killed by Jon Venables and Robert Thompson," All That's Interesting, October 14, 2021, https://allthatsinteresting.com/james-bulger-case.

95. Mariah Timms and Zusha Elinson, "More Cities Turn to Surveillance Cameras, Like One that Caught Tyre Nichols Beating," *Wall Street Journal*, February 3, 2023, https://www.wsj.com/articles/cameras-like-one-that-captured-tyre-nichols-beating-are-multiplying-across-u-s-11675398852?mod=djem10point.

96. Closed-circuit Television (CCTV), Coll. of Policing (Oct. 1, 2021), https://www.college.police.uk/research/crime-reduction-toolkit/cctv [https://perma.cc/5TSD-GENM].

97. https://www.comparitech.com/blog/vpn-privacy/us-surveillance-camera-statistics

98. Jennifer Brett, "Real-Time Crime Fighting in Atlanta. Around 11,000 Security Cameras Keep Watch," *The Atlanta Journal Constitution*, November 1, 2019.

99. Ignacio Munyo and Martin Rossi, "Police-Monitored Cameras and Crime," June 30, 2019, https://cepr.org/voxeu/columns/police-monitored-cameras-and-crime.

100. Sidney Fussell, "When Private Security Cameras Are Police Surveillance Tools," *Wired*, August 11, 2020, https://www.wired.com/story/private-security-cameras-police-surveillance-tools/.

101. Ibid.
102. Ibid.
103. Ibid.
104. Emma Freire, "Bring Your Own Camera," *City Journal*, August 19, 2022, https://www.city-journal.org/baltimore-residents-use-security-cameras-to-catch-thieves.
105. "Guidance on the Use of Domestic CCTV," Gov.UK, August 2019, https://www.gov.uk/government/publications/domestic-cctv-using-cctv-systems-on-your-property/domestic-cctv-using-cctv-systems-on-your-property.
106. Peter French, "The CCTV Crime Prevention Bubble Is Set to Burst Unless Extra Money Can Be Found to Maintain Public Systems," March 7, 1998, https://www.1in12.com/publications/cctv/bubble.html.
107. "Pricing a CCTV Maintenance Contract (Annual Contract)," Learn CCTV, 2022, https://learncctv.com/pricing-a-cctv-maintenance-contract/.
108. Uses of ALPR include: "traffic enforcement, parking management, tollbooth operations, secure area access control, collection of delinquent taxes and fines, homeland security and terrorist interdiction, AMBER alerts, gang and narcotic interdiction, the identification of suspended and revoked drivers, and the recovery of stolen vehicles." See Murat Ozer, "Automatic License Plate Reader (ALPR) Technology: Is ALPR a Smart Choice in Policing?" *The Police Journal* 82, no. 2 (June 2016): 117.
109. See, for example, Police 1 Staff, "7 Cases Solved Thanks to ALPR Data," Police 1, June 12, 2018, https://www.police1.com/police-products/traffic-enforcement/license-plate-readers/articles/7-cases-solved-thanks-to-alpr-data-doayALt3VGwqCIN5/; Police 1 Staff, "News Stories about Law Enforcement ALPR Successes September 2017–September, 2018," https://www.theiacp.org/sites/default/files/ALPR%20Success%20News%20Stories%202018.pdf;

Pennsylvania District Attorneys Association Hearing on HB 317 and HB 1509 Before the House Transportation Committee, August 13, 2019, https://www.pdaa.org/pdaa-testimony-on-hb-317-and-hb-1509-before-the-house-transportation-committee/.
110. David J. Roberts and Meghann Casanova, "Automated License Plate Recognition (ALPR) Use by Law Enforcement: Policy and Operational Guide, Summary," US Department of Justice Document No. 239605, September 2012, 6.
111. As of 2022, at least sixteen states had statutes that directly regulated ALPR usage in some way. For a list of states statutes that explicitly address the use of ALPR, see National Conference of State Legislatures, "Automated License Plate Readers: State Statutes," February 3, 2022, https://www.ncsl.org/technology-and-communication/automated-license-plate-readers-state-statutes.
112. Ibid.
113. Mike Maharrey, *Massachusetts Bill Would Limit ALPR Data Use and Retention, Help Block National License Plate Tracking Program*, Tenth Amend. Ctr. (Apr. 10, 2023), https://blog.tenthamendmentcenter.com/2023/04/massachusetts-bill-would-limit-alpr-data-use-and-retention-help-block-national-license-plate-tracking-program.
114. Roberts, supra note 110, at 8–9. A significant number of states only store data for less than six months. Id. Currently, 8 states legally limit how long data can be retained, while other states discard data due to space constraints.; National Conference of State Legislatures, "Automated License Plate Readers: State Statutes."
115. Roberts and Casanova, "Automated License Plate Recognition (ALPR) Use by Law Enforcement," 6.
116. For a description of ALPR's rapid growth in the United States, see Ángel Díaz and Rachel Levinson-Waldman,

"Automatic License Plate Readers: Legal Status and Policy Recommendations for Law Enforcement Use," Brennan Center for Justice, September 10, 2020.

117. Jasmine, "ANPR Cameras: What Are They and What Do They Do?" Fluxposuer, April 20, 2021, https://www.adrianflux.co.uk/blog/2021/04/what-are-anpr-cameras.html; National Police Chiefs' Council, "Automatic Number Plate Recognition (ANPR): Use of ANPR by Police Forces and Other Law Enforcement Agencies (LEA)," 2019, https://www.met.police.uk/advice/advice-and-information/rs/road-safety/automatic-number-plate-recognition-anpr/.

118. Irmin M. Cohen et al., "A Report on the Utility of the Automated License Plate Recognition System in British Columbia," University College of Fraser Valley, 2007, 2.

119. Heath, "Police Secretly Track Cellphones to Solve Routine Crimes."

120. Policy Directive 047-02, Department Policy Regarding the Use of Cell-Site Stimulator Technology, US Department of Homeland Security, October 19, 2015, 1.

121. Heath, "Police Secretly Track Cellphones to Solve Routine Crimes."

122. Carpenter v. United States, 138 S. Ct. 2206 (2018); United States v. Jones 565 US 400 (2012); Nina Totenberg, "High Court: Warrant Needed for GPS Tracking Device," NPR, January 23, 2012, https://www.npr.org/2012/01/23/145656654/top-court-police-need-warrant-for-gps-tracking.

123. Carpenter 138 S. Ct. 2206, 2223; Nina Totenberg, "In Major Privacy Win, Supreme Court Rules Police Need Warrant to Track Your Cellphone," NPR, June 22, 2018, https://www.npr.org/2018/06/22/605007387/supreme-court-rules-police-need-warrant-to-get-location-information-from-cell-to.

124. Deepali Lal, "Criminal Procedure—Technology in the Modern Era: The Implications of Carpenter v. United States and the Limits of the Implications of Carpenter v. United States and the Limits of the Third-Party Doctrine as to Cell Phone Data Gathered Through Third-Party Doctrine as to Cell Phone Data Gathered Through Real-Time Tracking, Stingrays, and Cell Tower Dumps Real-Time Tracking, Stingrays, and Cell Tower Dumps," University of Arkansas at Little Rock Law Review 43, no. 4 (2022): art. 3, https://lawrepository.ualr.edu/cgi/viewcontent.cgi?article=2088&context=lawreview

125. Lisa Myers, "Four Law Enforcement Terms that Every Legal Secretary Should Know," Northwest Career Blog, March 4, 2021, https://www.northwestcareercollege.edu/blog/four-law-enforcement-terms-that-every-legal-secretary-should-know/.

126. Bryan McMahon, "How the Police Use AI to Track and Identify You," The Gradient, October 3, 2020, https://thegradient.pub/how-the-police-use-ai-to-track-and-identify-you/.

127. Ibid.

128. Leslie Corbly, "Geofences Aren't the Only Reverse Warrants," Libertas Institute, July 1, 2022, https://libertas.org/justice-and-due-process/geofences-arent-the-only-reverse-warrants/

129. Kayla Matthews, "How Data Analytics Is Solving Murders," Towards Data Science, July 22, 2019, https://towardsdatascience.com/how-data-analytics-are-solving-murders-1cdac5432d6e.

130. John Buntin, "Social Media Transforms the Way Chicago Fights Gang Violence," Governing, September 26, 2013, https://www.governing.com/archive/gov-social-media-transforms-chicago-policing.html.

131. Ibid.

132. Heath, "Police Secretly Track Cellphones to Solve Routine Crimes."

133. Adrianna Rodriguez, "Cold Case Solved 22 Years Later after Google Earth Satellite Image Shows Missing Man's

Car," *USA Today*, September 13, 2019, https://www.usatoday.com/story/news/nation/2019/09/13/google-earth-helps-solve-missing-florida-man-cold-case-22-years-later/2309070001/.

134. See chapter 3 of Nathan Judish, *Searching and Seizing Computers and Obtaining Electronic Evidence in Criminal Investigations*, third edition (Office of Legal Education Executive Office for United States Attorneys, Department of Justice, 2019).

135. Ibid.

136. Jose Pagliery, "Tech Companies Are Hindering Criminal Investigations, Under Outdated Law," CNN, October 19, 2017.

137. See, for example, Nola Valente, "City of Katy to Implement New Technological Layer of Security," *Community Impact Newspaper*, March 19, 2020; Police Executive Research Forum, "How Are Innovations in Technology Transforming Policing?" January 2012, 28–34.

138. Díaz and Levinson-Waldman, "Automatic License Plate Readers."

139. Landler and Sussman, "Poll Finds Strong Acceptance for Public Surveillance."

140. It makes sense to leave the decision up to elected representatives as opposed to direct ballot initiatives because elected legislators are more likely to be able to review the empirical evidence in favor of CCTV than the population at large while still being aware of their communities' valuation of privacy. Municipal leaders can also decide what sort of conditions or guidelines should be applied to the use of CCTV footage when making the decision to install more cameras.

141. Thomas Abt, "Solving America's One-of-a-Kind Murder Problem," Carnegie Endowment, May 17, 2022, https://carnegieendowment.org/2022/05/17/solving-america-s-one-of-kind-murder-problem-event-7877.

142. "Criminal Justice Expenditures: Police, Corrections, and Courts," The Urban Institute, 2020, https://www.urban.org/policy-centers/cross-center-initiatives/state-and-local-finance-initiative/state-and-local-backgrounders/criminal-justice-police-corrections-courts-expenditures#Question1Police.

143. "How to Find Grants for Mobile Surveillance Cameras," Wireless CCTV, 2021, https://www.wcctv.com/how-to-find-grants-for-mobile-surveillance-cameras/.

144. Ibid.

145. Federal Ministry of the Interior and Community of Germany, "The Federal Government and Deutsche Bahn Agree on Additional Measures to Step Up Security in Railway Stations," December 13, 2020.

146. See Philipp Olterman, "Germany to Expand CCTV Network in Wake of Berlin Attack," *The Guardian*, December 21, 2016, https://www.theguardian.com/world/2016/dec/21/germany-to-expand-cctv-network.

147. The expectation of privacy test originated from *Katz v. United States* where Justice Harlan created a two-part test: (1) an individual has exhibited an actual (subjective) expectation of privacy, and (2) the expectation is one that society is prepared to recognize as reasonable. Katz v. United States, 389 US 347 (1967).

148. Matthews, "How Data Analytics Is Solving Murders,"

149. Amy Harmon, "As Cameras Track Detroit's Residents, a Debate Ensues over Racial Bias," *New York Times*, July 8, 2019, https://www.nytimes.com/2019/07/08/us/detroit-facial-recognition-cameras.html.

150. Samantha Parry, "'Stop Lying, You Knew What You Were Doing': Tinder Serial Killer's Ex-Girlfriend Says His Claims 'Voice' Made Him Do It Is Just a Ploy for Insanity Plea," MailOnline, August 1, 2018, 2.

151. https://news.bloomberglaw.com/privacy-and-data-security/california

-at-crossroads-over-policing-and-facial
-recognition

152. See James O'Neill, "Opinion—How Facial Recognition Makes You Safer," *New York Times*, June 9, 2019.

153. See, for example, Bosman et al., "Facial Recognition—Dawn of Dystopia or Just the New Fingerprint?" *New York Times*, May 18, 2019.

154. A program used in Florida, for example, reports one hundred useful investigative tips a year. Jennifer Valentino-DeVries, "How the Police Use Facial Recognition Software," *New York Times*, January 12, 2020, https://www .nytimes.com/2020/01/12/technology /facial-recognition-police.html.

155. Samuel Woodhams, "London Is Buying Heaps of Facial Recognition Tech," *The Wire*, September 27, 2021, https://www .wired.co.uk/article/met-police-facial -recognition-new.

156. Irakli Beridze et al., "A Policy Framework for Responsible Limits on Facial Recognition Use Case: Law Enforcement Investigations," World Economic Forum, October 2021, 4.

157. Harmon, "As Cameras Track Detroit's Residents, a Debate Ensues over Racial Bias"; Miriam Marini, "Farmington Hills Man Sues Detroit Police After Facial Recognition Wrongly Identifies Him," *Detroit Free Press*, April 13, 2021, https://www.freep.com/story/news /local/michigan/2021/04/13/detroit -police-wrongful-arrest-faulty-facial -recognition/7207135002/.

158. See, for example, "How Effective Is Facial Recognition," NEC, August 4, 2021, https://www.nec.co.nz/market -leadership/publications-media/how -effective-is-facial-recognition /#:~:text=According%20to%20research %20published%20in,a%2099.97 %25%20recognition%20accuracy%20 level; Miguel Cedeno Agamez, "Aging Effects in Automated Face Recognition," Dissertation Purdue University, 2016.

159. Lauren Feiner and Annie Palmer, "Rules Around Facial Recognition and Policing Remain Blurry," CNBC, June 12, 2021, https://www.cnbc.com /2021/06/12/a-year-later-tech-compa nies-calls-to-regulate-facial-recogni tion-met-with-little-progress.html. As of this writing, there is no indication that the ban has been renewed.

160. Denise Lavoie, "Virginia Lawmakers OK Lifting Ban on Facial Technology use," AP News, March 10, 2022, https://apnews.com/article/tech nology-virginia-crime-legislature-f3f 2af850745911014b950d951c3c464.

161. Drew Harwell, "Senators Seek Limits on Some Facial-Recognition Use by Police, Energizing Surveillance Technology Debate," *Washington Post*, April 21, 2021, https://www.washingtonpost .com/technology/2021/04/21/data-sur veillance-bill/.

162. "State Facial Recognition Policy," Electronic Privacy Information Center, https://epic.org/state-facial-recogni tion-policy/; Nathan Sheard and Adam Schwartz, "The Movement to Ban Government Use of Face Recognition," The Electronic Frontier Foundation, May 5, 2022, https://www.eff.org/deeplinks /2022/05/movement-ban-government -use-face-recognition.

163. Edward Graham, "House Dems Seek Guardrails for Law Enforcement Use of Facial Recognition," Nextgov/FCW (Oct. 30, 2023), https://www.nextgov .com/emerging-tech/2023/10/house -dems-seek-guardrails-law-enforce ments-use-facial-recognition/391619.

164. Jay Greene, "Microsoft Bans Police from Using Its Facial Recognition Technology, Following Similar Moves by Amazon and IBM," *Washington Post*, June 11, 2020, https://www.washingtonpost .com/technology/2020/06/11/micro soft-facial-recognition/.

165. Feiner and Palmer, "Rules Around Facial Recognition and Policing Remain Blurry."

166. Brendan F. Klare et al., "Face Recognition Performance: Role of Demographic Information," Institute of Electrical and Electronics Engineers, 2012, 10.

167. Jacqueline G. Cavazos et al., "Accuracy Comparison Across Face Recognition Algorithms: Where Are We on Measuring Race Bias?" *Institute of Electrical and Electronics Engineers Transactions on Biometrics, Behavior, and Identity Science* 3, no. 1 (September 2020).

168. "How Effective Is Facial Recognition"; Agamez, "Aging Effects in Automated Face Recognition."

169. McLaughlin and Castro, "The Critics Were Wrong: NIST Data Shows the Best Facial Recognition Algorithms Are Neither Racist Nor Sexist."

170. As of April 2024, the ACLU was aware of only seven wrongful arrests in the United States due to facial recognition technology—a trivially small number. Nathan F. Wessler, "Police Say a Simple Warning Will Prevent Face Recognition Wrongful Arrests. That's Just Not True," ACLU, April 30, 2024, https://www.aclu.org/news/privacy-technology/police-say-a-simple-warning-will-prevent-face-recognition-wrongful-arrests-thats-just-not-true.

171. Robert Kolker, "Serial Killers Should Fear This Algorithm," Bloomberg Businessweek, February 8, 2017, https://www.bloomberg.com/news/features/2017-02-08/serial-killers-should-fear-this-algorithm.

172. Kolker, "Serial Killers Should Fear This Algorithm"; see James S. Liebman, Shawn Blackburn, David Mattern, and Jonathon Waisnor, "The Evidence of Things Not Seen: Non-Matches as Evidence of Innocence," *Iowa Law Review* 98, no. 2 (January 2013).

173. L. J. Kangas, "Artificial Neural Networks System for Classification of Offenders in Murder and Rape Cases," US Department of Justice, October 25, 2001.

174. Andrew Guthrie Ferguson, "Big Data Prosecution and Brady," *UCLA Law Review* 67, no. 1 (April 2020): 198.

175. Robert Garcia, "Garbage In, Gospel Out: Criminal Discovery, Computer Reliability, and the Constitution," *UCLA L. Rev.* 38, 1043 (1990).

176. Ferguson, "Big Data Prosecution and Brady."

177. Ibid., 192.

178. Ibid., 191.

179. Police Executive Research Forum, "COMPSTAT: Its Origins, Evolution, and Future in Law Enforcement Agencies," 6.

180. Dan Hunter, Mirko Bagaric, and Nigel Stobbs "A Framework for the Efficient and Ethical," *Florida State University Law Review* 47, no. 4 (2020): 765.

181. T. Christian Miller, "DOJ to Give Financial Boost to FBI's Violent Crime Database," *ABA Journal*, May 4, 2018; T. Christian Miller, "The FBI Built a Database that Can Catch Rapists—Almost Nobody uses it," ProPublica, August 3, 2015.

182. Ibid.

183. Ibid.

184. Ibid.

185. Feiner and Palmer, "Rules Around Facial Recognition and Policing Remain Blurry."

186. O'Neill, "How Facial Recognition Makes You Safer."

187. Julie Wartell and J. Thomas McEwen, "Privacy in the Information Age," US Department of Justice, Crime Mapping Research Center, July 2001.

188. Brian Finch, "The Trouble with Facial Recognition Doesn't Justify a Ban," *Wall Street Journal*, December 15, 2020.

189. Beridze et al., "A Policy Framework for Responsible Limits on Facial Recognition Use Case."

190. About the COPS Office, Department of Justice, https://cops.usdoj.gov/about cops.

191. "Facial Recognition Technology," US Department of Justice, September 6, 2016.

192. Benjamin Conarck, "How an Accused Drug Dealer Revealed JSO's Facial Recognition Network," *The Florida Times*, November 11, 2016.

193. "Facial Recognition Technology: City of Jacksonville Award," Bureau of Justice Assistance, US Department of Justice, September 26, 2016.

194. Samuel Woodhams, "London Is Buying Heaps of Facial Recognition Tech," *The Wire*, September 27, 2021.

195. Ibid.

CHAPTER 8

1. Government Printing Office, Fourth Amendment: Search and Seizure 1197, at 1210.

2. Ronald F. Wright, "Book Review: The Constitution and Criminal Procedure: First Principles," review of *The Constitutionals and Criminal Procedure: First Principles* by Akil Reed Amar, *Constitutional Commentary* 14 (1997): 560, https://scholarship.law.umn.edu/concomm/957

3. Adams v. People of State of New York, 192 US 585 (1904).

4. Weeks v. United States, 232 US 383 (1914); American Civil Liberties Union, "ACLU History: Mapp v. Ohio," last accessed March 10, 2023, https://www.aclu.org/other/aclu-history-mapp-v-ohio.

5. Silverthorn Lumber Co., Inc. v. United States, 251 US 383 (1914); Stephen J. Kaczynski, "The Admissibility of Illegally Obtained Evidence: American and Foreign Approaches Compared," *Military Law Review* 101 (July 1983): 87.

6. Mapp v. Ohio, 367 US 643 (1961); Kaczyinski, "The Admissibility of Illegally Obtained Evidence," 87–88.

7. Miranda v. Arizona, 384 US 436 (1966); Kaczyinski, "The Admissibility of Illegally Obtained Evidence," 118.

8. Paul H. Robinson and Sarah M. Robinson, *Shadow Vigilantes: How Distrust in the Justice System Breeds a New Kind of Lawlessness* (Prometheus Books, 2018), 71–73.

9. State v. Ellis, 351 Mont. 95 (2009).

10. People v. Skinner, 71 A.D.2d 814 (1979); "Court Frees Suspect Queried Sans Lawyer," *The Post Star*, December 23, 1980.

11. People v. Skinner, 52 N.Y.2d 24 (1980).

12. Timothy L. Perrin et al., "If It's Broken, Fix It: Moving Beyond the Exclusionary Rule a New Extensive Empirical Study of the Exclusionary Rule and a Call for a Civil Administrative Remedy to Partially Replace the Rule," *Iowa Law Review* 83 (May 1998): 674.

13. United States v. Calandra, 414 US 338, 339 (1974).

14. See, for example, Commonwealth v. Johnson, 86 A.3d 182 (Pa. 2014) (Pennsylvania); State v. Guzman, 842 P.2d 660 (Idaho 1992) (Idaho); State v. Cline, 617 N.W.2d 277 (Iowa 2000) (Iowa); Megan McGlynn, "Competing Exclusionary Rules in Multistate Investigations: Resolving Conflicts of State Search-and Seizure Law," *The Yale Law Journal* 172, no. 2 (November 2017): 246–489.

15. Matthew D. Kim, "The Exclusionary Rule and Judicial Integrity: An Empirical Study of Public Perceptions of the Exclusionary Rule," *Missouri Law Review* 87, no. 4 (2023): 1071.

16. There are around twenty-one million criminal cases each year in the United States, and suppression motions are filed in around 10 percent of those cases. Oren Bar-Gill and Barry Friedman, "Taking Warrants Seriously," *Northwestern University Law Review* 106, no. 4 (2012): 1669.

17. United States v. Walker (D. Md. January 28, 2013).

18. "The United States stands alone among common law countries in mandating the exclusion of relevant evidence seized in violation of individual rights. England, Canada, Australia and New Zealand all give courts discretion to exclude illegally seized evidence in certain circumstances, but none mandate exclusion." Timothy Perrin et al., "Symposium on Reform of the Exclusionary Rule: Introduction: An Invitation to Dialogue: Exploring the

Pepperdine Proposal to Move Beyond the Exclusionary Rule," *Pepperdine Law Review* 26, no. 4 (1999): 792.

19. Ibid., 792.

20. The United Kingdom's Police and Criminal Evidence Act of 1984 (PACE) established that the court has discretion regarding evidence and the exclusionary rule. See Yue Ma, "Comparative analysis of exclusionary rules in the United States, England, France, Germany, and Italy," *PIJPSM* 22, no. 3 (1999): 285.

21. "The burden of proof in a court's application of its discretion to exclude illegally obtained evidence lies with the person seeking exclusion: the accused.... The Australian judge's decision as to whose rights deserve protection is exercised on a case-by-case basis. This results in protection of not only the rights of the accused, but also the rights of the victim and the public at large. The rights of the latter two are not even considered under the American Exclusionary Rule." Harry M. Caldwell and Carol A. Chase, "The Unruly Exclusionary Rule: Heeding Justice Blackmun's Call to Examine the Rule in Light of Changing Judicial Understanding About Its Effects Outside the Courtroom," *Marquette Law Review* 78, no. 1 (Fall 1994): 64.

22. Israeli appellate court case CrimA 5121/98 Yissascharov v. Chief Military Prosecutor et al., 2006; see Amit Pundik and Uri Preisman, Prohibited Methods of Obtaining and Presenting Evidence: Israeli Report, International Association of Procedural Law, XIV World Congress, July 2011.

23. "The discretion given to British judges, requiring them to consider the probative weight of the evidence prior to ruling upon its admissibility, offers a distinct advantage over the American rule of per se exclusion: It avoids a result that is not proportional to the underlying wrong. Under the American Rule, the 'smoking gun' may be excluded from a murder trial, making conviction impossible, solely because a police officer has made a minor blunder with respect to Fourth Amendment law.... We lack the ability, unlike our British counterparts, to make the remedy proportional to the type of wrongful conduct involved and to the remedy's overall effect on the truth-finding process of the criminal justice system." Caldwell and Chase, "The Unruly Exclusionary Rule," 58–59.

24. Yuval Merin, "Lost Between the Fruits and the Tree: In Search of a Coherent Theoretical Model for the Exclusion of Derivative Evidence," *New Criminal Law Review: An International and Interdisciplinary Journal* 18, no. 2 (Spring 2015): 275.

25. Gordon V. Kessel, "The Suspect as a Source of Testimonial Evidence: A Comparison of the English and American Approaches," *Hastings Law Journal* 38, no. 1 (November 1986): 29; Peter Ashford, "The Admissibility of Illegally Obtained Evidence," *Arbitration* 85, no. 2 (2019): 387.

26. Merin, "Lost Between the Fruits and the Tree," 312.

27. Walter Pakter, "Exclusionary Rules in France, Germany, and Italy, Hastings," *International and Comparative Law Review* 9, no. 1 (Fall 1985): 52.

28. See, for example, England and Wales Court of Appeals, R. v. Ismail Abduraham, Case No: 201900493 C5, Dec. 12, 2019; R. v. Ismail Abdurhman, Summary: Court of Appeal Dismisses Appeal against Conviction, Judiciary of England and Wales.

29. Ibid.

30. "As of 2007, the highest courts of fourteen states had rejected the so-called 'good faith' exception, which prohibits the exclusion of evidence obtained in violation of the Fourth Amendment if the police act in good-faith reliance on a search warrant that later proves to be defective." McGlynn, "Competing Exclusionary Rules in Multistate Investigations," 410.

31. Ibid., 417–18.

32. Chapter 1, Section F, 22.

33. Brian A. Sutherland, "Whether Consent to Search Was Given Voluntarily: A Statistical Analysis of Factors that Predict the Suppression Rulings of the Federal District Courts," *New York University Law Review* 81, no. 6 (2006): 2214–17.

34. A 1965 study found that suppression motions were filed in 4 percent of the felony charges for assault, rape, and homicide in the District Court for the District of Columbia. Dallin H. Oaks, "Studying the Exclusionary Rule in Search and Seizure," *The University of Chicago Law Review* 37, no. 4 (Summer 1970): 686. Similar results were found in a 1991 study of anonymized jurisdictions in urban, industrial, and commercial US cities that found that motions to suppress evidence were filed in roughly 4 to 5 percent of felony cases. In River City, 4.5 percent of cases involve motions to suppress physical evidence, 0 percent in Mount City, 4 percent in Plains City, 0.4 percent in Border City, 2.3 percent in Hill City, 8.9 percent in Forest City, and 1.6 percent in Harbor City. Out of those 4 percent of charges with a motion to suppress, 27 percent of motions were granted. Craig D. Uchida and Timothy S. Bynum, "Search Warrants, Motions to Suppress and 'Lost Cases': The Effects of the Exclusionary Rule in Seven Jurisdictions," *Journal of Criminal Law & Criminology* 81 (1991): 1060. A 1987 study found that up to 8.8 percent of all cases involve the filing of a motion to suppress physical evidence. Peter F. Nardulli, "The Societal Costs of the Exclusionary Rule Revisited," *University of Illinois Law Review* (1987): 228. While other sources suggest around 10 percent of all criminal cases involve some suppression motion, whether aimed to exclude physical evidence or a confession. Bar-Gill and Friedman, "Taking Warrants Seriously," 1669.

35. There are around twenty-one million criminal cases each year in the United States (including around 5 million felony cases), and suppression motions are filed in around 10 percent of felony cases (and likely a similar number of criminal misdemeanor cases). Even if the filing rate is less for misdemeanor cases, the court system is still swamped with hundreds of thousands of suppression motions each year. Bar-Gill and Friedman, "Taking Warrants Seriously," 1669.

36. In a study using a sample of cases from federal district courts, the defense counsel's motion to suppress data from lack of voluntary consent (most likely invalidated by police violation of the Fourth Amendment) was granted in 35 of 142 cases—around 25 percent of the time. In the Fourth Amendment violation cases, the motion to suppress is granted 23 out of 28 times. Sutherland, "Whether Consent to Search Was Given Voluntarily," 2214. (See also Uchida and Bynum, "Search Warrants, Motions to Suppress and 'Lost Cases,'" 160. Table 7 depicts the percent of motions to suppress in different types of cases. For our focus on violent crimes, in River City, 4.5 percent of cases involve motions to suppress physical evidence, 0 percent in Mount City, 4 percent in Plains City, 0.4 percent in Border City, 2.3 percent in Hill City, 8.9 percent in Forest City, and 1.6 percent in Harbor City. Out of those 4 percent of charges with a motion to suppress, 27 percent of motions were granted.)

37. "As to motions to exclude physical evidence in the merged pool of cases for nine counties, the percent of motions granted was 16.9%; for the Chicago cases, it was almost 64%. The success rate for motions to exclude identifications for the nine counties was 1.7%; in Chicago, it was nearly 48%." Nardulli, "The Societal Costs of the Exclusionary Rule Revisited," 228–29.

38. Ibid., 229.

39. Ibid., 233 (see table 8).

40. Michael Kinsley, "When the Constable Blunders Crime and the Exclusionary Rule," *Washington Post*, April 19, 1991.
41. A National Institute of Justice study found that 4.8 percent of all felony arrests rejected prosecution because of search and seizure problems and that 50 percent of defendants freed from the exclusionary rule were arrested again within two years of their release. However, Davies criticizes this study for inappropriate samples and that the 4.8 percent should actually be a 0.8 percent, which more recent studies tend to agree with. Uchida and Bynum, "Search Warrants, Motions to Suppress and 'Lost Cases,'" 1044.
42. The NIJ looks at the effect of the exclusionary rule on state court cases in California. It concluded that of all felony arrests rejected for prosecution in California in 1976–1979, 4.8 percent were rejected because of the exclusionary rule, which was significantly higher than the 0.4 percent reported for federal cases in a different study. The National Institute of Justice, "The Effects of the Exclusionary Rule: A Study in California," Criminal Justice Research Report, December 1982, 2.
43. Thomas Y. Davies, "A Hard Look at What We Know (and Still Need to Learn) About the 'Costs' of the Exclusionary Rule: The NIJ Study and Other Studies of 'Lost' Arrests," *American Bar Foundation Research Journal* 8, no. 3 (1983): 620; Uchida and Bynum, "Search Warrants, Motions to Suppress and 'Lost Cases.'"
44. Nicole L. Waters, NCJ 248874, "Criminal Appeals in State Courts," Bureau of Justice Statistics, September 2015.
45. "This article examines the costs of three exclusionary rules using data collected for 7,500 cases in a nine-county study of criminal courts in three states. It emphasizes motions to suppress physical evidence but for comparative purposes also includes motions to suppress confessions and identifications. The results show that the various exclusionary rules

exact only marginal social costs. Motions to suppress physical evidence are filed in fewer than 5% of the cases, largely drug and weapons cases, while serious motions to suppress identifications and confessions are filed in 2% and 4% of the cases. The success rate of motions to suppress is equally marginal. Successful motions to suppress physical evidence occur in only 0.69% of the cases, while successful motions to suppress identifications or confessions occur much less often. Moreover, not all who successfully suppressed evidence escaped conviction, especially when only an identification or a confession was suppressed. In all, only 46 cases—less than 0.6% of the cases studied—were lost because of the three exclusionary rules." Nardulli, "The Societal Costs of the Exclusionary Rule Revisited," 585.
46. D. Lowell Jensen, "The Exclusionary Rule's Many Undeserving Beneficiaries," *New York Times*, May 27, 1983.
47. According to FBI data, there were a total of 495,871 arrests for violent crimes across the United States in 2019. 2019 Crime in the United States, Federal Bureau of Investigation, https://ucr.fbi.gov/crime-in-the-u.s/2019/crime-in-the-u.s.-2019/tables/table-29.
48. Christopher Slobogin, "Why Liberals Should Chuck the Exclusionary Rule," *University of Illinois Law Review* 1999 (1999): 443. Other studies suggest this rate or even higher. In California between 1976 and 1979, 4,130 defendants (though comprising only 0.78 percent of all defendants) escaped prosecution due to motions to suppress the evidence against them. The same California study also found that many of the defendants released under the exclusionary rule went on to commit more crimes. In fact, in 1976 and 1977, 2,141 defendants were not prosecuted due to the exclusionary rule and 981 of them were rearrested within the next two years, accounting for 1,270 new felonies. Jensen, "The Exclu-

sionary Rule's Many Undeserving Beneficiaries," Section A Page 22.

49. "The exact number of suppression motions filed in the United States is difficult to figure, though multiple scholars have estimated that suppression motions are filed in about 10% of criminal cases. There are approximately 21 million criminal cases in the United States each year." Bar-Gill and Friedman, "Taking Warrants Seriously," 1669.

50. Paul Cassell, "Tradeoffs Between Wrongful Convictions and Wrongful Acquittals: Understanding and Avoiding the Risks," *Seton Hall Law Review* 48 (2018): 1488.

51. Ibid.

52. Raymond A. Atkins and Paul H. Rubin, "Effects of Criminal Procedure on Crime Rates: Mapping Out the Consequences of the Exclusionary Rule," *The Journal of Law & Economics* 46, no. 1 (April 2003): 157–79; "The filing of these motions has driven up the cost of processing cases, and it is beyond dispute that a number of apparently guilty defendants go free as a result of the rule. Many of those set free by the operation of the rule will continue their pattern of criminal activity, compounding the high social costs of the rule." Perrin et al., "It's Broken, Fix It," 711.

53. "Looking at aggregated state data, Mapp increased crimes of larceny by 3.9 percent, auto theft by 4.4 percent, burglary by 6.3 percent, robbery by 7.7 percent, and assault by 18 percent. Moreover, these results mask larger impacts in suburban cities-where the imposition of the exclusionary rule increased violent crimes by 27 percent and property crimes by 20 percent." Atkins and Rubin, "Effects of Criminal Procedure on Crime Rates," 174.

54. Ibid.

55. The government's victimization statistics prepandemic showed about two million violent crimes excluding simple assault. Rachel E. Morgan and Alexandra Thompson, Bureau of Justice Statistics, NCJ 301775, "Criminal Victimization: 2020," October 2021, https://bjs.ojp.gov/library/publications/criminal-victimization-2020.

56. Dallin H. Oaks, "Studying the Exclusionary Rule in Search and Seizure," *The University of Chicago Law Review* 37 (1970): 75.

57. Ibid.

58. See Myron W. Orfield Jr., "The Exclusionary Rule and Deterrence: An Empirical Study of Chicago Narcotics Officers," *University of Chicago Law Review* 54, no. 3 (1987): 1017; United States v. Janus, 428 US 433 (1976); Stone v. Powell 428 US 465 (1976), United States v. Leon, 486 US 897 (1984), Elkins v. United States, 364 US 206 (1960); Bivens v. Six Unknown Names Agents of Federal Bureau of Narcotics, 403 US 388, 411 (1971).

59. "In Bivens v. Six Unknown Named Agents of Federal Bureau of Narcotics, Chief Justice Burger . . . argued that the exclusionary rule has not accomplished its stated objective of deterrence and that there is no reason why the exclusionary rule should be preserved if an effective alternative can be developed." Randy E. Barnett, "Resolving the Dilemma of the Exclusionary Rule: An Application of Restitutive Principles of Justice," *Emory Law Journal* 32 (1983): 942; see Yue Ma, "The American Exclusionary Rule: Is There a Lesson to Learn From Others?" *International Criminal Justice Review* 22, no. 3 (2012): 309–2; Mark Phillips et al., "The Exclusionary Rule and Social Science," Cornell Law Student Projects, 2010.

60. Some have urged that the justification for the exclusionary rule be shifted to one based upon promoting judicial integrity. See, for example, Kim, "The Exclusionary Rule and Judicial Integrity."

61. Christopher Slobogin, "The Exclusionary Rule: Is It on Its Way Out? Should It Be?" *Ohio State Journal of Criminal Law* 10 (2013): 341–55.

62. Scott Howe, "A Sixth Amendment In-clusionary Rule for Fourth Amendment Violations," *Connecticut Law Review* 53, no. 3 (May 2022): 613–54.

63. Paul H. Robinson, *Intuitions of Justice and the Utility of Desert* (Oxford University Press, 2013), chap. 2.

64. Stuart Taylor Jr., "Exclusionary-Rule Fight Moves to the Supreme Court," *New York Times*, January 26, 1983.

65. See, for example, Roger Simon, "Exclusionary Rule Is Aimed at Procedure, Not the Truth," *Baltimore Sun*, July 6, 1994; Thomas Weigend, "Should We Search for the Truth, and Who Should Do It," *N.C. J. INT'L L.* 36, no. 2 (2010): 389, https://scholarship.law.unc.edu/ncilj/vol36/iss2/6.

66. Taylor, "Exclusionary-Rule Fight Moves to the Supreme Court."

67. Nix v. Williams Exclusionary Rule Offends Law and Order Supporters, JRank Articles, 2021, https://law.jrank.org/pages/24074/Nix-v-Williams-Exclusionary-Rule-Offends-Law-Order-Supporters.html.

68. Taylor, "Exclusionary-Rule Fight Moves to the Supreme Court."

69. U.S. v. Leon, 468 US 897 (1984); Nix v. Williams Exclusionary Rule Offends Law and Order Supporters.

70. Taylor, "Exclusionary-Rule Fight Moves to the Supreme Court."

71. Spencer Sherman, "Supreme Court Ends Term with Reagan Victory," UPI Archives, July 5, 1984.

72. See, for example, chapter 3.C.2.

73. Orfield, "The Exclusionary Rule and Deterrence," 1053.

74. Testimony of Alan M. Dershowitz Before the Committee on the Judiciary House of Representatives, The Consequences of Perjury and Related Crimes, December 1, 1998.

75. Dru Stevenson, "Judicial Deference to Legislatures in Constitutional Analysis," *N.C.L. Rev.* 90 (2012): 2083–2141.

76. See William J. Stuntz, "The Political Constitution of Criminal Justice," *Harvard Law Review* 199, no. 3 (2006): 781–82; "Overcriminalization, excessive punishment, racially skewed drug enforcement, overfunding of prisons and underfunding of everything else—these familiar problems are as much the consequences of constitutional regulation as the reasons for it." Further, "The Court drove legislators, along with the dollars they control, away from those areas where legislation might have done the most good (policing and procedures), and into those areas where it is bound to do the more harm (crime definition and sentencing)." Ibid., 792.

77. Ibid., 823.

78. See McGlynn, "Competing Exclusionary Rules in Multistate Investigations," 410; Leigh A. Morrissey, "State Courts Reject 'Leon' on State Constitutional Grounds," *Vanderbilt Law Review* 47, no. 3 (1994): 941.

79. Hudson v. Michigan, 547 US 586 (2006).

80. Arizona v. Evans, 115 US 1 (1995); Laurence Naughton, "Taking Back Our Streets: Attempts in the 104th Congress to Reform the Exclusionary Rule," *Boston College Law Review* 38 (December 1996): 206.

81. Perrin et al., "It's Broken, Fix It," 740–41.

82. Ibid.

83. The exclusionary rule in other countries, particularly the United Kingdom, is discussed in further detail in the "Nature and Extent of the Problem" subsection of this chapter.

84. Gregory D. Totten et al., "Symposium on Reform of The Exclusionary Rule: Article: The Exclusionary Rule: Fix It, But Fix It Right," *Pepperdine Law Review* 26 (1996): 914–15. The proposed test was as follows:

(1) The magnitude of the illegality: For example, an unjustified intrusion into a private home at night where a number of people were present is an illegality of far greater magnitude than an entry during the day into an unoccupied garage.

(2) The good faith of the officers: Analogous to the present rule regarding search warrants. An officer's honest, but erroneous belief in the legality of his conduct would mitigate in favor of admission of the evidence. This criteria could take into account the extent to which the belief was reasonable, even if later determined to be erroneous.

(3) The importance and probative value of the evidence: This assumes that evidence which is essential should be subject to suppression less than evidence which may constitute additional corroborative evidence.

(4) The degree to which the admissibility of the evidence is likely to affect the integrity and validity of the fact finding process: Similar to criterion number three, this would require an assessment of the risk of a factually and legally erroneous verdict were the evidence to be excluded.

(5) The seriousness of charged offenses: This consideration would include, but not be limited to, the extent of harm suffered by innocent victims, for example, serious physical injuries or death, amount of theft, or fraud, the level of the accused's sophistication and planning, and the nature of the charged offense.

(6) The likely effect of inadmissibility on public safety: This criterion would require examination of public safety concerns which represent a significant and legitimate factor for consideration. For example, on the extreme, the possible release of a clearly guilty serial killer or habitual child molester would strongly mitigate against suppression of vital evidence.

(7) The extent to which a serious injustice would result from admissibility: For example, acquittal of a rapist or a child molester would rate much higher on the scale than the possible unjustified acquittal of a shoplifter or a possessor of minor amounts of dangerous drugs.

(8) Clarity of the law: This criterion would take into account factors such as complexity of the law, the extent to which the law was clear, and the uniformity of past judicial decisions regarding the specific search and seizure or interrogation issue under review in a given case.

(9) The extent to which the officers should have known at the time of their conduct that it was illegal: Besides some of the criteria mentioned above, this would include assessing the amount of time the officers had to weigh and consider their actions, the officer's experience, and the extent of training the officer has received. These factors might either account for the officer's failure to know the precise Fourth Amendment law or suggest that they should have known the specific rule at issue.

(10) The extent to which the officers' conduct was an invasion of personal privacy and the magnitude of that invasion: For example, the presence or absence of unjustified harm to innocent citizens would be a relevant consideration.

(11) The extent to which good faith consideration of public safety and officer safety influenced police decision: For example, in New York v. Quarles, 135th United States Supreme Court created a public safety exception for the Miranda warnings requirement.

85. Ibid.
86. Civilian review boards (or civilian commissions) are municipal boards composed of citizens that review policies, activities, and complaints against police officers in their community. The utility of civilian commissions is discussed further in the recommendations for chapters 15 and 16.
87. For example, between 1958 and 1967, Philadelphia's civilian review board only recommended punitive sanctions in 6 percent of cases it reviewed. Vanessa Taylor, "Civilian Review Boards Are Touted as an Essential Piece of Police Reform. Are They?" Impact, October 12, 2021, https://www.mic.com/impact/what-are-civilian-review-boards-and-can-they-actually-fix-policing.
88. "Abolition of the rule and replacing it with a system of civil damage remedies has been advocated by such distinguished legal figures as Chief Justice Warren Burger, Dallin Oaks, Akhil Amar, Bill Pizzi, and Paul Robinson . . . there is

some tradeoff in the current regime favoring procedural claims over substantive ones." Cassell, "Tradeoffs Between Wrongful Convictions and Wrongful Acquittals," 1469–470.

89. Kim, "The Exclusionary Rule and Judicial Integrity," 1–3.

90. Legal Information Institute, Federal Rules of Evidence, https://www.law.cornell.edu/rules/fre.

91. FRE 403 provides in full: "The court may exclude relevant evidence if its probative value is substantially outweighed by a danger of one or more of the following: unfair prejudice, confusing the issues, misleading the jury, undue delay, wasting time, or needlessly presenting cumulative evidence." Fed. R. Evid. 403.

92. FRE 401 defines evidence to be "relevant" if it has "any tendency to make a fact [of consequence] more or less probable than it would be without the evidence." Fed. R. Evid 401. The Advisory Committee Notes to FRE 403 indicate that "unfair prejudice . . . means an undue tendency to suggest decision on an improper basis, commonly, though not necessarily, an emotional one."

93. Christopher B. Mueller et al., *Evidence Under the Rules*, sixth edition (Aspen Publishing, 2018), 81; Material cites Ritchie v. State, 632 P.2d 1244, 1245–46 (Okla. Crim. 1981).

94. So, for example, the admission of prior criminal convictions for the purpose of impeaching witnesses is most directly controlled by FRE 609. However, even if evidence of a prior conviction would be admissible under Rule 609, a judge could still exclude the prior conviction based on a finding that the evidence's probative value was substantially outweighed by one of the dangers listed in FRE 403. See, for example, Fed. R. Evid. 609.

95. In theory, evidence with high probative value should very rarely be excluded under FRE 403 because even if the evidence carried a danger of significant prejudicial effect, the prejudicial effect would

not substantially outweigh the evidence's high probative value.

96. Abuse of discretion review can act as "a virtual shield from reversal." Roger Park et al., Evidence Law § 12.01, 540–41 and n.6 (1998). See also C. Wright and K. Graham, Statutory History: Rule 403, 22 Fed. Prac. & Proc. Evid. § 5211 (first edition 2009) ("Seldom have the appellate courts insisted on the careful balancing envisaged by Rule 403; instead, they rely on a sloppy, free-floating conception of discretion as a magic elixir to resolve all issues of admissibility").

97. "Steps in a Trial: Appeals," American Bar Association, November 28, 2021, https://www.americanbar.org/groups /public_education/resources/law_re lated_education_network/how _courts_work/appeals/.

98. Edward J. Imwinkelried, "The Meaning of Probative Value and Prejudice in Federal Rules of Evidence 403: Can Rule 403 Be Used to Resurrect the Common Law of Evidence?" *Vanderbilt Law Review* 41, no. 5 (October 1988): 880.

99. Kenneth S. Klein, "Why Federal Rule of Evidence 403 Is Unconstitutional, and Why That Matters," *University of Richmond Law Review* 47 (2013): 1078.

100. State v. Westpoint, 404 Md. 455, 2008, 46.

101. WomensLaw.org, Legal Information: Maryland, § 3-307. "Sexual Offense in the Third Degree," last accessed March 17, 2023, https://www.womenslaw.org /laws/md/statutes/ss-3-307-sexual-of fense-third-degree#node-52184.

102. State v. Westpoint, 404 Md. 455, 459–460 (2008).

103. Ibid., 495.

104. People v. Thigpen, 306 Ill. App.3d 29, 34 (1999).

105. Ibid., 35.

106. Ibid., 36.

107. "The two crimes did not have the requisite degree of similarity." Ibid., 108.

108. See, for example, Lee J. Curley, "Cognitive and Human Factors in Legal Lay-

person Decision Making: Sources of Bias in Juror Decision Making," *Medicine, Science, and the Law* 62, no. 3 (February 2022): 206–15.

109. Klein, "Why Federal Rule of Evidence 403 Is Unconstitutional, and Why That Matters," 1078; see also Donald A. Dripps, "Relevant but Prejudicial Exculpatory Evidence: Rationality Versus Jury Trial and the Right to Put on a Defense," *Southern California Law Review* 69 (1996): 1400–1402.

110. Klein, "Why Federal Rule of Evidence 403 Is Unconstitutional, and Why That Matters," 1080.

111. Ibid., 1078.

112. See Stephen Landsman and Richard F. Rakos, "A Preliminary Inquiry into the Effect of Potential Biasing Information on Judges and Jurors in Civil Litigation," *Behavioral Science & Law* 12, no. 2 (1994): 113.

113. Todd E. Pettys, "The Immoral Application of Exclusionary Rules," *Wisconsin Law Review* 2008 (2008): 463–513.

114. Note that the appellate decisions reversing convictions for improperly admitting prejudicial evidence represent relatively exceptional cases, given the broad discretion afforded to trial judges in evidentiary decisions. But this goes both ways—in many cases where the trial court excludes evidence that probably should have been admitted, the deferential standard of appellate review shields the defendant from ever having to be retried with the evidence admitted against them.

115. Mueller et al., *Evidence Under the Rules*, 74–78.

116. Ibid., 71–74.

117. Christopher B. Mueller, Laird Kirkpatrick, and Liesa Richter, §4.10 "Unfair Prejudice, Confusion, Delay, Collateral," GW Law Faculty Publications, 2018.

118. This list was found at James A. Tanford, "The Prejudice Rule," in *Everything You Ever Wanted to Know About Evidence* (Maurer School of Law, 2003), chap. 5, https://law.indiana.edu/instruction/tanford/b723/05prej/T05.pdf.

119. Peter Yesko, "How Can Someone Be Tried Six Times for the Same Crime?" In the Dark, July 16, 1996.

120. Lauren Tallent, "Through the Lens of Federal Evidence Rule 403: An Examination of Eyewitness Identification Expert Testimony Admissibility in the Federal Circuit Courts," *Washington & Lee Law Review* 68 (2011): 778 (citing C. Wright and K. Graham, Statutory History: Rule 403, 22 Fed. Prac. & Proc. Evid. § 5211 [first edition, 2009]).

121. Laura Gaston Dooley, "Our Juries Our Selves: The Power Perception and Politics of the Civil Jury," *Cornell Law Review* 80, no. 2 (1995): 3.

122. Diana Friedland, "27 Years of 'Truth-in-Evidence': The Expectations and Consequences of Proposition 8's Most Controversial Provision," *Berkeley Journal of Criminal Law* 14 (Spring 2009): 1.

123. The act, which passed by a margin of 56 percent to 44 percent, stipulated as follows: "Except as provided by statute hereafter enacted by a two-thirds vote of the membership of each house of the Legislature, relevant evidence shall not be excluded in any criminal proceeding, including pretrial and post-conviction motions and hearings, or in any trial or hearing of a juvenile for a criminal offense, whether heard in juvenile or adult court. Nothing in this section shall affect any existing statutory rule of evidence relating to privilege or hearsay, or Evidence Code, Sections 352, 782, or 1103. Nothing in this section shall affect any existing statutory or constitutional right of the press." Ibid., 1; see Cal. Const. art. I § 28(d) (1982).

124. Larry Laudan, *Truth, Error, and Criminal Law: An Essay in Legal Epistemology* (Cambridge University Press, 2006), 24.

125. The United Kingdom, Italy, Germany, and France are among the countries that allow an appeal after an acquittal,

See for example, "Prosecution Rights of Appeal, Health and Safety Executive," Health and Safety Executive, https://www.hse.gov.uk/enforce/enforcement guide/court/appeals-prosecution.htm#p9cja2003; Massima Bolognari, "The Appeal in the Italian Criminal Legal System: Legislative Reforms and Case Law," *Ceza Hukuku ve Kriminoloji Dergisi-Journal of Penal Law and Criminology* 6, no. 1 (2018): 15–26; "German Prosecutors Drop Appeal of ex-President Christian Wulff's Acquittal," *Deutsche Welle*, June 13, 2014, https://www.dw.com/en/german-prosecutors-drop-appeal-of-ex-president-christian-wulffs-acquittal/a-17705670; Bryan Colton, "French Criminal Procedures—Surprising Features of a French Trial," Bloomberg News, July 12, 2019, https://news.bloomberglaw.com/white-collar-and-criminal-law/insight-french-criminal-procedures-surprising-features-of-a-french-trial.

CHAPTER 9

1. Allie Preston and Rachel Eisenberg, "Profit over People: Primer an U.S. Cash Bail Systems," Center for American Progress, July 6, 2022, https://www.americanprogress.org/article/profit-over-people-primer-on-u-s-cash-bail-systems/#:~:text=Cash%20bail%20practices%20undermine%20the,racially%20and%20economically%20disparate%20outcomes.
2. Ibid.
3. Brian Reaves, "Felony Defendants in Large Urban Counties, 2009—Statistical Tables," December 2013, US Department of Justice, table 16, https://bjs.ojp.gov/content/pub/pdf/fdluc09.pdf.
4. "Bail Bond Cost Calculator," Bail Agent Network, https://www.bailagentnetwork.com/bail-bond-cost-calculator/; Van Brunt and Locke Bowman, "Toward a Just Model of Pretrial Release: A History of Bail Reform and a Prescription for What's Next," *Journal of Criminal Law & Criminology* 108, no. 4 (2018): 715; Eleanor Coggins, "An Overview of the Bail System in the United States and Its Discriminatory Components," *The Mid Southern Journal of Criminal Justice* 19, no. 4 (2020): 5.
5. Paul Cassell and Richard Fowles, "Does Bail Reform Increase Crime? An Empirical Assessment of the Public Safety Implications of Bail Reform in Cook County" Illinois, S.J. Quinney College of Law, Research Paper No. 349, 2020, 1–45; Brian H. Bornstein et al., NCJRS 234370, "Reducing Courts' Failure to Appear Rate: A Procedural Justice Approach," Department of Justice, May 2011, 5.
6. National Conference of State Legislatures, "Pretrial Release: State Constitutional Right to Bail," last modified June 20, 2022, https://www.ncsl.org/civil-and-criminal-justice/pretrial-release-state-constitutional-right-to-bail.
7. 42 Pa. C.S. §5701 Right to Bail (1978).
8. "New York is the only state in the country that does not allow a judge to detain a defendant who poses a threat to the community. 49 other states, as well as the federal system, allow judges to consider a defendant's dangerousness." Josiah Bates, "Eric Adams Wants 'Dangerousness' Factored into New York's Bail Laws. Advocates Say It Will Only Bring More Bias," *Time Magazine*, February 10, 2022, https://time.com/6146431/eric-adams-bail-reform-dangerousness/.
9. Three factors many jurisdictions use to predict dangerousness include prior criminal record, seriousness of the current offense, and judicial discretion. See Jeffrey Fagan and Martin Guggenheim, "Preventive Detention and the Judicial Prediction of Dangerousness for Juveniles: A Natural Experiment," *The Journal of Criminal Law & Criminology* 86, no. 2 (1996): 422.
10. "Statutory Framework of Pretrial Release," NCSL, November 18, 2020, https://www.ncsl.org/civil-and-criminal-justice/statutory-framework-of-pretrial-release.

11. Thomas H. Cohen and Brian A. Reaves, NCJ 214994, "Pretrial Release of Felony Defendants in State Courts," US Department of Justice, November 2007, 1, https://bjs.ojp.gov/content/pub/pdf/prfdsc.pdf.

12. "Warrants Ordered between Arraignment and Disposition," New York State Unified Court System, 2021, https://app.powerbigov.us/view?r=eyJrIjoiOGRmOTU3ZTQtZDVkYy00YjEzLWEwN2UtZWY3M2YzZmE1OTA4IiwidCI6IjM0NTZmMTkyLWNiZDEtNDA2ZC1iNWEzLTU4NjNjZWMwYTTgzMyJ9&pageName=ReportSection0d92f92c611463f2a05f.

13. Cohen and Reaves, "Pretrial Release of Felony Defendants in State Courts."

14. Preston and Eisenberg, "Profit over People."

15. Jillian Melchior, "How a Nonprofit Bail Fund Frees Violent Criminals," Wall Street Journal, December 30, 2022, https://www.wsj.com/articles/how-a-nonprofit-bail-fund-frees-violent-criminals-defund-police-seattle-crime-convictions-defendant-riots-11672415159.

16. Jason Riley, "It Doesn't Make Sense to Blame Crime on Poverty," Wall Street Journal, February 28, 2023, https://www.wsj.com/articles/it-doesnt-make-sense-to-blame-crime-on-poverty-eric-adams-new-york-bail-reform-shoplifting-public-safety-61209f0b.

17. US Marshals subsequently arrest Waynewood in Arizona. Jonathan Hogan, "Local Man Accused of Child Sex Abuse Arrested in Arizona After Four Months on the Run," Post Register, October 21, 2021, https://www.idahostatejournal.com/news/crimes_court/local-man-accused-of-child-sex-abuse-arrested-in-arizona-after-four-months-on-the/article_cf6594ea-93f9-5180-bce8-648ce1a760a2.html.

18. John Paul Wright, "Bail Reform in Chicago: Un-Solving Problems in Public Safety and Court Financing," City Journal, November 22, 2022, https://www.manhattan-institute.org/bail-reform-in-chicago?utmsource=mailchimp&utm_medium=email.

19. Ibid. Also see 112.1 Pretrial Release: C 5, NC Prosecutors' Resource Online, November 30, 2022, https://ncpro.sog.unc.edu/manual/112-1.

20. Cohen and Reaves, "Pretrial Release of Felony Defendants in State Courts," 1.

21. Jim Quinn, "More Criminals, More Crime: Measuring the Public Safety Impact of New York's 2019 Bail Law," Manhattan Institute, July 28, 2022.

22. Ibid.

23. Dan Frosch and Ben Chapman, "New Bail Laws Leading to Release of Dangerous Criminals, Some Prosecutors Say," Wall Street Journal, February 10, 2020, https://www.wsj.com/articles/bail-reform-needs-reform-growing-group-of-opponents-claim-11581348077.

24. Elizabeth Berger, "The Impact of Bail Reform in the United States," Crime and Consequences, December 14, 2021, https://www.crimeandconsequences.blog/?p=5263.

25. Jesse McKinley, Alan Feuer, and Luis Ferré-Sadurní, "Why Abolishing Bail for Some Crimes Has Law Enforcement on Edge," New York Times, December 31, 2019, https://www.nytimes.com/2019/12/31/nyregion/cash-bail-reform-new-york.html.

26. Ibid.

27. Quinn, "More Criminals, More Crime."

28. John Ketcham, "Correcting Course," City Journal, April 11, 2022, https://www.city-journal.org/ny-state-budget-negotiations-yield-criminal-justice-changes.

29. Creek was found by authorities and killed himself, ending a three-hour standoff with police. Gary Creek, "Alleged Founder of the 'Triple-C' Gang, Dead in Georgia After 3-Hour Barricade," CBS Baltimore, June 8, 2021, https://www.cbsnews.com/baltimore/news/gary-creek-triple-c-dead-barricade/.

30. The Professional Bail Agents of Idaho, "A Review of Failed Bail Reform: An

Analysis of States," https://pbtx.com/files/2019/11/PBT-LinkedBooklet2.pdf.

31. Ibid.
32. Ibid.
33. Ibid.
34. Ibid.; Aileen B. Flores, "El Paso County Commissioners Court Approves Establishment of Pretrial Services Office," *El Paso Times*, May 4, 2015, https://www.elpasotimes.com/story/news/local/2015/05/04/county-commissioners-court-approves-establishment-pretrial-services-office/31262993/.
35. Lisa Hagen, "6 Months in, the Battle for Atlanta Bail Reform May Just Be Starting," WABE, September 26, 2018, https://www.wabe.org/6-months-in-the-battle-for-atlanta-bail-reform-may-just-be-starting/.
36. Ibid.
37. Leonard Adam Sipes, "Is Bail Reform Dying? 43 Percent of Murder Suspects Bailed or Out," Crime in America, November 29, 2021, https://www.crimeinamerica.net/is-bail-reform-dying-43-percent-of-murder-suspects-bailed-or-out/.
38. Cortney Crown, "40% of Indy Murder Suspects in 2021 Were on Pretrial Release, Sentencing at Time of Crime," Fox 59, November 15, 2021, https://fox59.com/news/indycrime/significant-number-of-homicide-victims-suspects-on-pre-trial-release-sentencing-at-time-of-crime/.
39. Ibid.
40. Taylor Bisacky, "Half of People Released from Jail Before Trial Accused of New Crime While Free in San Francisco: Study," Kron 4, July 13, 2021, https://www.kron4.com/news/bay-area/new-legislation-introduced-to-better-track-criminal-re-offenders-in-san-francisco/.
41. Barnini Chakraborty, "Bail Reform Laws Let Alleged Criminals Back on the Streets Within Hours," Fox News, June 3, 2020, https://www.foxnews.com/us/bail-reform-laws-let-alleged-criminals-back-on-the-streets-within-hours-threatening-public-security.

42. Jim Quinn, "The Truth: 43% of People Let Go with No Bail on a Serious Charge in NYC Were Rearrested—the 'Reform' Is a Disaster," *New York Post*, February 14, 2022, https://nypost.com/2022/02/14/43-of-people-let-go-with-no-bail-on-a-serious-charge-in-nyc-were-rearrested/.
43. Chakraborty, "Bail Reform Laws Let Alleged Criminals Back on the Streets Within Hours."
44. Ibid.
45. Frosch and Chapman, "New Bail Laws Leading to Release of Dangerous Criminals, Some Prosecutors Say."
46. William J. Bratton and Rafael A. Manguel, "'Bail Reform' Is Killing New Yorkers as Eric Adams Pushes for Change," *Wall Street Journal*, February 16, 2022, https://www.wsj.com/articles/bail-reform-killing-new-yorkers-violence-convictions-criminals-judges-court-order-release-murder-stabbing-assault-violent-crime-11645029571.
47. Nicole Hensley and Samantha Ketterer, "As Killings Tied to Defendants Out on Bond Rise in Houston, Crime Data Reveals a Crisis in Courts," *The Houston Chronicle*, July 13, 2021, https://www.houstonchronicle.com/news/investigations/article/crime-murder-bonds-defendants-courts-crisis-16302521.php.
48. Louis Casiano, "Texas' Largest County Sees More than 150 Killed by Suspects Out on Bonds, Victims Group Says," Fox News, January 4, 2022, https://www.foxnews.com/us/150-killed-bonds-texas-victims.
49. Cassell and Fowles, "Does Bail Reform Increase Crime?" 3.
50. Ibid., 23.
51. Ibid., 28.
52. Audrey Conklin, "California County Saw 70% of Criminal Suspects Released on $0 Bail Commit New Crimes: DA," Fox News, August 23, 2022, https://www.foxnews.com/us/california-county-saw-70-criminal-suspects-released-0-bail-commit-new-crimes-da.

53. Thomas Hogan, "Guaranteed Murder," *City Journal*, November 26, 2021, https://www.city-journal.org/from-waukesha-to-new-york-lax-bail-assures-homicides.

54. Bryan Polcyn, "Darrell Brooks Freed on Bond Before Parade, No Record of Bail Hearing," Fox 6 Milwaukee, November 30, 2021, https://www.fox6now.com/news/darrell-brooks-freed-on-bond-before-parade-no-record-of-hearing.

55. Bruce Vielmetti, "A Suspect in a Domestic Homicide Posted $250 Bail After a Previous Violence Case. Here's How Wisconsin Lawmakers Plan to Prevent Repeats," *Milwaukee Journal Sentinel*, January 5, 2022, https://www.jsonline.com/story/news/crime/2022/01/04/dennis-kurasz-charged-killing-girlfriend-milwaukee-business/9095156002/.

56. See, for example, Ari L. Maas and Hannah E. Meyers, "Losing Control," *City Journal*, February 4, 2022, https://www.city-journal.org/nyc-losing-control-of-crime; Michael Ruiz, "Waukesha Christmas Parade Horror: Milwaukee DA Announces Internal Review of Darrell Brooks Bail Recommendation," Fox News, November 22, 2021, https://www.foxnews.com/us/waukesha-christmas-horror-milwaukee-darrell-brooks-bail-review; Carol Robinson, "South Carolina Man Killed by Alabama Police Had 48-Page Rap Sheet, Should Have Been in Jail, Chief Says," AL.com, February 14, 2022, https://www.al.com/news/2022/02/south-carolina-man-killed-by-alabama-police-had-48-page-rap-sheet-should-have-been-in-jail-chief-says.html.

57. "Americans Favor Expanded Pretrial Release, Limited Use of Jail," Pew Trusts, November 21, 2018, https://www.pewtrusts.org/en/research-and-analysis/issue-briefs/2018/11/americans-favor-expanded-pretrial-release-limited-use-of-jail.

58. Mary Chappell, "Families of Violent Crime Victims Gather at Criminal Courthouse to Protest Release of Defendants on Bond," *Chicago Sun Times*, July 31, 2021, https://chicago.suntimes.com/metro-state/2021/7/31/22603702/families-of-violent-crime-victims-gather-protest-electronic-monitoring-and-low-bonds.

59. Robinson, "South Carolina Man Killed by Alabama Police Had 48-Page Rap Sheet, Should Have Been in Jail, Chief Says."

60. Frosch and Chapman, "New Bail Laws Leading to Release of Dangerous Criminals, Some Prosecutors Say."

61. Ibid.

62. Ibid.

63. Chakraborty, "Bail Reform Laws Let Alleged Criminals Back on the Streets Within Hours."

64. Zachary Faria, "Soft-on-Crime Policy Emboldens Criminals to Commit More Dangerous Crimes," *Washington Examiner*, July 29, 2022, https://www.washingtonexaminer.com/opinion/soft-on-crime-policy-emboldens-criminals-to-commit-more-dangerous-crimes.

65. Joshua Chaffin, "'The Issue Is Crime: Kathy Hochul in Trouble in New York Governor's Race," *Financial Times*, October 26, 2022, https://www.ft.com/content/6ea86abc-e636-4acc-b779-e84d9d286e7d.

66. Chappell, "Families of Violent Crime Victims Gather at Criminal Courthouse to Protest Release of Defendants on Bond."

67. Caroline Beck, "House Unanimously Passed 'Aniah's Law' and Sexual Assault Survivor 'Bill of Rights' on Tuesday," *Anniston Star*, February 24, 2021, https://www.annistonstar.com/news/state/house-unanimously-passed-aniah-s-law-and-sexual-assault-survivor-bill-of-rights-on-tuesday/article_fe2bd2f4-76c8-11eb-ac1a-dfbed8b3aad5.html; Ken Curtis, "Dale County Judge First to Rule on Aniah's Law," News 4, December 7, 2022, https://www.wtvy.com/2022/12/08/dale-county-judge-first-rule-aniahs-law/.

68. Will Dobbie and Crystal Yang, "Proposals for Improving the U.S. Pretrial

System," The Hamilton Project, March 2019, 17–19.

69. Brice Cooke et al., "Using Behavioral Science to Improve Criminal Justice Outcomes," Ideas42, January 2018, https://www.ideas42.org/wp-content/uploads/2018/03/Using-Behavioral-Science-to-Improve-Criminal-Justice-Outcomes.pdf.

70. Dobbie and Yang, "Proposals for Improving the U.S. Pretrial System," 17.

71. Dylan Ashdown, "The End of Cash Bail: As Simple as Sending a Text Message?" *SLU Law Journal Online*, September 7, 2020; Massachusetts Probation Services, "Text Message Notification for Those on Pretrial Probation Is Underway in Every Court Across the Commonwealth," Mass.gov, January 14, 2021, https://www.mass.gov/news/text-message-notification-for-those-on-pretrial-probation-is-underway-in-every-court-across-the-commonwealth.

72. Dobbie and Yang, "Proposals for Improving the U.S. Pretrial System," 18.

73. Karla Dhungana Sainju et al., "Electronic Monitoring for Pretrial Release: Assessing the Impact," *United States Courts, Statistics and Reports* 82, no. 3 (December 2018): table 8. See also Matt Barno et al., "Exploring Alternatives to Cash Bail: An Evaluation of Orange County's Pretrial Assessment and Release Supervision (PARS) Program," *American Journal of Criminal Justice* 45, no. 3 (2020): 363–78.

74. NCJ 234460, "Electronic Monitoring Reduces Recidivism," National Institute of Justice, September 2011, 2.

75. Janet Portman, "Consequences of Violating Bail: Revocation and Bond Forfeiture," Lawyers.com, December 30, 2021, https://www.lawyers.com/legal-info/criminal/criminal-law-basics/revoking-bail-and-forfeiting-bond.html.

76. Luis Ferre-Sadurni, Grace Ashford, and Jonah Bromwich, "Push for More Restrictive Bail Law Gains a Key Ally: Gov Hochul," *New York Times*, March 17, 2022, https://www.nytimes.com/2022/03/17/nyregion/bail-reform-hochul-ny.html; Rafael A. Mangual, "Reforming New York's Bail Reform: A Public Safety-Minded Proposal," Manhattan Institute, March 5, 2020.

77. Mangual, "Reforming New York's Bail Reform," 9.

78. Ibid., 10.

79. Isabella Jorgensen and Sandra Susan Smith, "The Current State of Bail Reform in the United States," Harvard Kennedy School, December 2021, 18.

80. Reuven Blau, "New Jersey No-Bail System Eyed by New York Leaders Reckons with Bias Risk," The City, March 6, 2020, https://www.thecity.nyc/justice/2020/3/6/21210469/new-jersey-no-bail-system-eyed-by-new-york-leaders-reckons-with-bias-risk.

81. Dobbie and Yang, "Proposals for Improving the U.S. Pretrial System," 20.

82. Ibid., 21.

83. Adam Neufeld, "In Defense of Risk-Assessment Tools," The Marshall Project, October 22, 2017, https://www.themarshallproject.org/2017/10/22/in-defense-of-risk-assessment-tools.

84. Ibid.

85. Marie VanNostrand et al., "Pretrial Risk Assessment in the Federal Court," *Federal Probation Journal* 73, no. 2 (September 2009): 3.

86. Lauryn P. Gouldin, "Disentangling Flight Risk from Dangerousness," *BYU Law Review* 2016, no. 3 (2016): 867.

87. There is an important distinction to be made between flight risk assessment and dangerousness assessment tools. In this proposal, we primarily address the former and the failures of justice they may mitigate. Dangerousness assessments, on the other hand, target an individual's chance of committing another crime if released. While both algorithms share some metrics relied upon to produce a final score, they are different in terms of their final usage and the assessments that may be made as a result. Generally, however, those individuals who do reof-

fend on pretrial release are also much less likely to reappear, so assessment tools targeting flight risk will likely reduce recidivism as well. Ibid.

88. Shima Baradaran and Frank McIntyre, "Predicting Violence," *Texas Law Review* 90, no. 3 (2012): 502.

89. Neufeld, "In Defense of Risk-Assessment Tools."

90. Ibid.

91. Ibid.

92. A 2014 study found that the popular PSA did nothing to reduce the amount of crime committed by those released pretrial. Cindy Redcross and Brit Henderson, "Evaluation of Pretrial Justice System Reforms that Use the Public Safety Assessment," MDRC Center for Criminal Justice Research, March 2019, 2. However, other studies have shown some risk assessment tools do result in modest reductions in recidivism for pretrial releases. John Monahan and Jennifer Skeem, "Risk Assessment in Criminal Sentencing," *Annual Review of Clinical Psychology* 12 (2016): 489–513.

93. "By 2015, approximately ten percent of jurisdictions in the United States had adopted some sort of empirically-based risk assessment tool, and that number continues to rise." Gouldin, "Disentangling Flight Risk from Dangerousness," 841.

94. "Mapping Pretrial Injustices: A Community-Driven Database, What Are Risk Assessment Tools?," Mapping Pretrial Injustices, https://pretrialrisk.com /#:~:text=Learn%20More,The%20 Danger,inflate%20and%20over%2D predict%20risk.

95. Oliver F. Wellinston, "Risk Assessment Algorithms in the New Zealand Criminal Justice System," *New Zealand Law Journal* (March 31, 2022).

96. See, for example, Klopfer v. North Carolina, 386 US 213 (1967).

97. Gregory Joseph, "Speedy Trial Rights in Application," *Fordham Law Review* 48, no. 5 (1980): 613.

98. Barker v. Wingo, 407 US 514, 530–32 (1972).

99. Brian P. Brooks, "A New Speedy Trial Standard for Barker v Wingo: Reviving a Constitutional Remedy in the Age of Statutes," *The University of Chicago Law Review* 61, no. 2 (Spring 1994): 588–89.

100. Joseph, "Speedy Trial Rights in Application," 17–18.

101. CO Rev Stat § 18-1-405 (2016).

102. Fla. R. Crim. P. 3.191, section (3).

103. 2006 Ohio Revised Code § 2945.73.

104. See, for example, CO Rev Stat § 18-1-405 (2016), sec 6 (Colorado); Criminal Procedure (CPL) Chapter 11-A, Part 1, Title C, Article 30, Section 30(4) (New York).

105. Nancy L. Ames, Department of Justice no. 98295, "The Impact of the Speedy Trial Act on Investigation and Prosecution of Federal Criminal Cases," June 1985, 29–30.

106. State v. Collins, 91 Ohio App. 3d 10 (1993).

107. Ibid., 17.

108. Logan Smith, "Truck Driver Sentenced to Life in Prison for Sexually Assaulting Boys on Road Trips," CBS Colorado, March 10, 2023, https://www.cbsnews .com/colorado/news/truck-driver-sen tenced-to-life-in-prison-for-sexually -assaulting-boys-on-road-trips/.

109. "Trial Set for Sex Offender Michael McFadden, Man Let Out of 316-Year Sentence," KKTV, last modified June 25, 2018, https://www.kktv.com/con tent/news/Colorado-man-sentenced -to--475480273.html. Subsequently, he was convicted in federal court. In March 2023, McFadden was sentenced to life in prison. "Grand Junction Man Sentenced to Life in Federal Prison for Sexually Abusing Two Children," March 9, 2023, https://www.justice.gov/usao-co /pr/grand-junction-man-sentenced-life -federal-prison-sexually-abusing-two -children.

110. Gary Harmon, "DA Appalled at Ruling that Frees Man," *The Daily Senti-*

nel: Grand Junction, Colorado, March 1, 2018, https://www.gjsentinel.com/news/western_colorado/da-appalled-at-ruling-that-frees-man/article_bec7f5d6-1d1e-11e8-ace5-10604b9f7e7c.html.

111. Subsequently, he was convicted in federal court. In March 2023, McFadden was sentenced to life in prison. "Grand Junction Man Sentenced to Life in Federal Prison for Sexually Abusing Two Children," March 9, 2023, https://www.justice.gov/usao-co/pr/grand-junction-man-sentenced-life-federal-prison-sexually-abusing-two-children.

112. In addition to a speedy trial time limit, Congress in 1979 created a minimum preparation period that prohibits trials starting "less than 30 days from the date the defendant first appears in court, unless the defendant agrees in writing to an earlier date." This amendment aimed to ensure legal teams would be adequately prepared for trial. However, it has likely made the problem of failures of justice worse by preventing prosecutors from quickly resolving some cases where the evidence is incontrovertible. 18 U.S.C. §§ 3161-3174 (1979).

113. Cal Penal Code § 1382.

114. PKN Law, "What Are My Speedy Trial Rights in Pennsylvania?" August 16, 2021, https://patricknightingale.com/2013/02/speedy-trial-rights/.

115. "Delaware Appendix D-2 Policy on Speedy Trial Guidelines," Delaware.gov, https://courts.delaware.gov/forms/download.aspx?id=83548.

116. "See Sex Offender Released 297 Years Early Due to Technicality," CNN, March 1, 2018, https://www.wgal.com/article/sex-offender-released-297-years-early-due-to-technicality/18933449.

117. Joseph, "Speedy Trial Rights in Application," 611–12. Dismissal of the charges is also the only remedy for violating the constitutional right as the Supreme Court in Barker held.

118. Ames, "The Impact of the Speedy Trial Act on Investigation and Prosecution of Federal Criminal Cases," 29–30.

119. "Sex Offender Released 297 Years Early Due to Technicality," CNN, March 1, 2018, https://www.wgal.com/article/sex-offender-released-297-years-early-due-to-technicality/18933449.

120. Ibid.

121. Gary Horcher, "Speedy Trial Denied: Murder Charges against Convicted Killer Dropped in Port Angeles Strangulation," KIRO 7 News, November 23, 2019, https://www.kiro7.com/news/local/speedy-trial-denied-murder-charges-against-convicted-killer-dropped-in-port-angeles-strangulation/1011613137/.

122. Marie Zoglo, "Statutory Speedy Trial Period Calculations for Dismissed and Refiled: A Case Study of Colorado's Approach," *Washington University Law Review* 97, no. 3 (2020): 911.

123. Rule 3.191, Speedy Trial, Fla. R. Crim. P. 3.191.

124. Abbe David Lowell et al., "Problems with Tolling the Speedy Trial Act During Pandemic," Law360.com, May 6, 2020, https://www.law360.com/articles/1270308/problems-with-tolling-the-speedy-trial-act-during-pandemic.

125. Ibid.

126. Klein Burdett and Associates, "Coronavirus and Its Effect on the Pennsylvania Criminal Justice System," August 6 2021, https://www.elliskleinlaw.com/coronavirus-and-its-effect-on-the-pennsylvania-criminal-justice.html.

127. Carlos Ballesteros, "Illinois Speedy Trial Rights Ordered Reinstated—But Not Until October," Injustice Watch, June 30, 2021, https://www.injusticewatch.org/news/2021/speedy-trial-rights-reinstated-illinois-supreme-court/.

128. Lowell et al., "Problems with Tolling the Speedy Trial Act During Pandemic."

129. R. Robin McDonald, "Defense Bar Frets that Proposed Speedy Trial Suspension

Will Become 'New Normal,'" Law.com, December 21, 2020, https://www.law.com/dailyreportonline/2020/12/21/defense-bar-frets-that-proposed-speedy-trial-suspension-will-become-new-normal/.

130. Joseph, "Speedy Trial Rights in Application," 615.

CHAPTER 10

1. John Gramlich, "Only 2% of Federal Criminal Defendants Go to Trial, and Most Who Do Are Found Guilty," Pew Research Center, June 11, 2019, https://www.pewresearch.org/fact-tank/2019/06/11/only-2-of-federal-criminal-defendants-go-to-trial-and-most-who-do-are-found-guilty/; Jeffrey Q. Smith and Grant R. Macqueen, "Trials Continue to Decline in Federal and State Courts. Does It Matter?" *Judicature* 101, no. 4 (2017): 28 .

2. See, for example, David A. Starkweather, "The Retributive Theory of 'Just Deserts' and Victim Participation in Plea Bargaining," *Indiana Law Journal* 67, no. 3 (1992): 858.

3. Lucian E. Durvan and Vanessa A. Edkins, "The Innocent Defendant's Dilemma: An Innovative Empirical Study of Plea Bargaining's Innocence Problem," *Journal of Criminal Law and Criminology* 103, no. 1 (2013): 10.

4. Cynthia Alkon, "What's Law Got to Do with It? Plea Bargaining Reform After Lafler and Frye," *Yearbook on Arbitration and Mediation* 7 (2015): 5; Brady v. United States 397 US 742, 751–52 (1970).

5. Starkweather, "The Retributive Theory of 'Just Deserts' and Victim Participation in Plea Bargaining," 871.

6. Fourteen states (New York, Arizona, Idaho, North Carolina, Massachusetts, Oregon, Minnesota, Montana, Vermont, Connecticut, Florida, Indiana, Oklahoma, and Alabama) encourage judges to be involved in the plea process. Eighteen states (Illinois, Maryland, Missouri, Maine, Hawaii, New Jersey, Louisiana, Michigan, California, South Carolina, Nebraska Ohio, Delaware, Iowa, Kentucky, New Hampshire, Rhode Island, and Wyoming) either allow but discourage or have not ruled on judicial participation in plea bargaining, thus meaning that it can be done but it is very uncommon. Eighteen states (Colorado, North Dakota, South Dakota, West Virginia, Arkansas, Tennessee, Pennsylvania, Utah, Georgia, Mississippi, New Mexico, Virginia, Alaska, Kansas, Texas, Washington, Wisconsin, and Nevada), the federal government, and the District of Colombia have outright prohibited judicial participation in plea bargaining. Rishi Batra, "Judicial Participation in Plea Bargaining: A Proposal for Plea Reform," Casetext, September 2, 2015, https://casetext.com/analysis/judicial-participation-in-plea-bargaining-a-proposal-for-plea-reform.

7. Dylan Walsh, "Why U.S. Criminal Courts Are So Dependent on Plea Bargaining," *The Atlantic*, May 2, 2017, https://www.theatlantic.com/politics/archive/2017/05/plea-bargaining-courts-prosecutors/524112/.

8. Douglas D. Guidorizzi, "Should We Really Ban Plea Bargaining: The Core Concerns of Plea Bargaining Critics," *Emory Law Journal* 47, no. 2 (Spring 1998): 770.

9. Ibid., 771.

10. Smith and Macqueen, "Trials Continue to Decline in Federal and State Courts. Does It Matter?" 27–28.

11. Courtney Hessler, "Man Convicted of Incest Accused of Violating Probation Again, Back in Jail," *Herald-Dispatch*, April 7, 2021, https://www.herald-dispatch.com/news/man-convicted-of-incest-accused-of-violating-probation-again-back-in-jail/article_def489be-fe68-5fdc-9091-2f7cb307153f.html.

12. Paul H. Robinson and Mitchell T. Cahill, *Law Without Justice: Why Criminal Law Doesn't Give People What They Deserve* (Oxford University Press, 2006), 74–86.

13. A Rand Corporation study concluded that the cost per reported murder averages out as $33,000, and $3,500 for each

reported rape/sexual assault. But as most reported crimes are not prosecuted, and most prosecutions end with a plea deal, the cost for trials must be at least a factor of ten higher. See Priscillia Hunt et al., "The Price of Justice: New National and State-Level Estimates of the Judicial and Legal Costs of Crime to Taxpayers," *American Journal of Criminal Justice* 42, no. 2 (2017): 231–51.

14. "State Studies on Monetary Costs," Death Penalty information Center, https://deathpenaltyinfo.org/policy-issues/costs/summary-of-states-death-penalty. (For example, in Maryland the costs for a non-death-penalty murder case is $1.1 million [$870,000 in imprisonment, $250,000 in trial]).

15. National Institute of Justice, "Five Things About Deterrence," June 5, 2016, https://nij.ojp.gov/topics/articles/five-things-about-deterrence.

16. Beth Schwartzapfel et al., "The System: The Truth About Trials," The Marshall Project, November 4, 2020, https://www.themarshallproject.org/2020/11/04/the-truth-about-trials.

17. In addition to allowing lenient sentences and failures of justice, plea bargaining also worries those concerned about injustices in the form of wrongful convictions. The threat of a greater sentence if convicted at trial makes a guilty plea more appealing than maintaining innocence for some defendants. Notably, prosecutors' increased "reliance on plea bargaining has created incentives for innocent people to plead guilty and almost certainly led to an increase in the number of Americans with criminal records." Ibid. Guilty pleas are not always a valid substitute for truth. "Though it was once believed that a confession in open court—a guilty plea—was proof-positive of a person's guilt," that is no longer the case in the US criminal justice system due to how guilty pleas are now a strategy in a game instead of a confession. Clark Neily, "Prisons Are Packed Because Prosecutors Are Coercing Plea Deals. And, Yes, It's Totally Legal," Cato Institute, August 8, 2019, https://www.cato.org/commentary/prisons-are-packed-because-prosecutors-are-coercing-plea-deals-yes-its-totally-legal. In fact, 18 percent of known exonerees pleaded guilty to crimes they did not commit. #GuiltyPleaProblem, "Why Do Innocent People Plead Guilty to Crimes They Didn't Commit?" https://www.guiltypleaproblem.org/#about. Thus, prosecutors' prioritization of clearing cases with guilty pleas instead of pursuing truth and justice significantly undermines the criminal justice system by benefitting criminals and putting innocent defendants at risk.

18. "The National Registry of Exonerations," https://www.law.umich.edu/special/exoneration/Pages/Exonerations-in-the-United-States-Map.aspx. Calculations were done based on the data present on April 4, 2023: eighty-eight exonerations were obtained for murder convictions that were based on guilty pleas in the thirty-three years that the registry covers, yielding 1.09 annual occurrences.

19. Shi Yan, "Pandemic Pushed Defendants to Plead Guilty More Often, Including Innocent People Pleading to Crimes They Didn't Commit," *The Conversation*, August 2, 2021, https://www.yahoo.com/video/pandemic-pushed-defendants-plead-guilty-123803135.html?guccounter=1&guce_referrer=aHR0cHM6Ly93d3cuZ29vZ2xlLmNvbS8&guce_referrer_sig=AQAAAK_mkJBhNrDkrNdxt_IRK31r9BoJi4DfXJuXL52W7dvUrHAqii6H3xbJQLNAqu-mWa-LxpbhLTef29SWWA_2vCENCkf.

20. Paul H. Robinson and Lindsay Holcomb, "The Criminogenic Effects of Damaging Criminal Law's Moral Credibility," *Southern California Interdisciplinary Law Journal* 31 (2022): 303; Jonathan Casper, *American Criminal Justice: The Defendant's Perspective* (Prentice Hall, Inc., 1972), xii.

21. Miriam H. Baer, "Cooperation's Cost," *Washington University Law Review* 88, no. 4 (2011): 903–67.

22. "Recidivism Rate by State 2023," https://worldpopulationreview.com/state-rankings/recidivism-rates-by-state.

23. Matthew R. Durose, NCJ 255947, "Recidivism of Prisoners Released in 34 States in 2012: A 5-Year Follow-Up Period (2012–2017)," US Department of Justice, July 2021, https://bjs.ojp.gov/library/publications/recidivism-prisoners-released-34-states-2012-5-year-follow-period-2012-2017.

24. Mariel Alper et al., NCJ 250975, "2018 Update on Prisoner Recidivism: A 9-Year Follow-Up Period (2005–2014)," Bureau of Justice Statistics, May 2018, 1.

25. Gramlich, "Only 2% of Federal Criminal Defendants Go to Trial, and Most Who Do Are Found Guilty."

26. Bureau of Justice Statistics, NCJ 226846, "Felony Sentences in State Courts, 2006—Statistical Tables," December 2009, 1.

27. Emilio C. Viano, "Plea Bargaining in the United States: A Perversion of Justice," *Revue Internationale de Droit Penal* 83, no. 1 (2012).

28. Ibid.

29. Gramlich, "Only 2% of Federal Criminal Defendants Go to Trial, and Most Who Do Are Found Guilty."

30. Francis A. Allen, "The Erosion of Legality in American Criminal Justice: Some Latter-Day Adventures of the Nulla Poena Principle," *Arizona Law Review* 29, no. 3 (1987): 393.

31. "The Troubling Spread of Plea-Bargaining from America to the World," *The Economist*, November 9, 2017, https://www.economist.com/international/2017/11/09/the-troubling-spread-of-plea-bargaining-from-america-to-the-world?ppccampaignID=&ppcadID=&ppcgclID=&utm_medium=cpc.adword.pd&utm_source=google&ppccampaignID=17210591673&ppcadID=&utm_campaign=a.22brand_pma.

32. Joseph Georges Dusek, "The Effect of Plea Bargaining vs. Trial Conviction on the Sentencing of Offenders Charged with a Drug Offense in Cook County, Illinois" (Dissertation, Loyola University Chicago).

33. Paul J. Hofer, "Federal Sentencing After Booker," *Crime and Justice* 48 (January 2019): 154.

34. Brian A. Reaves, "Felony Defendants in Large Urban Counties, 2009—Statistical Tables," Department of Justice, December 2013, chrome-extension://efaidnbmnnnibpcajpcglclefindmkaj/https://bjs.ojp.gov/content/pub/pdf/fdluc09.pdf.

35. Selwyn Raab, "Plea Bargains Resolve 8 of 10 Homicide Cases," *New York Times Archives*, January 27, 1975, 1.

36. Franklin Zimring, Joel Eigen, and Sheila O'Malley, "Punishing Homicide in Philadelphia: Perspectives on the Death Penalty," *The Chicago Law Review* 43, no. 2 (Winter 1976): 227–52.

37. Yan, "Pandemic Pushed Defendants to Plead Guilty More Often, Including Innocent People Pleading to Crimes They Didn't Commit."

38. Kayli Reese, "The Art of the Deal," *Telegraph Herald*, June 6, 2021.

39. Noelle Crombie, "Justice Delayed or Justice Denied? Some Fear Spike in Plea Deals to Clear COVID-Caused Court Backlog," *The Oregonian/Oregon Live*, March 17, 2021, https://www.oregonlive.com/crime/2021/03/i-lost-nothing-i-thought-was-going-to-happen-happened.html.

40. Ronald W. Fagan, "Public Support for the Courts: An Examination of Alternative Explanations," *Journal of Criminal Justice* 9, no. 6 (1981): 407.

41. Simmrin Law Group, "Does California Ban Plea Bargaining in Any Criminal Cases?" last modified March 31, 2023, https://www.simmrinlawgroup.com/faqs/does-california-ban-plea-bargains-in-any-criminal-cases/.

42. Thea Johnson, "Public Perceptions of Plea Bargaining," *American Journal of Criminal Law* 46, no. 1 (2019): 141.

43. David Reutter, "Plea Bargaining: Prosecutors Leave Trail of Injustice When Playing Hardball with Defendants," *Criminal Legal News*, April 12, 2019; Missouri v. Frye, 566 US 134, 143 (2012).

44. Reutter, "Plea Bargaining"; Lafler v. Cooper 566 US 156 (2012).

45. Lafler v. Cooper 566 US 156 (2012).

46. Ibid.

47. "'End Victim Blaming': Protesters Gather Outside of Philadelphia District Attorney Larry Krasner's Office," 6abc Philadelphia, October 9, 2019.

48. Kyle Kaminski, "Man Behind 'Heinous' Murders Takes Plea Deal for Lesser Sentence," *Lansing City Pulse (MI)*, July 27, 2020.

49. Lauren Pack, "Guilty Pleas: Recent Cases Highlight Deals that Sometimes Anger Public," *Butler County Journal News*, January 18, 2020.

50. Richard A. Oppel Jr., "Court Approves Plea Deal with No Jail Time in Baylor Rape Case," *New York Times*, December 11, 2018, https://www.nytimes.com /2018/12/11/us/baylor-rape-plea-proba tion-jacob-anderson.html.

51. Lance Benzel, "Guard Assigned to El Paso County District Judge Threatened over Rape Sentences," *Colorado Spring News*, April 27, 2018, https://gazette .com/news/guard-assigned-to-el-paso -county-district-judge-threatened-over -rape-sentences/article_643d171d-e032 -5728-813a-486546f09d92.html.

52. Guidelines Manual 2021, §3E1.1. Acceptance of Responsibility, United States Sentencing Commission, November 2021, at 376 .

53. "Guilty Plea: Plea Bargaining Abolition and Reform Efforts," JRank Articles, June 2021, https://law.jrank.org/pages/1290 /Guilty-Plea-Plea-Bargaining-Abolition -reform-efforts.html.

54. Walsh, "Why U.S. Criminal Courts Are So Dependent on Plea Bargaining."

55. Teresa W. Carns and John Kruse, "A Re-Evaluation of Alaska's Plea Bargaining Ban," *Alaska Law Review* 8, no. 1 (1991): 28.

56. Ralph Adam Fine, "Plea Bargaining: An Unnecessary Evil," *Marquette Law Review* 70, no. 4 (Summer 1987): 615–32.

57. Simmrin Law Group, "Does California Ban Plea Bargaining in Any Criminal Cases?"

58. Ibid.

59. Carns and Kruse, "A Re-Evaluation of Alaska's Plea Bargaining Ban," 27–28.

60. Ibid., 28.

61. "Guilty Plea: Plea Bargaining Abolition and Reform Efforts"; Carns and Kruse, "A Re-Evaluation of Alaska's Plea Bargaining Ban," 42–43.

62. Carns and Kruse, "A Re-Evaluation of Alaska's Plea Bargaining Ban," 34–35.

63. Ibid., 28.

64. Guidelines Manual 2021, 376.

65. See generally Paul H. Robinson, Matthew Kussmaul, and Muhammad Sarahne, "How Criminal Code Drafting Form Can Restrain Prosecutorial and Legislative Excesses: Consolidated Offense Drafting," *Harvard Journal on Legislation* 58, no. 1 (2020): 69–102.

66. Ibid., 69–102. For example, whatever grading scheme is used for the general damage to property offense, one would logically expect it to bear some relation to the grading scheme used in other kinds of damage to property offenses. In Delaware, a person who causes damage to property, whether intentionally or recklessly, is guilty of criminal mischief. The offense is classified as a Class G felony if it is committed intentionally, and the monetary loss exceeds $5,000 or if it impairs one from a list of essential services. Damage valued at more than $1,000, caused intentionally or recklessly, is classified as a Class A misdemeanor. Any other criminal mischief is an unclassified misdemeanor. However, the offense grading of other offenses addressing particular property damage in

Delaware's code is highly inconsistent with the grading set forth by the criminal mischief offense. An act of graffiti is a Class A misdemeanor, and it becomes a Class G felony if the damage to the property exceeds $1,500—significantly less than the threshold of a Class G felony according to the criminal mischief offense. The offense of destruction of computer equipment, which criminalizes causing damage to equipment used in a computer system, inexplicably adopts a different grading scheme, contingent upon the amount of damage or the value of the property affected: the offense is a Class D felony if it exceeds $10,000; a Class E felony if it exceeds $5,000; a Class G felony if it exceeds $1,500; and a Class A misdemeanor in any other case.

67. Ibid., 85–86; Paul H. Robinson et al., Report of the Delaware Criminal Law Recodification Project 114–15, 2017, 400–402.

68. Paul H. Robinson and Michael T. Cahill, "Final Report of the Illinois Criminal Code Rewrite and Reform Commission," 2003, 23–31, https://scholarship.law.upenn.edu/faculty_scholarship/291; Paul H. Robinson and Kentucky Criminal Justice Council Staff, "Final Report of the Kentucky Penal Code Revision (2003)," https://scholarship.law.upenn.edu/faculty_scholarship/294.

69. Robinson, Kussmaul, and Sarahne, "How Criminal Code Drafting Form Can Restrain Prosecutorial and Legislative Excesses: Consolidated Offense Drafting."

70. "Compare id. § 771(a)(1) (providing a higher grade of rape where the victim is less than fourteen years of age, and the offender is at least nineteen years of age), and Id. § 773(a)(5) (providing an even higher grade of rape where victim is less than twelve years of age, and the offender is at least eighteen years of age), with id. § 769(a)(3) (providing a higher grade of unlawful sexual assault where the victim is less than thirteen years of age, regardless of the offender's age). Note

also that the relevant age of the victim—less than twelve or less than thirteen years of age—varies between the two sets of offenses, see id. §§ 773(a)(5), 769(a)(3), but it is not clear that these different distinctions are meaningful, or whether the Delaware General Assembly was even aware of this apparent discrepancy." Ibid., 802.

71. United Nations Development Programme Maldives, "Options for Legal Aid Programming in The Maldives," 2016, 1–3; Paul H. Robinson, Final Report of the Maldivian Penal Law & Sentencing Codification Project: Text of Draft Code (Volume 1) and Official Commentary (Volume 2)," January 2006, https://ssrn-com.proxy.library.upenn.edu/abstract=1522222 .

72. "PG Considering the Introduction of Plea Bargain," PSM News, December 18, 2019, https://psmnews.mv/en/61522.

CHAPTER 11

1. Lili Loofbourow, "Why Society Goes Easy on Rapists," Slate, May 30, 2019, https://slate.com/news-and-politics/2019/05/sexual-assault-rape-sympathy-no-prison.html.

2. Joshua Divine, "Booker Disparity and Data-Driven Sentencing," Hastings Law Journal 69, no. 3 (April 2018): 778.

3. Michael Tonry, "Fifty Years of American Sentencing Reform: Nine Lessons," Crime and Justice 48 (2019): 21.

4. See, for example, Louis Aguilar, "Estate of Vincent Chin Seeks Millions from His Killer," The Detroit News, June 24, 2017; Associated Press, "Slayer Is Acquitted of Civil Rights Violation," New York Times, May 2, 1987, Section 1, 28; Josh Holusha, "2 Fined in Detroit Slaying Are Indicted by Federal Jury," New York Times, November 3, 1983; UPI, "U.S. Appeals Court Reverses Conviction in Michigan Slaying," New York Times, September 13, 1986; "The $3,000 License to Kill," Washington Post, April 30, 1983.

5. See, for example, Celestine Bohlen, "Holtzman May Appeal Probation for Immigrant in Wife's Slaying," *New York Times*, April 5, 1989; Doriane Lambelet Coleman, "Culture, Cloaked in Mens Rea," *The South Atlantic Quarterly* 100, no. 4 (Fall 2001): 981–1004; Aahren R. DePalma, "I Couldn't Help Myself—My Culture Made Me Do It: The Use of Cultural Evidence in the Heat of Passion Defense," *Chicana/o Latina/o Law Review* 28, no. 1 (2009): 7–8; Leslie Gevirtz, "Immigrant Gets Probation for Killing Wife," UPI, March 31, 1989; Leti Volpp, "(Mis) identifying Culture: Asian Women and the 'Cultural Defense,'" *Harvard Women's Law Journal* 17 (1994): 57–101; Marianne Yen, "Refusal to Jail immigrant Who Killed Wife Stirs Outrage," *Washington Post*, April 10, 1989.

6. Susan Rinkenas, "Illinois Judge Reverses Conviction of 18-Year-Old Rapist So He Won't Have to Go to Prison," Jezebel, January 12, 2021, https://jezebel.com/illinois-judge-reverses-conviction-of-18-year-old-rapis-1848344571.

7. Note, for example, the Supreme Court case of *Rummel v. Estelle* in which the Court approved a mandatory life sentence for a habitual offender who had committed three felonies amounting to stealing $230. Rummel v. Estelle, 445 US 263 (1980).

8. Griffin Edwards, Stephen Rushin, and Hoseph Colquitt, "The Effects of Voluntary and Presumptive Sentencing Guidelines," *Texas Law Review* 98, no. 1 (2019): 12.

9. See, for example, Ted Alcorn, "Judge Who Keeps People Out of Jail," *Washington Post*, November 30, 2021; Eric Westervelt, "To Save Opioid Addicts, This Experimental Court Is Ditching The Delays," NPR, October 5, 2017; Jennifer Smith, "Nearly 100 People Charged with Murder Are Free to Walk Streets of Chicago Thanks to Woke Bail Reform: Judge REFUSES to Jail Suspects Accused of Violent Crimes Despite Pleas from Cops and the Mayor," *Daily Mail*, January 11, 2022.

10. See Richard S. Frase, "Forty Years of American Sentencing Guidelines: What Have We Learned?" *Crime and Justice* 48 (February 2019): 102–3.

11. Marvin E. Frankel, *Criminal Sentences: Law Without Order* (Hill and Wang, 1972); James R. Thompson and Gary L. Starkman, "Reviewed Work(s): Criminal Sentences: Law without Order by Marvin E. Frankel," *Columbia Law Review* 74, no. 1 (January 1974): 152–58.

12. Stephen Breyer, "Federal Sentencing Guidelines Revisited," PBS, November 1998, https://www.pbs.org/wgbh/pages/frontline/shows/snitch/readings/breyer.html.

13. Divine, "Booker Disparity and Data-Driven Sentencing."

14. End Mandatory Minimums, "Brennan Center for Justice," October 18, 2021, https://www.brennancenter.org/our-work/analysis-opinion/end-mandatory-minimums.

15. Erica Zunkel and Alison Siegler, "The Federal Judiciary's Role in Drug Law Reform in an Era of Congressional Dysfunction," *Ohio State Journal of Criminal Law* 18, no. 1 (2020): 295; see Harrison Narcotics Tax, Pub. L. No. 63-223, 38 Stat. 278, 1914.

16. End Mandatory Minimums, "Brennan Center for Justice."

17. Breyer, "Federal Sentencing Guidelines Revisited."

18. "National Assessment of Structured Sentencing," Department of Justice, Bureau of Justice Assistance, 1996, 22.

19. Ibid., 24–45.

20. See Rummel v. Estelle, 445 US 263 (1980).

21. Breyer, "Federal Sentencing Guidelines Revisited."

22. Ram Subramanian and Ruth Delaney, "Playbook for Change? States Reconsider Mandatory Minimum Sentences," February 2014, 8.

23. The United States Sentencing Commission is made up of seven voting members who are appointed by the president. The members serve staggered six-year terms

and no more than four members can be from a single political party, and at least three must be federal judges. United States Sentencing Commission, "Organization," https://www.ussc.gov/about/who-we-are/organization.

24. "An Overview of the United States Sentencing Commission," United States Sentencing Commission, 2.

25. United States Sentencing Commission, "Federal Sentencing: The Basics," 2018, 3.

26. Divine, "Booker Disparity and Data-Driven Sentencing," 776.

27. United States v. Booker, 543 US 220 (2005).

28. Ibid. Justice Breyer's opinion.

29. Ibid.

30. "Fact Sheet: The Impact of United States v. Booker on Federal Sentencing," Department of Justice, March 15, 2006, 2.

31. Ibid.

32. Divine, "Booker Disparity and Data-Driven Sentencing," 773–76. Apparently, a small group of lenient judges choose lenient sentences and a small group of harsh judges choose harsh sentences, thus significantly increasing the inter-judge disparity while not affecting average sentences very much.

33. NCSC's 2008 publication profiles twenty-one state sentencing guideline systems: Alabama, Alaska, Arizona, Delaware, Kansas, Louisiana, Maryland, Massachusetts, Michigan, Minnesota, Montana, North Carolina, Ohio, Oregon, Pennsylvania, Tennessee, Utah, Virginia, Washington, Wisconsin, and Washington, DC. Neal B. Kauder and Brian J. Ostrom, "State Sentencing Guidelines—Profiles and Continuum," National Center for State Courts (NCSC), July 2008, 4.

34. The six questions were: 1. Is there an enforceable rule related to guideline use? 2. Is the completion of a worksheet or structured scoring form required? 3. Does a sentencing commission regularly report on guideline compliance? 4. Are compelling and substantial reasons required for departures? 5. Are written reasons required for departures? 6. Is there appellate review of defendant-based challenges related to sentencing guidelines? Ibid., 5.

35. Ibid.

36. Ibid., 19.

37. Ibid., 20.

38. Ibid.

39. Edwards, Rushin, and Colquitt, "The Effects of Voluntary and Presumptive Sentencing Guidelines," 1.

40. "Voluntary guidelines are 'a starting point or suggestion for sentencing,' while presumptive or mandatory guidelines 'connote that the sentences established by the guidelines are required.'" Ibid., quoting Kelly Lyn Mitchell, "State Sentencing Guidelines: A Garden Full of Variety," *Fed. Probation*, September 2017, 34.

41. Edwards, Rushin, and Colquitt, "The Effects of Voluntary and Presumptive Sentencing Guidelines," 39; Paul J. Hofer et al., "Effect of the Federal Sentencing Guidelines on Interjudge Sentencing Disparity," *Journal of Criminal Law & Criminology* 90, no. 1 (1999): 239; James M. Anderson et al., "Measuring Interjudge Sentencing Disparity: Before and After the Federal Sentencing Guidelines," *Journal of Law & Economics* 42, no. S1 (April 1999): 271. (Finding average interjudge sentencing disparity dropped from around 4.9 months to around 3.9 months after the passage of the Federal Sentencing Guidelines.)

42. Edwards, Rushin, and Colquitt, "The Effects of Voluntary and Presumptive Sentencing Guidelines," 1.

43. Ibid., 1 and 4.

44. Ibid., 1.

45. Brenda Sims Blackwell, David Holleran, and Mary A. Finn, "The Impact of the Pennsylvania Sentencing Guidelines on Sex Differences in Sentencing," *Journal of Contemporary Criminal Justice* 24, no. 4 (November 2008): 399, https://doi.org/10.1177/1043986208319453.

46. Edwards, Rushin, and Colquitt, "The Effects of Voluntary and Presumptive Sentencing Guidelines," 34–35.

47. "Sentencing Guidelines Around the World," Scottish Sentencing Council, https://www.scottishsentencingcouncil.org.uk/media/1109/paper-31a-sentencing-guidelines-around-the-world.pdf.

48. In re Disciplinary Proceedings Against Addison, 340 Wis.2d 16 (2012); Erika Slife, "Chicago Attorneys Are Charged in Rape of Wisconsin Woman," *Chicago Tribune*, September 21, 2005, https://www.chicagotribune.com/news/ct-xpm-2005-09-21-0509210225-story.html.

49. Cary Spivak, "Lawyers' Licenses Suspended by State Supreme Court," *Milwaukee Journal Sentinel*, April 4, 2012, https://archive.jsonline.com/news/wisconsin/lawyer-accused-of-rape-has-license-suspended-for-two-months-vd4sarq-146092705.html/.

50. Izabelle B. Reyes, "The Epidemic of Injustice in Rape Law: Mandatory Sentencing as a Partial Remedy," *UCLA Women's Law Journal* 12, no. 2 (2003): 356–57.

51. Ibid.

52. Ibid.

53. Ibid.

54. Ibid.

55. Bill Otis, "When a 12 Year-Old Girl Can Be Considered the 'Aggressor' in Attempted Rape, You Can See Why We Need Mandatory Minimums," *Crime and Consequences*, December 20, 2017.

56. Meghan Keneally, "Inappropriately Light Sentences in Sexual Assault Cases Can Hurt Reporting of Future Crimes: Experts," ABC News, December 20, 2018, https://abcnews.go.com/US/inappropriately-light-sentences-sexual-assault-cases-hurt-reporting/story?id=59748226.

57. Ibid.

58. Ibid.

59. "Criminal Justice System: Statistics," Rape, Abuse, & Incest National Network, https://www.rainn.org/statistics/criminal-justice-system.

60. Liam Stack, "Light Sentence for Brock Turner in Stanford Rape Case Draws Outrage," *New York Times*, June 6, 2016, https://www.nytimes.com/2016/06/07/us/outrage-in-stanford-rape-case-over-dueling-statements-of-victim-and-attackers-father.html.

61. Richard Gonzales and Camila Domonoske, "Voters Recall Aaron Persky, Judge Who Sentenced Brock Turner," NPR, June 5, 2018, https://www.npr.org/sections/thetwo-way/2018/06/05/617071359/voters-are-deciding-whether-to-recall-aaron-persky-judge-who-sentenced-brock-tur.

62. "Plea Deal for Okla. Child Rapist Prompts Outrage," NBC News, June 16, 2009, https://www.nbcnews.com/id/wbna31395402.

63. Eric Fish, "35 Years After Vincent Chin's Murder, How Has America Changed?" Asia Society, June 16, 2017, https://asiasociety.org/blog/asia/35-years-after-vincent-chins-murder-how-has-america-changed.

64. United States v. Waters, 437 F.2d 722, 723 (D.C. Cir. 1970).

65. Karen Gelb, "Public Opinion About Sentencing," in *Encyclopedia of Criminology and Criminal Justice*, ed. Gerben Bruinsma and David Weisburd (Springer, 2014).

66. Julian V. Roberts, "Public Opinion, Crime, and Criminal Justice," *Crime and Justice* 16 (1992): 147.

67. Gelb, "Public Opinion About Sentencing." For example, a 1996 survey in the United Kingdom found that people who believed that sentencing was too lenient "were more likely to believe that judges were out of touch with society and were doing a poor job."

68. Princeton Survey Research Associates International, "The NCSC Sentencing Attitudes Survey: A Report on the Findings," July 2006, 3.

69. Ibid.

70. Ibid.; see, for example, Mark A. Cohen, Roland T. Rust, and Sara Steen, NCJRS

199364, "Measuring Public Perceptions of Appropriate Prison Sentences: Executive Summary," October 2002.

71. Megan Brenan, "Fewer Americans Call for Tougher Criminal Justice System," Gallup, November 16, 2020, https://news.gallup.com/poll/324164/fewer-americans-call-tougher-criminal-justice-system.aspx.

72. Michael M. O'Hear and Darren Wheelock, "Public Attitudes Toward Punishment, Rehabilitation, and Reform: Lessons from the Marquette Law School Poll," *Federal Sentencing Reporter* 29, no. 1 (2016): 51.

73. Subramanian and Delaney, "Playbook for Change?" 8.

74. Evan Bernick and Paul J. Larkin Jr., "Reconsidering Mandatory Minimum Sentences: The Arguments for and Against Potential Reforms," No. 114 Legal Memorandum, The Heritage Foundation, February 10, 2014.

75. Karol Markowicz, "A String of Murders Shows We Must Give Violent Offenders Harsher Sentences," *New York Post*, December 12, 2021, https://nypost.com/2021/12/12/a-string-of-murders-shows-we-must-give-violent-offenders-harsher-sentences/.

76. Reyes, "The Epidemic of Injustice in Rape Law," 372–78.

77. If mandatory minimums include exceptions to try to avoid this problem, they become simply less nuanced mandatory sentencing guidelines.

78. Michael Tonry, "Sentencing in America, 1975–2025," *Crime and Justice* 42, no. 1 (August 2013): 159, https://doi.org/10.1086/671134.

79. See "Sixth Amendment—Right to Jury Trial—Mandatory Minimum Sentences—Alleyne v. United States," *Harvard Law Review* 127, no. 1 (November 2013): 256–57.

80. Hans Zeisel and Shari Seldman Diamond, "Sentencing Councils: A Study of Sentence Disparity and Its Reduction," *University of Chicago Law Review* 43, no. 1 (Fall 1975): 109.

81. Breyer, "Federal Sentencing Guidelines Revisited."

82. United States v. Greenlaw, 481 F. 3d 601, vacated and remanded.

83. Carissa B. Hessick, "Appellate Review of Sentencing Policy Decisions After Kimbrough," *Marquette Law Review* 93, no. 2 (2009): 74.

84. H.R.5773—98th Congress (1983–1984): Sentencing Reform Act of 1984. Congress.gov, Library of Congress, October 12, 1984.

85. United States Sentencing Commission, Guidelines Manual, Ch.5 Pt.A, November 2021, at 407.

CHAPTER 12

1. Timothy A. Hughes, Doris James Wilson, and Allen J. Beck, NCJ 184735, "Trends in State Parole 1990–2000," US Department of Justice Bureau of Justice Statistics, October 2001, https://bjs.ojp.gov/content/pub/pdf/tsp00.pdf.

2. Danielle Kaeble, NCJ 252205, "Time Served in State Prison," US Department of Justice Bureau of Justice Statistics, November 2018, 1.

3. Ibid.

4. Matthew R. Durose, NCJ 255947, "Recidivism of Prisoners Released in 34 States in 2012: A 5-Year Follow-Up Period (2012–2017)," US Department of Justice Bureau of Justice Statistics, July 2021, https://bjs.ojp.gov/library/publications/recidivism-prisoners-released-34-states-2012-5-year-follow-period-2012-2017.

5. Hughes, Wilson, and Beck, "Trends in State Parole 1990–2000," 10.

6. Shelley Murphy and Andrea Estes, "Twenty-One First-Degree Murderers Set Free Under State's New Compassionate Release Law," *The Boston Globe*, March 14, 2021, https://www.bostonglobe.com/2021/03/14/metro/twenty-one-first-degree-murderers-set-free-under-states-new-compassionate-release-law/.

7. Paul H. Robinson, "One Perspective on Sentencing Reform in the United States," *Criminal Law Forum* 8, no. 1 (1997): 7–9.

8. See chapter 3, "Reforms."

9. Charles Doyle, RS21364, "Supervised Release (Parole): An Abbreviated Outline of Federal Law," Congressional Research Service, last modified September 28, 2021, 6.

10. "States Can Shorten Probation and Protect Public Safety," Pew Charitable Trust, April 2021, https://www.pewtrusts.org/en/research-and-analysis/reports/2020/12/states-can-shorten-probation-and-protect-public-safety.

11. Ibid.

12. Some may argue that the one exception to this is the offender who after the offense expresses genuine and heartfelt remorse and seeks to atone for his crime. See Paul H. Robinson, Sean Jackowitz, and Daniel M. Bartels, "Extralegal Punishment Factors: A Study of Forgiveness, Hardship, Good-Deeds, Apology, Remorse, and Other Such Discretionary Factors in Assessing Criminal Punishment," *Vanderbilt Law Review* 65, no. 3 (2012): 737. However, a clemency system is arguably a better mechanism for reducing the sentences of such unusually repentant offenders than a parole system. See chapter 13 for a discussion of executive clemency.

13. Section 235(b) of the Sentencing Reform Act of 1984 (98 Stat. 2032) called for the elimination of the Federal Parole Commission.

14. Hughes, Wilson, and Beck, "Trends in State Parole 1990–2000," 10.

15. J. J. Prescott et al., "Understanding Violent-Crime Recidivism," *Notre Dame Law Review* 95, no. 4 (2020): 1667.

16. See, for example, Louise Continelli, "A Serial Killer's Lessons Learning from the Atrocities of Arthur Shawcross," *The Buffalo News*, April 13, 1993, https://buffalonews.com/news/a-serial-killers-lessons-learning-from-the-atrocities-of-arthur-shawcross/article

_d17ecf2d-6b5c-5d5d-ab38-518e525fdefb.html; "Keep Convicted Killers in Prison," *The Daily News*, January 9, 2013; William DeLong, "Inside the Mind of Arthur Shawcross, The 300-Pound 'Genesee River Killer,'" All That's Interesting, August 28, 2020, https://allthatsinteresting.com/arthur-shawcross; Michael Keene, "The Genesee River Killer," *Rochester Examiner*, November 25, 2009; Michael Keene, "The Genesee River Killer," *The Times Union*, September 19, 1994; Gina Tron, "'He Should Suffer': Why Was Serial Killer Arthur Shawcross Paroled Before Murder Spree?" True Crime Buzz, November 20, 2020.

17. Shawcross is sentenced to 250 years and dies in prison nineteen years later.

18. Ilyana Kuziemko, "How Should Inmates Be Released from Prison? An Assessment of Parole Versus Fixed Sentence Regimes," *Quarterly Journal of Economics* 128, no. 1 (2013): 372.

19. Michael Tonry, "Predictions of Dangerousness in Sentencing: Déja Vu All Over Again," *Crime and Justice* 48, no. 1 (2019): 439–82.

20. Durose, "Recidivism of Prisoners Released in 34 States in 2012."

21. Allison Lawrence, "Making Sense of Sentencing: State Systems and Policies," National Conference of State Legislatures, 2015, 5, https://documents.ncsl.org/wwwncsl/Criminal-Justice/sentencing.pdf.

22. Paula Ditton and Doris Wilson, NCJ 170032, "Truth in Sentencing in State Prisons," US Department of Justice Bureau of Justice Statistics, January 1999.

23. Lawrence, "Making Sense of Sentencing: State Systems and Policies," 6–7.

24. Ditton and Wilson, "Truth in Sentencing in State Prisons," 3.

25. Caitlin Curley, "Truth in Sentencing: Why America Locks People Up and Throws Away the Key," Gen Biz, December 17, 2015, https://genbiz.com/truth-in-sentencing-america-america-locks-people-up-throws-away-key-16856-2.

26. Alexis Watts et al., "Profiles in Parole Release and Revocation: Examining the Legal Framework in the United States: Texas," Robina Institute of Criminal Law & Criminal Justice, July 15, 2016, 8.

27. Ibid.

28. Those serving life for crimes committed after July 1, 2006, will need to serve thirty years under a newer law. State Board of Prisons and Parole, Life Sentences,https://pap.georgia.gov/parole -consideration/parole-process-georgia /life-sentences.

29. "California Parole Law—How It Works," Shouse Law Group, https://www.shouse law.com/ca/defense/parole/. Variations also apply in states with mandatory parole where some crimes may not be eligible for any early release or even good time discount. For example, in Illinois, which abolished discretionary parole in 1978, murderers are required to serve 100 percent of their sentence, while other violent offenders are only required to serve 85 percent of their sentence. Ditton, Ditton and Wilson, "Truth in Sentencing in State Prisons." Other states have similar 100 percent time served requirements for some especially serious crimes. Curley, Curley, "Truth in Sentencing."

30. "How Long Is a Life Sentence? Shortest, Longest, and Everything in Between," Recording Law, January 24, 2022, https:// recordinglaw.com/how-long-is-a-life -sentence/.

31. Kaeble, "Time Served in State Prison," 4. (The maximum sentence is either the actual determinate sentence or the upper bound of a sentencing range in an indeterminate sentence.)

32. Hughes, Wilson, and Beck, "Trends in State Parole 1990–2000," 5.

33. David P. Farrington, "Homicide in Eight Countries From 1980 to 2000: The Flow from Crimes Committed to Time Served in Prison," Homicide Studies 24, no. 3 (2020): 276, https://doi.org /10.1177/1088767920916914.

34. Kaeble, "Time Served in State Prison," 4.

35. Ibid., table 2.

36. Hughes, Wilson, and Beck, "Trends in State Parole 1990–2000," 4.

37. "Earned and Good Time Policies: Comparing Maximum Reductions Available," Prison Fellowship, 2018, https:// www.prisonfellowship.org/wp-content /uploads/2018/04/GoodTimeChartUS _Apr27_v7.pdf.

38. Ibid.

39. Jeffrey A. Meyer and Linda Ross Meyer, "Abolish Parole," New York Times, October 28, 2007.

40. National Criminal Justice Reference Service, "Crime and the Criminal Justice System in the State of Maryland," US Department of Justice, November 1974, 85.

41. Gary Craig, "Poll: Parole Concerns Still Ride High," Democrat and Chronicle, October 29, 2014, https://www .democratandchronicle.com/story/news /2014/10/29/voice-voter-parole-poll /18142215/.

42. John Doble and Judith Greene, "Attitudes Towards Crime and Punishment in Vermont: Public Opinion about an Experiment with Restorative Justice," National Institute of Justice, March 2000, 11.

43. Paul H. Robinson, "Punishing Dangerousness: Cloaking Preventive Detention as Criminal Justice," Harvard Law Review 114, no. 5 (March 2001): 1429–59; "Don't Blame Parole for Murders," New York Times, August 8, 1992; James Wootton, "Truth in Sentencing—Why States Should Make Violent Criminals Do Their Time," University of Dayton Law Review 20, no. 2 (1995): 779–80.

44. "Don't Blame Parole for Murders," New York Times, August 8, 1992.

45. Paul H. Robinson and Sarah M. Robinson, Shadow Vigilantes: How Distrust in the Justice System Breeds a New Kind of Lawlessness (Prometheus Books, 2018), 15.

46. Julian V. Roberts, "Public Opinion, Crime, and Criminal Justice," Crime and Justice 16 (1992): 101.

47. For a discussion of punishment equivalencies, see, for example, Paul H. Robinson, "Restorative Processes and Doing Justice," *University of St. Thomas Law Journal* 3, no. 3 (Spring 2006): 426.

48. See the recommendation for chapter 11.

49. As quoted directly from 18 US Code § 3624, "a prisoner who is serving a term of imprisonment of more than 1 year other than a term of imprisonment for the duration of the prisoner's life, may receive credit toward the service of the prisoner's sentence of up to 54 days for each year of the prisoner's sentence imposed by the court, subject to determination by the Bureau of Prisons that, during that year, the prisoner has displayed exemplary compliance with institutional disciplinary regulations." See 18 US Code § 3624.

50. See Lindsey E. Wylie and Alexis K. Knutson, "Extraordinary and Compelling: The Use of Compassionate Release Laws in the United States," *Psychology, Public Policy, and Law* 24, no. 2 (2018): 216–34.

51. Mary Price, "Everywhere and Nowhere: Compassionate Release in the States," FAMM, 2018, 12.

52. Christie Thompson, "Frail, Old and Dying, but Their Only Way Out of Prison Is a Coffin," *New York Times*, March 7, 2018, https://www.nytimes.com/2018/03/07/us/prisons-compassionate-release-.html.

53. "Families Against Mandatory Minimums, Compassionate Release and the First Step Act: Then and Now," FAMM, https://famm.org/wp-content/uploads/Compassionate-Release-in-the-First-Step-Act-Explained-FAMM.pdf.

54. Attorney General's First Step Act Section 3634 Annual Report, United States Department of Justice, December 2020, 8.

55. John Annese, "Mobster and Drug Gang Killer Ordered Released by Federal Judge: 'I Am Letting Two Murderers Sentenced to Life Out of Prison,'" *Daily News*, November 2, 2022, https://www.nydailynews.com/new-york/nyc-crime/ny-nyc-mobster-drug-gang-killer-released-early-judge-20221103-52zenynwgvfrld5yeael63ehem-story.html.

56. Price, "Everywhere and Nowhere," 12.

57. Families Against Mandatory Minimums, Compassionate Release State by State, https://famm.org/wp-content/uploads/CCR-State-Chart-2022indd-03-18-22.pdf.

58. Kristin Brown Parker et al., Increasing Alternative Care Options for Terminally and Chronically Ill Prisoners, October 2017, 17, https://drexel.edu/~/media/Files/law/academics/clinical/Compassionate%20Release%20Report%20by%20Community%20Lawyering%20Clinic.ashx?la=en.

59. TCR Staff, "'Paroling Grandpa': Study Finds 3% Recidivism Rate Among Elderly Ex-Inmates," The Crime Report, November 19, 2018, https://justiceroundtable.org/news-item/paroling-grandpa-study-finds-3-recidivism-rate-among-elderly-ex-inmates/.

60. Rebecca Silber, Alison Shames, and Kelsey Reid, "Aging Out: Using Compassionate Release to Address the Growth of Aging and Infirm Prison Populations," Vera Institute of Justice, December 2017, 3.

61. "Prison Inmate Release Responses in Response to the Coronavirus (COVID-19) Pandemic, 2020," Ballotpedia, July 1, 2020, https://ballotpedia.org/Prison_inmate_release_responses_in_response_to_the_coronavirus_(COVID-19)_pandemic,_2020.

62. Wendy Sawyer, "New Date: The Changes in Prisons, Jails, Probation, and Parole in the First Year of the Pandemic," Prison Policy Initiative, January 11, 2022, https://www.prisonpolicy.org/blog/2022/01/11/bjs_update/. Reporting and analyzing data is from the Bureau of Justice Statistics. To be clear, these numbers account not only for inmates granted compassionate release but all inmates who were "released" from detention for any reason, including due to death. Because the most recent BJS data is only for the year 2020,

it also includes temporary releases during the initial waves of the pandemic.

63. Sarah N. Lynch, "U.S Justice Dept. Says Inmates Sent Home Due to COVID Will Not Be Returned to Prison," Reuters, December 21, 2021, https://www.reuters.com/world/us/us-justice-dept-says-inmates-sent-home-due-covid-19-will-not-be-returned-prison-2021-12-21/.

64. Murphy and Estes, "Twenty-One First-Degree Murderers Set Free Under State's New Compassionate Release Law."

65. Ibid.

66. Corin Hoggard, "Are Violent Criminals Getting Out in Second Wave of Early Prison Release?" ABC30 Fresno, July 27, 2020, https://abc30.com/prison-central-valley-coronavirus-early-release/6337687/.

67. Ibid.

68. Ibid.

69. See, for example, Hollie McKay, "Public Health Versus Public Safety: Confusion Looms as Sex Offenders Are Released from Incarceration Across the Country," Fox News, May 14, 2020, https://www.foxnews.com/us/public-health-public-safety-sex-offender-release-incarceration.

70. See, for example, April Baumgarten, "Man Who Plotted 'Second American Revolution' Sentenced to Five Years," Herald, December 14, 2018; Herald Staff, Life, "Uneasily, Goes on in Oklee, Minn., as Eric Reinbold Remains at Large," Herald, July 13, 2021; Daniel Horowitz, "Horowitz: MN Man Caught Building Pipe Bombs for 'Revolution' Released for COVID 'Compassion.' Now He's Wanted for Murder," Blaze Media Op-Ed, July 13, 2021; "Compassionate Release During the COVID-19 Pandemic in Minnesota," Meshbesher & Associates Attorneys at Law, May 19, 2020, https://www.stevemeshbesher.com/blog/2020/may/compassionate-release-during-the-covid-19-pandem/; "Manhunt Continues for Reinbold," Thief River Falls Times & Northern Watch, July 14, 2021;

Adam Kurtz, "MN Man Who Did Time for Pipe Bombs Now Wanted in Homicide Case," Forum News Service, July 9, 2021; "Oklee Man Sentenced to Five Years in Federal Prison for Possessing Unregistered Pipe Bombs," US Department of Justice, US Attorney's Office District of Minnesota, December 14, 2018; Adam Kurtz, "Pennington County Sheriff's Office Searching for Homicide Suspect," Yahoo! News, July 9, 2021; Adam Uren, "Bomb Maker Recently Released from Prison Now Wanted for Murder," Bring Me The News, July 10, 2021; see also the Minnesota Conditional Medical Release program (Minn. Stat. § 244.05, Subd. 8).

71. Matt Miller, "Victim's Family Opposes 'Compassionate' Release of Dying Killer Who Murdered Steelton Man in 1974," PennLive News, April 9, 2021, https://www.pennlive.com/news/2021/04/should-a-dying-killer-who-murdered-a-steelton-man-in-1974-receive-a-compassionate-release-from-his-life-prison-sentence.html.

72. Mensah M. Dean, "A Judge Let a Terminally Ill Killer from Philly Leave Prison to Die at Home. The Victim's Daughter Calls It a Miscarriage of Justice," The Philadelphia Inquirer, August 12, 2020, https://www.inquirer.com/news/compassionate-release-deferred-sentence-jessie-alexander-alicia-russell-jenkins-prison-20200812.html.

73. Christina Carrega, "Victim's Family Says They Weren't Told of Violent Offender's Release Amid COVID-19," ABC News, April 7, 2020, https://abcnews.go.com/Health/crime-victim-calls-slap-faces-violent-offenders-released/story?id=69957568.

74. Murphy and Estes, "Twenty-One First-Degree Murderers Set Free Under State's New Compassionate Release Law."

75. "California COVID Pison Releases Catching Victims of 'Non-Violent' Crimes Off-Guard," ABC 30 Action News, August 28, 2020, https://abc30.com/daniel-mendez

-ramona-fresno-drunk-driving-deadly
-accident/6394106/.

76. Lindsey Van Ness, "COVID-19 Extends Sentences for Some Incarcerated People," Pew Charitable Trusts, January 20, 2021, https://www.pewtrusts.org/en/research-and-analysis/blogs/stateline/2021/01/20/covid-19-extends-sentences-for-some-incarcerated-people.

77. Sam Stanton, "Prosecutors Want to Halt New Good-Time Release Credits for 76,000 California Inmates," *The Sacramento Bee*, May 13, 2021, https://www.sacbee.com/news/local/article251392873.html.

78. Ibid.

79. Murphy and Estes, "Twenty-One First-Degree Murderers Set Free Under State's New Compassionate Release Law."

80. B. Jaye Anno, Camelia Graham, and James E. Lawrence, "Correctional Health Care: Addressing the Needs of Elderly, Chronically Ill, and Terminally Ill Inmates," National Institute of Corrections, February 2004.

81. "Interstate Corrections Compact," Ballotpedia, https://ballotpedia.org/Interstate_Corrections_Compact.

82. "Interstate Transfer of Prison Inmates in the United States," National Institute of Corrections, February 2006.

CHAPTER 13

1. P. S. Ruckman Jr., "Executive Clemency in the United States: Origins, Development, and Analysis (1900–1993)," *Presidential Studies Quarterly* 27, no. 2 (1997): 252.

2. US CONST. art. II, §2.

3. Margaret Colgate Love, "50-State Comparison: Pardon Policy & Practice," Restoration of Rights Project, October 2022, https://ccresourcecenter.org/state-restoration-profiles/50-state-comparisoncharacteristics-of-pardon-authorities-2/.

4. "Clemency Statistics," Department of Justice, https://www.justice.gov/pardon/clemency-statistics; "Executive Clemency and Presidential Pardons," Ballotpedia, last modified March 15, 2023, https://ballotpedia.org/Executive_clemency_and_presidential_pardons; Anne McMillian, "The Pardon: Politics or Mercy?" International Bar Association, https://www.ibanet.org/article/465431E6-8846-4A89-BA0A-6A8B85E5ED1D.

5. Love, "50-State Comparison." The estimate of ten thousand annually derived from adding up the state pardon statistics using annual averages and the middle of ranges.

6. Jessica Weil, "Controversial Clemency: The President's Problematic Power to Pardon" (Master of arts thesis, Case Western Reserve University, 2017), 12.

7. Kristen H. Fowler, "Limiting the Federal Pardon Power," *Indiana Law Journal* 83, no. 4 (2008): 1652.

8. Weil, "Controversial Clemency," 12.

9. Ibid.

10. Ibid., 8.

11. Ibid., 16–17.

12. Ibid., 13.

13. Ibid.

14. US Department of Justice, Office of the Pardon Attorney, "Frequently Asked Questions," last accessed April 13, 2023, https://www.justice.gov/pardon/frequently-asked-questions.

15. Love, "50-State Comparison."

16. Ibid.

17. "50-State Comparison: Pardon Policy and Practice, Restoration of Rights Project," October 2022, https://ccresourcecenter.org/state-restoration-profiles/50-state-comparisoncharacteristics-of-pardon-authorities-2/. Note that of the fourteen states that require the approval of the pardon board, four include the governor on the board, but a majority of the board must still concur with any proposed clemency.

18. Love, "50-State Comparison."

19. "50-State Comparison."

20. Love, "50-State Comparison."

21. "50-State Comparison."

22. Ibid.

23. Love, "50-State Comparison."

24. "50-State Comparison."

25. North Dakota Century Board, Chapter 12-55.1, Pardon Advisory Board.

26. North Dakota Corrections and Rehabilitation, "Pardon Advisory Board," https://www.docr.nd.gov/pardon-advisory-board.

27. Ibid.

28. Ibid.

29. Milana Bretgoltz et al., "An Absolute Power, or a Power Absolutely in Need of Reform?" Proposals to Reform the Presidential Pardon Power, Democracy and the Constitution Clinic: Fordham University School of Law, January 2021, 10–11.

30. Carol J. Williams, "End-of-Term Clemency Is a Centuries-Old, Often Vilified Tradition," *Los Angeles Times*, January 10, 2011, https://www.latimes.com/archives/la-xpm-2011-jan-10-la-me-pardon-power-20110111-story.html.

31. Love, "50-State Comparison."

32. Ibid.

33. "The Clemency Application Process," Clear Up My Record, https://www.clearupmyrecord.com/the-clemency-application-process.php.

34. Nicholas M. Pace et al., NCJ 300116, "Statistical Analysis of Presidential Pardons," Bureau of Justice Statistics, June 2021.

35. Love, "50-State Comparison."

36. "Frequently Asked Questions," Arizona Board of Executive Clemency, https://boec.az.gov/helpful-information/faq.

37. State of California, Office of the Governor, "How to Apply for a Pardon," https://www.siskiyou.courts.ca.gov/system/files?file=governors-pardon.pdf.

38. Ibid.

39. Colorado, Hawaii, Illinois, Michigan, Montana, New Jersey, New York, Pennsylvania, Washington, and West Virginia have no eligibility criteria. Love, "50-State Comparison."

40. Paul H. Robinson et al., "Extralegal Punishment Factors: A Study of Forgiveness, Hardship, Good-Deeds, Apology, Remorse, and Other Such Discretionary Factors in Assessing Criminal Punishment," *Vanderbilt Law Review* 65, no. 3 (2012): 737–826.

41. Kenneth P. Cohen and Glenn R. Schmitt, "An Analysis of the Implementation of the 2014 Clemency Initiative," United States Sentencing Commission, September 2017.

42. Julia Dahl, "8 of the Murderers Haley Barbour Pardoned Killed Their Wives, Girlfriends," CBS News, January 13, 2012, https://www.cbsnews.com/news/8-of-the-murderers-haley-barbour-pardoned-killed-their-wives-girlfriends/.

43. Joseph Gerth, "How the Courier Journal Won a Pulitzer Prize for Digging into Matt Bevin's Pardons," *Courier-Journal*, May 10, 2020, https://www.courier-journal.com/story/news/politics/2020/05/09/pulitzer-prize-2020-how-courier-journal-won-covering-bevins-pardons/5179802002/.

44. Bevin claimed, but provided no evidence to support, the notion that Jones was targeted by prosecutors because of a political vendetta against his grandparents.

45. George Lardner Jr., "A Pardon to Remember," *New York Times*, November 24, 2008, https://www.nytimes.com/2008/11/22/opinion/22lardner.html; Kelly Phillips Erb, "Marc Rich, Famous Fugitive & Alleged Tax Evader, Pardoned by President Clinton, Dies," *Forbes*, June 27, 2013, https://www.forbes.com/sites/kellyphillipserb/2013/06/27/marc-rich-famous-fugitive-alleged-tax-evader-pardoned-by-president-clinton-dies/#166703613187.

46. The key difference is that an amnesty prevents politically and societally contentious prosecutions for conduct that may not have been criminal in motivations (for example, Confederate soldiers believed they were discharging a duty to their states and many Vietnam War draft dodgers were conscientious objectors). The problematic mass clemency discussed here is postconviction resentenc-

ing or pardoning of offenses that were undoubtedly criminal in motivation.

47. Joseph N. Rupcich, "Abusing a Limitless Power: Executive Clemency in Illinois," *Southern Illinois University Law Journal* 28, no. 1 (2003): 131.

48. Ibid.

49. He argued that these individuals were non-violent offenders who "would have received substantially lower sentences if convicted for the same offense" under new laws. Cohen and Schmitt, "An Analysis of the Implementation of the 2014 Clemency Initiative," 1.

50. Joseph Biden, "A Proclamation on Granting Pardon for the Offense of Simple Possession of Marijuana," Presidential Actions, October 6, 2022, https://www.whitehouse.gov/briefing-room/presidential-actions/2022/10/06/granting-pardon-for-the-offense-of-simple-possession-of-marijuana/.

51. Christina Wilkie, "Biden Pardons Thousands of People Convicted of Marijuana Possession, Orders Review of Federal Pot Laws," CNBC, October 6, 2022, https://www.cnbc.com/2022/10/06/biden-to-pardon-all-prior-federal-offenses-of-simple-marijuana-possession-.html.

52. Stephanie Armour and Laura Kusisto, "Biden Pardoning Thousands Convicted of Marijuana Possession Under Federal Law," *Wall Street Journal*, October 6, 2022, https://www.wsj.com/articles/biden-plans-to-pardon-people-convicted-of-simple-marijuana-possession-11665083338.

53. In April 2022, the House voted to nationally legalize marijuana, but the Senate did not take up the bill and some members specifically requested more research be done on long-term health issues before such legalization moved forward. See Kyle Jaeger, "GOP Senator Blocks Bipartisan Marijuana Research Bill from Expedited Thursday Vote Despite Calling for More Studies," Marijuana Moment, September 29, 2022, https://www.marijuanamoment.net/gop-senator-blocks-bipartisan-marijuana-research-bill-from-expedited-thursday-vote-despite-calling-for-more-studies/; Armour and Kusisto, "Biden Pardoning Thousands Convicted of Marijuana Possession Under Federal Law."

54. Martin Pengelly, "Trump Considered Blanket Pardon for Capitol Insurrectionists—Report," *The Guardian*, February 2, 2022, https://www.theguardian.com/us-news/2022/feb/02/trump-blanket-pardon-capitol-attack-january-6.

55. Sarah Lucy Cooper and Daniel Gough, "The Controversy of Clemency and Innocence in America," *California Western Law Review* 51, no. 1 (2014): 56.

56. Mark Osler, Review of *Mass Pardons in America: Rebellion, Presidential Amnesty, & Reconciliation*, by Graham G. Dodds, *Criminal Law and Criminal Justice Book Reviews*, January 2022, https://clcjbooks.rutgers.edu/books/mass-pardons-in-america-rebellion-presidential-amnesty-and-reconciliation/.

57. Laura Benshoff, "With Commutation, the Window to Freedom Opens a Crack for Lifers in PA," WHYY, May 31, 2016, https://whyy.org/articles/with-commutation-the-window-to-freedom-opens-a-crack-for-lifers-in-pa/.

58. Budd N. Shenkin and David I. Levine, "Should the Power of Presidential Pardon Be Revised?" *Hastings Constitutional Law Quarterly* 47, no. 1 (2019): 1–18.

59. Sam Amico, "Oklahoma Man Who Got Early Release Commits Triple Homicide, Cuts Out Woman's Heart," Rare, March 16, 2023, https://rare.us/crime/oklahoma-man-who-got-early-release-commits-triple-homicide-cuts-out-womans-heart/.

60. Human Rights Council, "Annual Report of the United Nations High Commissioner for Human Rights and Reports of the Office of the High Commissioner and the Secretary-General," September 15, 2021.

61. John Gramlich, "Trump Used His Clemency Power Sparingly Despite a Raft of Late Powers and Commutations," Pew Research Center, January 22, 2021, https://www.pewresearch.org/fact-tank/2021/01/22/trump-used-his-clemency-power-sparingly-despite-a-raft-of-late-pardons-and-commutations/ft_21-01-20_trumpclemencyrecord_1/.

62. Some examples illustrate these percentages: Truman granted 41 percent of clemency requests (1,913 total); Taft granted 39 percent of clemency requests (383 total); and Nixon granted 36 percent of clemency requests (863 total). President Franklin Roosevelt granted the greatest number of absolute requests, granting clemency to 3,756 individuals. Ibid.

63. Ibid.

64. Ibid.

65. Ibid.

66. Ibid.

67. "Obama Administration Clemency Initiative," United States Department of Just. Archives, last modified January 12, 2021, https://www.justice.gov/archives/pardon/obama-administration-clemency-initiative.

68. "Clemency Statistics"; Ruckman, "Executive Clemency in the United States."

69. See Love, "50-State Comparison," for an explanation of how this number was derived.

70. Ibid.

71. Ibid.

72. Christopher Reinhart, "Office of Legislative Research Report 2005-R0065, Pardon Statistics from Other States," January 14, 2005.

73. Rosalio Ahumuda, "Newsome Grants Clemency for 20, including California Inmates with Elevated COVID-19 Risk," *The Sacramento Bee*, March 12, 2021, https://www.sacbee.com/news/local/crime/article249906578.html.

74. Reinhart, "Office of Legislative Research Report 2005-R0065."

75. "I firmly believe there are thousands of Ohioans, maybe tens of thousands of Ohioans, who—if we had all the facts in front of us—would be granted a pardon." Mike DeWine (@GovMikeDeWine), Twitter, January 19, 2021, 9:59 am.

76. Office of the Governor State of Ohio, "Ohio Governor's Expedited Pardon Project," https://governor.ohio.gov/priorities/expedited-pardon-project.

77. Christopher Zoukis, "State Governors Grant over 500 Pardons, Commutations," Prison Legal News, December 5, 2017, https://www.prisonlegalnews.org/news/2017/dec/5/state-governors-grant-over-500-pardons-commutations/.

78. Restoration of Rights Project, "New York Restoration of Rights & Record Relief," https://ccresourcecenter.org/state-restoration-profiles/new-york-restoration-of-rights-pardon-expungement-sealing/.

79. Restoration of Rights Project, "Colorado Restoration of Rights & Record Relief," https://ccresourcecenter.org/state-restoration-profiles/colorado-restoration-of-rights-pardon-expungement-sealing-2/#II_Pardon_policy_practice.

80. Restoration of Rights Project, "Connecticut Restoration of Rights & Record Relief," https://ccresourcecenter.org/state-restoration-profiles/connecticut-restoration-of-rights-pardon-expungement-sealing/.

81. Margaret Love, "Delaware Pardon Statistics 1988–2019 (First Quarter)," Collateral Consequences Resource Center, November 9, 2019, https://ccresourcecenter.org/delaware-pardon-statistics-1988-present/.

82. Restoration of Rights Project, "Virginia Restoration of Rights & Record Relief," https://ccresourcecenter.org/state-restoration-profiles/virginia-restoration-of-rights-pardon-expungement-sealing/.

83. Brian Naylor, "Preemptive Pardons by Trump Raises Questions: What Can He Do?" NPR, December 2, 2020, https://www.npr.org/2020/12/02/941290291/talk-of-preemptive-pardons-by-trump-raises-questions-what-can-he-do.

84. Janice Broach, "Victim's Sister Angry After Ozment's Miss. Pardon," Action 5 News, January 31, 2012, https://www.actionnews5.com/story/16636298/victims-sister-angry-after-miss-pardon/.

85. Mario F. Cattabiani, "Victim's Daughter Questions Pardon in McFadden Case," *The Morning Call*, February 7, 1995, https://www.mcall.com/news/mc-xpm-1995-02-07-3022213-story.html

86. Clay Bennett, "Trump Demonstrates the Need for Pardon Reform," *Press Democrat*, January 3, 2021, https://www.pressdemocrat.com/article/opinion/pd-editorial-trump-demonstrates-the-need-for-pardon-reform/?sba=AAS.

87. Austin Sarat, "Putting a Square Peg in a Round Hole: Victims, Retribution, and George Ryan's Clemency," *North Carolina Law Review* 82, no. 4 (2004): 1348.

88. Maggie Haberman and Michael Schmidt, "Trump Gives Clemency to More Allies, Including Manafort, Stone and Charles Kushner," *New York Times*, December 23, 2023, https://www.nytimes.com/2020/12/23/us/politics/trump-pardon-manafort-stone.html.

89. Kathryn Watson, "Can a President Pardon Himself?" CBS News, June 18, 2023, https://www.cbsnews.com/news/can-a-president-pardon-himself/.

90. "Ford lost the 1976 election, and many believed—himself included—that it was due to his controversial pardon of Nixon, issued on September 8, 1974, a decision met with significantly negative responses in the media both nationally and internationally." Liz Tracey, "The Pardon of President Nixon: Annotated History," JSTOR Daily, September 8, 2022, https://daily-jstor-org.proxy.library.upenn.edu/the-pardon-of-president-nixon-annotated/.

91. Frank Newport and Joseph Caroll, "Americans Generally Negative on Recent Presidential Pardons," Gallup, March 9, 2007, https://news.gallup.com/poll/26830/americans-generally-negative-recent-presidential-pardons.aspx.

92. "Hill-Harris Poll: 76 Percent Oppose Trump Pardoning Former Campaign Aides," *The Hill*, March 19, 2019, https://thehill.com/hilltv/what-americas-thinking/434756-poll-76-percent-of-americans-oppose-trump-pardoning-former/.

93. Cattabiani, "Victim's Daughter Questions Pardon in McFadden Case."

94. Commonwealth of Pennsylvania, Legislative Journal, Senate, No. 9 First Special Session, Monday, February 13, 1995.

95. See Ex Parte Garland, 71 US 333 (1866); United States v. Klein, 80 US 128 (1871); Colleen Shogan, "The History of the Pardon Power—Executive Unilateralism in the Constitution," White House Historical Association, December 2, 2020, https://www.whitehousehistory.org/the-history-of-the-pardon-power.

96. Congressional Research Service, S. 2042 (106th), Pardon Attorney Reform and Integrity Act, https://www.govtrack.us/congress/bills/106/s2042/summary.

97. Kery Murakami, "Democrats Offer Plan to Free More Prisoners by Overhauling Presidential Clemency Process," *The Washington Times*, December 10, 2021.

98. Bretgoltz et al., "An Absolute Power, or a Power Absolutely in Need of Reform?" 11–18.

99. Shenkin and Levine, "Should the Power of Presidential Pardon Be Revised?" 5.

100. Cooper and Gough, "The Controversy of Clemency and Innocence in America," 56.

101. Paul H. Robinson and Mahammad Sarahne, "The Opposite of Punishment: Imagining a Path to Public Redemption," *Rutgers University Law Review* 73 (2020): 101–31.

102. "50-State Comparison."

103. Linda Dale Hoffa, "Pa. Is Leading the Way on Pardon Reform," *The Inquirer*, June 30, 2021, https://www.inquirer.com/opinion/commentary/pa-is-leading-way-pardon-reform-opinion-20210630.html.

104. In Delaware, clemency claims usually require a psychiatric assessment before the hearing occurs in order to determine whether the offender is psychologically ready to reenter society. Additionally, in Indiana, a parole agent is assigned to conduct an investigation into the possibility of pardoning the offender and its impact on the community. Love, "50-State Comparison."

105. Catherine Green Tree, "Retaining the Royal Prerogative of Mercy in New South Wales," *UNSW Law Journal* 42, no. 4 (2019): 1328.

CHAPTER 14

1. Peter Greenwood et al., "The Criminal Investigation Process Volume III: Observations and Analysis," Department of Justice, 1975, 9, https://www.ojp.gov/pdf files1/Digitization/148118NCJRS.pdf.

2. P. Jeffrey Brantingham and Craig Uchida, "Public Cooperation and the Police: Do Calls-for-Service Increase After Homicides?" *Journal of Criminal Justice* 73 (2021), https://doi.org/10.1016/j.jcrimjus .2021.101785.

3. NCJ 247350, "Five Things About Deterrence," National Institute of Justice, May 2016.

4. Michael H. Graham, "Witness Intimidation," *Florida State University Law Review* 12, no. 2 (Summer 1984): 241.

5. David Kocieniewski, "With Witnesses at Risk, Murder Suspects Go Free," *New York Times*, March 1, 2007, https://www .nytimes.com/2007/03/01/nyregion /01witness.html.

6. Arlen Egley and Mehala Arjunan, "Highlights of the 2000 National Youth Gang Survey, #4," Department of Justice, February 2002, https://www.ojp.gov/pdffiles1 /ojjdp/fs200204.pdf.

7. Kelly Dedel, "Witness Intimidation," COPS Problem-Oriented Guides for Police, Problem-Specific Guides Series No. 42, 2006, 5.

8. Wesley Lowery and Dalton Bennett, "Witness to the Killing," *Washington Post*, October 12, 2018, https://www.wash ingtonpost.com/news/national/wp/2018 /10/17/feature/witness-to-the-killing/.

9. Carl R. Peed and Chuck Wexler, "The Stop Snitching Phenomenon: Breaking the Code of Silence," Department of Justice, 2009, 14, https:// portal.cops.usdoj.gov/resource center/RIC/Publications/cops-p158-pub .pdf.

10. John Browning, "#Snitches Get Stitches: Witness Intimidation in the Age of Facebook and Twitter," *Pace Law Review* 35, no. 1 (2014): 192.

11. "Probe into New Jersey Street Gang Ends with 71 Arrests," CBS News New York, May 20, 2015, https://www.cbsnews.com /newyork/news/grape-street-crips -arrests.

12. Antoinette DelBel, "Park Dedicated to Latasha Shaw, Mother Murdered More than a Decade Ago," WHAM 13abc, September 29, 2018, https://13wham .com/news/local/park-dedicated-to-lata sha-grayson-shaw-who-was-murdered -more-than-a-decade-ago; Jordan Mazza, "Eight Years Later: Community Remembers Latasha Shaw," Spectrum Local News, September 30, 2015, https://spec trumlocalnews.com/news/2015/09/30 /latasha-shaw-death-remembered; Latasha Shaw, "Longtime Food Service Employee, Dies," University of Rochester, October 2, 2007, https://www.rochester .edu/news/printable.php?id=2995.

13. Graham, "Witness Intimidation," 242.

14. "Victims of Sexual Violence: Statistics," Rape, Abuse & Incest National Network, https://www.rainn.org/statistics/vic tims-sexualviolence#:~:text=Sexual%20 Violence%20Affects%20Millions%20 of,year%20in%20the%20United%20 States; "The Criminal Justice System: Statistics," Rape, Abuse & Incest National Network, https://www.rainn.org/statis tics/criminal-justice-system.

15. "The Criminal Justice System: Statistics."

16. Ibid.

17. Graham, "Witness Intimidation," 241.

18. National Institute of Justice, NCJ 163067, "Preventing Gang and Drug-Related Witness Intimidation," November 1996, 5, https://www.ojp.gov/pdffiles/163067.pdf.

19. Katie Manzi McDonough, "Comment: Combating Gang-Perpetrated Witness Intimidation with Forfeiture-by-Wrongdoing," *Seton Hall Law* 11 (2013): 1294.

20. Large jurisdictions are defined as counties with populations over 250,000 and small jurisdictions are defined as populations between 50,000 and 250,000. National Institute of Justice, NCJ 151785, "Prosecuting Gags: A National Assessment," Department of Justice, 1995, 2, https://www.ojp.gov/pdffiles1/Digitization/151785NCJRS.pdf.

21. National Institute of Justice, NCJ 15655, "Victim and Witness Intimidation: New Developments and Emerging Responses," Department of Justice, 1995, 2.

22. Kocieniewski, "With Witnesses at Risk, Murder Suspects Go Free."

23. Ryan Martin and Tim Evans, "He Helped IMPD Put Away a Killer. Then His Death Became a Warning: Don't Talk to Police," Indystar, October 19, 2017, https://www.indystar.com/story/news/crime/2017/10/19/dont-snitch-witness-intimidation-witness-protection-indiana-indianapolis-murder-homicide/653056001/.

24. Ibid.; Justin L. Mack and Ryan Martin, "Indianapolis Homicides Down for the First Time in Years. Here's Why No One Is Celebrating," *Indianapolis Star*, January 10, 2020, https://www.indystar.com/story/news/crime/2020/01/08/homicides-indianapolis-down-but-there-no-time-celebrate/2793754001/.

25. NCJ 250183, "Federal Justice Statistics, 2014—Statistical Tables," Department of Justice Bureau of Justice Statistics, March 2017, 4.

26. National Institute of Justice, "Preventing Gang and Drug-Related Witness Intimidation," 1–15.

27. Margaret O'Malley, "Witness Intimidation in the Digital Age," *The Prosecutors' Center for Excellence* 14 (2014): 21; Conor Gallagher, "Just 27% of Witness or Jury Intimidation Cases Result in Conviction," *The Irish Times*, July 6, 2021, https://www.irishtimes.com/news/crime-and-law/just-27-of-witness-or-jury-intimidation-cases-result-in-conviction-1.4612182.

28. National Institute of Justice, "Victim and Witness Intimidation," 2.

29. Julie L. Whitman and Robert C. Davis, "Snitches Get Stitches: Youth, Gangs, and Witness Intimidation in Massachusetts," The National Center for Victims of Crime, 2007, 10, https://archives.lib.state.ma.us/bitstream/handle/2452/38544/ocn137337215.pdf?sequence=1&isAllowed=y.

30. Dedel, "Witness Intimidation," 5.

31. National Institute of Justice, "Victim and Witness Intimidation," 2.

32. Jim Haner et al., "Cases Crumble, Killers Go Free," *Baltimore Sun*, September 29, 2002, https://www.baltimoresun.com/bal-te.murder29sep29-story.html.

33. Whitman and Davis, "Snitches Get Stitches," 10.

34. Anthony Braga et al., "The Influence of Investigative Resources on Homicide Clearances," *Journal of Quantitative Criminology* 35, no. 2 (June 2018): 360–61.

35. Kocieniewski, "With Witnesses at Risk, Murder Suspects Go Free."

36. "Breaking the Wall of Silence to Fight Crime: Allentown, Like Other Cities Across the Nation, Is Struggling to Break Through the 'Code of the Street' to Solve Homicides and Other Offenses. Authorities Are Turning to Discreet Ways for Cooperation," Morning Call, October 5, 2021, https://www.mcall.com/2007/08/19/breaking-the-wall-of-silence-to-fight-crime-Allentown-like-other-cities-across-the-nation-is-struggling-to-break-through-the-code-of

-the-street-to-solve-homicides-and
-other-offenses-authorities-are-tu.

37. Peed and Wexler, "The Stop Snitching Phenomenon," 18.

38. Alexandra Natapoff, *"Stop Snitching" in Snitching: Criminal Informants and the Erosion of American Justice* (New York University Press, 2009), 134.

39. Peed and Wexler, "The Stop Snitching Phenomenon,"18.

40. "The campaign began as a partnership of the FBI Philadelphia Field Office's Community Relations Unit, Mothers in Charge, and Clear Channel Outdoor, but has 'grown to include 26 partners from federal and state government, the news media, private businesses, and religious organizations'" (Peed and Wexler, "The Stop Snitching Phenomenon," 35).

41. Peed and Wexler, "The Stop Snitching Phenomenon," 18.

42. Ladel Lewis, "Stop Snitching: Hip Hop's Influence on Crime Reporting in the Inner City," Western Michigan University, April 2012, 7.

43. "Witness Security Program," US Marshal Service, https://www.usmarshals.gov/witsec/.

44. Lewis, "Stop Snitching," 38–39.

45. Peter Finn and Kerry M. Healey, National Institute of Justice, NCJ 15655, "Victim and Witness Intimidation: New Developments and Emerging Responses," Department of Justice, 1995, 12–13.

46. Ibid., 139.

47. Peed and Wexler, "The Stop Snitching Phenomenon,"18.

48. Susan Clampet-Lundquist, Patrick J. Carr, and Maria J. Kefalas, "The Sliding Scale of Snitching: A Qualitative Examination of Snitching in Three Philadelphia Communities," *Sociological Forum* 30, no. 2 (June 2015): 282.

49. Peed and Wexler, "The Stop Snitching Phenomenon," 28.

50. Ibid., 17.

51. Julie Bykowicz, "As Boston Boosts Witness Protection, Baltimore Takes the Legal Route."

52. Amaris Elliot-Engel, "Proposals Touted to Combat Witness Intimidation; Increased Resources, Grand Juries Eyed," *The Legal Intelligencer* 241, no. 74 (April 2010): 1; Craig R. McCoy, "Panel Urges Funding of a Witness-Intimidation Crackdown for Phila. Courts," *The Inquirer*, January 8, 2013.

53. Ibid.

54. Ibid.

55. Finn and Healey, "Victim and Witness Intimidation,"12–13. Some important points to consider in an anti-gang law enforcement strategy include:

- Find a highly qualified leader for witness security and assistance programs who is knowledgeable about the local gang problem and needs of concerned intimidated communities.

- Have program protocols endorsed by public officials at the highest level to get cooperation from public and private agencies (local police, public housing, schools, churches, etc.).

- Design a manual that clearly outlines the witness security plans, such as sample court papers for prosecutors, resource and contact lists for witnesses.

- Build evaluation designs to survey attitudes in gang-dominated communities to measure program's effectiveness to tell whether the city needs to increase funding or other improvements.

- Police should be familiar with the most current literature on gangs and gang suppression. They can also use gang-tracking software and computerized identification of bullets in gang incidents to link crimes in communities, target gang leaders, which will help disrupt gang activity in intimidated neighborhoods, maximize number of defendants indicted in each gang case, focus on truancy reduction (consider truancy reduction programs)—addressing the problem of gangs addresses the problem of gang witness intimidation. The mentioned "gang tracking software" is the "Gang Tracking System" developed by the Los Angeles County Sheriff's Department (14).

- Seek long-term, renewable funding for witness protection programs.

56. Ibid., 84. The effort seems to be a municipal effort rather than larger bodies: Downey California Municipal Code § 4107.5; North Las Vegas Code of Ordinances § 9.16.020; Auburn Washington Municipal Code § 9.24.010.
57. Ibid., 81.
58. Ibid., 79.
59. Ibid., 80.
60. Ibid., 84. Also see John E. Floyd, Editorial Chair, "Introduction," in *RICO State by State: A Guide to Litigation Under the State Racketeering Statutes*, second edition, 2(4) GPSolo eReport, American Bar Association, November 2012.
61. Richard D. Friedman, "Confrontation and the Definition of Chutzpa," *Cambridge University Press*, no. 1–3 (1997): 507.
62. Tom Lininge, "The Sound of Silence; Holding Batterers Accountable for Silencing Their Accusers," *Texas Law Review* 87, no. 5 (April 2009): 1. Prosecutors now have to show the victim was killed specifically to silence them as opposed to some other reason.
63. Coroners and Justice Act 2009, c. 25 (UK), https://www.legislation.gov.uk/ukpga /2009/25/part/3/chapter/2/crosshead ing/witness-anonymity-orders.
64. Charlene Ellis and Letisha Shakespeare, "Murders: Legal Challenge of Key Witness," BBC News, September 21, 2018, https://www.bbc.com/news/uk-england -birmingham-45601867.
65. "Witness Anonymity (The Director's Guidance)," cps.uk.gov, December 2009, https://www.cps.gov.uk/legal-guidance /witness-anonymity-directors-guidance.
66. Ibid.
67. Smith v. Illinois, 390 US 129, 133 (1968).
68. Ibid.
69. United States v. Gutierrez De Lopez, 761 F.3d 1123, 1140 13-2141 (10th Cir. 2014).
70. Ibid., 1141; United States v. Palermo 410 F.2d 468, 472 (7th Cir. 1969).

71. Rod K. Brunson and Brian A. Wade, "Oh Hell No, We Don't Talk to Police," *Criminology and Public Policy* 18, no. 3 (2019): 627.
72. Rachael A. Woldoff and Karen G. Weiss, "Stop Snitchin': Exploring Definitions of the Snitch and Implications for Urban Black Communities," *Journal of Criminal Just and Popular Culture* 17, no. 1 (2010): 189–90.
73. McDonough, "Comment," 13.
74. Susan Clampet-Lundquist, "The Sliding Scale of Snitching: A Qualitative Examination of Snitching in Three Philadelphia Communities," *Sociological Forum* 30, no. 2 (June 2015): 266.
75. Peed and Wexler, "The Stop Snitching Phenomenon," 17.
76. Ibid.
77. Whitman and Davis, "Snitches Get Stitches," 5.
78. See, for example, Lisa Munoz, Adam Nichols, and Alison Gendar, "His Poetic 'Justice' Rhymes Consoles Sis of Slain Guard with Pledge—But Won't Talk to Cops," *New York Daily News* (online), February 8, 2006, https://infoweb-news bank-com.proxy.library.upenn.edu/apps /news/document-view?P=AWNB&docr ef=news/10FA8F10B09506E8.
79. Ibid.
80. Brunson and Wade, "Oh Hell No, We Don't Talk to Police," 624.
81. Emily Ekins, "Policing in America: Understanding Public Attitudes toward the Police: Results from a 2016 Cato Institute Criminal Justice Survey," December 7, 2016, 14, https://www.cato.org/sites /cato.org/files/survey-reports/pdf/polic ing-in-america-august-1-2017.pdf.
82. Natapoff, *"Stop Snitching" in Snitching*.
83. Peed and Wexler, "The Stop Snitching Phenomenon," 12.
84. Ibid., 16.
85. Ibid., 15.
86. Daniel Schorn, "Stop Snitchin'," CBS News, April 19, 2007, https://www.cbs news.com/news/stop-snitchin/.

87. Kevin McCorry, "Witness Intimidation at Near Epidemic Level," NBC10 Philadelphia, June 8, 2021, https://www.nbcphiladelphia.com/news/local/witness-intimidation-near-epidemic-level/2087038.

88. Ted Scouten, "Video Murder of Suspect Released as Dying Mother Asks Public to Forget 'No Snitch Code,' Bring Killer to Justice," CBS Miami, June 8, 2021, https://www.cbsnews.com/miami/news/murder-suspect-video-dying-mother-no-snitch-code-justice.

89. Ibid.

90. "Mothers Over Murder," Nashville Peacemakers, https://www.nashvillepeacemakers.org/copy-of-back-to-basics.

91. Levi Ismail, "Grieving Parents Upset over Signs Promoting a Song About Not Snitching in Nashville," News Channel 5 Nashville, June 8, 2021, upset-over-signs-promoting-a-song-about-not-snitching-in-nashville.

92. Peed and Wexler, "The Stop Snitching Phenomenon," 32.

93. Ibid., 20.

94. Ibid., 24.

95. See section II.A.6.

96. David S. Kirk and Mauri Matsuda, "Legal Cynicism, Collective Efficacy, and the Ecology of Arrest," Criminology 49, no. 2 (2011): 444.

97. See Alex R. Piquero et al., "Criminology: Developmental Trajectories of Legal Socialization Among Serious Adolescent Offenders," Journal of Criminal Law & Criminology 96, no. 1 (Fall 2005): 267.

98. Matt O'Connor, "Cook Pleads Guilty to Five Felony Counts, Forced to Register as Sex Offender," The Badger Herald, February 21, 2018, https://badgerherald.com/news/2018/02/21/cook-pleads-guilty-to-five-felony-counts-forced-to-register-as-sex-offender/.

99. Shaymus McLaughlin, "One Survivor's Story Leads to More Sexual Assault Accusations Against UW-Madison Student," Bring Me the News, October 26, 2016, https://bringmethenews.com/minnesota-news/one-survivors-story-leads-to-more-sexual-assault-accusations-against-uw-madison-student.

100. Pat Schneider, "Outrage Grows over 3-Year Sentence for 'Privileged' Alec Cook in Sex Assaults Case," The CAP Times, June 27, 2018, https://captimes.com/news/local/education/university/outrage-grows-over-3-year-sentence-for-privileged-alec-cook-in-sex-assaults-case/article_86bc27d808ed-5fdb-8f09-f93d849b8882.html; Michelle J. Anderson, "Women Do Not Report the Violence They Suffer: Violence Against Women and the State Action Doctrine," Villanova Law Review 46, no. 5 (2001): 909.

101. See McLaughlin, "One Survivor's Story Leads to More Sexual Assault Accusations Against UW-Madison Student."

102. See Schneider, "Outrage Grows over 3-Year Sentence for 'Privileged' Alec Cook in Sex Assaults Case."

103. Ibid.

104. "Criminal Victimization, 2016," Bureau of Justice Statistics, https://bjs.ojp.gov/content/pub/pdf/cv16_sum.pdf.

105. Kirk and Matsuda, "Legal Cynicism, Collective Efficacy, and the Ecology of Arrest," 451–52.

106. See Matthew Desmond et al., "Police Violence and Citizen Crime Reporting in the Black Community," American Sociological Review 81, no. 5 (2016): 857–76.

107. Kirk and Matsuda, "Legal Cynicism, Collective Efficacy, and the Ecology of Arrest," 462.

108. Ibid., 444.

109. See Ashley M. Mancik, "Neighborhood Context and Homicide Clearance: Estimating the Effects of Collective Efficacy," Homicide Studies 22, no. 2 (2018): 188–213.

110. Giffords Law Center, "In Pursuit of Peace: Building Police-Community Trust to Break the Cycle of Violence," September 9, 2021, 38, https://giffords

.org/lawcenter/report/in-pursuit-of
-peace-building-police-community
-trust-to-break-the-cycle-of-violence,
citing David S. Kirk and Andrew V.
Papachristos, "Cultural Mechanisms
and the Persistence of Neighborhood
Violence," *American Journal Sociology*
116, no. 4 (2011): 1221.

111. Ibid., 42.

112. Michael D. Reisig et al., "Legal Cynicism, Legitimacy, and Criminal Offending: The Nonconfounding Effect of
Low Self-Control," *Criminal Justice and
Behavior* 38, no. 12 (December 2001):
1265–79.

113. Emily Etkins, "Policing in America: Understanding Public Attitudes Towards
the Police. Results from a National Survey," Cato Institute, 2016, 1.

114. Ibid.

115. David Nather, "Axios-Ipsos Poll: Black
Americans' Police Experiences Are
Getting Worse, Axios," May 22, 2021,
https://www.axios.com/2021/05/22
/axios-ipsos-poll-black-americans
-police.

116. 64% of African Americans say police
are generally not held accountable for
misconduct, compared to 43% of white
Americans. Etkins, "Policing in America," 4.

117. Lana M. Browning et al., "Citizen Journalism and Public Cynicism toward Police in the USA," *Journal of Police and
Criminal Psychology* 36, no. 3 (2020):
373.

118. Ibid., 374.

119. See, for example, Corey Rayburn Yung,
"Rape Law Gatekeeping," *Boston College Law Review* 58 (2017): 205.

120. While there is no single agreed-upon
statistic indicating the percentage of
rapes that are reported, all estimates
range roughly between 30 and 40 percent. RAINN (Rape, Abuse & Incest
National Network) estimates that 31
percent of rapes are reported. "The
Criminal Justice System: Statistics."

121. NCJ 253043, "Criminal Victimization,
2018," US Department of Justice, Bureau of Justice Statistics, September
2019, table 5.

122. David Weisburd et al., "The Abuse of
Police Authority—A National Study of
Police Officers' Attitudes," Police Foun-
dation, 2001, 26.

123. German Lopez, "Police Have to Repair
Community Trust to Effectively Do
Their Jobs," VOX, November 14, 2018.

124. WISH-TV, "Prosecutor Talks of Indy's
Cycle of Violence, Lack of Trust in Law
Enforcement," 93.1FM WIBC, June 24,
2021.

125. "N. Charleston Police to Public: Let's
Talk—Department Launching Effort to
Improve Ties with Residents," *The Post
and Courier*, March 21, 2008.

126. Ibid.

127. Ibid.

128. Debo P. Adegbile, "Policing Through
an American Prism," *Yale Law Journal*
126, no. 7 (May 2017): 2222.

129. Ibid.

130. Abene Clayton, "Distrust of Police Is
Major Driver of US Gun Violence, Report Warns," *The Guardian*, January 21,
2020.

131. Elizabeth Weise, "'All Lives Matter' a Creed for Richmond, Calif. Police," *USA Today*, September 24, 2015,
https://www.usatoday.com/story/news
/nation/2015/09/23/richmond-com
munity-policing/72563038/.

132. Ibid.

133. Ibid.

134. Ibid.

135. Ibid.

136. Hannah Shirley, "Grand Forks Police
'Safe Spaces' Program Aims to Encourage LGBTQ People to Report Hate
Crimes," *Grand Forks Herald*, July 19,
2021.

137. Ibid.

138. COPS Office, "FY 2017 Strategy," US
Department of Justice. https://www
.justice.gov/jmd/file/822291/download.

139. Kyle Peyton, Michael Sierra-Arévalo, and David G. Rand, "A Field Experiment on Community Policing and Police Legitimacy," PNAS, October 1, 2019.

140. Adegbile, "Policing Through an American Prism."

141. Department of Justice Open Government Progress Report April 2015, US Department of Justice Archives.

142. See Tosha Childs, "Building Police-Community Trust in Illinois: Will We Ever Get There? An Examination of the Illinois Police and Community Relations Act," *Southern Illinois University Law Journal* 43 (2019): 675.

143. See chapter 4.

144. Ronald G. Fryer, "An Empirical Analysis of Racial Differences in Police Use of Force," *Journal of Political Economy* 127, no. 3 (2019): 1239.

145. Candice Norwood, "Can Use of Force Restrictions Change Police Behavior? Here's What We Know," PBS News Hour, July 23, 2020, https://www.pbs .org/newshour/politics/can-use-of -force-restrictions-change-police-be havior-heres-what-we-know (describing movement demanding an end to excessive use of force by police following George Floyd's death).

146. While Blacks accounted for 13 percent of the population in 2005, they were the victims of nearly half of all homicides. Bureau of Justice Statistics, NCJ 214285, "Black Victims of Violent Crime," August 2007.

147. "Department of Justice Report Regarding the Criminal Investigation into the Shooting Death of Michael Brown by Ferguson, Missouri Police Officer Darren Wilson," March 4, 2015, 12–17, https://www.justice.gov/sites/default /files/opa/press-releases/attach ments/2015/03/04/doj_report_on _shooting_of_michael_brown_1.pdf.

148. Ibid., 13.

149. Ibid.; also see Peter Eisler, "Ferguson Case: By the Numbers," *USA Today,* November 25, 2014, https://www.usa today.com/story/news/nation/2014 /11/25/ferguson-case-by-the-numbers /70110614/

150. Fryer, "An Empirical Analysis of Racial Differences in Police Use of Force," 13.

151. Ibid., 13–14.

152. Ibid.

153. Ibid.

154. Ibid.

155. Ibid., 25. Later test show that "Brown tested positive for the presence of cannabinoids, the hallucinogenic substances associated with marijuana use. . . . This concentration of THC would have rendered Brown impaired at the time of his death. As a general matter, this level of impairment can alter one's perception of time and space, but the extent to which this was true in Brown's case cannot be determined."

156. See ibid., 26, for Witness 102's account. "Witness 102 was in disbelief that Wilson seemingly kept missing because Brown kept advancing forward. Witness 102 described Brown as a 'threat,' moving at a 'full charge.' Witness 102 stated that Wilson only fired shots when Brown was coming toward Wilson. It appeared to Witness 102 that Wilson's life was in jeopardy. Witness 102 was unable to hear whether Brown or Wilson said anything."

157. Ibid., 15.

158. Ibid.

159. Ibid., 16. "Wilson's account was consistent with those results, and consistent with the accounts of other independent eyewitnesses, whose accounts were also consistent with the physical evidence. Wilson's statements were consistent with each other in all material ways, and would not be subject to effective impeachment for inconsistencies or deviation from the physical evidence. Therefore, in analyzing all of the evidence, federal prosecutors found Wilson's account to be credible."

160. For example, here is a quote from the Obama US Department of Justice Report: "Witness 104 knew that Brown's arms were inside the SUV, but she could not see what Brown and Wilson were doing because Brown's body was blocking her view. Witness 104 saw Brown run from the SUV, followed by Wilson, who 'hopped' out of the SUV and ran after him while yelling 'stop, stop, stop.' Wilson did not fire his gun as Brown ran from him. Brown then turned around and 'for a second' began to raise his hands as though he may have considered surrendering, but then quickly 'balled up in fists' in a running position and 'charged' at Wilson. Witness 104 described it as a 'tackle run,' explaining that Brown 'wasn't going to stop.' Wilson fired his gun only as Brown charged at him, backing up as Brown came toward him. Witness 104 explained that there were three separate volleys of shots. Each time, Brown ran toward Wilson, Wilson fired, Brown paused, Wilson stopped firing, and then Brown charged again. The pattern continued until Brown fell to the ground, 'smashing' his face upon impact. Wilson did not fire while Brown momentarily had his hands up. Witness 104 explained that it took some time for Wilson to fire, adding that she "would have fired sooner." Ibid., 30.

161. Ibid., 28.

162. Ibid.

163. Ibid.

164. Cheryl Corley, "Whether History or Hype, 'Hands Up Don't Shoot Endures,'" NPR, August 8, 2015, https://www.npr.org/2015/08/08/430411141/whether-history-or-hype-hands-up-dont-shoot-endures.

165. Ibid.

166. "Timeline of Events in Shooting of Michael Brown," AP, August 8, 2019, https://apnews.com/article/shootings-police-us-news-st-louis-michael-brown-9aa32033692547699a3b61da8fd1fc62.

167. Ibid.

168. Ibid.

169. Eliott McLaughlin, "What We Know About Michael Brown's Shooting," CNN, August 15, 2014, https://www.cnn.com/2014/08/11/us/missouri-ferguson-michael-brown-what-we-know/index.html.

170. "Department of Justice Report Regarding the Criminal Investigation into the Shooting Death of Michael Brown by Ferguson, Missouri Police Officer Darren Wilson," 25.

171. Colleen Curry and Sabina Ghebremedhin, "Michael Brown Could Have Survived First 5 Shots, Last Shot Killed Him, Autopsy Says," ABC News, August 18, 2014, https://abcnews.go.com/US/michael-brown-survived-shots-shot-killed/story?id=25017247Curry.

172. Ibid.

173. See "Department of Justice Report Regarding the Criminal Investigation into the Shooting Death of Michael Brown By Ferguson, Missouri Police Officer Darren Wilson," at 17–18 and 25.

174. Rajini Vaidyanathan, "Ferguson Riots: Ruling Sparks Night of Violence," BBC, November 25, 2014, https://www.bbc.com/news/world-us-canada-30190224.

175. "Timeline of Events in Shooting of Michael Brown."

176. Ibid.

177. John Eligon, "No Charges for Ferguson Officer Who Killed Michael Brown, New Prosecutor Says," *New York Times*, July 30, 2020, https://www.nytimes.com/2020/07/30/us/michael-brown-darren-wilson-ferguson.html.

178. Darren Wilson, "Former Ferguson Cop Who Shot Unarmed Teen, Won't Receive Severance Package or Pension," *The National Post*, January 24, 2015, https://nationalpost.com/news/darren-wilson-former-ferguson-cop-who-shot-unarmed-teen-wont-receive-severance-package-or-pension.

179. Larry Buchanan et al., "Black Lives Matter May Be the Largest Movement in U.S. History," *New York Times*, July 3, 2020, https://www.nytimes.com/interactive/2020/07/03/us/george-floyd-protests-crowd-size.html.

180. Ibid.

181. Aimee Ortiz, "Confidence in Police Is at Record Low, Gallup Survey Finds," *New York Times*, August 12, 2020, https://www.nytimes.com/2020/08/12/us/gallup-poll-police.html; Zach Goldberg, "Is Defunding the Police a 'Luxury Belief'?: Analyzing White vs. Nonwhite Democrats' Attitudes on Depolicing," Manhattan Institute, September 8, 2022.

182. Kevin McCaffree and Anondah Saide, "How Informed Are Americans About Race and Policing?" Skeptic Research Center, CUPES-007, February 20, 2021.

183. https://www.washingtonpost.com/graphics/investigations/police-shootings-database/Unarmed, as categorized by the *Washington Post*, "includes suspects grabbing an officer's gun or fleeing in a stolen car with a loaded pistol on the car seat." For a complete discussion of the "unarmed category," see Heather Mac Donald, *The War on Cops: How the New Attack on Law and Order Makes Everyone Less Safe* (Encounter Books, 2016), 74; Heather Mac Donald, "Team Biden Finally Admits There Is a War on Cops—Which It Is Inflaming," *New York Post*, April 28, 2022, https://nypost.com/2022/04/28/team-biden-finally-admits-theres-a-war-on-cops/.

184. Mac Donald, "Team Biden Finally Admits there is a War on Cops."

185. "Majority of Public Favors Giving Civilians the Power to Sue Police Officers for Misconduct," Pew Research Center, July 9, 2020, https://www.pewresearch.org/politics/2020/07/09/qualified-immunity-acknowledgments/.

186. Nather, "Axios-Ipsos Poll."

187. Kat Stafford and Hannah Fingerhut, "AP-NORC Poll: Police Violence Remains High Concern in U.S.," AP News, May 21, 2021, https://apnews.com/article/politics-violence-race-and-ethnicity-racial-injustice-death-of-george-floyd-b74d3005500397c850ab3c116cf69ea0.

188. Robert VerBruggen, "Fatal Police Shootings and Race: A Review of the Evidence and Suggestions for Future Research," Manhattan Institute, March 9, 2022, https://www.manhattan-institute.org/verbruggen-fatal-police-shootings. For the deaths in auto accidents the actual numbers are: "Blacks, particularly black men, were at increased risk of dying relative to whites when traveling in motor vehicles (rate ratio (RR) for black men=1.48; 95% confidence interval (CI)=1.42-1.54)." Elisa R. Braver, "Race, Hispanic Origin, and Socioeconomic Status in Relation to Motor Vehicle Occupant Death Rates and Risk Factors Among Adults," National Library of Medicine, https://pubmed.ncbi.nlm.nih.gov/12643947/. Black men die in fatal traffic accidents at a rate of 52.1/1,000 and from police-related encounters the rate is 3.4/1,000; see Amina Khan, "Getting Killed by Police Is a Leading Cause of Death for Young Black Men in America," *Los Angeles Times*, August 16, 2019, https://www.latimes.com/science/story/2019-08-15/police-shootings-are-a-leading-cause-of-death-for-black-men.

189. Sarah Butrymowicz, "They Only Kill Us Because of Our Skin Color and Our Race," The Hechinger Report, September 22, 2016, https://hechingerreport.org/kill-us-skin-color-race/.

190. Brian Burghart, "Fatal Encounters: A Step Towards Creating an Impartial, Comprehensive and Searchable National Database of People Killed During Interactions with Police," Fatal Encounters, https://fatalencounters.org/view/person/?gv_search=&filter_2=&filter_41=&filter_42=&filter_10=&filter_13=&filter_46=&filter_16=&filter_1=&filt

er_28%5Bstart%5D=&filter_28%5Bend
%5D=&mode=all.

191. Ibid.

192. Julie Tate et al., "Police Shootings Database 2015–2021," *Washington Post*, June 2, 2022, https://www.washington post.com/graphics/investigations/po lice-shootings-database/. Since January 1, 2015, 6,471 people were shot and killed by police, or still about one thousand people each year.

193. See "Table 1: Crime in the United States," FBI, https://ucr.fbi.gov/crime -in-the-u.s/2019/crime-in-the-u.s. -2019/tables/table-1.

194. See Tate et al., "Police Shootings Database 2015–2021."

195. Ibid.; John Sullivan, "Fatal Police Shootings of Unarmed People Have Significantly Declined, Experts Say," *Washington Post*, May 7, 2018, https://www.washingtonpost.com/in vestigations/fatal-police-shootings -of-unarmed-people-have-significantly -declined-experts-say/2018/05/03 /d5eab374-4349-11e8-8569-26fd a6b404c7_story.html.

196. George Fachner and Steven Carter, "Collaborative Reform Initiative: An Assessment of Deadly Force in the Philadelphia Police Department," US Department of Justice, Community Oriented Policing Services, 2015.

197. Fryer, "An Empirical Analysis of Racial Differences in Police Use of Force," 26.

198. Heather Mac Donald, "The Myth of Systemic Police Racism," *Wall Street Journal*, June 2, 2020; "Police Use of Deadly Force Is Not About Racism," Self Educated American, October 12, 2020.

199. Dan O'Donnell and Daunte Wright, "The Truth About Police Shootings in America," MacIver Institute, April 14, 2021, https://www.maciverinstitute.com /2021/04/the-truth-about-police -shootings-in-america/.

200. "Murder in the U.S. Number of Victims By Race/Ethnicity and Gender 2019," Statista Research Department, Febru-

ary 2, 2021, https://www.statista.com /statistics/251877/murder-victims-in -the-us-by-race-ethnicity-and-gender.

201. "Crime in the United States: 2019," FBI, https://ucr.fbi.gov/crime-in-the -u.s/2019/crime-in-the-u.s.-2019/tables /expanded-homicide-data-table-6.xls.

202. CDC Wonder, "Underlying Cause of Death 2018–2021, Single Race Results: Deaths Occurring through 2021."

203. Khaleda Rahman, "Full List of Black People Killed by Police in 2021," *Newsweek*, December 28, 2021, https://www .newsweek.com/black-people-killed -police-2021-1661633.

204. The 1.2 percent is derived by dividing the number of Black homicides in 2021 (CDC Wonder, "Underlying Cause of Death 2018–2021, Single Race Results") by the number of Black individuals killed by police.

205. O'Donnell and Wright, "The Truth About Police Shootings in America."

206. Mac Donald, "Team Biden Finally Admits There Is a War on Cops."

207. Keith Humphreys, "How Fatal Shootings by Police Were Cut in Half—And How We Might Do It Again," *Washington Post*, July 9, 2018, https://www .washingtonpost.com/news/wonk /wp/2018/07/09/how-fatal-shootings -by-police-were-cut-in-half-and-how -we-might-do-it-again/.

208. Jack Moore, "NYPD Officers Shot the Lowest Number of People Ever in 2017," *Newsweek*, December 24, 2017, https://www.newsweek.com/nypd -officers-shot-lowest-number-people -ever-2017-758205.

209. See Eric Levenson and Aaron Cooper, "Derek Chauvin Found Guilty of All Three Charges for Killing George Floyd," April 21, 2021, CNN, https:// www.cnn.com/2021/04/20/us/derek -chauvin-trial-george-floyd-delibera tions/index.html.

210. Akshita Jain, "George Floyd's Killing Not a Hate Crime," *Independent*, April 26, 2021, https://www.independent.co

.uk/news/world/americas/george
-floyd-killing-hate-crime-b1837419
.html.

211. Since 2005, 139 officers have been arrested on charges of murder or manslaughter due to an on-duty shooting,
representing an arrest rate of 1 or 2
percent of police shootings each year.
Of those officers arrested, forty-four
were convicted while forty-two cases
remain pending. German Lopez, "Police Officers Are Prosecuted for Murder
in Less than 2 Percent of Fatal Shootings," VOX, April 2, 2021, https://www
.vox.com/policy-and-politics/2017
/7/17/15985442/minneapolis-police
-shooting-justine-damond-video. See
Amelia Thomson-DeVeaux, Nathaniel Rakich, and Likhitha Butchired-
dygari, "Why It's So Rare for Police
Officers to Face Legal Consequences,"
FiveThirtyEight, June 4, 2020, https://
fivethirtyeight.com/features/why-its
-still-so-rare-for-police-officers-to-face
-legal-consequences-for-misconduct/.
Prosecutors normally work very hard
to try only cases that they believe they
will win, and yet when prosecuting police involved deaths more cases fail than
succeed, suggesting that prosecutors are
pursuing cases they know they cannot
win. In a 2015 *Washington Post* article,
Doug Friesen, a defense lawyer, said,
"Anytime you have politicians that have
to make charging decisions, realistically
that (race) is part of their decision-
making process, They are asking themselves, 'Is there going to be rioting out
in the streets?'" Kimberly Kindy and
Kimbriell Kelly, "Thousands Dead, Few
Prosecuted," *Washington Post*, April 11,
2015.

212. O'Donnell and Wright, "The Truth
About Police Shootings in America."

213. Ibid.

214. Leila Mitchell, "Intentional Police Deaths
at 20 Year High Due to Distrust and
Other Factors," KMIZ, March 29, 2022,
https://abc17news.com/news/2022

/03/29/intentional-police-deaths-at
-20-year-high-due-to-distrust-and
-other-factors/.

215. Sullivan, "Fatal Police Shootings of Unarmed People Have Significantly Declined, Experts Say."

216. Tina Moore, Larry Celona, and Melissa Klein, "Actress Fired After Rant-
ing About Street Closures for NYPD
Detective Jason Rivera's Funeral," *New
York Post*, January 29, 2022, https://
nypost.com/2022/01/29/actress-fired
-after-ranting-about-street-closures-for
-jason-riveras-funeral/.

217. Lisa M. Graziano, "News Media and
Perceptions of Police: A State-of-the-
Art Review," California State University
Los Angeles, February 22, 2018.

218. Christopher J. Ferguson, "Negative
Perceptions of Race Relations: A Brief
Report Examining the Impact of News
Media Coverage of Police Shootings,
and Actual Fatal Police Shootings," *The
Social Science Journal* (2021): 6.

219. Mac Donald, *The War on Cops*.

220. See Fryer, "An Empirical Analysis of
Racial Differences in Police Use of
Force," 26.

221. Rob Montz, "Why Did Harvard University Go After One of Its Best Black Professors?" Quillette.com, April 15, 2022.

222. Zac Kriegman, "I Criticized BLM. Then
I Was Fired," *The Free Express*, May 12,
2022.

223. Ibid.

224. Jukka Savolainen, "Give Criminology a
Chance," *City Journal*, May 12, 2023.

225. Ibid.

226. Ray Arora, "Feelings over Facts: A Police Shooting in Minneapolis Reveals
the Misplaced Priorities and Misguided
Policies of the Defund-the-Police Left,"
City Journal, July 21, 2022.

227. Heather Mac Donald, "Is the Criminal-
Justice System Racist?" *City Journal*,
Spring 2008, https://www.city-journal
.org/html/criminal-justice-system-rac
ist-13078.html.

228. German Lopez, "Obama Is Right about the Criminal 'Injustice System': 7 Ways It's Racially Skewed," VOX, July 15, 2015, https://www.vox.com/2015/5/29/8687205/criminal-justice-racism.

229. Mac Donald, "Team Biden Finally Admits There Is a War on Cops."

230. David Siders, "Warren, Hinting at 2020 Run, Slams 'Racist' Criminal Justice System," Politico, August 4, 2018, https://www.politico.com/story/2018/08/04/elizabeth-warren-2020-criminal-justice-system-racist-762428.

231. Mac Donald, "Team Biden Finally Admits There Is a War on Cops."

232. For 2019 arrest data: "2019: Crime in the United States," FBI: UCR, https://ucr.fbi.gov/crime-in-the-u.s/2019/crime-in-the-u.s.-2019/tables/table-43. This table shows the number of crimes committed and race of offender. For 2018 incarceration data: John Gramlich, "Black Imprisonment Rate in the U.S. Has Fallen by a Third Since 2006," Pew Research Center, https://www.pewresearch.org/fact-tank/2020/05/06/share-of-black-white-hispanic-americans-in-prison-2018-vs-2006/.

233. Allen Beck, "Race and Ethnicity of Violent Crime Offenders and Arrestees, 2018," US Department of Justice, January 2021, https://bjs.ojp.gov/content/pub/pdf/revcoa18.pdf.

234. Ibid.

235. Different numbers exist for the Black share of America's population. The most reliable census data puts the share at 13.6 percent, but other sources may put the number as high as 14.2 percent or as low as 12 percent. See "QuickFacts," United States Census, 2022, https://www.census.gov/quickfacts/fact/table/US/RHI225222.

236. Aleksander Tomic and Jahn K. Hakes, "Case Dismissed: Police Discretion and Racial Differences in Dismissals of Felony Charges," July 2, 2007; Mac Donald, "Team Biden Finally Admits There Is a War on Cops."

237. Some scholars suggest the lower rate of conviction for Black offenders is evidence that they are more likely to be unjustifiably arrested in the first place (thus naturally leading to a higher rate of case dismissal). However, on a system-wide level, this seems unlikely. If the percentage of arrestees who are Black matches the percentage of reported criminal offenders who are Black, it is hard to argue the justice system is overarresting Black offenders. Additionally, the higher rate of dismissals for Black arrestees could equally be taken to show that prosecutors or judges are more likely to dismiss a case against Black arrestees because they are eager to reduce any appearance of racism in the system—and not that the evidence against Black arrestees is weaker because Blacks are overarrested. We do not make such a claim; we merely point out that assuming a higher dismissal rate for Black arrestees is proof of racism is dubious. Of course, in localized areas there may be instances of apparently biased arrest patterns—for example, police are ordered to "crack down" on crime in a high-crime minority community while doing nothing to increase enforcement in lower-crime non-minority communities. Additionally, officers may conclude that targeting minority suspects is more likely to produce evidence of a crime because of racial differences in crime rates (for example, consider certain stop and frisk policies). We do not seek to minimize local concerns about police-community interactions that may be seen as racially biased. The police-community commission we propose at the end of this chapter would be the proper place to discuss and resolve such legitimate concerns.

238. Rachel Morgan, "Criminal Victimization, 2020—Supplemental Statistical Tables," US Department of Justice, February 2022, https://bjs.ojp.gov/content/pub/pdf/cv20sst.pdf.

239. Ibid.

240. "Drug Related Crime Statistics," National Center for Drug Abuse Statistics.

241. Patrick Langan, "The Racial Disparity in U.S. Drug Arrests," National Criminal Justice Reference Center, October 1, 1995, https://bjs.ojp.gov/content/pub/pdf/rdusda.pdf.

242. In fact, this raises a broader challenge to the entire narrative of racial bias in incarceration rates. If Black incarceration rates were higher than Black crime rates, this would not be an argument to let more Black offenders go free but rather to ramp up policing in non-Black neighborhoods to catch more non-Black offenders who were escaping justice at greater rates. Yet virtually no proponents of the narrative of racism in incarceration rates call for a massive policing surge in non-Black neighborhoods.

243. Even if we assumed racially biased decision making at every level of the justice system, it is obvious targeting such "systemic racism" will barely affect outcomes for Black offenders on aggregate. Why? Because as mentioned previously, starting with criminal offender data and assuming perfectly race-neutral decision making in the justice system, one would arrive at expected arrest, conviction, and incarceration numbers for Black offenders that are extremely similar to the actual numbers. Unfortunately, we do not have the time or space to engage with every claimed piece of evidence for systemic racism in the justice system. We would merely note that the actual outcomes of such a claimed racist system are so similar to the predicted outcomes of a race-neutral justice system that reforms meant to reduce racism in the justice system will clearly do little to change Black arrest, conviction, or incarceration rates.

244. Conceptually, such activists would see it as a grave injustice against Black communities if the justice system punished 100 percent of Black offenders while punishing only 50 percent of White offenders. But because most crime is intraracial, one could argue such a situation would disproportionately benefit Black communities as Black victims would receive justice at twice the rate of White victims. But such activists almost never think from the perspective of innocent crime victims.

245. "Changes to Policing Policy in the States and 100 Largest Cities, 2020," Ballotpedia.

246. Mike Zaro, "The New Rules for Police," *The Suburban Times*, July 29, 2021.

247. Cameron Sheppard, "New State Police Reform Laws to Kick in on July 25," *Renton Reporter*, July 21, 2021.

248. Zaro, "The New Rules for Police."

249. Amber Widgery, "One Year After George Floyd's Death, Work Continues on Policing Policy," National Conference of State Legislatures, May 20, 2021.

250. Tate et al., "Police Shootings Database 2015–2021."

251. Nather, "Axios-Ipsos Poll."

252. Aaron Chalfin and Jacob Kaplan, "How Many Complaints Against Police Officers Can Be Abated by Incapacitating a Few 'Bad Apples,'" *Criminology & Public Policy* 20, no. 2 (June 2021).

253. Jamiles Lartey and Abbie VanSickle, "'That Could Have Been Me': The People Derek Chauvin Choked Before George Floyd," MPR News, February 5, 2021.

254. Ibid.

255. "People with Untreated Mental Illness 16 Times More Likely to Be Killed by Law Enforcement," Treatment Advocacy Center, https://www.treatmentadvocacycenter.org/key-issues/criminalization-of-mental-illness/2976-people-with-untreated-mental-illness-16-times-more-likely-to-be-killed-by-law-enforcement-

256. Paul H. Robinson, "A Right to Bear Firearms But Not to Use Them? Defensive Force Rules and the Increasing Effectiveness of Non-Lethal Weapons," *Boston University Law Review* 89 (2009).

257. Jo Ciavaglia, Josh Salman, and Katie Wedell, "The April 11 Shooting Death of Daunte Wright Highlights Problems with Police Use of Tasers that Have Contributed to at Least 500 Deaths Since 2010," *USA Today*, April 23, 2021.

258. Thomas Brewster, "Taser Found and CEO Says Police Won't Need Guns in Ten Years," Forbes, April 14, 2021.

259. Another common police commission form is that of the official police commission, but such commissions are simply a form of group leadership of the police department. Such commissions do not provide civilian oversight at all but rather are simple a part of the official police hierarchy, in some cases acting as a board of directors overseeing the police chief as chief executive. See, for example, https://www.lapdonline.org/police-commission/ (Los Angeles); https://en.wikipedia.org/wiki/New_York_City_Police_Commissioner (New York); https://stlouiscounty police.com/who-we-are/board-of-police -commissioners/ (St. Louis).

260. See, for example, Michael Vitoroulis, "NACOLE Case Studies on Civilian Oversight Atlanta Citizen Review Board Atlanta, Georgia Investigative-Focused Model," COPS, 2021, 6; "Kentucky Law Enforcement Council," Commonwealth of Kentucky: Kentucky Justice and Public Safety Cabinet, https:// justice.ky.gov/Boards-Commissions /pages/klec.aspx.

261. Sam Sinyangwe, the creator of Mapping Police Violence and creator of Campaign Zero, a group that lays out police reform policies to reduce officer violence. Marlene Lenthang, "Police Oversight Boards Are Proliferating, But Do They Actually Work?" ABC News, June 4, 2021, https://abcnews.go.com/US /police-oversight-boards-proliferating -work/story?id=77919091.

262. Jim Pasco, Nicole Dungca, and Jenn Abelson, "When Communities Try to Hold Police Accountable, Law Enforce-ment Fights Back," *Washington Post*, April 27, 2021, https://www-washing tonpost-com.proxy.library.upenn.edu /investigations/interactive/2021/civil ian-oversight-police-accountability /tigations/interactive/2021/civilian -oversight-police-accountability/.

263. Anthony Perez, "More Data, Better Policy," *City Journal*, September 19, 2022, https://www.city-journal.org/po lice-transparency-bills-produce-better -policy.

CHAPTER 15

1. Justin Wise, "Bobby Rush Likens Chicago Police Union to KKK: 'Racist Body of Criminal Lawlessness,'" *The Hill*, June 15, 2020, https://thehill.com/homenews /house/502709-bobby-rush-likens-chi cago-police-union-to-kkk-racist-body-of -criminal/.

2. Alana Goodman, "Incitement: Johnson Blames Deadly Kenosha Riots on Barnes's Anti-Police Rhetoric," *Washington Free Beacon*, October 7, 2022, https://freebeacon.com/latest-news/incite ment-johnson-blames-barness-anti-po lice-rhetoric-for-deadly-kenosha-riots/.

3. Alex Lang, "'I'm Scared of Cops, Bro': Florida Officer Dragged by Car as Suspect Flees Traffic Stop," KNEWZ, https:// knewz.com/florida-officer-dragged-traf fic-stop/.

4. "Law Enforcement Officer Deaths," FBI Crime Data Explorer, https://crime-data -explorer.app.cloud.gov/#.

5. "Union Head Blames Anti-Police Rhetoric After NYC Cop Stabbed in Neck," CBS News, June 4, 2020, https://www.cbsnews .com/news/union-head-blames-anti-po lice-rhetoric-after-nyc-cop-stabbed-in -neck/.

6. Victoria Spartz, "Anti-Police Rhetoric Must Stop and We Have to Support Our Police Officers on the Frontlines Daily," August 22, 2022, https://spartz.house.gov /media/press-releases/spartz-anti-police -rhetoric-must-stop-and-we-have-sup port-our-police-0).

7. See Mark Memmott, "15 Years Later, Tawana Brawley Has Paid 1 Percent of Penalty," NPR, August 5, 2013, https://www.npr.org/sections/thetwo-way/2013/08/05/209194252/15-years-later-tawana-brawley-has-paid-1-percent-of-penalty; Alexandra Hutzler, "Who Is Tawana Brawley? As Al Sharpton Feuds with Trump, False Rape Accusation Against Law Enforcement Officials Resurfaces," Newsweek, July 29, 2019, https://www.newsweek.com/tawana-brawley-al-sharpton-rape-145159.

8. Ibid.

9. Corey Dade, "The Rev. Al Sharpton, in Six True-False Statements," NPR, January 19, 2013, https://www.npr.org/2013/01/19/169734710/the-rev-al-sharpton-in-six-true-false-statements,

10. Steven J. Allen, "Al Sharpton Liar, Liar, Cities on Fire," Capital Research Center, October 6, 2015.

11. See Jonathan Allen and Laila Kearney, "New York Mayor Calls for Pause in Protests After Police Killings," Reuters, December 22, 2014, https://www.reuters.com/article/uk-usa-police/new-york-mayor-calls-for-pause-in-protests-after-police-killings-idUKKBN0K01HZ20141222.

12. Benjamin Mueller and Al Baker, "2 N.Y.P.D. Officers Killed in Brooklyn Ambush; Suspect Commits Suicide," New York Times, December 20, 2014, https://www.nytimes.com/2014/12/21/nyregion/two-police-officers-shot-in-their-patrol-car-in-brooklyn.html.

13. See Allen and Kearney, "New York Mayor Calls for Pause in Protests After Police Killings."

14. Transcript of remarks on television program of David Ashman, China; Sony's Next Move, December 22, 2014.

15. Seth Mandel, "Al Sharpton Is Not a Lifelong Fighter for Justice," Washington Post, August 28, 2019, https://gogale com.proxy.library.upenn.edu/ps/i.do?p=STND&u=upenn_main&id=GALE|A597671011&v=2.1&it=r&sid=summon.

16. Frank James, "Obama and Al Sharpton: An Odd Couple Who Make Political Sense," NPR, April 10, 2014; Ross Barkan, "Defying Critics, Bill de Blasio Embraces Al Sharpton on His Home Turf," Observer, January 19, 2015; Robert W. Wood, "Defends Al Sharpton's Ties to White House, Despite Tax Debts," Forbes, February 28, 2015; Michael Gartland, "NYC Mayor Adams Lauds Rev. Al Sharpton for His Friendship, Advocacy Work," New York Daily News, April 6, 2022.

17. Scott Davis, "Defunded Minneapolis to Bring in Outside Help to Deal with Surge in Violence Amid Police Shortage," Law Enforcement Today, May 24, 2021, https://www.lawenforcementtoday.com/minneapolis-to-bring-in-outside-help-to-deal-with-surge-in-violence/.

18. https://www.washingtonpost.com/graphics/investigations/police-shootings-database, as categorized by the Washington Post, "includes suspects grabbing an officer's gun or fleeing in a stolen car with a loaded pistol on the car seat." For a complete discussion of the "unarmed category," see Heather Mac Donald, The War on Cops (Encounter Books, 2016), 74; Heather Mac Donald, "Team Biden Finally Admits There Is a War on Cops—Which It Is Inflaming," New York Post, April 28, 2022, https://nypost.com/2022/04/28/team-biden-finally-admits-theres-a-war-on-cops/.

19. See Nicholas Kulish, "After Raising $90 Million in 2020, Black Lives Matter Has $42 Million in Assets," New York Times, May 17, 2022, https://www.nytimes.com/2022/05/17/business/blm-black-lives-matter-finances.html.

20. Ibid.

21. William Saletan, "Democratic Candidates Are Misrepresenting Michael Brown's Death," Slate, September 20, 2019, https://slate.com/news-and-politics/2019/09/warren-michael-brown-ferguson-misrepresenting-death.html.

22. Ronn Blitzer, "Biden Has Called to Redirect Police Funding, but Stopped Short of 'Defund' Embrace," Fox News, July 20, 2020, https://www.foxnews.com/politics /biden-has-called-to-redirect-funding -from-police-but-stopped-short-of-de fund-embrace.

23. Ryan Mills, "Where Have All the Officers Gone?" National Review, October 4, 2021, https://www.nationalreview.com /magazine/2021/10/04/where-have-all -the-officers-gone/.

24. Ibid.

25. Heather Mac Donald, "What Killed Tyre Nichols," *City Journal*, February 19, 2023, https://www.city-journal.org /what-killed-tyre-nichols.

26. Tyler Kingkade, "Black Lives Matter Activist Wins in Iowa on a 'Defund the Police' Platform," NBC, November 3, 2021, https://www.nbcnews.com/news/us -news/black-lives-matter-activist-wins -iowa-defund-police-platform-rcna4460.

27. Retraction for Johnson et al., "Officer Characteristics and Racial Disparities in Fatal Officer-Involved Shootings," PNAS, July 10, 2020, https://www.pnas .org/doi/10.1073/pnas.2014148117.

28. The opportunity was provided by a Title IX investigation into sexual harassment allegations against Fryer. An investigation by Harvard recommended Fryer merely receive workplace conduct training. However, the committee that actually decided the punishment was staffed with academics who had been outspoken against Fryer's work, and they chose to punish Fryer far more harshly, even attempting to have his tenure revoked. See Rob Montz, "Why Did Harvard University Go After One of Its Best Black Professors?" *Quillette*, April 15, 2022.

29. Paulina Dedaj, "LeBron James Sponsors, Lakers, NBA Silent in Wake of Controversial Tweet that Targeted Ohio Cop," Fox News, April 22, 2022, https://www .foxnews.com/sports/lebron-james -sponsors-lakers-nba-silent-tweet-ohio -cop.

30. Ibid.

31. Manny Fernandez et al., "Five Dallas Officers Were Killed as Payback, Police Chief Says," *New York Times*, July 7, 2016, https://www.nytimes.com/2016/07/09 /us/dallas-police-shooting.html.

32. Melinda Urbina and Katie Chaumont, "FBI Releases Statistics for Law Enforcement Officers Assaulted and Killed in the Line of Duty," October 22, 2021.

33. Patrick Yoes, "Monthly Update: Law Enforcement Officers Shot and Killed in the Line of Duty," National Fraternal Order of Police, April 1, 2022, https:// national.fop.net/report-shot-killed -20220401#page=1.

34. Mac Donald, "Team Biden Finally Admits There Is a War on Cops."

35. Harold Hutchison, "Attacks on Police Hit Record Highs; Last Year Saw a Record Number of Attacks on Police Officers, According to a Study Released by a National Law-Enforcement Advocacy Group," *The Daily Caller*, January 4, 2022,

36. Josh Delaney, "Why Are Attacks on Cops in Oklahoma and the Nation on the Rise?; Says One Expert: 'It's Escalating to the Point of No Return,'" *The Daily Oklahoman*, December 18, 2021; also see, for example, Gian Carlo Camparo and Amy Swearer, "Ambush Attacks on Police: Sadly Predictable Result of Lies, Overheated Rhetoric," The Heritage Foundation, September 29, 2020, https://www .heritage.org/crime-and-justice/com mentary/ambush-attacks-police-sadly -predictable-result-lies-overheated.

37. Delaney, "Why Are Attacks on Cops in Oklahoma and the Nation on the Rise?"

38. Michelle Price and Ken Ritter, "Vegas Officer on Life Support After Attack During Protests," *The Seattle Times*, June 3, 2020; James Gordon, "Man Is Charged with Attempted Murder for Throwing Molotov Cocktails at Police During Last Summer's Portland Protests After He Left Evidence on Unexploded Bomb," MailOnline, April 6, 2021.

39. Price and Ritter, "Vegas Officer on Life Support After Attack During Protests."

40. Lucas Aulbach, "Arrest Citation Details Charges against Larynzo Johnson, Suspect Accused in LMPD shooting," *Louisville Courier Journal*, September 24, 2020, https://www.courier-journal.com/story/news/local/breonna-taylor/2020/09/24/larynzo-johnson-charged-shooting-louisville-police-officers-protest/3514621001/.

41. KIRO 7 News Staff, "47 Arrested, 59 Officers Injured in Seattle Protests that Turned Violent," KIRO 7 News, July 25, 2020, https://www.kiro7.com/news/local/thousands-gather-capitol-hill-solidarity-with-demonstrations-portland/STVDEK5XUJHWLL2HQZT2NWDYVY/.

42. Tom Winter and Jonathan Dienst, "Nearly 400 NYPD Cops Hurt During NYC's Two Weeks of Protest Over George Floyd's Death," NBC, June 10, 2020, https://www.nbcnewyork.com/news/local/nearly-400-nypd-officers-hurt-during-nycs-two-weeks-of-protest-over-george-floyds-death/2455285/.

43. "Los Angeles Police Officers Shot in 'Ambush,'" BBC News, September 13, 2020, https://www.bbc.com/news/world-us-canada-54137838.

44. "The Siege of Atlanta's 'Cop City,'" *Wall Street Journal*, March 7, 2023, https://www.wsj.com/articles/atlanta-cop-city-attacks-georgia-police-training-site-63c4cf40.

45. Urbina and Chaumont, "FBI Releases Statistics for Law Enforcement Officers Assaulted and Killed in the Line of Duty."

46. Heather Mac Donald, "Where Is the Outrage Over the Killing of Baltimore Police Officer Keona Holley?" *New York Post*, December 29, 2021, https://nypost.com/2021/12/29/where-is-the-outrage-over-the-killing-of-keona-holley/.

47. Ibid.

48. Ibid.

49. Ibid.

50. Ibid.

51. Ibid.

52. Aleksandra Bush and Dan Abrams, "Why No Nationwide Protests When Police Officers Are Killed?" News Nation, January 24, 2022, https://www.newsnationnow.com/danabramslive/why-no-nationwide-protests-when-police-officers-are-killed/.

53. Mac Donald, "Team Biden Finally Admits There Is a War on Cops."

54. See Paul H. Robinson, "Why Police Should See the 'Defund' Movement as a Golden Opportunity," *Newsweek*, July 21, 2020, https://www.newsweek.com/why-police-should-see-defund-movement-golden-opportunity-opinion-1519099.

55. Ibid.

56. See Tim Arango and Matt Furber, "Where George Floyd Was Killed: Solemn by Day, Violent by Night," *New York Times*, August 11, 2020, https://www.nytimes.com/2020/07/29/us/george-floyd-memorial.html.

57. Ibid.

58. Megan Burks, "George Floyd's Square Offers an Alternative to Police—Though Not All Neighbors Want One," MPR News, December 12, 2020.

59. See Imez Wright, "Fatally Shot in George Floyd Square, Was 'One of the Leaders of Change,'" CBS Minnesota, March 16, 2021, https://www.cbsnews.com/minnesota/news/shantaello-christianson-charged-with-second-degree-murder.

60. Ibid.

61. See David Griswold, "Traffic Resumes at George Floyd Square," KARE 11, June 21, 2021, https://www.kare11.com/article/news/local/george-floyd/traffic-resumes-at-george-floyd-square/89-8c7d1e73-b8a7-422d-b459-027659f36a9b.

62. Nigel Jaquiss, "Portland on Pace to Record Fewest Number of Murders Among Nation's 30 Largest Cities," *Willamette Week*, December 22, 2018, https://www.wweek.com/news/2018/12/22/portland-on-pace-to-record-fewest-number-of-murders-among-nations-30-largest-cities/.

63. "Portland Police Bureau officials say that's because of legislation passed by Oregon lawmakers this year, which restricts the tools they can use to confront people vandalizing buildings and causing mayhem. 'The reason that we did not intervene goes back to . . . House Bill 2928 and the restrictions placed on us in a crowd control environment,' KOIN reports that Portland Police Lt. Jake Jensen said in a neighborhood meeting Thursday." Sarah Cline, "Lawless City? Worry After Portland Police Don't Stop Chaos," Associated Press, October 15, 2021.

64. Michael Totten, "Portland Sobers Up," *City Journal*, 2023, https://www.city-journal.org/article/portland-sobers-up.

65. The constant riots and protests are devasting to city businesses and terrifying to residents. By the end of 2021, one report estimates that since 2019, Portland's metropolitan area has lost ten thousand tourism jobs, at least in part due to the seemingly constant protesting. See Taxpayers Association of Oregon, "Portland Loses 10,000 Tourism Jobs Due to Riots, Homeless Camps," *The Guardian*, November 16, 2021, https://oregoncatalyst.com/56087-portland-loses-10000-tourism-jobs-due-riots-homeless-camps.html.

66. Jarrett Stepman, "Anarchy Reigns in Portland," *The Daily Signal*, October 27, 2021, https://www.heritage.org/progressivism/commentary/anarchy-reigns-portland.

67. Adriana Diaz and David Averre, "'Lawless' Portland Sets New Homicide Record with over 66 Killings This Year and More than 1,000 Shootings," Daily Mail, October 19, 2021, https://www.dailymail.co.uk/news/article-10106211/A-dangerous-time-Portland-Oregon-sees-record-homicides.html.

68. Maxine Bernstein, "Portland's 101 Homicides in 2022 Set New Record: 'At Some Point, We Have to Be Tired of Burying Our Children,'" Oregon Live, February 3, 2023, https://www.oregonlive.com/crime/2023/01/portlands-101-homicides-in-2022-set-new-record-at-some-point-we-have-to-be-tired-of-burying-our-children.html.

69. Hannah Meyers, "Public Safety on the Ballot in Portland," *City Journal*, October 28, 2022, https://www.city-journal.org/public-safety-on-the-ballot-in-portland-oregon.

70. Totten, "Portland Sobers Up."

71. Ibid.

72. Liz Burch, "Businessowners Implore City Leaders to Do More to Fix 'Lawless' Portland After Protest," KOIN 6, July 6, 2022, https://www.koin.com/news/portland/business-owners-implore-city-leaders-to-do-more-to-fix-lawless-portland-after-fourth-of-july-protest/.

73. Laurel Duggan, "'No Consequences': Residents Reveal How Portland Has Become Plagued by Crime, Filth and Fear," *Daily Caller*, October 18, 2022, https://dailycaller.com/2022/10/18/portland-oregon-crime-filth-drugs-residents/.

74. Ibid.

75. Jared Cowley, "Multiple People Shot Near Illegal Street-Racing Takeovers in Portland," KGW8, August 29, 2022, https://www.kgw.com/article/news/crime/shootings-illegal-street-racing-portland-oregon/283-b0e27fee-0372-47f4-9a41-2a110c51b3fe.

76. Alma McCarty, "Portland Man Assaulted During Illegal Street Takeover," KGW, September 3, 2022, https://www.kgw.com/article/news/local/portland-man-assaulted-illegal-street-racing-sandy-blvd/283-8043ebc1-2a39-415d-9a41-cfff5e6aa51.

77. Totten, "Portland Sobers Up."

78. Zane Sparling, "Rising 'Fear of Violence' in Old Town, Pearl Spurs Patrols," *Portland Tribune*, May 12, 2020, https://pamplinmedia.com/pt/9-news/466367-377925-rising-fear-of-violence-in-old-town-pearl-spurs-patrols.

79. Totten, "Portland Sobers Up."

80. Ibid.

81. Ashitha Nagesh, "This Police-Free Protest Zone Was Dismantled—But Was It the End," BBC, July 12, 2020, https://www.bbc.com/news/world-us-canada-53218448.

82. Ibid.

83. Ibid.

84. Jillian Kay Melchoir, "A Black Life Lost in Seattle's No-Cop Zone," *Wall Street Journal*, May 7, 2021, https://www.wsj.com/articles/a-black-life-lost-in-seattles-no-cop-zone-11620412478.

85. Ibid.

86. Ibid.

87. Ibid.

88. Nagesh, Nagesh, "This Police-Free Protest Zone Was Dismantled."

89. Ibid.

90. In February 2023, Seattle settled with victims, residents, and businesses in the zone for $3.65 million as evidence showed that the city had actively participated in the disruptions. Six hundred thousand dollars of the settlement were penalties for the illegal destruction of evidence by the city. See, "The Price of Anarchy in Seattle," *Wall Street Journal*, February 19, 2023, https://www.wsj.com/articles/the-price-of-anarchy-in-seattle-capitol-hill-autonomous-zone-settlement-lawsuit-business-9ade3e33.

91. Ibid.

92. Fola Akinnibi, Sarah Holder, and Christopher Cannon, "Cities Say They Want to Defund the Police. Their Budgets Say Otherwise," Bloomberg News, January 12, 2021, https://www.bloomberg.com/graphics/2021-city-budget-police-funding/.

93. Sam Levin, "These US Cities Defunded Police: 'We're Transferring Money to the Community,'" *The Guardian*, March 11, 2021, https://www.theguardian.com/us-news/2021/mar/07/us-cities-defund-police-transferring-money-community#:~:text=city%20councils%20responded.-,In%202020%20budget%20votes%2C%20advocacy%20groups%20won%20over%20$4840m,

Center%20for%20Research%20on%20Women.

94. Jason Johnson, "Why Violent Crime Surged After Police Across America Retreated," *USA Today*, April 9, 2021, https://www.usatoday.com/story/opinion/policing/2021/04/09/violent-crime-surged-across-america-after-police-retreated-column/7137565002/.

95. Ibid.

96. Adam Manno, "Portland REFUNDS the Police: Department Gets an Extra $5.2M as City Faces Greatest Cop Shortage in Decades and Record Number of Homicides After Slashing $150M from the Budget over Defund the Police Movement," *Daily Mail*, November 17, 2021, https://www.dailymail.co.uk/news/article-10214459/Portland-US-cities-looking-refund-police.html.

97. Marlene Lenthang et al., "What We Know About the 5 Memphis Police Officers Charged with Beating Tyre Nichols to Death," NBC News, January 29, 2023, https://www.nbcnews.com/news/us-news/what-we-know-about-memphis-police-officers-tyre-nichols-death-rcna67861.

98. CST Editorial Board, "City Must Find Answers for Unwise Policy of Overworking Cops," *Chicago-Sun Times*, August 31, 2022, https://chicago.suntimes.com/2022/8/31/23331220/chicago-police-department-canceled-days-off-schedule-editorial.

99. Steve Friees, "'Defund the Police' Is Dead But Other Reform Efforts Thrive in U.S. Cities," *Newsweek*, May 24, 2022, https://www.newsweek.com/2022/06/24/defund-police-dead-other-reform-efforts-thrive-us-cities-1709393.html.

100. Section III.C.

101. Levin, "These US Cities Defunded Police."

102. Robert L. Woodson, "The Deadly Results of Defunding the Police," *Wall Street Journal*, June 9, 2021.

103. Levin, "These US Cities Defunded Police."
104. Abene Clayton, "Distrust of Police Is Major Driver of US Gun Violence, Report Warns," *The Guardian*, January 21, 2020.
105. Sarah Elbeshbishi and Mabinty Quarshie, "Fewer than 1 in 5 Support 'Defund the Police' Movement," *USA Today*, March 8, 2021.
106. Ibid.
107. Zach Goldberg, "Is Defunding the Police a 'Luxury Belief'?: Analyzing White vs. Nonwhite Democrats' Attitudes on Depolicing," Manhattan Institute, September 8, 2022, https://www.manhattan-institute.org/is-defunding-the-police-a-luxury-belief?utm_source=mailchimp.
108. Heather Mac Donald, "Minneapolis Voters Saw Life Without Police—and Soundly Rejected a Defund Ballot Initiative," *New York Post*, November 3, 2021, https://nypost.com/2021/11/03/minneapolis-voters-soundly-rejected-a-defund-ballot-initiative/.
109. Ailan Evans, "Rising Crime Forces Liberals to Reckon with Their Stance on the Police," *The Daily Caller*, June 26, 2021.
110. Shane D. Kavanaugh, "How Portland Leaders Fumbled Through a Historic Year of Disorder, Violence and Despair," *Oregonian*, January 2, 2022.
111. Matthew Yglesias, "The Case for Hiring More Police Officers," VOX, February 13, 2019, https://www.vox.com/policy-and-politics/2019/2/13/18193661/hire-police-officers-crime-criminal-justice-reform-booker-harris.
112. Ibid.
113. Larry Sand, "Cops Out: After School Police Are Cut Back, Campus Crimes Increase," *City Journal*, November 30, 2021.
114. Ibid.
115. Ibid.
116. Aaron Chalfin et al., "Police Force Size and Civilian Race," National Bureau of Economic Research, December 2020, 42, https://www.nber.org/papers/w28202.
117. Ibid., 12.
118. Reid J. Epstein, "These Top Democrats Go Further than Biden on Diverting Police Funds," *New York Times*, June 26, 2020, https://www.nytimes.com/2020/06/26/us/politics/defund-police-protests-democrats.html
119. See Michael Balsamo, "When Protesters Cry 'Defund the Police,' What Does It Mean?" NBC L.A., June 7, 2020, https://www.nbclosangeles.com/news/when-protesters-cry-defund-the-police-what-does-it-mean/2376366.
120. Editorial Board, "Refunding the San Francisco Police: Mayor London Breed Undergoes a Law-and-Order Conversion," *Wall Street Journal*, December 16, 2021, https://www.wsj.com/articles/refunding-the-san-francisco-police-london-breed-crime-11639696468.
121. Sarah Westwood, "Refund the Police: Cities Backtrack on 2020 Clarion Call Amid Crime Spikes," *Washington Examiner*, August 24, 2021, https://gazette.com/refund-the-police-cities-backtrack-on-2020-clarion-call-amid-crime-spikes/article_2787b0f3-6ccf-5d4d-9ab9-710426b8d45f.html.
122. Ibid.
123. Ibid.
124. David Cohen, "'Defund the Police' Is Not the Policy of the Democratic Party, Pelosi Says," Politico, February 13, 2022, https://www.politico.com/news/2022/02/13/pelosi-defund-police-democrats-00008449.
125. Aaron Blake, "Biden Tries to Nix 'Defund the Police,' Once and for All," *Washington Post*, March 2, 2022, https://www.washingtonpost.com/politics/2022/03/02/biden-nix-defund-police/.
126. Scott McClallen, "Judge Rules Minneapolis Residents Have Standing to Sue over Police Reduction," The Center Square, November 24, 2020. Also see Charles Fain Lehman, "America's

Shrinking Police Forces Could Spell Trouble for Our Safety," The Manhattan Institute, February 9, 2020, https:// www.manhattan-institute.org/amer icas-shrinking-police-forces-could -spell-trouble-for-our-safety.

127. "Crime in the United States 2011," FBI, https://ucr.fbi.gov/crime-in-the-u.s /2011/crime-in-the-u.s.2011/tables /table8statecuts/table_8_offenses _known_to_law_enforcement_minne sota_by_city_2011.xls.

128. McClallen, "Judge Rules Minneapolis Residents Have Standing to Sue over Police Reduction"; Bret Baier, "Police Department in Minneapolis Facing Continuing Officer Shortage," Fox News, August 28, 2019.

129. Curtis Gilbert, "Documents Show Rift Between Minneapolis Police, Top Brass," Minnesota Public Radio News, February 25, 2015, https://www .mprnews.org/story/2015/02/25/min neapolis-police-survey.

130. Ibid.

131. Baier, "Police Department in Minneapolis Facing Continuing Officer Shortage."

132. McClallen, "Judge Rules Minneapolis Residents Have Standing to Sue over Police Reduction"; Doug Seaton and James Dickey, "Minneapolis Needs a Fully Funded Police Department," Minneapolis Post, December 7, 2022, https://www.minnpost .com/community-voices/2022/12/min neapolis-needs-a-fully-funded-police department/#:~:text=The%20Minnea polis%20City%20Charter%20requires ,to%20560%20in%20August%202022.

133. Jamiles Lartey and Abbie VanSickle, "'That Could Have Been Me': The People Derek Chauvin Choked Before George Floyd," Minnesota Public Radio News, February 5, 2021, https:// www.mprnews.org/story/2021/02/05 /that-could-have-been-me-the-people -derek-chauvin-choked-before-george -floyd.

134. Jennifer Mayerle, "Former Minneapolis Police Officer Talks About His Decision to Leave: 'I Did It Out of Principle,'" CBS Minnesota, May 16, 2021, https:// minnesota.cbslocal.com/2021/05/16 /former-minneapolis-police-officer -talks-about-his-decision-to-leave/.

135. Matt Sepic, "A Year After George Floyd's Death, Plans for Minneapolis Police Reform Have Softened," NPR, May 25, 2021, https://www.npr.org /2021/05/25/1000298293/a-year-after -george-floyds-death-plans-for-minne apolis-police-reform-have-soften.

136. Deena Winter, "Minneapolis Council Member Says He 'Got' at Defund Police Rally," Minnesota Reformer, October 8, 2021, https://minnesotareformer .com/2021/10/08/minneapolis-council -member-says-he-got-got-at-defund -police-rally/.

137. Davis, "Defunded Minneapolis to Bring in Outside Help to Deal with Surge in Violence Amid Police Shortage."

138. McClallen, "Judge Rules Minneapolis Residents Have Standing to Sue over Police Reduction."

139. Ibid.

140. Mayerle, "Former Minneapolis Police Officer Talks About His Decision to Leave."

141. Ibid.

142. Scott A. Mourtgos et al., "Elevated Police Turnover Following the Summer of George Floyd Protests: A Synthetic Control Study," Journal of Criminology and Public Policy 21, no. 1 (2021): 4.

143. Andy Mannix and Jeff Hargarten, "Minneapolis Closes in on Homicide Milestone at End of Violent Year," Star Tribune, December 30, 2020, https:// www.startribune.com/a-most-violent -year-in-minneapolis/600131444/.

144. "Most Dangerous Cities in Minnesota," PopulationU.com, https://www.popu lationu.com/gen/most-dangerous-cit ies-minnesota.

145. Mannix and Hargarten, "Minneapolis Closes in on Homicide Milestone at End of Violent Year."

146. Bill Otis, "Defunding the Police, Minneapolis Edition," Crime and Consequences, November 16, 2020, https://plus.lexis.com/document?crid=08c52aea-417e-428c-8357-c46b621d96a4&pddocfullpath=%2Fshared%2Fdocument%2Fnews%2Furn%3Acontentitem%3A619P-G3G1-F03R-N4TS-00000-00&pdsourcegroupingtype=&pdcontentcomponentid=299488&pdmfid=1530671&pdisurlapi=true.

147. "Minneapolis MC Crime Rate 2004–2008," Macro Trends, https://www.macrotrends.net/cities/us/mn/minneapolis/crime-rate-statistics.

148. Emma Freire, "Police by Another Name: Demand for Private Security Is Booming in Minneapolis," *City Journal*, September 16, 2022, https://www.city-journal.org/in-minneapolis-private-security-replaces-police.

149. Otis, "Defunding the Police, Minneapolis Edition."

150. Davis, "Defunded Minneapolis to Bring in Outside Help to Deal with Surge in Violence Amid Police Shortage."

151. Brady Slater, "After George Floyd: Northland Colleges, Police Recruiting Suffer," *Duluth News Tribune*, January 22, 2022, https://www.duluthnewstribune.com/news/local/after-george-floyd-northland-colleges-police-recruiting-suffer.

152. Mayerle, "Former Minneapolis Police Officer Talks About His Decision to Leave."

153. Elissa Salamy, "'Crime Will Go Up' If Minneapolis Votes to Replace Police Dept, Says Ex-NYC Police Commish," ABC 4 News, November 2, 2021, https://abcnews4.com/news/nation-world/crime-will-go-up-if-minneapolis-votes-to-replace-police-dept-says-ex-nyc-police-commish.

154. Mills, "Where Have All the Officers Gone?"

155. Heather Mac Donald, "Biden Wants to Boost Policing—After Spreading Toxic Lies that Tore It Down," *New York Post*, July 13, 2021, https://nypost.com/2021/07/13/biden-wants-to-boost-policing-after-spreading-toxic-lies-that-tore-it-down/.

156. Robert Woodson, "Hold Anti-Police Activists Accountable for the Harm They've Done to Black America," *Washington Examiner*, February 23, 2022, https://www.washingtonexaminer.com/restoring-america/fairness-justice/hold-anti-police-activists-accountable-for-the-harm-theyve-done-to-black-america.

157. Brianna Lyman, "NYPD Sees Surge in Retirement Amid Rise in Violent Crime, Anti-Police Rhetoric," *The Daily Caller*, October 9, 2020, https://plus.lexis.com/document?crid=84bd3643-7cc4-4999-b65e-1d9d4ab16e8b&pddocfullpath=%2Fshared%2Fdocument%2Fnews%2Furn%3AcontentItem%3A611K-CD61-DXXD-7547-00000-00&pdsourcegroupingtype=&pdcontentcomponentid=470729&pdmfid=1530671&pdisurlapi=true.

158. Mac Donald, "Biden Wants to Boost Policing."

159. Ibid.

160. Lehman, "America's Shrinking Police Forces Could Spell Trouble for Our Safety."

161. Ibid.

162. Ibid.

163. Libor Jany, "Police Call Officer Shortage a 'Crisis,'" *Star Tribune*, December 13, 2020, https://www.startribune.com/police-staffing-issues-are-at-a-crisis-duluth-police-chief-says/600165492/.

164. Lehman, "America's Shrinking Police Forces Could Spell Trouble for Our Safety."

165. US Census Bureau, https://www2.census.gov/programs-surveys/popest/tables/.

166. Martin Kaste, "America's Growing Cop Shortage," NPR, December

12, 2018, https://www.npr.org/2018/12/12/675359781/americas-growing-cop-shortage.

167. Lehman, "America's Shrinking Police Forces Could Spell Trouble for Our Safety"; Mourtgos et al., "Elevated Police Turnover Following the Summer of George Floyd Protests."

168. Chalfin et al., "Police Force Size and Civilian Race."

169. Ibid., 4.

170. Kaste, "America's Growing Cop Shortage."

171. Sean Kennedy, "'The Wire' Is Finished, But Baltimore Still Bleeds," *Wall Street Journal*, May 10, 2019, https://www.wsj.com/articles/the-wire-is-finished-but-baltimore-still-bleeds-11581119104.

172. Paul G. Cassell, "Explaining the Recent Homicide Spikes in U.S. Cities: The 'Minneapolis Effect' and the Decline in Proactive Policing," *The Federal Sentencing Reporter*, 2020, 51.

173. Keith Griffith, "New Orleans Overtakes St. Louis as Become the MURDER CAPITAL of America," *Daily Mail*, September 16, 2022.

174. Ibid.

175. Cassie Schrim, "Leaders Call New Orleans' Violent 2022 a 'Horrific Year,'" WDSU, January 4, 2023, https://www.wdsu.com/article/leaders-call-new-orleans-violent-2022-a-horrific-year/42390054.

176. Murder Rate by Country 2023, World Population Review, https://worldpopulationreview.com/country-rankings/murder-rate-by-country.

177. Kavanaugh, "How Portland Leaders Fumbled Through a Historic Year of Disorder, Violence and Despair."

178. Ibid.

179. Mourtgos et al., "Elevated Police Turnover Following the Summer of George Floyd Protests."

180. Lyman, "NYPD Sees Surge in Retirement Amid Rise in Violent Crime, Anti-Police Rhetoric."

181. Carma Hassan, Omar Jimenez, and Ray Sanchez, "Judge Orders Minneapolis to Add More Police Officers," CNN, July 2, 2021.

182. Kim Parker and Kiley Hurst, "Growing Share of Americans Say They Want More Spending on Police in Their Area," Pew Research Center, October 26, 2021.

183. Ibid.

184. Ibid.

185. Ibid.

186. Dara Lind, "The 'Ferguson Effect,' a Theory that's Warping the American Crime Debate, Explained," VOX, May 18, 2016, https://www.vox.com/2016/5/18/11683594/ferguson-effect-crime-police.

187. Heather Mac Donald, "The New Nationwide Crime Wave," *Wall Street Journal*, May 29, 2015, https://www.wsj.com/articles/the-new-nationwide-crime-wave-1432938425.

188. Ross Deuchar, Seth Wyatt Fallik, and Vaughn J. Crichlow, "Despondent Officer Narratives and the 'Post-Ferguson' Effect: Exploring Law Enforcement Perspectives and Strategies in a Southern American State," *Policing and Society* 29, no. 9 (2019): 1–16.

189. German Lopez, "A Continuing Drop in Murders," *New York Times*, December 30, 2022.

190. Heather Mac Donald, "The Unwinding of Law and Order in Our Cities Has Happened with Stunning Speed," *City Journal*, July 1, 2020, https://www.city-journal. sporg/ferguson-effect-in ner-cities; Aamer Midhani, "'Ferguson Effect': 72% of U.S. Cops Reluctant to Make Stops," *USA Today*, January 11, 2017, https://www.usatoday.com/story/news/2017/01/11/ferguson-effect-study-72-us-cops-reluctant-make-stops/96446504/; Tanaya Devi and Roland G. Fryer Jr., "Policing the Police: The Impact of 'Pattern-or-Practice' Investigations on Crime," National Bu-

reau of Economic Research, Working Paper 27324, 2020.

191. TRC Staff, "Can Police Cope with the Surge in Violent Crime," *The Crime Report*, June 23, 2021.

192. Stephen Walters, "Anatomy of a Crime Wave," *City Journal*, May 5, 2021, https://www.city-journal.org/baltimore-failed-de-policing-experiment.

193. Ibid.

194. Ibid.

195. Alec MacGillis, "What Can Mayors Do When the Police Stop Doing Their Jobs?" ProPublica, September 3, 2020, https://www.propublica.org/article/what-can-mayors-do-when-the-police-stop-doing-their-jobs.

196. Ibid.

197. Ibid.

198. Walters, "Anatomy of a Crime Wave."

199. Amy Lu, "Residents Call for Action as Baltimore Records More than 300 Homicides," WBAL tv, December 31, 2021, https://www.wbaltv.com/article/baltimore-more-than-300-homicides-2021/38647379#.

200. Aimee Ortiz, "What to Know About the Death of Rayshard Brooks," *New York Times*, May 6, 2021; "Fellow Officer Charged with Murder of Rayshard Brooks Report Says," Nexstar Media Wire, June 18, 2020; Christian Boone, "We Feel Like We've Been Abandoned.' Atlanta Suffers a Deadly July 4," *Atlanta Journal-Constitution*, July 10, 2020; Joshua Sharpe, "Atlanta Wendy's Protesters Decry Secoriea Turner's Killing," *Atlanta-Journal Constitution*, July 6, 2020.

201. Cheng Cheng and Wei Long, "The Effect of High Publicized Police Killings on Policing: Evidence from Large US Cities," *Journal of Public Economics* 206 (February 2022).

202. Ibid.

203. Jamiles Lartey et al., "Fergerson Effect Is a Plausible Reason for Spike in Violent US Crime, Study Says," *The Guardian*, July 15, 2016, https://www.theguardian.com/us-news/2016/jun/15/ferguson-effect-homicide-rates-us-crime-study.

204. National Institute of Justice, "Assessing and Responding to the Recent Homicide Rise in the United States," November 2017.

205. Rich Morin et al., "Police, Fatal Encounters and Ensuing Protests," Pew Research Center, January 11, 2017, https://www.pewresearch.org/social-trends/2017/01/11/police-fatal-encounters-and-ensuing-protests/.

206. Ibid.

207. Ibid.

208. Morin et al., "Police, Fatal Encounters and Ensuing Protests."

209. Mara Gay, "Why Did the NYPD Solve Fewer Crimes Last Year," *New York Times*, February 11, 2021, https://www.nytimes.com/2021/01/29/opinion/nypd-crime-murder.html.

210. Cassell, "Explaining the Recent Homicide Spikes in U.S. Cities," 49.

211. Johnson, "Why Violent Crime Surged After Police Across America Retreated."

212. Gay, "Why Did the NYPD Solve Fewer Crimes Last Year."

213. Ibid.

214. Ibid.

215. Annie Sweeny and Jeremy Gorner, "Chicago Police's Homicide Clearance Rate Dips in 2020 After Improvement in Recent Years," *Chicago Tribune*, December 15, 2020, https://www.chicagotribune.com/news/criminal-justice/ct-chicago-police-2020-clearance-rates-20201215-2evyuaybxbcvxex7s4wlvrx62q-story.html.

216. Johnson, "Why Violent Crime Surged After Police Across America Retreated."

217. Devi and Fryer, "Policing the Police."

218. Ortiz, "What to Know About the Death of Rayshard Brooks."

219. Morin et al., "Police, Fatal Encounters and Ensuing Protests."

220. Yglesias, "The Case for Hiring More Police Officers."

221. Ibid.

222. Brooke Singman, "Biden Calls for Hiring More Police, Cracking Down on Illegal Guns to Combat Crime," Fox News, July 12, 2021.

223. Alanea Cremen, "'The Solution Can't Solely Be More Police'—DC Council Approves Compromise Budget, Splits $11M Between Police and Violence Prevention Programs," WUSA 9, August 4, 2021.

224. Ibid.

225. "Durkan Seeks to Lift $7.5 Million Budget Restriction to Hire More Seattle Police Officers," King 5, July 30, 2021.

226. Ibid.

227. Jonathan Klick and John M. Mac Donald, "Hire More Cops," *City Journal*, August 4, 2020.

228. Ibid.

229. Chalfin et al., "Police Force Size and Civilian Race."

230. Ibid.

231. Ibid.

232. Katja Ridderbusch, "Violence, Stress, Scrutiny Weigh on Police Mental Health,"PBS,June14,2021,https://www.gpb.org/news/2021/06/14/violence-stress-scrutiny-weigh-on-police-mental-health.

233. Joseph De Angelis, Richard Rosenthal, and Brian Buchner, "Civilian Oversight of Law Enforcement: Assessing the Evidence," OJP Diagnostic Center, September 2016.

234. Mike Nolting, "Morgantown Council Approves Court Ordered Changes to Police Oversight Board," WAJR, June 21, 2022.

235. John G. Reece and Judy Macy, "Citizen Advisory Boards in Contemporary Practice: A Practical Approach in Policing," *The Police Chief*, October 2015.

236. Ibid.

237. Char Adams, "In St Louis, a Battle Is Brewing over Police Accountability," NBC News, September 2, 2022, https://www.nbcnews.com/nbcblk3/st-louis-battle-brewing-police-accountability-rcna46123.

CHAPTER 16

1. Paul H. Robinson and John M. Darley, "Intuitions of Justice: Implications for Criminal Law and Justice Policy," *Southern California Law Review* 81, no. 1 (2007): 1–68.

2. The Constitution gives the police power to the states; the federal government has criminalization authority only over matters that involve some special federal interest. Grace Benton, "The Legality of Sanctuary Cities," *Georgetown Immigration Law Journal* 33, no. 1 (2018): 139–44.

3. Dorothy Roberts, "Foreword: Abolition Constitutionalism," *Harvard Law Review* 133, no. 1 (2019): 1–22; Rebecca Goldstein, "The Politics of Decarceration," *The Yale Law Journal* 129, no. 2 (November 2019): 308–611.

4. "2018 Crime in the United States: Texas," FBI, https://ucr.fbi.gov/crime-in-the-u.s/2018/crime-in-the-u.s.-2018/tables/table-8/table-8-state-cuts/texas.xls; Brian Manley, "Austin Police Department: Annual Crime and Traffick Report: 2018 Preliminary Report," June 20, 2019.

5. "Austin TX Crime Rate 1999–2018," Macrotrends, https://www.macrotrends.net/cities/us/tx/austin/crime-rate-statistics.

6. "2018 Crime in the United States: Texas."

7. Mark Pulliam, "Woke City," *City Journal*, June 25, 2018, https://www.city-journal.org/article/woke-city.

8. Mary Tuma, "A Year After Austin's Passage of the Freedom Cities Policies, Activists Urge APD to Do Better," *The Austin Chronicle*, June 21, 2019, https://www.austinchronicle.com/news/2019-06-21/a-year-after-austins-passage-of-the-freedom-cities-policies-activists-urge-apd-to-do-better/.

9. Mariska Lee, "Is Austin, TX Safe to Visit—2022 Crime Rates and Crime States," Van Life Wanderer, https://vanlifewanderer.com/2021/10/07/is-austin-safe/.

10. Sally Hernandez, "Austin Saw a Record Number of Homicides in 2021. How

Many Did Police Solve?" KXAN, January 7, 2022, https://www.kxan.com/news/crime/austin-saw-a-record-number-of-homicides-in-2021-how-many-did-police-solve/.

11. Morgan O'Hanlon, "Rising Crime Around UT has Safety Organizations Demanding Answers," *Austin Monthly*, April 2022, https://www.austinmonthly.com/rising-crime-around-ut-has-safety-organizations-demanding-answers/.

12. Jaqulyn Powell, "Austin Business Owner Repeatedly Burglarized—Here's Why She's Not Reporting It Anymore," KXAN, October 11, 2021, https://www.kxan.com/news/crime/austin-business-owner-repeatedly-burglarized-heres-why-shes-not-reporting-it-anymore/.

13. Daranesha Herron, "North Austin Business Owner Was Told by Police to Gather His Own Evidence After a Burglary at His Store," KVUE, October 21, 2021, https://www.kvue.com/article/news/crime/north-austin-business-burglarized-caught-on-camera/269-5a8eb3f7-48a1-4082-aeef-5da915c68372.

14. Daniel Van Oudenaren, "Do Austin Police Investigate Property Crimes," *The Austin Bulldog*, July 23, 2021, https://theaustinbulldog.org/do-austin-police-investigate-property-crimes/.

15. Candy Rodriguez, "Auto Thefts up 40% Across Austin, Downtown Cases Nearly Doubled," KXAN, May 20, 2022, https://www.kxan.com/news/crime/auto-thefts-up-40-across-austin-downtown-cases-nearly-doubled/.

16. Elliot Kauffman, "'Criminal (In)Justice' Review: In Defense of Policing," *Wall Street Journal*, August 17, 2022, https://www.wsj.com/articles/criminal-in-justice-review-in-defense-of-policing-11660774344.

17. "decarceration," Merriam-Webster, https://www.merriam-webster.com/dictionary/decarceration#:~:text=Decarceration%20is%20the%20effort%20to

,release%20people%20already%20in%20custody.

18. See, for example, Carl Takei, "From Mass Incarceration to Mass Control, and Back Again: How Bipartisan Criminal Justice Reform May Lead to a For-Profit Nightmare," *University of Pennsylvania Journal of Law and Society Change* 20, no. 2 (2017): 126–83; Mirko Bagaric and Daniel McCord, "Decarcerating America: The Opportunistic Overlap Between Theory and (Mainly State) Sentencing Practice as a Pathway to Meaningful Reform," *Buffalo Law Review* 67, no. 2 (2019): 230–309.

19. It should be noted that decarceration draws far from unanimous support among conservatives, and some believe "more criminals should be behind bars today, not fewer." See Tom Cotton, "Our Under-Incarceration Problem," *The National Review*, August 11, 2021, https://www.nationalreview.com/2021/08/our-under-incarceration-problem/.

20. Martha T. Moore, "Conservatives, Liberals Unite to Cut Prison Population," *USA Today*, March 17, 2014, https://www.usatoday.com/story/news/politics/2014/03/16/conservatives-sentencing-reform/6396537/; also see Bagaric and McCord, "Decarcerating America," 252.

21. Ben Grunwald, "Toward an Optimal Decarceration Strategy," *Stanford Law & Policy Review* 33 (September 2021): 1.

22. See, for example, "Decarceration Strategies: How 5 States Achieved Substantial Prison Population Reductions," National Institute of Corrections, https://nicic.gov/decarceration-strategies-how-5-states-achieved-substantial-prison-population-reductions-2018.

23. Alexandra Natapoff, "Atwater and the Misdemeanor Carceral State," *Harvard Law Review* 133, no. 6 (April 2020): 147–78.

24. John Gramlich, "America's Incarceration Rate Falls to Lowest Level Since 1995," Pew Research Center, August 16, 2021, https://www.pewresearch.org

/fact-tank/2021/08/16/americas-incarceration-rate-lowest-since-1995/.

25. Jacob Kang-Brown, Chase Montagnet, and Jasmine Heiss, "People in Jail and Prison in Spring 2021," Vera Institute, June 2021, https://www.vera.org/publications/people-in-jail-and-prison-in-spring-2021.

26. See, for example, "The Drug War, Mass Incarceration and Race," Drug Policy Alliance, June 2015; Nkechi Taifa, "Race, Mass Incarceration, and the Disastrous War on Drugs," The Brennan Center for Justice, May 10, 2021, https://www.brennancenter.org/our-work/analysis-opinion/race-mass-incarceration-and-disastrous-war-drugs; "A Brief History of Civil Rights in the United States: The War on Drugs and Mass Incarceration," Howard University School of Law, https://library.law.howard.edu/civilrightshistory/blackrights/massincarceration.

27. "Drug Related Crime Statistics," National Center for Drug Abuse Statistics, 2023, https://drugabusestatistics.org/drug-related-crime-statistics/.

28. Ibid.

29. Sam Taxy et al., NCJ 248648, "Drug Offenders in Federal Prison: Estimates of Characteristics Based on Linked Data," Bureau of Justice Statistics, October 2015.

30. "The Truth About Trials," The Marshall Project, https://www.themarshallproject.org/2020/11/04/the-truth-about-trials.

31. Wendy Sawyer and Peter Wagner, "Mass Incarceration: The Whole Pie 2020," Prison Policy Initiative, March 24, 2020, https://www.prisonpolicy.org/reports/pie2020.html.

32. ProCon.org, "Incarcerated Population by Type of Crime Committed," ProCon.org, last modified March 23, 2023, https://felonvoting.procon.org/incarcerated-felon-population-by-type-of-crime-committed/.

33. Ibid.

34. Ibid.

35. Sawyer and Wagner, "Mass Incarceration."

36. Kauffman, "'Criminal (In)Justice' Review."

37. John Dilulio, "The Numbers Don't Lie; It's the Hard Core Doing Hard Time," Brookings Institute, March 17, 1996, https://www.brookings.edu/opinions/the-numbers-dont-lie-its-the-hard-core-doing-hard-time/. "Nationally representative BJS data indicate that about one in four criminal cases, including nearly one in three violent criminal cases, is dismissed, and just 54 percent of violent offenses result in prison confinement. Most traffic, misdemeanor, and nonviolent felonies that end in conviction bring their perpetrators fines, restitution, deferred sentences, day reporting, home confinement, electronic monitoring, community service, or the ubiquitous probation. Less serious offenders comply well with these sanctions, complete their sentences, and exit the justice system, but even serious offenders receive these opportunities if their underlying charges are not grave." Matt DeLisi and John Paul Wright, "Mass Incarceration Hysteria," City Journal, Spring 2022, https://www.city-journal.org/article/mass-incarceration-hysteria.

38. Allen Beck, "Race and Ethnicity of Violent Crime Offenders and Arrestees, 2018," US Department of Justice, January 2021, https://bjs.ojp.gov/content/pub/pdf/revcoa18.pdf.

39. Sandy Banks, "Prop. 47 Is Achieving Its Main Goal, But with Unintended Consequences," Los Angeles Times, January 30, 2015, https://www.latimes.com/local/california/la-me-banks-prop-47-fallout-20150131-column.html.

40. Christopher Rufo, "The 'Supermarket Sweep,'" City Journal, October 21, 2019, https://www.city-journal.org/west-coast-shoplifting-boom.

41. Kyle Wang, "Second Chances: The Enduring Empathy of Prop 47," Stanford Politics, 2018, https://stanfordpolitics.org/2018/12/10/second-chances-the-enduring-empathy-of-prop-47/.

42. Christopher F. Rufo, "The New Untouchables," *City Journal*, December 3, 2020, https://www.city-journal.org/article/the-new-untouchables.

43. Ibid.

44. David Kroman, "Seattle's Controversial 'Poverty Defense' Proposal Stalls Out," Crosscut News, February 23, 2021, https://crosscut.com/news/2021/02/seattles-controversial-poverty-defense-proposal-stalls-out.

45. Ruth Wilson Gilmore and James Kilgore, "The Case for Abolition," The Marshall Project, June 19, 2019, https://www.themarshallproject.org/2019/06/19/the-case-for-abolition; Angela Y. Davis and Dylan Rodriquez, "The Challenge of Prison Abolition: A Conversation," *Social Justice* 27, no. 3 (2000): 212.

46. Roberts, "Foreword," 7–8.

47. Paul H. Robinson and Sarah M. Robinson, *Pirates, Prisoners, & Lepers: Lessons from Life Outside the Law* (Potomac Books, 2015), 45.

48. See, for example, Keeanga-Yamahtta Taylor, "The Emerging Movement for Police and Prison Abolition," *The New Yorker*, May 7, 2021, https://www.newyorker.com/news/our-columnists/the-emerging-movement-for-police-and-prison-abolition; Rachel Kushner, "Is Prison Necessary? Ruth Wilson Gilmore Might Change Your Mind," *New York Times*, April 17, 2019, https://www.nytimes.com/2019/04/17/magazine/prison-abolition-ruth-wilson-gilmore.html; Gabriella Paiella, "How Would Prison Abolition Actually Work," *GQ*, June 11, 2020, https://www.gq.com/story/what-is-prison-abolition; Joshua Dubler and Vincent Lloyd, "Think Prison Abolition in America Is Impossible? It Once Felt Inevitable," *The Guardian*, May 2018, https://www.theguardian.com/commentisfree/2018/may/19/prison-abolition-america-impossible-inevitable.

49. Rachel Barkow, "Promise or Peril? The Political Path of Prison Abolition in America," *Wake Forest Law Review* (forthcoming).

50. Rachel E. Barkow, *The Politics of Decarceration* (Harvard University Press, 2019).

51. German Lopez, "Want to End Mass Incarceration? This Poll Should Worry You," Vox, September 7, 2016, https://www.vox.com/2016/9/7/12814504/mass-incarceration-poll.

52. Ibid.

53. Jason L. Riley, "San Francisco Has Become a Shoplifter's Paradise," *Wall Street Journal*, October 19, 2021, https://www.wsj.com/articles/san-francisco-shoplifters-theft-walgreens-decriminalized-11634678239.

54. Mallory Moench, "'Out of Control': Organized Crime Drives S.F. Shoplifting, Closing 17 Walgreens in Five Years," *San Fransisco Chronicle*, May 15, 2021, https://www.sfchronicle.com/local-politics/article/Out-of-control-Organized-crime-drives-S-F-16175755.php.

55. Atavia Reed, "Auburn Gresham Aldi Abruptly Closes, Leaving South Siders With 1 Less Grocery Store: 'It's One Hit After Another,'" Block Club Chicago, June 20, 2022, https://blockclubchicago.org/2022/06/20/auburn-gresham-aldi-abruptly-closes-leaving-south-siders-with-1-less-major-grocerits-one-hit-after-another/. The trend appears to be getting worse in Chicago. Walmart announced that four Chicago locations will be closing with four days' notice. Chris Tye, "Big Voids Will Emerge as Walmart Pulls Out of Chicago Neighborhoods, Community Leaders Say," CBS, April 12, 2023, https://www.cbsnews.com/chicago/news/big-voids-walmart-pulls-out-chicago-neighborhoods/.

56. Lauren Lewis, "Aldi Closes Store in Crime-Ridden Chicago Neighborhood Without Notice After 13 Years Blaming 'Repeated Burglaries,'" *Daily Mail*, June 21, 2022, https://www.dailymail.co.uk/news/article-10938217

/Aldi-closes-store-crime-ridden-Chi cago-neighbourhood-without-notice -blaming-repeated-burglaries.html.

57. Nathaniel Meyersohn, "Here's What Happens When a Neighborhood's Only Grocery Store Closes," CNN Business, July 1, 2020, https://www.cnn.com /2020/07/01/business/grocery-store-in equality-norfolk/index.html.

58. Will Glaser, "American 'Food Des- erts' Are Getting Worse. Here's How Technology Will Fix Them," Grabango, August 11, 2020, https://www.grabango .com/food-deserts/.

59. Annie E. Casey Foundation, "Food Des- erts in the United States," Annie E. Casey Foundation, February 13, 2021, https:// www.aecf.org/blog/exploring-americas -food-deserts.

60. Kelly M. Bowe et al., "The Intersection of Neighborhood Racial Segregation, Poverty, and Urbanicity and Its Impact on Food Store Availability in the United States," *Preventative Medicine* 58 (Janu- ary 2014): 33–39.

61. Aila Slisco, "Two-Thirds of American Voters Support Decriminalizing All Drugs: Poll," *Newsweek*, June 10, 2021, https://www.newsweek.com/two-thirds -american-voters-support-decriminaliz ing-all-drugs-poll-1599645.

62. "Prison Condition," Equal Justice Initia- tive, https://eji.org/issues/prison-condi tions/.

63. Christy Visher and John Eason, "A Better Path Forward for Criminal Jus- tice: Changing Prisons to Help People Change," Brookings Institution, April 2021, https://www.brookings.edu/re search/a-better-path-forward-for-crim inal-justice-changing-prisons-to-help -people-change/.

64. Office of the Inspector General, "Re- view of the Federal Bureau of Prisons' Monitoring of Contract Prisons," August 2016; Sean Bryant, "The Business Model of Private Prisons," Investopedia, Au- gust 25, 2021, https://www.investopedia

.com/articles/investing/062215/busi ness-model-private-prisons.asp.

65. See M. Keith Chen and Jesse M. Shapiro, "Do Harsher Prison Conditions Reduce Recidivism? A Discontinuity-Based Ap- proach," April 16, 2007, https://www .brown.edu/Research/Shapiro/pdfs /prison041607_web.pdf.

66. Dan M. Kahan, "What Do Alternative Sanctions Mean?" *The University of Chi- cago Law Review* 63, no. 2 (Spring 1996): 591–653.

67. Beatrix Lockwood and Nicole Lewis, "The Hidden Costs of Incarceration," The Marshall Project, December 17, 2019, https://www.themarshallproject .org/2019/12/17/the-hidden-cost-of -incarceration.

68. Robert E. Harlow, John M. Darley, and Paul H. Robinson, "The Severity of In- termediate Penal Sanction: A Psycho- physical Scaling Approach for Obtaining Community Perceptions," *Journal of Quantitative Criminology* 11, no. 1 (March 1995): 72.

69. Ibid., 71 and 86.

70. Ibid., 76.

71. United Nations Office on Drugs and Crime, "Executive Global Study on Ho- micide," 2019.

72. Barry Latzer, "It's Possible to Reduce Imprisonment and Crime Rates," *Wall Street Journal*, October 27, 2022, https://www.wsj.com/articles/its-pos sible-to-reduce-incarceration-and -crime-gps-ecarceration-parolee-pro bationer-prison-ankle-bracelet-privacy -offender-recidivism-11666896237

73. Paul H. Robinson and Jeffrey Seaman, "Electronic Prison: A Just Path to Decar- ceration" (forthcoming 2025).

74. David McNeill, "Life in Japan: The Softer Corners and Harder Edges of the Japa- nese Justice System," *The Mainichi*, April 3, 2022, https://mainichi.jp/english/ar ticles/20220402/p2a/00m/0op/017000c; Mari Kita, "Proxy Punishment: Conse- quences of Informal Sanctions Among

Families of Offenders in Japan," *Qualitative Criminology* 6, no. 1 (2018).

75. NCJRS 147416, "Commentary on the United Nations Standard Minimum Rules for Non-Custodial Measures (The Tokyo Rules)," National Institute of Justice, 1993, 1–39.

76. United Nations Office on Drugs and Crimes, "Handbook of Basic Principles and Promising Practices on Alternatives to Imprisonment," 2007, 41.

77. Policies of nonenforcement can extend even backward in time when prosecutors decide to exonerate convicted criminals based on dubious claims of innocence if it serves their ideological agenda. Thomas Hogan, "The Exoneration Hustle," *City Journal*, July 5, 2022, https://www.city-journal.org/article/the-exoneration-hustl.

78. Snejana Farberov, "Moment Shoplifter Struts Behind Counter of Bay Area Walgreens, Fills Huge Bag Full with Stolen Goods, Then Hurls BANANAS at Fellow Shopper Who Stood Up to Him," *Daily Mail*, March 4, 2022, https://www.dailymail.co.uk/news/article-10578235/Shoplifter-struts-counter-Bay-Area-Walgreens-fills-bag-stolen-goods.html; Madeline Wells, "A Second Downtown San Francisco Walgreens to Close This Month," SF Gate, February 10, 2022, https://www.sfgate.com/bayarea/article/Another-San-Francisco-Walgreens-closing-16848319.php. These policies have forced companies like Walgreens to face unprecedented security challenges; Walgreen reported that in 2021, retail theft in San Francisco was five times the chain average, and security costs were forty-six times the chain average. The problem has been so pervasive that the company has had to close ten of its stores in San Francisco since 2019, and seven since November 2021. Riley, "San Francisco Has Become a Shoplifter's Paradise."

79. Thomas Fuller, "Voters in San Francisco Topple the City's Progressive District Attorney, Chesa Boudin," *New York Times*, June 8, 2022, https://www.nytimes.com/2022/06/07/us/politics/chesa-boudin-recall-san-francisco.html; Joshua Rhett Miller, "Replacement Named for Ousted San Francisco DA Chesa Boudin," *New York Post*, July 8, 2022, https://nypost.com/2022/07/08/brooke-jenkins-replacing-ousted-san-francisco-da-chesa-boudin/.

80. John E. Foster, "Charges to Be Declined: Legal Challenges and Policy Debates Surrounding Non-Prosecution Initiatives in Massachusetts," *Boston College Law Review* 60, no. 9 (2019): 2534.

81. There is reason to doubt progressive prosecutors who enact policies of non-prosecution are truly representing the people, however. For example, Chesa Boudin was recalled in 2022. "When Mr. Boudin was elected in 2019 he received only 36 percent of the vote in the first round of voting. In the third round of that election, under the city's ranked choice system, he ultimately inched ahead of his main rival for the job, Suzy Loftus, by a few thousand votes." Fuller, "Voters in San Francisco Topple the City's Progressive District Attorney, Chesa Boudin." Additionally, primary systems in other cities allow more extreme candidates to win office who do not necessarily represent the beliefs of the majority of city residents.

82. Heaven LaMartz, "Progressive Prosecution—Fewer Felonies or More Murders?" National Criminal Justice Association, September 22, 2022, https://www.ncja.org/crimeandjusticenews/the-effects-of-progressive-prosecution.

83. Michelle Bolger, "Predicting Arrest Probability Across Time: An Exploration of Competing Risk Perspectives," *Journal of Criminal Justice* 59 (November–December 2018): 92.

84. See, for example, Rand Corporation, "The Relationship Between Firearm Prevalence and Violent Crime," March 2, 2018, https://www.rand.org/research

/gun-policy/analysis/essays/firearm
-prevalence-violent-crime.html; "Homicide, Harvard Injury Control Research
Center," Harvard T. H. Chan School of
Public Health, https://www.hsph.har
vard.edu/hicrc/firearms-research/guns
-and-death/.

85. Daniel E. Martínez et al., "Providing
Sanctuary or Fostering Crime? A Review
of the Research on 'Sanctuary Cities' and
Crime," Sociology Compass, 2017.

86. Kassra A. R. Oskooii et al., "Partisan Attitudes toward Sanctuary Cities:
Asymmetrical Effects of Political Knowledge," *Politics & Policy* 46, no. 6 (December 2018): 951–84.

87. The eleven states are California, Colo-
rado, Connecticut, Illinois, Massachu-
setts, New Jersey, New Mexico, New
York, Oregon, Vermont, and Washing-
ton; see Jessica M. Vaughan and Bryan
Griffith, "Map: Sanctuary Cities, Coun-
ties, and States," Center for Immigration
Studies, March 22, 2021, https://cis.org
/Map-Sanctuary-Cities-Counties-and
-States.

88. Raina Bhatt, "Pushing an End to Sanctuary Cities: Will It Happen?" *Michigan
Journal of Race & Law* 22, no. 1 (2016):
144.

89. Vaughan and Griffith, "Map."

90. Bill McCarthy, "Fact-Checking Trump's
State of the Union Claim on Sanctuary
Cities, Criminals," POLITIFACT, February 5, 2020, https://www.politifact.com
/factchecks/2020/feb/05/donald-trump
/fact-checking-trumps-state-union
-claim-sanctuary-c/.

91. Erica Turret, Chelsea Parsons, and Adam
Skaggs "Second Amendment Sanctuaries: A Legally Dubious Protest Movement," *The Journal of Law, Medicine &
Ethics* 48, no. 4 (2021): 105.

92. Brady, "So-Called 'Second Amendment
Sanctuaries' Are Troubling Attacks on
Gun Safety Laws Across the Country,"
2019, https://www.bradyunited.org/act
/second-amendment-sanctuaries.

93. The Wall Street Journal Editorial Board,
"Second Amendment 'Sanctuaries,'"
Wall Street Journal, December 29, 2019,
https://www.wsj.com/articles/second
-amendment-sanctuaries-11577661926.

94. Bethany Blankley, "61% of U.S. Counties Now 'Second Amendment Sanctuaries,'" The Center Square, July 4,
2021, https://www.thecentersquare.com
/national/61-of-u-s-counties-now-sec
ond-amendment-sanctuaries/article
_12565326-d82b-11eb-8b83-8713ae
288961.html. But note that it's unclear how many of these counties actually have "effective" sanctuary laws.
See, for example, Tim Dodson, "Second
Amendment 'Sanctuary' Resolutions
'Have No Legal Effect' in Virginia, Attorney General Mark Herring Writes
in Advisory Opinion," *The Bristol
Herald Courier*, December 20, 2019,
https://heraldcourier.com/news/local
/second-amendment-sanctuary-resolu
tions-have-no-legal-effect-in-virginia
/article_3f618f70-234b-11ea-9704-ff40
e2b891d2.html.

95. Shawn E. Fields, "Second Amendment
Sanctuaries," *Northwestern Univer-
sity Law Review* 115, no. 2 (2020): 439.
Also see, for example, Luke X. Martin,
"New 2nd Amendment Protections in
Missouri Split Law Enforcement," NPR,
June 28, 2021, https://www.npr.org
/2021/06/28/1010320106/new-2nd
-amendment-protections-in-missour
-split-law-enforcement.

96. North Dakota Office of the Governor,
"Burgum Designates North Dakota as a
'Second Amendment Sanctuary State,'
Signs Bill Protecting Gun Rights," April
26, 2021, https://www.governor.nd.gov
/news/burgum-designates-north-dakota
-second-amendment-sanctuary-state
-signs-bills-protecting-gun; Office of the
Texas Governor, Greg Abbot, "Governor Abbott Signs Second Amendment
Legislation into Law," June 17, 2021,
https://gov.texas.gov/news/post/gover
nor-abbott-signs-second-amendment

-legislation-into-law-2021; "Missouri Governor Michael L. Parson, Governor Parson Signs HB 85 Establishing Second Amendment Preservation Act," June 14, 2021, https://governor.mo.gov /press-releases/archive/governor-par son-signs-hb-85-establishing-second -amendment-preservation-act.

97. Shannon Najmabadi, "Some Red States Weigh Bans on Enforcing U.S. Gun Laws," *Wall Street Journal*, February 26, 2023, https://www.wsj.com/articles /some-red-states-weigh-bans-on-en forcing-u-s-gun-laws-201e4719.

98. Emma Colton, "California 'Sanctuary City' Declares Itself a Constitutional Republic to Fight COVID Mandates," Fox News, November 15, 2021, https:// www.foxnews.com/politics/oroville -california-city-council-votes-constitu tional-republic-city-mandates.

99. Sarah Holder, "Local Officials Beef Up Abortion Sanctuary Cities," Bloomberg, June 24, 2022, https://www.bloomberg .com/news/articles/2022-06-24/from -washington-d-c-to-seattle-cities-es tablish-abortion-sanctuaries.

100. Megan Messerly, "Austin Pushing to Effectively Decriminalize Abortion Ahead of Ruling on Roe," Politico, May 30, 2022, https://www.politico.com/news /2022/05/30/austin-decriminalize -abortion-roe-00035791.

101. United States Attorney's Office: Southern District of California, "U.S. Attorney Highlights Danger of Sanctuary Laws; Urges Change to Enhance Public Safety," February 10, 2020, https://www .justice.gov/usao-sdca/pr/us-attorney -highlights-danger-sanctuary-laws -urges-change-enhance-public-safety.

102. Marta Ascherio, "Do Sanctuary Policies Increase Crime? Contrary Evidence from a County-Level Investigation in the United States," *Social Science Research* 106 (August 2022).

103. George Copplo, "States that Elect Their Chief Prosecutors," OLR Research Report, February 24, 2003, https://www .cga.ct.gov/2003/rpt/2003-R-0231.htm.

104. Bruce A. Green and Rebecca Roiphe, "When Prosecutors Politick: Progressive Law Enforcers Then and Now," *Journal of Criminal Law & Criminology* 110, no. 4 (2020): 719–68.

105. Josh Christensen, "Report: Soros Prosecutors Run Half of America's Largest Jurisdictions," *The Washington Free Beacon*, June 8, 2022, https:// freebeacon.com/democrats/report-so ros-prosecutors-run-half-of-americas -largest-jurisdictions/.

106. Ibid.

107. Alyssa Shea Daley and Jacob Carruthers, "Judicial Review of Prosecutorial Blanket Declination Policies," *Ohio State Journal of Criminal Law* 20, no. 1 (2022): 179–207.

108. Eric Burk, "Loudoun County Board of Supervisors Criticizes Commonwealth's Attorney for Handling of Domestic Violence Cases," *The Tennessee Star*, March 30, 2021.

109. Julie Carey, "Mother Says System Failed Her Daughter After Domestic Violence Killing in Sterling," NBC, February 15, 2022, https://www.nbcwashington .com/news/local/northern-virginia /mother-says-system-failed-her-daugh ter-after-domestic-violence-killing-in -sterling/2972705/.

110. Matthew Barakat, "Democrat Bideraj Concedes in Hard-Fought Northern Virginia Prosecutor Race," AP News, November 15, 2023, https://apnews .com/article/virginia-loudoun-pro secutor-buta-biberaj-anderson-d6c e394a14e5fafb396d37992048d7a5.

111. See Thomas P. Hogan, "De-Prosecution and Death: A Synthetic Control Analysis of the Impact of De-Prosecution on Homicides," *Criminology and Public Policy* 21, no. 3 (2022): 491.

112. Edwin Meese III, "Prosecutorial Malpractice: Progressive Prosecutors, Public Safety, and Felony Outcomes," Law Enforcement Legal Defense Fund, 4.

113. Glenn Minnis, "Report: Foxx Dismissed 30% of Felony Charges in First Three Years as State's Attorney," *Chicago City Wire*, August 14, 2021, https://chicago citywire.com/stories/606581092-re port-foxx-dismissed-30-of-felony -charges-in-first-three-years-as-state -s-attorney. In fact, Foxx has dropped 9.5 percent of cases involving felony sex crimes and 8.1 percent of homicide cases. See David Jackson et al., "Kim Foxx Drops More Felony Cases as Cook County State's Attorney than Her Predecessor, Tribune Analysis Shows," *Chicago Tribune*, August 10, 2020, https://www.chicagotribune.com/in vestigations/ct-kim-foxx-felony -charges-cook-county-20200810-ld vrmqvv6bd3hpsuqha4duehmu-story .html.

114. Charles D. Stimson and Zack Smith, "'Progressive' Prosecutors Sabotage the Rule of Law, Raise Crime Rates, and Ignore Victims," The Heritage Foundation Legal Memorandum No. 275, October 29, 2020, 25.

115. Chicago Police, "2021 Ends as Chicago's Deadliest Year in a Quarter Century," NBC 5 Chicago, January 1, 2022, https://www.nbcchicago.com/news /local/2021-ends-as-chicagos -deadliest-year-in-a-quarter-century /2719307/.

116. Thomas P. Hogan, "De-Prosecution and Death: A Synthetic Control Analysis of the Impact of De-Prosecution on Homicides," *Criminology and Public Policy* 21, no. 3 (2022): 492.

117. Thomas Hogan, "Death and De-Prosecution in Philadelphia," *City Journal*, May 13, 2021, https://www.city-journal .org/article/death-and-de-prosecution -in-philadelphia#:~:text=In%202021 %2C%20the%20body%20count ,the%20authority%20to%20de%2D prosecute.

118. Michael D'Onofrio, "Philadelphia Homicides Surge Hit 30-Year High in 2020," *Philadelphia Tribune*, January 4, 2021, https://www.phillytrib.com /news/local_news/philadelphia-homi cides-surge-hit-30-year-high-in-2020 /article_0b9b8851-5aa1-5517-8b5a -5b93786fe7de.html.

119. The Editors, "To Stop Philly's Cycle of Violence, D.A. Krasner Must Prosecute Gun Crimes," Broad and Liberty, August 8, 2021, https://broadandliberty .com/2021/08/08/stop-phillys-cycle-of -violence-d-a-krasner-must-prosecute -gun-crimes/.

120. Hogan, "Death and De-Prosecution in Philadelphia."

121. In 2022 impeachment proceeding were opened against Krasner. The impeachment effort is headed by State Representative John Lawrence: "In light of the city's crisis, it would be dereliction of duty if we did not take action." Alejandro A. Alvarez, "Mothers of Homicide Victims Testify During First Day of Hearings in Effort to Impeach DA Larry Krasner," *Philadelphia Inquirer*, September 29, 2022, https://www.inquirer .com/news/philadelphia/philadelphia -district-attorney-larry-krasner-im peachment-hearing-20220929.html.

122. D'Onofrio, "Philadelphia Homicides Surge Hit 30-Year High in 2020."

123. Larry Platt, "The Buck Stops Elsewhere," *The Philadelphia Citizen*, April 9, 2021, https://thephiladelphiacitizen .org/larry-krasner-accountability/.

124. Ibid.

125. Claudia Vargas, "A Record 559 Murders in Philly in 2021 Scrapes Scars into the City's Psyche," NBC 10 Philadelphia, December 31, 2021, https:// www.nbcphiladelphia.com/news /local/a-record-murders-in-philly-in -2021-scrapes-scars-into-the-citys -psyche/3093658/.

126. United States Attorney's Office, Eastern District of Pennsylvania, "Feds Step Up Focused Effort to Deter Violent Crime in Philadelphia," January 21, 2022, https://www.justice.gov/usao-edpa/pr

/feds-step-focused-effort-deter-violent
-crime-philadelphia.

127. Cleve R. Wootson, "The White DA, the Black Ex-Mayor and a Harsh Debate on Crime," *Washington Post*, December 28, 2021, https://www.washingtonpost.com/politics/2021/12/28/krasner-nutter-philadelphia-crime/.

128. Jason L. Riley, "The Pursuit of 'Social Justice' Is Getting People Killed," *Wall Street Journal*, July 12, 2022, https://www.wsj.com/articles/the-pursuit-of-social-justice-killed-testing-stop-frisk-gun-policy-biden-administration-11657658420.

129. "Philadelphia County," 2020 Criminal, The Unified Judicial System of Pennsylvania, https://www.pacourts.us/courts.

130. Hogan, "The Exoneration Hustle."

131. Ibid.

132. Isaac Avilucea, "Pennsylvania Senate Postpones Krasner Impeachment Trial Indefinitely," *Axios Philadelphia*, January 12, 2023, https://www.axios.com/local/philadelphia/2023/01/12/larry-krasner-impeachment-trial-postponed.

133. Scott Calvert, "Cherelle Parker Wins Democratic Nomination in Philadelphia Mayoral Primary," *Wall Street Journal*, May 16, 2023, https://www.wsj.com/articles/philadelphia-democratic-mayoral-primaries-elections-voting-d26de88a.

134. Maura Ewing, "Philadelphia's Progressive Movement Aims for the Mayor's Office," Bolts, May 2, 2023, https://boltsmag.org/philadelphias-progressive-movement-aims-for-the-mayors-office/; also "Mayoral Election in Philadelphia, Pennsylvania (2023)," Ballotpedia, May 16, 2023, https://ballotpedia.org/Mayoral_election_in_Philadelphia,_Pennsylvania_(2023).

135. Elizabeth McCormick, "Federal Anti-Sanctuary Law: A Failed Approach to Immigration Enforcement and a Poor Substitute for Reform," *Lewis and Clark Law Review* 20, no. 1 (2016): 192–93. While the family members' legal case was ultimately lost because a causal link could not be proved in court, the families believed that their loved ones would be alive had their murderers been previously deported.

136. Good Morning America, "Cop Killing Sparks Immigration Debate," ABC News, September 25, 2006, https://abcnews.go.com/GMA/story?id=2487004.

137. For example, the Trump White House condoned sanctuary cities in a statement that said in part, "Sanctuary cities . . . block their jails from turning over criminal aliens to Federal authorities for deportation." Conservative media outlet Breitbart characterized sanctuary cities as "the counties and cities that refuse to hand over criminal illegal aliens to ICE to be detained and deported from the US. Instead, these illegal aliens are released back into American communities." Kit Johnson, "The Mythology of Sanctuary Cities," *Southern California Interdisciplinary Law Journal* 28 (2019): 589–90.

138. Joel Shannon, "'Second Amendment Sanctuary' Movement Called a 'Childish Pity Party' by Democratic Governor," *USA Today*, February 28, 2019, https://www.usatoday.com/story/news/politics/2019/02/28/new-mexico-governor-criticizes-second-amendment-sanctuary-movement/3022175002/.

139. Ibid.

140. Vaughan and Griffith, "Map."

141. Helen Ubiñas, "Angry Families of Murder Victims Protest DA Larry Krasner," *Philadelphia Inquirer*, last modified October 11, 2019, https://www.inquirer.com/opinion/helen-ubinas-larry-krasner-murder-crime-exoneration-district-attorney-philadelphia-20191011.html.

142. Ibid.

143. Katie Meyer, "As Critics Slam Him on Gun Violence, Philly DA Larry Krasner Looks Past Election to Next Term," WHYY, October 27, 2021, https://whyy.org/articles/as-critics-slam-him-on

-gun-violence-philly-da-larry-krasner
-looks-past-election-to-next-term/.

144. Platt, "The Buck Stops Elsewhere."

145. Daniel Duane, "Everyone in San Francisco Has Something to Say About Chesa Boudin," *New York Magazine*, August 3, 2021, https://nymag.com /intelligencer/2021/08/chesa-boudin -recall-san-francisco.html.

146. "San Francisco Population," PopulationU.com, https://www.populationu .com/cities/san-francisco-population #:~:text=San%20Francisco%20popula tion%20in%202022,fourth%20popu lous%20in%20California%20state; "Chesa Boudin recall, San Francisco, California (2021–2022," Ballotpedia, https://ballotpedia.org/Chesa_Boudin _recall,_San_Francisco,_California _(2021-2022).

147. Astead W. Herndon, "They Wanted to Roll Back Tough-on-Crime Policies. Then Violent Crime Surged," *New York Times*, February 18, 2022, https://www .nytimes.com/2022/02/18/us/politics /prosecutors-midterms-crime.html.

148. Kimberley A. Strassel, "The 2022 Referendum on Crime," *Wall Street Journal*, July 14, 2022, https://www.wsj .com/articles/the-2022-referendum -on-crime-alvin-bragg-justice-prose cute-violence-midterms-11657836128.

149. Kevin Held, Chris Hayes, and Joey Schneider, "St Louis Circuit Attorney Kim Gardner Resigns, Effective June 1," Fox2, May 4, 2023, https://fox2now .com/news/missouri/st-louis-circuit -attorney-kim-gardner-resigns-effec tive-june-1/.

150. McCormick, "Federal Anti-Sanctuary Law," 178–79.

151. Adam Klasfeld, "Sanctuary States, City Lose Appeal on Federal Grant Cuts," Courthouse News Service, February 26, 2020, https://www.courthousenews .com/second-circuit-lets-doj-withhold -funding-to-sanctuary-states-and-city/.

152. Burk, "Loudoun County Board of Supervisors Criticizes Commonwealth's Attorney for Handling of Domestic Violence Cases."

153. Zach Williams, "How Manhattan DA Alvin Bragg Could Get Removed from Office," *New York Post*, June 8, 2022, https://nypost.com/2022/06/08/how -manhattan-nyc-da-alvin-bragg-could -get-removed-from-office/.

154. Tierney Sneed and Steve Contorno, "Judge Criticizes DeSantis Firing of Democratic Prosecutor But Declines to Reinstate Andrew Warren," CNN, January 20, 2023, https://www.cnn .com/2023/01/20/politics/florida-ron -desantis-democratic-prosecutor-law suit/index.html; Laura Kusisto, "Liberal Prosecutors Tussle with State Officials over Abortion, Drug Crimes," *Wall Street Journal*, May 2, 2023, https:// www.wsj.com/articles/liberal-pros ecutors-tussle-with-state-officials-over -abortion-drug-crimes-6fd04e64.

155. Alabama (Ala. Code § 36-15-14); Arizona (Ariz. Rev. Stat. Ann. § 41-193(A) (2)); California (Cal. Const. art. V § 13); Hawaii (Haw. Rev. Stat. Ann. § 46-1.5(17)); Iowa (Iowa code ann. § 13.2(1) (b)); Maine (ME. Rev. Stat. Ann. Tit 5, § 199); Michigan (In re Watson, 291 N.W. 652, 655 (Mich. 1940)); Montana (Mont. Code. Ann. § 2-15-501(5)); Nebraska (Neb. Rev. Stat. § 84-203); Nevada (Nev. Rev. Stat. Ann. § 228.120(3)); New Hampshire (N.H. Rev. Stat. Ann. § 7:11); New Jersey (N.J. Stat. Ann. § 52:17B-107); New Mexico (N.M. Stat. Ann. § 8-5-3); North Dakota (N.D. Cent. Code. Ann. § 54-12-03); Oklahoma (Okla. Stat. Ann. Tit 74 § 18b(A) (3)); South Dakota (S.D. Codified Laws § 1-11-1(2)); Vermont (3 V. S. A. § 152 & 157); Washington (Tyler Yeargain, "Discretion Versus Supersession: Calibrating the Power Balance Between Local Prosecutors and State Officials," *Emory Law Journal* 68, no. 1 [2018]: 112); Alaska, Rhode Island, and Delaware do not have local prosecutors and

the attorneys general are responsible for criminal prosecutions in the state.

156. As in Arkansas, Connecticut, Illinois, Indiana, Massachusetts, Mississippi, Missouri, North Carolina, and West Virginia.

157. Colorado (Colo. Rev. Stat. Ann. § 24-31-101(1)(a) "when required to do so by the governor"); Florida (Fla. Stat. Ann. § 27. 14(1)) "the Governor determines that the ends of justice would be served"); Georgia (GA. Const. Ann. Art. V, § 3, paragraph IV "when required by the Governor"); Idaho (Idaho Code § 31-2227(3) "when in the judgment of the governor the penal laws of this state are not being enforced as written"); Kansas (Kan. Stat. Ann. § 75-702 "when required by the governor or either branch of the legislature"); Kentucky (Ky. Rev. Stat. Ann. § 15.200(1)); Louisiana (LA. Const. art. IV, § 8 "when authorized by the court which would have original jurisdiction"); Maryland (MD. Const. art. V, § 3(a)(2) "which the General Assembly by law or joint resolution, or the Governor"); Minnesota (Minn. Stat. Ann. § 8.01 "upon request of the county attorney" or "whenever the governor shall so request"); New York (N.Y. Exec. Laws § 63(2) "whenever required by the governor"); Ohio (Ohio Rev. Code §109.02 "upon the written request of the governor") Oregon (OR. Rev. Stat. Ann. § 180.070(1)); Pennsylvania (PA. Stat. and Const. Stat. Ann. § 732-205(a)(4) "The Attorney General may petition the court having jurisdiction"); South Carolina (S. C. Code of Laws tit. 1, ch. 7, art. 1, § 1-7-40 "when required by the Governor or either branch of the General Assembly"); Tennessee (TN. Const. art. VI § 5 "the court has the power to appoint an attorney pro tempore in all cases where the attorney for any district fails or refuses to attend and prosecute according to the law"); Texas (Tex. Code Crim. Proc.

art. 207—the court may appoint an attorney from any county/district, or an attorney from the state or an assistant attorney general, "whenever an attorney for the state is disqualified to at in any case or proceeding, is absent from the county or district, or is otherwise unable to perform the duties of the attorney's office, or in any instance where there is no attorney for the state"); Utah (Utah Code Ann. § 67-5-1(8) "when required by the public service or directed by the governor" the attorney general may assist a local prosecutor in discharging his duties); Virginia (VA. Code Ann. § 2.2-511 "unless specifically requested by the Governor"); Wisconsin (Yeargain, "Discretion Versus Supersession," 119); Wyoming (WYO. Stat. Ann. § 9-1-603(c) "at the request of the board of county commissioners of the county involved or of the district judge of the judicial district involved"). See, for example, Saldano v. The State of Texas 232 S.W.3d 77 (2007).

158. NCJ 13878, "The Prosecution Function: Local Prosecutors and the Attorney General," US Department of Justice, 1974.

159. Mariah Timms, "Tennessee Lawmakers Approve New Check on Powers of 'Rouge' Local Prosecutors," *The Tennessean*, October 28, 2021, https://www.tennessean.com/story/news/politics/2021/10/28/tennessee-lawmakers-advance-bill-check-powers-local-prosecutors/6177872001/.

160. Attorney General's Office, "The Government of the UK Office of the Attorney General," last accessed April 26, 2023, https://www.gov.uk/government/ministers/attorney-general#:~:text=Victoria%20Prentis%20was%20appointed%20Attorney,2022%20to%2025%20October%202022.

161. Elwyn Jones, "The Office of the Attorney General," *The Cambridge Law Journal* 27, no. 1 (1969): 43–53.

CHAPTER 17

1. See chapter 1, section C; chapter 2; chapter 3, section C; chapter 5, note 31; chapter 6, note 8; chapter 7, note 156; chapter 9, notes 22 and 29; chapter 12, note 50; chapter 14, notes 106, 110, and 130; chapter 15, notes 2, 5, 181, 207, and 220; chapter 16, notes 14, 56, and 117.

2. See chapter 1, notes 108 and 109; chapter 7, note 13 and 148; chapter 14, notes 106, 196, 219, and 221; chapter 15, note 1, 185, and 189; chapter 16, note 60 and 125.

3. Chapter 14, note 143.

4. Rafael Mangual, "Democrats Champion 'Equity' But Shrug as Radical Criminal Justice Reforms Hit Minorities the Hardest," Fox News, February 2, 2023, https://www.foxnews.com/opinion/democrats-champion-equity-shrug-radical-criminal-justice-reforms-minorities-hardest.

5. "These Are Nine Stories from America's Homicide Crisis," *Washington Post*, November 27, 2022, https://www.washingtonpost.com/nation/interactive/2022/america-homicide-victim-stories/.

6. Chapter 1, note 108.

7. Chapter 1, note 109.

8. Richard Florida, "The High Cost of Fear in America," Bloomberg, September 30, 2015, https://www.bloomberg.com/news/articles/2015-09-30/how-america-s-fear-of-crime-leads-to-bad-policy-decisions. Also see Matthew Yglesias, "A Really Boring Way to Solve More Serious Crime," Slow Boring, August 31, 2021, https://www.slowboring.com/p/a-really-boring-way-to-solve-more.

9. "FBI's National Crime Data Found to Be Flawed, Manipulated," *Prison Legal News*, April 15, 2013, https://www.prisonlegalnews.org/news/2013/apr/15/fbis-national-crime-data-found-to-be-flawed-manipulated/.

10. Ibid.

11. Michael D. Maltz, NCJ 215343, "Analysis of Missingness in UCR Crime Data," Department of Justice, 2006.

12. "Bureau of Justice Statistics: Data to Keep Our Communities Safe," https://www.amstat.org/docs/default-source/amstat-documents/pol-bjs-priorities-2021plus.pdf.

13. Mitchell Langbert, "Homogenous: Political Affiliations of Elite Liberal Arts Faculty," Academic Questions, Summer 2018, https://www.nas.org/academic-questions/31/2/homogenous_the_political_affiliations_of_elite_liberal_arts_college_faculty

14. Ibid.

15. John Paul Wright and Matt DeLisi, "What Criminologists Don't Say, and Why," *City Journal*, Summer 2017, https://www.city-journal.org/article/what-criminologists-dont-say-and-why.

16. Ibid.

17. Ibid.

18. See Greg Lukianoff and Jonathan Haidt, *The Coddling of the American Mind: How Good Intentions and Bad Ideas Are Setting Up a Generation for Failure* (Penguin Books, 2018).

19. See chapter 15.

20. See chapter 14, note 221.

21. Kyle Peyton, Michael Sierra-Arévalo, and David G. Rand, "A Field Experiment on Community Policing and Police Legitimacy," PNAS, October 1, 2019.

22. See chapter 5, section B; chapter 6, notes 30, 36, and 60; chapter 7, notes 38, 51, 159, and 160; chapter 8, note 64; chapter 9, notes 4, 7, and 91–94; chapter 10, notes 6–7, 15–16, 38–39, and 64; chapter 11, notes 22–24; chapter 12, notes 43 and 63; chapter 13, notes 36, 38, 43, 46, 48, and 72; chapter 16, section C.

23. Chapter 1, sections D and F.

24. See chapter 2, note 20; chapter 12, section C, "Reforms."

25. Paul Robinson, "Symposium on Victim's Rights (Leadership Issues in Criminal Justice)," *McGeorge Law Review* 33 (2002): 749–58.

26. Notice, however, that we do support the use of restorative justice processes that do directly involved both victim and offender, under certain circumstances. See Paul H. Robinson, "Restorative Pro-

cesses & Doing Justice," *University of St. Thomas Law Journal* 3, no. 3 (2006): 421; Paul H. Robinson, "The Virtues of Restorative Processes, The Vices of Restorative Justice," *Utah Law Review* (2003): 37–88.

27. See chapter 2; chapter 7; chapter 8; chapter 9.
28. Chapter 2, note 109.
29. Chapter 2, note 123.
30. Chapter 2, section D, "A Closer Look at the Doctrines of the Legality Principle."
31. Chapter 7, section D, "State Diversity in Collection of DNA."
32. One of us was the only dissenting commissioner to the original USSC Guidelines. That dissent did not contest important value of sentencing guidelines generally but rather reflected a view that the federal guidelines could and should been drafted in a more workable in principle form. See Paul H. Robinson, Dissenting View of Commissioner Paul H. Robinson to the Promulgation of Sentencing Guidelines by the United States Sentencing Commission, 52 Fed. Reg. 181 21 (1987), reprinted in *Crim. L. Rep.* 41, no. 3174 (1987); Dissenting View of Commissioner Paul H. Robinson to the Proposed Sentencing Guidelines for United States Courts, 52 Federal Register, 1987, at 3986–88, reprinted in *Journal of Criminal Law and Criminology* 77: 1112–25.

Selected Bibliography

Adegbile, Debo P. "Policing through an American Prism." *Yale LJ* 126 (2016): 2222.

Ames, Nancy L. "The Impact of the Speedy Trial Act on Investigation and Prosecution of Federal Criminal Cases." US Department of Justice, Office of Legal Policy, June 1985. https://www.ojp.gov/pdffiles1/Digitization/98285NCJRS.pdf.

Anderson, James M., Jeffrey R. Kling, and Kate Stith. "Measuring Interjudge Sentencing Disparity: Before and After the Federal Sentencing Guidelines." *The Journal of Law and Economics* 42, no. S1 (1999): 271–308.

Armour, Marilyn Peterson. "Experiences of Covictims of Homicide: Implications for Research and Practice." *Trauma, Violence, & Abuse* 3, no. 2 (2002): 109–24.

Ascherio, Marta. "Do Sanctuary Policies Increase Crime? Contrary Evidence from a County-Level Investigation in the United States." *Social Science Research* 106 (2022): 102743.

Atkins, Raymond A., and Paul H. Rubin. "Effects of Criminal Procedure on Crime Rates: Mapping Out the Consequences of the Exclusionary Rule." In *Economics, Law and Individual Rights*, edited by Hugo Mialon and Paul Rubin, 238–63. Routledge, 2008.

Auxier, Brooke, and Lee Rainie, "Key Takeaways on Americans' Views about Privacy, Surveillance and Data-Sharing." Pew Research Center, November 15, 2019. https://www.pewresearch.org/fact-tank/2019/11/15/key-takeaways-on-americans-views-about-privacy-surveillance-and-data-sharing/.

Baer, Miriam Hechler. "Cooperation's Cost." *Wash. UL Rev.* 88 (2010): 903.

Baradaran Baughman, Shima. "How Effective Are Police? The Problem of Clearance Rates and Criminal Accountability." *Ala. L. Rev.* 72 (2020): 47.

Bar-Gill, Oren, and Barry Friedman. "Taking Warrants Seriously." *Nw. UL Rev.* 106 (2012): 1609.

Barkow, Rachel E. "Promise or Peril?: The Political Path of Prison Abolition in America." *Wake Forest L. Rev.* 58 (2023): 245.

Barnett, Randy E. "Resolving the Dilemma of the Exclusionary Rule: An Application of Restitutive Principles of Justice." *Emory LJ* 32 (1983): 937.

Barno, Matt, Deyanira Nevárez Martínez, and Kirk R. Williams. "Exploring Alternatives to Cash Bail: An Evaluation of Orange County's Pretrial Assessment and Release Supervision (PARS) Program." *American Journal of Criminal Justice* 45 (2020): 363–78.

Bastomski, Sara, and Marina Duane. "Losing a Loved One to Homicide: What We Know About Homicide Co-Victims from Research and Practice Evidence." Center for Victim Research, July 2019. https://justiceresearch.dspacedirect.org/server/api/core/bitstreams/879bb0ce-3fc7-4215-b2ba-68dc3bae9090/content.

Beck, Allen. "Race and Ethnicity of Violent Crime Offenders and Arrestees, 2018." US Department of Justice, Bureau of Justice Statistics, January 2021, https://bjs.ojp.gov/content/pub/pdf/revcoa18.pdf.

Benton, Grace. "The Legality of Sanctuary Cities." *Geo. Immigr. LJ* 33 (2018): 139.

Bhatt, Raina. "Pushing an End to Sanctuary Cities: Will It Happen." *Mich. J. Race & L.* 22 (2016): 139.

Bowers, Josh, and Paul H. Robinson. "Perceptions of Fairness and Justice: The Shared Aims & Occasional Conflicts of Legitimacy and Moral Credibility." *Wake Forest Law Review* 47 (2012): 11–13.

Bradley, Craig M. "Exclusionary Rule in Germany." *Harv. L. Rev.* 96 (1982): 1032.

Braga, Anthony A., and Desiree Dusseault. "Can Homicide Detectives Improve Homicide Clearance Rates?" *Crime & Delinquency* 64, no. 3 (2018): 283–315.

Braga, Anthony A., Brandon Turchan, and Lisa Barao. "The Influence of Investigative Resources on Homicide Clearances." *Journal of Quantitative Criminology* 35 (2019): 337–64.

Brantingham, P. Jeffrey, and Craig D. Uchida. "Public Cooperation and the Police: Do Calls-for-Service Increase After Homicides?" *Journal of Criminal Justice* 73 (2021): 101785.

Bretgoltz, Milana, Albert Ford, and Alicia Serrani. "An Absolute Power, or a Power Absolutely in Need of Reform? Proposals to Reform the Presidential Pardon Power." 2021. https://ir.lawnet.fordham.edu/cgi/viewcontent.cgi?article=2106&context=faculty_scholarship.

Brown, Darryl K. "Permitting Post-Miranda Questioning in Exchange for Regulating Interrogation Tactics." *Tex. Tech L. Rev.* 54 (2021): 1.

Browning, John. "# Snitches get stitches: Witness Intimidation in the Age of Facebook and Twitter." *Pace L. Rev.* 35 (2014): 192.

Browning, Lana M., Mara Merlino, and Johnathon Sharp. "Citizen Journalism and Public Cynicism Toward Police in the USA." *Journal of Police and Criminal Psychology* 36 (2021): 372–85.

Brunson, Rod K., and Brian A. Wade. "'Oh hell no, we don't talk to police': Insights on the Lack of Cooperation in Police Investigations of Urban Gun Violence." *Criminology & Public Policy* 18, no. 3 (2019): 623–48.

Carling, Duncan. "Less Privacy Please, We're British: Investigating Crime with DNA in the UK and the US." *Hastings Int'l & Comp. L. Rev.* 31 (2008): 487.

Carlsmith, Kevin M. "On Justifying Punishment: The Discrepancy between Words and Actions." *Social Justice Research* 21 (2008): 119–37.

Carlsmith, Kevin M., John M. Darley, and Paul H. Robinson. "Why Do We Punish? Deterrence and Just Deserts as Motives for Punishment." *Journal of Personality and Social Psychology* 83, no. 2 (2002): 284.

Carpenter v. United States, 138 S. Ct. 2206 (2018).

Cassell, Paul G. "Explaining the Recent Homicide Spikes in US Cities: The 'Minneapolis Effect' and the Decline in Proactive Policing." *Federal Sentencing Reporter* 33, nos. 1–2 (2020): 83–127.

Cassell, Paul G. "Miranda's Social Costs: An Empirical Reassessment." *Nw. UL Rev.* 90 (1995): 387.

Cassell, Paul G. "The Mysterious Creation of Search and Seizure Exclusionary Rules Under State Constitutions: The Utah Example." *Utah L. Rev.* (1993): 751.

Cassell, Paul G. "Tradeoffs between Wrongful Convictions and Wrongful Acquittals: Understanding and Avoiding the Risks." *Seton Hall L. Rev.* 48 (2017): 1435.

Cassell, Paul G., and Richard Fowles. "Does Bail Reform Increase Crime? An Empirical Assessment of the Public Safety Implications of Bail Reform in Cook County, Illinois." *Wake Forest L. Rev.* 55 (2020): 933.

Cassell, Paul G., and Richard Fowles. "Handcuffing the Cops—A Thirty-Year Perspective on Miranda's Harmful Effects on Law Enforcement." *Stan. L. Rev.* 50 (1997): 1055.

Cassell, Paul G., and Richard Fowles. "Still Handcuffing the Cops: A Review of Fifty Years of Empirical Evidence of Miranda's Harmful Effects on Law Enforcement." *BUL Rev.* 97 (2017): 685.

Cassell, Paul G., and Bret S. Hayman. "Police Interrogation in the 1990s: An Empirical

Study of the Effects of Miranda." *UCLA L. Rev.* 43 (1995): 839.

Center for Disease Control and Prevention Wonder. "About Underlying Cause of Death, 1999–2000 Results: Deaths Occurring Through 2020." https://wonder.cdc .gov/controller/datarequest/D76;jsessioni d=F40BCB177B9B04859F3B1983F725.

Chalfin, Aaron, Benjamin Hansen, Emily K. Weisburst, and Morgan C. Williams Jr. "Police Force Size and Civilian Race." *American Economic Review: Insights* 4, no. 2 (2022): 139–58.

Chalfin, Aaron, and Jacob Kaplan. "How Many Complaints against Police Officers Can Be Abated by Incapacitating a Few 'Bad Apples'?" *Criminology & Public Policy* 20, no. 2 (2021): 351–70.

Chemerinsky, Erwin, "Why Have Miranda Rights Failed." Democracy a Journal of Ideas, June 27, 2016. https://democrac yjournal.org/arguments/why-have-mi randa-rights-failed/.

Chen, M. Keith, and Jesse M. Shapiro. "Do Harsher Prison Conditions Reduce Recidivism? A Discontinuity-Based Approach." *American Law and Economics Review* 9, no. 1 (2007): 1–29.

Cheng, Cheng, and Wei Long. "The Effect of Highly Publicized Police Killings on Policing: Evidence from Large US Cities." *Journal of Public Economics* 206 (2022): 104557.

Childs, Tosha. "Building Police-Community Trust in Illinois: Will We Ever Get There: An Examination of the Illinois Police and Community Relations Act." *S. Ill. ULJ* 43 (2018): 675.

Clampet-Lundquist, Susan, Patrick J. Carr, and Maria J. Kefalas. "The Sliding Scale of Snitching: A Qualitative Examination of Snitching in Three Philadelphia Communities." *Sociological Forum* 30, no. 2 (2015): 265–85.

Cohen, Kenneth P., and Glenn R. Schmitt, "An Analysis of the Implementation of the 2014 Clemency Initiative." United States Sentencing Commission, September 2017. https://www.ussc.gov/sites/default/files /pdf/research-and-publications/research -publications/2017/20170901_clemency .pdf.

Cohen, Mark A., Roland T. Rust, and Sara Steen. "Measuring Public Perceptions of Appropriate Prison Sentences, Final Report." 2002. https://www.ojp.gov/pdf files1/nij/grants/199365.pdf.

Cohen, Thomas H., and Brian A. Reaves, "Pretrial Release of Felony Defendants in State Courts." US Department of Justice, Bureau of Justice Statistics, 2007. https:// bjs.ojp.gov/content/pub/pdf/prfdsc.pdf.

Costa, Daniella Harth da, Kathie Njaine, and Miriam Schenker. "Repercussions of Homicide on Victims' Families: A Literature Review." *Ciencia & saude coletiva* 22 (2017): 3087–97.

Creekpaum, Kyden. "What's Wrong with a Little More Double Jeopardy—A 21st Century Recalibration of an Ancient Individual Right." *Am. Crim. L. Rev.* 44 (2007): 1179.

Daley, Alyssa Shea, and Jacob Carruthers. "Judicial Review of Prosecutorial Blanket Declination Policies." *Ohio State Journal of Criminal Law* (forthcoming 2022).

Darley, John M., Kevin M. Carlsmith, and Paul H. Robinson. "Incapacitation and Just Deserts as Motives for Punishment." *Law and Human Behavior* 24 (2000): 659–83.

Desmond, Matthew, Andrew V. Papachristos, and David S. Kirk. "Police Violence and Citizen Crime Reporting in the Black Community." *American Sociological Review* 81, no. 5 (2016): 857–76.

Deuchar, Ross, Seth Wyatt Fallik, and Vaughn J. Crichlow. "Despondent Officer Narratives and the 'Post-Ferguson' Effect: Exploring Law Enforcement Perspectives and Strategies in a Southern American State." *Policing and Society* 29, no. 9 (2019): 1042–57.

Devi, Tanaya, and Roland G. Fryer Jr. *Policing the Police: The Impact of "Pattern-or-Practice" Investigations on Crime.* No. w27324. National Bureau of Economic Research, 2020.

Diamond, Shari Seidman, and Hans Zeisel. "Sentencing Councils: A Study of Sentence

Disparity and Its Reduction." *U. Chi. L. Rev.* 43 (1975): 109.

DisasterCenter. "United States Crime Rates 1960–2019." https://www.disastercenter .com/crime/uscrime.htm.

Dobbie, Will, and Crystal S. Yang. "Proposals for Improving the US Pretrial System." Washington: The Hamilton Project, Brookings Institution, 2019.

Doleac, Jennifer L. "The Effects of DNA Databases on Crime." *American Economic Journal: Applied Economics* 9, no. 1 (2017): 165–201.

Doyle, Charles. *Statutes of Limitation in Federal Criminal Cases: An Overview.* Congressional Research Service, 2007.

Dripps, Donald A. "Relevant But Prejudicial Exculpatory Evidence: Rationality Versus Jury Trial and the Right to Put on a Defense." *S. Cal. L. Rev.* 69 (1995): 1389.

Duke, Steven B. "Does Miranda Protect the Innocent or the Guilty?." *Chap. L. Rev.* 10 (2006): 551.

Durose, Matthew R., "Recidivism of Prisoners Released in 34 States in 2012: A 5-Year Follow-Up Period (2012–2017)." US Department of Justice, Bureau of Justice Statistics, July 2021. https://bjs.ojp.gov /library/publications/recidivism-prisoners -released-34-states-2012-5-year-follow -period-2012-2017.

Edwards, Griffin, Stephen Rushin, and Joseph Colquitt. "The Effects of Voluntary and Presumptive Sentencing Guidelines." *TEx. L. REv.* 98 (2019): 1.

Ekins, Emily, "Policing in America: Understanding Public Attitudes toward the Police. Results from a National Survey." Cato Institute, December 7, 2016. https://www.cato.org/sites/cato.org/files /survey-reports/pdf/policing-in-america -august-1-2017.pdf.

Elbeshbishi, Sarah, and Mabinty Quarshie, "Fewer than 1 in 5 Support 'Defund the Police' Movement." *USA Today*, March 9, 2021. https://www.yahoo.com/now/fewer -one-five-support-defund-233140592 .html.

Englebrecht, Christine, Derek T. Mason, and Margaret J. Adams. "The Experiences of Homicide Victims' Families with the Criminal Justice System: An Exploratory Study." *Violence and Victims* 29, no. 3 (2014): 407–21.

Fachner, George, and Steven Carter. "Collaborative Reform Initiative: An Assessment of Deadly Force in the Philadelphia Police Department." Washington, DC: Community Oriented Policing Services, US Department of Justice, 2015. Retrieved from ric-zai-inc. com/ric. php.

Fagan, Ronald W. "Public Support for the Courts: An Examination of Alternative Explanations." *Journal of Criminal Justice* 9, no. 6 (1981): 403–17.

FBI. "The Transition to the National Incident-Based Reporting System (NIBRS): A Comparison of 2020 and 2021 NIBRS Estimates." https://kfor.com/wp-content /uploads/sites/3/2022/10/NIBRS-Trend -Analysis-Report.pdf.

Federal Bureau of Investigation Crime Data Explorer. Law Enforcement Officer Deaths. https://crime-data-explorer.app .cloud.gov/#.

Feld, Barry C. "Real Interrogation: What Actually Happens When Cops Question Kids." *Law & Society Review* 47, no. 1 (2013): 1–36.

Ferguson, Christopher J. "Negative Perceptions of Race Relations: A Brief Report Examining the Impact of News Media Coverage of Police Shootings, and Actual Fatal Police Shootings." *The Social Science Journal* (2021): 1–7.

Fields, Shawn E. "Second Amendment Sanctuaries." *Nw. UL REv.* 115 (2020): 437.

Fine, Ralph Adam. "Plea Bargaining: An Unnecessary Evil." *Marq. L. Rev.* 70 (1986): 615.

Finn, Peter, and Kerry Murphy Healey, "Preventing Gang and Drug-Related Witness Intimidation." National Institute of Justice, November 1996. https://www.ojp .gov/pdffiles/163067.pdf.

Foster, John E. "Charges to Be Declined: Legal Challenges and Policy Debates Surrounding Non-Prosecution Initiatives in Massachusetts." *BCL Rev.* 60 (2019): 2511.

Fowler, Kristen H. "Limiting the Federal Pardon Power." *Ind. LJ* 83 (2008): 1651.

Frankel, Marvin E. *Criminal Sentences: Law Without Order.* Hill and Wang, 1973.

Frase, Richard S. "Forty Years of American Sentencing Guidelines: What Have We Learned?" *Crime and Justice* 48, no. 1 (2019): 79–135.

Fryer Jr., Roland G. "An Empirical Analysis of Racial Differences in Police Use of Force." *Journal of Political Economy* 127, no. 3 (2019): 1210–61.

Garrett, Brandon L. "The Costs and Benefits of Forensics." *HOuS. L. REv.* 57 (2019): 593.

Garrett, Brandon L., and Gregory Mitchell. "Error Aversions and Due Process." *Mich. L. Rev.* 121 (2022): 707.

Gebreth, Vernon J. "10 Most Common Errors in Death Investigations." *Law and Order* 55, no. 11 (2007): 84–89.

Gershowitz, Adam M., and Laura R. Killinger. "The State (Never) Rests: How Excessive Prosecutorial Caseloads Harm Criminal Defendants." *Nw. UL Rev.* 105 (2011): 261.

Giannelli, Paul C. "Crime Labs Need Improvement." *Issues in Science and Technology* 20, no. 1 (2003): 55–58.

Giffords Law Center. "In Pursuit of Peace: Building Police-Community Trust to Break the Cycle of Violence." September 2021. https://giffords.org/lawcenter/report/in-pursuit-of-peace-building-police-community-trust-to-break-the-cycle-of-violence.

Gilmore, Ruth Wilson, and James Kilgore. "The Case for Abolition." The Marshall Project, June 19, 2019. https://www.themarshallproject.org/2019/06/19/the-case-for-abolition.

Goldberg, Zach. "Is Defunding the Police a 'Luxury Belief'? Analyzing White vs. Nonwhite Democrats' Attitudes on Depolicing." Manhattan Institute, September 2022. https://media4.manhattan-institute.org/sites/default/files/is-defunding-the-police-a-luxury-belief.pdf.

Goldenberg, Rina. "Abuse of Diplomatic Immunity: Is the Government Doing Enough?" *ILSA J. Int'l & Comp. L.* 1 (1995): 197.

Goldstein, Rebecca. "The Politics of Decarceration." *Yale L.J.* 129, no. 2 (2019): 308–611.

Graham v. Florida, 560 US 48, 71 (2010)

Graham, Michael H. "Witness Intimidation." *Fla. St. UL Rev.* 12 (1984): 239.

Green, Bruce A., and Rebecca Roiphe. "When Prosecutors Politick: Progressive Law Enforcers Then and Now." *J. Crim. L. & Criminology* 110 (2020): 719.

Gromet, Dena M., and John M. Darley. "Restoration and Retribution: How Including Retributive Components Affects the Acceptability of Restorative Justice Procedures." *Social Justice Research* 19 (2006): 395–432.

Grunwald, Ben. "Toward an Optimal Decarceration Strategy." *Stan. L. & Pol'y Rev.* 33 (2022): 1.

Guidorizzi, Douglas D. "Should We Really Ban Plea Bargaining: The Core Concerns of Plea Bargaining Critics." *Emory Lj* 47 (1998): 753.

Harmelin v. Michigan, 501 US 998-999 (1991).

Heather MacDonald, "Team Biden Finally Admits There Is a War on Cops—Which It Is Inflaming." *New York Post*, April 28. 2022. https://nypost.com/2022/04/28/team-biden-finally-admits-theres-a-war-on-cops/.

Hofer, Paul J., et al. "Effect of the Federal Sentencing Guidelines on Interjudge Sentencing Disparity." *J. Crim. L. & Criminology* 90, no. 1 (1999): 239–306.

Hogan, Thomas P. "De-Prosecution and Death: A Synthetic Control Analysis of the Impact of De-Prosecution on Homicides." *Criminology & Public Policy* 21, no. 3 (2022): 489–534.

Howe, Scott W. "Moving Beyond Miranda: Concessions for Confessions." *Nw. UL Rev.* 110 (2015): 905.

Hunt, Kim Steven, and Robert Dumville. *Recidivism among Federal Offenders: A*

Comprehensive Overview. United States Sentencing Commission, 2016.

Jensen, D. Lowell. "The Exclusionary Rule's Many Undeserving Beneficiaries." *New York Times*, May 27, 1983. https://www.ny times.com/1983/05/27/opinion/l-the-ex clusionary-rule-s-many-undeserving-ben eficiaries-193315.html.

Johnson, Jason. "Why Violent Crime Surged After Police Across America Retreated." *USA Today*, April 9, 2021. https://www.usatoday.com/story/opinion /policing/2021/04/09/violent-crime -surged-across-america-after-police-re treated-column/7137565002/.

Johnson, Kit. "The Mythology of Sanctuary Cities." *S. Cal. Interdisc. LJ* 28 (2018): 589.

Johnson, Thea. "Public Perceptions of Plea Bargaining." *Am. J. Crim. L.* 46 (2019): 133.

Kahan, Dan M. "What Do Alternative Sanctions Mean?" *U. Chi. L. Rev.* 63, no. 2 (1996): 591–653.

Kail, Shelby. "The Unintended Consequences of California Proposition 47: Reducing Law Enforcement's Ability to Solve Serious, Violent Crimes." *Pepperdine Law Review* 44, no. 5 (2017): 1039–82.

Kamisar, Yale. "Mapp v. Ohio: The First Shot Fired in the Warren Court's Criminal Procedure 'Revolution.'" In *Criminal Procedure Stories*, edited by Carol S. Steiker. Foundation Press, 2006.

Kirk, David S., and Mauri Matsuda. "Legal Cynicism, Collective Efficacy, and the Ecology of Arrest." *Criminology* 49, no. 2 (2011): 443–72.

Klein, Kenneth S. "Why Federal Rule of Evidence 403 Is Unconstitutional, and Why That Matters." *U. Rich. L. Rev.* 47 (2012): 1077.

Kuziemko, Ilyana. "How Should Inmates Be Released from prison? An Assessment of Parole versus Fixed-Sentence Regimes." *The Quarterly Journal of Economics* 128, no. 1 (2013): 371–424.

Lee, Yung Hyeock. "How Police Policies and Practices Impact Successful Crime Investigation: Factors that Enable Police Depart-

ments to 'Clear' Crimes." *Justice System Journal* 41, no. 1 (2020): 37–62.

Li, Weihua, and Jamiles Lartey. "As Murders Spiked, Police Solved About Half in 2020." The Marshall Project, January 12, 2022. https://www.themarshallproject.org /2022/01/12/as-murders-spiked-police -solved-about-half-in-2020.

Lininger, Tom. "The Sound of Silence: Holding Batterers Accountable for Silencing Their Victims." *Tex. L. Rev.* 87 (2008): 857.

Lorenz, Katherine, Anne Kirkner, and Sarah E. Ullman. "A Qualitative Study of Sexual Assault Survivors' Post-Assault Legal System Experiences." *Journal of Trauma & Dissociation* 20, no. 3 (2019): 263–87.

Ma, Yue. "Comparative Analysis of Exclusionary Rules in the United States, England, France, Germany, and Italy." *Policing: An International Journal of Police Strategies & Management* 22, no. 3 (1999): 280–303.

Ma, Yue. "The American Exclusionary Rule: Is There a Lesson to Learn from Others?" *International Criminal Justice Review* 22, no. 3 (2012): 309–25.

MacDonald, Heather. "Biden Wants to Boost Policing—After Spreading Toxic Lies that Tore It Down." *New York Post*, July 13, 2021. https://nypost.com/2021/07/13/biden -wants-to-boost-policing-after-spreading -toxic-lies-that-tore-it-down/.

MacDonald, Heather. "Is the Criminal-Justice System Racist?" *City Journal*, Spring 2008. https://www.city-journal.org/html /criminal-justice-system-racist-13078.html.

MacDonald, Heather. "The Myth of Systemic Police Racism." *Wall Street Journal*, June 2, 2020. https://www.wsj.com /articles/the-myth-of-systemic-police-rac ism-11591119883.

MacDonald, Heather. "The New Nationwide Crime Wave." *Wall Street Journal*, May 29, 2015. https://www.wsj.com/articles/the -new-nationwide-crime-wave-1432938425.

MacDonald, Heather. *The War on Cops: How the New Attack on Law and Order Makes Everyone Less Safe*. Encounter Books, 2016.

MacDonald, Heather. "Where Is the Outrage Over the Killing of Baltimore Police Officer

Keona Holley?" *New York Post*, December 29, 2021. https://nypost.com/2021/12/29/where-is-the-outrage-over-the-killing-of-keona-holley/.

Mancik, Ashley M., Karen F. Parker, and Kirk R. Williams. "Neighborhood Context and Homicide Clearance: Estimating the Effects of Collective Efficacy." *Homicide Studies* 22, no. 2 (2018): 188–213.

Martínez, Daniel E., Ricardo D. Martínez-Schuldt, and Guillermo Cantor. "Providing Sanctuary or Fostering Crime? A Review of the Research on 'Sanctuary Cities' and Crime." *Sociology compass* 12, no. 1 (2018): e12547.

McCaffree, Kevin, and Anondah Saide. "How Informed Are Americans About Race and Policing?" *Skeptic Research Center, CUPES-007* (2021).

McCormick, Elizabeth M. "Federal Anti-Sanctuary Law: A Failed Approach to Immigration Enforcement and a Poor Substitute for Real Reform." *Lewis & Clark L. Rev.* 20 (2016): 165.

Morgan, Anthony, and Christopher Dowling. "Does CCTV Help Police Solve Crime?" *Trends and Issues in Crime and Criminal Justice [electronic resource]* 576 (2019): 1–16.

Morgan, Rachel, and Jennifer Truman, "Criminal Victimization, 2019." US Department of Justice, Bureau of Justice Statistics, September 2020. https://bjs.ojp.gov/content/pub/pdf/cv19.pdf.

Mourtgos, Scott M., Ian T. Adams, and Justin Nix. "Elevated Police Turnover Following the Summer of George Floyd Protests: A Synthetic Control Study." *Criminology & Public Policy* 21, no. 1 (2022): 9–33.

Murder Accountability Project. "America's Declining Homicide Clearance Rates 1965–2020." https://www.murderdata.org/p/reported-homicide-clearance-rate-1980.html.

Murder Accountability Project. "Black Murders Accounted for All of America's Clearance Decline." February 18, 2019. https://www.murderdata.org/2019/02/black-murders-account-for-all-of.html#:~:text=Declining%20homicide%20clearance%20rates%20for,Murder%20Accountability%20Project%20(MAP).

Nadler, Janice. "Flouting the Law: Does Perceived Injustice Provoke General Non-Compliance?" *Northwestern Law & Econ Research Paper* 02-9 (2002).

Nardulli, Peter F. "The Societal Costs of the Exclusionary Rule revisited." *U. Ill. L. Rev.* (1987): 223.

Natapoff, Alexandra. *Snitching: Criminal Informants and the Erosion of American Justice*. New York: New York University Press, 2009.

Oaks, Dallin H. "Studying the Exclusionary Rule in Search and Seizure." *U. Chi. L. Rev.* 37 (1969): 665.

O'Donnell, Dan, and Daunte Wright, "The Truth About Police Shootings in America." MacIver Institute, April 14, 2021. https://www.maciverinstitute.com/2021/04/the-truth-about-police-shootings-in-america/.

Orfield, Myron W. "The Exclusionary Rule and Deterrence: An Empirical Study of Chicago Narcotics Officers." *The University of Chicago Law Review* 54, no. 3 (1987): 1016–69.

Oskooii, Kassra AR, Sarah K. Dreier, and Loren Collingwood. "Partisan Attitudes toward Sanctuary Cities: The Asymmetrical Effects of Political Knowledge." *Politics & Policy* 46, no. 6 (2018): 951–84.

Osler, Mark Osler. "Mass Pardons in America: Rebellion, Presidential Amnesty, & Reconciliation." 2022. https://clcjbooks.rutgers.edu/books/mass-pardons-in-america-rebellion-presidential-amnesty-and-reconciliation/.

Parker, Kim, and Kiley Hurst, "Growing Share of Americans Say They Want More Spending on Police in Their Area." Pew Research Center, October 26, 2021. https://www.pewresearch.org/fact-tank/2021/10/26/growing-share-of-americans-say-they-want-more-spending-on-police-in-their-area/.

Peed, Carl R., and Chuck Wexler. "The Stop Snitching Phenomenon: Breaking the Code of Silence." US Department of Justice,

Office of Community Oriented Policing Services, Februar 2009. https://portal.cops .usdoj.gov/resourcecenter/RIC/Publica tions/cops-p158-pub.pdf.

Perrin, Andrew. "About Half of Americans Are OK with DNA Testing Companies Sharing User Data with Law Enforcement." Pew Research Center, February 4, 2020. https://www.pewresearch.org/fact -tank/2020/02/04/about-half-of-ameri cans-are-ok-with-dna-testing-companies -sharing-user-data-with-law-enforcement/.

Perrin, L. Timothy, H. Mitchell Caldwell, Carol A. Chase, and Ronald W. Fagan. "If It's Broken, Fix It: Moving Beyond the Exclusionary Rule: A New and Extensive Empirical Study of the Exclusionary Rule and a Call for a Civil Administrative Remedy to Partially Replace the Rule." *Iowa L. Rev.* 83 (1997): 669.

Pettys, Todd E. "Immoral Application of Exclusionary Rules, The." *Wis. L. REv.* (2008): 463.

Pew Research Center. "Majority of Public Favors Giving Civilians the Power to Sue Police Officers for Misconduct." July 9, 2020. https://www.pewresearch.org /politics/2020/07/09/majority-of-public -favors-giving-civilians-the-power-to-sue -police-officers-for-misconduct/.

Piquero, Alex R., Jeffrey Fagan, Edward P. Mulvey, Laurence Steinberg, and Candice Odgers. "Developmental Trajectories of Legal Socialization among Serious Adolescent Offenders." *The Journal of Criminal Law & Criminology* 96, no. 1 (2005): 267.

Piza, Eric L., Brandon C. Welsh, David P. Farrington, and Amanda L. Thomas. "CCTV Surveillance for Crime Prevention: A 40-Year Systematic Review with Meta-Analysis." *Criminology & Public Policy* 18, no. 1 (2019): 135–59.

Police Executive Research Forum. "Promising Strategies for Strengthening Homicide Investigations, Findings and Recommendations from the Bureau of Justice Assistance's Homicide Investigations Enhancement Training and Technical Assistance Project." https://www.police

forum.org/assets/homicideinvestigations .pdf.

Prescott, J. J., Benjamin Pyle, and Sonja B. Starr. "Understanding Violent-Crime Recidivism." *Notre Dame L. Rev.* 95 (2019): 1643.

Price, Zachary. "The Rule of Lenity as a Rule of Structure." *Fordham L. Rev.* 72 (2003): 885.

Project: Cold Case. "Cold Case Homicide Statistics: Breakdown of Homicide Clearance Rates." https://projectcoldcase.org /cold-case-homicide-stats/.

Quinn, Jim. "More Criminals, More Crime: Measuring the Public Safety Impact of New York's 2019 Bail Law." *Manhattan Institute, July* 28 (2022).

RAINN. "The Criminal Justice System: Statistics." https://www.rainn.org/statistics /criminal-justice-system.

RAINN. "Perpetrators of Sexual Violence: Statistics." https://www.rainn.org/statistics /perpetrators-sexual-violence.

RAINN. "State by State Guide on Statutes of Limitation." https://www.rainn.org /statutes-limitations.

RAINN. "Victims of Sexual Violence: Statistics." https://www.rainn.org/statistics/vic tims-sexual-violence#:~:text=Sexual%20 Violence%20Affects%20Millions%20 of,year%20in%20the%20United%20States.

Reisig, Michael D., Scott E. Wolfe, and Kristy Holtfreter. "Legal Cynicism, Legitimacy, and Criminal Offending: The Nonconfounding Effect of Low Self-Control." *Criminal Justice and Behavior* 38, no. 12 (2011): 1265–79.

Restoration of Rights Project. "50-State Comparison: Pardon Policy & Practice." October 2022. https://ccresourcecenter.org /state-restoration-profiles/50-state-com parisoncharacteristics-of-pardon-author ities-2/.

Robb, Gary C. "Police Use of CCTV Surveillance: Constitutional Implications and Proposed Regulations." *U. Mich. JL Reform* 13 (1979): 571.

Roberts, Aki. "Explaining Differences in Homicide Clearance Rates between Japan and the United States." *Homicide Studies* 12, no. 1 (2008): 136–45.

Roberts, Julian V. "Public Opinion, Crime, and Criminal Justice." *Crime and Justice* 16 (1992): 99–180.

Roberts, Paul. "Double Jeopardy Law Reform: A Criminal Justice Commentary." *The Modern Law Review* 65, no. 3 (2002): 393–424.

Robin, Lily, et al. "Public Surveillance Cameras and Crime: The Impact of Different Camera Types on Crimes and Clearance." Urban Institute, February 8, 2020. https://www.urban.org/sites/default/files/publication/101649/public_surveillance_cameras_and_crime.pdf.

Robinson, Paul H. "Competing Conceptions of Modern Desert: Vengeful, Deontological, and Empirical." *The Cambridge Law Journal* 67, no. 1 (2008): 145–75.

Robinson, Paul H. "Criminal Law's Core Principles." *Wash. U. Jurisprudence Rev.* 14 (2021): 153.

Robinson, Paul H. *Distributive Principles of Criminal Law: Who Should Be Punished, How Much?* Oxford University Press, 2008.

Robinson, Paul H. "Empirical Desert." In *Criminal Law Conversations*, edited by Paul H. Robinson, Stephen Garvey, and Kimberly Kessler Ferzan, 29–66. Oxford University Press, 2009.

Robinson, Paul H. "Fair Notice and Fair Adjudication: Two Kinds of Legality (2005)." *University of Pennsylvania Law Review* 154: 335.

Robinson, Paul H. *Intuitions of Justice and the Utility of Desert.* Oxford University Press, 2013.

Robinson, Paul H. "The Moral Vigilante and Her Cousins in the Shadows." *U. Ill. L. Rev.* (2015): 401.

Robinson, Paul H. "One Perspective on Sentencing Reform in the United States." *Criminal Law Forum* 8, no. 3 (1997): 1–41.

Robinson, Paul H. "Punishing Dangerousness: Cloaking Preventive Detention as Criminal Justice." *Harvard L. Rev.* 114, no. 5 (2001): 1429–56.

Robinson, Paul H. "Report on Offense Grading in Pennsylvania." *Paul H. Robinson and the University of Pennsylvania Criminal Law Research Group, REPORT ON OFFENSE GRADING IN PENNSYLVANIA* (2009): 10–01.

Robinson, Paul H. "Why Does the Criminal Law Care What the Layperson Thinks Is Just? Coercive versus Normative Crime Control." *Virginia Law Review* (2000): 1839–69.

Robinson, Paul H., and Michael T. Cahill. *Criminal Law.* Wolters Kluwer Law & Business, 2012.

Robinson, Paul H., and Michael T. Cahill. "Final Report of the Illinois Criminal Code Rewrite and Reform Commission." *PH Robinson, ILLINOIS CRIMINAL CODE REWRITE AND REFORM COMMISSION* (2003): 09–40.

Robinson, Paul H., and Michael T. Cahill. *Law without Justice: Why Criminal Law Doesn't Give People What They Deserve.* Oxford University Press, 2005.

Robinson, Paul H., and John M. Darley. "The Utility of Desert." *Nw U. L. Rev.* 91 (1997): 453.

Robinson, Paul H., and John M. Darley. "Intuitions of Justice: Implications for Criminal Law and Justice Policy." *S. Cal. L. Rev.* 81 (2007): 1.

Robinson, Paul H., and Markus D. Dubber. "The American Model Penal Code: A Brief Overview." *New Criminal Law Review* 10, no. 3 (2007): 319–41.

Robinson, Paul H., Geoffrey P. Goodwin, and Michael D. Reisig. "The Disutility of Injustice." *NYUL Rev.* 85 (2010): 1940.

Robinson, Paul H., and Lindsay Holcomb. "The Criminogenic Effects of Damaging Criminal Law's Moral Credibility." *S. Cal. Interdisc. LJ* 31 (2021): 277.

Robinson, Paul H., Sean E. Jackowitz, and Daniel M. Bartels. "Extralegal Punishment Factors: A Study of Forgiveness, Hardship, Good Deeds, Apology, Remorse, and Other Such Discretionary Factors in Assessing Criminal Punishment." *Vand. L. Rev.* 65 (2012): 737.

Robinson, Paul H., Matthew G. Kussmaul, and Muhammad Sarahne. "How Criminal Code Drafting Form Can Restrain Prosecutorial and Legislative Excesses: Consolidated Offense Drafting." *Harv. J. on Legis.* 58 (2021): 69.

Robinson, Paul H., Matthew Kussmaul, and Ilya Rudyak. "Report of the Delaware Criminal Law Recodification Project." *Report of the Delaware Criminal Law Recodification Project to the Delaware General Assembly's Criminal Justice Improvement Committee (2017), U of Penn Law School, Public Law Research Paper* 17–19 (2017).

Robinson, Paul H., Rebecca Levenson, Nicholas Feltham, Andrew Sperl, Kristen-Elise Brooks, Agatha Koprowski, Jessica Peake, Benjamin Probber, and Brian Trainor. "Report on Offense Grading in New Jersey." *U of Penn Law School, Public Law Research Paper* 11–03 (2011).

Robinson, Paul H., and Sarah M. Robinson. *Crimes that Changed Our World: Tragedy, Outrage, and Reform.* Rowman & Littlefield, 2018.

Robinson, Paul H., and Sarah M. Robinson. *Pirates, Prisoners, and Lepers: Lessons from Life Outside the Law.* Universary of Nebraska Press, 2015.

Robinson, Paul H., and Muhammad Sarahne. "The Opposite of Punishment: Imaging a Path to Public Redemption." *Rutgers UL Rev.* 73 (2020): 1.

Robinson, Paul H., and Tyler Scot Williams. *Mapping American Criminal Law: Variations Across the 50 States.* Bloomsbury Publishing USA, 2018.

Rosenfeld, Richard, et al. "Assessing and Responding to the Recent Homicide Rise in the United States." National Institute of Justice, November 2017. https://www.ojp .gov/pdffiles1/nij/251067.pdf.

Rosenmerkel, Sean, Matthew Durose, and Donald Farole, "Felony Sentences in State Courts, 2006—Statistical Tables." US Department of Justice, Bureau of Justice Statistics, December 2009. https://bjs.ojp.gov /library/publications/felony-sentences -state-courts-2006-statistical-tables-stan dard-error-tables#:~:text=In%202006%20 an%20estimated%2069,and%2011%20 months%20in%202006.

Ross, Mitchell S. "Rethinking Diplomatic Immunity: A Review of Remedial Approaches to Address the Abuses of Diplomatic Privileges and Immunities." *Am. UJ Int'l L. & Pol'y* 4 (1989): 173.

Rupcich, Joseph N. "Abusing a Limitless Power: Executive Clemency in Illinois." *S. Ill. ULJ* 28 (2003): 131.

Rushin, Stephen, and Roger Michalski. "Police Funding." *Fla. L. Rev.* 72 (2020): 277.

Sackett, Chase. "Neighborhoods and Violent Crime." Office of Policy Development and Research, Summer 2016. https://www .huduser.gov/portal/periodicals/em/sum mer16/highlight2.html.

Sainju, Karla Dhungana, Stephanie Fahy, Booz Allen Hamilton, Katherine Baggaley, Ashley Baker, Tamar Minassian, and Vanessa Filippelli. "Electronic Monitoring for Pretrial Release: Assessing the Impact." *Fed. Probation* 82 (2018): 3.

Sawyer, Wendy, and Peter Wagner. *Mass Incarceration: The Whole Pie 2023.* March 14, 2023. Prison Policy Initiative, March 14, 2023, Slideshow 1. www.prisonpolicy.org /reports/pie2023.html.

Scarman, Justice. "Codification and Judge-Made Law: A Problem of Coexistence." *Ind. LJ* 42 (1966): 355.

Schulhofer, Stephen J. "Miranda's Practical Effect: Substantial Benefits and Vanishingly Small Social Costs." *Nw. UL Rev.* 90 (1995): 500.

Shenkin, Budd N., and David I. Levine. "Should the Power of Presidential Pardon Be Revised." *Hastings Const. LQ* 47 (2019): 3.

Slobogin, Christopher. "Comparative Empiricism and Police Investigative Practices." *NCJ Int'l L. & Com. Reg.* 37 (2011): 321.

Slobogin, Christopher. "The Exclusionary Rule: Is It on Its Way Out: Should It Be." *Ohio St. J. Crim. L.* 10 (2012): 341.

Slobogin, Christopher. "Why Liberals Should Chuck the Exclusionary Rule." *U. Ill. L. Rev.* (1999): 363.

Starkweather, David A. "The Retributive Theory of Just Deserts and Victim Participation in Plea Bargaining." *Ind. LJ* 67 (1991): 853.

Statista. "Number of Murder Victims in the United States in 2022, by Race." October 20, 2023, https://www.statista.com/statistics/251877/murder-victims-in-the-us-by-race-ethnicity-and-gender/.

Stevenson, Dru. "Judicial Deference to Legislatures in Constitutional Analysis." *NCL Rev.* 90 (2011): 2083.

Stimson, Charles D., and Zack Smith, "'Progressive' Prosecutors Sabotage the Rule of Law, Raise Crime Rates, and Ignore Victims." The Heritage Foundation, October 29, 2020. https://www.heritage.org/crime-and-justice/report/progressive-prosecutors-sabotage-the-rule-law-raise-crime-rates-and-ignore.

Strom, Kevin J., and Matthew J. Hickman. "Unanalyzed Evidence in Law-Enforcement Agencies: A National Examination of Forensic Processing in Police Departments." *Criminology & Public Policy* 9, no. 2 (2010): 381–404.

Strom, Kevin J., et al. "Survey of Law Enforcement Forensic Evidence Processing 2007." US Department of Justice, Office of Justice Programs, October 2009. https://www.ojp.gov/ncjrs/virtual-library/abstracts/survey-law-enforcement-forensic-evidence-processing.

Stuntz, William J. "The Political Constitution of Criminal Justice." *Harvard Law Review* 119, no. 3 (2006): 780–851.

Sutherland, Brian A. "Whether Consent to Search Was Given Voluntarily: A Statistical Analysis of Factors that Predict the Suppression Rulings of the Federal District Courts." *NYUL Rev.* 81 (2006): 2192.

Takei, Carl. "From Mass Incarceration to Mass Control, and Back Again: How Bipartisan Criminal Justice Reform May Lead to a For-Profit Nightmare." *U. Pa. JL & Soc. Change* 20 (2017): 125.

Thompson, James R., and Gary L. Starkman. "Book Review." *Review of Criminal Sentences: Law without Order*, by Marvin E. Frankel. *Columbia L. Rev.* 74 (1974): 152–58.

Totten, Gregory D., Peter D. Kossoris, and Ebbe B. Ebbesen. "The Exclusionary Rule: Fix It, But Fix It Right—A Critique of If It's Broken, Fix It: Moving Beyond the Exclusionary Rule." *Pepperdine Law Review* 26, no. 4 (1999): 7.

Tyler, Tom R. "Procedural Justice, Legitimacy, and the Effective Rule of Law." *Crime and Justice* 30 (2003): 283–357.

Tyler, Tom R. *Why People Obey the Law.* Princeton University Press, 2006.

Uchida, Craig D., and Timothy S. Bynum. "Search Warrants, Motions to Suppress and Lost Cases: The Effects of the Exclusionary Rule in Seven Jurisdictions." *J. Crim. L. & Criminology* 81 (1990): 1034.

United States v. Jones 565 US 400 (2012).

US Department of Justice. "Department of Justice Report Regarding the Criminal Investigation into the Shooting Death of Michael Brown By Ferguson, Missouri Police Officer Darren Wilson." March 4, 2015, https://www.justice.gov/sites/default/files/opa/press-releases/attachments/2015/03/04/doj_report_on_shooting_of_michael_brown_1.pdf.

US Department of Justice, Bureau of Justice Statistics. "National Judicial Reporting Program (NJRP)—2006." https://www.bjs.gov/index.cfm?ty=dcdetail&iid=241.

US Department of Justice, Office of the Pardon Attorney. "Clemency Statistics." https://www.justice.gov/pardon/clemency-statistics.

Van Kessel, Gordon. "The Suspect as a Source of Testimonial Evidence: A Comparison of the English and American Approaches." *Hastings LJ* 38 (1986): 1.

van Wijk, Anton, Ilse van Leiden, and Henk Ferwerda. "Murder and the Long-Term Impact on Co-Victims: A Qualitative, Longitudinal Study." *International Review of Victimology* 23, no. 2 (2017): 145–57.

Visher, Christy, and John Eason. "A Better Path Forward for Criminal Justice: Changing Prisons to Help People Change." The Brookings Institution, April 2021. https://www.brookings.edu/research/a-better-path-forward-for-criminal-justice-changing-prisons-to-help-people-change/.

Westera, Nina J., Mark R. Kebbell, and Becky Milne. "Want a Better Criminal Justice Response to Rape? Improve Police Interviews with Complainants and Suspects." Violence against Women 22, no. 14 (2016): 1748–69.

Woldoff, Rachael A., and Karen G. Weiss. "'Stop snitchin': Exploring Definitions of the Snitch and Implications for Urban Black Communities." Journal of Criminal Justice and Popular Culture 17, no. 1 (2010): 184–223.

Woodson, Robert L. "The Deadly Results of Defunding the Police." Wall Street Journal, June 9, 2021. https://www.wsj.com/articles/the-deadly-results-of-defunding-the-police-11623259226.

Wylie, Lindsey E., Alexis K. Knutson, and Edie Greene. "Extraordinary and Compelling: The Use of Compassionate Release Laws in the United States." Psychology, Public Policy, and Law 24, no. 2 (2018): 216.

Yung, Corey Rayburn. "Rape Law Gatekeeping." BCL Rev. 58 (2017): 205.

Zizumbo-Colunga, Daniel. "Crime, Corruption and Societal Support for Vigilante Justice: Ten Years of Evidence in Review." AmericasBarometer Insights 120 (2015).

Index

About the Authors

Paul H. Robinson is one of the world's leading criminal law scholars. A prolific writer and lecturer, Robinson has published twenty books and articles in virtually all of the top law reviews, lectured in more than 110 cities in thirty-four states and twenty-seven countries, and had his writings appear in fifteen languages.

He is a former federal prosecutor and counsel for the US Senate Subcommittee on Criminal Laws and Procedures. Robinson's books include the standard lawyer's reference on criminal law defenses, three Oxford monographs on criminal law theory, a highly regarded criminal law treatise, and an innovative case studies course book. He has authored more than a hundred scholarly articles that have appeared in essentially every major law review and his work has been published in fifteen languages.

A member of the American Law Institute, Robinson is the lead editor of *Criminal Law Conversations* (Oxford), with contributions from more than one hundred scholars around the world, and the author of *Intuitions of Justice and the Utility of Desert* (Oxford); *Mapping American Criminal Law* (Praeger, also in Chinese); *Distributive Principles of Criminal Law* (Oxford, also in Spanish and Chinese); and *Structure and Function in Criminal Law* (Oxford, Clarendon, also in Chinese). Robinson recently completed three criminal code reform projects in the United States and two modern Islamic penal codes, including one under the auspices of the UN Development Programme. He also writes popular books for general audiences, such as *Would You Convict?* (New York University), *Law Without Justice* (Oxford), *Crimes that Changed Our World* (Rowman & Littlefield), *Shadow Vigilantes* (Prometheus), *American Criminal Law: Its People, Principles & Evolution* (Routledge), and *Pirates, Prisoners & Lepers: Lessons from Life Outside the Law* (Potomac).

Jeffrey Seaman is a researcher and writer on the US criminal justice system. He holds a bachelor of arts in philosophy, politics, and economics (2022) and a master's of science in behavioral and decision sciences (2023) from the University of Pennsylvania. He is committed to bringing an interdisciplinary approach to the problem of criminal justice reform to make the system more just for all.

Muhammad Sarahne, SJD 2020 and LLM 2017, University of Pennsylvania Law School; LLB (law) and BA (psychology), Hebrew University of Jerusalem, 2011, is currently an attorney in the Criminal Department of the State Attorney's Office in Israel, representing the state in criminal matters before the Israeli Supreme Court. He previously worked as a prosecutor in the Economic Crime Department and was an assistant to the Israeli Deputy Attorney General (Criminal). He is an adjunct teacher at the Law School of the Hebrew University of Jerusalem and has published a number of articles in American and British law reviews.

www.ingramcontent.com/pod-product-compliance
Lightning Source LLC
Chambersburg PA
CBHW051427290326

41932CB00049B/3259